TIMES SQUARE ROULETTE

TIMES SQUARE ROULETTE

REMAKING THE CITY ICON

LYNNE B. SAGALYN

The MIT Press
Cambridge, Massachusetts
London, England

Library of Congress Cataloging-in-Publication Data

Sagalyn, Lynne B.

　　Times Square roulette: remaking the city icon / Lynne B. Sagalyn

　　　　p. cm.

　　Includes bibliographical references and index.

　　ISBN 0-262-19462-7 (hc. : alk. paper)

　　1. City planning—New York (State)—New York. 2. Urban renewal—New York (State)—New York. 3. Tourism and city planning—New York (State)—New York. 4. Times Square (New York, N.Y.) 5. New York (N.Y.)—politics and government. I. Title.

HT168.N5 S24 2001

307.1'216'097471—dc21

　　　　　　　　　　　　　　　　　　　　　　　　　　2001034276

SOURCES FOR CHAPTER OPENING IMAGES: 1: Enrico Ferorelli; 2: NYC Economic Development Corporation; 3: Collection of the author; 4: Maggie Hopp; 5: Collection of Bruce J. McCuen; 6: Gary Hack; 7: Michael Peters, Newsday; 8: Gary Hack; 9: Collection of the author; 10: Collection of Bruce J. McCuen; 11: Identity Map Company, Inc.; 12: Gary Hack; 13: Maggie Hopp; 14: Collection of the author; Epilogue: Lynne B. Sagalyn

To G. H.

Contents

PREFACE

Not long into the research for this book during the prelude of an interview when one sets the stage for questioning by explaining purpose and, one hopes, elicits interest and enthusiasm beyond mere recall of events, I encountered a type of skepticism that had come to mark the notion of a transformation of West 42nd Street as quixotic. Before I asked my first question, my subject posed a friendly challenge: "You have two problems," he said. "First, the Times Square redevelopment project is sui generis; second, it's not likely ever to get done." The time was 1991, and after a decade of concerted effort the redevelopment project was stalled indefinitely, perhaps decisively, by the collapse of the Manhattan real estate market.

What was not a propitious time for this public-private project, however, turned out to be a fine time to begin unraveling a story of development politics and power. Among insiders, the recall of events was still relatively fresh, not yet clouded by hazy memories or shaded by altered perceptions that might creep in later if, as proved to be the case, subsequent events led to a dramatic turnaround. As with any case study, the potential sui generis problem did exist, yet notwithstanding the unique attributes of the New York real estate market, I believed an intense examination of the Times Square project would offer meaningful insights into the process and risks confronting public officials when taking on the deliberate task of transforming a large, distinctive area of a city, a political task made all the more difficult in the absence of federal dollars from Washington. By focusing on an urban icon such as Times Square I hoped to reach a broad audience interested in cities and explain how the existing fabric of a district changes—in perception as well as physical reality (figure P.1). The idea was to build an appreciation of how outcomes evolve by looking at the ways in which large-scale plans interface with unintended events, political needs interact with economic mandates, and design principles intersect (or not) with market-driven development pressure to reshape the physical and social contours of an urban district. As to whether the 42nd Street

P.1
The former Times Tower, 2001:
icon transformed, once again.
(Gary Hack)

P.2
Cleanup goals underground as
well as above: Times Square subway station mosaic newly fashioned. (Gary Hack)

Development Project (42DP) would ever get done, "That doesn't matter,"
I replied a bit defensively. "I'm an academic; we study things because they
hold the prospect of revealing meaningful insights whether or not they
succeed." Fortunately, not having to make a crystal-ball judgment on the
project's future trajectory allowed me to push forward with the interview
and a decade of research and writing. By the time I finished, the earlier
doom-and-gloom consensus about the 42DP had become a piece of project lore and the turnaround a much noted success story.

The historically intractable character of the civic problem and the
contentious complexity of the promises for a cleanup of West 42nd Street
contributed research drama (figure P.2). Unexpected events and continual
twists and turns meant that the story was never static. The scope expanded
beyond my initial intent; what started as a focused analysis of the policy
implications of New York's innovative scheme for financing the multibillion redevelopment project turned into a broad profile of development
politics in New York in the last quarter of the twentieth century. The
issues raised by the project compelled a larger treatment. In the aftermath
of the city's mid-1970s fiscal crisis any large-scale public development represented an ambitious political undertaking; the particular plans for cleaning up Times Square made the task more of a challenge in the absence of
the type of command-and-control powers formerly wielded by Robert
Moses, the man who more than any other sculpted the physical face of
twentieth-century New York. Only as the research progressed would I
come to understand the true measure of how both these legacies recast
the context of public development.

Explanations of what makes for place-defining physical change
could be found in volumes about city planning, political decision making,

urban economics, and real estate development, each oriented toward its own specialized audience, academic or practitioner. My objective was to link these audiences and bridge disciplines by making connections between the political, economic, and social forces that shaped development in New York during an era of aggressive public deal making. Being multi-disciplinary, the book focuses more on explaining the complexity of practice than on testing alternative theories, though the analysis starts from the theoretical premise that politics matters—not just in formulating policy but in shaping implementation. Since the publication of Paul E. Peterson's award-winning *City Politics* in which he put forth the policy-formulates-politics argument, a debate has ensued about the role of conflict in urban politics. Given the difficulties, conflicts, and escalating costs expected in executing public projects, however, "governing officials *may shape policies to facilitate the political task*—that is, they may adopt politics that contribute to both building and maintaining coalitions and to managing conflict."[1]

Times Square Roulette* falls solidly in this alternative politics-shapes-policy camp articulated by Clarence H. Stone and Heywood T. Sanders. Using the 42DP as a case study, it first argues that the political imperatives facing the administration of Mayor Edward I. Koch post–fiscal crisis and the politics of historic preservation as played out in Times Square directly shaped the policy strategy for this high-profile project in two commanding ways: first, by making firm a financial ground rule that the city would take no risk for escalating costs for land acquisition and second, by eliciting guarantees from public officials that the 42nd Street theaters would be protected from the bulldozer slated to clear nearly the rest of the block. The book further argues that the politically treacherous task of implementing the first corporate-oriented vision begat a level of contention and conflict so deep and threatening as to cause a rare reversal of the planning program—all but for the economic dependence on the four high-density office towers, the project's financial generator.

The pieces of Peterson's argument—development policy has a consensual quality, group conflict is minimal, support is broad and continuous, and there is no need for bargaining over value trade-offs or mutual adjustments because development is in the unitary interest of the whole community—define away conflict. The case of Times Square proves otherwise. While support for the plan was broad, it would be hard to conclude that it was continuous. Likewise, support did not grow over time as the "benefits" became clearer. Rather than dissolving "conflicts in a sea of collective economic well-being," the move to implementation seemed "to heighten controversy and to compound problems."[2] By explaining how conflict and controversy shaped the task of implementation, *Times Square Roulette* contributes to the theoretical dialogue on the politics of urban development. At the same time, it addresses the practical question, how do public officials get big plans implemented in a political context?

As a case study, the Times Square story offers lessons about several aspects of the political economy of urban development: on how a city is forced to take risks—both financial and political—to foster large-scale physical redevelopment; on how divergent forces of opposition to a high-profile project—litigation and civic activism—rescripted a flawed plan; on how a city's cleverly constructed—but untried and unconventional—effort to shift the financial risk of redevelopment to the private sector succeeded, but not before turning back on itself, exacerbating the political risks of what many perceived to be a discredited policy of large-scale condemnation; on how the very complexity of the off-budget financing resulted in impossible accountability, inflexibility in dealing with a changing market, unreasonable private risks that would only be carried out by naive institutional investors with deep pockets, and most probably higher costs than piecemeal development.

Deal making for urban development takes place in a planning context void of overarching theories or singularly dominant prescriptive approaches to building better cities. The grand theories and comprehensive plans have been forsaken by city officials who are focused on pragmatic and concrete results within their tenure of office. Some in New York, Mayors Koch and Giuliani in particular, have been openly hostile to planners and grand plans, favoring the directness and control of entrepreneurial deal making from city hall. Whether to prime the pump of real estate development, foster economic development, or retain corporate jobs, policy is being made through deal making, and the scope and character of that policy making is embedded in the terms and conditions of the public's deals with private developers and corporate chief executives. In other words, the details of a deal matter. Because every possible contingency cannot be specified upfront, policy choices evolve over the course of implementation in the political and financial trade-offs that each side must make along the way in reaching agreements or renegotiating deals. These too reveal themselves through detail. The fragmented and often attenuated process of decision making, the necessary and endless coordination by both city and state development officials responsible for the project, and the fragile balance of execution—so dependent upon the timely alignment of public leadership, political savvy, and market feasibility—similarly explain themselves through the accumulation of story details. The details establish context, explain the varying motivations of the cast of players, and add depth of understanding to the nuances of a complex and often shifting tableau of economic and political forces. In short, the story of Times Square's transformation depends upon understanding the colorful and contextual contours of detail.

What are the lessons of public development when a high-profile project with the concentrated powers of a public-entity coalition and the deep financial resources of a private company such as Prudential Insurance Company of America, financial partner for the development of the four office towers, gets humbled by opposition lawsuits and market events? Market forces ultimately define the timetable for implementing ambitious city plans. Cities can push and prod in a number of ways to alter and adjust market signals, but with large-scale projects, even though a city often starts out ahead of the market, intense controversy and attention to procedural diligence often alter the timetable such that it ends up following the market. Also, public interventions and market dynamics are intimately interwoven, symbiotic forces in the process of urban transformations. The Times Square story details this complex relationship between planning and politics and the role of market forces in shaping redevelopment opportunities, and reveals the way in which the interaction altered the course of revitalization in Times Square. It also illustrates the power of symbolism as a mediating force among contending, fractious interests in shaping the changing fabric of cities, as laid out in chapter 1.

From its beginning as Longacre Square, Times Square quickly evolved into an icon as the place's symbolic associations—garish commercialism, spectacular signage, cultural diversity, and social tolerance—embedded themselves deep into the city's psyche. More than the city's center of entertainment, more than a commercial marketplace capable of satisfying diverse consumer needs, Times Square has been a public place of high symbolic importance, as explained in chapter 2. This role guaranteed that any plan for its "renewal" would arouse fierce debate and fractious opposition from a range of interests. It was contested turf (figure P.3).

P.3
Looking east toward the Chrysler Building, the iconic vision of West 42nd Street, 1982. (Collection of the author)

Though not oblivious to the iconic quality of place, city and state officials saw West 42nd Street as a civic embarrassment, in moral terms, as a cesspool of epic proportions in need of thorough sanitization. To advance his vision of cleanup—Koch had just rejected *The City at 42nd Street,* an ambitious Disneyish large-scale vision, put forth by a private redevelopment group supported by the Ford Foundation and big business—the mayor took charge, entered into a powerful coalition with the state's entrepreneurial Urban Development Corporation (UDC), and put in place policies that departed from precedents, as described in chapter 3. What the project's planners produced as a new vision for West 42nd Street—a corporate-dominated district of "good" uses—however, was perceived by most interests other than real estate developers as "alien" to Times Square, in the term of meaning first put forth by John Costonis in *Aliens and Icons: Law, Aesthetics, and Environmental Change.* During this period, a strongly negative reaction to the first "helpful" alien intervention in Times Square, the Portman/Marriott Marquis Hotel, intensified the unfolding aesthetic drama of the controversy. Though economically rational, the first 42DP plan was politically misguided in its singular development focus on commercial uses. In quest of economic marketability, it made only the slightest of rhetorical bows toward preserving the street's nine historic theaters—its historic legacy—as explained in chapter 4. This symbolic but empty bow did not fool the performing-arts or theater-preservation interests, who had lost patience as well as belief in the city's ability or willingness to ever do the right thing for its underappreciated Broadway heritage.

Reflecting the city's zeal to clear away social problems, the corporate character of the first plan—four massive office towers dreamed up for developer George Klein by architects Philip Johnson and John Burgee and a huge merchandise mart that would also support a large business-oriented hotel—appeared arrogantly and brutally insensitive to the cultural symbolism of the place. Despite a clever financial strategy, analyzed in chapter 5, progress proved elusive for more than eight years. Driven by the city's political mandate to avoid all financial risk, the strategy shifted the risk for condemnation to private developers. The trade-offs embedded in this ingenious arrangement would become politically troublesome, however. In addition, the goals of the project were at odds with one another, which exacerbated the task of holding together what from the start was a tenuous constituency for the project. Disregard of its own design guidelines for the project furthered the growing distrust of the city/state's behavior as a public developer. In the interests of development feasibility, city officials were even ready to allow demolition of the former Times Tower, the physical icon of the place's symbolic importance. As a replacement, Pritzker-Prize-winning architect Robert Venturi proposed a "Big Apple for Times Square." This monumental element was brilliant, given that Venturi had to work with Johnson and Burgee's towers. Symbolically right, it was, nevertheless, politically impossible, as well as aesthetically difficult for his client, George Klein. The alien character of the Johnson/Burgee office towers begat an all-out open battle for the soul of the place over the issue of aesthetics, as detailed in chapter 6.

To the continual frustration of the city and state's development officials, a tangle of implementation problems plagued the first 42DP plan. The troubles amounted to a recitation on the political risks of large-scale public development and the conflicting demands of managing such a high-profile project. Programmatically, the ambitions of the plan overreached its feasibility, and clashing internal agendas exacerbated its vulnerability to crippling litigious opposition, as discussed in chapter 7. While opposition was to be expected, the unexpected play was the change in policy direction, and more notably, the way it came about—through the actions of the civics, a politically weak but influential elite voice of opposition, who skillfully deployed the symbolic images of Times Square to change the dialogue of redevelopment planning, the pivotal piece of the transformation described in chapter 8.

The new and third vision for an entertainment and tourist-oriented mecca that emerged in 1993 in the rescripted plan, *42nd Street Now!*, was still nothing more than a blueprint, but one as economically in sync with the changing real estate market in Times Square in the early 1990s as it was culturally in sync with its iconic legacy. Nostalgia-inspired, this plan made direct references to the street's historic past through visual images that sought to bring a contemporaneous flair to the street and an emphasis on popular forms of entertainment that would appeal to the middle class, especially families (figure P.4). Cast back in time to the dark days of the 1980s, such a program would have been an unlikely vision of economic success because the market for popular entertainment in cities simply was not there, as argued in chapter 9.

Until the street's negative activities had been shut down the perception of the place did not change; throughout the early 1990s, sex shops were still opening. And until investment perceptions began to change, there was little hope of attracting the large corporations that were producing and distributing entertainment for they are unlikely candidates to pioneer change in sleazy urban areas notorious for crime, pornography, and prostitution. Only the real estate recession of the early 1990s, which delivered irresistible building bargains, made buying into a marginal location a reasonable risk to take and an economically smart thing for corporations to do, for the long term, a turn of events analyzed in chapter 10. This opportunistic buying created the critical mass of investment activity needed to assure players like Disney that West 42nd Street could once again function as a place for family-oriented popular entertainment. Disney made the planning vision real: Its commitment signaled deliverance, as told in chapter 11. Disney's decision to come not just to a big-city downtown but to Times Square was rich in symbolism as well as irony—squeaky clean, family-oriented Disney on the infamous 42nd Street!

The public initiative transforming Times Square was one of several big public projects that, over the past two decades, heightened the stakes of big development in New York and raised serious questions of policy—

P.4
Middle-class appeal: popular entertainment on the new 42nd Street. (Gary Hack)

about planning strategy and democratic accountability. *Times Square Roulette* examines these policy issues using the 42DP as an illustrative case. Although the long-term spillovers of the project are still unfolding, the physical and cultural redevelopment of the street represents a public-sector success story. That success did not come without substantial public risk taking. As argued in chapter 12, risk taking demands camouflage because cities are not supposed to gamble with taxpayer's dollars; they are reluctant risk takers. Providing political protection from the short-term winds of change, the mechanisms of camouflage—off-budget financing and quasi-autonomous single-purpose agencies—have proven to be remarkably resistant to reform, notwithstanding the policy need for procedural safe-guards and greater accountability. Suggestions for reform are not hard to come by. Rather the problem stems from the fact that there is no con-stituency for reform. For politicians, the bet in public development is all about achieving visible results within a time frame that lets the public to forget about the costs of achieving the benefits, as argued in chapter 13.

The new Times Square is not without its critics. Ambivalence exists amid the cheers. Assertions of Disneyfication and complaints of cultural dumbing down reveal the critics' class and cultural biases. A type of nostalgic angst wafts through other critiques, as explained in chapter 14. What the arguments of the cultural criticisms and romanticized nostalgia deny is that the new 42nd Street reflects changing middle-class consumer tastes, a desire for more "going out," and a new perception of cities as safer places to go for that entertainment (figure P.5). Moreover, both miss one of the most salient messages of renewal: the revisionist record of public success in the post-Moses landscape of development politics.

P.5
Tourist-friendly place: bronze sculptures by Tom Otterness in the Hilton Times Square Hotel. (Gary Hack)

A large number of people became involved with the transformation of Times Square as public officials, developers, consultants, civic players, critics, commentators, and community activists—all of whom when asked graciously shared their experiences and opinions with me, both on and off the record. Their strong personal as well as professional perspectives on events added intensity and color to the narrative. I am deeply grateful to these many players and to my colleagues who gave generously of their time in helping me with this book, but I want to single out several for their efforts. The first round of appreciation goes to Sally Goodgold who as president of the City Club of New York secured early funding from the J. M. Kaplan Fund to support the policy piece of this project. Support for the second phase of work came from my own institution, Columbia University Graduate School of Business. I am especially grateful to Carl Weisbrod and Rebecca Robertson, both of whom spent innumerable hours with me over the course of many years so that I might understand as much of the inside story as possible without ever asking how I viewed or would record these events in which they figured prominently. Cora Cahan, Craig Hatkoff, Con Howe, Tibor Kalman, and Jay Walder offered special insights into critical episodes of the story without which this book would be less connected to the larger tangents of development politics, design, and planning policy.

No book such as this would have been possible without access to primary documents and supporting data; Deborah Allee; Geoffrey Baker of the Department of City Planning; Wendy Cohn, formerly of the office of Manhattan Borough President Ruth Messinger; Louis D'Avanzo, Jason Spicer, and Lee Winter of Cushman & Wakefield; Donald Elliott; Martin Gold; Bruce Nelligan; Frederic Papert; Gary Rosenberg; Robin Stout of the Empire State Development Corporation; Emanuel Tobier; and the Municipal Art Society, among others, generously supplied research materials. Madelyn Kent of the Seymour B. Durst Old York Library of the Graduate School of the City of New York guided me through a treasure trove of New York memorabilia and graciously assisted with photographic images for the book. The otherwise tedious process of securing permissions became a personal pleasure as photographers, artists, and illustrators generously opened up their files to search for images of the past and extended professional courtesies. I am grateful to all, but especially Enrico Ferorelli, Arnoldo Franchioni, Richard Haas, Maggi Hopp, and Charles M. Weiss, who offered telling vignettes about capturing images of Times Square. John Vickers and Paul Diamond of Tishman Realty & Construction guided me and my students through several field trips of construction sites on the street, as did William Rudin of the Rudin Organization. Peter Beck, Vanessa Brakhan, Christine Bubrick, Alicia Glen, Craig Harte, Scott Lotikis, Rachel Miller, Amy Segal, Wendy Shafran, Sarah Stonehart, Phyllis Toeh Su-Yin, Mitchell Yentis, and Anthony Yoseloff offered valuable research assistance as graduate students at Columbia; Morgan Fleming painstakingly transformed the project's episodes into readable maps. Several colleagues reviewed earlier versions of the manuscript or individual chapters; Eugenie Birch, Barbara Chu, Martin Gold, Gary Hack, Craig Hatkoff, and three anonymous referees raised critical questions and offered substantive suggestions that led me to clarify particular facts and refine some of the trickier issues of interpretation. Their efforts notwithstanding, I am responsible for any remaining errors.

At MIT Press I had the good fortune of working with a team of talented and dedicated professionals, a couple of whom made commitments beyond their normal responsibilities to work on this manuscript because of their strong interest in the topic. To Jane Macdonald, who expertly managed the process, Michael Sims, who skillfully edited the manuscript with the extra care and knowledge of a theater enthusiast, and Yasuyo Iguchi who envisioned the imagery and designed the layout for the book with sophistication, my lasting appreciation for enhancing every aspect of the final publication and making the production process a memorable experience.

Some insights about one's methods of inquiry come slowly. It was years before I realized that it was my late father who had first taught me how to persistently pursue a research trail and search for revealing details of importance. As a life-long book collector and avocational scholar of John Steinbeck, he believed passionately in the importance of ephemera and its role in reading context. By example, he passed that to me, as well as to numerous doctoral researchers of Steinbeck, along with his enthusiasm for the quest.

The time it took to complete this book exceeded my expectations twice over. I am deeply indebted to the support of family and friends who listened seemingly without end to my work stories and boosted my spirits when I realized it would take "one more year" to finish. Always, the burden of deferred time together fell on Gary Hack, with whom I share life and a love of cities. The unique combination of his love, professional perspective, and critical intelligence was essential to the task.

PART I

PLANNING: CREATING AGENTS OF CHANGE

CHAPTER 1

Staging a Transformation

The children squealed with delight. The parents endured hours of waiting and aching shoulders, many thrilled by the spectacle and sounding suspiciously like the real parade enthusiasts. Motorists in Manhattan maneuvered around the closed streets and coped with parking bans in midtown on that "gridlock-alert day." The thousands of businesses along the 1.8-mile route turned off their lights, as requested, as the parade passed so the 30 floats, with their 566,000 lights, would shine more brightly. Peep Land, a 25-cent peep show on that part of the street not yet recast into corporate form, turned off its "Live Girls" neon sign. One hundred and thirty city lights along the route went dark at second-by-second choreographed magic moments. City crews laid new asphalt on the famous (and infamous) one-block stretch of West 42nd Street and filled potholes along the parade route. They painted the street in front of the newly refurbished New Amsterdam Theater gold with the lightning-bolt logo of the *Hercules* animated feature, put up 300 sound towers along the route to trumpet Disney songs as floats went by, and erected nearly eight miles of police barricades, and set out 350 litter baskets. Nearly 2,000 police officers lined the route for crowd control and crime prevention. These were but the most visible preparations from among the welter of details executed by a cast of thousands during three months of planning by city officials and corporate executives from the Walt Disney Company on that summer evening of June 14, 1997, for the Hercules Electrical Parade (figure 1.1).

Parades are nothing new in New York; more than 650 are staged in any given year. They represent a form of self-affirmation for the hundreds of ethnic groups that have continuously brought energy, hope, and pride into the city's economic and social life. If not ethnicity, New York's parades annually celebrate history or holiday or home-town major-league sports triumphs, and, on occasion, national events deemed to hold special importance for its citizens. For parades, the city usually closes streets, assigns extra police officers to line the route and sanitation workers to

1.1
Celebrating the transformation as a civic event: The Hercules Electric Parade, June 14, 1997. (Frances M. Roberts)

restore the streets to their prior state of normalcy. Motorists prepare for gridlock headaches—which are not as bad as the pain of getting ticketed for "blocking the box," those zebralike markings on many of midtown's heavily trafficked intersections designed to minimize actual gridlock. And since the Hercules parade, like others, was as much a political event as a celebration, at least one group, union members on strike against Disney-owned ABC, used the event as a stage to protest, while some businesses would not put Disney's commercial interests above their own—advertisers who wanted their billboards in the landscape of snapshots taken home and were, therefore, unwilling to turn off their lights.

Still, the Hercules parade was unprecedented, in a way. Lavish celebrations had long been a part of New York's eighteenth-century history and a vital part of life of the city in the nineteenth century. Then, too, they were staged performances to mark a political event, honor outstanding citizens or distinguished visitors, or signal completion of great projects; then, too, they were designed to illustrate a theme or reinforce a point of view.[1] This parade appeared to strike a different chord. "This is the first one with no historic constituency in the city," said the chairman of the Fifth Avenue Business Improvement District.[2] It was not, though, Disney's first hyped commercial event in New York: Two years earlier, amid a storm of controversy, Mayor Rudolph W. Giuliani allowed the media giant to stage its premier of *Pocahontas* in the city's most coveted public place, Central Park. As a commercial event, Disney's Hercules Parade may have seemed akin promotionally to the Macy's Thanksgiving Day Parade without, however, the transcendent nature associated with a national holiday; its "civic" purpose was purely political. Moreover, Disney's brand of corporate commercialization fueled strong fears of what was called Disneyfication, especially among those who worried about the disappearance of the city's legendary "ethnic moxie" and feared that it might lose as well its special status as a cultural outsider to the American experience—that New York might not be New York anymore.

Ostensibly a premier-night celebration to promote its newest animated movie, the parade played to many levels of interpretation. On one level, it was, as a *New York Times* reporter put it, the "ultimate corporate-coming-out bash" for a company seeking to establish a new market niche in the nation's largest city,[3] the media capital of the world. On another level, it was a civic celebration, with Mayor Giuliani lauding the new Times Square as a sign of the "rebirth of the city."[4] To open the event, Disney CEO Michael Eisner presented "hero awards" to Olympic gold medalists in a red-carpeted outdoor ceremony on West 42nd Street, though the subtext of the event was to give his company a hero award for igniting the street's redevelopment. In both deed and word, the event was a joint civic-corporate rite of passage baptizing the transformation of West 42nd Street from a once-deviant zone of extreme permissiveness and rampant pornography into a revitalized zone of family entertainment.

Because it was Disney, the event was national news deemed worthy of a worldwide live broadcast and attended by reporters from as far away as Japan. Because it was in a place known internationally for decades as a sleazy crime-ridden sexual playground, the event marked a transformation as symbolically important as it was physically profound: The middle class had reclaimed the city's iconic location, its symbolic soul. No more a matter of clever marketing, the redevelopment of West 42nd Street had entered the realm of the real. Although the idea for the celebration parade came from the media giant, what better way for the mayor to celebrate the city's achievement, for which he was taking full credit, in turning around this long-festering civic embarrassment? What more appropriate way to inaugurate a new image? "You can't buy this type of advertising," boasted Mayor Giuliani. "This says to people all over the world, 'Come to New York. It's a friendly place.'"[5] The dramatic turnaround in perception hit with a force like Hercules' lightening bolt itself.

Throughout the 1970s New York had been linked synonymously with every big urban problem of the times. Though hardly the only big city where poverty, crime, racial tension, economic distress, and social pessimism defined the civic profile, New York served as a metaphor for all of the nation's intractable urban ills. Cities were viewed as ungovernable, out of control—socially, politically, and fiscally—and New York's problems loomed menacingly as the most threatening. Its house was in disarray, the 1975 fiscal crisis and brush with bankruptcy having cost Mayor Abraham D. Beame political control in a forfeiture that gave the bankers who held the city's bonds, and then the state-created Municipal Assistance Corporation, decision-making powers over the life of the city. The budget

1.2
The sign of city malaise: subway graffiti. (© Lou Stoumen Trust, courtesy of the Barry Singer Gallery, Petaluma, Calif.)

was slashed. Services were cut back. Capital expenditures continued to be deferred. Transit service deteriorated further, accompanied by a decline in ridership that simultaneously signaled the city's weakening economy. Graffiti materialized everywhere, overnight (figure 1.2). The middle-class flight to suburbs, an established post–World War II trend, accelerated; corporate executives could not flee fast enough to Connecticut and New Jersey, where they reestablished headquarter operations. "When can a city be said to be dying?" columnist Herb Caen asked in 1976. "For one thing, when its past far outshines its present and overwhelms the future, and New York is at that point. The giants have gone, along with the good days and easy nights."[6] Doom and gloom prevailed. Nothing captured the mood of the times better than the oft-cited October 30, 1975, banner headline on the front page of the *New York Daily News*: "FORD TO CITY: DROP DEAD." The message carried meaning beyond New York. The nation's largest city might be on the verge of bankruptcy because of a larger-than-life fiscal crisis, but its survival held no economic or political consequences to the nation. Cities had ceased to be a national issue. They were expendable. They were being "written off" as obsolete anachronisms of an earlier age before the technological advances of the automobile and new forms of communications turned the distinctly urban advantages of density, agglomeration, and specialization into competitive disadvantages.

If New York served a metaphor for the nation's urban ills, the most visual consequences of that disease found concentrated social expression in Times Square. Decline was no stranger to West 42nd Street; it had started in the 1920s and in later decades mirrored the decline of public forms of amusement and the withdrawal of the middle class from city life. The particular permissive sociological context of the 1970s, however, drew to the street, like moths to street lights, a motley cross-section of people— social misfits, sexual deviants, plain down-and-outers, alcoholics, druggies, teenage runaways, panhandlers, hustlers of all types, pimps, and buyers of sex, along with the unwary and unprotected, as well as average lower- and middle-class moviegoers. By middle-class standards, it was an intense scene of social depravity: sin in depth. "Along Forty-second, you don't have to exercise the imagination," wrote a reporter for the sex magazine *Rouge* in 1962, "you walk and see it all."[7]

The tawdry concentration of social ills on West 42nd Street was both a symptom and a cause of Times Square's decline as a place of public play. In 1971, the editors of the *Times*, which had an obvious interest in its namesake neighborhood, called Times Square "a midtown perversion of 'Fun City'"; in 1972, "a boulevard of filth instead of a Great White Way"; in 1974, "a textbook of social pathology"; in 1975, "sick, criminal, aberrant and offensive to even the most tolerant sensitivity"; in 1976, "a sordid and dangerous place where legitimate businesses are hardly able to survive."[8] At the start of 1977—after an estimated tally of those in Times Square for New Year's Eve revealed that the annual civic rite drew a crowd in excess of 50,000, compared with an estimated one million 25 years earlier—they wrote: "So when the crowds fail to assemble in Times Square we worry about the future of cities whose people have lost the habit of meeting (except perhaps in protest), or the sense of the importance of meeting."[9] The civic script of Times Square was not merely a morality play; First-Amendment rights hold too much significance in New York for that to be the case. Rather, because Times Square held symbolic significance as the heart of the city, city life itself was at risk. The pathology of the street was not hard to diagnose: In terms of policy, the problem was that the city's past cleanup efforts had failed to amount to anything more than an "exercise in redundant futility."[10]

Advance the clock twenty years to the time of the Hercules Parade. Signs of resurgence in Times Square are strikingly evident throughout the 20-plus-block district. By millennium New Years Eve 2000, which drew a crowd of revelers estimated at a dubious two million, the transformation was visible, surprising, and worth understanding, regardless of whether one looked favorably upon the reshaped landscape or considered it in terms of nostalgic loss. The new Times Square was now home to the most unlikely tenants: Morgan Stanley, a white-collar, blue-chip investment banking firm, and Condé Nast, a trendy, upscale publishing giant; soon they would welcome Reuters American Holdings, Inc., a conservative U.K. communications company, and Ernst & Young, Inc., a giant tax-and-audit firm. International media giants Bertelsmann, A.G. and Viacom headquartered there as well. In short, West 42nd Street was morphing into a ribbon of popular-entertainment venues capitalized by the biggest corporate names in businesses: Disney, Warner Brothers, Sony, AMC, Madame Tussaud's, SFX Entertainment. MTV Networks and ABC's "Good Morning America" were broadcasting live a few blocks away from sidewalk-fronting television studios. The sidewalks commonly overflowed to the point of pedestrian gridlock—investment bankers, lawyers, accountants, and media types angling to get somewhere in a hurry, mixed together with camera-totting tourists and teenage tourist-truants looking about and lolling around more casually. Real estate values had skyrocketed. Economic pressures had ignited changes in land use on seedy Eighth Avenue and in the aged Garment District. The street that *Rolling Stone* magazine in 1981 called the "sleaziest block in America" was now a family-entertainment venue. The "magical" transformation of West 42nd Street had even become a model for other cities. City and state officials' hopes at the start of the 42nd Street Development Project (42DP) in 1980 were high, but these results were improbable. It was time to revise one's mental map of Times Square (figures 1.3–1.6, plates 5–8).

How did this all happen? How is it that a high-profile development project well on its way to being labeled a "great planning disaster" turned into an internationally recognized symbol of urban redemption? How did the icon of sleaze and pornography transmute back into the icon of popular entertainment and glitzy commercialism? What is it about the character of the transformation of place that derivatively wiped away New York's image as a "big, bad city" and, in the process, put a shine on city life in general?

1.3
The new Times Square as a home
for high-rise media headquarters.
(Gary Hack)

1.4
The Lyric Theater, view of West
43rd Street entrance, 1903.
(Museum of the City of New
York Theater Collection)

1.5
The Lyric Theater recast as part
of the Ford Center for the
Performing Arts, 2001. (Gary
Hack)

1.6
Signs of the new Times Square.
(Gary Hack)

Five myths have had a commanding influence upon the perception of the transformation story: It happened overnight; Disney the "handsome prince" waved a magic wand and awakened West 42nd Street; Mayor Giuliani deserves the credit—only a bold mayor could make it happen; it took only minimal public investment—$75 million to stimulate $2.5 billion of private investment; the market could have done it on its own without the intervention of the public sector. West 42nd has always been a place marked by the tremendous power of mythology. Indeed, as a historic force, myth kept Times Square alive, for decades. How West 42nd Street and Times Square got to where they are today cannot be understood without undoing these misconceptions. Why are they wrong?

For starters, the transformation was 20 years in the making. It was the result of an arduous process that involved intense public controversy, continuous litigation, and interminable delay. Jointly managed by city and state officials and their redevelopment specialists, the process was fraught with political tensions, especially in the mid-1990s when success, finally, was close at hand. Though the physical landscape appeared to change in quick time-lapse sequence, the basis for that change came about slowly, and then somewhat fortuitously. The entertainment focus was almost accidental. The legacy of West 42nd Street should have precluded any other programmatic mandate, but this vision was a stepchild of the first redevelopment plan. The troubled execution of that plan provided a serendipitous opportunity for revision, a rare second chance in charting the course of public development, which was masterfully choreographed by Rebecca Robertson, president of the 42nd Street Development Project, Inc. Mass-market entertainment on West 42nd Street could not have happened in the 1980s. Neither consumers nor the city's planners were ready for it. The market was not there. In the mid-1990s, the timing was right for the new vision known as *42nd Street Now!* because it coincided with international corporate interest in cities as a mecca for mass-market entertainment and synergistic merchandising.

Second, Disney got to the party just in time to have the first dance. Its decision to renovate the legendary Art-Nouveau New Amsterdam Theater (figures 1.7, 1.8) created a strong momentum for the entertainment-focused plan by sparking a swift 180-degree shift in the perception of investment possibilities among private developers and brand-name corporations. It was the catalyst for other big-name commitments to West 42nd Street. Disney was not, however, the pioneer. That role belongs to the nonprofit entity entrusted with overseeing and protecting the street's historic theaters, The New 42nd Street, Inc., which, under the leadership of Cora Cahan, brought children's theater to the former street of porn in the refurbished New Victory Theater (plates 14, 15). Also, safety on West 42nd Street had been established by the early 1990s, after more than thirty years of effort and condemnation of two-thirds of the property on the block. Viacom, Bertelsmann, A.G., and The Gap, all had taken up

highly visible positions in Times Square before Disney's CEO stepped into
the ruined, rain-soaked New Amsterdam. The big Japanese brand names
had led the way back to Times Square years before that, in the 1970s, and
the domestic brand advertisers had followed suit by the early 1990s. Still,
clustered at its western end, the infamous block housed more than 20 sex-
related businesses—which meant Disney staked its prized reputation more
than its capital to venture onto West 42nd Street.

Third, while it did take a bold mayor to face the political risks of
pushing through such a large-scale public project, that mayor was Edward
I. Koch, whose ten years of continuous support was followed by four years
of support from Mayor David N. Dinkins. As the next elected to govern
the city, Mayor Giuliani has taken the credit for making the transformation
happen because the announcement of the Disney deal and the ribbon-
cutting opportunities materialized at the start of his administration (figure
1.9). "It was Giuliani and Pataki who were there when it opened," said
David L. Malmuth who was general manager of Disney's development

1.8
The legendary New Amsterdam
Theater nine decades later,
renovated, 1997. (Whitney Cox
Photographer)

company at the time, "but without the support of Dinkins and [Governor
Mario] Cuomo, it wouldn't have happened"[11] (figure 1.10). Times Square
has become the emblem of Giuliani's safe, clean, family-friendly New York
and his quality-of-life campaign helped make the city a more hospitable
place for corporate habitation, but he inherited the political benefits of the
42DP's rapidly accelerating momentum. The "'misappropriated saga' was a
familiar story in Rudy Giuliani's life," wrote veteran *Village Voice* reporter
Wayne Barrett in his biography *Rudy!* In the book's opening pages Barrett
covers each aspect of Giuliani's grab for credit, concluding that "Instead of
Times Square savior, he was its beneficiary, the almost accidental hero to
the glory of a booming new street, propelled by two mayors he maligned
and a governor who shared the Disney catalyst with him."[12]

More important to the transformation's story line, though, it was
an unusual continuity of political support and leadership—across three
mayoral administrations and two governorships—that defined the difference between success and failure of the 42DP. Major public-development

projects happen because of the people involved, their skills, and the strength of their commitments to the task, over time.

The myth that it took minimal public investment is to the most misleading, but this myth holds a political pedigree rooted in the time-tested tradition of off-budget financing. Asserting that the costs "will be," "are," or "were" minimal allows mayors to finesse the true economic cost of a city's incentive package and to camouflage the extent of the public sector's risk-taking. The true cost picture remains unknown as long as the only costs tallied are the out-of-pocket costs—without the off-budget tax abatements and rent credits given to developers and corporations and the dollars contributed by other agents of the public sector whose budget decisions take place beyond the domain of the city council. To finance its bold initiative, New York constructed an ingenious and complex financial arrangement through which city officials "privatized" the public costs of land acquisition for the 13-acre project area, as well as other public costs of development, shifting the financial risk of rising condemnation costs to private developers—ultimately, the Prudential Insurance Company of America, which would be repaid for its "loan advances" through rent credits on the underlying lease payments for its development sites. The political mandate of the times demanded that the city make no out-of-pocket expenditures, take no financial risk. The city's strategy for funding condemnation nevertheless created unique risks for both public and private players in the project, even as it kept the true economic costs off the budget.

Ideology rules the last myth, that the market could have effectuated the transformation without public intervention. Years of aggressive law enforcement and policing had failed to change the deviant social behavior of West 42nd Street or dent its heavy crime statistics, essential preconditions for attracting private developers and the institutional lenders who were needed to finance long-term investment. (At the start of the 42DP, no new construction had taken place on West 42nd Street for more than 40 years; by the end, private investment will exceed $4 billion.) Profits from pornography made vested economic interests slow to relinquish their prime real estate in midtown Manhattan, which was after all was an ideal location for businesses whose main customers were white, middle-aged, middle-class men. Land assembly loomed as a formidable obstacle. Most significantly, the public agenda was ambitious—beyond the capacity of what passive zoning incentives, the city's traditional means of influencing development patterns, could deliver.

The policy-driven transformation of West 42nd Street became a dual test of political power and market imperatives. Left solely to its own dynamic, the market could not have effectuated physical and social change on such a large scale within a time frame deemed acceptable by most mayors, especially New York's Ed Koch. The transformation had to be invented, and even the first invention failed before the planners moved away from their initial over-ambitious program for commercial development—ever unpopular and tortured for ten years. Lawsuits, long delays, and market reversals defined the 42DP's every key episode. Yet the high-profile public controversies significantly shaped the rescripting process and gave the new vision for West 42nd Street much of its acclaimed character. From a policy perspective, the rescripted plan marked an unusual inversion of intended influence: The broader renewal of Times Square was supposed to spark from the catalytic 42DP; instead, it led the way to the new 42nd Street. To understand the transformation of Times Square, one has to understand the role of the public sector—as developer—in effectuating that change. What one sees in Times Square is the result of successful public intervention, testimony that runs counter to the prevailing notion that cities do not have the capacity to effect large-scale change.

BEYOND CONTROL

The common perception of Times Square among New York's mayors and governors and the majority of their middle-class constituency was aptly summed up years later by the urbanist Marshall Berman: "a human sinkhole, a civic disgrace, a place where no decent person would willing go, and where the only helpful thing would be to blow it all away,"[13] a place, in other words, that demanded immediate attention. Still, an exotic seediness kept the "pilgrims coming to Times Square," as one *Times* header put it. Pleasure-seekers and tourists came to ogle, see the bright lights of Times Square, say they'd been there. Titillation. The allure of danger and desire for a new experience involving some degree of risk-taking or thrill-seeking also attracted many to the "night frontier." This was "a place where the laws of conventional society are suspended, people come to seek adventure, to take risks in dealing in the fast life . . . to con and to be conned," wrote sociologists William Kornblum and Vernon Boggs.[14]

It was also a place definitively marked: Day or night, it was "male turf," a world of sex shops, action movies, and retail stores that catered to primarily male tastes (figure 1.11). The street's sexist and pornographic visual imagery provided a prime field site for the 1970s activist group Women Against Pornography, which ran twice-weekly bus tours of West 42nd Street. For New Jersey commuters or New York subway riders with jobs in midtown Manhattan, however, West 42nd Street was simply the most efficient route to work, a place to pass through, quickly. With support provided by the Ford Foundation, Kornblum and Boggs studied the area intensively in the late 1970s as part of major project undertaken by the Graduate School and University Center of the City University of New York (CUNY). They considered the street's heavy pedestrian traffic one of "unparalleled complexity," even to those familiar with the "wonderful layering and stacking of Manhattan neighborhoods."[15] Yet its social behavior, so vividly portrayed in John Schlesinger's Academy-Award-winning film *Midnight Cowboy* (1969), a then-shocking tale of the dark side of the street's squalid subculture, not only offended middle-class sensibilities but offered up a powerful and sad indictment of urban depravity.

The sociological context of the place was not without its special twist. The audience for West 42nd Street's existing businesses was not visi-

1.11
West 42nd Street as male turf.
(© Lou Stoumen Trust, courtesy
of the Barry Singer Gallery,
Petaluma, Calif.)

bly deviant, in no small part because what Kornblum and Boggs found
was that the deviants in the area were not likely to be paying customers
of the XXX-rated entertainment establishments. Rather, the area drew
together a "loosely connected society of people 'in the life,' " a subterranean economy with its own status-ranking system, specialized language,
and value system. Joining the "regulars" on a daily basis were scores of
transient youth, runaways, and adults—hustlers, chickens and chicken
hawks, johns, and simps (small-time pimps). Regular "places" for street
behaviors and illicit markets made the block a reliable economic market
for every possible human need. Because of that, it was a street most New
Yorkers, especially women, wanted to avoid.

In their comprehensive and insightful report of the "Bright Light
Zone," Kornblum and his colleague Boggs explained the place-specific
dynamic of these markets: They depended upon "the actions of buyers
who seek loose joints and other drugs along the north side of 42nd Street
because they recognize this block as a reliable market; or on the behavior
of tricks who are familiar with the Eighth Avenue prostitute's stroll; or on
the actions of the patrolmen who attempt to disperse the hustlers and
street loiters."[16] It was perfectly sited for crime, as one young entrepreneur
explained:[17]

If you city planners set out to make a place for dope peddlers, you couldn't plan anything as good as Times Square. I get off the bus from Detroit without a penny in my pocket. I walk up to the blood bank on Forty-second Street, where I sell a pint of my blood, take the money, and go just four doors away where I can buy me a knife. I use the money left over to go into one of them all-night movies, where I slit open the back pocket of the first sleeping drunk I see. I take his money down to the street, buy myself an ounce of smoke, find myself a doorway, and begin selling. I've been in town less than an hour and I'm already in business.

The underclass structure of the street became, in the eyes of many sociologists, the police, and city officials, the most problematic feature of the area. Heavy police resources were being devoted to the district. Signaling a new approach to the cleanup effort, Mayor Abraham D. Beame set up a special task force, the Mayor's Office of Midtown Enforcement (OME), in 1976. The policy prescription was code enforcement based on a real estate strategy, and the goal of the OME was to return Times Square real estate to "good commercial uses." Designed to enforce existing laws against obscenity with the use of heavy fines and to shut down commercial establishments that did not conform with city fire, health and building codes, and zoning-law amendments, the OME—described with style as a "twenty-member legal swat team" and a "grey-flannel vice squad"[18]—under the direction of Carl B. Weisbrod from 1978 to 1984 succeeded in virtually banning massage parlors—so-called "adult physical cultural establishments"—pinball arcades, topless bars, and peep shows, and it worked diligently to improve street conditions on the Deuce—argot for the infamous block of West 42nd Street between Seventh and Eighth Avenues. It was never, however, successful in eliminating street prostitution. By law, the city could deal with prostitution only on a legal, not a moral, basis, and since street prostitution was not directly connected to the real estate-based strategies of the OME, it was not susceptible to standard legal harassments.[19] Two years later, in 1978, to increase police presence on the street the city set up the Operations Crossroads Police Substation at 42nd Street and Broadway.

The city's stepped-up police activities brought approximately 100 additional police personnel to the Times Square area. Notwithstanding these high-profile initiatives, law-enforcement efforts to control street behaviors were perceived by the police and others to be of limited efficacy because constitutional safeguards and judicial practices constrained police efforts to control street traffic in drugs, remove alcoholics and vagrants, and prevent loitering in the area. On a practical level, even holding down street peddling and other nuisances to a minimum seemed daunting at the peak hours of pedestrian traffic on the street when the ordinary demands on police for surveillance and assistance to citizens was so great. And as

recent indictments and guilty pleas have shown, some police were beneficiaries of services in the neighborhood, in uniform and while on patrol—
"Police Used Brothel So Often, Madam Got Worried" the *Times*
headlined—while others were trying to root them out.

Loitering presented the police with a special problem—the
"indiscernible mix of those engaged in, or about to engage in, illegal
activities and those the *Draft Environmental Impact Statement* (*DEIS*)
described as just 'hanging around' to experience the excitement of 42nd
Street."[20] The street population of the Deuce was an "outdoor circus of
people" made up of several groups: the regulars "in the life" at their hang-
outs, on their "strolls," or on their "hustles"; the winos, vagrants, derelicts,
and other street people ambling about or lying in doorways in one state or
another; the pedestrians on their way somewhere; movie goers; and the
tourists, joined by street-preaching revivalists, peddlers, and errant window
shoppers. As the *DEIS* went on to explain:[21]

> There are, after all, no laws in our society which fore-
> close standing on public sidewalks to watch those pass-
> ing by, but on the contrary, the ability to assemble freely
> is constitutionally-protected. The police cannot arrest
> people simply because they are standing around—and
> this is a good deal of what takes place on 42nd Street.
> Yet it is also in [this] context . . . that the illegal activities
> function and are able to function. The crowds provide
> the market and the screen for the hustlers and pushers—
> the market in the sense of potential customers and the
> screen in the sense that those hanging around are often
> indistinguishable from criminals.

Beyond creating difficulty for law enforcement, this confusion, sociologists
argued, had a psychological impact on the public, which came to bias the
policy prescription for West 42nd Street.[22]

In confronting the problems of Times Square, the mayor and the
professionals he selected to lead law enforcement in midtown west were
dealing with an intractable situation where the prescriptive solution had to
change public perception as well as reality. The conclusion from years of
heavy-duty but essentially ineffectual law enforcement—occasionally
things could be closed down because of the carelessness or stupidity of an
operator—was that "nothing could be changed in Times Square unless
42nd Street changed." It was an issue of "image and reality. Most visible
was the sex business, but that was only one element of a larger gestalt:
crime. Sex was the springboard to bigger issues of crime, not only on
42nd Street but beyond, into Times Square. You had to deal with 42nd
Street in the whole if you were ever to address the whole Times
Square."[23]

In the late 1970s, when city officials and urban planners considered ambitious plans to renew and rehabilitate the Deuce, the public's

perception of the bright-light zone was clear and unambiguous. A large segment of the New York metropolitan population saw the block as dangerous and morally repulsive, a place with "safety hazards that have nothing to do with OSHA [Occupational Safety and Hazards Act]," said one respondent to the CUNY survey.[24] Social conditions had deteriorated beyond acceptable standards. Crime on the street seemed increasingly random and violent. Ordinary people knew of the street violence or had witnessed it; the sense of danger, of menace, was real.

Race and class also played an important part in how the middle class perceived the area. Although whites dominated the block at all times of the day, except after midnight, the "street people" were predominately black and Hispanic, which, the two CUNY sociologists noted, added considerably to the insecurity and fear of the white middle class:[25]

> For them the loiterers on the street seemed alien, unre-
> strained by conventional social codes, and filled with a
> pent-up rage which could explode at any moment....
> Most certainly it [racism] enhanced racial stereotypes as
> innocent Blacks and Hispanics on 42nd Street were
> given wide berth by wary whites.... The belief that
> 42nd Street's decline was a result only of social change
> and hence represented a microcosm of the city's fall
> from grace was widespread.

That the racial element affected the public's perception of Times Square was hardly unique to the place or the city. As urban historian Kenneth T. Jackson wrote, "After World War II, the racial and economic polarization of large American metropolitan areas became so pronounced that downtown areas lost their commercial hold on the middle class. Cities became identified with fear and danger rather than glamour and pleasure."[26] This is what Koch sought to reverse with a transformation.

The Gamble

The transformation of Times Square poses questions of planning and policy broader in import than the domain of New York. Is it possible for cities to reshape what the market is likely to deliver in an area? What set of policy tools is best suited to large-scale development ambitions? Is the ambition of large-scale development a plausible political objective in the post–federal urban-renewal policy environment, especially when aggressive actions like condemnation are deemed a necessary part of the strategy? In New York, for example, where city officials and redevelopment specialists operate under the ever-present shadow of Robert Moses, New York's legendary master builder, and the haunting legacy of failure of the Westway highway project, large-scale ambitions have been handicapped from the start. "Public Projects: Are They Viable in the City Anymore?," asked seasoned *Times* reporter Martin Gottlieb in 1985. "Can a city that often has trouble running its subways smoothly or keeping its streets clean perform important public services adequately? Can a city whose sense of identity is enhanced by such hallmark public projects as the Brooklyn Bridge, Central Park and the Gothic-style campus of City College still build functionally, elegantly and with civic purpose?"[27] The presumed answer was no. Confidence in government performance in New York and elsewhere had been falling for years and had not yet hit its nadir.

As a class, large-scale public projects have been considered an endangered species for a number of compelling reasons. They often demand the use of condemnation powers, yet since the passing of the federal urban-renewal program—"synonymous in the popular mind with bulldozers and heartless displacement of the poor and the powerless"[28]— its characteristic heavy-handed tactic of wholesale clearance has been a political taboo. "Its enduring lessons were negative," wrote urban historian Jon C. Teaford. "It taught America what not to do in the future."[29] Large-scale projects are also often prohibitively expensive without federal subsidy. And they are guaranteed targets of intense and continuous litigation, by which opponents can kill a project without ever winning a lawsuit. The scale of their ambitions typically aims to wipe away the investment negatives of an urban environment—age, dilapidation, disorder, social problems—yet context and the need to conform with the urban physical context had become the new orthodoxy of postmodern architecture, that buildings should fit into, not clash with, the existing environment. Again, the federal urban-renewal benchmark is relevant. "For most urban renewal planners," said Teaford, "there was no reason to conform to the urban context. That context was the very thing they were trying to destroy."[30] Because they take so long to execute, large-scale public projects typically suffer what one city official called the "disease of bureaucracy," getting passed around from staff person to staff person "with none of them having more than limited concern for its overall well-being" and no institutional knowledge to inform their efforts.[31] In short, embarking on large-scale long-term complicated development projects is a gamble—potential political suicide for mayors or governors with a "normal" time horizon for tenure in office. Such ambition does not fit with the conventional notion that "mayors, especially, want quick results and viable successes."[32]

In New York and elsewhere across the nation, problems of project implementation during the 1960s and 1970s bequeathed a general lack of faith in the capacity of government to influence change, which led many a mayor to focus on small-scale discrete projects like downtown shopping malls.[33] The success of the 42DP upset all the reasonably pessimistic explanations for why the pursuit of large-scale development was an improbable goal for a city's highest elected official at the same time that it confirmed the high selectivity of the effort. Cities are continually shaped by large-scale gestures, in no small part because politicians continue to pursue ambitions of growth, progress, and economic development through physical change. Also, business interests who often seek large-scale solutions are a powerful constituency. In other words, despite their risks, large-scale projects have remained politically alluring (plate 2).

The desire to control development directly and thus shape the broad canvas of city growth was central to the public-development strategy as executed in big cities throughout the nation. To do so, cities typically needed to act ahead of market demand, which they did by absorbing the front-end risks of market-shaping development; an institutional mechanism, deal making, which provided for expanded governmental influence over the development process; and a means of fiscal independence from the annual budget appropriations process to empower long-term decision making over development, which in practical terms meant a politically viable plan for self-sufficient project financing and revenue generation from privately owned commercial uses on the site. In an era when most big cities operated with dwindling sources of federal aid and constant fiscal pressures to maintain existing levels of municipal services, public spending for large-scale development projects also demanded a form of government intervention that could capture enough of the appreciation in land values to finance the needed up-front public investment, or else other means around this most essential precondition for action. Regulatory policies requiring subway improvements or public amenities could generate the public benefits—when developers initiated projects and, most successfully, in strong real estate markets. Yet the sums needed to redirect the pattern of development in ways envisioned by cities generally exceed the financial capability of any single-building development, even a large one.

From its beginning in 1980, New York's cleanup strategy for West 42nd Street grabbed center stage as a high-profile public initiative. Aggressively pushed forward by both the mayor and the governor, it reflected in both real and symbolic terms the city's agenda—and constant efforts—to rebuild itself, economically as well as physically, and stem the continuous flight of its middle class to the suburbs. By the end of the decade, the effort had reached a stalemate, bogged down by litigation and a real estate downturn. The question of whether it was possible to execute a project as large and with as many components as the 42DP—simultaneously—seemed to have been answered in the negative. By the mid-1990s, economic and social forces had recast the long-running pessimistic prognosis for the 42DP: Opportunity born of excessive office overbuilding coincident with a shift in tastes favorable to cities fused with a new entertainment-oriented vision for West 42nd Street and turned this second plan into reality. As the use activity on the street shifted dramatically from drug dealing, prostitution, and pornography to legitimate theater, family entertainment, tourism, and office employment, ironies of change defined the transformation—in symbolic as well as physical terms.

From a planning perspective, several big-picture issues are significant: How can the unique history of a place be capitalized upon to make distinct places? What are the associations that give identity to a place and bind people to its legacy, its memories, even in the midst of decay? To phrase it another way, to what extent can city planning rewrite a place's legacy? The answer is firmly embedded in the Times Square saga—not a lot and only at great political cost.

Three sets of economic interests were actively battling for this prized—and from a real estate perspective, underdeveloped—turf in the heart of Manhattan: the sex industry, which sought to retain its position of location centrality; the performing-arts industry, which sought to preserve its Broadway brand; and the real estate industry, which sought assistance in clearing the investment bottleneck that held in check westward expansion of the central business district. (The street's economic fundamentals had been strong enough by the 1920s to put in play real estate pressures that ultimately might have reshaped the area, if not for three unpredictable intervening events: Prohibition, the Great Depression, and World War II.) A cast of community groups and civic interests also held strong opinions of what a cleanup should amount to. Some interests wanted to clean out and clear out the "garbage"; others, to do something directly about the area's social problems; and still others, to reconstruct the "verve" and "raciness" of the legendary place.

The bricks-and-mortar strategy adopted by the city and state did not aim to deal directly with the social disorder and dysfunction that prevailed on West 42nd Street; rather, it would clear out the "bad" uses by substituting "good" uses. In deal-making terms, this meant granting most-favored status to development of four extraordinarily high-density office towers. In Times Square, such a singular use focus was untenable and, therefore, unsustainable, politically. Years of tortured execution finally gave way under the weight of a dramatic city-wide market collapse. The strong and clear lesson on programming from that experience is that planners cannot make plans, big or small, that explicitly or implicitly destroy what is special about a place, then hope to steamroll through their implementation as did Robert Moses. This, more than wholesale clearance per se, is the real lesson of four decades of experience with urban renewal.

When long-term large-scale projects get carried over one or more real estate cycles and multiple political administrations, what holds a project together? What keeps an often diverse and fragile coalition from fragmenting? Implementation is not static. It takes alliances, and these alliances often shift; at times, even die-hard opponents sign on to back the effort. How do public servants bridge the gap between big vision and slow progress? How do they maintain the momentum of a project when nothing is happening? How can they avoid (or finesse) failure that comes, not from a single, massive blow of a show of opposition, but from what Gerald D. Suttles describes as the slow destruction of the political and economic conditions that gave rise to the initiative?[34] How do public officials minimize political exposure when thinking big requires taking equally big risks? How can the public sector use public power to command resources not of its own to take unprecedented risk? What can private developers do that the public sector would otherwise have to take on? These are all tactical questions that critically shape the management of large-scale projects. How skillfully—or not—public officials managed the politics of the process would emerge as one of the most striking lessons of the 42DP experience. Visions depend upon people, and in executing a vision the planner may need to form the public interest, develop a consensus, and persuade people.[35] Specific individuals, as "leaders," can make things happen apart from market and political forces and institutional context, especially when opportunity presents itself.

Though the initial plan was conventional in its vision of urban renewal, the 42DP was an atypical redevelopment project. Not for its size, though it was the nation's largest urban project. Not for its cleanup focus, nor its programmatic content (corporate financial services, theater preservation, infrastructure improvement), for these were conventional elements of urban-redevelopment strategies. Rather, its status as an atypical project derived from the defining spatial centrality of West 42nd Street and Times Square—as a vital transportation node in the heart of midtown Manhattan, as the ever-pulsating entertainment center of the city, as a built-up district dense with First-Amendment protected uses, as the place of civic celebrations—and derivative of the past and present legacy, its role as the symbolic soul of the city. It has been an enduring icon of city life (figure 1.12).

The iconic value of the place represented an idealized holdover from the boogie-woogie, prepornography 1930s to 1950s (figures 1.13, 1.14), before the images so vividly captured in the movie *Midnight Cowboy* came to define the reality of the street in the 1960s and 1970s. The image, however, was out of sync with the reality of the place, and remained ahead

1.12
Postcard image of the Times Tower, 1904. (Collection of the author)

TIMES BUILDING,
NEW YORK

1.13
West 42nd Street as a historic
theater street, 1924. (B'Hend-
Kaufman Archives, Academy of
Motion Picture Arts and Sciences)

1.14
Broadway brand: west side of
Broadway between 47th and 48th
Streets, 1930s. (Milstein Division
of United States History, Local
History and Genealogy, The New
York Public Library, Astor, Lenox
and Tilden Foundations)

of the reality of change until the late 1990s. The degraded social environment placed the district outside the mainstream of market-driven economic development. Always seemingly prime real estate, the Deuce, also
known as "the strip," had long been a physical and psychological bottleneck constraining the westward expansion of midtown business activity.
New zoning incentives put in place at about the same time as the 42DP
altered the market dynamic of the area's quiescent commercial potential.
The range of social, civic, and economic interests challenged by the public
sector's proposed changes for West 42nd Street immediately triggered
every hot button of public controversy in America: free speech, property
taking through eminent domain, development density, tax subsidy, historic
preservation.

Throughout the twenty-year development period, symbolism was used by all of the drama's players to shape the debate and promote alternative visions of what the new 42nd Street should be. For the project's promoters, it served as a rationale for advancing a large-scale development strategy predicated on condemnation, a cleanup designed to return the street to its former legendary glory. Promising that the midblock historic theaters would be preserved, city officials used symbolism as political leverage to build a coalition of support among preservationists, culturally minded civic groups, and performing artists. Developers too, fearing a return to the days of porn, evoked symbolic as well as real images of the past as an argument against allowing movies on the street. The argument against demolition of the architecturally defaced former Times Tower rested solely on symbolism: It was revered not as architecture, but as an irreplaceable icon of the place, of New York. Civic groups in pushing forth their agenda for strong urban-design controls in Times Square vociferously argued in terms calculated to evoke symbolic meaning: Don't let corporate culture dull and dim the Great White Way. And finally, the project's planners evoked the razzle-dazzle visual images of the Great White Way to promote *42nd Street Now!* (figure 1.15).

What was the public good represented by the project—clearing a moral eyesore, accelerating development in a key transit location, preserving cultural institutions, improving infrastructure, helping to develop the cultural/services economy, recasting the civic psyche? Could these goals have been accomplished by targeting public efforts more cheaply? What were the alternatives—wait until land values drifted low enough at some indefinite time in the future for the market to effect piecemeal change? How critical was the public effort toward attracting Disney and other entertainment giants such as Madame Tussaud's? Where did the porn go? What are the spillover effects of such large-scale change?

The symbolism embedded in the transformation goes beyond the immediate context of New York. If festival marketplaces such as Boston's

1.15
Visual image for *42nd Street Now!*
(© Robert A. M. Stern Architects)

1.16
Celebrating Broadway's 300th birthday with a parade through Times Square, 1926. (New York Times Pictures)

Faneuil Hall were "half-way house[s] for people from the car culture who are trying to learn to love cities again,"[36] then successfully reestablishing pornography-ridden Times Square as an entertainment center for the middle class twenty years later signifies the full-scale reemergence of cities as places of public entertainment—going out, seeing others and being seen by others, experiencing night life, courting a little danger and naughtiness. Times Square is not "a theatrical presentation of street life." It is New York's reincarnated center of popular entertainment—unvarnished, unabashedly commercial, and branded with corporate capital.

Entertainment—legitimate or sub rosa, cultured or streetwise, elite or popular—has long been one of the defining characteristics of cities. For many, cities in themselves are entertainment. Behind the rescripted vision of West 42nd Street, city and state officials staked a big gamble on the middle class—if Times Square could be made safe and, once again, attractive to the middle class, metropolitan residents from the city's other boroughs, New Jersey, and Connecticut as well as tourists from around the nation and the world—then New York could reposition itself to benefit from its singular competitive advantage: agglomerations of pleasure-seeking activity (figure 1.16, plate 13). It was a big gamble the city could not afford not to take. It could become, once again, a metaphor for the allure of city life.

1.17 Entertainment's many formats: New York
Living Sculpture. (Gary Hack)

CHAPTER 2

THE LATE GREAT WHITE WAY

The Deuce reeked of moral decay. By 1960, the once-proud public playground had become infamous as the home of vice, crime, and seemingly
uncontrollable social behaviors. Prostitution of all gender affiliations, hustling of all kinds, open drug trade, alcoholism, vagrancy, and con games
like three-card monte and clio ruled the street. Criminal activity thrived
nearby, inside the underground corridors of the subway stations in Times
Square and on the corners of the nearby Port Authority Bus Terminal.
When in 1961 the administration of Mayor Robert F. Wagner, urged on
by the press, sealed up the entrance to the IRT subway through the Rialto
Arcade—"the Hole," notorious as a pickup point where adult homosexu-
als found complicitous teenagers—the action amounted to a tacit admission that the city's police department was unable to control the
sex-for-sale in Times Square. Known in police circles as Midtown South,
this hard-edged area ranked first in the city for felony and net crime complaints by the late 1970s. Forty-second Street itself recorded more than
twice as many criminal complaints as any other street in the area, with
drug offenses, grand larceny, robbery, and assault topping the list. This
malignancy, so disturbing to authorities, grew rapidly, notwithstanding significantly heightened police protection from a variety of police forces: foot
and car patrols of uniformed officers, mounted police, plainclothes and
anticrime units, and special forces including the police department's Public
Morals Squad and its Pimp Squad for Manhattan South, and the police
patrols of the Port Authority and the Transit Authority. On West 42nd
Street, even the police did not walk alone.

Illicit sexual activity was not limited to any one neighborhood in
New York, but during the 1970s and 1980s, West 42nd Street became synonymous in the minds of a worldwide public with violence and crime,
flaunted deviance and pornography, and urban decay. "The Great White
Way is now a byword for ostentatious flesh-peddling in an open-air meat
rack," one scholar later wrote in influential retrospective review of the

city's sexual underground.[1] The libertarianism of the sixties, instructed by a series of U.S. Supreme Court rulings narrowing the definition of "obscene," broke the physical constraints on what had been a subterranean world of hustling. Sex became an industry "as entrepreneurs began purveying allurements to the libido on a grand scale," and massage parlors, live-nude shows, peep shows, topless bars, hard-core sex films, porn emporiums, and bookstores now called "adult" turned the street into a supermarket for sex and sleaze. With the instant success of the twenty-five-cent peep show introduced in 1966, small businesses converted to arcades featuring film loops and explicit magazines; higher profits sent the cost of leases skyward and attracted the mob, which "muscled in around 1968."[2] By the late 1970s, the best-known parcel of real estate in America was, depending upon one's perspective, "a bazaar for human ungodliness," "a catalogue of degradation open to view," "a regional drug mart," "an infrastructure for crime," or "a drugs-and-sex half-world."

What would it take to cleanup the pathology of West 42nd Street and, by extension, Times Square? How could the unique history of the place—the symbolic soul of the city—be capitalized upon to make a distinctive place? With so many different interests in the neighborhood, how would the inevitable social tensions shape the political stakes of the redevelopment effort? Which players—private businesses or public planners—would define the new vision for West 42nd Street?

FROM BRIGHT LIGHTS TO NIGHT FRONTIER

The enduring image of Times Square as "The Great White Way" locked into place during a relatively short period of time, from the 1890s to 1929. Between 1899 and 1920, 13 theaters were built on West 42nd Street, beginning with impresario Oscar Hammerstein I's theaters, the Victoria (figure 2.1) and the Republic,[3] and including the most lavish of all now on the National Register of Historic Places, the legendary New Amsterdam, an elaborate Art-Nouveau theater designed by Herts & Tallant

2.1
Hammerstein's Victoria Theater at the northwest corner of 42nd Street and Seventh Avenue, 1904. (The Museum of the City of New York, Byron Collection)

30028 - Roof Garden. Hotel Astor, New York.

2.2
Postcard aerial perspective of the
Astor Hotel roof garden, place of
"frivolous informality" in an era
of "starchy public occasions."
(Collection of Bruce J. McCuen)

and constructed in 1903. Many more theaters were constructed on nearby
streets, driven by a fierce competitive war between the six-member
Theatrical Syndicate, a trust owning numerous theaters, and independent
producers, in particular the Shubert Brothers, who set out to challenge
the Syndicate.[4] Fashionable hotels such as the Astor, the Claridge, the
Knickerbocker, and the Rossmore came soon after, as did elaborate roof
gardens, racy cabarets and fancy restaurants catering to upper-class patrons
(figures 2.2, 2.3). Between 1893 and 1927, at least 85 theaters were constructed in an area from 38th to 63rd Streets from Sixth to Eighth Avenues
(figure 2.4) before the Theater District consolidated around Times Square,
which at its height—theatrical activity peaked during the 1927–1928 season when 264 shows opened in the district—drew in 68 theaters. Forty-
second Street was the most central and fashionable of theater streets, the
meaning of its address so vital to commercial success that as land values
rose only narrow entrances and marquees fronted 42nd Street while the
theater auditoriums were housed behind on 41st Street or 43rd Street.

The dramatic excitement and syncopated dazzle of the district
were expressed in the blaze of lights affixed to marquees, theater signs, billboard advertisements, and promotional displays that lined 42nd Street and
Broadway. The city's competitiveness knew few bounds, especially in Times

30023
Ladies and
Gentlemen's
Restaurant.
Hotel Astor,
New York.

2.3
Postcard image of Times Square
upper-crust restaurant. (Collection
of Bruce J. McCuen)

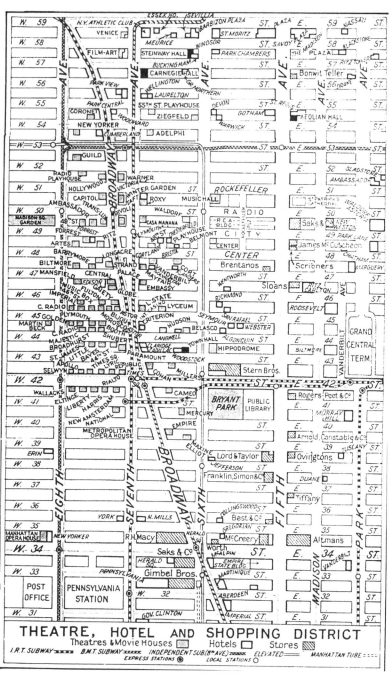

2.4
The Theater District, 1938. Rand McNally's Geographic Atlas of Greater New York, 1938. From the collection of Charles Knapp. (William R. Taylor, ed., *Inventing Times Square.* © 1991 Russell Sage Foundation, New York, N.Y.)

Square, where promoters of all kinds produced a bewildering array of garish lights that created a renowned trademark some would claim played an even greater role in attracting crowds than the theaters. "Mildly insane by day, the square goes divinely mad by night," wrote Will Irwin in 1927.[5] Enraptured by the magic and lushness of city lights, an ancient symbol of the contrast between city life and rural areas, writers of all genres who also seemed to know no limit gushed forth with vivid descriptions of Times Square's visual mystique. They "exhausted their vocabularies trying to capture the blazing, multicolored, dazzling, animated, fantastic, monstrous, absurd spectacle," remarked Irwin Lewis Allen in his engaging sociological study of the origins of New York slang[6] (figures 2.5, 2.6).

2.5
Times Square at night, 1923.
(Photograph by Irving Browning.
© Collection of The New-York
Historical Society)

2.6
The syncopated dazzle of signs in
Times Square, looking north from
about 44th Street, 1919. (The
Museum of the City of New York,
Print Archives)

During the first quarter of the twentieth century the world of legitimate theaters and bright lights centered on West 42nd Street defined not just the block but the entire district surrounding Times Square stretching north to 53rd Street from Broadway to Eighth Avenue. Commercial extravagance rather than aesthetic discipline set the prevailing tone for Times Square, and it was precisely this tone that gave the district its legendary distinctiveness and, most important, national influence. The distinctiveness arose, as historian David Hammack explained, not just from the success and centrality of the legitimate theater business, but from the unique role Times Square attained during this period as America's great central marketplace for commercial culture.[7] As fashions in popular entertainment evolved over time in response to changes in popular tastes and the novelty of new technology, a succession of new businesses moved into Times Square: first film, then movies, vaudeville, cabaret, popular music—"Tin Pan Alley" as the industry was known—then radio. Times Square evolved into a national showcase for popular music, vaudeville turns, Broadway plays, mass-market fashions and consumer goods, which, even when challenged by Hollywood, held its position for many years thereafter.

The scope and depth of its entertainment infrastructure was vast: numerous large theaters, nearby network radio producers and national print-news houses, dance studios, rehearsal halls, musical-instrument shops, costumers, theatrical agents, publicity brokers, and other ancillary show-business activities. The city's large and growing metropolitan market gave New York, and Times Square in particular, a commanding edge over other big cities. Its position as the largest and brightest stage for the presentation and sale of commercial culture in the United States evolved from these local and national forces, but perhaps as important in establishing its power, Hammack argued, was the sociological fact still true today that "to the extent Americans increasingly defined themselves through the items they bought on the market rather than through inherited or workplace identities, the commercial fashions and icons marketed through Times Square took on added importance."[8] The popular entertainments of Times Square were particularly urban in form and the source of a rich slang lexicon that came to form a distinct body of American popular speech. They were also a centerpiece for New York's growing tourism business.

Times Square's growth and prosperity as a national entertainment center were directly tied to the city's newly emergent midtown business district. Its development in the early part of the twentieth century took place at a time when, nationally, tourism was simultaneously expanding the market for entertainment and the drawing power of Times Square. As social historian Neil Harris explained in an expansive essay on urban tourism, for the businessmen and their entourages coming to New York, the buying trips, conventions, trade shows, or financial transactions provided the pretext for visiting, but they were not the sole reason for doing so. Rather, it was the combination of business contacts and personal pleasure that brought New York so many tourists. Moreover, what tourists wanted was not always the uplifting art galleries, historical monuments, and parks, but the satisfactions of good plays, enjoyable food, jolly rides about town, memorable views from observation decks, and live music and entertainment at nightclubs and roof gardens. "This was not high culture, but in its concern for information, mundane experience, corporate celebration, and broad urban vistas, it reflected a set of metropolitan values that were easily comprehensible"[9] (plate 1),

Before Times Square was Times Square it was Longacre (sometimes Long Acre) Square, a name taken from a commercial street in central London. The moniker was a logical one stemming from the land use common to the district in both cities. Horse dealerships, carriage factories, and stables constituted the area's main businesses in the second half of the nineteenth century, when the area of former Dutch farms was undergoing its first development transition from residential to commercial use. The commercial concentration itself hardly made for public value at the time; rather it was a history of amusement and the characters in the areas surrounding the square, even before theaters became its main attraction, that defined the place (figures 2.7, 2.8). It was associated with horseplay, on

2.7
Longacre Square's billboards, 1898. (Courtesy Seymour B. Durst Old York Library at The Graduate Center of The City University of New York)

2.8
Longacre Square, the view south, 1900. (The Museum of the City of New York, Byron Collection)

several levels, and given an early nickname, "Thieves Lair"; the American Horse Exchange built by William K. Vanderbilt and completed in 1893 was where some of the city's largest and most famous horse sales took place. (Now the Winter Garden Theater and, until recently, home to the long-running musical *Cats!*, outlines of the original structure's arched windows and corner towers can been seen on the 50th Street and Seventh Avenue facades.) In physical terms, Longacre Square in the late 1880s was "a monotonous open space bordered by rows of drab apartment houses and dingy dwellings" (figure 2.9). Theaters were relatively dispersed at the time; in other words, "Broadway frontage was not then the precious possession it is to-day," one observer wrote in 1923.[10] Two events were principally responsible for the area's turn-of-the-century change in character: the illumination of the theaters in the late 1880s, followed shortly thereafter by outdoor lamps, street signs, and lighted entrances to public places, and the decision in 1901 by August Belmont to build New York's first rapid transit system, the Interborough Rapid Transit Company (IRT).

Designated a crosstown thoroughfare when the city's grid network of streets was first laid out in 1811, 42nd Street was not officially opened until 1837. It evolved into a crossroads—shortly to become *the* crossroads—of the city only after the subway opened in 1904, with a key station at 42nd Street and Broadway. In the half century from 1850 to 1900, the city's major east-west thoroughfare had moved northward three times, from 14th Street to 23rd Street, then to 34th Street, before settling for good, in 1915, at the crossing of Broadway and Seventh at 42nd Street. The subway would prove to be pivotal to 42nd Street's centrality because the path of the IRT would traverse a broad swath of Manhattan, from City Hall up the East Side to Grand Central Station, then west across 42nd Street to Times Square, and up Broadway to the Upper West Side, where it divided into two branches that continued north and terminated in the Bronx. By 1928, West 42nd Street was accessible to the furthest points of the city, with five subway lines, four elevated lines, five bus lines, eleven surface lines, and a ferry having stations, stops, or a terminal there. Such access gave West 42nd Street an incomparable advantage as a location for servicing three distinct groups of the metropolis: city residents, affluent suburbanites, and visitors. Superior transit also gave it a lock on the "Rialto," as the Theater District was called. Whereas Hammerstein's construction of two theaters around the turn of the century made West 42nd Street an important theater street overnight, it was the subway that finally stopped the Rialto's continuous move uptown on Broadway. Times Square would attract its great concentration of theaters because entertainment districts require a centrality of location in terms of population and transportation, and the Times Square station carried almost five million customers in 1905, its first year of operation (figure 2.10).

Much as the transportation nexus at 42nd Street and Broadway defined a centrality that would shape the real estate history of Times Square, the public character of the space afforded businesses strategic advantages that entrepreneurs of the era were quick to grab on to. The

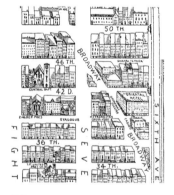

2.9
Broadway at Longacre Square, 1890. (Sun Manhattan Map Company. Courtesy Seymour B. Durst Old York Library at The Graduate Center of The City University of New York)

wave of real estate speculation set off by the announcement of IRT subway construction attracted, among others, Adolph S. Ochs, owner and
publisher of the *New York Times*, who succeeded through a series of adroit
actions to forge a public identity between his newspaper and what he perceived could be the renown of an "internationally celebrated crossroad."[11]
First, Ochs selected the area's most visible site, the small triangular piece of
the block at the southern end of the Times Square "bow tie" created by
the now-familiar X-crossing of Broadway and Seventh Avenue;[12] he then
tore down the Pabst Hotel and built for his headquarters a 25-story building in Italian-Renaissance style—a modern version of Giotto's campanile
in Florence, New York style—faced in limestone, terra-cotta and brick.
Appropriately named the Times Tower, it was the second tallest building in
the city at the time and, reportedly, visible from a distance of twelve miles.
A booster for the growing city as well as for his paper, Ochs reversed the
downtown orientation of the earlier structure and had the Times Tower's
entrance face uptown (figure 2.11).

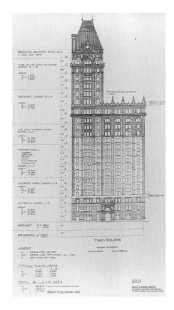

2.11
Elevation of the Times Tower,
design with a mansard roof. (HLW
International)

Second, upon completion of the landmark tower in 1904,
Longacre Square was renamed Times Square to mark the newspaper's
importance to the city. Initiated by Belmont, it was a repeat action by the
city following a precedent that assured the *Times* of equal footing with its
rival, the *Herald*, located in Herald Square eight blocks to the south. "The
fact that the renaming of the square owed as much to the assiduous promotion of the new underground rail lines and the stunning real estate
opportunities they opened as to the structure being celebrated, was quintessential New York style," remarked architectural critic Ada Louise
Huxtable. "And if the Times Tower was more of a lumpenskyscraper than
Louis Sullivan's ideal of a proud and soaring thing, it was destined for an
enduring role."[13]

With the building's dedication timed to welcome in the New Year, on December 31, 1904, the *Times* staged a carefully orchestrated gala attended by thousands of New Yorkers who watched a fireworks display launched from the still-unfinished tower. This was Ochs's third, but not final, signature move. The New Year's Eve event, refined a year later with the addition of a giant electrically lighted ball dropped from the 70-foot flag pole of the Times Tower, immediately marked the site as a stage for municipal celebrations, and over the years increasing popularity and promotion turned the annual rite into a beloved national custom. A few years later, the paper of record that pledged to publish "All the News That's Fit to Print" offered passing pedestrians and waiting crowds instant information about election results or other major events through "news signs" posted in windows. The news signs preceded the *Times*'s more lasting contribution to the square, which debuted in 1928: the famous Motogram "zipper," a five-foot-high, 360-foot long ribbon of 14,800 electric-light bulbs that wrapped around the base of the building and spelled out the news in traveling headlines (figure 2.12).

2.12
The "zipper" still bringing news to the square in the 1970s, as it first did in 1928. (Jill Stone)

THE LONG SLIDE

By the early 1920s economic forces made West 42nd Street the city's preeminent entertainment district—numerous legitimate theaters, transit centrality, a burgeoning midtown commercial district. The growth of a commercial business district in midtown brought big crowds of pedestrians to the street, during the day as well as at night. Forty-second Street between Seventh and Eighth Avenues became known as "the street that never sleeps," and its intersection with Broadway, as "the 24-hour corner." With the crowds came the potential for new and expanded businesses. As land values soared to reflect this business potential, rising rents gave way to more intense uses. The legitimate theaters, low in density and dedicated to a single use that had a short season of nine or ten months and a schedule

of nine plays a week, found it difficult to generate sufficient revenues to retain command over the street. High production costs further contributed to the economic squeeze. Raising the price of theater tickets would only go so far before it self-defeatingly cut into the theater audience.

The solutions adopted by various owners differed. Several theaters leased part of their space to restaurants, roof gardens, and night clubs, though this strategy failed without the sale of liquor once Prohibition took effect in 1920. Others switched from drama to light entertainment structured for multiple daily shows, for example, vaudeville and burlesque. By 1925, proposed new theaters such as the Paramount were combined with office buildings or, in the case of the Roxy, joined with hotels. The construction of Radio City Music Hall, part of Rockefeller Center, in 1928 evidenced a further extension of this trend. Yet the most common solution was conversion to a movie house, and the first on West 42nd Street to do so was the Liberty in 1927, "without notice or fanfare an irrevocable trend had begun," as one historian of the area remarked. By 1934 only three legitimate theaters remained on West 42nd Street; five had been converted to movie houses and three others were dark. The last to convert, in 1937, was the New Amsterdam, widely considered the "flagship theater of Forty-second Street."[14]

The 1930s proved to be the turning point for West 42nd Street as a "class" entertainment district. Legitimate theater was still the signature activity of Broadway, but the social and economic power of the medium had begun to fade years earlier. The new economic formula for popular entertainment demanded continuous play and large turnover, which meant business strategies based on volume and lower prices and an emphasis on off-the-street trade. Changes in tastes for public entertainment also pushed forward the rapid rise of motion-picture audiences in cities all over the nation and with it the decline of legitimate theater. Movies merged extraordinarily well with the nation's demographics because they occupied an economic niche between audiences for whom theater was too expensive, vaudeville too crude, and nickelodeons too dark, dirty, and cheap. Price and reputation were equally important to urban residents. Making movies more expensive than storefront nickelodeons yet affordable made them more desirable. Priced for a "middling" audience, David Nasaw wrote, movies also had tremendous success in attracting the female audience, which testified to its newfound reputation as respectable entertainment for a broad range of city folk.[15]

Though lined with theaters ripe for conversion to movie houses, West 42nd Street suffered the fate of rapid obsolescence. Lacking the size and

2.13
The visual expanse of Times Square at 46th Street, 1911. (Photograph by William Hassler. The Museum of the City of New York)

splendor of the many new movie places being built on or near
Broadway—"monuments of ostentation so stupendous that customers
willingly paid the price of admission to get a peak inside"[16]—the theaters
on West 42nd Street specialized in "grinders" (figure 2.14), reruns of older
movies emphasizing action and violence that appealed to a male rather
than a family audience. The grinders brought a new kind of commercial
promotion to the street: garish marquees, sexually suggestive posters,
bizarre devices to lure crowds, and gravel-voiced "barkers" to induce
passers-by into the movies. This more than the movies per se is what
"detracted from the reputation and appearance of the street" and set in
motion a chain sequence of declining fortunes. On the eve of World War
II, West 42nd Street was "undeniably an unaesthetic street of sordid establishments and garish displays: it was also a street viewed by many as inde-
cent and unsafe."[17] It was not yet, however, infiltrated by the drug trade.

The slide downhill from grinders to burlesque to grit to commercialism to honky-tonk debauchery to sex on the hoof to a marketplace for pornography is a story in itself, a moving montage of cultural
images, societal mores, and sexual boundaries. The vice was nothing new.
Its antecedents went back to the turn of the century, as did its links with
theater and a honky-tonk atmosphere. In fact, as hotels and theaters
moved up Broadway into Longacre Square, so did the brothels. They were
an accompaniment of growth, so much so that a former police chief had
concluded in 1906 "the city is being rebuilt, and vice moves ahead of
business."[18] Longacre Square at the turn of the century had become a

center of prostitution thick with streetwalkers prowling West 42nd Street between Sixth and Ninth Avenues. "Commercial sex seemed to define the midtown area," wrote a historian of the subject, his point made quite clear by a map of the houses of prostitution in Longacre Square in 1901 (figure 2.15). "By 1901, the sobriquet of 'Soubrette Row' [the moniker for the French-run bordellos of West 39th Street] had moved to West Forty-third Street, a block where almost every house was a brothel and directly across from the future site of the *New York Times*."[19] This infamous block too was one of those targeted for cleanup as part of the 42DP.

Critical reaction to the changes of the 1960s and 1970s spanned the spectrum. Not everyone saw the street's decline as a disgrace. Some appreciated the "fine-grained detail" of street life, while others saw its danger and vice as an attraction forming a new part of the street's mythos. And, in a chain of writings that continues today, still others pined nostalgically for the street's lost past, whether its years as a district for legitimate theater, or its recent role as a unique sexual playground for the city. None of these observers, however, was reacting to an immediately noticeable change. Though seemingly inexorable, the street's decline occurred not as a fast-paced movie clip but rather as a series of slow-motion events and market responses reducing the district's draw as a middle-class entertainment center, a role Lincoln Center, as the largest performing-arts complex in the United States, had taken over in the mid-1960s. By 1980, when the city and state started to formulate plans for West 42nd Street, the tally of years added up to more spent down-at-the-heels than in commercial glory.

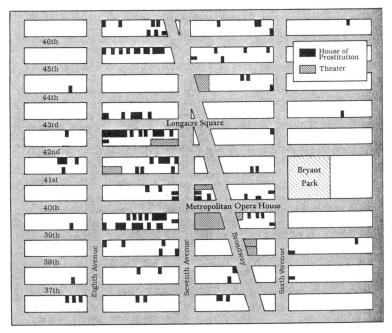

2.15
Houses of prostitution in Longacre Square, 1901. (Timothy Gilfoyle. William R. Taylor, ed., *Inventing Times Square* © 1991 Russell Sage Foundation, New York, N.Y.)

Not surprisingly, the perception of widespread decline and depravity exceeded the territorial scope of "contagion," which appeared to be concentrated in an irregular **L**-shaped run from both sides of 42nd and 43rd Streets between Seventh and Eighth Avenues, up along Eighth Avenue from 42nd to 51st Street, with a jump to the street fronts surrounding the islands on Broadway between 47th and 49th Streets, where the Pussycat Lounge and Cinema and Kitty Kat and Mardi Gras Topless Disco did a booming XXX-rated business (figure 2.16). In the early 1970s, the heaviest concentration of heterosexual prostitution activity clustered between 49th and 51st Streets on Eighth Avenue, conveniently right across from the "pross" hotels of "Hell's Bedroom." This was the territory Gail Sheehy described so vividly in her 1972 exposé of the city's perpetual efforts to clean up midtown's sex industry. As heterosexual prostitution shifted northwest, West 42nd Street became primarily a center for male prostitution. Despite continual anxiety and self-interested fears among theater owners and restaurateurs throughout the 1970s, the area's sex business was

2.16
Vice Map of Times Square, 1973.
(NYC Office of Midtown
Planning and Development)

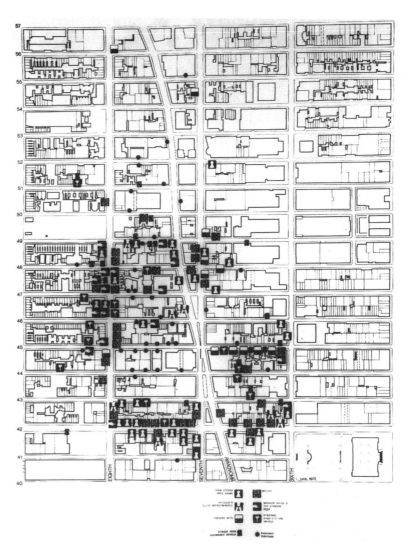

not keeping Broadway dark. Historically volatile, the theater industry in New York appeared to be in relatively good shape in 1980. After a tough 1973–1974 season, when the city itself was suffering from a near-brush with bankruptcy, box-office receipts soared throughout the rest of the decade, as did the number of total playing weeks. Tourists packed the streets at night. That would change almost as quickly after the record 1980–1981 season of eleven million attendees, but at the time, confidence on Broadway was strong. The area's urban ills seemed only to keep people from staying longer and frequenting the restaurants, especially after hours.

Ironically, with ten of its fourteen movie theaters showing first-run releases of general and action-adventure movies at low prices several times a day, West 42nd Street also functioned as a unique movie center for the city, drawing ethnic audiences from all of its boroughs. In terms of paying customers, the action movies were probably the largest single attraction of the street in the late 1970s, according to the CUNY sociologists. The diverse draw, in concert with the equally diverse fare, made for a "cross-cultural event," Mark Jacobson wrote a decade later. "And that's why you have to have grind theaters on Forty-second Street," he told Weisbrod, then head of the OME. "It's New York's drive-in circuit. You can't make every movie theater like Cinema One. If the city is really interested in the occult vibe in this country, they ought to nationalize Forty-second Street as a center for sleazological cinema studies"[20] (figures 2.17, 2.18).

From a real estate perspective, the problem appeared obvious if also somewhat ironic: On a street long touted for its high land values in a city that constantly tore down to rebuild, a Sodom-and-Gomorrah form of social ecology inhibited new investment. Only one new building had been built on 42nd Street between Seventh and Eighth Avenues after 1920, the Rialto, which was designed exclusively for movie programs, and none after 1937. The Great Depression and then the restrictions on construction during World War II brought to a halt the city's 1923–1929 building boom, preventing major redevelopment of West 42nd Street and also of Eighth Avenue from 40th to 50th Streets, which was in the works, according to one historian of the area. Change reshaping Times Square along the lines of Rockefeller Center no longer seemed inevitable. During the 1960s, when a building boom reshaped Sixth Avenue into a 14-block stretch of office towers—over 20 million square feet of new space erected between 56th and 42nd Streets between 1959 and 1974—Broadway found builders "scarce." Real estate sources cited three reasons for the dormant state of activity in the Times Square district: small parcels that made land assembly difficult, exceedingly costly acquisitions owing to high rents augmented by income from advertising signs, and the proliferation of pornography and crime, which made the entertainment district inhospitable to business tenants.

If the *Times* reporter had cast a wider net for his story, a fourth reason would have emerged: huge weekly gross revenues and out-sized profits gleaned from the operation of "grinder" houses, porn bookstores,

sex emporiums, massage parlors, and peep shows. The configuration of
parcels in this area looked no different than that in any other commercially underdeveloped—meaning low-density—area of midtown Manhattan,
where as many as 80 small parcels might make up a single block. The
nature and pattern of the sex industry, however, cast a particular and complex imprint on the structure of property control: In the environs of Times
Square, real estate activity resembled a byzantine underworld of covert
ownership. Seeking anonymity and the ability to claim "no responsibility,"
landlords put a lot of distance between their title to the bricks and mortar
and the ultimate operator of the businesses within. The chain of ownership and leasehold interests aimed to confuse, if not obfuscate. It was a
business predicated on speculative profits. Legitimate owners of the buildings housing message parlors—"hit-and-run brothels combining the

2.18
Still, decades later, a movie haven,
1986. (Enrico Ferorelli)

virtues of low overhead and high turnover"[21]—adult bookstores and peep shows commonly net leased (leased without loss) the properties for ten years or more to others (often organized crime interests, according to the New York State Select Committee on Crime's investigative work) who might operate the sex-related business directly but who, in turn, were just as likely to sublease the premises on a short-term basis, even month-to-month, to small-time, generally fly-by-night operators. Not atypically, property was purchased because the building was scheduled to be demolished in the next couple of years; in the interim, nominal improvements, if any, would be made. The short-terms leases made it easy to vacate tenants quickly while the sex-related businesses generated a lucrative source of short-term income pending demolition.[22] "An ugly cow gives a lot of milk," remarked one broker.[23] In 1969, he noted, the street's ten grinder movie houses drew nine million customers while highly profitable sex bookstores could pay as much as $32,000 a year for a small sliver of street frontage. Milking, in other words, was a low-cost high-revenue holding action among speculative owners until conditions ripened for redevelopment and property sold for substantial gains.[24]

In 1970 the pornography business in midtown Manhattan had just begun to locate its best customers—the vast population of office workers proximate to West 42nd Street, who on either side of the journey home were within striking distance of Times Square. The people count was higher than that of Rockefeller Center, by a great deal: 49,000 persons entered 42nd Street between Sixth Avenue and Eighth Avenue during the morning rush hours compared with about 12,000 at Rockefeller Center. "An Environmental and Economic Survey of Times Square and Mid-Manhattan" commissioned by the West Side Association of Commerce, one of the area's several business groups, reported that "it was not as inevitable as frequently assumed that new office buildings will 'sweep' across 42nd Street."[25] Nor would an increase in land values, in itself, eliminate the pornographic bookstores or movies, which, because of their exceptionally high gross revenues and expected returns, appeared to face no economic constraints. Prepared by urban designer and consultant Arthur B. Zabarkes, the report put forth a number of development proposals aimed at an upgrade of West 42nd Street: office construction, more intensive development of Times Square as a cinema center, expansion of the garment center to include retail and office facilities on and near 42nd Street, construction of a major retail shopping center, and intensification of the 'super-graphics' of Times Square. Serious obstacles in the path of redevelopment existed, he conceded, including the complex ownership of many of the small properties, the unwillingness of many small businessmen to give up the advantage of their present sites and, most significantly, the increasing growth of the pornography industry on the street, which could only be expected to increase since pedestrian access was high.

Well positioned, erotica could afford to pay high rents, rents sometimes as much as twice the front-foot rate prevailing for an ordinary store on West 42nd Street. Operating on a 24-hour basis, the theaters and especially the peep shows generated heavy gross revenues; for instance, in 1978, when they studied the scene, CUNY researchers estimated that the weekly gross of peep shows ranged from $74,000 to $106,000 or roughly $5 million a year. This represented a tremendous profit since the establishments, comprising a few dozen cheaply made booths with small film machines, needed only a few low-paid employees to run them. While it is true that a multiplicity of small parcels made the task of land assembly exceedingly difficult, it is also true that at this time three corporations with major holdings of theater and small-shop properties in the district controlled about 80 percent of the available land and buildings on West 42nd Street. This concentration, however, would not necessarily make land assembly by private interests any easier or any more manageable. There were still more than 27 landlords and multiple layers of fragmented property interests on the street to complicate the task immensely. The block seemed immune to change without deliberate intervention to alter the market dynamic.

By middle-class standards of behavior, the depravity and intensity of the conditions on West 42nd Street provided a ready consensus for a cleanup and the assemblage problems of private market-driven redevelopment, a strong rationale for aggressive public intervention. Based on their survey of metropolitan residents—a cross section of the city's "prime demographics," what marketers call that portion of the population with the most disposable income and the greatest inclination to spend it on goods and services, in this case, entertainment; plus the region's cultural leaders, those who would bring out-of-towners and tourists to the district[26]—Kornblum and Boggs found "an immense public desire to see the area brought back to its former greatness." Yet they also found a deep pessimism about the area's future in the fact that a large proportion of New Yorkers doubted that, "short of massive intervention and rebuilding, the District could ever become a safe, enjoyable place for family entertainment."[27] Just what this "rebuilding" would mean in terms of a new 42nd Street was unclear. Nevertheless, given the symbolic significance of the area and the gathering storm over theater preservation, the ambiguity of vision was purposeful: It served as a necessary precondition for moving forward, that is, for doing something to remove the blight. That vision would have to be clarified, soon. Given the highly contentious and fragmented character of development interests in New York, the process for doing so was likely to be played out, with controversy, in the public arena.

SYMBOLIC SOUL OF THE CITY

Throughout the 1960s and 1970s the unvarnished and unromantic truth about Times Square contrasted sharply with the historic image and myth about the place. It was no longer the nation's central production center for popular entertainment, yet it remained its preeminent icon and symbol of show business. It was no longer the city's creative core nor its trend-setting scene, yet it remained its symbol of "golden potential" and a "testing ground of the limits of fantasy and fulfillment." It was no longer coining revolutionary vernacular speech, yet the place maintained its hold on the mental imagination of tourists and city dwellers alike. Even when the energy crisis dimmed the dramatic displays and bright lights of the district in the early 1970s, the legendary vision of "spectaculars" continued to shine brightly in the minds and imaginations of those who visualized the past. Even in civic disgrace and criminal distress when in 1981 West 42nd Street was billed by *Rolling Stone* as "the sleaziest block in America" and identified in the national press with the general woes of New York, the "local" nature of the place continued to be eclipsed by its larger role as a powerful national metaphor, this time, however, for urban pathology and decline. Hopeful words attached themselves to negative realities: "gloriously vulgar," "decedent raffishness," "seedy grandeur," "tawdry glamour," "a junkyard for dreams." The Great White Way might now be "a byword for ostentatious flesh-peddling in an open-air meat rack," but it was still the "crossroads of the world."[28] The illustrious memory of glory was not to be erased.

One did not have to look too far for an explanation of this paradox. For New Yorkers, 42nd Street and Times Square had become synonymous with the city itself, its commercialism, intense energy, urban insouciance, cultural and economic diversity—a constantly changing stage for urban life. Writers sharpened their pencils when evoking the romance and importance of the place, especially in the 1980s when all seemed threatened by the city and state's redevelopment plan which most critics disfavored intensely: Times Square, they said, was "a bubbling up of human nature. Its chronometer is on perpetual Night Saving Time"; "A giant blinking toy, an entertainment in itself"; "The most fragile kind of urban fabric, in a constant state of change"; "The most dynamic and intense urban space of the twentieth century, America's gift to the modern world, a home for magic realism, the commercial sublime"; "Times Square is not just a place, it's a backdrop, a colorful, ironic setting that symbolizes the round-the-clock vibrancy of New York City."[29]

In short, Times Square served as the symbolic soul of New York. Its chaotic action, dense and diverse pedestrian activity, continuous role as the key entertainment district—in a city defined by creative juices—immutable prime location as the city's transit hub, and unique physical "experience of place," which derived from its small-scale buildings, open space, and illuminated lights, made it a public place overendowed with meaning or, as the cultural commentators saw it, drenched in semiotic meaning. Times Square was a stage for urban life to one group, a state of mind to another, and a danger zone to still another. Its seediness was considered integral to New York.

Symbolic meanings of place took center stage in the campaign to garner support for the city's aggressive plans for redevelopment. Symbolic rhetoric dominated the many sets of public hearings on the 42DP during the 1980s. The depth of symbolic significance underscored the objections of civic groups, architectural critics, and cultural commentators who later made strong appeals to preserve Times Square's values, past and present, which they believed were being cast aside in the pursuit of a comprehensive cleanup that would use "good" activities—offices, hotels, restaurants, theaters—to drive out the "bad"—drug dealing, prostitution, vagrancy, and homeless congregations. And as controversy and complexity continuously spawned lawsuits and produced years of delays throughout the decade, the symbolism of the place grew ever more sophisticated and elaborate.

Meaning permeates a city incrementally. Over time, out of the specialness of memorable events as well as the commonality of daily experiences, an overlay of meanings accumulates. It maps the evocative content of place from a generalized perspective, though casts, shadows, and weights of meaning differ across groups of city residents. At least five meanings fashioned the symbolism of place of Times Square for New Yorkers.

First, as "The Theater District," Times Square lay claim to an exceedingly proud history renowned throughout the world. Embodied in a tradition of legitimate theater that in its time represented the leading edge of show business, this story glorified a type of urban energy characterized by the city's own special ethnic "moxie."

Second, as "The Turf of Promoters and Showmen," Times Square had nurtured the nation's first great "entrepreneurs of entertainment"— Oscar Hammerstein I, David Belasco, Florenz Ziegfeld, Samuel "Roxy" Rothafel, Irving Berlin, Damon Runyon, the Minsky Brothers, Billy Rose (figure 2.19). Legendary as larger-than-life showmen, they left an enviable legacy of "financial shrewdness with a remarkable sensitivity to new markets and changing public tastes,"[30] a general point of business pride whose currency has never lost value among the city's immigrants or its movers and shakers.

Third, as "The Great White Way," Times Square could take credit for inventing the "commercial aesthetic"—bright carnivalesque signs of color, light, and glass designed to thrill, excite, and awe onlookers while convincing them to buy. Visually, the commercial aesthetic came to define and dominate not only Times Square but much of American culture in a

2.19 Postcard view of entertainment entrepreneur S. L. Rothafel's luxurious Rialto Theater, built exclusively for movie programs (1916) on the site of Hammerstein's Victoria. It lasted nineteen years before being torn down for a four-story combination of shops and offices, including a small movie theater known as the Rialto. (Collection of Bruce J. McCuen)

FOYER – THE RIALTO "THE TEMPLE OF THE MOTION PICTURE"
BROADWAY AT 42ND ST. NEW YORK. DIRECTION S.L. ROTHAPFEL.

way few cities in the world could match. Through the medium of promotion, it created super-sized evocative images of desire on billboards and brilliantly lit "spectaculars," and these reinforced the city's own sense of self-importance—that it was setting the pace for the nation, that Times Square was an index of cultural changes.

Fourth, as "The Testing Ground," Times Square had a reputation as a place without limits where "anything goes." This was rooted in the historically close association between theater and vice, but the tales of deviant excesses on West 42nd Street during the 1960s, 1970s, and 1980s bequeathed an especially distinctive legacy of sexual theater. It was theater that continually tested the limits of social tolerance, even that of New Yorkers who habitually exhibit a liberal, if ambivalent, social tolerance—part pure disgust, part hardened acceptance, part perverse pride: "I can handle anything; there isn't anything I haven't seen in this city; nothing is newly shocking." Indeed, as Ada Louise Huxtable wrote, the city requires a "testing ground of limits," a place dealing with fantasy and fulfillment, and this has been Times Square's unique societal and urban role. Speaking about architecture with words whose meaning extended beyond the tangibility of bricks and mortar she said: "When conventional sources [of eclecticism] have been rung dry, the door is opened to no-style and free-style, to increasingly hyped effects, and to the shock value of those things usually considered taboo."[31] Life in Times Square was prescient, she implied, for by the 1950s and 1960s, a similar testing was taking place in society at large. This was no less true in the 1970s and 1980s when an unbridled market created a unique drugs-and-sex half-world that, when threatened with extinction by the public's power of condemnation, acquired a new-found mythic status in what would be irrevocably lost.

Finally, as "Quintessential New York," Times Square provided a city image for the nation at large. That image took shape from the experience of being in Times Square and sampling its particular brand of city life—going to the theater, joining the crowds, vicariously partaking of Broadway's success. Constant promotion made it part of the national mythology. While the reality of Times Square was changing, especially after the 1930s, Hollywood defined Broadway for America and kept alive the aura of its old image. As cast on the west coast, Broadway meant the musical: "production numbers of dazzling, almost surreal beauty," and "an enchanted place where talent and hard work could lead to undreamed-of success."[32] The list of "Broadway" movies is long and includes, among many others: *Broadway Melody of 1929* (with later editions in 1938 and 1940), *Glorifying the American Girl* (1929), *42nd Street* (1933), *Dames* (1934), *The Great Ziegfeld* (1936), *Stage Door* (1937), *Footlight Serenade* (1942), *Babes on Broadway* (1942), *Broadway Rhythm* (1943), *The Band Wagon* (1953), *Main Street to Broadway* (1953), *Guys and Dolls* (1955), *Sweet Smell of Success* (1957), *The Producers* (1968), *Funny Girl* (1968), *All That Jazz* (1979), *Fame* (1980), *Staying Alive* (1983), *The Muppets Take Manhattan* (1984), *Breakin'* (1984), and *A Chorus Line* (1985).

This image of Times Square from the glory days of the 1920s was important symbolically, even if it was out of date, for this was also the high point of urban growth in America, when cities all over the country boasted of their progressive achievements in architecture, engineering, culture, and community. It was also a time when being in public, especially in Times Square, and being a part of the mixed crowd—not as just a spectator but simultaneously as a participant—symbolized the ultimate city experience for visitors and residents alike. Cities glowed in "the spectacle of urban life" in a way that they have sought to recapture ever since.

Cleaning up West 42nd Street, and by extension Times Square, promised to put the shine back on the "big apple," the city's universally known booster nickname.[33] The historic legacy of Times Square should have made entertainment the obvious planning priority of redevelopment because the area's intrinsic character, still evident beneath the sleaze, did not have to be invented, as had been the monumental task with the creation of Lincoln Center. It was already in place. It was known worldwide. Yet even had that been the city and state's initial planning agenda, the stage for controversy was set. The heavy multifaceted symbolism of Times Square, forged over a period of more than 60 years, was embedded with sensitive associations that touched an especially broad range of interests; it was a heavy political load for any redevelopment plan. The politics of the 42nd Street Development Project would be symbolic politics. What other scenario could possibly prevail?

CALLING TIMES SQUARE A NEIGHBORHOOD

In the everyday world, Times Square was home to more than Broadway and sleaze, its two most conspicuous industries. Families and single residents lived in nearby Clinton, the neighborhood of working-class ethnic roots formerly called "Hell's Kitchen" stretching north from 38th Street to 59th Street and west from Eighth Avenue to the Hudson River. Performers and producers assembled nearby in rehearsal halls, dance studios, restaurants, bars, and clubs for practice, production, and play, as did the vast specialized business network that made up the entertainment industry—designers, costumers, musicians, agents, photographers, and suppliers of gels, sets, props, lights, and amplifiers—who crowded into the area's low-rent offices. The pool halls and game rooms and gyms that had once made up the neighborhood's low-cost entertainment venues were long gone, but vestiges of this past remained in a few boxing clubs housed in upper-story locations (figure 2.20), the sporting-good stores, and the New York Chess and Checkers Club on West 42nd Street, still next to the New Amsterdam Theater as it was in the late 1940s. Also remaining were the show-business supply stores—costume rentals, lighting suppliers, and the like on Tenth Avenue in the 20s and 30s.

Working, living, and playing surrounded by the drug and sex trade and XXX-rated entertainments did not immunize any of these groups from the daily sights, sounds, smells, and hustles of West 42nd Street. The

2.20
The street grain of West 42nd Street: bar & grill, formal wear, Times Square Boxing Club, 1978. (Manny Millan/*Sports Illustrated*)

residents, restaurant and theater businesses, churches, civic groups, and real estate operators of existing properties of the area all found offensive and threatening the street conditions that law-enforcement efforts failed to control. As early as 1975 they demanded that the city commit itself to doing something about the Times Square area, and in response Mayor Abraham D. Beame set up the Midtown Citizens Committee. The consensus around which these groups, normally skeptical of one another, found a way to work together was the pragmatism of need mirroring the dependency of interrelated land uses that made up the fragile fabric of the Times Square district. The low rents of the area seemed to promise neighborhood stability for Clinton's low-income and elderly households and performing artists who valued its walk-to-work accessibility, as well as the small business owners and service providers who tenanted the small offices of Times Square. Much as this unlikely coalition might be in favor of a cleanup, each group harbored serious concerns about how they would be affected by economic pressures likely to result from any kind of large-scale redevelopment.

Clinton was no stranger to large-scale public actions. In the 1930s and 1940s huge land takings necessary for the elaborate entry/exit networks of the Lincoln Tunnel and the Port Authority Bus Terminal radically truncated the neighborhood, leaving in its scarred path speculative land holdings, vacant plots, and a proliferation of parking lots. It was now officially smaller, as the DEIS map revealed (figure 2.21). In 1968, Mayor John V. Lindsay announced plans for a West Side convention center at the Hudson River and 42nd Street. Although alternative West Side locations emerged during the protracted years of planning, any one of these sites, except the one at Battery Park City, threatened to further decimate this "transitional" neighborhood dominated by five-story walk-up buildings. In a bargain struck with the neighborhood, in 1974 the city set up the Special Clinton District to preserve and stabilize its low-density residential character and prevent it from becoming an upper-middle income area of high-rise apartments, but this became something of a rear-guard action as other projects, many publicly funded, eventually led to an upgrading of the area.

Most notable was the eventual success in 1977 of Manhattan Plaza, a twin-tower apartment complex of 1,688 units operated under a federal subsidy program and rented mainly to performing artists, which increased pressures for housing conversions and renovations. (When completed, the market-rate project could not rent up. With the addition of federal rent subsidies, it became noted for its ground-breaking role as a performing arts residential community.) Two other housing-conversion projects in the area nearing completion, along with several others proposed, were projected to add 1,126 residential units to the neighborhood. Private investments had enhanced the Art-Deco McGraw-Hill building (42nd Street and Eighth Avenue), Restaurant Row (46th Street between Eight and Ninth Avenues), and Theater Row I (42nd Street between 9th and Dyer Avenues). Completed in 1978, Theater Row I converted derelict tenements, empty lots, and abandoned buildings into six small Off-Off

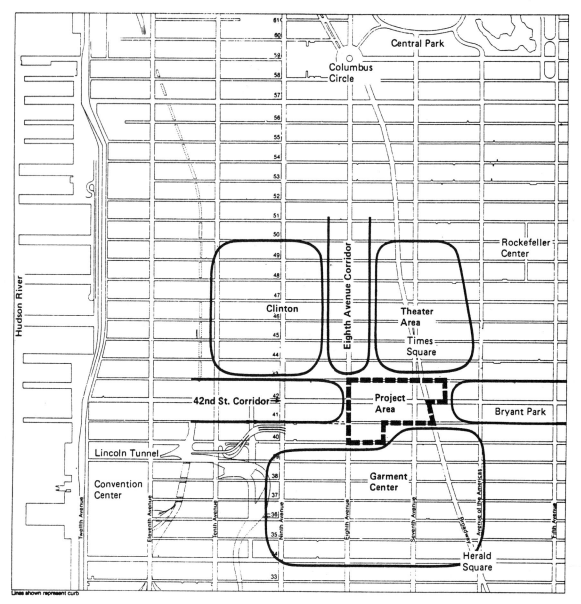

Map labels: Central Park, Columbus Circle, Rockefeller Center, Hudson River, Clinton, Eighth Avenue Corridor, Theater Area, Times Square, Bryant Park, 42nd St. Corridor, Project Area, Lincoln Tunnel, Garment Center, Convention Center, Herald Square, Avenue of the Americas, Broadway, Fifth Avenue, Seventh Avenue, Eighth Avenue, Ninth Avenue, Tenth Avenue, Eleventh Avenue, Twelfth Avenue

Lines shown represent curb

2.21
Secondary impact areas abutting
the 42DP. (42nd Street
Development Project, Inc.)

Broadway theaters, twelve floors of supporting space, and a restaurant. Plans for a Theater Row II were on the drawing boards.

Once an isolated neighborhood "decidedly deficient in political power," Clinton displayed a new-found optimism from its social position as a locale of choice for the arts-oriented community and others who liked to be near restaurants and entertainment. Still, heavy fears tinged this optimism. Residents definitively supported a 42nd Street cleanup, yet they were equally apprehensive of its displacement impacts, fearing an intensification of real estate pressures even more than an expansion of porn shops, street crime, and hustling that might spill over into the neighborhood's streets. However much exaggeration seemed to accompany their testimony at public hearings, their fears were well founded. So were those of the small businesses in Times Square.

To the real estate community, development opportunity in Times Square had standing as a dream long deferred. Great real estate plays from new, higher-density office uses on West 42nd Street had tantalized investors as early the 1920s when modern office buildings began to line the street in a march across town from Second Avenue to Sixth Avenue. In 1927, with the announcement of plans for two skyscrapers on the block between Seventh Avenue and Eighth Avenue, the move westward appeared imminent. Although the depression and World War II thwarted any plans for the area's redevelopment, during the 1950s and 1960s notable land assemblages in the Times Square district, from Sixth Avenue to the Hudson River, were in the making. Underneath the derelict buildings and surface parking lots lay a potential gold mine for those with long-term vision and the patience to hold property until public action or market trends swept away obstacles to development. The best way to acquire a site for new development was to acquire an existing theater or a series of store-front walk-ups and fill it with ground-floor "taxpayers," tenants that paid at least enough rent to cover the property taxes. Eventually, so the logic went, these obsolete structures could be torn down to make way for much more lucrative office towers.

Postwar building on Broadway remained rare until the celebrated Astor Hotel, a landmark since its opening in 1905, was torn down in 1969 and the site redeveloped into a 1.4-million-square-foot office tower. This event signaled just how precarious the future would be for a Times Square district singularly dedicated to entertainment. The development of One Astor Place (1515 Broadway, now the home of Viacom), covered the western Broadway block between 44th and 45th Streets, and is most notable as the defining event that led to the creation of the city's first special zoning district, the Special Theater District, although the 54-story building itself is ordinary. After much negotiation, the new zoning offered the tower's developers, the Minskoffs, a 20-percent zoning bonus in exchange for a 1,621-seat theater suitable for large-scale "legitimate" theatrical performances and a 1,500-seat movie theater. Its opening in 1971 marked the completion of a development concept put forth as early as 1947 to turn

2.22
Postcard perspective of the new Port Authority Bus Terminal, built 1947-50, shielding from view its connecting ramps to the Lincoln Tunnel entrance plaza, its 450-car rooftop parking lot and multilevel accommodation for 2,500 buses per day. (Collection of the author)

the old hotel site into new offices for Hollywood movie maker Metro-Goldwyn-Mayer; it also marked the "dramatic acceleration in the shift from Times Square's principal role as a nighttime world of entertainment to its hitherto secondary daytime role as an office district."[34] Before the collapse of the city's office market in 1973–1974, development in the Times Square district produced several other new towers: 1411 Broadway (1969), 1500 Broadway (1970), 1633 Broadway (1971), and 1700 Broadway (1969).

So it was familiar news in 1978 when the CUNY survey reported a "new sense of optimism": The mood among local investors was "decidedly upbeat" and commercial lenders with business interests in midtown Manhattan regarded Times Square as a "prime location for investment."[35] A knowledgeable observer of real estate trends would have readily recognized a resurgence of the industry's decades-dormant expectations. Neither time nor physical decay nor public policy had altered the strategic centrality of Times Square as a business and transportation hub for midtown Manhattan. In fact, intense high-density development on the East Side during the intervening years made the move west even more logical. "Plans and projects are simmering all over the Midtown West Side," Huxtable wrote in 1979. "A surprising number of these are aimed at the Times Square area, in spite of its unsavory state and reputation. . . . And these schemes don't appear, with builders expressing interest in them, unless there is a reasonable expectation of success and profit."[36] On the wall in the West 42nd Street office of the director of the Mayor's Office of Midtown Planning and Development, Kenneth Halpern, was a map showing more than 20 development projects from 40th to 54th Street between Sixth and Eighth Avenues. These included the 2,020-room Portman hotel and the entertainment center proposed by the City at 42nd Street group, discussed shortly, as well as a pedestrian mall down Broadway, a giant discotheque, two theaters, an apartment building, a revitalized restaurant row on West 46th Street, and the expansion and modernization of the Port Authority Bus Terminal.

With all these different interests in the neighborhood—vocal residents anxious about their future, healthy small businesses and shops catering to the entertainment industry, civic groups with a mission to protect the past and future cityscape, profitable porn enterprises on short-term leases, waiting real estate speculators, and city officials eager to clean up a civic disgrace with an international reputation—the political stakes, inevitably, were high. The diversity of interests acting against the backdrop of West 42nd Street's symbolic meaning set up social and political tensions that would hamper implementation of any redevelopment plan, but especially one that turned its back on the area's raffish and glitzy character in an effort to clear away the sleaze. The early efforts almost oozed with an optimism that, in retrospect, was living on borrowed time. Still held at bay was the cynicism and intense opposition to large-scale development from New York's fragmented and contentious interest groups that emerged so forcefully in the 1980s.

Moreover, it was not at all clear whether the cleanup forces would succeed. They would have to prevail over what CUNY researchers found to be powerful sociologically driven market forces ruling West 42nd Street in the late 1970s. Their informed assessment of the prospects was not terribly sanguine:[37]

> At present time there is a battle going on between the middle class of the city, and particularly its cultural inno-vators (architects, businessmen, planners, local residents, and clergymen), and the street culture class over who will control the street and gather its gold. . . . Presently the street people are extracting a small-time "nickel-and-dime" profit while the owners of theaters and peep shows are claiming the larger stakes. Would an even larg-er staking out of the territory by big business eliminate the penny ante dealer and street hustlers? . . . probably not likely.

Intense field observation had convinced them that the street performed a therapeutic function. During the period of great social unrest in the 1960s and 1970s, the permissive chaos and amoral climate of West 42nd Street operated as a local outlet for broad-based societal tensions, which were manifesting themselves most acutely in urban areas—in the drugs, crime and violence, and general lawlessness that seemed to prevail and con-tributed to the flight of white middle-class households to the suburbs. In that context, West 42nd Street served not only as a metaphor for New York's ills but as a unique icon of urban distress, which was how the national press and movie industry vividly portrayed the situation. To this way of thinking, the street was administering to the needs of the suffering urban psyche of the twentieth century.

Private Beginnings

Throughout the 1960s and 1970s, public actions to deal with pornography and prostitution in Times Square and its associated criminal activity were continuous: vice cleanups, prostitution crackdowns, massage-parlor sweeps, more stringent licensing requirements, surveillance and law-enforcement efforts, antisleaze laws, porn-zone ordinances, antiporn zoning amend-ments, special citizen councils and civic committees, planning studies. (See appendix C for a list of public strategies and policy actions designed to improve conditions in Times Square.) A succession of mayors—Robert F. Wagner (1954–1965), John V. Lindsay (1966–1973), Abraham D. Beame (1974–1977)—and their city planning commissioners revisited ever-worsening conditions, effectuating little positive change. Others preceded them—Fiorello H. LaGuardia (1934–1945) and William O'Dwyer (1946–1950)—a period that became legendary for its ineffectualness. Reporting in April 1977 on Mayor Beame's new campaign against vice, the *Economist* interpreted it as a "clear signal that he is in the race [for mayor]." It was, the influential London-based weekly explained, "little more than an election gambit," the most recent in a long line of such publicity-seeking efforts no more likely to have permanent or serious impact than those of the past. "Mayor Fiorello LaGuardia banned burlesque performances in 1937, when he was first up for reelection. Mayors Robert Wagner and John Lindsay tried to clean up Times Square every four years, prodding the police to arrest prostitutes and to clear the streets of other 'undesirables.' But these flurries have always failed, partly because the courts found the evidence inadequate, partly because porn is an industry that attracts tourists and provides jobs."[38] Cleaning up West 42nd Street, another reporter similarly concluded, was something of "a long-running joke in New York City politics: Everyone who ever runs for anything in the city has promised to do 'something' about The Street. No one ever really does."[39]

If the city seemed stymied in its efforts to stem the swelling tide of social decay, the U.S. Supreme Court decision in 1974 upholding citizens' First-Amendment rights to publish, sell, or buy pornographic literature as well as to present pornographic theatrical entertainment further constrained policy choices. Acting in accord with conventional planning roles, public policy was avowedly passive. "We applaud, but we cannot initiate. It [redevelopment] has to be a private enterprise effort," remarked City Planning Commissioner James Felt in response to the announcement in 1962 that the Broadway Association had hired architect Richard W. Snibbe to blueprint a new 42nd Street.[40] More than the plan itself, the ambitions and logic of the private-business group would ultimately set the stage for the upgrading agenda, though it would take nearly thirty years to get there.

Founded in 1911 by a group of prominent Times Square businessmen, the Broadway Association sought a revival of "class" in Times Square, and not for the first time. Once it realized that the brief prosperity of postwar victory would not rid the street of its sleazy establishments, the group convinced the city to amend the zoning code—twice, in 1947 and 1954—with antisleaze provisions designed to prevent the opening of penny arcades and "sucker-auction" establishments. More than a decade later, the association switched tactics and aimed to reclaim the entire block for "the cause of legitimate theater." Seriously concerned that the decline of West 42nd Street would jeopardize the Theater District as a whole, their 1962 plan called for the remodeling of ten run-down movies houses, with some converted into stylish supper clubs for dining, cabaret entertainment, and gambling. Victorian-inspired sidewalk arcades with second-story pedestrian overpasses would cross the street at several points and a mall landscaped with seasonally appropriate potted plants would stretch down the length of the block (figure 2.23). How this would all come into being was unclear, but as one set of architectural historians noted, "With its mix of planning ideas taken from suburban shopping malls and a sense of glittering urbanity that was difficult to reconcile with the street's ugly realities, Snibbe's unrealized scheme was at least provocative."[41]

2.23
The Broadway Association's plan
for the redevelopment of West
42nd Street, 1962. (Richard W.
Snibbe, FAIA Architect. George
Rudolph, delineator)

The association's vision of a new 42nd Street might have taken
its cues from the activities of maverick realtor Irving Maidman, who pioneered a new location for the city's experimental Off-Broadway theater
(traditionally located in Greenwich Village) on the 400 block of 42nd
Street between Ninth and Tenth Avenues, two blocks removed from the
historic and troubled core of Times Square. Between 1960 and 1962, he
opened a series of small theaters, some with restaurants, and all with
rehearsal halls and workshops for building and storing sets, props, and costumes—critically important space in short supply throughout the entire
Theater District. While Maidman hoped to showcase the theaters, in line
with classic real estate logic, he also hoped to boost the value of his other
real estate holdings in the neighborhood.[42]

Maidman's activities were prophetic, though his timing suffered.
More than 15 years would lapse before the appearance of the next phase
of this Off-Off-Broadway investment, Theater Row I (1978) and II
(1982). Developed as an incubator for the performing arts, Theater Row
resulted from the vision and dogged persistence of another maverick,
Frederic S. Papert, a former president of the Municipal Art Society, who
founded the not-for-profit 42nd Street Development Corporation (42RC)
in 1976 "to reverse 42nd Street's fall from grace" by upgrading, restoring,
and redeveloping the street "from river to river." (figure 2.24). The opportunity to turn seedy buildings into attractive entertainment venues in that
stretch of 42nd Street just blocks away from the heart of Times Square,
which both Maidman and Papert exploited ingeniously, owed a lot to
two key market fundamentals: depressed property values and the lack of
competing land uses for the sites.[43] In short, the development path of
commercial real estate did not get in the way of pioneering their risky
concept.

The distance east to Broadway was only two blocks, but it
loomed as a chasm in terms of development potential. Although Broadway
north of West 42nd Street had remained virtually unchanged for nearly 25
years after World War II, it still held its position as the next logical place

for future office, retail, and hotel development. The psychological barrier
of Sixth Avenue had been breached, as the development of One Astor
Place made clear, if ever so slightly. Economic events may have thwarted
redevelopment in the past, but the vicissitudes of the real estate cycle
rarely alter the path of growth, only its timing. Broadway was where the
competitive race for new skyscraper development would be staged. It was
where land assemblages were proceeding quietly with the expectation of
an expanding midtown office district. It was where the underused zoning
capacity of the district's low-density theaters and five-to-seven story buildings created "soft spots"—large parcels of land awaiting redevelopment.
From this perspective, adding some office buildings to the mix of Times
Square would not deviate from established mixed usage. Since the early
part of the century, "large office buildings fronted and interspersed with
great theater marquees" defined the "classic" shape of Times Square.[44]
Following the dictates of market opportunities in the 1980s, however, the
meaning of "large" would change dramatically. The threat to the Theater
District lay not in the new office buildings per se, but in the loss of existing theaters and the urban-design implications of a Broadway refashioned

by high-density office buildings. Out of these uncertainties came a series
of visions for West 42nd Street.

Vision #1: The City at 42nd Street

Redevelopment along the seedy streets of Times Square during the 1960s
and 1970s reflected the incremental decisions of a handful of private
developers and investors acting in response to announcements of major
public investments such as the convention center or speculating on the
eventual expansion of the office district and the timing of neighborhood
change. These were not coordinated actions, nor even actions coincident
in time, but rather a series of maverick forays and isolated speculations.
When, however, the double whammy of a national economic recession
and a local fiscal crisis brought the city to the brink of default in the mid-
1970s, a chill descended on this small-scale investment activity.

   Into a semicomatose state of market inertia in the late 1970s
stepped Papert and his not-for-profit organization with a bold and comprehensive plan, *The City at 42nd Street* (figure 2.25). The ambitious plan
aimed to transform the entire three-block area from 41st Street to 43rd
Street between Seventh Avenue and Eight Avenue into a combined world's
fair, theme park, and cultural showcase for New York. "It was a garbage
dump, a bad business, and city suicide not to do anything about it. A

2.25
The City at 42nd Inc.'s plan for
the redevelopment of West 42nd
Street, 1978. (Design: Chermayeff
& Geismar)

cleanup was necessary. The city's brightest memory was living like a bum," he remarked in an interview echoing one of his catchy marketing slogans for the effort.[45]

Fresh from his success with Theater Row, Papert was ready to tackle his next 42nd Street project, which he firmly believed should also be anchored by the performing arts. The idea for both projects had been to proceed with "one-small-scale capital-intensive project at a time," he wrote Louis Winnick, then president of the Ford Foundation, which was underwriting the major predevelopment expenses for the venture, to an eventual total of $600,000. They planned to start with the block's cornerstone, the New Amsterdam Theater, because it possessed the second-best stage for dance in town after the New York State Theater at Lincoln Center. Economic reality, however, quickly altered the feasibility of this strategy: Real estate on the hard-core block of West 42nd Street had become too expensive. The New Amsterdam's owner wanted eight million dollars for the theater, yet, as Papert explained to Winnick, the owner cited a value of only $700,000 in legal papers appealing for a reduction in the theater's property-tax assessment. This led Papert "to conclude that a bigger idea was needed, one that provided condemnation powers, and that led to *The City at 42nd Street*."[46]

Papert shaped his plan to accommodate economic realities and the rules of potential private investors. On the basis of strong advice from real estate experts at Equitable Life Assurance Society of America, a senior day-to-day adviser on the marketing and financial aspects of the plan and a potential lender on the project, he came to understand that revenues from theme-park admissions could not possibly support the debt needed to carry the project. To meet conventional lending standards, Equitable's people argued definitively, meant greater emphasis on commercial real estate development, in particular office space. The die for shaping the future 42nd Street had been cast.

Papert's revised vision for *The City at 42nd Street* was indeed large. Working with a consortium of "concerned and talented New York architects and designers under the design direction of Richard Weinstein,"[47] former director of the Mayor's Office of Lower Manhattan Planning and Development and a winner of the Prix de Rome in architecture, Papert and former City Planning Commission chairman Donald H. Elliott aimed to restore and redevelop this "deteriorated and blighted" stretch of 42nd Street.[48] The group's plan called for a $600-million development program composed of six interrelated elements: the restoration of five architecturally and historically important theaters for legitimate stagehouse productions (the New Amsterdam and the Victory for nonprofit companies; the Selwyn, the Apollo, and the Harris for commercial operators) and facade preservation of three others (the Lyric, the Times Square, and the Empire); the creation of a 500,000-square-foot "educational, entertainment and exhibit center" designed to "extend the tradition of entertainment which is rooted in the history of the Street, and builds on recent developments in the theater, cinemas, and popular entertainment";

400,000 square feet of retail shops and restaurants arranged on two levels and connected to the Port Authority Bus Terminal and across 42nd Street by second-level bridges; four million square feet of office space in three 42-story towers (one would be increased to 70 stories) on sites surrounding the former Times Tower, which would be torn down and "replaced by a major public open space furnished with an electronic display that will update the news with pictures and text"; a 2.1-million-square-foot merchandise mart to provide garment manufacturers with modern and conveniently arranged showroom space under one roof (an idea that came from people in the fashion industry who believed new space would bring together foreign and domestic designers and shows); and a renovated subway connection in the Times Square station built in conjunction with the project's office towers. The office space and merchandise mart pieces of the program were huge. Overall, with nearly seven million square feet of new and renovated building proposed for the project area's eight acres, the massing promised to be dense, especially around the public open space that marked the Times Square intersection.[49]

Entertainment for the middle class made up the programmatic centerpiece of *The City at 42nd Street*. The planned exhibition center would examine life in New York and make it "more understandable to visitors"; exhibit designers would create "unique attractions for large numbers of people" employing the newest of media technologies already pioneered at world's fairs and theme parks. An IMAX Theater would provide "a unique trip around the world." The "Slice of the Apple" would "simulate the experience of rising from the subterranean depths of New York City up to the top of the tallest skyscrapers." "The Vertical Theater" would "give a balloon rider's view of public celebrations in great public spaces around the world."[50] None of this would be free, however. In order to cover operating costs and finance the building program, an expected three-and-a-half to five million visitors would pay an average admission charge pegged at $4.00 per head. Papert's group also planned to sell $40 million in corporate sponsorships, taking a lesson from Disney's Epcot Center.

This vision of a new 42nd Street was not for everyone. Huxtable was characteristically sharp and on point:[51]

> To fund the displays, which to some minds, are not all
> that wonderful an idea, would require the construction
> of three very large office towers that would be partly
> located on non-blighted land ... [and] include the dem-
> olition of the much-remodeled, little old Times Tower
> between them. This is unnecessary nonsense. The pro-
> posed construction is an overly brutal scheme tacked
> onto a questionable land use for Midtown, as well as
> more theater destruction on the 42d Street block than
> some of the city planners think necessary. The project is
> far more intriguing as a legal and financial exercise than

it is admirable as design. With all of its expertise, the
scheme has an unhappy resemblance to a discredited
tradition of urban renewal.

Nostalgia for the street's seediness and danger also held strong appeal for
those who believed that grit was an integral part of what made a city,
especially New York: "Do planners know how hard it is to achieve a visual
clutter so extreme that it makes the simple traversal of one city block as
adventurous as passing through a gauntlet?" (figures 2.26, 2.27) asked
author Philip Lopate in a *New York Times* op-ed titled "42d Street You Ain't
No Sodom." "Sure, there are hustlers, thieves, prostitutes, cripples, derelicts,
winos, molesters, monsters, droolers, accosters. I'm not denying it. Would
you prefer to cement over the whole beehive with a dipsy-doodle exhibition hall and kick out those people so they'll congregate on another block
and make a new heaven and hell somewhere else, maybe not as bright and
never as satisfyingly central?"[52]

The forces behind *The City at 42nd Street* represented a significant sampling of the corporate, civic, and cultural elite of the city, and they
had been marshaled expressly for the formidable task at hand. Papert's
group created a separate nonprofit entity, The City at 42nd Street, Inc.
(CA42), with its own powerhouse board of directors headed by John
Gutfreund, managing partner of Salomon Brothers.[53] "We needed a board
of impeccable character to do this," Elliott recalled.[54] CA42 was spun off
by the 42RC to establish financial credibility for the project, whose much
expanded scope was now critically dependent upon the development
massing of "excess" air rights—about 3.4 million square feet—from the
street's low-density theaters in order to guarantee its financial viability.
Elliott's group prepared an extraordinarily well documented set of materials in support of the proposal they would submit to the city for assistance
in implementing their plan. CA42 spent time at Disney studying its operations, planning, and people. They also approached the company about participation, but Disney "didn't want to be involved with any idea that was
controversial; they only wanted a visual story, not a talk or text story,"
Elliott recalled. "We were told, Disney didn't do these things downtown,
in New York City."[55]

Papert promoted the project tirelessly, briefing a broad range of
cultural and arts entities as well as the city's fiscal monitors and a roster of
blue-chip corporations. With the Ford Foundation leading the way, initial
funding in excess of one million dollars came from public and private
sources, including the Port Authority of New York and New Jersey, the
City of New York, the Rockefeller Brothers Fund, I.B.M., The Chase
Manhattan Bank, Exxon, Equitable Life Assurance Society, Morgan
Guaranty Trust, the National Endowment for the Arts, and the New York
Times Foundation. Contrary to what Huxtable concluded, the obvious
thoughtfulness and professionalism of preparation mirrored the seriousness
of their efforts: "*The City at 42nd Street* was not a planning exercise, but a
development exercise," Elliott emphasized.[56]

As sponsor of the development project, CA42 projected an ambitious vision with substantial financial backing. It passed the first test of feasibility when it lined up major-name private firms with "demonstrated capacity" to develop the project's commercial components—Olympia & York (O&Y) from Canada to build the three office towers, all at once, and New York's Helmsley-Spear Inc. to build the fashion mart. But the big development could not go forward without the city; it had to be a public-private venture. Elliot and his group needed the city's full political and legal support to secure the necessary approvals for zoning changes allowing the critically important transfer of development rights from one parcel to another, bridges across streets, and designation as an urban-renewal plan authorizing the acquisition of all property in the project area by condemnation or negotiated purchase. They also needed tax abatements and the city's help to secure approximately $40 million in federal grant funds to finance the land acquisitions for the theater restorations and the education/entertainment/exhibit center. The scope and character of the plan was bigger than any private development proposal ever put before the city; moreover, it called for aggressive public-development actions.

Elliot directed his discussions with the city through the chairman of the City Planning Commission, Robert F. Wagner, Jr. (later a deputy mayor), with a copy of written correspondence going to Koch's key advisor and deputy mayor for economic development, Peter J. Solomon. In addition to "repeated consultations" with Wagner and Solomon, he and Weinstein were meeting with staff from six city agencies and Kenneth Halpern and John West of the city's Office of Midtown Planning and Development to review the project in detail. Although the city would not be at risk for any land acquisition or construction, official encouragement remained lukewarm, at best. In a progress memo to the CA42 board of directors, Elliott reported that city officials expressed basic support for the project but remained skeptical of its scale and financing plan, the usefulness of a fashion mart, and the requirement by O&Y that the former Times Tower be demolished. Persistent, persuasive and ever the optimist, Papert explained the problem to Winnick:[57]

> What had seemed an unassailable, even heroic, plan to
> remove blight was sounding more like yet another, mas-
> sive, insensitive Urban Renewal scheme. In fact, market
> economics will dictate how and where air rights will be
> developed, and if bulk (especially tax and revenue-gen-
> erating bulk) is the price the City has to pay to physical-
> ly upgrade its most famous Street, that would be a small
> price, indeed. In any case, adjustments are being made,
> the good but badly introduced idea of demolishing the
> Times Tower has been shelved, and City approvals are
> expected shortly.

2.26
West 42nd Street scene, 1970s.
(NYC Economic Development
Corporation)

2.27
Live adult shows, West 42nd
Street, 1978. (© 2001 Maggie
Hopp)

City officials asked for demonstrable evidence that air-rights development was essential to finance the project and satisfaction on other items as well, nominally. What Mayor Koch really wanted soon revealed itself: total control over the project. And in June 1980, to the chagrin of the business supporters who believed that the mayor had been in their corner from the time the project was announced in 1978, Koch withheld support, derisively dismissing *The City at 42nd Street* as "Disneyland on 42nd Street." He called for "seltzer instead of orange juice."[58] It was "awful: Ferris-wheel image, Disney, hanging gardens of Babylon," he said in retrospect.[59] He did not want an urban theme park on West 42nd Street, but his main point of opposition was the awarding of an exclusive contract to the CA42 and its development partners. Gutfreund, according to Koch, said he was not to be stopped. In response, Koch replied, "No, not with your money, but there will be no city money." In rejecting the proposed program with its emphasis on commercial culture and tourism, Koch used the opportunity to announce a city commitment to do the project his way—publicly. He believed that the city would get the best deal only through an open competitive-bidding process and that the blighted area had enough profit potential to attract other developers. Koch wanted the city to draw up guidelines, advertise for proposals and elicit community commentary and city-agency participation. He agreed with Elliott's assessment that such a process would kill the CA42's plan "because the commitments of the developers were not eternal."[60] City Hall, the *Wall Street Journal* reported, sees itself in an adversarial position with real estate interests and "doesn't want to be at the mercy of the sharks—the developers."[61]

To this day, Elliot remains convinced that politics, not feasibility, killed the plan. "This was a Lindsay project. Koch pulled the plug on *The City at 42nd Street* because he wanted nothing to do with Lindsay or Lindsay people. We came very close to pulling it off," he emphasized several times in an interview. "The lost beauty of this proposal was that the land values were depressed and we had Olympia & York ready to finance and build the office towers, Helmsley-Spear to do the same with the fashion mart and Rockefeller Center, Inc., ready to participate. We also had widespread support in the business and civic community."[62]

Times Square's location as a mass-transit crossroads and juncture of several midtown commercial districts had long defined an infrastructure centrality that historically shaped its development and early reputation as a mixed-class area tolerant of diversity. It was notably different from nineteenth-century residential neighborhoods where restricted access had brought about uniformity and control over urban space as a means of realizing new economic value. From the start, its popular commercial culture was out of sync with the prevailing investment logic of real estate development. The positive legacy of innovation, cultural unpredictability, and risk that evolved over decades and distinguished Times Square had all but been lost, however, in the conspicuous transformations that turned West 42nd

Street into a tawdry concentration of action-movie theaters and sex shops and a haven for drug transactions and threateningly deviant behavior. If Times Square nevertheless remained a metaphor for the city's changing dynamics, it was stuck in a warp of immobility, unable to push itself forward as it had in the early part of the twentieth century.

2.28
Souvenirs (© 2001 Maggie Hopp)

It had become clear to the mayor and his advisors that neither the public efforts to date (recurrent prostitution and drug sweeps, inspired cleanups, dedicated code enforcement) nor the private efforts (Theater Row, Ford Foundation-driven CA42) would be able to restore the luster of Times Square. The market might be "simmering" on its own in selected areas of the district, but the Deuce itself appeared resistant to change. Moreover, consumer demand for the street's sex-for-sale and porn businesses seemed undiminished by porn's move into private bedrooms made possible by video technology. The street's access as a business location remained as central as ever. And, in the perverse way that public policy can often have unintended consequences, putting more cops on the beat was making the place "safer" for all sorts of drunks and other "undesirables."

Change on West 42nd Street was a matter of scale and timing. Incremental investment could not promise to drive out the "bad" uses; wholesale change would not happen by itself, at least within the time frame of a typical mayor. And Koch was not a typical mayor, even for New York. Two years into his first term, with the city on an economic upswing after a debilitating fiscal crisis, he was ready to take on the big project, even though the city appeared pushed into it as a defensive reaction to the CA42. A couple of elements were in place: OME's success with code enforcement, in effect, promoted real estate development as the strategy of choice and the goal of "good commercial uses" as a programmatic prescription; and the marketing efforts of the CA42 indicated that corporate power and big-name developers were ready to play roulette under the right conditions. As a politician, Koch wanted the credit and the glory that would come from cleaning up the intractable civic disgrace. Now he had to figure out how to do it.

While the Department of City Planning would shortly release its draft report on new zoning regulations for midtown Manhattan, which had been in the works for some time, public development was the emerging strategy of choice for cities around the country trying to rebuild their downtowns. New York would be no exception. In several key ways the city's plan for redeveloping West 42nd Street resembled the private blueprint for *The City at 42nd Street*. That was only natural since the latter functioned as the foundation for the city's plan. High-density office development at the intersection of 42nd Street, Seventh Avenue, and Broadway would continue to drive the city's development program. The reason was simple: It was necessary to pay the bill for the rest of the street's renovation—in the absence of federal grants or city funds for land condemnation.

C H A P T E R 3

THE PUBLIC TAKES CHARGE

If Mayor Koch's dismissal of *The City at 42nd Street* cast an intense limelight on the city to do something about Times Square, a blunt assessment
of the situation just as readily revealed a scarcity of resources, financial and
institutional, for moving forward with the task. "They didn't have a clue
about how to do it, nor did it have a vehicle," recalled one close participant.[1] The redevelopment of West 42nd Street, however, fit snugly within
Koch's ambitious plans to revitalize the economy of New York, an essential
policy priority given that he assumed office just as the city was emerging
from a traumatic fiscal crisis and near brush with bankruptcy. "Default
fears" were "seared into the mayor's mind,"[2] and he had to operate under
a strict mandate to balance the budget imposed by special state authorities
created to bail out the city. The changing character of the city's economy—the decline of its industrial sector with its serious loss of revenue and
job opportunities for blue-collar workers, the loss of white-collar jobs to
outlying metropolitan areas, and the repeated threats of corporations to
move their office activities from the city—also weighed heavily on the
mayor. Economic development emerged quickly as a top priority in the
early days of his administration as the mayor sensed opportunity in the
growing strength and continual expansion of the city's financial-services
sector, long recognized as the world's largest. The corollary to the policy
strategy came easily: If financial services held potential as an indispensable
source of city revenue, then commercial real estate development, the traditional stimulant to economic good fortune, could be made into a turbocharged fiscal generator for the city. "To grow and build the city-physical
became the centerpiece of the mayor's program," wrote political scientist
Jewel Bellush in an insightful review of the emergence of "tower power"
during the Koch era. "Development not only provided new sources of
municipal revenue, it served, in a very concrete and visible way, to symbolize New York's fiscal recovery and renewed vitality."[3]

Abetted by extraordinarily favorable real estate fundamentals, the twelve years of Koch's mayoralty became "the era of big development." Strong control over the reigns of city government afforded many channels through which the mayor could foster his build-and-grow priority—financial assistance (budget allocations for capital improvements, assessments, property taxes, subsidy and loan programs, and tax abatements), supportive land-use policies (negotiated development deals, midtown rezoning), special institutional arrangements (enlisting state government in for large-scale projects like the 42DP)—and Koch used them all to position his administration "as a willing partner with development." The 42DP in particular sent a "clear signal to developers that new space was being created for them."[4]

The aggressiveness with which the Koch administration pursued growth-oriented development throughout the 1980s set the critics to wondering aloud whether there were any control mechanisms governing the city's sale of development rights. In a city known for its aggressive developers, the city itself, acting as public developer, became one of the most aggressive players, negotiating complex deals with private firms for development on city-owned land and pushing hard for financial returns as well as public amenities. The limits on growth seemed few and far between. "The city is not likely to collapse this year or this decade, if 10 new skyscrapers are built, or 100," wrote *Times* architectural critic Paul Goldberger in 1982. "New York is remarkably resilient, and its total strangulation is not the issue. What is likely to happen is not collapse, but something far less dramatic—a slow, steady increase in noise and the tension and the crowding and the shadows. Such changes are impossible to quantify, impossible to measure in absolute terms. But they are certain to come—if they are not already here."[5] Other critics and journalists railed that the city was pursuing short-term gain at the expense of long-term public interest. "Creeping giantism," Ada Louise Huxtable termed the city's seemingly addictive proclivity for favoring high towers and big bucks; *City for Sale* shouted newsmen Jack Newfield and Wayne Barrett's more general investigative exposé of greed and corruption during the Koch era.

It was in this context that the city tackled the largest and inherently most controversial redevelopment project of its history. The 42DP required large-scale condemnation—in midtown Manhattan. It was predicated on commercial land uses and was destined to carry over one or more real estate cycles. What would hold it together? How would city officials manage the political exposure to shifting alliances, escalating costs, and continuous litigation, all of which spelled potential failure? How would the city finance its big ambitions when it was still a little shaky financially and, for both political and fiscal reasons, it could take no financial risk?

SEARCHING FOR CAPACITY

Mayor Koch's gambit discarding the Ford Foundation's plan raised the ante of earlier cleanup efforts because in 1980 New York's capacity to execute public-development projects or complex city-planning objectives was decidedly deficient. The Department of City Planning (DCP), which during the Lindsay era had built a reputation for innovation and excellence in urban design, had almost ceased functioning and could now do little more than react to events. Debilitating staff cutbacks brought on by the city's fiscal belt-tightening and a severe backlog of work triggered by new environmental-regulation requirements and community-review processes severely compromised its ability to handle any initiatives beyond the ordinary processing of approvals. In the heyday of development during the Koch years, the city was processing over 10,000 major building permits a year, more than enough to keep the planning staff occupied. Also, Koch's deputy mayor for policy and physical development, Robert Esnard, was an architect and planner, and he wanted to make key decisions himself. Agency morale suffered from the reductions of staff, and clarity of direction was missing as well. Koch's less-than-favorable disposition toward "egghead planners" and his strong belief in the private marketplace tipped his administration's hand toward entrepreneurial deal making.

Managing the first half of the era's aggressive deal making was Herbert J. Sturz, chairman of the City Planning Commission (CPC). A top adviser to Mayor Koch since the inception of his administration, Sturz had been deputy mayor for criminal justice before being appointed to chair the CPC in 1980. Early in his career he helped found and directed the Vera Institute of Justice, a foundation dedicated to the improvement of the criminal justice system. As chairman of the CPC, Sturz pushed forward the city's aggressive pursuit of private investment until he left government service in 1986 to join the editorial board of the *Times*. Although new to the field of real estate development, he was a fast learner who surrounded himself with good people. On taking over as chairman of the CPC, the 49-year old Sturz saw that *The City at 42nd Street* was "dead." He believed that the plan was not feasible and objected to the private group's decision to entrust the project to a singular "master" developer. After rejecting the Ford Foundation's proposal, Sturz wanted the city to do 42nd Street alone, without the state's involvement, but did not think the city could do it, and he agonized over how best to proceed with implementation. He sensed this project, this decision, demanded new directions in policy.

The city's entrepreneurial arm, the Public Development Corporation (PDC), was the logical choice to lead the redevelopment project, but it "did not have the power nor the track record and credibility to do the job, though it had some good people," Sturz remarked.[6] Created in 1966 as a not-for-profit corporation to serve as the city's lead real estate entity, PDC had the unique ability to dispose of land acquired from the city on a sole-source basis, rather than through a competitive-bid process or auction. On paper, its special position within city government afforded flexibility to advance projects more quickly than city agencies since it could structure deals and pursue its mission largely unfettered by red-tape constraints of the public bureaucracy. Expertise was another matter, however. Only later, in the mid-1980s, did PDC command the capacity, after it had developed a reputation as an experienced, decisive operator able to move fast on construction projects. Even so, its role as a public developer was first defined by industrial projects such as the suburban-style Bathgate Industrial Park, not high-density commercial real estate development. And when PDC became focused on more complex commercial development projects, in Brooklyn, for example, the subtext of its activity was to create a track record, "to prove that the city could get things done," recalled Steven Spinola, who led the agency from 1983 through 1986.[7] Capacity was not the only problem: PDC did not have the clear statutory authority to undertake condemnation—and land-use experts considered the city's process for land taking to be relatively slow—or the ability to do customized deals for tax abatements as did the state's public-benefit corporations, particularly, the New York State Urban Development Corporation (UDC). When Koch announced that the city had joined forces with UDC, the reasoning was straightforward: "They have the expertise, and they know how to move fast."[8]

While the city needed the full strength of UDC's statutory powers, the clarity of that need did not make the decision any easier for Sturz, who thought long and hard about the potential loss of control accompanying such an institutional coalition. Bringing in the state as lead agency for the project marked the first of several unusual twists of public policy distinguishing the 42DP from other big projects in the city. Combining these public players paired the city's chief regulator (CPC) with two entrepreneurial entities (PDC and UDC) to spearhead a proprietary project. It meant that the city be would be simultaneously playing the role of regulator and developer. It was a turn of direction in planning practice bound to increase the political risks of the initiative (as happened so dramatically several years later in another large-scale project, the redevelopment of the Coliseum site at Columbus Circle). Twice before the city had paired up with UDC to prime the pump of private investment with catalytic projects, notably for Donald Trump's renovation of the Commodore (Grand Hyatt) Hotel (on East 42nd Street) and John Portman's revived efforts to build a hotel in Times Square. In these instances urban-renewal powers were used, but relatively selectively. Application of condemnation powers to the 42DP put the initiative in a different league because scope alone—a 13-acre project in midtown Manhattan—made the redevelopment far more complex than either of those single-building projects. In terms of investment ambitions, the then-$1.6-billion project was the largest proposed redevelopment initiative in the country. From a political perspective, the 42DP was the most visible of several large-scale public developments in the city being undertaken by a coalition of powerful public entities.[9] As a prototype for tackling ambitious and complicated redevelopment efforts, city/state coalition deal making would come to dominate big planning initiatives in New York.

The new policies put in place to implement the 42DP reflected the demands of the project's double-barreled political agenda: to sweep clean the moral mess that ruled West 42nd Street in a way that did not expose

the city to any financial risk and put in place new activity consonant with
the mayor's economic goal of growing the city's financial-services sector.
Some goals, such as the replacement of "bad" land uses with "good" land
uses, could be specified immediately. Others—the program for revitalizing
the midblock theaters—could only evolve over time, as the city gauged
the scope and feasibility of what the market would support in this location. The early years of execution from 1981 to 1984—during which time
city and state planners put together a redevelopment plan, issued requests
for proposals (RFPs), designated private developers, and presented and
secured approval for the project from the city's Board of Estimate
(BOE)—proved formative. The public-private deals for the 42DP that
came to fruition during this time represented a clever packaging of the
city's limited resources. Over time they would prove to be a little too
clever in terms of the political risks that attached themselves to the project
because the complexity of the city's strategy for financing the costs of
redevelopment and the primacy of the office-development agenda unwittingly held the seeds of costly controversy.

THE COALITION

Turning to UDC was purely pragmatic, for the city did not have what it
took "to deal the deal," as one player put it. Until Koch created the position of deputy mayor for economic development, to which he appointed
an investment banker, Peter J. Solomon, and beefed up capacity at PDC,
headed by Philip E. Aarons, "UDC as well as BPCA [a UDC subsidiary
singularly focused to the development of Battery Park City in lower
Manhattan] filled a vacuum for things the city wasn't doing," recalled
Stephen A. Lefkowitz, the city's outside counsel for the 42DP who had
been in on the drafting of the original UDC legislation.[10] Created in
1968, almost overnight in the aftermath of the assassination of Martin
Luther King, Jr., UDC owed its existence, in large part, to the enormous
pressure exerted by Governor Nelson A. Rockefeller. Endowed with
extraordinary and controversial development powers, UDC under the creative leadership of the late city planner Edward J. Logue ushered in the era
of public-entrepreneurial ventures with its statewide development of well-
designed subsidized housing, new towns, and urban projects.[11] During the
early 1970s, the public authority acquired an outstanding "can-do" reputation for getting the job done. By 1980, however, its political status had
been greatly diminished as a result of a traumatic bankruptcy/default crisis
in 1975, from which it had barely recovered. Despite being in something
of a down mode, in terms of institutional capacity, no other state agency
had as seasoned a team of in-house development professionals—in construction, finance, urban planning, engineering, architecture, law, public
approvals, and management—as did UDC.

The force behind its institutional personality came from a combination of powers only UDC could bring to the deal-making process: the
legal status as would-be landowner to negotiate customized tax agreements

for commercial projects, the police power of eminent domain to condemn land, and a unique statutory power to override local land-use regulations. The scope of authority was why the agency had received uncommon attention from every governor since Rockefeller.[12] Using these extraordinary powers, UDC could take title to the property, package the financial deal for the city, then transfer the parcels' development rights to private developers through long-term lease arrangements. The agency did not need to provide any financing, just supply its tax-exempt status and real estate expertise.[13]

With UDC's designation as "lead agency" for the 42DP, city officials were counting on fewer delays and more certainty with the approvals process because the project would come under the state's environmental review processes (SEQR) rather than the more stringent environmental review process governing the city's statute (CEQR). Even more important, bringing UDC into the process meant that the project would bypass the maze of local approvals—zoning, building codes, review by the community board under the city's Uniform Land Use Review Process (ULURP), which includes a nonbinding vote by the community board within whose jurisdiction the project falls, and additional hearings before the CPC. Presumably, this would also shorten the period of approval preceding development, which political scientist John Mollenkopf's research indicated had lengthened from 18 months to five years for large projects owing to the interacting layers of regulation. Legally, a UDC project did not even need approval from the BOE, the city's now-defunct unique executive board made up of the comptroller, the city council president, and the five borough presidents with whom the mayor was forced to share power.[14] But that was not a feasible end-run, politically. The BOE imprimatur was necessary, Lefkowitz emphasized in an interview, and, following Koch's decision on the issue, its review became part of the process, voluntarily.

In June 1980 the city and UDC signed a "Memorandum of Understanding" (MOU) setting forth the intention of the parties "to cooperate in the preparation and implementation of a plan for the redevelopment of the area around 42nd Street in Manhattan." The agreement defined relations, formally. The four-page document contained a lot of "joint language" outlining general responsibilities for planning, project management, developer selection, and project implementation and defining turf along what one participant described as a "natural division of responsibility." Acting on the premise that city land, city tax dollars, and city interests were at stake, city officials took the lead on the financial aspects of the deal. As the designated lead agency, UDC held responsibility for project implementation. For planning, design, and development programming, a joint structure was set up, though responsibility in this area would, in effect, become "a function of the people involved, their personalities, and their strengths in light of the tasks to be done."[15] In practice, "the clear line between issues of finance and process was not that simple; it was more of a joint effort," Sturz recalled.[16] Still, as an exercise in joint power, the 42DP existed within the bigger political orbit of city/state relations. And while the city/state partnership may have been a pragmatic choice based UDC's unique powers, it was not an easy relationship for the city.

What city officials feared most was that the state would grab control for its own purposes. UDC's role, by design, was only that of a broker and a vehicle for process. In negotiations, it was to throw everything back to the city because it was not positioned to take risks, but rather shift them to the city. As a matter of course, the state and the city—represented three ways, by the mayor's office, CPC, and PDC—acted in response to different agendas, needs, and constituencies. Despite consensus on the overall strategic goals of the project, tensions within the institutional coalition inevitably arose and as city and state officials worked through the concrete details of how to meet their mutual goal, tactical differences emerged, dramatically in some instances. Nowhere were such governance tensions more apparent than in the political standoff over the selection of a developer for a 2.4-million square-foot wholesale trade mart in 1983, a key episode in the project's life.

After the first team selected to develop the mart (Richard Reinis and David Morse, members of the family that owned the California Mart in Los Angeles) was removed in November 1982 for failure to deliver on administrative payments to UDC, the site was once again put out to bid. UDC invited 49 organizations to submit proposals for development, but none responded. After a three-month search proved fruitless, UDC approached New York developer Paul Milstein, the unsuccessful bidder for the four office sites, as explained in the next chapter, who had joined with an owner of property in the Garment District, Alan Weiler, for the development of this site, and entered into exclusive negotiations with the developers. By June 1983, talks had progressed to the point whereby UDC was able to send Milstein a proposed Memorandum of Terms for development of the mart site; two months later they had reportedly reached a negotiated agreement, in principle. During this time, UDC also advised the Milstein-led team, now joined by A. Alfred Taubman, one of the nation's most prominent shopping center developers, to purchase a tract of land within the project area (on the southeast corner of 42nd Street and Eighth Avenue) on which the state corporation held an expiring option "on the assurance that it would soon be officially designated as the Mart developer."[17] To avoid getting preempted by someone else, the developer group went ahead with the purchase, which represented approximately 25 percent of the land necessary for developing the mart, at a price of approximately $5 million.[18]

In the meantime, George Klein, the developer conditionally designated to build the four office sites on the eastern end of the project area, phoned Milstein asking for—or, depending upon the source of information, "demanding"—a half-interest in the mart project. Milstein's predictable response: "no way". Klein, in turn, reportedly threatened Milstein, saying "I'll make sure you don't get the project."[19] Relations between these two New York developers were strained, at best. Klein did not really want to build the mart as much as he wanted to protect his controlling position as developer of the four office sites. Wary of what he believed to be Milstein's ulterior motive—that he would somehow contrive to turn the mart structure, which had a much bigger footprint, into low-cost back-office space much in demand at the time, thereby undercutting the appeal of Park Tower's office towers, all of which had small footprints ill suited for back-office space—Klein exercised a clause in his agreement with the city/state giving him the option to take on the mart if the original developer defaulted. He teamed up with the Trammell Crow, the legendary developer from Houston—"a Texas billionaire making his New York debut," as the *Times* later put it. A former bank teller who had become one of the nation's largest commercial developers with control over an empire valued at $4.5 billion, the 69-year-old Crow was one of the handful of people who could claim credit for perfecting the concept of a merchandise mart; he had guided the expansion of the Dallas Mart from its beginning as a single 217,000-square-foot building into a seven-building complex of 8.3 million square feet; Crow marts existed in Atlanta and Brussels, as well. "There wasn't a list in which his name wasn't No. 1 or No. 2," said Sturz in reference to the discussion stages of the Times Square project.[20]

Meanwhile, in January 1983, the governor's office in Albany changed hands, as Mario M. Cuomo succeeded Hugh L. Carey. The changeover affected UDC immediately. It was the "most tumultuous transition of the Cuomo administration," veteran *Times* reporter Martin Gottlieb wrote. Cuomo considered UDC to be too separate. There was, the governor later said, "a general lack of responsiveness to the rules that the rest of the government lives by . . . a certain elegance of manner more befitting a very successful private business than a state agency, a certain duplication and excessiveness."[21] Not wanting the agency "to serve as a place for a quasi-governmental elite," Cuomo directed his newly appointed chairman, the former finance chairman of his election campaign William J. Stern, to "start cleaning the agency out." A self-made millionaire whose fortune was made in the computer-software field, the 46-year old Stern had a reputation as "an elephant in a china shop." He was a tough man assigned to a highly political job, and he lost no time dismissing senior executives, accepting resignations and, generally, shaking things up. He ordered audits of two UDC subsidiaries, one of which was the Times Square Redevelopment Corporation (TSRC), the specially formed entity for the 42DP, and moved quickly to cut the agency's heavy use of highly paid consultants, some of whom, he believed, had too strong an influence over the agency's decisions. He was the first person to serve as both chairman and president of UDC; he also was the first of its four leaders not to have a background in construction. To his way of thinking, the agency maintained "a radical position" by devoting all its activity to one facet of economic development, commercial real estate development. His no-nonsense bottom-line orientation was what Cuomo was counting on to redirect the agency's resources and get more things done: "Physical development in some cases is appropriate, so is high technology in some cases. I asked him [Stern] to widen the agency's scope so that U.D.C. is on line with our vision of the future."[22] Stern started off following the governor's agenda, but his tenure as UDC chairman, characterized by some observers as lacking in focus, would last only two years.

UDC also had moved away from its original notion of designating a master developer for the entire 42DP. In this sense, going with Milstein was consistent with its position of not wanting one person to control the whole project. "This issue became diversity versus Crow's mart experience," one official said.[23] The city insisted on the Klein/Crow team, so an inevitable split in the vote occurred. Governor Cuomo's three directors on the board of TSRC—UDC chairman William J. Stern; Abraham D. Beam, former mayor of New York; and William I. Spencer, former chairman of Citibank—backed Milstein, while the mayor's two appointees—CPC chairman Herbert J. Sturz and Philip E. Aarons, president of PDC— backed the Klein/Crow team. In a protest designed to mark the record, Koch's appointees abstained from the formal board decision, making for a three-to-zero vote, then briskly walked out of the meeting.[24]

However much the city/state coalition represented a formal sharing of power, the question of control always lurked in the background. Neither Stern nor Sturz wanted to relinquish command. Adjudging the city's autonomy to be at stake by an action he charged was an attempt to usurp its role, Koch announced that the city would no longer participate with UDC on the project and would get the job done without the state authority. "The City of New York is not a vassal city," he declared. "What you always have with these independent authorities is they want to do it their own way. But it's always going to be 50-50, never 60-40. Unless it's 60-40 for us."[25] Responding to a letter from the mayor announcing the city's termination of the agreement, Stern also announced that his agency intended to carry out the plan by itself. "I can assure you that no unilateral action on your part will dissuade us from meeting out statutory obligations," he wrote.[26] Koch's position prevailed, and having gotten a message that the state would respect the city, a few days later the mayor reentered the negotiations.

In a forty-minute private meeting—only their second—at the governor's office in the World Trade Center on a Sunday evening, Koch and Cuomo worked out their differences, with the governor making concessions. The priorities, in Cuomo's words: "One, we must do the project. Everybody else had failed. Two, the city must be respected. Three, nobody has an agenda other than getting the best developers. Four, we should not give any group too much control over the project." After what Gottlieb described as "colorful, convoluted, and often desperate negotiations, the rift was resolved through compromise."[27] In a something-for everyone deal, Koch and Cuomo came to an agreement on a mart developer. Neither Klein nor Milstein would be designated as developer of the mart, although Milstein was invited to acquire a passive, minority investment in the partnership that would be designated. Instead, a new consortium was cobbled together by bringing in a third major developer, Jerry I. Speyer, the managing partner of Tishman Speyer Properties, to oversee development of the $400-million trade mart along with Trammell Crow and Equitable Life Assurance Society.[28] The context of the institutional rift was shaded by a personal one: "Remember," Tese said in an interview, "there had just been an election [the September 1982 Democratic gubernatorial primary], with Koch and Cuomo running against one another, and Koch lost. He's not a good loser. Feelings amongst the staff were not good either. These are people issues; there was a lack of trust."[29]

When asked about the governance tension that existed between the city and the state, Sturz characterized it as "typical." He was not evasive as much as nondescript and full of innuendo, and he brought up the mart flap as an example, noting that the city walked out of the deal, temporarily. He offered little more than body language in explanation, but did remark to the author: "Afterward, Stern came to my office frequently."[30]

Even before the mart dispute, the city's fear of losing control was not unfounded. While the state may not have had compelling economic interests in the project per se, its power in city affairs had grown tremendously through its public authorities, in particular, the Municipal Assistance Corporation (MAC), which managed the city's fiscal affairs through the 1974–1975 fiscal crisis and retained political power as a monitor charged with carefully scrutinizing the city's expenses and limiting its debt for some time thereafter. Numerous other state public authorities including the Metropolitan Transit Authority (MTA) and Robert Moses's powerful Triborough Bridge and Tunnel Authority spent billions annually within the boundaries of the city and had tens of billions invested there. "The complicated and often stormy relationship," wrote Gottlieb in a follow-up story about the turf battle over the mart designation, "has shaped New York to an unparalleled degree. Cooperation between the city and a variety of agencies has brought forth the George Washington, Verrazano-Narrows and Triborough Bridges, all the tunnels under the Hudson and East Rivers, the World Trade Center, the consolidated subway and bus system, Battery Park City, tens of subsidized housing units, a good portion of the public college campuses and the New York City Convention Center still under construction."[31] With the redevelopment of West 42nd Street under the aegis of UDC, the state's presence dominated the West Side of Manhattan, almost continuously, from the Battery to Times Square.

The state's portfolio of power could be read as a potential threat to municipal sovereignty, even as it grew out of what one scholar characterized as "an attempt by the State to take a creative and positive role in addressing seemingly intractable urban problems with resources beyond those available to the City alone."[32] Distrust on the part of city officials prevailed, despite notable public works produced by state agencies. "Elected officials often look at the authorities as arrogant, unfairly removed from the sturm und drang of New York's freewheeling politics and more interested in building empires than serving the public," wrote Gottlieb, who saw the mart flap as "a modern version of the often bitter and colorful turf battles that for half a century have pitted New York City's mayors against the powerful and charismatic men who have run the region's public authorities."[33] An "institutionalized attitude"—"I am the State"—influenced the politics of implementation in city/state projects, one city negotiator recalled. Despite what the city feels, the state is the superior entity, and, legally, municipal powers flow from the state, which is sovereign. Nonetheless, when major disputes arise in one project, as in the case of the mart episode, the solution often is to be found in political compromises involving other initiatives in the joint-governmental portfolio.

The coalition of city and state entities backing New York's big public developments represents an uncommon institutional alliance that the city has repeatedly found to be to its advantage in implementing complex large-scale projects. This type of joint-governmental working relationship appears in few other big-city development projects across the nation. As New York's legacy of long-standing suspicion attests, joining forces begets inherent political tensions. This seemed to be a manageable gamble for the city to take at the time in exchange for the enhanced probability of getting the 42DP done. It allowed the city to overcome the political difficulties of such a massive public intervention, what political scientists Michael Danielson and Jameson Doig identified as constraints on the ability of cities in general to concentrate resources. They argued persuasively that the complexity of political action among the many competing constituent interests and the broad functional scope of services in cities made the achievement of development goals intensely problematic for city governments compared to their suburban counterparts. The development initiatives that were most successful in overcoming this structural hurdle were those carried out elsewhere beyond the domain of general-purpose governments, the region's public authorities being instructive examples.[34]

The city/state coalition concentrated power in formidable ways. That was its compelling strategic advantage. In the case of the 42DP, the main advantage was political, according to Weisbrod, whose skillful leadership spanned both sides of the public coalition for five years, from 1987 through 1993, first as president of the UDC subsidiary for the project, then as president of PDC (later renamed the Economic Development Corporation, EDC):[35]

> When the mayor and governor are joined at the hip, it is a difficult powerhouse to dismantle. Opponents find it difficult to upset that stability, that political force. . . . The perception of opposition doesn't come across as forcefully as in other instances. Developers and others, particularly sophisticated players at the trough, like to play off the city and the state. Inability to do that when they are joined closes off an avenue of tactical maneuver. The second advantage flows from the combination of city and state resources that can be deployed to that end—dollars and powers. The city has a more flexible budget, but the state's powers and processes are more important than any dollars it might potentially contribute.

Vincent Tese, who headed UDC for nine years (1985–1994) under Governor Cuomo, was even more direct, downright blunt, in his assessment: "I can't stress enough the importance of being UDC," he said in an interview. "The advantage of being UDC is that you are UDC—that's it. That's why everyone hates you. There is no vote on your actions, the vote is the board. People say, UDC is usurping their rights. But that's the only way things get done. There is only one who matters, the governor."[36]

Sanitizing Clearance

The area's profile of chronic blight, detailed in UDC's findings and reported in the *General Project Plan for the 42nd Street Development Land Use Improvement Project* (*GPP*), read like a text-book set of preconditions for urban renewal—underutilization of land, high building vacancies, low and declining tax assessments, obsolete and deteriorating buildings, low employment, low office rents, high crime rates, and a diversity of land ownership that would make private-sector land assemblage "virtually impossible." Similarly, the response nearly resembled a blueprint from the pages of the federal urban-renewal handbook—clearance and relocation, except for the nine historic theaters lining the midsections of the block, which would be preserved. This was as it had to be for the "findings of blight" required to justify a UDC condemnation project mirrored the standards of the federal urban-renewal program. There was one key difference, however, and it was a matter of local policy: Until the 42DP, New York had refused to use the urban-renewal strategy for a commercial project in midtown Manhattan.

The city's policy stance had been firmly grounded in the belief that the market through private development could lead redevelopment on its own in midtown Manhattan. Public development, particularly if it involved land condemnation, was to be reserved for specific areas or projects where the market clearly needed assistance, to create a cultural arts complex for the city at Lincoln Center, for example. In two earlier 1970s planning studies, a short-term "action plan" for Times Square and a physical "comprehensive analysis" of 42nd Street, the recommendations of the planning staff reflected an approach of relatively passive "encouragement." There were no calls for aggressive action. The planning proposals—long-range zoning proposals, street improvements, preservation and planning controls, and selective tax incentives—would work only generally toward a cleanup of Times Square.[37]

By 1980, however, city officials believed the cleanup of West 42nd Street called for the kind of comprehensive and simultaneous action achievable only through the broad use of condemnation powers. The failure of earlier approaches—policing and law enforcement, pedestrian malls, streetscape improvements, private redevelopment plans—which the city attributed to "the intransigence of the blight that pervades the area," created the context for the 180-degree shift in city policy. And the CA42's urban-renewal strategy, a statement that zoning alone would not accomplish the task and itself a rejection of earlier incrementalist development approaches, provided the model that it was necessary to take on the whole block.

Condemnation and clearance were the conventional approaches to urban renewal, though discredited by this time. Throughout the 1950s and 1960s, the federal program cleared thousands of acres in center cities through wholesale bulldozing. New York officials considered their plan for sanitizing West 42nd Street to be more sensitive than indiscriminate razing because it incorporated selective preservation and restoration of the small-scale midblock theaters for legitimate entertainment. Together with four office towers, a merchandise mart, a hotel, and ancillary retail, the program would put in place "good" white-collar professional uses." Social clearance—of the con artists, drug hawkers, thieves, hustlers, and hangers-out—would come about by imposing a high-caliber new economic order inhospitable for the return of the sex trade, XXX-rated entertainment shops, loitering, and drug trade—the "bad" uses. The plan envisioned intense pedestrian usage. City and state officials wanted to reclaim this most centrally situated block in midtown from the crime and sordidness that had made it off limits to so many New Yorkers. They wanted to attract a more affluent crowd than the threatening denizens drawn to the street for the last twenty years. They wanted to flood the place with thousands of middle-class pedestrians—office workers, wholesale buyers, tourists, theatergoers. These were the types of people that had made Manhattan street life vibrant and abundant—and relatively safe; these "planners' people" were also the prototypes that habitually showed up in artists' renderings of redevelopment schemes. Redevelopment via selective condemnation would, as the *DEIS* aptly put it, "effect a transfer of turf to the new uses."[38] In this most forthright of statements, the planners unabashedly put forth the project's social agenda.

The nearly 800 pages of the *DEIS* made the case that the project's goal was to "return the area to productive use for New York City as a whole."[39] From a planning perspective, that meant targeting the full stretch of West 42nd Street from the northeast corner of Broadway to the southwest end at Eighth Avenue, a project area composed of twelve sites, ten of which would be the focus of the 42DP, as shown in figure 3.1. The redevelopment effort centered on the two 800-foot blockfronts along West 42nd Street, but as the *DEIS* argued, "blighted conditions are not limited to the blockfaces alone. For that reason, and to make the redevelopment effort economically feasible, the project area extends northward, southward and eastward as well"; thirteen acres in all: a project midway in size between the 12-acre Rockefeller Center and the 14-acre Lincoln Center complex. Describing the redevelopment plan and attempting to gauge its expected impacts were monumental jobs. Developed over three years by the consulting firm of Parsons Brinckerhoff Quade & Douglas, the environment impact study required by law as the basis for public hearings and final governmental consideration of the project took the task to a new level of thoroughness. It was a state EIS, and the only one done before was

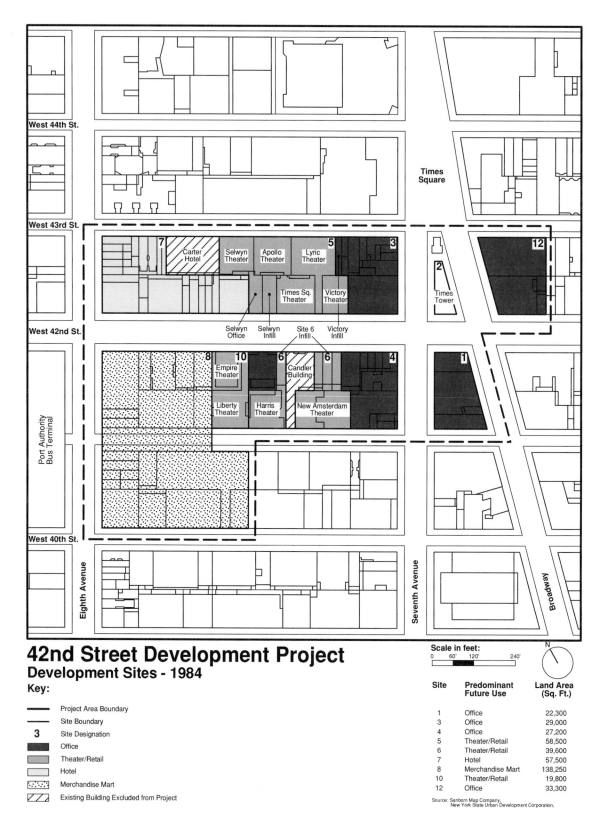

42nd Street Development Project
Development Sites - 1984

Key:

———	Project Area Boundary
———	Site Boundary
3	Site Designation
■	Office
▨	Theater/Retail
□	Hotel
▦	Merchandise Mart
▧	Existing Building Excluded from Project

Scale in feet:
0   60'   120'   240'

N

Site	Predominant Future Use	Land Area (Sq. Ft.)
1	Office	22,300
3	Office	29,000
4	Office	27,200
5	Theater/Retail	58,500
6	Theater/Retail	39,600
7	Hotel	57,500
8	Merchandise Mart	138,250
10	Theater/Retail	19,800
12	Office	33,300

Source: Sanborn Map Company,
New York State Urban Development Corporation,

3.1
The land-use plan for a new West
42nd Street, 1984. (Morgan Fleming
for the author)

that for the Jacob K. Javits convention center; no other EIS had a section on the "impacts on social and street conditions." The final version required two volumes, exceeding anything that had been done before. For the 1981 loft rezoning, for example, there was a "negative declaration" finding, meaning the existence of no significant environmental impacts; for the 1982 Midtown Zoning Resolution, the EIS, which one mild critic called a "shoestring study,"[40] came to only 20 pages. Each of these policy actions had a profound impact on the city. The EIS for the 42DP was reportedly expected to cost a total of $1.5 million; the bill for the 1,100-page final version presumably came in higher.

The "advanced stages of blight" that the *DEIS* described as "decay without the wrecker's ball" chronicled the gestalt of the area, in real estate terms.[41] While the existing buildings were functionally obsolete and physically deteriorated, the *DEIS* found the ground-floor uses of buildings on West 42nd Street—"where the image of the area is established"—most detrimental to desired new economic activity. The impact of face-to-face storefronts promoting adult entertainment (figure 3.2) was as visually arresting as it was inhibiting of long-term capital investment. Although the adult-entertainment movie theaters, video and book stores, peep parlors, and live shows represented little more than half of the block's storefronts, the pervasive character of the pattern perceptually blanketed the block. Eighteen of the area's 22 sex businesses fronted on the Deuce (figure 3.3). The character of the street stood in sharp contrast to others in the project area (40th, 41st, and 43rd) and the avenues (Broadway, Seventh, and Eighth). There, while sex-related businesses and movie theaters similarly occupied more than half the blockfronts, the visual impact was considerably reduced.

The buildings in the project area would never meet the standards of conventional commercial activity. Economically worthless, they were all scheduled for demolition, except for the symbolic and architecturally significant nine theaters in the midblock and three major high-rise buildings: the Carter Hotel (Site 9), the Candler Building (Site 11), and the former Times Tower, also known as One Times Square (Site 2). Most of the block would be razed, but compared with the historic pattern of urban renewal, there would be relatively little wholesale bulldozing (figure 3.4). Ironically, while both the north and south sides of the midblock would be preserved, because the frontage of the midblock theaters measured out to be relatively small, the visual impact of their preservation on the new streetscape was likely to be minor—a point few proponents wanted to make and few critics seemed to realize. But keeping the bulldozer away from the theaters served other, political purposes, as we will see.

If the large-scale clearance strategy seems outdated by the today's planning norms, or even those of the late 1970s and early 1980s, the way Sturz and Stern and their staff planners saw it, the social environment of West 42nd Street at that time held out few other options. The market fundamentals were not considered, nor were they in fact, strong enough to deliver replacement uses on a scale sufficiently broad and deep to reverse

3.2
The commerce of adult entertainment in Times Square, mid-1980s. (Jeff Goodman. Josh Allen Friedman, *Tales of Times Square*, Feral House Press)

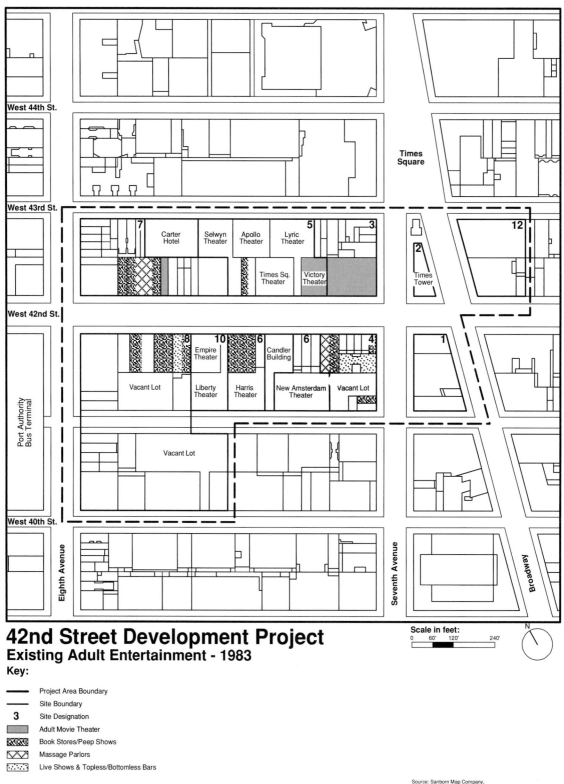

42nd Street Development Project
Existing Adult Entertainment - 1983

Key:

──── Project Area Boundary

──── Site Boundary

3 Site Designation

▨ Adult Movie Theater

▨ Book Stores/Peep Shows

▨ Massage Parlors

▨ Live Shows & Topless/Bottomless Bars

Scale in feet:
0   60'   120'   240'

N

Source: Sanborn Map Company,
New York State Urban Development Corporation

3.3
Adult uses in the 42DP project
area, 1983. (Morgan Fleming for
the author)

the dysfunctional social dynamic of the street; the negative vibes (external-
ities, in economic terms) of the place were just too formidable. Add to
that the well-known problems of assembling the 74 parcels (with a larger,
unknown number of ownership and tenant interests) that comprised the
tightly packed project area, and the practical policy result equaled condemnation (figure 3.5). In other cities, fragmented land ownership patterns
were in themselves considered evidence of blight—the inability of neighborhoods to renew themselves. Incremental action, as the privately funded
CA42 concluded, was unlikely to ensure the street's physical and moral
turnaround, even though it was the "right" approach by then-prevailing
notions of good city planning.

Critical writings on urban renewal, especially Jane Jacobs's *The Death
and Life of Great American Cities,* had long propounded a new orthodoxy of
small-scale renewal and neighborhood-based rebuilding that had found
widespread acceptance among city planners. About these planning merits
there was no fundamental policy disagreement, in general; that strategy just
did not fit the prescriptive needs of West 42nd Street. In practice, the clear
failings of large-scale clearance seemed only to apply to "good" neighborhoods—even if poor or dilapidated or obsolete—not "bad" environments,
which is to say, those tolerant of sexual deviance, hustling, pornography, and
drug dealing. Where these conditions existed on a such a scale as to dominate turf, especially within the central business district, the policy logic of
large-scale clearance still held sway. And, in line with the new orthodoxy
that emerged from the lessons of past experience, the plan put forth for
West 42nd Street mixed clearance and selective rehabilitation within the
framework of comprehensive and simultaneous condemnation.[42]

The programmatic imperatives of the 42DP *DEIS* were but one
reading of the data amassed for the exercise. Columbia University professor
Herbert J. Gans interpreted the environmental conditions of West 42nd
Street from a considerably different perspective than that of the project's
planners. Gans, an expert on the social destructiveness of comprehensive
schemes for urban renewal, exposed the strategy's most strident failure as
social policy in the early 1960s. His book *The Urban Villagers* had schooled
a generation of city planners on the not-so-readily visible social networks,
sense of community, and intrinsic values sustaining attachment to neighborhoods that, because of their aged tenements and other marks of physical dilapidation, appeared to be in a desperate and irreversible cycle of
decline. His work had made suspect deterministic theorizing, which, he
now argued in a 14-page report prepared for the BOE on behalf of the
Brandt Organization (which controlled many of the street's theaters), false-
ly underlay the planners' justification for condemnation and demolition of
much of West 42nd Street:[43]

> The analysis proceeds on the basis of a mixture of an esthetic and an
> architectural determinism, by which land uses deemed esthetically
> and otherwise undesirable are thought to produce undesirable social
> effects. . . . However, the report's approach conveniently forgets that

42nd Street Development Project
Structures to Be Demolished - 1984
Key:

——	Project Area Boundary
—	Site Boundary
3	Site Designation
▓	Building to be Demolished
░	Existing Building to be Retained or Renovated
⠿	Vacant Lot
▨	Existing Building Excluded from Project
▨	Status Uncertain

Source: Sanborn Map Company,
New York State Urban Development Corporation

3.4
Sanitizing clearance: 42DP plan
for clearance and retention.
(Morgan Fleming for the author)

buildings are only physical shells for human actions, and that whatever takes place on 42nd Street is the end product of a set of markets, in the case of commercial activities, legal and criminal; and of
human failures, social and individual, in the case of the alcoholics,
the poor and other helpless people for whom the street is now
home.

The DEIS, Gans concluded, was primarily a "commercial" for the
project because while the report "seeks to show that the Development
Project will cause the negative social conditions to disappear," it fails to
make the case. To support this conclusion, Gans highlighted some of the
"many errors of commission, omission, fact and prediction, as well as the
exaggerations, contradictions and biases" he found in the report and its
manipulation of statistics designed to prove the state and city's case. With
clear logic and unadorned but sharp prose, his critique laid bare the class
bias of the report and, by clear extension, the 42DP as planning policy.
In his general comments on the report's "Impacts on Social and Street
Conditions," he took pains to point out the problems of defining loiterers,
especially in New York, which is full of those who congregate in a variety
of entertainment and cultural districts:[44]

This entire sector of the EIS is an attempt to justify class-displace-
ment in the project area: to move out lower-income citizens and
taxpayers and to replace them with more affluent ones. This bias is

3.5
The land assembly task: lots and
plots of fragmented ownership in
the 42DP project area. (42nd
Street Development Project, Inc.)

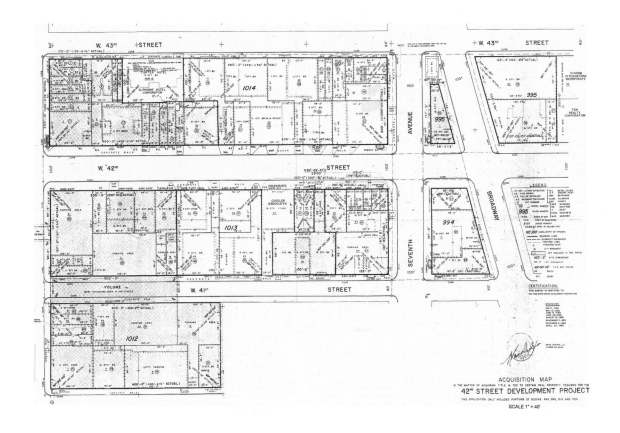

so extensive that it even pervades the architectural jargon. For example, the bright lights that are now condemned as "garish," will after redevelopment supply "glitter and excitement"; and at that time, the project area will exhibit "an active pedestrian environment," the report's architectural euphemism for affluent loitering.

The most problematic contradiction of the report, he believed, was that except for the low-cost movie theaters, the "undesirable" facilities, land uses, criminals, and low-life types that state and city officials sought to eliminate would not disappear but rather would find their way to other parts of Times Square or nearby Clinton, as the *DEIS*, in fact, concluded. If the problem was crime and threatening street life, the proper and rational prescriptions were crime prevention and law enforcement, as well as social-welfare programs for the alcoholics, the homeless, and others who made up the West 42nd Street population—not redevelopment. Gans was most concerned that the city and state develop further mitigation measures for the major victims of the project.

Though his analysis was intensely critical, Gans was not suggesting maintenance of the status quo on West 42nd Street, nor was he opposed to its redevelopment. He objected to the heavy tax subsidies and the extreme bulk and density of the office towers, designs that represented "architectural ego-trips." To his way of thinking, the scope and importance of the project demanded more economic and social planning, especially on the programmatic side. With prescience, but too quietly, he noted that "An entertainment district with skyscrapers on top is different than an office-block with entertainment facilities on the first floors."[45] Picking up on his analysis, others would later argue that the class- and race-based agenda of the 42DP—the conversion of one particular kind of commercial entertainment district to another—foreclosed alternative planning options: Just how the problem of West 42nd Street got defined in public discourse and official reports, that is, precluded incremental private redevelopment through zoning and tax incentives.

Most urban and real estate experts, however, would have concluded at the time, as did CPC chairman Sturz, that "zoning alone would not have done it."[46] Though the 42DP was an important part of the city's 1982 Midtown Development Plan, this regulatory initiative, discussed shortly, served a different purpose: It enabled the city to deal with the overconcentration of high-density buildings and negative impacts resulting from intense office development of the east side of midtown Manhattan. Experience had proven that zoning incentives could trigger substantial private investment, but there were two problems with this policy approach as it might apply to West 42nd Street.

The first problem was one of means: Given its passive character, regulation was a limited form of market intervention because the initiative for change depended upon developers who are typically slow to establish new areas of desirability, even as prime sites run out. The second problem was one of ends: City and state officials were after something more than uncoordinated construction of new tax-generating office towers. They wanted to establish a critical mass of new economic activity on the street, broad in scope and deep in impact. They also wanted the terribly worn and depressingly dilapidated Times Square subway station complex renovated and the prized historic midblock theaters rehabilitated—public pieces of the project agenda that had to be linked to and financed by private investment, given the city's barely recovered fiscal condition. While the corners of Broadway and Seventh Avenue might eventually have attracted new office construction without public development, the value of the development opportunity created by bulking up the street's permitted density and shifting it to office use was considered critical leverage for bringing back legitimate theater to West 42nd Street, as well as for securing private proposals for the more difficult western end of the area. Although some housing, notably the twin high-rise towers of Manhattan Plaza further west on 42nd Street, had been built by this time, to both city planners and real estate practitioners alike, the western edges near the Port Authority Bus Terminal presented the toughest sell. At the same time, development of those sites was deemed absolutely necessary to stabilize Eighth Avenue and guarantee the street's physical rebirth. Zoning, even when done well, could not serve this ambitious agenda. The mandate called for simultaneous condemnation of the parcels and comprehensive redevelopment of the entire project area.

Keeping Risk at Bay

When condemnation anchors the strategy for cleaning up blight, the effort is inevitably costly. Beyond the cost of purchasing individual parcels, the expenses of acquiring land include appraisals, title reports and surveys, payments for business terminations, relocation of existing tenants, demolition, and legal fees associated with the condemnation process. Some types of cost are mandated by condemnation and relocation statutes; the magnitudes of others, such as relocation, if not statutorily mandated are dictated by political needs to manage the situation sensitively, a legacy of disastrous performance from the early days of the federal urban-renewal program. The process of taking land through eminent domain is lengthy and delays are inevitable. These time lapses expose a project to inflationary cost increases and changing land values. Consequently, the final cost of land acquisition for the 42DP would remain open-ended and unknown for an uncertain, but likely long, period of time. Traditionally federal underwriting of the cost protected cities from this risk exposure, but New York could not do the project in the old way with federal funds because Washington had shut down its urban-renewal program in 1974. So, how to do it?

"Religious principle number one at the time: the city should not be at risk for buying land in midtown Manhattan," recalled Paul A. Travis, PDC's first project director for the project. This position did not spring from the pain of the city's 1974–1975 fiscal crisis as much as it was "a policy position set in relative terms—private office buildings in the context of all the needs of the city."[47] Practically as well as politically, fiscal conditions reinforced this policy position and shaped the solution—full funding from private developers. The fiscal crisis made a deep impression on city officials, and the local economy remained vulnerable in its aftermath. New York was hard hit by a national recession in the early 1980s; the impact on employment and corporate profits resulted in a shortfall in tax revenues to which Mayor Koch responded by imposing a temporary hiring freeze. It was difficult, if not impossible, at the time to use current budget dollars or to float bonds for the project. (New York did not reenter the bond market with an offering of short-term notes until 1979, and it was not until fiscal year 1981 that the city budget finally achieved balance.)

Politics even more than pragmatic considerations hung heavy over city decision making during this period. The fiscal crisis had exacted big political costs. A period of austerity marked by significant cutbacks in public-sector jobs, postponements of capital improvements, and reductions in basic services as well as redistribution prevailed throughout the second half of the 1970s, while the state's imposition of fiscal monitoring and management systems effectively stripped the mayor of control over fiscal policy. More than anything, the city needed to regain control of its internal and fiscal affairs. The need to once again gain access to the capital markets imposed political restraints on the growth of municipal spending because city officials had a clear and pressing stake in attaining fiscal stability and regaining the capacity to balance the budget. In that context, large expenditures for land condemnation to promote commercial redevelopment in midtown Manhattan, whether through bonding or on a pay-as-you-go basis, would not have fit anyone's definition of a budget priority, certainly not one worth risking the disapproval of the city's fiscal monitors or a rejection by Wall Street financiers. Not surprisingly, capital spending had been shut down during the fiscal crisis, and it did not resume with any consequence until Koch prepared his first ten-year capital-budget plan for $35 billion in May 1982. By this time, New York had regained the confidence of the bond-rating agencies, all of whom restored an investment-grade rating to the city's bonds, as had the federal bank regulators.

City and state officials were not inexperienced with the risks of large-scale public development in Manhattan. When Koch committed, politically, to do something about Times Square in June 1980, the ink had barely dried on the work-out agreement between the city and the state for the troubled Battery Park City (BPC). Now a highly acclaimed model of how the public sector succeeded in creating land value and capturing that value for public gain, BPC had first to live through a rocky financial history, including its own brush with bankruptcy. In this joint venture between the city and state, which started in the mid 1960s, $200 million of state moral-obligation bonds had been at risk for close to a decade before the private office buildings and residences expected to repay the indebtedness materialized. Bedeviled by a misconceived master plan, a depressed real estate market, the default of UDC, and a political environment in which was the city was steadily sliding into fiscal crisis, BPC's development followed no smooth progression. Rather, for a decade the project proceeded through a series of false starts until a new legal framework, master plan, financial-workout arrangement, and takeover by the state—fortuitously coincident with a revived real estate market—yielded the building cranes that catapulted the project into blinding reality in the mid-1980s. In Times Square, because the public sector did not own the land and did not have the money to buy it, the task would be far trickier.

DENSITY FINANCING

The financial imperative that the city take no risk meant that it spend no major capital funds on the project. As with many big-city public-development projects across the nation in the 1980s, the financial strategy city officials devised relied on techniques designed to make the project self-financing: Advances from private developers would fund the costs of land acquisition, and these, in turn, would be paid back with the incremental gain in property taxes generated by the project as well as other project-specific revenues. In concept, it was a bit like tax-increment financing, without the public issuance of bonds and the transparency of fiscal plan and market rigor that come with that formal process.

As a form of off-budget financing, New York's self-financing approach was singular because it relied 100 percent on the private sector to fund the public costs of redevelopment. But New York was more constrained than many other cities because the state constitution limits public contributions to private projects and, unlike other cities, New York could float revenue bonds only through state-authorized special entities of which there were very few in the city. "In its inception, the device was very simple," remarked one of the city's attorneys on the deal. "The city could make up the developer's advance [of front-end costs] with the tax money the developer would be paying the city. It got much more complicated as time went on, and the idea had to be put into draft language."[48]

Forty-second Street was still a secondary location, and to deal with that risk and attract developers, city officials relied on two other tried-and-true off-budget tools: property tax abatements and increased building densities. "We had to come up with a tax deal that was better than any other in midtown, with certainty up-front in terms of the dollar amount of taxes that would have to be paid," Travis recalled. The abatements would attract developers by conferring a competitive advantage upon the project's office towers, but preparatory to that, according to Sturz, the city "had to create values on the corners because that was what was of interest to the developers."[49] For that reason, the density tool was by far the more important of the two.

Office development was the linchpin of the financial strategy, as it had been in *The City at 42nd Street*. Even though the development program of the *GPP* allowed developer proposals that included retail and entertainment uses, a hotel, a residential building, and a wholesale mart, office towers drove the economics of the project. The logic was easy: Office development promised the most in terms of business profitability. Only the development values of the office sites could underwrite the privatization of the public's ambitious financing needs—not merely for the costs of land acquisition, but also for the subway improvements and the theater acquisitions. The overall land-use plan for the project area called for approximately 8 million square feet of developable floor area, a significant ramping up from the 2.1 million square feet in place in existing structures, though less than the maximum 8.8 million square feet achievable with bonus permits for theater preservation and subway improvements under the special midtown zoning put in place in 1982. Office uses accounted for more than 51 percent of the land-use plan. While market studies indicated the potential for as much as 5.1 million square feet on the five office sites in the area, including in this calculation the former Times Tower, the 42DP plan provided for 4.1 million square feet. The fate of the tower remained ambiguous, but should that icon be replaced with a smaller structure or a plaza—under "serious consideration" at the time—total office use allowed in the project area would have been 4.4 million square feet.

To understand the physical implications attached to the city's decision to privatize the funding of land condemnation, one only had to look at the spatial pattern of development densities across the project area. Making the numbers work for office development meant transferring project-wide development rights to the four office sites, thereby permitting enormous bulk—on relatively small sites—to encircle the iconic symbol of Times Square. These transferred development rights were far in excess of the maximum developers might have achieved on any one individual site under current zoning, that is, absent UDC's special override powers; the transfer of development rights also exceeded what was allowed under existing law.[50] How the buildable floor area of a site relates to the size of the land parcel is commonly spoken of in terms of floor-area ratio (FAR). As the architectural elevations published in the *DEIS* shown in figures 3.6 and 3.7 reveal, the FARs embedded in the plan presented a dramatic visual story. For the office towers (Sites 1, 3, 4, and 12), they ranged from 24.3 to 46.3, whereas for both the mart (Site 8, an FAR of 15.3) and the hotel and retail site (Site 7, an FAR of 12.6) they were less than the as-of-right FAR of 18 and a fraction of the maximum permitted with bonuses under current zoning (an FAR of 21.6). The *DEIS* explained:[51]

> The inclusion in the project of the high-density office buildings on Sites 1 and 12 results primarily from economic necessity (i.e., the substantial difficulty in attracting developers willing to risk new construction within the project area), the importance of generating funds sufficient to finance essential public improvements, and the decision to maintain, to the greatest extent possible, the low-rise theater structures on the 42nd Street midblocks.

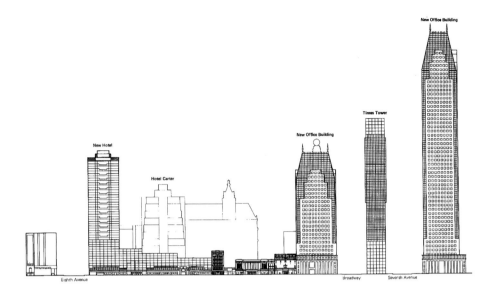

3.6
Architectural elevation of the
north side of West 42nd Street to
be redeveloped under the *GPP*.
(42nd Street Development
Project, Inc.)

The office densities were enormous, by any standard, even for
Manhattan. As one architectural critic pointed out at the time, "Even the
original Equitable Building downtown, which is credited with inspiring
New York's first zoning ordinance in 1916, had an F.A.R. of only 30."[52]

Because the UDC-based powers embedded in the 42DP's institutional structure allowed the city to set development parameters outside
existing zoning, using density financing to meet its fiscal objectives did not
pose the same type of legal conflict of interest that ultimately turned the
city's management of the first-round of the Columbus Circle project into
such a policy scandal. The self-financing of the 42DP project created
another distinctive difference between the city's use of density financing
for these two high-profile developments. In the Columbus Circle project,
a 4.5-acre development on the site of the old Coliseum on the southwest
corner of Central Park, the court characterized the 1985 development
transaction as a cash sale for a zoning bonus. The deal between the
city and Boston Properties, which won a city-sponsored competition

3.7
Architectural elevation of the
south side of West 42nd Street to
be redeveloped under the *GPP*.
(42nd Street Development
Project, Inc.)

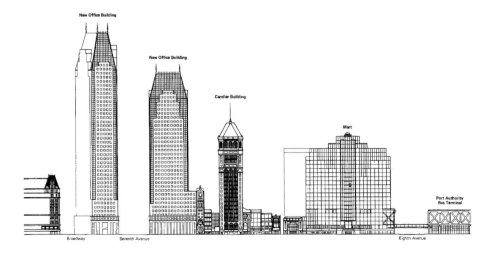

to develop the site, exchanged the publicly owned site (the MTA was the parent owner of the parcel) and permission to exceed the zoning by 20 percent for a payment by the developer of $455.1 million and a commitment of up to $40 million for improvements to the nearby Columbus Circle subway station. With the bonus, the allowable FAR increased from 15 to 18, allowing 2.7 million square feet of commercial space to be built. The design would have produced one of the biggest private buildings in the world, a 925-foot-high structure. The MAS and other civics filed suit, arguing that the city's financial stake in the sale tainted the approval process and that the environmental analysis of traffic and light and air quality was not adequate. In late 1987, the judge found that the city had exchanged density bonuses for money. The pivotal issue was the contractual clause that allowed Boston Properties to cut its payment by $57 million—intended to be used for off-site purposes—should the city withhold the bonus of 448,500 square feet. In the decision, the judge wrote "A proper quid pro quo for the grant of the right to increase the bulk of a building may not be the payment of additional cash into the city's coffers for citywide use." His definitive conclusion was that "government may not place itself in the position of reaping a cash premium because one of its agencies bestows a zoning benefit upon a developer. Zoning benefits are not cash items."[53]

Financing urban redevelopment in the post–federal-funds era demanded that cities search for new sources of capital. Using density financing and relying on developers to advance funds for condemnation evidenced a shift toward greater involvement of the private sector in solving public problems, which was part of a broad national policy trend growing in prominence since the 1970s. New York's type of fiscal privatization went beyond the self-financing trend, displacing, in part, direct public capital investments by the city. Through its deal making, New York was not just using tax abatements to attract private investment. As was the case in other big cities, it was using development rights as currency to buy a whole range of public benefits—subway renovations, streetscape improvements, parks—to be supplied by private firms. Inherently, this linked the provision of public benefits to the timing and specific place of private investment. In exchange for no capital outlay, public improvements that might otherwise pave the way for new private investment by making marginal locations attractive and increasing land values ran the risk of becoming captive to that same investment, a potential catch-22 and a reversal of the traditional public-works-as-catalyst strategy.

As a form of public "investment," density financing stands in direct contrast to the type of direct public investment that made Battery Park City a planning success beyond the wildest expectations of public officials. The revised plan for BPC placed considerable emphasis on the role of open space and public amenities—waterside esplanade, indoor winter garden, neighborhood parks, a program of public art—in shaping the image of the project to city residents and potential private investors alike. From the start, the project's public-authority developer planned to build the public spaces itself, as it would do for the project's other infrastructure: site improvements, utilities, streets, and blocks. There was nothing unusual about the need for timely provision of such a public capital investment. Large-scale urban developments, whether public or private, impose a requirement for major public works early in the development process. Without new infrastructure, transit facilities, and open-space amenities, the transformation of raw acreage into an attractive location for long-term private investment would inevitably come to a standstill.[54]

Privatizing the cost of public infrastructure, by requiring private developers to either build, finance, and deliver to the city specific infrastructure works or public amenities, or to pay the costs for the city to construct those improvements, is a strategy that works best when strong real estate market conditions prevail. Inevitably, it is a strategy that begets political risk. City and state officials would learn this firsthand years later, when, as a victim of a dramatically collapsed real estate market, the prospects for the 42DP's office development disappeared along with the significant developer funding for the long-awaited renovation of the Times Square subway station complex.

Shifting Office Development

Relying upon density financing for the 42DP was not out of line programmatically with the city's major planning initiative for Manhattan, the Midtown Development Project, begun in 1980 under Herb Sturz's predecessor, Deputy Mayor Robert F. Wagner, Jr. Prompted by widespread dissatisfaction on all sides—civic groups, planners, and real estate interests—and supported by five of the city's most prominent foundations, the DCP study set out to deal with "the development needs, problems and potential of Midtown Manhattan." To the planners in charge of the work, this meant changing what was generally wrong with the city's existing zoning resolution of 1961 plus correcting the unintended but misguided regulatory incentives governing development in the Special Theater District that had been put in place in 1967. While West 42nd Street was not explicitly on the regulatory agenda, it did not need to be because the city/state MOU for the project had been signed barely a month before the CPC released its 300-page *Midtown Development Project Draft Report* for public review and comment. The role of the 42DP, along with the new convention center and a planned pedestrian mall for Broadway, was to help turn around the West Side, making it more competitive with the East Side as a location for office construction; without upgrading the Times Square area, the planners reasoned it would be difficult to lure development away from the East Side, regardless of the generous zoning incentives provided on the West Side. From this perspective, the 42DP was a key element in the city's larger agenda for redirecting commercial real estate development. Yet how zoning was used to reshape development rights in midtown and how developers responded to the new incentives would directly affect the 42DP, in a completely unanticipated way.

The immediate push for the change in zoning policy came from the rash of immense new towers on the East Side in midtown, among them the 62-story Trump Tower on Fifth Avenue and the towering headquarters of IBM (43 stories) and AT&T (47 stories), monoliths on Madison Avenue built side by side that rose up straight from street and threatened to overwhelm Manhattan, if that was possible. Size was not the irritating factor per se, but rather the aggregate impact of density and the "shoehorning" of so many skyscrapers "into tight sites that would have been considered unbuildable a few years ago," wrote *Times* architectural critic Paul Goldberger. "The result," he concluded, "is a real concern that density may reach intolerable levels."[55] Transit was another issue: Most of the subway lines lay west of Fifth Avenue, while most of the development was taking place east of Fifth Avenue. The existing zoning code did not work, period, let alone in ways that fostered growth in line with any rational plan. It was functionally inoperative, and in its place an uncertain and unpredictable "negotiation syndrome" ruled development permissions. This discretionary decision-making process produced buildings that many experts felt were too big for their sites. Moreover, the urban-design incentives built into the zoning code that had produced many of the tallest buildings did not seem to work either, because the amenities were of questionable value. The "system" was a mess, the discretion excessive, its critics claimed. Administratively, the goal was to reform it and make as-of-right development the norm rather than the exception to zoning practice.[56]

Instead of merely amending zoning maps, the strategy aimed to replace "old zoning concepts" with an overall policy framework to guide development in midtown, unarguably of critical importance to the local economy and tax base of the entire city. Using a range of tools, including zoning incentives, public projects, and tax incentives, the proposed zoning aimed "to ease the pressure on the crowded, valuable East Side office core by helping to shift new development west and south." In place of the uniform limits of an FAR of 15 to 18 that blanketed midtown, the new midtown strategy established geographic districts, each with its own development criteria. It down-zoned the East Side (the "stabilization" area) midblocks to an FAR of 12 to 13, keeping the avenue frontages at an FAR of 15 to 16; whereas on the West Side (the "growth" area) the principal avenue frontages (Sixth, Seventh, and Broadway) were up-zoned to an 18 FAR (with opportunities to reach a 21.6 FAR) for a six-year period, with the midblocks remaining at a 15 FAR (figure 3.8). These changes aimed to provide a clear distinction between the East and West Sides, while helping to retain New York City's traditional development pattern of higher density on the avenues and lower ones on the side streets. Urban-design regulations were also restructured, including special incentives for theater preservation, and bonuses for amenities were sharply reduced. "The cumulative effect" of these proposals, the DCP report stated, "would go a long way toward eliminating negotiated zoning. They would permit development to proceed on a more predictable and as-of-right basis."[57] Adopted by the BOE in May 1982, the Midtown Zoning

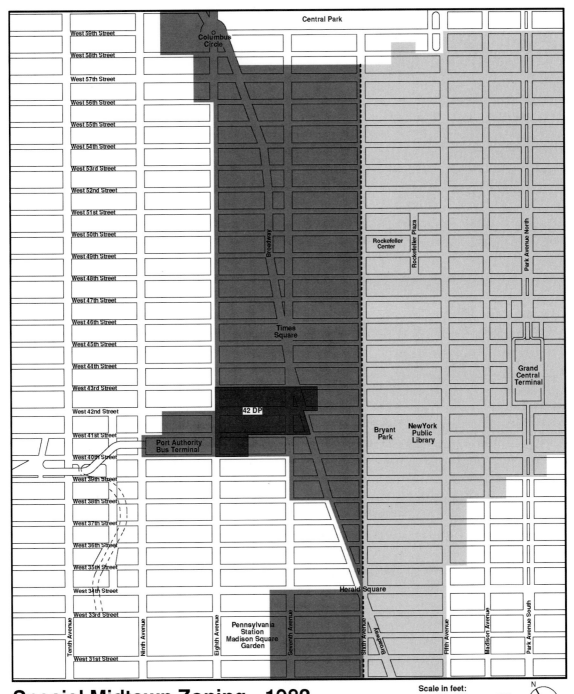

Special Midtown Zoning - 1982

Key:

- ▪ ▪ ▪ ▪ District Boundary
- ▪ Upzoned or "Growth" Area
- ▫ Downzoned or "Stablization" Area
- ▪ 42nd Street Development Project (42DP)

Source: Sanborn Map Company,
New York State Urban Development Corporation,
New York City Development Corporation,
New York Department of City Planning.

3.8
Zoning to shift midtown
office development westward.
(Morgan Fleming for the
author)

Resolution marked the first time New York adopted an overall policy on the location of new office buildings. As a policy initiative, it would test the city's resolve—in the midst of a building boom and perceived shortage of prime sites on the avenues—in controlling the congestion that was clogging the midtown sidewalks of the East Side.

At the time, neither urban experts nor architectural critics questioned whether the 42DP was a redundant policy initiative because few expected zoning modification to reverse the unsavory social patterns in the Times Square district or on Eighth Avenue. Their tune would change less than five years later when a race against the clock to beat the deadline of the Midtown Zoning's sunset provision threatened the Times Square district with millions of square feet of new office and hotel projects, ironically calling into question the logic of the still-unbuilt 42DP. When the new zoning policy was being debated, however, West 42nd Street was "the cork in the bottle of development in its move westward," as urban designer Jonathan Barnett put it.[58] The designers of the plan consciously used regulation for up-zoning and bonuses: "To make the area safe for corporate buildings, the social culture of Times Square had to be sanitized," recalled one of the CPC's consultants, Michael Kwartler.[59] More to the point, in the early 1980s, it would have been hard to view the special Midtown Zoning as immediately competitive with the 42DP because expectations among developers and realty professionals were not high that the experimental plan would succeed in shifting development to the West Side.

The talk of the time questioned whether anyone would take advantage of the new incentives. Office developers are rarely pioneers. Typically, they build where there is clear acceptance for their product, exploiting every opportunity for development until they are unable to do so anymore. The East Side was still the natural spot for office development: Rents were high enough and demand strong enough to support new construction; the zoning changes seemed unlikely to forestall development on sites already assembled. Not surprisingly, the new regulations were not welcomed by the developers who, according to Sturz, disliked the plan because it down-zoned at the same time it up-zoned parts of midtown. When first proposed in 1980, the president of the Real Estate Board of New York responded that "the excessively complex zoning system might go unused."[60] Two years later, before adoption, he argued that it would do little to encourage development on the West Side because corporate tenants would continue to insist on East Side locations. Developers held up ratification by the BOE for two weeks, pushing, to no avail, for a liberal grandfather clause that would have exempted projects in the planning stage.

To those developers quietly focused on finding opportunity in the Times Square market, the 42DP signified serious public intent. "The project gave heart to people like me," remarked Jeffrey Katz, developer of Two Times Square, the slim building between Broadway and Seventh Avenue at 47th Street ablaze with supersigns. "We believed it would happen, even if it was having trouble getting started. The state's intervention was important. The first move was so big that it couldn't be turned back; the scale of the activity was terribly important to the change."[61] From the start, the need for a critical mass of new investment led policy makers to reject the idea that the market could effect a makeover of West 42nd Street on its own. And the "success" attributed, in hindsight, to the rezoning's impact on the shift in midtown development toward the West Side needs to be considered in context. As Mollenkopf cautioned in his review of New York's city planning experience of the 1980s, the CPC "actively encouraged the construction of 15.2 million square feet of office space in East Midtown during the 1980s by granting discretionary bonuses."[62] So, while the new zoning policy may have merely accelerated the timing, pace, and volume of an inevitable shift in office development to the West Side, the combination of regulatory and proprietary initiatives served to radically alter the perceptions of investment opportunity around Times Square. And, like politics, real estate development is very much a business of perception.

THE DISCRETIONARY VOTE

The project Mayor Koch finally brought to the BOE for approval in October 1984 had been over four years in the making, and the cast of elected city officials—who usually sent surrogates—and other governmental notables in attendance signified the high stakes: For the first time in five years, the mayor presided over the BOE; for the first time in 35 years, the governor made a personal appearance; one of the state's U.S. senators spoke in favor of the project, as did two former mayors. Preparation had been similarly intense. For six to eight weeks prior to the hearings, high-level staff working on the project had been selling it to public officials on the BOE, explaining the deal and going over the financials. From the beginning, nobody wanted the project to fail—to be one more articulate plan that would go nowhere (figure 3.9).

The program approved by the BOE two weeks later allowed city and state officials to sign 99-year leases with four sets of developers. The

3.9
The political players waiting for the Board of Estimate to okay the plan for the 42DP (l to r): city planning commissioner Herbert J. Sturz, assistant to the mayor, Rosemary Ginty, comptroller Harrison J. Goldin, Governor Mario M. Cuomo, Mayor Edward I. Koch, U.S. senator Daniel Patrick Moynihan, UDC chairman William J. Stern, Queens borough president Donald Manes, Bronx borough president Stanley Simon, and PDC president Steven Spinola. (Holland Wemple)

deals promised to resurrect five legitimate theaters and transform four others (two for nonprofit theaters) and construct four new office towers totaling nearly 4.1 million square feet, a 2.4-million-square-foot whole-sale-merchandise mart and a mixed-use complex with a hotel of up to 750 rooms and related commercial use. The deals would effect an upgrading of public improvements, including the badly needed renovation of the Times Square subway station complex and construction of a pedestrian bridge spanning Eighth Avenue as well as amenity improvements to the streetscape. To get to this point, UDC had taken the project through detailed "findings of blight" pursuant to the Eminent Domain Procedure Law and a series of lengthy environmental impact reviews, including those pertaining to the state's Historic Preservation Act. If, however, there had been general agreement all along that something had to be done to clean up West 42nd Street, there was considerable dissension on the specifics of the plan and intense distress about the projected impacts of such massive redevelopment, in particular, the four high-density office towers designed by Philip Johnson and John Burgee. These points of opposition crystallized in last-minute maneuvers and political compromises by city officials with neighborhood representatives, Garment District interests, and major civic organizations—the week before the critical executive session.

More than 200 people testified at the public hearings held in the magnificent City Hall room where the BOE convened, 15 percent of them residents, small-business owners, and community representatives from the Clinton neighborhood. Clinton, where ethnic pockets of Hispanics, Greeks, and blacks had replaced the Irish, remained the main stumbling block. Though divided in their opinions of the project, the community's residents and local merchants were united in wanting protection from being "pushed out" of Clinton by rising housing costs brought about by the area's continuing gentrification and the "spillover effect" of real estate speculation. They were skeptical that the project would thoroughly eliminate the crime and sex businesses of West 42nd Street and fearful of its more likely displacement to Clinton.[63] All but two of the 31 from the community who testified at the public hearings spoke in opposition to the project. The community had already won a commitment from city and state officials, after weeks of negotiation, to spend $15 million in budget funds over five years; still, the BOE vote approving the project came only after 12 hours of back-room negotiations in City Hall offices and an agreement from city and state officials to add $10 million to this neighborhood mitigation fund. "We had to buy Clinton twice," said Koch. "It was an outrage" he thought "wrong," but something done to move the project foreword.[64] The funds would go toward the rehabilitation of several hundred apartments, aid for small business, and efforts to fight the spread of juvenile prostitution and pornography from Times Square to Clinton. That these funds would not come from the developers but rather pass through city and state budgets—which meant forcing legislators to set one group of constituents against another—left some local legislators who strongly opposed the project unsatisfied, but the remaining opposition was not enough to jeopardize a unanimous approval by the BOE—at 1:20 A.M.—for the $1.6-billion plan to rebuild West 42nd Street.[65]

The project finally had secured the necessary BOE votes, but the underlying public support was far from unqualified. It was broad, but not deep. Firm opposition to the project—from vested business interests, the residents of Clinton, the civics, and the performing-arts community—that emerged during the *DEIS* public hearings in the spring of the year seemed to have hardened during the intervening six months leading up to the late-fall public hearings before the BOE. It undermined the strength of the progrowth coalition of government and business; public officials could not push this project through without broadening the coalition of support. Public hearings bring out those who actively seek to make a public statement about the issues under review by public officials; the openness of the procedure is no guarantee that the opinions of those testifying will match the results of a representative sample of public opinion as measured against the standards of professional opinion polls. The tally of positions is, nonetheless, an important political barometer of changes in the public debate about controversial development projects. Over a period of months, the lines had hardened. Set side by side, the positions of speakers testifying at the two sets of public hearings strongly suggest that the middle ground of those offering qualified support had just about disappeared: you were either strongly for or strongly against the project, as indicated in table 3.1. Those opposed to the project came out in greater force for the BOE hearings; this might have been a harbinger of events to come—if city officials did not already believe that the biggest hurdle had been cleared.[66]

As testimony before the BOE revealed, the political problem of rebuilding West 42nd Street involved an extraordinarily delicate act of balancing the city and state's aggressive plan for large-scale ground-up development ("to remove blight and physical decay") with its other goals for preserving the historic midblock theaters and their symbolic sense of place ("to revitalize the area as a theater and entertainment center") while accommodating the intense community and business concerns of Clinton and the Garment District (to restore "a positive influence" and create a "productive link among these communities and the expanding midtown office district"). With BOE approval, the balancing act did not end; in fact, it had just begun, for the multiple goals driving the project were somewhat contradictory. The office-tower designs of Johnson and Burgee, first

TABLE 3.1. POSITIONS OF SPEAKERS TESTIFYING AT 1984 PUBLIC HEARINGS

	DEIS HEARINGS: MARCH/APRIL 1984	BOE HEARINGS: OCTOBER/NOVEMBER 1984
Supportive	36.5%	54.0%
Qualified support	33.3%	9.4%
Opposed	30.1%	36.6%
Total	100.0%	100.0%
Number testifying	156	202

SOURCE: Author's calculations.

revealed to the public in late 1983, signaled the appearance of a new corporate aesthetic on Broadway that threatened to destroy the area's cultural symbolism. Moreover, the westward office expansion stimulated by the city's own zoning policy would inevitably compound development pressure on the surviving legitimate Broadway theaters.

The city's financial strategy for cleaning up West 42nd Street—density financing and private funding of the public costs of condemnation—represented a resourceful packaging of its limited resources. It was an inventive solution to a major funding problem and it shielded the city from financial risk, a rabbit-in-the-hat at one of the most difficult times in the city's fiscal history when municipal treasuries all across the nation were losing more and more of their federal-dollar flows. The complexity of the financing task and the scale of redevelopment ambitions eventually undercut the initial, delicate consensus city officials so laboriously cultivated for that critical BOE meeting. In part, the strategy of the big deal unwittingly held the seeds of controversy because it created a set of political risks that became exceedingly treacherous for city officials to navigate. In other words, the complexity of the financial structure compounded the politics of making it work. The tensions between public and private parties and the rivalries between developers would put more emphasis on UDC's role, as H.V. Savitch insightfully pointed out with an apt metaphor describing the public authority as a "hinge" between public and private interests. UDC might have the ability to "swing past the ordinary process of government, thereby circumventing all kinds of local opposition. But the hinge was fastened by the tenuous glue of politicians and developers."[67] City and state officials were not unaware of the political challenges ahead. They believed that by trading financial risk for political risk, they were assuming their legitimate role in the public-private partnership.

Based on the city's history of contentious development politics, opposition and litigation from diverse interests could readily be anticipated, so tactics for coping with the anticipated controversy were factored into the details of project implementation. The financial underpinnings of the deal, explained in the next chapter, were not so tight or so refined at the start as to cave in at the first crisis. Also, it was protectively structured with what might be called "financial expansion joints." Politically sensitive and skilled public entrepreneurs would manage the day-to-day technical issues of development, including litigation, and orchestrate the complex negotiations leading up to final lease agreements. Though the implementation task would be full of tensions, economic and political, what mattered at this point was that a deal had been struck, finally. Lingering in the background was a big problem: Driven by the city's financial mandate, the development deal dismissed the symbolic impact of the proposed radical physical changes—a shortcoming that would ultimately undo the consensus.

C H A P T E R   4

DEALS FOR DEVELOPMENT

"Over ninety-nine percent of the $1.5-billion budget for the entire proj-
ect will be funded by the private sector," Mayor Koch boasted at the
Board of Estimate hearings. "This means for an investment of $7 million
the city will realize $570 million in rent and public improvement commit-
ments in the next fifteen years, and annual tax revenues thereafter of $116
million. This is indeed a handsome return on a modest investment."[1] The
figuring that led to that conclusion was right only in the legal sense—
the private sector was *funding* the out-of-pocket costs for the project.
Conceptually and financially, however, Koch's boast was dead wrong. As a
statement of public policy, it was misleading.

    The public investment was not only much larger, it was hidden,
embedded within the business terms of the individual deals with private
developers and discernable only through careful analysis. What was, for
example, the true cost of the incentives required to induce private
investors to front-end such a risky, open-ended commitment? Also less
than clear was how the financial calculus of these deals would drive decisions about the development program and shape its execution. How
would it affect realization of the project's conflicting goals and the public
sector's ability to manage the politics of the process? The policy implications of what the business terms meant were not so buried, however, even
at the time of the BOE hearings, so as to obscure the favored position of
office development or the minimal provision for theater restoration and
entertainment uses. But ferreting out these implications called for a reading of the deals as policy documents, which was not part of the official
disclosure agenda.

    Taken at face value, the individual elements of any of the 42DP
deals did not readily add up to an understanding of the long-term financial
commitments, subsidies, or benefits, to either public or private parties. Nor
did the final terms of the deals presented in the BOE resolution illuminate
the tradeoffs, political and financial, made along the way in reaching

agreements with the project's designated developers. This was not unusual; rarely are these tradeoffs explicit. Except for general statements of intent early in the process, the practice of public deal making offers few policy guidelines for making tradeoffs among competing objectives. Rather, policy choices evolve during the process of implementation—initially through developer selection and later through lease negotiations—and they take on explicit meaning only when drafted into the contractual responsibilities and cost-sharing arrangements that define the risks and contingencies borne by each party to the deal. The tradeoffs are denominated in the technical terms of real estate finance; they are embedded in the details of a deal. That is why casting public commitments in the form of business agreements presents a difficult, if not awkward, problem of analysis: It demands translations from one realm to another, from the technical jargon of business to the vernacular of public policy. This means that public debate over development deals often overlooks the real policies being established and focuses on the symbolic aspects of the project.

Translated, the 42DP deals revealed a set of development policies fully consistent with the overarching character of the city's financial imperative: Shift all financial risk to the private sector. As a singular driver of the redevelopment project, this policy principle governed far more than which party signed the checks for acquiring the sites, refurbishing the subway station, making streetscape improvements, preserving the midblock theaters, and underwriting a portion of the public's soft costs and expenses for the project. It conferred a most-favored-nation status to the office uses, in effect, downgrading the "priorities" attached to the project's other proposed land uses. The primacy of keeping risk at bay became one of the decisive factors, for example, in the selection of George Klein of Park Tower Realty as a master developer for the four office sites. And in a move by public officials that sparked the beginning of a long-running aesthetic controversy over the project, it further defined a logic for subordinating the project's design guidelines to the commercial dictates of marketing space to corporate tenants in so uncertain and, hence, risky a location. Because the office towers could become the financial Achilles' heel of the project, they commanded a priority; when the time for making tradeoffs arrived, less emphasis would be placed on the project's public objectives. Inherently a strong force in speculative development projects, the marketability focus of private investment was elevated in importance by the demands of the city's financial imperative. In the end, it became the ultimate price paid by the city for having what Richard A. Kahan, president of UDC from 1979 until early 1984, later described in an interview as a weak "public side of the balance sheet."[2]

However reasoned the city's financial caution and prudence, its singular focus on commercial uses for West 42nd Street was politically misguided. The heavy commercial bias sowed the seeds of discontent and controversy; it intensified the nature of the redevelopment gamble. Deals that favored office developers made the other pieces of the ambitious plan—restoring the midblock theaters and attracting viable activity to the western end of the project area—even harder to achieve than otherwise would have been the case. It held the public-benefit agenda—renovation of the city's busiest and thoroughly deteriorated Times Square subway station complex—hostage to the timing of private office development. Restoring the golden legacy of the midblock theaters was inevitably held out as the olive branch of peace, the public-good compensation for the city's emphasis on commercial development. The gesture was symbolic, however, for years. In the quest for economic feasibility the city made only the slightest of bows toward the street's historic trademark. Rhetoric, not substance, defined the theater agenda. This reflected a general carelessness about the midblock portion of the project that prevailed until 1987, when Rebecca Robertson, an experienced planner with a deep commitment to urban design, was hired to create a funding plan for the theater agenda. It would take nearly a decade for these lessons to lead to a rescripted plan for the project, which, in turn, led to a new round of deals for development. Until then, deal making commanded the front-and-center position.

PRECEDENT MATTERS

As policy, deal making differs in form and intent from regulation. First, the public's deals with private developers are custom-tailored agreements that target planning goals beyond the scope of what can be achieved through uniform zoning ordinances or programmatic incentives. Second, these public-policy objectives are linked to business practices rather than regulatory rationales or legal principles. Third, under the terms of most public-private development agreements, what the public is selling and the developer buying is not simply land per se, but rather a development opportunity—rights to build hedged with complex obligations to perform and responsibilities to produce, including a package of public benefits. Fourth, unlike the incentives embedded in zoning ordinances, deals are based on mutual business interests designed to keep each side performing throughout the agreement period. In short, deal making is more targeted, is full of mutual obligations, and commits the public sector to taking risks for the rewards it seeks. These differences define the opportunistic and aggressive character of public development. They also challenge established policy principles that call for uniformity in implementation and clarity of accountability, a constant charge of critics who railed against the subsidies of the 42DP deals.

Deal making demands that public officials be given broad scope to negotiate business agreements with private parties. The process is incremental. With increasing specificity, decisions are made and commitments accumulate as a project moves through the steps of implementation— from *policy principles* first articulated in initial plans, design guidelines, and requests for proposals, to *business terms* defined and negotiated through the process for selecting a developer (memorandums of understanding), to *contractual obligations* drafted into legal documents (land and disposition agreements, leases). Exact and complete terms and conditions of a deal cannot be laid out ahead of time because the strategy demands operational flexibility—the public sector is, after all, opening a dialogue with the private sector about what is economically feasible, subject to the mandates of articulated policy principles. Practical problems presented by uncertain large-scale transformations such as the redevelopment of West 42nd Street lead public and private players alike to adopt the pragmatic, businesslike view that the plan might fail if they waited until each and every problem was solved before acting. To critics of the process, such flexibility pejoratively equates to "ad-hoc policy making." Yet, even as project-specific deal making detours from public administration's norm of uniformity, the route follows an internal and consistent logic of its own—precedent.

Precedents are key to understanding how mayors manage the politics of economic development and, by extension, deal making. Faced, on the one hand, with corporations threatening to move out of the city unless they receive retention subsidies and, on the other, with critics charging that policy is being made anew each time and that the deal is a "giveaway," local officials need a defensible policy-making framework that is politically deft. Moreover, since one subsidy decision is rarely isolated from all others, thereby increasing the likelihood that other firms will demand similar deals, the framework must also be economically restraining.

"Land deals nearly always have a unique quality about them that requires you to have a hook explaining why the deal is different," remarked Carl Weisbrod. "If the deal is to be made on any basis other than [competitive] bidding, it must be based on precedent, rationale, antecedents, policy—just like a legal decision. To do otherwise is to run the risk of the special becoming the standard." A tension exists, moreover, between the normative demands of public administration that call for uniform and consistent policy making and the exposure to unlimited and expensive subsidies that uniform deal making would impose, especially for economic development. As a result, coming to terms on new deals involves a delicate balancing act: "You need to protect against the last deal being subject to charges of ad hocism [sic] and against future deal exposure by not setting public giving in stone. Deals must be sufficiently different but not too different."[3]

The deals for the redevelopment of West 42nd Street were no exception to this pragmatic rule. Despite complex and clever financial structures, they drew heavily upon elements of earlier public-private projects. The coalition execution structure, for example, first appeared in 1977 in the Commodore/Grand Hyatt hotel project, as did the ground-lease arrangement whereby UDC, acting as intermediary, negotiated tax abatements for projects (known as payments in lieu of taxes, or PILOTs) and the provision for self-financing of public costs with dedicated project revenues. Ground leases with PILOT payments were similarly a key feature of the deals for Battery Park City in the early 1980s and the 1978 deal for the Portman/Marriott Marquis Hotel in Times Square.

Profit sharing also had been a part of earlier deals, in particular, the Marriott deal, which for the first time provided for the city to receive a share of future revenues in the event of refinancing or sale of the hotel's ownership interests—an "equity kicker." (In the Commodore deal, the city shared project risk on the downside through a percentage-rent formula, but without the exchange of a potential upside return.) These capital-transaction equity "kickers" were essential for winning federal dollars for the redevelopment project under the criteria established by the Urban Development Action Grant (UDAG) Program, which awarded grants on a nationwide competitive basis. With most federal subsidy programs shut down in the late 1970s as Washington's funding for cities shifted to generalized Community Development Block Grants, UDAG offered cities a rare form of targeted but flexible assistance for entrepreneurial public-private projects; the program lasted 11 years, from 1978 until 1989, until it was shut down. In March 1981, on its second round of application—and after considerable controversy over political lobbying to further the hotel project—New York finally captured $21.5 million for the then-$292.5-million Marriott Marquis Hotel project, the city's largest UDAG award at the time. This equity-gap financing was deemed essential for the project to go forward, yet the profit-sharing element so necessary for securing federal funds had been staunchly resisted by the developer, who thought the city should be a cheerleader for the project rather than a coinvestor. According to one public-private development expert who represented the city as counsel, these kickers set a new precedent: "Without bearing any obligation to share in any losses, without having contributed any of its own money or land, the public sector was given a share in profits as if it were a limited partner."[4]

Just as each of these prior deals established new precedents, so did the deal for the 42DP with its distinctive privatization of the public costs of land acquisition. As argued in the previous chapter, this off-budget arrangement deftly fit the financial imperative of the time. It also served to counterbalance political risks the city was taking with this particular large-scale urban-renewal project. After all, as PDC's project manager Paul A. Travis noted at the BOE hearings, the project demanded that its private developers take on risks not typically associated with redevelopment: timing risk—not knowing when in fact they would be able to start construction; funding risk—the open-ended nature of land acquisition; and public-benefit risk—[inflation-adjusted] investment in public improvements that amounts to $15 per square foot—"a great deal of cost."[5]

Precedents go largely unnoticed, yet they play a key role in the incremental process through which deals come to define city policies. They provide a framework for public risk-taking. Political and pragmatic needs require that the crafting of public-private deals build on enough precedents to make each new deal familiar, without being wedded to absolutely uniform application to every new project. Precedents make deals easier to defend, negotiate, and finalize. Institutional knowledge of past deals, both successes and failures, therefore becomes crucial because the skill with which local officials use or reject existing precedents to legitimize their deals undergirds the politics of the process.[6]

That legitimacy is especially important because, as a policy strategy, deal making challenges the conventions of public administration. Custom-tailored deals lack clear, uniform standards of review and so create a heavier burden of democratic accountability than what is typically required of regulation. If there are sound reasons for deal making, then the public's business arrangements with private developers should be subject to an analysis that reviews the fairness of terms, the feasibility of public financial commitments, and the net cost/revenue relationship—hard bottom-line analysis notably missing from the process for the 42DP, as argued in chapter 13, though the omission was not atypical of the public-development process in New York.

Deal making as policy would be less of a problem if cities were simply selling a commodity to the highest bidder, then stepping away from the disposition with no need for further involvement. But through their deals city governments offer prime business opportunities in exchange for future benefits and specific performance objectives, not just incremental tax revenues. In response to a Request for Proposals (RFP), private firms bid for development opportunities but the public offering demands more than a money-based bid. Typically, it calls for a developer to assume ongoing responsibilities and make guarantees over the life of the agreement. When a project involves substantial uncertainty, as in the case of large-scale redevelopment such as the 42DP, additional financial risks and contingencies must be factored into the terms of the bid. And assurances on the intangibles of a deal, so often a bottleneck in otherwise reasonable negotiations between public officials and private developers, are critical to city interests. Even if the public sector is not an active partner in every piece of the project, it must still actively monitor the project to account for its interests, or foolishly expose itself to the charge that it "gave away the store."

The privatized-financing arrangement for the 42DP entailed a subtle distinction between private risk for immediate cash funding and public liability for ultimate economic cost, one easily blurred in public hearings. Its complexity would cause even the most interested reporter or committed commentator to move on to less technical and more comprehensible, and therefore more compelling, aspects of the project. Pitched to a general audience, the daily newspapers' early reporting of the project focused primarily on its symbolic importance, with exceptions only for scandal and political intrigue. Consequently, what the public understood about the city's real financial commitments to the project was minimal. Ironically, what it understood quite well from the 42DP's singular architectural vision of the four high-density office towers presented by the project's officials with forthright clarity was the singular priority of the city's financially driven commercial agenda for West 42nd Street.

DEAL FUNDAMENTALS

One of Mayor Koch's publicly stated reasons for rejecting *The City at 42nd Street* had been his belief that the city would get the best deal on this prime target for redevelopment only through an open competitive bidding process. Open competitive bidding on a public-private project did not, however, mean a sealed-bid, auction-type process. While the city did use the bidding process to better the initial deal terms received in response to its RFP, the developer-selection process itself left city officials much room for discretion. For example, the RFP presented the "criteria for selection of project developers"; the listing was a general one, with the factors neither ranked nor prioritized, which was and continues to be typical of the public deal-making practice.[7] Acting in entrepreneurial fashion, cities generally seek to preserve options, to choose the bid with the greatest overall benefit package defined as some combination of financial returns, public improvements, and social benefits. They also look for financial strength, ability and experience in raising capital, and a track record developing complex projects, along with a host of other, intangible, factors. From a proprietary perspective, it is not in the city's interest to define precisely the terms of sale, but rather to let competitive forces operate. An open developer-selection process for the 42DP was mandatory from Koch's perspective because, as the chairman of PDC at the time said, "it would guarantee that the public would be getting the highest possible financial return, through payments in lieu of taxes and funding for subway and theater improvements from a project that would be consistent with the city's overall plan for the area."[8]

New York's established developers had been slow to accept the new procedures that accompanied large-scale development in which the public sector took on the role of an entrepreneurial partner. The shift from a traditional auction-bid procedure to a negotiated-development process via an RFP was in the early stages of what would become a learning curve when the selection process for the developers of the 42DP got underway. Under an RFP approach, developers are asked to submit proposals along with financial packages for the development of a property rather than just a sealed, one-time bid for a parcel of land. The developer-selection process for the rights to build the commercial center of Battery Park City, for example, caused some consternation among the city's largest developers after Olympia & York was selected to be master developer for the four buildings making up the 6-million-square-foot World Financial Center. Procedures for this selection were perceived by some developers to be unclear and complex. The developer-selection process for the 42DP, initiated only a year later in mid-1981, went forward before the complexities of the BPC experience had been reworked into systematic procedures for selection based on financial and design criteria. In other words, if procedures were hazy, developers were operating without firm footing.

The RFP for the 42DP did, however, lay out the policy mandates that would drive the deal making. There were four fundamentals: (1) the financial imperative that the public bear none of the cash outlay for site acquisition; (2) the public-works decision to do a full-scale renovation of the Times Square subway station complex; (3) the planning goal to renovate all nine theaters; and (4) the programmatic decision to seek commercial uses for the Eighth Avenue corridor. As the project labored to fulfill these mandates, hindsight later revealed three of the four to be "heavy prices to the deal," according to Travis: "Full renovation of the subway station foisted a public project onto the private sector and may have been a mistake. It had a heavy impact on the deal structure, though no one knew how really expensive the job would be; they were thinking in terms of $15 million to $20 million." The goal of renovating all nine theaters was another heavy burden. It was driven, in part, by the legacy of the fierce battle over the demolition of the Helen Hayes and Morosco Theaters, to be discussed shortly. "There was no market for this scope of theater renovation—throughout most of the 1980s, demand was insufficient for all of the city's existing theaters—but the deal had to support it," Travis recalled. "And the uses on Eighth Avenue, they were never really viable." Housing was considered, but again, Travis said, "it was not marketable, not feasible on an unsubsidized basis. Also, there was a policy issue about whether public resources should be used to foster market-rate, that is, luxury, housing in Manhattan."[9] As it would turn out, of the four fundamentals, only the financial imperative for private funding of land condemnation survived the first decade of controversy before the other policy fundamentals had to be completely reworked or scrapped.

The process of selecting developers presented the first test of these fundamentals. In June 1981 the RFP was mailed to approximately 500 developers with public notices placed in various periodicals and trade publications. Because they considered the area's redevelopment a "unified undertaking," city and state officials initially hoped for "coordinated" project-wide proposals, that is, a master developer for all of the nine sites being solicited for new private investment. In September, UDC and PDC officials announced that 26 proposals had been received from private developers, including such giants as Cadillac Fairview and O&Y, both from Canada, and Helmsley Properties of Manhattan; several proposals were for more than one site, but only two covered the entire project. Both of these were submitted by New York developers: George Klein of Park Tower Realty and a consortium headed by Paul Milstein of Milstein Properties. Of the 62 proposals for the nine individual sites, 30, or nearly half, were for the four office sites.

Winnowing the list of potential developers through a competitive-bid process established a platform for negotiating the 42DP deals. During the seven months in which the UDC/PDC/CPC project team, with the aid of its economic consultant, Eastdil Realty, evaluated the proposals, intense negotiations ensued with those developers "who submitted the most attractive proposals." Somewhere in the middle of this process, city and UDC officials changed their minds about the bidding structure because, "although it was difficult to compare the project-wide proposals with the individual site proposals, the Eastdil analysis concluded that the individual proposals were more advantageous to the City than the project-wide proposals."[10]

Based on Eastdil's conclusion, the public entities for the 42DP rejected both project-wide proposals and requested new proposals for individual sites. Five proposals were submitted, and after several weeks of round-by-round negotiations during which all "were pushed to improve their proposals," the short list for the set of office sites included but two bidders: Park Tower Realty and a group led by New York developer Larry A. Silverstein, which Milstein later joined near the end of the process. Given both the size and significance of the development opportunity, this was a surprisingly abbreviated short-list of finalists; the context of the times and the magnitude of the project narrowed the field considerably. Also, those involved with the failed *City at 42nd Street* effort had withdrawn; the exception was O&Y, which agreed to bid, but only on the condition that the former Times Tower could be torn down. When the decision was made, at least temporarily, to retain the icon—a condition O&Y believed would destroy its concept for the project—the firm withdrew. Symbolic politics determined that the former Times Tower be preserved: "It was a lightning rod; razing it would not [have been] worth the political heat," said Travis, who believed "this was a mistake, however."[11]

The power dynamics of the public players also defined the negotiation process. Since PDC had no capacity to execute the project alone— it was "a mouse until 1981," said Travis; "when we asked a question, UDC was God"—a joint structure was set up in which Travis, along with UDC's Larry F. Graham and James Hunter reported to a three-party board. Developing the RFP was a "model" group effort for which the team met once a week.[12]

When it came to negotiating with the bidding developers over the financial terms of the deal, PDC took the lead. UDC's attitude: "It's your money, we'll give advice."[13] PDC's negotiating lead, however, reflected its role as the city's technician for the project. The real power lodged with Herb Sturz, who, independent of the city's deputy mayors, ran the 42DP for Mayor Koch. It was Sturz who brought in UDC, kept control, defined the roles of each side, and was responsible for bringing in the people who would subsequently execute the project, Carl Weisbrod and his hire, Rebecca Robertson.

In seeking the "maximization through negotiation of primary financial contributions and responsibilities of each developer/operator," the city at times played one bidding developer against the other. "It was heavy negotiation," Travis recalled. The financial aspects of the bid proposals for each office site included six core elements: a base ground rent, an incentive ground rent based on operating performance, a site acquisition price, contributions for public improvements, financial guarantees, and a profit-sharing component from any sale or refinancing transaction. Early on the city requested that the bids be recast to include greater financial support for the midblock theater sites. As negotiations with each of the developers proceeded, a main stumbling block emerged over property taxes or PILOTs, a figure that equated to the base ground rent.[14] After intense rounds of negotiations, the city "went for broke" and told developers

Milstein and Klein "to make their best and final offer" by a certain date (March 22, 1982). Klein, Travis recalled, "jumped; his tax offering went up five cents. Milstein didn't move."[15] In the end, the city ultimately got higher PILOT/base ground rent dollars.

Since each developer was required to fund all site costs, regardless of their magnitude, the pivotal financial element became the amount of site acquisition payment a developer was willing to guarantee and secure by a letter of credit (the "secured site acquisition price"). The deal, according to a former city official, was "safety driven versus maximum profits driven."[16] The base ground rent developers were prepared to pay was almost as important to the selection, though it was not decisive. In a reaction to losing the designation that eventually led to an unsuccessful suit against the city, a disgruntled Milstein claimed that his bid offered the city greater overall returns than that of George Klein.

His disgruntlement may, in fact, have stemmed from a big-picture view of his bidding position. Milstein had been an early and singular pioneer of serious investment in Times Square, when in 1978 he bought the moribund Royal Manhattan Hotel on Eighth Avenue between 44th and 45th Streets for $3.5 million, intending to convert it to apartments. Persuaded by theater owners and city officials that a hotel would do more to improve the seedy neighborhood, with the aid of tax abatements, he changed course, and two years later the building reopened as the Milford Plaza Hotel (figure 4.1), with 1,310 medium-priced tourist hotel rooms. The project won him an award from Community Board 5 "for courageous reopening of a hotel on Eighth Avenue." That courage proved to be financially costly, however, and in the fall of 1981, shortly after the first round of RFP submissions, Milstein went on record saying that the decision had already cost him $5 million: "We felt we made a contribution to the City of New York by redeveloping that entire rundown area," he told a *Times* reporter. He was "rather disappointed" the city had not done more to advance rehabilitation of that stretch of Eighth Avenue farther north of 42nd Street.[17] There was no question that the Milford Plaza signaled a gutsy willingness to go where others feared to tread, but past high-profile skirmishes with the city's land-use regulators on other development projects had, nevertheless, given Milstein a reputation as a tough and bruising adversary.

The structure of Klein's bid, with its greater protection for the city, appears to have been the determining financial consideration. According to the final Eastdil analysis presented to UDC's board of directors, the Park Tower bid was "approximately equal to a competitor with regard to the net present value of normalized base ground rent. However, Park Tower's secured site acquisition price was $25 million greater than that of the other developer. Mr. Klein also agreed to provide funds for the acquisition of the theaters in Site 5 plus the Harris Theater in Site 6. He will also acquire the infill area of Site 6 and develop it for retail use."[18]

The selection decision was not as clear-cut as the Eastdil document would have suggested. At the time, George Klein had but a short

4.1
Postcard view of the Milford Plaza Hotel, Eighth Avenue between 44th and 45th Streets, as its original namesake, Hotel Lincoln, designed to serve "the better element of the Masses." ca. 1928. (Collection of Bruce J. McCuen)

track record of completed office towers: two in Brooklyn (among the first public-private redevelopment projects in the city) and two in Manhattan, the 27-story black-glass box at 499 Park Avenue and the 36-story aluminum tower at 535 Madison Avenue; a third in lower Manhattan, the 27-story fortresslike tower at 33 Maiden Lane, was under construction. Some real estate observers questioned whether he had the capability to undertake the role of master developer for an office complex of the size predicated by the 42DP. Known to some as "The Candy Man" in reference to his family's ownership of New York's once well-known Barton's candy chain, which had been sold in 1981, Klein had quickly developed a reputation as a builder from Brooklyn who set out to make his mark in Manhattan by creating a "quality image" for his firm. Park Tower consistently hired the nation's best-known architectural firms—I. M. Pei & Partners, Edward Larrabee Barnes & Associates, Philip Johnson & John Burgee Architects—to design its buildings, and the firm filled the towers with prestige credit tenants, among them, several foreign banks; the Wall Street investment bank of Dillion Read & Co.; IBM, with whom it developed several projects; and Chase Manhattan Bank.

"The mere act of hiring these three architects alone," *Times* architectural critic Paul Goldberger wrote in early 1981 several months before the RFP had been issued, "would set Mr. Klein apart from most New York real-estate developers," whom Goldberger criticized en mass for seeming "to operate on the principle that any architect good enough to be famous is too good to design a building for them."[19]

Klein's reputation for small, high-quality, architecturally conscious buildings carried significant weight with city and state officials. "He has a great eye for design, and we had a lot of confidence in him," Travis told *Forbes*, which published an innuendo-filled article,[20] "How to make it big in New York real estate," about Klein and the crossed paths of politics and real estate in New York in October 1984, the month before the project went up for review by the BOE.[21]

A conservative Republican, Klein was well connected, locally and nationally.[22] Designation as the developer of the office towers in the $1.6-billion Times Square project had made him the city's most prominent developer; he was not, however, a part of the closed circle of New York real estate families whose dominant ownership and social and political presence casts a unique character upon the city's real estate market. A private man and orthodox Jew, Klein did not socialize with or go to the same synagogue as the rest of the crowd. Except for his continuous civic and fundraising activities, he was nearly as much a real estate outsider as an out-of-town developer.

Flush with the success of his 499 Park Avenue building, for which he was signing leases with prestige-minded corporations at rents greatly in excess of the what had been projected, Klein had a big vision for West 42nd Street. He was attracted to the 42DP because it offered "economic opportunity," yet like most developers who seek out the big projects, he was strongly motivated by the special character this particular opportunity presented "to shape a city," as he explained in an interview.[23] In proposing to develop the entire 13-acre site, Klein acted on the belief that the master-developer approach was necessary to ensure success; Times Square was in such bad shape that construction of the project's many parts needed to move ahead together, all at the same time. If any one element of the project did not go ahead, the financial viability of any newly erected office tower would be compromised by the surrounding sea of blight. Klein's willingness to take on the risk of being a master developer for the 42DP differed markedly, however, from his bid on the office component of Battery Park City, where he, like most other developers, bid only on one development site. O&Y, Klein later remarked, "made the right strategic bet with their bid approach."[24] It does not seem like a stretch to conclude that in losing the office development opportunity at Battery Park City, George Klein had learned a lesson in how to bid big when a similar opportunity for the 42DP came along less than a year later. As the successful winner in this contest, he would seek to make his mark on Manhattan by building a trophy-quality office complex akin to Rockefeller Center. Once again he would hire Philip Johnson & John Burgee Architects to design the four towers, which he was targeting for high-profile corporate headquarter users. If the city was inclined to collect big-name architects for its high-profile public-private projects, Klein had served up the prestigious, enticing choice.

By his bidding stance and willingness to guarantee what the city wanted in terms of a large secured site acquisition price, Klein positioned himself as more of a risk taker than New York's more seasoned developers. This was consistent with his early start on the 499 Park Avenue project in 1978, the first speculative office building constructed in Manhattan following that period's real estate recession. If Klein was both bold and perceptive about the development opportunity at the "Crossroads of America," he would nevertheless realize, in time, that he had overestimated the public sector's ability to move the condemnation process forward in a timely manner—to manage the political risks of the public-private development process. As litigation delays multiplied and the full extent of his open-ended commitment to the city became increasingly evident in 1986, the maverick developer would have to seek out a deep-pocketed institutional partner to carry this risk, which he found in the Newark, New Jersey-based Prudential Life Insurance Company of America.

EXTRACTING PUBLIC BENEFITS

Preserving the landmark-quality theaters on West 42nd Street and renovating the Times Square subway station complex were the two big public-improvements on the city's agenda for the 42DP, as the RFP had made clear. The nine midblock theaters symbolized the historic heart of Broadway. By preserving and restoring these "extraordinary older theaters for theatrical and upgraded movie use," the plan was to revitalize the area "as a theater and entertainment center serving tourists and all New Yorkers."[25]

This logic was as essential politically as it was impeccable pro-grammatically. The city's performing theater artists were engaged in a bruising but ultimately unsuccessful battle to save the legendary Helen Hayes and Morosco Theaters from demolition deemed necessary to clear the way for construction of the Portman hotel on Broadway between 45th and 46th Streets. The theater-demolition issue was the last of many hurdles to be overcome before construction of the hotel could begin. Execution of this high-profile project had been choppy, from the city's perspective. First initiated by Atlanta architect-developer John Portman in 1973, the project was soon stymied by a collapsed local economy during the city's 1974–1975 fiscal crisis. Upon taking office in January 1978, Mayor Koch picked up the cause, and he sought to enhance the hotel's prospects finan-cially by applying to Washington for a $21.5-million grant under President Jimmy Carter's new "Urban Action Demonstration Grant" (UDAG) pro-gram. Using the hotel project, which at that point had received wide pub-lic support, as a way of pushing forward its own quest for a two-block pedestrian mall on Broadway, the city also had applied for two transporta-tion-based grants totaling $4.5 million[26] (figure 4.2). Most significantly, the mayor made a firm political commitment. "Implicit in the beginning was our willingness to accept demolition of the Helen Hayes," said

4.2
Proposed pedestrian plaza for Broadway, 45th to 49th Streets, ca. 1981. (NYC Office of Midtown Planning and Development)

4.3
Victim of the city's intent to rebuild Times Square: The Folies Bergère built as it appeared in 1911, a theater restaurant. Within months, this "magnificent flop" was converted to a theater and renamed the Fulton. In 1955, the Fulton became the Helen Hayes Theater in honor of the first lady of the American stage. (The Museum of the City of New York, Wurts Collection)

4.4
Victim of the city's intent to rebuild Times Square, The Morosco Theater, 1917. (*Architect's and Builder's Magazine*)

Kenneth Halpern, then director of the Mayor's Office of Midtown Development. "We were looking to do whatever was necessary to get the hotel built."[27]

Public opposition to the Hayes-Morosco demolition was late—the first organized rally took place in February 1980—but the all-out pitched battle persisted for two years until the last legal action in March 1982 lifted a temporary stay against demolition. Waves of protest struggled valiantly to make the case for the theaters' preservation, one of which ended with the arrest of scores of protestors the day the U.S. Supreme Court lifted the stay against demolition, setting in motion the steel wrecking balls. The arguments for preservation had merit—the Helen Hayes Theater had been designated eligible for the National Register of Historic Places in 1978—and special emotional significance. Using the power of their prestige, a cast of celebrity performers, playwrights, and producers (Jason Robards, Lauren Bacall, James Earl Jones, Martha Scott, Elizabeth Ashley, Christopher Reeve, Arthur Miller, Joseph Papp, and Alexander H. Cohen) passionately made the case in staged performances at both theaters. But as the first major show of private investment in Times Square—almost universally considered economically destitute—the effort to save the theaters proved to be a losing struggle of dramatic proportions. Despite skepticism about its architectural merit, the Portman hotel was being proclaimed by its private supporters and government promoters as a "linch-pin" in the effort to clean up Times Square. This public, intense furor threatened the delicate alignment of political support for the 42DP, which was in the early stages of coalition building. The city's promise to restore the historic theaters on West 42nd Street aimed to compensate the performing-arts interests for the loss of the Hayes and Morosco Theaters, a connection Koch confirmed years later (figures 4.3–4.6).

The battle over the Hayes and Morosco Theaters was a precursor to the one looming over the 42DP, in that the controversy reflected clashing values and competing visions. Preservationists were not against the development of the 2,020-room Portman hotel per se, they just wanted it to be built over the "intimate houses" where numerous legendary plays had been staged, without demolishing them; Actors' Equity Association went so far as to commission architect Lee Harris Pomeroy to study whether a hotel could be built using Portman's concepts. The Pomeroy scheme was reportedly feasible, if costly and architecturally challenging to construct, but it did not have even a small probability of execution. For one, Portman found preservation "impossible" to accommodate with his architectural vision and adamantly refused to consider any kind of shift in his plans. In that context, the city's commitment to "do whatever was necessary to get the hotel built" translated into an intransigence to consider alternatives to wholesale demolition of the theaters regardless of their symbolic or historical significance. Uncertainty prevailed over the actual economic viability of the older theaters—"I'm torn between sentiment versus good sense," said Helen Hayes herself[28]—and that only hardened the city's intractability. Like the 42DP, the hotel initiative was haunted by the ghost of Robert Moses and governed by symbolic politics: "Broadway traffics in such intangibles as tradition, mystery, atmosphere," the actor Bernard Hughes wrote in an op-ed for the *Times*. "If the Hayes and the Morosco are pulled down, the working capital of this city's theater will be considerably diminished."[29] The media-oriented protests and rallies, celebrity power, lawsuits, and landmarking efforts would be repeated in the bigger battle to preserve the character of Times Square. The preservationists' opposition to the demolition of the Hayes and Morosco Theaters might have been late, but as the story told in chapter 8 reveals, the opposition learned its lessons well. They saw the destruction of the theaters as a breach of trust; the battle became an "icon for the byzantine conflicts inherent in large-scale development," a symbol of government's determination to prevail.[30]

Renovating the Times Square subway station complex was a different matter completely. Whether tourist or commuter riding the subways, one did not need to spend more than a few minutes traversing the complex labyrinth of platforms, concourses, stairs, and ramps that make up the complex to know it needed a major overhaul. Odoriferous and distinctively unpleasant in general, it ranked as among the most dangerous of subway stations as well. "When the subway system is called 'the most depressing public environment found anywhere,'" the *DEIS* noted, "this station is often cited as evidence. Its physical condition is generally poor"[31]—a tremendous understatement of fact few riders would contest (figure 4.7). Sixteen subway lines converge in the project area, eight in the Times Square station, making it the best served and most heavily utilized mass-transit node in the country, the *DEIS* reported. By the early 1980s, almost 25 million people each year passed through the turnstiles below Times Square, a load the station was never designed to carry. Though this

4.7
(The New Yorker Collection ©
1993 Tom Cheney from cartoon-
bank.com. All Rights Reserved)

was a big number, subway ridership was in decline. The city's economic recession was partly to blame, but crime in the subways was a factor too, which, as the *DEIS* noted, made the quest for a significant renovation of the system's central node (figure 4.8) all the more pressing and important a goal for the city. As the chairman of the MTA, Robert Kiley, testified at the BOE hearings: "For anyone who ever uses it regularly, you know it could be disorienting and downright dispiriting. This project gives us an opportunity to correct many of the problems of congestion, crowding, rising traffic flows, dinginess, and problems of security and surveillance."[32] The renovation plan for the subway complex included new entrances, a reorganization of the circuitous mezzanine, increased retail space, and a modernization of all finishes.

The overall game plan for securing the theater and subway benefits—at no cash cost to the city—called for cross-subsidies from the three commercial uses: office, merchandise mart, hotel. While the MTA had committed some funds for station improvements from its five-year capital plan, most of the required modernization work, including the new mezzanine, would depend upon payments from the project's private developers. In the beginning, these were pegged at $25.6 million from the office sites and $7 million from the mart site, both to be adjusted for inflation until the date of actual payment. As Kiley explained, "The subway improve-

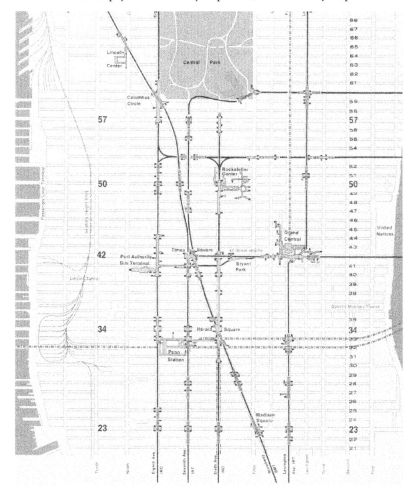

4.8
The centrality of Times Square as a transportation node. (Regional Plan Association)

ments in this sense are inextricably linked to the development project itself in two ways, funding and also the architectural and construction work [on the office towers] that has to go on in the project that is going to be so complex and is going to require extensive coordination."[33] It was clear to everyone that the improved efficiency and ambience of a newly renovated subway station would be essential to the economic success of four new Class A office towers in Times Square.

From a policy perspective, what was even more significant was that the public-benefit program—theaters and subway improvements—had been integrally tied to the timing of private development and, in turn, to the economic health of the city's real estate market. Such a connection was not unique to the 42DP, but rather a generic attribute of the privatization strategy. The strategy carried a clear political as well as financial risk: If the market tanked so severely that development was put on hold indefinitely, thereby jeopardizing revenues targeted for public infrastructure or amenities, the promised public benefits would disappear as well, unless public officials found alternative sources of funds to go forward with their plans.[34]

For the 42DP commercial sites to throw off the necessary dollars from private developers, at least one of two economic conditions had to prevail, initially: The sites would have to be economically attractive as development opportunities as dictated by conventional notions of real estate feasibility, or the development deal with the city had to be favorable enough to induce private capital to take on the risks of a disadvantageous site. To create development value, the bulk of the project-wide development rights had already been transferred to the four office sites, so the same strategy would not work to counteract the problems of the sites at the weaker western end of the project area.

Success for the western sites depended upon making the mart and hotel deals more economically attractive. That was always a tall order.

4.9
Fronting on Eighth Avenue, a merchandise mart, phase-one design by Kohn Petersen Fox Associates. (© Kohn Petersen Fox Associates PC)

Not only were these sites the toughest sell of the project, the hotel was feasible only if the merchandise mart could be put in place, and the mart was such a specialized use, there being only a few successful examples in the country, that it was a high-risk piece of the development program regardless of location (figures 4.9, 4.10). As one player put it, "no one really knew how or what to do with a mart."[35] The terms of the deal with the mart developers, the born-out-of-compromise joint venture of Equitable Life Assurance Society, Trammell Crow Company, and Tishman Speyer Properties described in the previous chapter, allowed for some flexibility of uses. This resulted from last-minute politicking in the early hours of the morning before the BOE vote in response to the Garment District industry's opposition to its use for apparel trade. That did not really change the fact, though, that the mart deal brought to the BOE for approval contained a weak set of economic incentives. Consequently, paying the bill for the public-benefit agenda depended much more heavily than was evident on paper upon development of the office towers—a fact that was, however, evident in the favored terms of that deal.

Vision #2: Corporate Square

Park Tower's designation as developer for the office sites carried with it the opportunity to build 4.1 million square feet of office space in four towers on sites covering 2.6 acres of land. Translated into the language of real estate development, this amounted to an average FAR of 36.6. Without minimizing the investment risk involved in what at the time was clearly a highly speculative endeavor, the option to develop four high-density towers under competitively advantageous conditions, and thus control the

100-percent corner at the city's mass-transit crossroads, was hardly an everyday real estate opportunity. The uncertainty of the development potential carried a high degree of risk, but in the mid-to-late 1980s, the deal "with all its government inducements" represented a "great profit opportunity."[36] Strategically, it was a singular opportunity to buy development rights for a location with a long-term probability of being a unique center of commercial activity.

From the developer's perspective, the deal promised to deliver three key economic benefits: a fixed site "price" (the "secured site acquisition price" now called the "offset amount") linked to UDC's powers of condemnation for assembling enough of West 42nd Street to reshape the tawdry environment for development, low PILOT payments (relative to taxes on comparable buildings), and fixed annual PILOT escalations (also, substantially below those anticipated for similar West Side buildings). Translated into dollars, the overall average annual savings for these buildings, as estimated by Park Tower's economic consultant, Landauer Associates, amounted to nearly $19 per square foot. Close to 75 percent of this differential was attributable to the PILOT subsidy, the rest to the writedown of land costs, as will be explained in the next chapter. According to that 1983 Landauer report, current property taxes for comparable buildings were running between $9 to $12 per square foot, compared to an initial PILOT of $3.60 per square foot for each of the four Times Square towers, regardless of when each might be completed.[37] This was a hefty competitive advantage. Because of the project's customized abatements, the annual savings in real estate taxes a tenant could obtain by leasing space in one of the four 42DP buildings rather than a new office building elsewhere in midtown Manhattan could "easily range from $13.00 to $22.00 per square foot per annum based upon when the buildings are completed."[38]

Equally attractive, the developer's fixed land cost mirrored the competitive advantage afforded by the PILOT subsidy. In 1984, when the BOE approved the deal, the full costs of the development opportunity (offset price plus public-improvement contributions) approximated $29 per square foot of FAR, which was 50 to 25 percent of the $58 to $120 per square foot of FAR land costs at other midtown locations. With land values increasing at approximately 6 percent per year, the differential between the market elsewhere in midtown and the second, third, and fourth 42DP buildings promised to become even more pronounced.[39]

The financial logic underlying the city's deal was deceptively simple: an exchange of government powers in the form of development rights for money, though that money would not flow directly into the city coffers. Rather, it would first go to cover site acquisition costs (SAC), thereby solving the city's immediate problem of finding dollars to cover the out-of-pocket costs of the development project. Open-ended payment of SAC would be the sole obligation of the developer and would be secured by an irrevocable letter of credit in favor of UDC for the appraised value of the properties, plus 20 percent. Through this funding arrangement, the private sector promised to absorb the condemnation risk commonly borne by the public sector under a conventional urban-renewal approach. From both sides' perspective, however, the risk was hedged over the 99-year term of the lease agreement. For the developer, government had fixed the site "price" at $88 million (with no inflation adjustment); if SAC exceeded this sum, he was obligated to fund the out-of-pocket cost, although the ultimate liability for this "loan" of "excess site acquisition costs" (ESAC) remained with the city, which was obligated to reimburse the developer's advance payments with interest.[40] A "cap" on the actual purchase price was necessary because there was no way any private developer would have taken on the responsibility without some kind of limit to its liability. "This project was conceived as a means of accomplishing a major public purpose at the same time as not having the city and public liable for a tremendous cash outlay up front," Weisbrod said later.[41] The cap was essential, he emphasized, because developers had to be assured that, beyond some point, they could recover their outlays for acquisition. The city would repay the developer for the ESAC with a "rent credit."[42]

The concept of ESAC is equivalent to the land-cost writedown employed in conventional urban renewal, only the risks of the players are reversed. Under this novel off-budget arrangement the developer would fund an open-ended loan to the city, accepting the risk of escalating land costs. The reversal of roles did not eliminate the public's ultimate responsibility for the land subsidy; it just reversed the timing. Instead of receiving the land writedown up front, the subsidy would flow over time through rent credits, as a payback for ESAC funds advanced. Moreover, this risk was hedged as well since the public's borrowing responsibility was nonrecourse: Unlike certain types of off-budget items that, as a practical matter, are recourse to the public treasury—for example, UDC's early "moral obligation bonds"—the nature of the 42DP deals precluded this type of ultimate recourse to taxpayer dollars.

At the time the office deal was inked, public officials did not expect ESAC to escalate dramatically, as it eventually did. In 1981, Park Tower's offset bid of $88 million appeared to provide a substantial cushion. According to the recollections of at least two key city players, the first internal appraisals put the land purchase costs for all but the mart and hotel sites in the $26 million to $30 million range. By the time of the BOE review in 1984, this figure had moved into a range of $40 million to $50 million. As to the related costs of condemnation, no one knew the likely tally, since no relocation activity had taken place in New York for a long time, and there were no real comparable transactions for the theaters. "The city really didn't see itself at risk," recalled Travis, "because its position was hedged by the expected increase in property taxes: property values, rents, taxes do track, even if with a lag."[43]

The deal, in essence, gave the developer an "option" on the four sites, an exclusive right to develop the sites short of an absolute obligation to do so. The cost of this option took several forms. First, Park Tower would pay a nonrefundable amount equal to 56 percent of costs and expenses associated with the project, beginning with a $700,000 "designation fee," with the balance capped at $2.52 million. Second, upon signing the leases, the developer would pay annual interim rent equivalent to the 1982–1983 property taxes attached to these sites. The third and heaviest cost flowed from the commitment to fully fund site acquisition costs: Should construction be delayed indefinitely beyond the deal's construction timetable—as ultimately proved to be the case—the funds advanced by the developer, as well as its own predevelopment expenses, would constitute a large and idle equity investment. Such a sunk investment would impose a huge opportunity cost on any developer, even a deep-pocketed financial institution such as Prudential. And the nature of the funding arrangement meant that this risk exposure would be open ended. "Accepting the funding exposure for site acquisition ran against the grain of private-development logic," remarked Veronica W. Hackett, former executive vice president for Park Tower in charge of the Times Square project. "A developer typically works with fixed land costs; the risk is in the construction phase."[44]

From the developer's perspective, the full set of financial obligations—option costs, offset amount, ground rents, transaction payments, and public-improvement costs—constituted the price of the development opportunity, however the individual parts were defined. The composition of that package, though, was key to the public sector whose financial perspective is always colored by political needs, as was so clearly revealed in the comparative evaluations of bids by prospective office developers. Typically, the public sector's analysis of the implications of a deal further varies from that of the private developer because each party uses different discount rates to value the same financial inputs. In short, the bottom line of a deal for a public developer, even one as focused on financial returns as was New York, reflects a political calculus.

The economics of the office deal were significantly better than those for the mart or hotel deals. First, if inflation produced increases in the site acquisition costs for the mart and hotel sites, the mart and hotel developers would pay accordingly, but that exposure did not exist for the office developers. Internally, among the city's people on the project, there was substantial discussion about whether this exposure should allowed to remain fixed, at least one negotiator recalled.[45] Second, under the terms of the mart and hotel deals, the period for repaying ESAC was relatively short, 15 years, compared to 99 years for the office deal. When the negotiators sat down to figure out the numerical implications of these terms, it quickly became apparent that the cash flows from the mart and hotel sites could never repay their ESACs. This made these deals nearly unworkable; there was not enough in the incentive pot for the mart, several players later stated. The office deal, in contrast, was, by most accounts, considered overly generous.

Reading the financial structure of the deals reveals that five distinct policy commitments were embedded in city's financial strategy for the redevelopment of West 42nd Street. First, the city committed to subsidize the costs of commercial redevelopment in midtown Manhattan, though it would take no direct financial risk for the costs of acquiring the land. To avoid the risk of escalating site acquisition costs, it required private developers to fund, in advance, both the public and private costs of land acquisition for the entire project area. Second, the city would use density, its off-budget currency, to create financially attractive development opportunities by transferring project-wide densities to the four office-tower sites, and it would enhance these development opportunities with competitively advantageous abatements of property taxes. Third, to meet the political need for a self-financed project, the city would channel the expected revenues from project sites to the repayment of the developers' funding advances. Fourth, as a tradeoff for its massive densities, the office sites would carry most of the financial burden associated with the city's symbolic mandate to revive the midblock theaters. In addition, the city assigned as much as possible of the costs of new infrastructure to private developers. Fifth, the city would trade lucrative short-term benefits (tax abatements) for long-term financial returns (percentage rents, profit-sharing transaction kickers, and spillover benefits) from the clean-up project. Linking each element and arching over the design of the financial strategy was a common denominator: The city was tying its ultimate financial liability for the land writedown to the health of the real estate market, through the timing of private construction and the profitability of the office towers.

These policy commitments were the ones approved by the BOE in 1984. A few years later, when negotiators for both sides sat down to translate them into contract language, the details of the lease agreements became exceedingly complex. Moreover, as explained in the next chapter, parts of the deal were being renegotiated under pressure from Mayor Koch, who wanted to tap the benefits of the big run-up in land prices triggered by the city's speculative office boom. Because the revised terms bettered the deal within the envelope of what the BOE had approved, no new review was called for. And although the financial implications of the changes turned out to be anything but superficial, the policy commitments revealed in the structure of the deal remained firmly in place.

Theater Rhetoric

The "revitalization of 42nd Street as a theater and entertainment center" was at the forefront of all of the earliest planning documents for the redevelopment project. While economic pragmatism might mean bending to the commercial profit motive of large-scale office development to pay the bill for cleaning up the street, city and state officials consistently argued that the task was being undertaken in service of the bigger goal: "to strengthen the existing Theater District and provide a strong anchor for it along 42nd Street." The GPP noted the neglected heritage of the street's great theaters with their "breathtaking architectural details" hidden by movie marquees that had been added in the 1930s, and explained the desire of the city and UDC "to seize the opportunity presented by this concentration of theaters to restore as many theaters as possible."[46] In brief prose the 1981 RFP similarly made the case: "A concentration of legitimate theater uses within the Project Area is possible and necessary to achieve the Project's goals." The words "possible and necessary" represented a telling combination of official encouragement and formal requirement for doing something extraordinarily difficult. The combination also signaled a weak beginning.

The importance of theater preservation was a political given: After withstanding the political heat surrounding the loss of the Helen Hayes and Morosco Theaters, Mayor Koch and city officials did not want a second bruising theater battle. "We had to preserve everything," Travis said.[47] Though not formally designated as architectural landmarks, save for the New Amsterdam Theater, which by 1982 had been designated as a New York landmark and placed on the National Register of Historic Places, the 42nd Street theaters were considered to be of landmark quality, worthy of preservation. Quality restoration was deemed as important as preservation, so, working with historians recommended by the Landmarks Preservation Commission, the project's planners developed design guidelines for interiors and exteriors of the street's nine theaters. If a full restoration of the theaters was not feasible, the RFP explained, the project's design guidelines had built in flexibility by permitting that "some of the existing theaters be restored and operated as commercial legitimate theaters and others be devoted to quality entertainment uses, such as multi-media, institutional theater or film."[48]

Nevertheless, throughout the 1980s, the task of recreating the street's historic entertainment focus presented a daunting programmatic and economic challenge. The decade would turn out to be one of the worst for the theater industry, with business conditions on a downward slide following the peak 1980–1981 season. "Urban entertainment," the concept that clusters of activity devoted to middle-class recreation could flourish in cities, had yet to see its moniker in lights. And movie uses— widely associated with what had made the street a mess—were not allowed in the long term under the terms of the theater deals approved by the BOE;[49] the RFP did not prohibit "film" uses per se, but private developers feared that movie theaters would turn West 42nd Street back to pornography. These factors—in short, poor timing—conspired against the success of a market-driven commercial strategy for theater preservation. Relying upon private developers to fill out this portion of the plan could not possibly alter that reality.

From the start, the theater sites struggled for attention. With no specially designed incentives to attract prospective bidders, it is hard to understand how public officials expected this difficult piece of the project to move forward. For three years city and state officials failed to attract prospective developers for Site 5, home of the Lyric, Selwyn, Apollo, Times Square, and Victory Theaters, and only in the month before the public hearing on the *FEIS* did they conditionally designate a developer/operator, Cambridge Investment Group, Ltd., headed by public-servant-turned-real estate developer Michael J. Lazar. Lazar's designation, the last of those made on the project, came only after city and state officials insisted that because of his lack of experience with theater operations he find an established theater company to run the houses, which he did in the Jujamcyn Company, a major New York theater operator. Then, less than twenty months later, when he was indicted on charges of racketeering and mail fraud stemming from a major scandal at the city's Parking Violations Bureau, the city and state revoked this conditional designation. Designation of a developer for the Site 5 theaters remained suspended for four years, until 1990, when a newly created nonprofit, the 42nd Street Entertainment Corporation, took over the theater agenda for the 42DP.

Preservation of the midblock theaters and the low-density character of the 42nd Street corridor was always put forth as the justification for the enormous densities of the office towers and the questionable inclusion of a wholesale mart on a historic entertainment street. The soundness of the policy logic lacked planning substance, however. Despite evidence of studies completed, theater planning was minimal, one knowing participant recalled. City and state officials were making decisions for the theaters on the basis of generalized ideas and stylized facts from feasibility studies conducted between 1980 and 1981, when the theater business was relatively robust. As summarized in a 1984 report on the "Status and Summary" of the Theater Preservation/Renovation Program, the 13-page "outline" fell far short of the type of overall vision and concrete economic strategy needed to energize the implementation of such a high-profile goal and historic theme for the street's revitalization. It suggested that thought had been given to regulatory issues of control—scale, prohibition of air-rights development, design, and use of the renovated spaces—designed to ensure the theaters' preservation. Nevertheless, missing were the detailed economics of how this "plan" would work. Indeed, the plan's program implicitly assumed that theater needed nothing more to stay alive in New York than a supply of adequate buildings in which to mount productions.

Responsibility for the cost of acquiring the theaters had been structured into the deals with private developers of the office, mart, and hotel sites, but these were capital subsidies for acquisition of the existing structures. They would only carry the theater agenda through the first act of the redevelopment play. Act two, renovation, could proceed only with private funding from the theater's designated developers. While the deal for the office sites allowed $4.2 million of its $9.45-million theater contribution to be used for the improvement and renovation of the five theaters packaged into Site 5 and the deal for Site 7 likewise provided for a $750,000 contribution, these amounts were intended not to cover the renovations but for property acquisition. More to the point, act three, theater operation, had to be self-sustaining: The seven theaters slated for profit-making uses were expected to make it on the strength of box-office revenues, helped along only by relatively low PILOTs in the deal approved by the BOE and favorable federal tax benefits for historic preservation.

Where operating funds were to come from for the Liberty and Victory Theaters, required by the *GPP* to be used only for "institutional" theater, was not dealt with at all.

The city's deal makers understood the self-sustaining mandate for the theaters to be a risky proposition. As an alternative for the Times Square Theater, the deal with Cambridge Investment Group allowed the developer to use the space for retailing; similarly, in the case of the Empire and Liberty Theaters (adjacent to the mart site on the south side of the street), some mart-related uses were permitted. Renovation of the street's crown-jewel, the Art-Nouveau New Amsterdam Theater—legendary even by the rich Broadway standards of the time—seemed more certain than the others, as it was to be redeveloped for legitimate theater independent of the project by the Nederlander Organization, the national's largest theater operator.[50] But for the more historically significant of the two theaters intended for use by nonprofit organizations, the Victory, uncertainty prevailed: no concept/feasibility plan for renovation and reuse had been prepared. Moreover, the earliest feasibility study commissioned by the city and UDC had identified the Victory and Liberty Theaters for nonprofit uses precisely because their physical characteristics limited the potential box-office revenues and, thus, their use for Broadway theater. The study called for subsidies to cover higher overhead necessary to book, manage, and raise funds for the Victory and Liberty operations. "The total annual deficit for these two houses may well reach $1 million, although as much as $500,000 of that might be offset by fund-raising," the report concluded. "Alternatively, this requirement could be met by diverting a small portion of the property tax revenues produced by the rest of the 42nd Street development apart from the ten theaters."[51] The deal for the theaters did not provide for any operating subsidies, however.

The precariousness of the theater-preservation strategy was not veiled. Rather, hope seemed to lie in by-the-by change, at least as presented in the official record. "Institutional operators have not yet been identified for either the Victory or Liberty," the *FEIS* reported. "UDC and the City are confident that, as the project moves ahead, the necessary commitments of funds will be forthcoming with respect to the renovation of the Victory and the nonprofit operation of both the Victory and the Liberty." The fall-back solution anticipated by the city's planners was first-run movie or theater-related uses, "until such renovation and theater operations become feasible."[52] In one of the last-minute compromises made prior to the BOE hearing on the 42DP, the city addressed mounting criticism of its theater "plan" with an announcement that a 14-person Theater Advisory Committee would be formed, according to a UDC update on the project, "to advise on the programming and management of the nonprofit theaters."[53] It would take another three years, however, and the hiring of Rebecca Robertson, for the 42DP to concentrate on how to meet its goals for the theater sites.

However persistent and strong the public sector's symbolic rhetoric on preserving the theaters was, it did not persuade the skeptics. At the public hearings, the incompleteness of the "plan" was called to task by the Regional Plan Association with an appeal to the BOE to withhold approval until assurances for the theaters and four other significant planning issues were forthcoming. The Actors' Equity Association and Save the Theaters, Inc., the city's major theater preservation organization, jointly withheld endorsement of the 42DP, firmly convinced after the demolition of the Helen Hayes and Morosco Theaters that the city and its planners did not really understand the elements needed to maintain the vitality of the Theater District. They had lost both patience and belief that the city would ever do the right thing for its underappreciated Broadway heritage. The promises to restore the 42nd Street movie houses to their historical roles as legitimate playhouses were "too vague" to be judged, Jack L. Goldstein, director of Save the Theaters, later wrote. "It is unclear whether funding for the theaters will be sufficient; it is unclear how they will be operated. Instead of a cohesive plan for the sensible management of the 42nd Street corridor as an entertainment complex of mixed performing arts uses, the plan simply proposes that some of the theaters be thrown into the competitive commercial market of Broadway."[54]

Though the city's goal was genuinely conceived, its initial execution was seriously flawed. It was crippled by the narrowness of what theater preservation meant at the time—"live" Broadwaylike productions—and a policy decision that commercial use of the theaters should prevail over other ways to preserve the structures (figure 4.11). The financial imperative remained dominant even in this most politically sensitive piece of the public agenda. Scenarios for reuse as film-revival houses or commercial-television production facilities had been briefly considered by UDC and PDC's consultants, who concluded that such uses were "not necessarily commercially feasible."[55] If the theaters could be commercially operated, there would be little need to spend scarce city resources to obtain the benefits their revitalization would bring to the street—middle-class pedestrian activity, ongoing employment, restaurant trade, and related retail sales. Entertainment in the most general sense was not encouraged in the redevelopment plan, though this would have been consistent with the cleanup strategy to put a new slate of "good" pedestrian-generating activities on the block in place the existing "bad" uses. "There seems never to have been a recognition that forms of entertainment other than theater are also 'legitimate,' " argued one architectural critic in an insightful review of the redevelopment plan for *Architectural Record* in 1984. "The [design] guidelines do not encourage movie theaters or nightclubs, rehearsal space, or stages for dance and music (except Broadway musicals). These uses frequently cannot generate the revenues per square foot that office or retail space can. They are, however, indispensable elements of what makes New York a center for the arts." The problem, he concluded, was the "giantism of the plan," which was "at odds with the idea of a coherent theater or entertainment district."[56] A more politically forthright assessment would have concluded that the theater "plan" amounted only to compensatory symbolism.

4.11
The intent of theater preservation for West 42nd Street: live Broadwaylike productions. (Gary Hack)

The hollowness of the policy effort would further weaken an already fragile consensus for the project. As revealed in the city and state's deals for development, the priority of the 42DP was singularly clear: commercial office development. The financial strategy of concentrating massive densities for office towers on all sides of the symbolic center of Times Square defined the 42DP in terms that became highly controversial, aesthetically as well as programmatically. In the absence of a substantive program for the theater agenda, the city's planning approach threatened the symbolic as well as physical character of West 42nd Street. Reflecting the city's zeal to clear away social problems, the corporate character of the initial plan appeared arrogantly and brutally insensitive to the cultural symbolism of the place.

Progress proved elusive for more than eight years, despite the city's clever funding strategy. By the time of the first condemnation takings in 1990, the funding strategy had become legally cumbersome as well as financially complex; by the time construction on the office sites finally began, in 1995, the complex mechanics of the arrangement had to be rebuilt to accommodate the unanticipated emergence of four separate development entities in place of a single, master developer. Still, at no point did the funding strategy fail to deliver on its promise. The fact that the terms of the office deal had provided the city with an open tab for spending, in the end, proved enduring, thanks to the deep pockets of Prudential.

a

b

4.12 Beginning to rebuild Times Square: a) Site preparation for the Portman-designed hotel, later designated
the Marriott Marquis Hotel, 1982. b) The structure of
change: Steel frame in place to the eighth floor of the
Marriott Marquis Hotel, 1983. (Charles M. Weiss)

CHAPTER 5

Run-away costs are what developers fear most about development. While they take risks and expect to be compensated for them, they fear unlimited risks. So, it had to be with great confidence that George Klein accepted the open-ended risk of funding UDC's condemnation of the office sites and midblock theaters. It was a statement of doubly great confidence that insurance giant Prudential Insurance Company of America reaffirmed that commitment in 1986 when it signed on to become Park Tower Realty's partner in the venture, formally known as Times Square Center Associates (TSCA). Though a practiced institutional developer, Newark-based Prudential had no New York "trophy project." It was not a New York player; its development record in the city was one of missed opportunities, as the real estate reporter for *Crain's New York Business* noted when he wrote that the 42nd Street Development Project gave Prudential "a historic opportunity to become a major player in city real estate through one mega-deal."[1] It was one of the city's highest profile development projects, along with Rockefeller Center, the World Trade Center, and Battery Park City. It offered a unique strategic opportunity to control midtown's commanding locations at the city's transit crossroads, and the fortunes of those sites promised to shape the broader West Side market.

All of these factors helped explain why Prudential remained committed to Times Square despite years of delay, dozens of lawsuits, and widespread doubts about whether midtown west could absorb so much more new office space. Where others saw a pending downturn in the real estate cycle as a looming problem, Prudential's top real estate decision maker at the time, Robert E. Riley, a stocks-and-bonds person who had taken over the development company in 1986, saw an opportunistic land play for localized market control. To his way of thinking, control was the strategic key that would get all interested tenants to come to Prudential, as the largest landlord in the area; it held out the promise of market-pricing power. If, as that reasoning goes, you are in Times Square and space gets tight, by controlling the available space, you could control rents—the classic capitalistic dream.

The city needed a deep-pocketed institutional player like Prudential so hungry for a high-profile success in Manhattan that it would take on the open-ended risk of condemnation. Did the senior executives at Prudential and the board of directors they would have to convince to make the big financial commitments, though, really understand the nature and extent of what the company was taking on? As a Newark-based insurance giant, could they understand the nuances and pockets of power of the closed world of New York family real estate? The lumbering giant had teamed up with a prescient entrepreneur, George Klein, who viewed real estate as "the last Mohican of the wildcatter."[2] Was this a marriage predicated on a solid foundation of trust and shared goals or was it one of convenience destined for tension from the start?

The city's cleverly constructed—but untried and unconventional—effort to shift all of the financial risk of redevelopment to the private sector would, in time, turn back on itself and exacerbate the political risks of what many perceived to be a discredited policy of large-scale land condemnation. And the very complexity of the off-budget financing resulted in a house of cards that in the end made for impossible accountability, inflexibility in dealing with a changing world, unreasonable private risks that could only be carried out by naive institutional players with deep pockets, and most probably higher costs than piecemeal development. It was an unprecedented journey, for all parties in the partnership.

INCREDULOUS OWNERS

When city and state officials and TSCA signed off on the more than 7,000 pages of leases and other accords that detailed their business agreement for the redevelopment of West 42nd Street, the path to ownership of nearly two-thirds of the project area seemed to be securely in place. Though the project was still tied up with significant litigation, finally, on that June day in 1988, UDC had what it needed to "immediately begin the process of acquiring properties in the project area." It was, the press release claimed, "day one of a revitalized 42nd Street" as "this agreement moves the 42nd Street Development Project dramatically closer to realization." City and state officials optimistically forecast that ground-breaking and construction would follow "soon afterwards."[3] A few days later, the condemnation process commenced with the mailing of offer letters to property owners, triggering a 90-day period during which UDC would carry out good-faith negotiations.

Getting to this stage of action had not been easy or timely. One complication was the city's strategy for financing the condemnation. Normally government does not have to declare how it will fund condemnation. Once the taking's public purpose has been established and the judicial scrutiny of the project deemed final, a map is filed and a petition for condemnation submitted to the court; if there is no opposition, the judge issues an order and the state takes title, a process known as "vesting." Afterward, valuation is determined (by appraisal) and, if contested, property owners litigate these valuations. The presumption is that government has the funds to pay condemnation costs. Given the uniqueness of the funding arrangement for the 42DP, however, the Land Acquisition and Development Agreement (LADA) called for the developers to post a financial guarantee 120 percent in excess of the appraised fee value of the condemnation parcels; the extra 20 percent would cover the additional costs of fixtures and furniture and relocation. With Prudential backing this pledge, in May 1989, nearly a year after the lease signing, TSCA delivered to UDC a standby letter-of-credit (L/C) for $155 million. The guarantee had been issued by Morgan Guarantee Trust Company, a AA-rated financial institution, the safety rating required by the state's obscure Public Authorities Control Board (PACB). This strong guarantee was needed, the PACB believed, to ensure "sure and certain condemnation" in accord with the constitutional requirements of due compensation. With delivery of the L/C, the project's complex funding seemed complete—that is, until an economic wake-up call in the form of a court-ordered reappraisal of the properties upped the required security to $241 million only six months later.

The new appraisal, at $193 million, was nearly 60 percent greater than the benchmark $120.7 million, and both figures greatly exceeded the rough estimates at the time of the BOE hearings that had pegged land acquisition costs within a $50-million range. At the start of the process, Klein considered costs much in excess of his $88-million capped price unlikely, but the high likely cost of the condemnation awards soon proved that assumption wrong. For city and state officials, the threatening issue was whether the cost escalation would turn out to be economically crippling. Notwithstanding the pledged security, TSCA's commitment to the 42DP was not yet irrevocable. Under the terms of an Escrow Agreement and a Side Letter to the Escrow Agreement, the developer still had the ability to walk away from its open-ended commitment to fund this first phase of condemnation (with a return of its security) if vesting did not occur within two years of the lease signings or if, under its determination, there existed conditions of "significant litigation," litigation pending or decided adversely to UDC beyond the right of further appeal.

In effect, TSCA held only an option to develop the office sites, which was a perfectly reasonable real estate position, particularly given the size and scope and risk of the project. Owing to a statutorily defined legal timetable—the essential deadline missed among the stacks and stacks of legal documents by Park Tower, Prudential, and TSCA's many lawyers—the window for this development option narrowed rapidly, much to Prudential's surprise. And in the context of Manhattan's dramatically weakening real estate market, the extraordinary dollar figure of the new appraisal made government officials, developers, and real estate experts alike question aloud whether the project could go forward on schedule, profitably, under the private burden of such high condemnation costs.

The unanticipated escalation in costs was linked, in part, to the belated date of condemnation, April 1990. Under New York State condemnation law, land owners are entitled to fair market value as of the date of vesting. Fair market value is based on current zoning, without consideration of any project impact, neither the positive effect of an improved future nor the negative effect of current blight. The volatility of land values in Times Square during the 1980s made valuation of the 34 parcels particularly tricky. First, soaring land prices in the mid-1980s, especially in midtown west where the 1982 Midtown Zoning Resolution had triggered construction of a rash of new office and hotel towers, complicated the business of determining what was driving the increase in values. According to the only known index of Manhattan land prices at the time, the average price of land in midtown had swung from roughly $24 per square foot of FAR in 1982 to $64 per square foot of FAR in 1986, the high end of this range being roughly $125.[4] Second, constant litigation continuously delayed filing the petition until the last possible moment. By the time title to the properties finally vested, massive overbuilding in midtown west had plunged the office market into a free fall. Real estate became totally illiquid. In such an uncertain market environment sales transactions cease, which meant there were no comparable sales to show that values had declined. Consequently, condemnation awards were based on sales drawn from 1989—the peak of the market. Moreover, the street's land uses—fast-food places, porn shops, and movie houses—proved to be veritable cash cows, which should not have surprised Park Tower's people, but did.[5]

When the new appraisals came in, Vincent Tese, UDC's forceful and effective chairman for nine years under Governor Cuomo, asked incredulously, "How could land values have gone up?" It wasn't real, he recalled. "We had hired the best in the business, and this guy was saying that real estate values never go down!" Tese wanted the appraisals redone because such values did not seem plausible after the 1987 stock-market collapse and obvious weakening of the real estate market. But the condemnation process was public, with the appraiser's working documents on file, so there was no way, he said in an interview, to go back on the formally reported appraised values. "The incredible thing" he recalled, "is that Prudential went along with the deal and put up the money. . . . I was amazed. We would have lost the project without this."[6] The *Times* titled its editorial on Pru's decision, "Miracle on 42d Street."

The unconventional funding arrangement for condemnation worked, if not exactly in the way city and state officials had intended. It enabled the public sector to take control of the open-air sexual playground and physical decay that defined West 42nd Street as a civic embarrassment and that had for so long frustrated cleanup efforts through conventional law-enforcement tactics. Closing down the street was a necessary prelude to the real estate–driven cleanup strategy, and after six years and more than 40 legal battles, the government finally got the land—nine of the 13 acres of the project area. "We own it. It's ours," Tese said at the time[7] (figure 5.1).

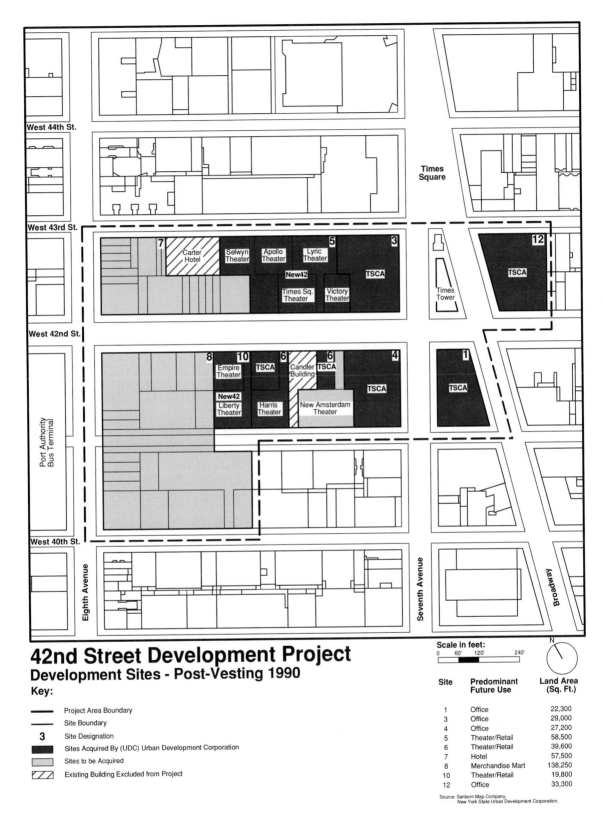

42nd Street Development Project
Development Sites - Post-Vesting 1990
Key:

——	Project Area Boundary
——	Site Boundary
3	Site Designation
■	Sites Acquired By (UDC) Urban Development Corporation
▨	Sites to be Acquired
▨	Existing Building Excluded from Project

Scale in feet:
0   60'   120'   240'

N

Site	Predominant Future Use	Land Area (Sq. Ft.)
1	Office	22,300
3	Office	29,000
4	Office	27,200
5	Theater/Retail	58,500
6	Theater/Retail	39,600
7	Hotel	57,500
8	Merchandise Mart	138,250
10	Theater/Retail	19,800
12	Office	33,300

Source: Sanborn Map Company,
New York State Urban Development Corporation.

5.1
The public takes control of two-thirds of
the project area. (Morgan Fleming for the
author)

Title was unquestionable proof that the strategy of privatizing the funding obligation had succeeded in accommodating the city's intense anxieties about a costly financial exposure to the condemnation process. The strategy, though, had not been without political cost. The complexity of what was, in essence, an open-tab arrangement created unique risks for both public officials and private developers. For the developer, the uncertain and open-ended financial exposure escalated to a point at which the loan, in effect, could never be repaid. In the meantime, the city was paying a premium for the funding arrangement, not just in economic terms, but in lost degrees of freedom in its ability to go forward with the subway and other public improvements at a time when this new infrastructure mattered most. These complications changed the stakes of development in significant ways neither side anticipated.

Addressing Political Needs

In 1986 a big run-up in land prices triggered by a speculative office boom sent PDC's president, James P. Stuckey, back to the negotiating table—on direct orders from Mayor Koch. Believing that the office deal was now unfavorable to the city and under growing criticism for the "loan" portion of the deal, Koch wanted to better the deal with TSCA. He was nervous about the political nature of the city's position now that the real estate market had turned hot, particularly, about the developers "making a killing." The mayor, Stuckey explained, "did not want to subsidize a windfall."[8] Real estate activity in midtown was nothing less than extraordinarily robust. The area immediately north of the Times Square intersection was changing so much and so fast that critics questioned why tax abatements were even necessary for office development in the 42DP. Koch was also driven by a desire to quell the growing chorus of architectural criticism from civic organizations, design critics, and what seemed to be every urban-affairs commentator with access to the printed media, all of whom loudly lambasted the design scheme of the office towers' architects, Philip Johnson and John Burgee.

After months of negotiation, the recut deal for the office sites bettered the city's position in two important ways: first, by providing for recapture of some previously lost revenues through "enhanced rents" and second, by extracting an additional $10 million in funding for public benefits, primarily subway and theater improvements. The "enhanced rents" would come from increasing the deal's profit-sharing arrangement to 10 percent from 5 and 7.5 percent. The logic for this "give" was somewhat obscure: It would reimburse the city for the rent credits given to TSCA as payment on the ESAC and so compensate the municipal treasury for that "rent erosion," a term used by the city's negotiators. Under the terms of the new deal, the burden of repaying the ESAC might be offset in the way-distant future to the extent the office towers proved to be profitable investments. For the moment, however, the larger public-benefit payments and greater profit-sharing percentages extracted from TSCA promised to counterbalance the weight of the city's growing financial liability for the loan portion of the deal. As Stuckey's counterpart on the state side, Carl Weisbrod, put it, "The new deal elegantly addressed Koch's political needs without spooking the developer to leave the project."[9]

However politically deft, the new financial terms merely tightened the city's tie to TSCA. The office sites were less problematic than the frustrations public officials experienced as they tried to line up developers for the two sites at western end of the project area. From the start, the mart and hotel sites, programmatically linked, presented the toughest planning problems, and the weak economics of those deals had not made the task any easier. Throughout the mid-1980s, as conditional development commitments for those sites fell by the wayside so did the economic logic of leveraging their market value to subsidize the costs of the theater program, subway improvements, and streetscape amenities. With no viable development proposals for either site, in 1987 the city made a highly significant tactical decision to go forward with the project, in phases, instead of continuing with its original, but now highly handicapped, comprehensive goal to redevelop the entire block simultaneously. The practical implication of this major policy decision was clear: Only TSCA remained on tap to fund the necessary costs.

The renegotiations with Park Tower that Stuckey had earlier concluded before Prudential joined on as developer were reopened. Public officials now pressed TSCA to fund the subway, theater, lighting, and streetscape obligations of Sites 7 and 8, as well as an additional contribution for the subway from the office sites—by adding these charges to the open tab. "It was tough," Stuckey recalled. "We were asking them to step up for the whole block, but were giving them no development rights. The plan might not even go forward as it was laid out on paper; it might not even succeed. The one thing we had over them, the leverage, was that they didn't want the rest of the block to go over to an office use," which was a possibility under the terms of the BOE-approved deal if it could be shown that a mart was not a feasible use for the site. The mart site's large footprint foretold of a serious competitive threat to TSCA's position should the west end of the project area be developed for office use (figure 5.2).[10] An office building, even in combination with a mart, could be designed to accommodate 40,000-to-60,000-square-foot floors, the type of large spaces desired by the type of tenants leaving New York for large blocks of less expensive back-office space. The sites at the east end of the project area were disadvantaged, which meant that TSCA's marketing strategy had to be focused on attracting corporate headquarters as opposed to back-office uses. In Stuckey's words, "The development of an office building on that site would have had a devastating effect on Park Tower's [TSCA] office towers."[11]

Hard-driving, focused, and aggressive, the 32-year-old Stuckey was the right city negotiator for the task at hand. Appointed president of PDC in May 1986, he had worked his way up through the organization, which he joined in 1980. He was experienced in the ways of public

development, having started his career in 1979 in the Mayor's Office of
Development (which was folded into PDC in 1980) working on the
South Street Seaport project. A graduate of St. John's University with both
a bachelor of science and a master of arts, he focused intently on the politics of feasibility, on getting things done. During his three-and-a-half year
tenure as PDC president, Stuckey was responsible for over $15 billion in
commercial, industrial, and waterfront real estate development projects. In
contrast to Weisbrod who cared greatly about planning policy, process, and
precedent, Stuckey's attitude toward deal making more closely matched
the maxim "the ends justify the means." When interviewed about his role
in the renegotiations, he recalled: "We were pulling down the gauntlet at
this time. We didn't want everything to get lost. We approached Pru, who
was more pregnant than [its executives] wanted to be. Prudential stepped
up to the plate, a real civic thing to do. They understood that they could
not jeopardize what they had in it [the 42DP] already. Once in with the
public sector," he concluded, "it is hard to pull out."[12]

When the lease agreements were finally completed in late 1987, the new, ever-more complex funding obligations known as "super" ESAC[13] totaled approximately \$40.7 million, which is to say that the new deal had increased the city's open tab by nearly 50 percent. Since four of every five dollars of the super ESAC would be used for the subway renovations, the renegotiations had effectively stretched the literal meaning of "excess site acquisition costs" to accommodate the city's policy position mandating near 100-percent private financing of the public's costs for the project. In political and practical terms, this meant that the entire public agenda for the 42DP was riding on the economic feasibility of developing the four office towers.

It is worth pausing to consider what the new deal with its "enhanced rents" really meant because the point bears directly on the issue of public accountability for deal making. From a political perspective, insiders considered the renegotiations brilliant because the enhanced rents appeared to give the city more, yet they did not call for anything immediate from the developers. This is what professional negotiators call a win-win situation. This deal, however, reflected not a lot of substance, just optics. As with movie deals, in real estate there is a vast divide between "net" and "gross" proceeds. In theory, the city was entitled to 5 percent of the profits ("net cash flow"). Even in 1987, though, it was apparent that the city would have to wait a long time to realize any of its share of profit. If the projected profit was virtually nonexistent, increasing the city's share to 10 percent from 5 percent was essentially cosmetic. The deal term, however, enabled the city's negotiator to tell the mayor the deal had been improved, without costing the developer much of anything. From the developer's perspective, this created a fiction as well: The distinction between regular ESAC and super ESAC was blurry at best. Moreover, it could not have provided TSCA much comfort to know that some of its ESAC loan was not subject to recovery by the city through a largely fictional profit-sharing payment.[14]

Because the 1986–1987 renegotiations—a city initiative UDC opposed—bettered particular details of the deal, city officials considered the revised deal to be within the envelope of what the BOE had approved. Not going back to the BOE was a political decision—a judgment call not to risk another test of the political will—since there was no legal requirement to do so. When timely development of the mart and hotel uses for the Eighth Avenue sites turned out to be infeasible, the subsequent decision to go forward with the project in a phased, rather than simultaneous, development process did require an amendment to the *GPP* and new public hearings. Yet this change, too, appeared to be within the scope of what the BOE approved.

The financial implications of the renegotiated positions were anything but superficial. With the office uses absorbing the big public-benefit obligations previously allocated to the mart and hotel sites, more than \$20 million had been added to the loan side of the public ledger. With land acquisition costs ever uncertain even at the time of vesting, the loan por-

tion of TSCA's funding obligation at that time—estimated by this author
at approximately $206 million, or $50 per square foot of FAR, after land
values pushed the L/C pledge up to $241 million—accounted for more
than 60 percent of the developer's full funding commitment, which had
soared to an estimated $343 million, or $84 per square foot of FAR. The
other 40 percent represented a pure-cost payment of $137 million—that
is, what the city would receive free and clear of financing encumbrances
for the four office sites and public-benefit obligations. Most of the estimated $343 million TSCA was putting at risk would go toward acquisition of
the office sites, though at the time roughly $82 million was slated for the
subway renovations. By June 1988, when the leases were signed, the dramatically enlarged ESAC liability had altered both the financial and political dynamic of the deal, though only those most familiar with the intimate
financial details understood just how (figure 5.3).

NO ONE'S MANDATE

Once the renegotiated deal for the office sites had been finalized, the procedural agenda next called for a public hearing on the "essential terms of
the leases." Serious delays owing to years of continuous litigation filed by
opponents with varied interests had already plagued implementation of
the redevelopment plan. The public hearing on the leases provided another
opportune forum for public comment and criticism, this time on the
detailed financials of the deal. The last airing of financial details had been
at the BOE hearings in the fall of 1984; since that time, UDC's press
releases on the project consistently presented, with no elaboration, a skele-
tal single sentence on the funding arrangement: "Construction of the
Project will be financed entirely by the developers, who will be responsible for all costs, including acquisition of the property."[15] In dramatic fashion, the lease-review process triggered a fundamental issue of democratic
accountability for public-private deal making. Opponents—especially the
Durst Organization, family real estate developers who held major real

estate interests in midtown—set their sights on a public debate about the financial arrangements: the true nature of the city's liability for the costs of redeveloping West 42nd Street embedded in the detailed business terms of the leases. It was, in other words, a direct challenge to examine the open-tab arrangement, though no one spoke of it in those terms.

Pursuant to New York State law governing UDC, the corporation scheduled a public meeting on the proposed leases for December 10, 1987, and published notice of the hearing in the *Times* on November 30, 1987. The public notice, costing in excess of $17,000, described in considerable detail the "essential" terms and conditions of the proposed leases with TSCA as they related to the lease term, rent (base and percentage rents), and other payments (alternative rent, transaction payments, purchase option, public-purpose payments, public costs), funding of site acquisition costs (including rent-erosion reimbursements), funding of public improvements (subway, theaters, streetscape), building design, general provisions of the agreements, and notice of negotiation of an affirmative action program, plus two 15-year rent (base and alternative) schedules. For Weisbrod, Stuckey, and other public officials involved in this project, a sense of obligation prevailed to provide sufficient detail on the office leases. So did pragmatism, since lawsuits were highly likely; providing a thorough overview of a such complex deal afforded defensive protection, especially since more than eight years had been spent getting the project to this point. Moreover, by 1987 public support—always broad but never deep—had eroded. Litigation loomed constantly. If the project's officials had not provided sufficient detail, or attempted to hide something "essential," the city and state would certainly have risked being overthrown by the courts. From any perspective, meeting the statutory standards of disclosure was a necessary prelude to successful execution.

Opponents, including two elected officials who filed a lawsuit less than 24 hours before the scheduled hearing, charged that the detailed published information on the "essential" proposed terms of the leases was insufficient for "intelligent and meaningful comment" (figure 5.4) No public hearing could take place before there was a written lease available for public scrutiny, the two legislators—State Senator Franz S. Leichter and City Councilwoman Carol Greitzer, whose districts included the project area—argued in seeking a temporary restraining order prohibiting UDC from closing the record of the lease hearing. The Durst Organization joined them as plaintiffs in the suit as did the Times Square Boxing Club, a gym on West 42nd Street, and an area resident, Shan Covey. Was publication of 128 lines of text setting forth the terms of the leases defective in that it failed to sufficiently disclose all the essential conditions of the deal, as the plaintiffs charged?[16] Would disclosure of the final leases prior to the hearing chill negotiations by undermining the confidence of the process, as UDC rebutted? Precedent existed protecting disclosure of documents reflecting "predecisional deliberations, opinions, and recommendations, so as 'to protect the deliberative process of the government by ensuring that persons in an advisory role would be able to express their opinion freely

5.4
Elected officials in opposition to
the 42DP outside city hall (l to r):
Councilwoman Carol Greitzer,
State Senator Franz S. Leichter,
Councilwoman Ruth W.
Messinger. (Neal Boenzi/New
York Times Pictures)

to agency decision makers,'" UDC counsel wrote to Durst counsel
Rosenberg and Estis.[17]

The legal question before the judge was the propriety of the
public notice issued prior to the hearing. The fundamental policy question
centered on the function of the public hearing: Was it supposed to be an
opportunity for comment and input into the process before the city and
state finalized its leases with private developers, or a forum for oversight
of the final terms and conditions of the leases? A first ruling of the court
made it clear that the purpose of the public hearing was input and that by
not explicitly calling for it, the statue did not require UDC to release
copies of the leases themselves.[18] In a second and key case surrounding
this episode, *Flynn v. N.Y.S. Urban Development Corporation*,[19] the court
addressed the disclosure issue directly by referencing the complex substance of the financial arrangements.

As in *Leichter*, the key issue in *Flynn* was whether UDC disclosed
enough information for meaningful comment to occur at the hearings.
On this, the judge reasoned that the public hearing could only consider
the proposed leases in broad terms, given "the complexity of the leases"—
some five thousand pages in the record. Moreover, the court explicitly
refused to "elevate" the role of the public hearing to that of final oversight. Rather, in keeping with the tenets of administrative law, it applied a
deferential standard of review: Only a "clear abuse of agency discretion"
would warrant court interference in a UDC deal. Although the court recognized the way in which the leases were being used to fund public costs,
it found this distinction unimportant, legally:[20]

> While we would go so far as to say that respondent
> [UDC] created some confusion by considering as site
> acquisition costs ("SAC") items which are clearly capital
> expenditures, such as subway construction expenses,
> there is no indication that the category to which these
> items were assigned is anything more than an account-
> ing convenience. . . . Whether subway improvements are

funded by revenues otherwise payable to the City as
taxes or monies otherwise payable to the City as rent is
not materially significant. . . . While the City may experience some reduction in revenue from respondent's
inclusion of subway improvements as costs associated
with the acquisition, the designation of those costs as
SAC cannot, without more, be said to constitute an
abuse of discretion by respondent.

For public officials, developers, and taxpayers, the complex payback mechanism had a clear and important function beyond mere
"accounting convenience." But adoption of a substantive policy review
traditionally lies outside the judiciary's narrow consideration of a case.
Case law is not comprehensive, except as a particular issue may evolve
incrementally into a fairly broad policy, and in the court's view, comprehensive policy is the role of the legislative and executive branches of government. Moreover, by practicing restraint in examining the substance of a
policy decision, courts evidence considerable respect for the expertise of
administrative agencies.

After the public hearing, drafts of the leases and related agreements, including the LADA, the Escrow Agreement, and the Side Letter,
were submitted as a package to the PACB whose review and approval was
required before UDC, the city, and TSCA could sign the final agreements.
Created in 1976 during the dire days of the city's fiscal crisis in response
to a recommendation by the state's Moreland Commission, which had
investigated UDC's financial default on its moral-obligation bonds, the
PACB was charged with reviewing applications from the state's public-
benefit corporations and ruling on whether "there are commitments of
funds sufficient to finance the acquisition and construction" of a project.
By statute, the board consists of three voting members appointed by the
governor, two of which are to be legislative appointments, one from the
senate and the other from the assembly; the third and chairperson, traditionally, has been governor's budget director. The vote to approve must be
unanimous. The singular question addressed: Is the state at risk?

A month after receiving the application, the PACB announced a
delay in the vote on UDC's leases with TSCA, an unusual event according
to Weisbrod, who had expected swift approval: "If ever there was a deal
which did not put the state's credit at risk, this was it."[21]

The delay signaled a more exhaustive review than was the
PACB's norm. The situation had become politicized. In two sets of tightly
targeted questions, which counsel for the Durst Organization claimed
came from his office,[22] assemblyman board member Mark Siegel, a
Democrat from Manhattan who had long been a vocal opponent of the
project, requested additional information and clarification from Weisbrod
and UDC staff. His request list was long: He wanted to know the substantive details of the state's financial obligation in the condemnation proceedings, the lease terms and related L/C to be pledged by TSCA as security

for the funding arrangement, and the availability of funds and obligations for the costs of the renovation and operation of the theaters and the subway renovations. Siegel and the PACB worried most about the state's exposure to downside financial risk: Would it incur any liability for the condemnation proceedings, especially if once the process started the project unwound? According the press reports at the time, Siegel saw the complexity of the leases as the key issue. "The panel cannot veto the entire deal," Siegel said, "but it could demand that officials alter certain aspects of the leases related to the financial risk the project would pose to taxpayers."[23]

Siegel pushed through the one substantive requirement imposed by the PACB—that the $155-million L/C, which he correctly viewed as the linchpin of the deal, be issued from a lending institution whose long-term corporate debt issues were rated AA or better by the rating agency Standard & Poor's. This was a subtle technicality with bite, for which he did not get credit: his constituency thought he "sold out," remarked one insider.[24] At the time, all over the country banks' balance sheets were beginning to deteriorate, and to the surprise of public officials, there were few so-rated banks in the city, the nation's undisputed financial center. On June 1, 1988, five months after receiving UDC's application, the PACB unanimously approved UDC's proceeding with the deal, conditional on the final documents being consistent with the terms of the PACB Resolution and containing the same provisions relating to the L/C as the draft leases and LADA submitted to the PACB.

In theory, the PACB served as a forum where the details of the financial transaction and the substantive meaning of the funding arrangement would be reviewed. And they were. Although the deal was closely examined by the PACB, its statutory mandate called for a narrow review in line with its limited agenda: to protect the state's financial exposure. The fact that UDC was acting as a broker for the city was reflected in the project agreements between the city and UDC, which provided for indemnities of specific project costs incurred by UDC. More to the point, the PACB review could not address the substantive implications of the open-tab funding arrangement—the city's contingent liability for the ESAC, the cost/benefit relationship of the overall deal, and the how the risks of a market downturn and indefinite delay might affect the project. As with the courts, these policy issues lay beyond its mandate.

PUBLIC LIABILITY AND PRIVATE RISK

Politically, the most attractive feature of the city's privatized-funding strategy was its flexibility. Without any of the tortuous bureaucratic procedures that would have accompanied federal urban-renewal financing (if it had been available) or the restraints Wall Street would have imposed on a bond issue (if the city could have issued project-specific bonds) or the limitations inherent in municipal capital-budget funding (if the city had the political will to allocate such funds), as costs for land condemnation, relocation, business buyouts, and related site acquisition costs escalated beyond the $88 million "cap" the developers would pay for the 42DP office sites, New York put the excess on its open tab—to be settled through an extended repayment plan. Nothing like this existed for other big public-private projects like California Plaza or Yerba Buena Gardens, as the costs of land acquisition for these initiatives had been borne decades earlier by the federal urban-renewal program.

The payback plan for the 42DP open tab mimicked the strategy's off-budget political logic: tapping future project revenues without recourse to other city-wide funds. It involved three fundamentals: First, monies to repay the outstanding ESAC would come, in theory, from the project's own sources of revenue—several of them, the last (but likely largest) of which would be the rent credits; second, no more than 50 percent of the annual base rents could be used as rent-credit reimbursements of the ESAC (the "maximum rent credit"), by which some PILOT revenues would flow into the city's general coffer; third, the rent credit would first pay down yearly interest accrual and then the ESAC principal. Interest accrual turned out to be the wild card of the repayment plan. The interest tab would start running on the actual date TSCA's payments moved into the realm of excess site acquisition costs; what could not be paid each year through the maximum rent credit would be added to the ESAC tab, and, in turn, repaid with interest. In other words, interest costs would compound. If, through compounding, interest charges grew large enough, the city might not be able to fully repay the ESAC within the 99-year term of its leases with TSCA, a situation wholly untenable for the developers.[25]

"In its inception, the payback device was very simple," Stephen A. Lefkowitz recalled. "The city would make up the developer's advance with the money from property taxes [PILOTs] the developer would be paying the city. It got much more complicated as time went on and they had to put the idea into draft language."[26] That language had to provide for risks and contingencies (developer delays, construction delays, default, termination) as well as the developer rights and obligations to commence construction and contribute to the subway renovations and other public amenities. Even the best drafting could not hedge the financial liabilities of the deal, for either side. At the start of the project, the exit was clear: Both sides expected the ESAC to be small and extinguishable within a few years. But with escalating condemnation costs and serious (soon to be indefinite) delays postponing construction, the math of compounding interest—the same mechanism that grows a savings account—threatened to implode the possibility of full repayment. Moreover, the payback depended upon a construction start, and in 1990 that seemed increasingly doubtful as the state of Manhattan's real estate market rapidly deteriorated.

Would assessed values for the parcels and the success of the office towers eventually boost rent revenues high enough to pay off the city's ESAC obligation? No, as projections by several third parties made clear.[27] Condemnation costs and other ESAC-denominated obligations of the deal had risen so much that the open tab could never be repaid under any reasonable set of assumptions. Given the size of the interest-bloated ESAC, what the city would owe TSCA simply swamped what TSCA would pay the city. Even under a more optimistic scenario, which projected payback within 40 to 60 years, the open tab had become, in the words of George Klein, "the longest municipal bond ever issued."[28]

The magnitude of the gap sent a clear and important message to those in the know: Under the terms of the deal, the city's financial liability for site acquisition and redevelopment of West 42nd Street could not reasonably meet the project's self-financing policy mandate. Yet, what did this really mean in practical terms? How might it change the dynamic of the office deal and the give-and-take of the public-private relationship?

The leases might have been signed and the land finally condemned, but rapidly weakening market conditions threatened a construction start in the near-term. Once two of the four sites had been cleared, TSCA was obligated to start construction of the first tower within one year, or 18 months from vesting, whichever came first. What would happen, however, if Prudential defaulted on the deal, forfeiting the $241 million rather than put more money at risk—at least $91 million in a letter of credit for the subway improvements and nearly $400 million for development of the first tower?

Up to this point in the development process, the ESAC loan had been performing the way city and state officials had intended, as a mechanism for keeping the city's risk exposure at bay. While, theoretically, the city had ultimate liability for the loan, no budget appropriation was at stake, nor would there be future budget exposure. Via the rent credit, "payment" was deferred, so public officials faced no immediate direct financial cost from the deferral. As a loan, the ESAC balance carried an interest cost, but during that period when construction might be delayed, it would accrue; the charge was not an out-of-pocket cost. In other words, repayment of the open-ended loan was painless politically, however large it got. Moreover, in the event TSCA defaulted on its obligations, the city, in effect, would acquire the land "free." With its unquestionable bet on the long-term value of the project's prime location, the public sector would have in its possession premium development sites, ready to go on the first swing of the next real estate cycle. At least that was the theory. That scenario, of course, assumed that there was no development opportunity cost to the public sector from an aborted project and, as we shall see, that was hardly the case.

For the private developer, the economic risk of an escalating ESAC exposure was real and immediate. Condemnation costs involved actual dollar outflows that had to be funded with either an equity investment or a loan from some institution, if not in the last resort from Prudential's own mortgage company. Moreover, because the insurance giant ultimately did act as both lender and developer—an exception to its policy—the deal put Prudential in a doubly risky position because repayment of the ESAC loan could not possibly start until its own development partnership, TSCA, started construction on at least one site, in accord with the deal's specific contractual fixed schedule. It also created an internal financial conflict of interest. Prudential, as lender, had no security behind its loan, leaving its lending arm with no ability to foreclose; even if there had been security, the possibility of foreclosing upon itself represents the ultimate nightmare for a financial institution.[29] By the conventional standards of commercial mortgage lending, this was a weird loan. Hence, when a weak market immobilized a pending construction start, Prudential faced a tremendous economic cost regardless of which option it chose—if it did the unthinkable and defaulted on the deal, or went ahead with development. It was caught between its own "rock" and a hard place, trapped in the economic downside of its agreement with the city and state. Without question, the private developer had become the major risk-taker in the 42DP.

PRUDENTIAL'S COSTLY EDUCATION

When Prudential first announced in October 1986 that its real estate subsidiary, Prudential Realty Group, would partner with Park Tower Realty, the excesses of new construction that had begun to slow office development in other parts of the country had not yet dimmed Manhattan's development prospects. New York appeared to be the nation's healthiest as well as its largest office market, with rents stabilizing at fairly high levels still supportive of new construction. This was especially true for midtown, which long had the highest concentration of U.S. real estate values. The Manhattan midtown market remained attractive to investors, in part because of premiums embedded in the price of its office buildings—the "Manhattan franchise," as Salomon Brothers' real estate experts termed the value attributable to the relative strength of the city's core as the location of choice for the financial-services industry. Robust demand by a broad set of investors—foreign institutional capital, wealthy individuals, and families—underpinned this bull market; in particular, a flood of Japanese investment during the mid-1980s did much to inflate office values.[30]

Only a few months before the October announcement, the president of Prudential Development Company, Arch K. Jacobson, had publicly discussed a commitment to a sharp cutback of development activity, though the insurance giant would still remain open to "selective" opportunities. As the *Financial Times* of London's aptly titled article "The Aftermath of Excess" explained: "Leaders like the Prudential are understandably cautious about new commitments in the current climate but remain totally confident about longer-term prospects and are poised to take advantage of buying opportunities."[31] The New York midtown market fit that description; moreover, an investment in Times Square presented a singular opportunity for a patient player.

Spurred by the 1982 zoning incentives for midtown west, the area around Times Square was full of "street talk" about pending projects and land assemblages that, if not yet actual projects under development in 1986, by 1991 resulted in more than 7.2 million square feet of new Class A office space and five new hotels with nearly 3,000 rooms. Among those circling the area in the early to mid-1980s were many of the city's major office developers—Durst, Rudin, Silverstein, Tishman Speyer, and Zeckendorf—whose interests signaled midtown west's ripeness as serious investment territory. Earlier, institutional capital—Metropolitan Life Insurance Company, New York State Common Retirement Fund, and Equitable Life Assurance Society of the United States—had gingerly stepped into the area with long-term financing for what was then a $292.5-million Marriott Marquis Hotel. Equitable also was investing nearly $200 million in a new 54-story headquarters tower in the Times Square vicinity, on Seventh Avenue between 51st and 52nd Street. This latest Equitable investment resounded with "historic import," Gottlieb of the *Times* wrote, because its earlier corporate decision in the late 1950s to move to midtown had hastened the growth of Sixth Avenue. While its newest headquarters might be construed as visually and geographically closer to Rockefeller Center than Times Square or the Theater District, the same could not be said for the 50-story Marriott Marquis Hotel, which sat squarely on Broadway at 45th Street, the heart of Times Square.

Still, in 1985 Times Square was unquestionably a "dicey" and "seedy" area for prospective corporate tenants and fiduciaries charged with making safe investments for pension beneficiaries and mutual shareholders. Between 42nd and 47th Streets, even along the well-established corporate boulevard that Sixth Avenue had become, the best that the Landauer market analysis commissioned by Klein could say of past experience was that the marketability of new buildings in this five-block area south of Rockefeller Center had been "varied." The lease-up experience along Broadway and Seventh Avenue had been worse: In the case of the 52-story tower at 1515 Broadway, large portions of the building remained unmarketable until the early 1980s, more than ten years since its construction in 1968. "Hard-edged wariness" about the area led Seymour Durst to remark: "Times Square became like a Bermuda Triangle—investments made there were never heard from again."[32]

Anticipated Position

The past, however, did not provide an exact blueprint for the future. The logic about location that had made the area well suited for development before became even more compelling in the mid-1980s. With all feasible development sites in the highly desirable midtown east either developed or under development, the ultimate necessity for midtown office growth to push west of Sixth Avenue appeared imminent: The large assemblages were there; the zoning was there; and with the new institutional players, so it seemed, was the right investment atmosphere. The long-term real estate play was in making an early—timely, in the jargon of real estate—speculative investment, then riding up the value curve as Times Square transformed itself into a mixed-commercial district of offices and entertainment activities. Combined, the four office sites represented an usually large assemblage by Manhattan standards. The built-out project, the Landauer report prepared for Klein suitably concluded, "will be the most important single real estate development in midtown Manhattan since Rockefeller Center opened in the early 1930s." The singular concentration of subway lines in Times Square, "better in this neighborhood than on the East Side where much higher rents prevailed," remained a most compelling feature of the area's long-term investment potential,[33] while the competitively advantageous financial package for the 42DP office sites (which had gotten larger as property values rapidly escalated between 1984 and 1986) reduced the short-term costs of taking a pioneering position. For all these reasons, Prudential considered the 42DP an unmatched development opportunity.

The property company was making a strategic gamble, for the economic risk of the long-term investment play remained large. At the time, Prudential's senior real estate executives considered it manageable because they confidently expected that financing construction would be easy. Operating with a powerful institutional franchise was one factor working in its favor. A second was fierce competition among lenders amid pressure to put out money, which made for liberal lending terms. The combination suggested that nearly all the development costs, including the ESAC, could be financed with construction debt, meaning that TSCA would only have to put in a small equity investment. Pru's real estate executives did foresee additional risk from the inevitable changes of such a complex project, but they just as confidently assumed that the insurance giant could get what would be needed to keep development viable—all the public agencies were in the project, and this, they believed, would keep a lever on getting things done. For the economics to work, though, TSCA needed to develop all four buildings, otherwise the $88-million offset price was steep for, say, any two buildings.[34] Pru's people did not consider the ESAC and the tax credits to be complicating problems because the partnership's pro-forma numbers presumably showed sufficient cash flow from the buildings to cover the debt service. (Whether the projected return was sufficient compensation for the risk is a different and truer financial criterion, as will be considered shortly.) For TSCA, the risk of escalating site acquisition costs appeared only as a cash-flow issue— assuming it could proceed with construction and fill the buildings with tenants. Only when the condemnation process and extraordinarily weak conditions in the real estate market eliminated the feasibility of development in a timely manner did the ESAC became something other than a cash-flow issue.

Selling the project to the board of directors of Prudential promised to be another matter, however. Donald R. Knab, Prudential's top real estate decision maker in the 1980s and the person who first negotiated with Park Tower for Prudential, felt he might have some trouble selling the board on the idea, according to a knowledgeable insider. To handle the politics of the process, he decided first to ask the board for approval to consider the deal, which he did and got; once in, he believed, the task of convincing the board would be manageable. As events turned out, Knab may not have been a totally disinterested player in his negotiations with

Klein, for whom he subsequently went to work after retiring from Pru not long after the company agreed to joint venture the project in Times Square. Knab had envisioned Pru as the premier development company in the world, and at the time of his retirement looked back on his tenure as chairman of Prudential Realty Group as being "responsible for developing and managing a real estate portfolio valued at over $33.5 billion."[35]

Prudential's real estate executives initially anticipated construction would start within eight to ten months, in mid-1987, with the first two towers set for completion two years later, in 1989, according to the company's public announcement of its entry into the Times Square project. This was wildy ambitious, even then, though such timing certainly would have been desirable considering the dark clouds visibly massing on the market horizon. Complying with the procedural requirements of the state's condemnation process might take as short a period as 25 to 35 days. The untried financial arrangement for privatizing the costs of land acquisition, however, added a unique twist to the condemnation process for the 42DP, one that could seriously jeopardize development timing. Weisbrod worried about this: "The type and complexity of the agreement with its private funding was all uncharted waters. Everyone was concerned. The fear was that something might go wrong."[36] New York had become a litigiousness battlefield of development politics; nearly every public action was almost certain to generate legal challenges, whether on legitimate grounds or as tactical means for opposing interests intent on thwarting or delaying the project. Pending litigation was the obvious wild card of the formal condemnation proceedings.

Prudential's real estate executives had good reason to believe that the project had already cleared most significant litigation. The starting point for condemnation proceedings had been in sight since the end of May 1986 when the *Jackson v. N.Y.S. Urban Development Corporation* decision finalized judicial scrutiny of the *42DP General Project Plan*, thereby settling litigation on the typically contentious environmental impacts of major land-use projects.[37] The project had also survived First-Amendment challenges in federal court and still other lawsuits in both federal and state courts attempting to stop or stall it, including a most significant case challenging UDC's ability to override the city's land-use review process, ULURP, *Waybro Corp. v. Board of Estimate*. By the close of 1986, the end of what UDC's former general counsel, Valerie Caproni, called the "Round I Phase," 27 cases had been filed within 13 months, all of which would be either dismissed or decided in UDC's favor.

UDC's record of judicial success was obvious, yet the question remained: How much more litigation might there be? A lot, it would turn out, as explained in chapter 7. The question was key because the timing of condemnation pivoted upon private funding, which TSCA, or any other investor, would understandably be reluctant to commit irrevocably to the project with "significant litigation" still pending. By the time the $155-million L/C was posted, the number of lawsuits challenging the project had grown to 43. The lawsuits "are the least of our concerns," Park Tower's executive vice president Veronica W. Hackett remarked at the time. What was of concern, however, was the frustration and financial toll the litigation was imposing upon TSCA: "If we had known what we were going to spend—the amount of money we put at risk before we even had title is quite extraordinary."[38]

The final costs of condemnation remained frustratingly uncertain for TSCA even after the state had title and possession of nearly all of the 34 parcels. The exact dollar amounts paid to property owners could not be known in advance, regardless of the effort or resources devoted to the task. Ensuring "just compensation" for a property taking carries an inherent element of uncertainty. The process is clear, though. Upon taking title, the state puts down a good-faith offer based on the fee estimate of the property value, which the owner can take while litigating for greater payment. With grinding slowness valuations are determined, settlements made, or litigation of condemnation awards resolved. "The problem for us as developers was in not knowing when we would get the sites, what the full costs of condemnation would be," Klein remarked with hindsight. "The process stretched over two economic cycles; it was open-ended, and we had no understanding of this, in general."[39] Indeed, the condemnation-award trials and private settlements for this first phase of the 42DP still had not ended as of June 1999 when the first tower was up and Condé Nast was moving into its new headquarters at Four Times Square, and only when they were would TSCA know the final cost figure for the 34 parcels. The uncertainty of the cost exposure was the worst part, Klein emphasized repeatedly in an interview. The issue was one of possession versus valuation: "The government allowed four years to pass for determination of value. Crazy! If this was their money would this have been allowed?"[40]

The open-ended nature of the condemnation risk turned the stakes in a way that also destroyed Prudential's initial plan to finance the cash-flow exposure. Condemnation costs simply became too large to finance out of the office towers' operating revenues, a problem exacerbated by softening market conditions that put downward pressure on any rental rates TSCA would be able to charge on the newly built office space—if the developer went ahead with construction. Such a scenario was growing increasingly risky, if not unrealistic in 1989: More than 2.65 million square feet of new office space going up in the bow-tie of Times Square in three major towers would be ready for occupancy in the next couple of years, but only a small percentage of that space had been preleased. This was painfully ironic for Prudential, whose commitment to the 42DP sent a strong signal to the investment community enabling the Times Square building boom. As litigation continued to thwart Prudential's withdrawal of a declaration of significant litigation, the economics of proceeding with construction—at least during the current real estate cycle—deteriorated inexorably. By late-summer 1992 when the formal decision to indefinitely delay construction was finally announced, Prudential's investment reportedly had reached $300 million. With no take-out in the near future, the present reality of the deal's opportunity costs overwhelmed the earlier promise of an "unmatched" development opportunity, even for this deepest-pocketed institutional investor.[41]

This was an embarrassing spot for a real estate developer of Prudential's experience and standing, not to mention leadership in the field of institutional real estate investment. During the early 1980s, the powerful property arm of the insurance giant had built a "towering reputation as a developer," after more than two decades as a mortgage lender and joint-venture player.[42] It was developing the full range of product—office towers, industrial parks, urban mixed-use complexes, hotels, and regional shopping malls.

As an institutional developer, Prudential was also something of a maverick, doing what others shied away from—controversial projects, those that involved political and community problems. In the late 1980s, while running with the Times Square project, its Boston-office executives working with an outside advisory planning team shepherded more than four years of community meetings and reviews in pursuit of its ambitious $390-million plan to redevelop and enlarge its flagship Prudential Center project. Similar community-relations challenges and political problems beset its efforts to develop Embarcadero Center in San Francisco, Town Center outside Detroit, and Century City in Los Angeles. In general, the powerful property company prided itself on doing complicated projects.

Prudential's long-term perspective, in addition to its central role as the deep-pocketed money partner, was what Klein sought for his Times Square venture. When Klein went looking for a partner after Manufacturers Hanover Trust Company pulled away from financing the 42DP towers, the field of potential players for such a gigantic project was slim. Yet in the final round, the out-of-town insurance giant was not alone; nor did its bid top that of the other out-of-town competitor, KG Land, the American subsidiary of Kumagai Gumi, the Japanese developer/construction concern. Significantly, Park Tower's decision making weighed in Prudential's favor because the company's domestic ties, its latent political power as a significant economic presence in New York, and its proximity to the city counted more than KG Land's extra bid dollars. These standby resources would matter a lot when, as Klein and his mortgage broker involved knew it would, the call came to renegotiate elements of the deal.

Pru also came to the table with the large-scale development experience Klein seemed to need. The defining contributions of the partners—Pru's financial resources and institutional staying power and Klein's control of a unique development opportunity and his New York knowledge and connections—appeared complementary. The joint venture got off to a rocky start, though, and as market conditions worsened and political pressures on TSCA from city and state officials intensified, the tense institution-entrepreneur marriage turned sour. It was shaping up as another painful lesson from the 1980s, common enough within the real estate industry by 1990 to have evolved into something of a mantra: At the beginning of an institutional development joint venture, the institutional partner holds the gold and the developer, the knowledge; at the end, after years of toil and trouble, time has reversed the positions—the institution now has the "experience" and the developer, the money. In the case of the 42DP, it was not possible to cite any pecuniary benefits garnered by Klein, who had come out of pocket with millions to fund predevelopment costs.

For all its development experience, Prudential was not accustomed to teaming up with local entrepreneurs. Unlike other insurance-company developers, it typically joint ventured with other major institutions like BetaWest Properties Inc. and Mitsubishi Estate Company, or wealthy family-based investors like the Rockefellers, or institutionally oriented developers like Hines Interests, whose cultures were more in sync with its own. Moreover, understanding development was not equal to understanding the structure of this deal, this project, this city. New York was fraught with land mines, and the partnership was venturing into midtown turf the Dursts had long considered their own. Pru's development knowledge of other markets and other government players was just not transferable to this market. New York's development rituals are a world apart from those of other cities across the nation. What sets the New York real estate market apart is scale and depth—and the power of insiders. In short, both the general terrain of a highly stylized real estate market and the specific complexity of this high-profile project posed exceedingly big risks for the Newark-based insurance giant. Its corporate headquarters was only across the river, but the distance amounted to a chasm in understanding.

Neither deep pockets, development experience, prudent business practices, nor a philosophy of long-term investing could protect the insurance giant from what it was not prepared for—the open-ended nature of the condemnation risk. This was the public-policy side of the equation. The privatized-funding arrangement spawned an uncontrollable business risk: The perils of condemnation were intricately intertwined with the delays and risks of litigation, which both public and private parties badly underestimated. Financial capacity aside, how long could Prudential stay in the deal before its position became economically untenable? When TSCA posted the first L/C for $155 million in May 1989 allowing the legal proceedings for condemnation to go forward at last, it still had the right to terminate the deal since along with the L/C it had delivered a declaration of "significant litigation." Until it formally waived this declaration, TSCA always had an "option" on project sites. The pivotal decision on whether to do so, however, came sooner than anticipated, exacerbating the condemnation risk in yet another unforeseen way.

Cold Reality

The terms of its 1988 Escrow Agreement with the city and state provided a two-year period during which TSCA could walk from the deal. As a practical reality Prudential's real estate executives again confidently expected the company would have not two years, but whatever time it wanted. While the company had the right to walk within that two-year period, it was not obligated to do so if the significant litigation was not resolved.

What went unrecognized by the small army of condemnation lawyers and remained unknown for some time after the project documents had been signed was a cold, hard, and unalterable legal reality: Quietly ticking away in the background was a three-year clock for filing the petition for condemnation, and it would run out the month before the two-year walk-away window lapsed. This invalidated the June 1990 date in the Escrow Agreement and with it, Prudential's perceived decision-making flexibility.

The unprecedented character of the funding arrangement must have overwhelmed the type of exacting legal due diligence commonly associated with deals of this magnitude where timing is key. Whatever the cause, this missed legal technicality dramatically changed the stakes, for all parties. Not meeting the critical date would have jeopardized the already delicate political balance of the project, unequivocally. It would have meant starting all over again, a high-risk gamble given the history of controversy and contention glued to the 42DP, which most probably would have ended it cold. But because market timing was clearly unfavorable for the developers, going forward did not eliminate the project's economic risks, even for the city.

When told about the problem Prudential's executives and Klein felt sandbagged. All parties understood this to be a serious problem, Weisbrod recalled, but, nonetheless, it created ill will. At the time the city's relations with Prudential were strained. The tangled internal politics of the joint venture also contributed to the misunderstanding between the city and its development partner. Weisbrod did not talk with Prudential directly, but let Klein, who may have had his own agenda, act as the interface. In retrospect, this was probably not in the city and state's best interests for the episode resulted in a lot of distrust of government on the part of Pru. It had become a sour deal in a sour market. There was a lot of pressure to resolve pending litigation and tension over whether all of it would be resolved by May 1990. Prudential felt pushed to make the final commitment to go ahead—the formal determination that there was no significant litigation pending—because the stakes of not doing so were so high. The significant litigation was really over (only two minor cases were still to be heard on appeal). Still, the company really did not want to make the go-ahead decision at this time: Vacancy rates for Class A space in midtown west in 1990 hit an extraordinary 33 percent as the glut of newly constructed office space reached the market, with no lessening in sight. "Klein, Pru Splitsville?" questioned *Newsday*.[43]

The number of Prudential senior staff who worked on the project intensively was small. In the property company, they included Brian P. Murphy, a West Point graduate with an MBA from Boston University who was a strong supporter and cheerleader for the project, and from corporate, Sharon Barnes, similarly a dedicated Prudential executive with an MBA from Columbia University though more skeptical of the company's full exposure to the project's multifaceted risks. Like the initial decision to enter the project, this one was accompanied by considerable internal debate. As the top decision maker for real estate, Riley's perspective on the long-term returns from the development opportunity ultimately prevailed. There was not much time for debate either, for the court order of April 6, 1990, granting the petition for condemnation was conditioned on TSCA's L/C being increased to $241 million; as the money partner, Prudential had only 20 days to make a decision.

Like all the other major company decisions regarding the 42DP, this one was presented to the finance committee of the insurance giant's board of directors for its final approval. Representing nearly 40 percent of the board, the committee's nine members included prominent business-men, academics, and distinguished New Jersey politicians, among them, Paul A. Volker, former chairman of the Federal Reserve Board and then chairman of the investment firm of James D. Wolfensohn, Inc.; Donald E. Procknow, former vice chairman and chief operating officer of AT&T Technologies, Inc.; John R. Opal, retired chairman of IBM; and Princeton University professor Burton G. Malkiel, who had invented the path-break-ing concept of a "random walk on Wall Street" to explain stock behavior. When this critical decision to irrevocably commit to the project came up for review, Times Square was a familiar project to these men. This commit-tee of the board, as one inside Prudential person requesting anonymity explained, "knew the broad outlines of how much money Pru had put in. . . . They understood the relations with George Klein. . . . They knew enough to ask the right questions."

Prudential's decision surprised city and state officials as much as it stunned the real estate community. The economic calculus of the decision was hard to grasp; at best, it was elusive. By conventional real estate criteria, the numbers could not possibly "pencil out" and produce a reasonable rate of return, and it is questionable whether, given the market risks attached to the project, the deal ever showed a sufficient risk-adjusted return. The eco-nomic parameters of the situation were relatively transparent: Assuming $55 per-square-foot pro-forma rents (after a five-year lease-up period), $425 per square foot in development costs and debt service at then-prevailing rates, an estimate of projected yield would fall within a 13-percent range, assuming favorable market conditions. As a development return, this is only a 2.5-percent spread above what a lender could expect on a mortgage loan at that time; it was, in other words, a thin premium for taking such a huge risk, and it is impossible to reconcile with then-prevailing economics. Such a modest yield projection could have been justified only in terms of the project's strategic value. An entrepreneurial developer at this time would have been looking for a yield in the range of 18 to 25 percent.

For the press, Prudential's spokesman explained: "Even though the short-term picture isn't rosy, we feel that by the time the office build-ings are constructed, there will be a new cycle and it will be a great opportunity."[44] At the press conference announcing the project victory, public officials had reason to cross their fingers behind the podium, for even then it was hard to image a construction start in line with the sched-ule called for in the agreement.

One has to ask how it was that an insurance company, typically so risk adverse, could take this enormous risk. "They kept stepping up to the plate with additional funds," remarked one still-disbelieving Prudential person close to the action. The company was initially confident that the $88-million offset price was a likely ceiling; they had been told that the condemnation would likely cost $77 million. When Prudential executives were ready to sign the document committing the company to the $155-million L/C, they were reminded that there was no backing out. The refrain of caution: "Chicken Little, what if the sky should fall?" One explanation for the course of events is that confidence born of prior success blinded Pru's top real estate professionals to the fundamental understanding that the key variables could change dramatically.[45] The lack of corporate accountability is an even more compelling factor in the equation. As a private mutual company owned by its policy holders rather than stockholders, Prudential did not face the same market discipline of a publicly traded company: There was no stockholder equity at risk, no required disclosure of future contingent commitments of this one real estate project in the consolidated financial statements of the insurance company. Serious disclosure about its long-term liabilities for the 42DP came only from the public sector, and then only when public procedures demanded such. It was a curious state of affairs for a 115-year-old blue-chip enterprise with more than $169 billion in assets, especially one with a highly polished marketing image of stability and trust personified by its trademark logo— "the Rock"—as in the Rock of Gibraltar.[46]

The go-ahead decision locking in the $241-million escrow money was but the first of two critical points of no return; the second would come more than two years later when two of the four sites could be delivered to TSCA in a condition of "vacant possession." Under the terms of the LADA, UDC's delivery of these sites triggered the developer's obligation to start construction on the first building and post another letter-of-credit to fund its commitment for improvements to the Times Square subway station complex. If Riley and the Prudential board underestimated the severity of the real estate cycle in Manhattan and the market worsened precipitously during the intervening period, the insurance giant would then have to decide whether to default on the deal or commit additional big sums to both the subway-station renovations and construction costs for the first building. By that time, Prudential would have completed its costly education: riding up the learning curve from an expectation of spending $88 million plus for the 42DP development opportunity to the reality of funding $241 million *plus*—with the open-tab still running—with nothing to show for the investment, for many more years at least.

However far into the future construction might be, the company's decision to fund the condemnation unconditionally guaranteed that the image of the street as an urban free-zone for drug dealing and pornographic sleaze would change—even if TSCA itself never built any of the four buildings. The money would clear the street of its undesirable activity.

The state had the $241 million at its disposal, and the tab would remain open until the last condemnation awards for the grinder theaters, adult bookstores, video peeps, T-shirt shops, camera and electronics shops, eateries, small clothing shops, and other businesses and properties compromising the nine-acre eastern portion of the project area had been resolved and paid. The largest and most significant phase of this extremely contentious land assembly was finally under UDC's control. For this act, Prudential singularly took the final bow; their capital sustained the redevelopment process throughout its darkest period of uncertainty. At the time, this was a dubious distinction.

MASQUERADING SUBSIDIES

The open-tab arrangement performed brilliantly, in line with its political promise, and the fiscal legacy of its innovative payback mechanism defined a new type of tax expenditure. Tax expenditure is a form of public spending that occurs painlessly through the loss of potential revenues; it can take many forms, property-tax abatement being most commonly used by local governments, especially New York, as a financial incentive for preferred types of housing, land-use, and economic-development projects. The 42DP rent credit is like a tax abatement, in the way it reduces the revenue that would otherwise flow to the city's general coffer. It is also akin to a capital-budget expenditure in that it is a "public investment" in a project that has been approved by the city's legislative body.

As a financing tool, the ESAC/rent-credit mechanism is distinctive for the way it remains hidden from any standard fiscal document or budget review. Though a tax expenditure, it will not show up in the city's *Annual Report on Tax Expenditures* as do others for assisted projects, including Battery Park City or South Street Seaport or the Marriott Marquis Hotel. It is a form of public investment, though it will not show up as an item in the city's *Capital Budget* as did the $106.5 million for condemnation and demolition, infrastructure improvements, and parking for Brooklyn's MetroTech project. It is repayment for a major city debt, though that liability will not be accounted for in the city's books or records of outstanding debt obligations. As with some types of public long-term leasing arrangements, the ESAC obligation and rent credits are a nonaccountable form of off-budget financing.

As a form of off-budget financing, the ESAC/rent-credit mechanism contained elements that made implementation relatively easy, politically. As consistently presented in the public announcements throughout this period, the package of 42DP benefits being promoted appeared to be without cost. In statements of the project's future fiscal benefits, public officials cited the expected increase in property taxes: "In the first year after completion the four office towers alone will pay more than double the approximately $5.8 million a year in tax revenues currently paid by the entire project area. . . . At the end of the 15-year base rent period, the project will provide approximately $50 million a year in payments-in-lieu-of-taxes. After year 15, each of the project sites will pay full property taxes."[47] No mention was made of the offsetting rent credit. The payback period, moreover, stretched over an extraordinarily long period; whether 55 years in the case of one optimistic scenario, or the 99-year lease term in the case of one pessimistic scenario, it was clearly far beyond the time horizon of any public official.

Most important, since the ESAC/rent-credit mechanism did not draw from either the city's operating or capital budget, local officials could readily support the project without diverting funds from other projects or city services. This had been essential in 1980, after public services had suffered continual cutbacks for the previous five years and no new capital investments had been made in more than a decade owing to the frail fiscal state of the city. The off-budget character of the payback endowed the privatized funding strategy with a distinct advantage over any other financing tool involving direct expenditures, bonds, or pay-as-you-go funding.

The city might have considered changing course in the latter 1980s when a booming economy had greatly enhanced its fiscal capacity. Yet, practically speaking, the prospects of allocating between $200 and $300 million to the 42DP remained slim. In the context of competing policy demands, the politics of defending such a proposal made it dead on arrival—implausibly self-defeating from either city or state perspective. "42nd Street was only one project," as Stuckey explained:[48]

> Refinancing the 42DP or other such redevelopment projects wasn't PDC's strategy at the time. The strategy was corporate retention—the Outer Borough Program. This was a higher priority. Plus, there was the waterfront. It didn't make sense, in terms of economic development, for the city as a whole to devote such large resources to this one project.

From the state's perspective, Tese echoed the same political impossibilities:[49]

> The city could never have justified that level of spending in midtown Manhattan. How about Harlem? Flushing? Brooklyn? No way there would be direct funding from the city. There's not enough money to go around. The city could also never have restructured the deal, admit to a mistake. Further, there was no agency to raise the dollars. Even the Port Authority [of New York and New Jersey] couldn't do it. Look at what it cost the city and state to build the convention center: $400 million with overruns when the initial figures were around $150 million, I believe. Could you imagine if they tried to build the 42nd Street project? They would have had to go to the state, and that's a political process. The

question there would have been, why should we do this? What about Syracuse. . . . But the bigger question is, why should it be public?

While the open-tab strategy protected the city from the direct exposure to escalating site acquisition costs, it did not keep at bay those critics who generally took aim at government's deals with private businesses. Heavy subsidies flowing to the 42DP grew to be a highly visible public issue as litigation and interminable time delays steadily undermined the fragile consensus for the project and increasing land values continually made for an ever-escalating ESAC. Project officials faced a troublesome problem of political management, which was only marginally accommodated by the revised terms of the renegotiated deal Koch had insisted upon. The bigger problem was that the public perception of the risk involved in transforming West 42nd Street, so real in 1980 when the project had been conceived, had reversed course dramatically over the intervening eight years. With developers putting up large office towers and hotels on the edges of the 42DP project area under a less generous tax-incentive regime, the heavily justified supposition supporting the early case for subsidies no longer appeared valid.

The problem, political scientist John Mollenkopf succinctly argued, had less to do with the subsidy per se and more to do with the changing implications of the policy intervention over time. "When the basic decisions about 42nd Street were made around 1980, these trends [development interest in midtown west] were not so clear. Although we can now see that such a massive project was probably not needed to encourage new investment in the area, it would have been hard then to second-guess these decisions." Acknowledging what prevailed at that time, he cited weak investment interest in the area and supporting market studies that showed that a subsidy would be required to produce competitive rental rates. "An argument can be made, therefore, that *some* public intervention was required to increase investment in the most squalid part of the Times Square area. But was this particular intervention the right one?"[50]

Critics charged that subsidies being given to the developers represented an oversized and overgenerous "give-away." Their language was positively florid. Announcing that "The total of the known subsidies flowing to George Klein is $1.4 billion," State Senator Franz S. Leichter asserted that the office deal was "a close second to Peter Minuet's purchase of Manhattan" and that it would make "Boss Tweed green with envy." Councilwoman Ruth W. Messinger called it "unquestionably the biggest raid ever on the public treasury."[51] After the thousands pages of leases had been made public following their June 1988 signing, Leichter once again, in chorus with other critics including attorneys for the Durst interests and Professor Emanuel Tobier of New York University, voiced outrage at the magnitude of subsidy, which by their estimates ranged from $626 million to $1.5 billion. "One hundred years of subsidy: do we really need century-long tax breaks in the heart of Manhattan?" asked the *Village*

Voice, reporting on Tobier's analysis. Since escalating land acquisition costs were ultimately the city's liability, the land-writedown subsidy inherent in the deal did grow along with the ESAC. Yet there was no easy way to resolve the numbers controversy. Weisbrod dismissed the Durst analysis as "patently ridiculous," and when UDC was asked for an estimate of the subsidies, he responded: "We can't tell you what the ultimate value is to the developer and nobody can, because we do not know what the ultimate cost of land will be."[52]

City and state officials laid out a rebuttal in unusual full fashion in a memo of February 1989 to the Piker Subcommittee of Community Board 5, which had tried to objectively analyze the TSCA/42DP funding agreements. The subcommittee had concluded that "the current 42nd Street property owners' charges of a 'billion dollar giveaway' are total fabrications and distortions." After commending the effort, the cogent and well-written memo, penned by Weisbrod, went on to correct "a number of significant factual errors, which have distorted the subcommittee's analysis and which require correction." Whereas the subcommittee accepted the current owners' "inflated assessment of their own land value to produce an ESAC of $100 million," the carefully considered text asserted that "In fact, total ESACS are unlikely to exceed $73 million, much of which will be spent some years after site acquisition (thus, substantially reducing interest accruals)." Just where this figure came from is unclear; Weisbrod was unsure when asked years later. The ESAC never worried him; the deal was a "classic" positive revenue producer for the city when considered in before-and-after terms:[53]

> The 42nd Street Project will directly create *23,500 full time* equivalent *jobs* and indirectly create *17,800 additional full time* equivalent *jobs* in New York.
>
> Upon reaching full taxes, the Project will provide almost *one quarter of a billion dollars annually* in taxes to the City and State treasuries.
>
> The City will receive in real estate taxes alone, *four times* as much on the office tower sites *during the tax abatement period* as it would have received in real estate taxes if the Project weren't built. According to *the property owners'* analysis, the four office sites alone will pay, *at a minimum,* $249.6 million in real estate taxes before going to full taxes. If the Project did not go forward, the same sites would pay a mere $66 million in real estate taxes over the same period.

"Is the glass half empty or half full," Weisbrod asked by way of explanation of his position on this issue years later: "Are you in favor of the project or against it?"[54]

The critics were wrong about their estimates of the "subsidy," but they were right about the economic inefficiency of city's payback arrangement. They argued that the ESAC was a costly device for the public treasury; government officials responded that it was a responsible method for shielding the city and state from financial exposure should the project fail. In truth, it was both. But the payback mechanism complicated the task of sorting out the subsidy elements in the deal because the off-budget rent credit obscured the real nature of the city's obligations for the redevelopment, much of which—except for the economically costly loan portion— could be deemed "public" responsibilities by conventional standards of what government has historically done to stimulate urban renewal.

The deal offered the office developers two subsidies common to urban renewal: a fixed purchase price for the development opportunity, expected to be lower than the reuse value of the land—this was the land "writedown"—and 15 years of generous tax abatements. A third subsidy linked to the privatized-financing arrangement existed, in theory, though it too was an empirical matter that could be determined only later, for it depended upon whether TSCA ended up earning money (a "spread") on the difference between its cost of funds and the rate it earned on the ESAC repayment. The actual subsidy the developers would receive did not, in any case, depend upon whether the city received positive cash flow after the ESAC accounting. The public subsidy in the office deal was not, as critics claimed, equivalent to the gap between the revenues going to the city and the interest charge on the outstanding ESAC balance. Because the rent-credit mechanism for repaying the ESAC would flow through the same channel—lease payments—as the tax abatements, it is easy to muddle the two and dramatically inflate the true tax savings available to TSCA, as did the critics' projections of the deal. Measuring the true magnitude of the subsidy remains a difficult task, but the flaws in the critics' studies stemmed from conceptual problems with the use of the cost-revenue gap as a measure of the city's subsidy to TSCA.

The terms of the financial payback created a costly economic inefficiency for the city. The city and UDC most likely prepared internal projections of the city's liability for the ESAC and its associated financial implications, but these were neither disclosed nor part of the public dialogue. How much interest would accrue on the tab or when it would be repaid did not seem material to either city officials or private developers when the deal's terms were first negotiated in the early 1980s; only with time did the ESAC liability take on meaning—one that was not there in the beginning. Notably, two policy decisions—targeting the rent credit at 50 percent and financing the ESAC at the private sector's cost of capital, which is almost always significantly more expensive that the interest rate on tax-exempt municipal bonds—shaped the size of the cost-revenue gap. Would the bottom line have been materially different if, instead of a 50-percent rent credit, the deal had specified that 100 percent of project rents be applied to repayment of the ESAC? In terms of project accounting, the outstanding ESAC would have been much lower at the end of the tax-abatement period, approximately half that otherwise (in nominal dollars, not present value) under the terms of the deal as of 1990. Total revenue dedication would have accelerated the payback, and hence, reduced the interest charge, but by diverting funds from the general coffer, it would also have completely preempted their future use for other city investments or services. This is how off-budget financing bypasses explicit spending decisions. Politically, there are limits to how a rent credit is deployed.

Next consider the cost of financing. What if, instead of long-term private financing of the ESAC, the city had used its bonding power to finance the ESAC at rates equivalent to its long-term borrowing for other capital investments? Assuming a 7.5 percent interest rate, the financials would have looked quite different: under this hypothetical scenario, over the course of the 15-year abatement period, interest payments on the ESAC would have been cut by nearly two-thirds, and the outstanding ESAC would have been reduced to $373.6 million from $1.1 billion.[55] Although in the early 1980s the city could not have financed the redevelopment by issuing its own bonds, at the time of the renegotiations in 1986–1987 its fiscal situation had greatly improved. Credibility in the long-term bond market had been fully reestablished for several years. More to the point, capacity would not have been a problem as the mayor's capital spending plans—$47 billion as laid out in the Ten-Year Capital Strategy for Fiscal Years 1987–1996—called for the city's largest-ever capital program. By staying on the course of what was politically and fiscally expedient policy in the early 1980s, the deal's financial strategy became visibly inefficient economically by the end of the decade. The short-term expediency increased costs and decreased future city revenues. For citizens and elected politicians, this would mean either higher taxes or lower levels of services to existing businesses and residents.

The masquerade surrounding the subsidy issue derived from the fact that the economic inefficiency of the financing arrangement, more than the economic costs of the tax abatement granted TSCA, was driving projections of a huge cost-revenue gap. Estimates of the true tax-abatement subsidy require assumptions about the amount of development that would have taken place in the absence of the financial inducement. All of the critics' reports defined the "subsidy" simply as the difference between the amount of payments-in-lieu-of-taxes (PILOTs) TSCA would pay and the amount the city would receive if the towers were fully taxed. This is equivalent to assuming that the market would have generated all 4.1 million square feet of office space *on those particular four sites during the same period*, without any government inducements. Such an assumption is implausible. As a result, the critics' calculations of this real estate tax differential, which ranged from $358.3 million to $459.1 million (unadjusted for the time value of money) overestimated the true tax abatement. Market conditions in the mid-to-late 1980s were sufficiently favorable to assume that some unknown amount of construction would have taken place on its own under the incentives afforded by the 1982 Midtown Zoning Resolution. Just how much, however, remains conjecture.

In assailing the "subsidies" of the deal, the critics correctly targeted the "spending" of so much of the city's future tax revenues on a single project. They went astray, however, with their exclusive focus on the cost-revenue gap, not just because it is technically the wrong concept by which to measure the subsidies, but rather because it is too narrow a measure of the city's true returns from a large-scale public-private redevelopment project such as the 42DP. It does not account for other tax revenues or economic or social benefits from the project, many of which, to be sure, defy easy quantitative analysis. This is critical. No accounting is complete without taking into consideration the two sides of this issue. First is the displacement of development that might have gone outside the city without the tax incentives; this represents the net loss to the city of tax revenues. Second is the economic growth through changing the character of West 42nd Street into an entertainment complex and cleaning up what had become a civic cesspool; this represents the net gain to the city. This piece of the analysis was missing; not until 1994 did the city and state produce a report germane to this issue, *Summary of Economic and Fiscal Benefits for New York from the 42nd Development Project*. But even this report represented a one-sided view; missing was any discussion of project costs. Consequently, throughout the 1980s when support for the project was deteriorating, officials remained politically vulnerable to hard questions of policy: In its effort to preserve the theater industry and help the corporate-service economy expand, was the city acting effectively and efficiently? Was such a large city investment needed to make the 42DP happen where it did? Was the city really going to get the public benefits it hoped would accrue from the project? Could these benefits have been achieved by less expensive and less disruptive means?

In the early 1980s the open-tab private-funding arrangement afforded many advantages. It solved the city's problem of finding funds to substitute for the demise of federal urban-renewal monies. It shifted the direct financial risk of escalating land costs to the private sector. It built in provisions for cost sharing the huge expense of improving the Times Square subway station complex and acquiring the symbolically important 42nd Street theaters. It deferred the city's liability for the land writedown and public improvements and dedicated project revenues to their repayment. It brought a strong private-sector commitment to the project and set up mutually binding incentives for both public and private parties to keep moving forward with the project.

Ironically, however, the political virtues of the city's funding strategy cast a haunting shadow, increasing the project's vulnerability to litigation and public controversy. The city was locked into the privatized-financing arrangement for the first, most significant, and most costly phase of condemnation. The political costs of switching gears prohibited any other solution, as Stuckey and Tese both made clear. That it was not an ideal strategy for all time seems evident by the city's later decision to use capital budget funds for the second and third phases of condemnation. By that time, the project's needs had changed, as had the investment climate of Times Square. The second-phase financing strategy did not have to accomplish what the first one did because Prudential's dollars had already cleared two-thirds of West 42nd Street. Ironically, in that stronger economic context, city and state officials could have chosen to leverage private funds, as they did initially. With Prudential's costly education so publicly evident, however, that would have been a difficult act to repeat. (Years later, however, they would do so for the development of the project's last remaining parcels requiring condemnation, Site 8S, site of the future headquarters for the New York Times.)

The complexity of the 42DP plan created inevitable problems of execution. Volatile market conditions, frustrating delays from litigation, and the crippling loss of viable development commitments for the mart, hotel, and theater sites compounded one another, thereby weakening the political and financial fabric of the deal, which was never tightly woven. The city was at risk, not withstanding the private funding of site acquisition costs. Managing the politics of the large financial liability reduced the degrees of freedom open to city officials, and the lack of transparency in the deal's financial obligations only served to intensify public mistrust.

Over the course of any large-scale project, unforeseen events inevitably force changes in the original development plan and the financial deal. When, however, these forces threaten to sink a high-profile initiative in which much political capital has been invested by a mayor and his agents, such events become political as well as policy. Continuous litigation, controversy over developer selection or architectural design, probing questions about the subsidies of financial deals, protracted delays in negotiation, and critical media attention—all of these erode public confidence and chip away at the base of support for a project, fragmenting what is often a diverse and fragile coalition. Typically, the losses result not from a single, massive blow or show of opposition, but rather from slow destruction of the political and economic conditions that gave rise to the initiative. Ultimately, the momentum is lost and a project becomes increasingly vulnerable to failure. In this first stage of planning, city and state officials had succeeded in creating agents of change for the 42DP. The next test would be whether they could manage the politics of their complex ambitions—execute the plan.

PART II

IMPLEMENTATION: THE POLITICS OF
COMPLEX AMBITIONS

C H A P T E R   6

TROUBLED EXECUTION

No one believed it would be easy. Development politics in New York is intense and fragmented. Numerous well-established civic associations, community-based organizations, special-purpose citizen groups, officially formed advisory committees, and vested economic interests regularly weigh in on matters of land development. In that context executing a large-scale plan for redevelopment of West 42nd Street meant clearing a formidable set of hurdles, legal and political. The planning strategy for the *42nd Street Development Land Use Improvement Project General Project Plan*—sanitization of the street's "bad" character through the substitution of "good" uses—further upped the ante of what was an inherently a contentious, complex, and challenging task. The ambitions of the plan revealed tensions and conflicting goals. Public officials attempted to resolve them, first, through political trade-offs embedded in compromises essential to forming a coalition of support and, second, through tactical maneuvers integral to implementing the development agenda. In 1984, the 42DP was acceptable to a broad set of diverse interests because it promised comprehensive cleanup, the need for which a widespread consensus existed. The plan's dramatic corporate vision for a new 42nd Street, however, was not firmly grounded, either in the prevailing planning ethos, historic legacy, or symbolic iconography of the place. Skillful as public management might be, it could not readily resolve the clash of values inherent in the plan. Consequently, this latest of cleanup attempts by the city, so different from earlier efforts, promised to be an impassioned battle.

From the start, the plan's comprehensive program of commercial development made only the slightest of bows to the prevailing entertainment character of Times Square, 42nd Street's symbolic and proximate identification worldwide. City and state officials promoted preservation and reuse of the midblock's nine historic theaters as an avowed top priority of the redevelopment project. Though rhetoric more than money defined this goal, in tangible ways, theater preservation linked entertainment and the performing arts to the city's financial-services strategy for economic development, more closely than public officials recognized at the time. It also linked the West 42nd Street renewal agenda to the broader fate of the 20-block Times Square district.

This was hardly the first time in the city's history that the performing-arts agenda had imposed itself. New York's grandest example is Lincoln Center, a 14-acre cultural center fashioned out of massive neighborhood displacement in the mid-1950s orchestrated by Robert Moses through his slum-clearance machine, also under a storm of controversy. As an entertainment center, Times Square stood apart, unique in ambience and diversity—a city icon despite of, and because of, its intensely chaotic and "naughty" character as a crossroads of theater, seduction, and sleaze. The physical place, defined so vividly in terms of a stage for commercialism, evoked a powerfully strong symbolism, which numerous dedicated interests vowed to protect. Many of these groups feared that a cleanup might too thoroughly sanitize West 42nd Street—the march, as one critic quipped, of thousands of "yuppie lawyers and accountants in Brooks Brothers suits"—wiping out the character of Times Square.[1]

Employing the language of theater preservation to promote its cleanup strategy, city officials knowingly activated the vested interests of the performing-arts community, as well as architectural preservation and civic groups, all of whom were still smarting from the unsuccessful battle to save the Helen Hayes and Morosco Theaters. In a gesture that turned out to be more than a symbolic bow, the early rhetoric of theater preservation reconfigured the conventional calculus of redevelopment politics. An alliance between business interests and city officials had long defined the redevelopment coalition throughout the post–World-War II period, in New York and elsewhere, particularly when white-collar financial services served as the engine of economic development. Because the cleanup rationale—in the absence of theater preservation and entertainment as part of the redevelopment agenda—could not guarantee the needed political support for the 42DP, the civics emerged as an important minority constituency whose buy-in to the project had to be ensured.

Through compromise and promise public officials finally succeeded in gathering the necessary support for an eleventh-hour approval by the BOE, yet given the tensions and fragmented interests embedded within the diverse coalition, the consensus was structurally fragile and vulnerable. Visible progress proved to be elusive for more than eight years. To the continual frustration of the city and state's skilled development officials, a tangle of implementation problems plagued the original plan. The troubles amounted to a recitation on the political risks of large-scale public development and the conflicting demands of managing such a high-profile project. Tellingly, they unexpectedly came to reveal the influential hand played by the opposition in shaping the city's public landscape.

Organized opposition from businesses to be condemned and competitive property and neighborhood interests uncertain of the future emerged immediately, in the form of 19 lawsuits. Expectations, first about the start of condemnation proceedings and construction, then about the settlement of yet another rash of lawsuits, so often failed to meet newly established deadlines that the heady optimism of early pronouncements by public officials steadily gave way to more modest press statements. Markers of time gone by were evident in the lengthening index of lawsuits, the extended timetables for ground breaking, the receding forecasts of completion, and the repeated lost commitments from corporate tenants for the office towers. Whether the 42DP had "an endless future,"[2] as Douglas Durst, a long-time critic of the project, put it or was merely in the first stage of a protracted multidecade effort so characteristic of large-scale redevelopment projects in big American cities, by 1987 it was obvious to most observers that the project had lost momentum. The loss of public confidence followed not far behind. Across the spectrum of news reports, headlines emphasized that the Times Square plan was "in jeopardy," "marked by delay," "taking more twists," "a shaky step forward," "bleeding," or "endangered."

The alien character of the Johnson/Burgee designs precipitated an all-out battle for the soul of the place over the issue of aesthetics. Barbed and pointed architectural criticism of the plan appeared with regularity in the city's most widely circulated papers, the *Times*, *Daily News*, and *Newsday*, as well as the national media and a wide range of professional journals. Disregard of its own design guidelines for the project furthered growing distrust of the city and state's joint behavior as a public developer. In the interests of feasibility, the city was even ready to allow demolition of the former Times Tower, the place's icon. While the public sector would succeed in winning all of the ensuing litigation—47 lawsuits—the powerful city/state coalition lost the battle for public confidence in the first go-around. Even before the real estate market collapsed in 1991 foreclosing near-term development of the commercial sites, the tide of public opinion had dramatically shifted against the project.

In varied ways and to different degrees, both opposition tacks—litigation and aesthetic criticism—pushed the redevelopment plan off course like a nor'easter. Following separate and unrelated strategies, each set of interests challenged the outcome of development as envisioned by the planners. Through printed criticism, high-profile publicity events, and cautiously husbanded regulatory change, civic organizations pushed for an alternative aesthetic vision of Times Square. In contrast, those most immediately threatened by change, the operators of adult-entertainment stores as well as other economic interests on West 42nd Street, and nearby property owners and residents of Clinton, maneuvered through aggressive litigation to stop or continuously delay condemnation. Though moving on widely spaced parallel tracks, these strategies of opposition eventually coalesced to effectuate a radical—and politically sustaining—shift in focus of the redevelopment plan. It was a stunning turnabout.

In a striking way in which few architectural visions ever grab public attention—as a statement of monumental and wrong-headed thinking—the Johnson/Burgee designs for Times Square emerged as the lightning rod for intense and unrelenting criticism of the 42DP for more than seven years. The four red polished granite and light-colored limestone buildings intending to rise 29, 37, 49, and 56 stories respectively as sheer clifflike walls from the street were to be topped by glass mansard roofs, crowned with ornamental iron finials, and lighted by formal lanterns and floodlights (plate 9). Their monolithic and monotonous style attracted wide derision from architects, conservationists, critics, and neighboring residents. They were seen as too big, bulky, bland, staid, stolid, lifeless, and alien to Times Square. Among the New York crowd, Ada Louise Huxtable first called them "enormous pop-up buildings with fancy hats" and, later, "oversized commercial packages wrapped in a bit of quasi-historical trim . . . a curious blend of the gross and effete." The *Times* architectural critic, Paul Goldberger, complained that the quartet had been "made with a cookie cutter." Another critic, Michael Sorkin, writing for the *Village Voice*, lambasted them as "extravagantly ugly and mercenarily large," and *New York* magazine's Carter Weisman, as corporate "architecture of authority." Brendan Gill, long-time drama and architecture critic for the *New Yorker* and the project's fiercest and most acerbic opponent, considered the whole to be "a heinous urban misadventure." The office towers were "exceptionally repellent," he said, "great gray ghosts of buildings, shutting out the sun and turning Times Square into the bottom of a well." The view was no different among those writing in professional journals or national weeklies or from afar. To *Architectural Record*'s James S. Russell, the Johnson/Burgee towers bespoke "button-down architecture." *Newsweek*'s Douglas Davis called them "strange invaders"—"hulking"; as did Kurt Anderson, *Time*'s design critic, who bemoaned the "loss of funk," noting that there was "nothing deft or original" about these office towers. The loss, wrote Benjamin Fogery of the *Washington Post,* was obvious: While the office towers might merit standing as "handsome structures in their own right," their "simplified profiles and exaggerated historical quotations" and "awesomely corporate character" would change forever the image and reality of Times Square. "When standing in that 'square,' simultaneously observing the nighttime spectacle of the great signs and trying to substitute the Burgee-Johnson vision, one would have to be hard-hearted or blind, or both, not to feel a sense of loss."[3]

From the street level pedestrians would not see the ornate mansard roofs that could make historical reference to the district's famous, but no longer standing, turn-of-the-century French-Renaissance area landmark, the flamboyant Astor Hotel on Broadway between 44th and 45th Streets (built in 1904 and torn down in 1960 to make way for a new office building) (figure 6.1) or the slightly more restrained shell of the Knickerbocker Hotel, where Enrico Caruso and George M. Cohan once

6.1
The celebrated Astor Hotel, 1907,
now the site of One Astor Place.
(Photograph by Frank M. Ingalls.
© Collection of The New-York
Historical Society)

lived, on the southeast corner of West 42nd Street (built in 1906, converted to office use during the era of Prohibition in the 1920s, then renovated
for condominium use in 1980) (figure 6.2). The monumental character of
these earlier buildings would carry over, however. Passing by any of the
four nearly identical Johnson/Burgee buildings, pedestrians would confront
overscaled ground floors and immense formal archways similar to what the
architects had chosen for the A&T building between 55th and 56th Streets
on Madison Avenue. The whole formal ensemble was designed to form an
overpowering spectacle. It appeared out of place in Times Square not
because of these grandiose and monumental gestures, but because the formal architectural devices employed in the service of corporate power stuck
a dissonant chord with the special legacy of the place. The formal postmodern buildings appeared not merely as contextual misfits, stylistically, but
as a deliberate and misdirected attempt to transform the historically bois-
terous and eclectic ambience of the entertainment district into an orderly
and decorous place for blue-chip business tenants. This view, put forth in
the country's most widely read weekly magazines—first in 1984 and again
in 1988—held that the greatest threat of the redevelopment scheme was
too much sanitization, that the commercial program, abetted by its corporate architecture, would make Times Square "square." "By consensus,"
wrote Franz Schulze in *Philip Johnson: Life and Work*, "the Times Square
design represented the worst of the architecture of the 1980s in general
and of the Johnson/Burgee partnership in particular."[4]

These style objections came forth at a time when the architecture
profession was thrashing out its own internal disagreements over postmodernism and its discomfort with the forces of corporate commercialism dom-
inating its drawing boards. The critics disagreed strongly about the criteria
for evaluating these designs because they saw the role of architecture from
distinctly differing perspectives. Some considered architecture in terms of
"stylistic" combinations of aesthetics and function, others as a creative social

6.2
The Knickerbocker Hotel with its
three-story copper mansard roof,
1986. (David W. Dunlap, *On
Broadway: A Journey Uptown Over
Time*)

and cultural force defining the future, not simply an embodiment of what is past or already there. Important commonalities existed in the subtext of the project's design critiques, however. These revealed deeper, unresolved issues of public policy: the need for large-scale intervention, the dependence on density financing, and the lack of substance behind the stated goal of preserving the 42nd Street theaters.

The imperative of large-scale intervention made many critics uneasy. The 42DP was only one of several massive initiatives being pursued aggressively by the city and state to transform midtown west. The 1982 Midtown Zoning Resolution was generating numerous proposals for new office towers and hotels. In addition, the 1.8-million square-foot convention center (to be named in memory of Senator Jacob K. Javits) that had been first discussed in the early 1970s was finally under construction on a huge site between 34th and 38th Streets and 11th and 12th Avenues. By the end of 1982, so was the 2,000-plus-room Portman hotel on Broadway between 45th and 46th Street.

When plans were first announced in 1973, city officials and critics alike viewed the Portman hotel as a crucial private-investment catalyst essential to the hoped-for cleanup and revitalization of Times Square. Critical reaction was generally favorable although not unanimous, even from critics who were not usually admirers of Portman's work. Huxtable, for one, wrote favorably on the flash and flamboyance that typified Portman's atrium-style hotels,[5] then the raging trend in hotel design. "The hotel appears to be the right building in the right place. Its flamboyance can bring back the kind of theater district glitter that the new theaters, understated to the point of dullness, conspicuously lack. . . . It can be the promise of appropriate new life."[6] The design, even then, was that of a "full-block bunker and beachhead," but, Huxtable wrote nearly two decades later, it promised "an infusion of new life and capital. Measured against the multiplying massage parlors, it was seen as a giant step toward salvation."[7] During the heat of controversy over the demolition of the Helen Hayes and Morosco Theaters, the "of-necessity" assessment of the Portman project still held sway, despite the design's obvious massive scale, heavy concrete form, and harsh facade: "The proposed Portman Hotel can do a great deal to reverse the fortunes of this part of town," wrote Goldberger. "Times Square remains one of the few places in which large-scale urban renewal—provided it is the right project in the right place—can still make sense"[8] (figures 6.3, 6.4).

Writing in the *Wall Street Journal* just a few days earlier, Sorkin offered an aggressively different opinion of the Portman hotel as "hopelessly self-centered" in its "shunning statement of isolation, of contempt" for its unique (even if tawdry) context: the mythic center of Manhattan and the nation. What Portman was proposing, he complained, was a quintessential Portman building: huge, soaring spaces, exclusively internal. "Paradoxically, his buildings, which practically scream their aspirations to urbanity, are virtually without a sense of urbanism," Sorkin lamented. "Grand spaces . . . in settings which practically barricade themselves against

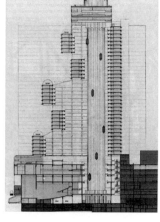

6.3
Cross-section of the proposed Portman hotel, 1973. (John Portman)

their surroundings. . . . Whatever their formal achievements, Mr. Portman's buildings are like giant spaceships, offering close encounters with the city, but not too close. The buildings are always adamant about their alien status." That the hotel signified a "vote of confidence in the area's commercial future" was notable, he conceded. "But that does not mitigate its architectural mediocrity. Instead of a building which adds to the fantasy of the skyline, it is a scaleless box. Instead of making a statement that reflects New York and the city's tradition, it speaks of an architecture of sameness."[9] This was unforgivable.

When the 50-story hotel finally opened in 1985 as the Marriott Marquis, it was universally considered to be disastrous and damaging to the visual character of Times Square. The project generated intense critical contempt: "bombastic," "out-of-touch," "antiurban," "antisocial," "a brooding,

6.4
The Marriott Marquis Hotel, 1985. (Charles M. Weiss)

ugly fortress that turns its back on Times Square and isolates its occupants from the urban environment." This had been Portman's objective: "I meant to create the antithesis to the confusion of Times Square."[10] City officials had been no less desperate for investment in Times Square than before when they dusted off plans for this on-again-off-again Times Square project, but by the late 1970s times had changed. So had architectural taste and prevailing planning theory, both of which had moved away from the type of large-scale urban-renewal intervention epitomized by the Portman hotel. Backpedaling, Goldberger called the Marriott Marquis an Edsel: "What might have looked spirited in the early 1970's," when it had a kind of "energetic swagger to it," now seems tired, worn-out and desperately overreaching."[11] The vitriol heaped upon the Marriott Marquis contrasted sharply with its economic success—an economic "jewel in a dunghill," according to *Engineering News-Record*—which proved that a first-class hotel could thrive in Times Square.[12]

Still, if this was what was needed to satisfy private investment, it was a truly worrisome portent: In the name of "saving" Times Square, the city/state coalition and the developers might end up destroying it. This was the oft-referenced urban equivalent of the Vietnam metaphor: bombing a village to save it. To the most thoughtful and balanced critical commentators, Times Square in the mid-1980s appeared trapped in a no-win situation: If the 42nd Street plan failed, the area would continue to deteriorate; if the plan realized its vision as a large-scale office district, the transformation would undermine the energy and unique qualities of Times Square. "The inability of both architects and urban designers to include gracefully the incompatible but moneymaking elements into the scheme," wrote Russell in an early and systematic evaluation of the 42DP full of cogent observations overlooked by many other reviewers, "demonstrates yet that, despite promises of politicians and experts, there is no such thing as a free lunch."[13]

Even more problematic than size was the density transfer built into the plan. The exceedingly large densities needed to secure the funds from private developers for land acquisition, subway-station renovation, and theater preservation seriously distorted the urban-design intentions. It was a Faustian bargain. "Can good architecture be made of this," Russell asked rhetorically? "Thirty-to-40-story street walls and a 300-foot tunnel [referring to the "windowless 'footprint'" for the 20-story mart at the western edge of the project area] speak for themselves"[14] (figure 6.5). In their intense critical reaction against density extraordinary even by Manhattan's oversized standards, the critics were right on target. Although it is easy to say in hindsight that such an outcry should have been expected, the economic forces and planning loopholes that made such transgressions a familiar critical refrain of development politics in New York in the 1980s intensified the angst among the cultural elite and the city's urbanists. Clustered together in midtown, a crop of giant new buildings, regardless of their architectural merit, threatened to damage the city fabric and its intense street life. The impact of less sunlight and more pedestrian conges-

6.5
The massing model of the 42DP.
(Cooper Robertson & Partners
and Johnson Burgee Architects)

tion seemed especially acute on Madison Avenue with the completion
of the 43-story IBM and 37-story AT&T buildings in 1983 and 1984,
respectively. Huxtable, who was writing compelling criticism about
"blockbuster" buildings as early as 1978, cast the planning dilemma in
political terms that were prescient and remained on point for West 42nd
Street years later:[15]

> New York is so anxious to have large-scale building
> resume that it is going to be very difficult for the City
> Planning Commission to set and maintain standards for
> these huge, innovative projects. . . . Can you refuse
> waivers of height and setback requirements, or increases
> in plot coverage, when the city's economy and image are
> dependent on going ahead? . . . Does one tell Philip
> Johnson to go back to the drawing board?

Johnson was the celebrated architect of the time, then at the
apogee of his career. Through his style-defining buildings, his image-making skills, his extensive social connections and networking, and his genuine
professional generosity, Johnson's influence was commanding. As the oft-
described "dean of American architecture," he had established for himself a
unique place in the cultural world of New York and had consolidated a
professional position many thought unrivaled in the architecture world at
the time. In 1978 alone, he won four of the profession's most prestigious
awards: the R. S. Reynolds Memorial Award for an outstanding building in
aluminum (Pennzoil), the City of New York's Bronze Medallion, the
University of Virginia's Thomas Jefferson Medal, and the American
Institute of Architect's Gold Metal. The next year, at age 73, he was named
the first winner of the new and highly publicized Pritzker Prize; granted
by a jury of peers, it is the Nobel prize of architecture. *Time* magazine fea-
tured him on the cover of its January 7, 1979, issue.

All of this followed a decade of notable commercial commissions that represented a professional rebound. In the late 1960s Johnson had formed a partnership with John Burgee, who brought a mastery of practical methods and working techniques from his years of practice in Chicago, and rebuilt the luster of his career. The IDS Center in Minneapolis (1973) and the twin towers built for Pennzoil in Houston (1976) redefined the style of the tall building through sculptural abstraction, while later corporate buildings of overwhelming power and impact—PPG Headquarters in Pittsburgh (1978–1983), Republic Bank (1980–1984) and Transco Tower in Houston (1980–1983), and AT&T in New York (1978–1983)—established Johnson as the acknowledged leader of postmodern design. The

6.6
Architects Philip Johnson and John Burgee with their model of the proposed 42DP office towers. (Bernard Godfryd)

Johnson/Burgee collaboration, Huxtable wrote, "produced a skyscraper line that exhibits a wide-ranging picturesque eclecticism."[16] To his critics, he was a dilettante of style who appropriated history in modern terms to realize the cultural aspiration of the era; "the style monger," one wrote stingingly.[17] The eclecticism and ever-changing character of these high-profile corporate buildings fueled much critical commentary, none more so than the controversial AT&T tower when its design was revealed in 1978. "Even before it was anything else," wrote Schulze, "the AT&T Building was a triumph of the image-making process that had increasingly taken command of the arts in the 1970s." The "Chippendale" skyscraper (so called because of the shape of its pediment) elevated Johnson "from star to superstar status." He became "the greatest architectural presence," though not, Goldberger would note, "the greatest architect of our time."[18] A "master of cultural politics" and "cultural king maker," Johnson the celebrity was as controversial for what he said as for what he designed.

Though critics commonly complained that Johnson/Burgee's work "represents too shallow, too broad-brush a rendition of history," that some of the work was "discouragingly ungainly and unbeautiful," or "impersonal," the architects could not "be dismissed as mere pasticheurs nor as mere popularizers of history," wrote Susan Doubilet for *Progressive Architecture*.[19] Not only was their impact on American city skylines too great, the power of their ideas to evoke heated commentary from critics and nonarchitects alike spoke to an engagement with both important and catchy ideas that she for one considered characteristic of the American scene. Johnson's name drew the clients, including George Klein, who insisted that Johnson be the major player in the project's overall planning. For the firm, the Times Square project was among its "most ambitious efforts," according to Schulze (figure 6.6). Yet neither Johnson's high professional standing nor the political support of Governor Cuomo and Mayor Koch, both of whom offered unqualified enthusiasm for the scheme, could shield him from the searing attacks of his critics and the unrelenting pressure from the city's civic elite to produce a design more in tune with the special legacy of Times Square. In time, Johnson would be asked, ever so reluctantly, by city and state officials, his ultimate client, "to go back to the drawing board."

The Public Stake

Even when defined by the new standards of scale, the wave of skyscrapers going up in Times Square in the 1980s exceeded the oversized buildings of midtown's East Side because the West Side's larger land parcels allowed for bigger building footprints, while the new zoning incentives permitted the building of more floors. In this emerging cityscape, Goldberger noted, even the Marriott Marquis "could begin to look like a medium-sized old friend."[20] Manhattan's physical identity had long been tied to the notion of density, yet the newest crop of super-buildings, far larger than those of earlier speculative booms, threatened the urban romanticism of the skyscraper. "Giantism" had come to replace density as a defining attribute of urban vitality, and there was nothing positive about the new label. Critics assailed the city for its lack of planning discipline and the "creeping giantism" resulting from its own roster of big public developments. The city seemed indifferent to a loss of its "public realm," they complained justly, with planning seemingly dictated by development feasibility.

If at other times public policy permitted significant zoning bonuses for large-scale development in the interests of gaining tax revenues and other public benefits for the fiscally taut city, this trade-off was far riskier in the unique urban district of Times Square. "The area's peculiar assets—a lively emphasis on continuous, varied, small-scale, fine-grained human activities and a constantly moving kaleidoscope of moving light and color—have overshadowed its liabilities," wrote Huxtable as early as 1968.[21] Its urban energy derived from its varied roles as a center of entertainment supportive of ancillary businesses, a historic home to illuminated-sign advertising—"the greatest of all Pop Art displays"—the symbolic meeting place for New Yorkers, and an internationally known mecca for tourists. Defined over decades, the urban fabric of this close-quartered diversity was fragile, intangible, and beloved. So too was the sense of social tolerance.

The public stake in the "character" and "ambience" of Times Square was immediately understandable, under either polar scenario: as status-quo district of porn-sleaze or future white-collar office district. The force of critical aesthetic opposition was not about whether to preserve the past or stop the clock of progress. Change, irreversible change, was already at work, especially after the 1982 Midtown Zoning Resolution juiced up the market pressures of speculative commercial development in the Theater District. Rather, opposition to the project's stylized architecture—whether in verbal sparring at public hearings or in printed critiques—centered on differing planning visions for the future. The complex issue framed a simple question: Would Times Square be recast as an extension of the central business district or could some "uneasy equilibrium" between commerce and culture be maintained? The answer was only too apparent: Without secure planning policies in place, office uses were likely to completely take over the turf as the economic laws of land-use Darwinism played themselves out in the Theater District.

The "giantism of the plan," Russell wrote, was at odds with the idea of a coherent theater or entertainment district. The massive densities at both ends of the block seemed to overwhelm the low-rise midblock theaters (see figures 3.6, 3.7). If it was necessary to transfer the maximum permissible building density of the entire block to the office sites in order to finance the preservation and redevelopment of the theaters, where, the critics asked, was the *quid* in the *quid pro quo?* City and state officials had put much time and energy into presenting and vetting the proposed office-tower designs, yet no design details for the culturally significant and politically important theaters had been put forward. The reason: There were none at the time. As a result, only one set of visuals dominated the discussion agenda, for years, which made it easy for critics to target the project's Achilles' heel: the lack of substance behind the theater agenda, not merely for West 42nd Street but for Times Square more generally. The larger planning problems remained "untouched," complained Huxtable, who, in 1989, published a searing *Times* op-ed piece out of deep frustration with what she felt to be the continual blunders of the city's planners who failed to understand the deep complexities of Times Square. The renewal of Times Square was "a farce" in which the real issues were overlooked in the "ludicrous debate about a 'suitable' style": the lack of construction commitment for Eighth Avenue, "where it is essential to stabilize the neighborhood"; the weak and uncertain plans for restoring and operating the 42nd Street theaters, which were symptomatic of massive new construction "already transforming and tipping the balance of the city's entertainment and tourist heart"; and the lack of justification for the huge public subsidies.[22]

Huxtable's frustration had grown from her repeated appeals to city officials to make sure the planning for Times Square was put into competent and sensitive hands, something she concluded had not happened. More than twenty years earlier, in a piece titled "Will Slab City Take Over Times Square?," she had written presciently about the "Dangers of Respectability" from the westward press of commercial construction that had already demolished such historic markers as the Astor Hotel, taken the theater out of the Paramount Theater Building to create additional space for offices, and fueled the transfer of property into developers' hands. She had argued persuasively for "Holding Off Conformity," fearing that without "thoughtful urban design" sanitary sterility would come to Times Square and make it a faceless single-purpose district, "as it had to so many once-colorful parts of the city." Just "walk down Third Avenue," she suggested. The city had an essential role to play in shaping new development in the area and "there is still time," she wrote:[23]

> There are ways of having open space, pedestrian pleasures and the visual fireworks and human scale and variety that is the best of Times Square in new development. But it will never happen by itself. It will take a planned framework, the establishment of principles and patterns for building, the coordination of private development and city tools, objectives and guidance. It will take a city that wants to do it.

Huxtable understood the economic and political forces that shaped cities: "No city ever got built on faith, hope and charity. The formula is profit," she wrote in 1967 in an article about the city's efforts "to save the Theater District from the perils of commercial blandness."[24] But she was also an optimist who, at the time, held great faith and hope in the ability of the city's newly formed Urban Design Group to provide the technical persuasion—"muscle"—necessary to effect better planning solutions for New York. She was an optimist, architectural critic Nicolai Ouroussoff emphasized, because of her "dogged search for a way out—for an option to the crass commercialism that is choking our cities."[25] Change, Huxtable argued, is an important component of Times Square, a force contributing to its particular character. What made her incessantly wary about the 42DP was the scale and density and character of the initial proposal; it threatened to destroy the fragile urban fabric of Times Square.

An internationally known voice of sharp but reasoned architectural criticism, Huxtable had been responsible for bringing "a public consciousness of architecture," and, by writing for a newspaper's general audience rather than only for professional journals, she determined to reach the people who made decisions about the environment: architects, planners, real estate developers, financial power brokers, and city officials. Her writing focused public opinion on the city's built environment in a way not seen before and with a style of prose as memorable for its literary devices as for its candid criticism and devastating wit. She was a major force on the New York scene.[26]

Goldberger was less forceful a voice at the *Times*. Wishing to appear balanced, he spoke in both a milder and more ambivalent tone; his reviews were "more carefully modulated," considered "prudent by some, noncommital by others." As to Times Square, ideologically, Goldberger appeared to believe that its character as an entertainment district with a strong street-life presence should be maintained, but he also believed that such a position could only be realized through a large-scale intervention such as the 42DP. As his early endorsement of the project, his waffling criticism, and his reluctance to universally condemn the Johnson/Burgee office towers revealed, he was less willing than Huxtable to take strong forthright positions.[27] For him, the real issue of architecture has been decoration, rather than the social and cultural forces behind architectural form. If this made Goldberger less effective as a critic, though, it was only for a short while. His influence increased steadily, due to his position of power as architectural critic for the *Times*, a voice able to set the tone of critical discourse for the profession.[28] Klein, reportedly, went to pains to get Goldberger's response before going public with a design.

Without a viable theater plan, the clash of values inherent in the promotion of a new high-density office district alongside the aging entertainment district was strikingly clear. Expansion of the midtown office district was the city's real script for cleaning up West 42nd Street. The 42DP aimed just to restore the street's theaters, which was not the same thing as rejuvenating the famed entertainment district. City and state officials offered no rebuttal. Nor did they apologize for either the central role of the office towers—always intended to be the economic machine of the project—or for their design. "The towers may be big and ugly," said UDC's head, Vincent Tese, for the record during an interview in Autumn 1988, "but the numbers work, and what's important to the developer is economics, not size."[29]

That no-nonsense emphasis on bottom-line business, and impolitic style, captured perfectly the essence of Tese's leadership of the state's economic-development activities. He understood the profit-oriented needs of the private businessmen with whom he had to make deals, and he knew how to create an atmosphere for investment. That understanding served him well during the years he consolidated power in state government[30] and became a close confident of Governor Cuomo. Trained as an accountant and tax attorney with degrees from Pace College, Brooklyn Law School, and New York University Law School, the 42-year-old Tese had achieved millionaire-level success by the age of 34 as a businessman and Wall Street commodities trader before he joined Governor Cuomo's administration as State Superintendent of Banks in 1983. He had been tapped to take over two key jobs, the newly created position of Director of Economic Development and the chairmanship of UDC from William J. Stern, after the latter's relatively brief service of two years, and given a mandate to streamline the state's economic-development program and reorder UDC's priorities from physical development to job creation, state-wide. Spending all of its money had been one of UDC's main problems in the past, but under Tese the record became one of steady spending for job creation and retention. Known for his expensive cigars, Italian-cut suits, and preference for pricier restaurants, Tese served in government because he loved it and thought he made a difference, and he donated his entire salary to charity. Though reportedly he did not make many friends in state government—and by one *Times* reporter's account was one of the most confrontational and least-liked people in Cuomo's administration—by and large his work was winning high marks from the business community.

When it came to the 42DP Tese saw any political problems UDC may have had with the project as being solved, ultimately, by UDC's power. He knew he held the powers, knew how special they were, and was not timid about using them because he had a "mission" on West 42nd Street, and this provided him with the certainty to act in the public interest. About this he was extraordinarily clear: "Projects of this size happen when people get committed. You have to have agency to do it, and then stick to doing it," he said in an interview.[31] While the 42DP was not the biggest project UDC had ever done—Roosevelt Island and the new towns program were larger—it was the biggest one of his tenure as chairman of the state corporation and special for him, absorbing half a day of his time each week. On the walls of his current office at Bear Stearns Companies Inc., an investment bank and brokerage concern where he serves on the board of directors, framed news articles—about his appointment as head of UDC (1985), UDC's authorization of the leases with TSCA (1988) (figure 6.7), and the success at reaching an interim agreement with TSCA that broke a two-year deadening impasse (1994)—marked highlights in his career as the state's leading public entrepreneur. "No one believed those buildings would get built," Tese recalled:[32]

> They were ugly. We were going to make the developers
> redesign them. But it was not where we were at the
> time. We were dealing with the square-footage space
> issue; that's at the heart here, and we weren't going to

give this up. The buildings had to have value; for all the
developers were putting up in terms of money and risk,
the public had to give something back. The bulk on the
site was dictated by the amenities to the public sector.

If Tese and other state and city officials did not seem overly concerned with the finer points of urban design or architecture, they did care
about image. Dealing constantly with negative publicity from the continual barrage of critical and public reactions—even from among some of the
more fervent backers of the plan—they felt compelled to change the perception of the long-stalled project, and they pressured Klein and
Prudential to prepare a new set of designs. "When they sent Mr. John
Burgee, the architect, back to the drawing board, they implicitly admitted
that the office blocks they first planned to build were as monumentally
boring as the critics said," the *Economist* reported from London.[33] State
and city officials had been talking to the developers for months about
revisions, but not until after the important lease documents had been
signed in June 1988 did the new designs appear publicly.

Released at the end of August 1989, Burgee's new designs (since
the partnership had been dissolved, Johnson was now formally acting only
as a "consultant," but Klein insisted that he remain a major player in the
overall planning) tried to appease public criticism by changing the aesthetics of the proposed office towers. Each of the four towers, now no longer
of "cookie-cutter classicism," presented itself as a "brash" reflection of
Times Square: colorful, full of signs and lights—in one case, a 27-story
cylindrical sign—reflective glass surfaces, asymmetrical grids, and angled
roofs. The visual transformation was received favorably by city and state
officials, and by the editorial page of the *Times*, because it appeared to take
into account the urban context of Times Square, at least as much as the
public could see of the building's exterior surfaces (figure 6.8). That said,
the critics and the public remained unconvinced of aesthetic improvement
and, therefore, unappeased.

Goldberger called the new designs "a stunning public reversal, less an architectural event than a marketing one, a sort of architectural equivalent to the Coca-Cola Company's abrupt replacement of New Coke. . . . These buildings try to be entertaining; they represent a serious attempt to evolve a viable new esthetic out of Times Square's tradition of lights and signs." That was the good news; the bad: It was just "cosmetics." The buildings themselves he described as "a head-on collision between a half-dozen architectural styles," including deconstructionism, modernism, and post-modernism. While stylistically different, the new designs were "merely token changes" as the headline of his appraisal made clear. The problem lay in the unchanged basic premises of the project—enormous size and imposing bulk—and the resulting prognosis for Times Square—"to be an office district with some theaters appended to it, not a neighborhood whose primary purpose is to provide entertainment and public space."[34] Huxtable, in characteristic style, painted a more vivid, critical vision of Burgee's "new costumes": "Quicker-than-the-eye transformations, like scene shifts in the dark. Abstract wall patterns, kinetic roof lines, state of the art illuminated displays. More surface skills, less historical malapropism. Shell games, so to speak. Give the architects a hand."[35] In other words, once again, optics, not substance.

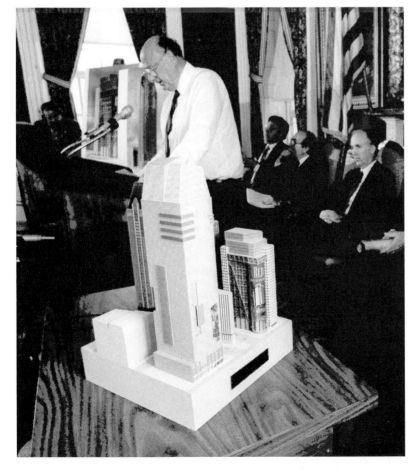

6.8
Mayor Koch, with the model in the foreground, announces new designs for the 42DP office towers. (Dan Brinzac, *New York Post*)

Could it have been otherwise? Could size have been changed as well, as Goldberger speculated? Not likely, not unless political winds shifted in such a dramatic (and uncharacteristic) manner as to displace the still-prevailing financial imperative of the plan. In addition, such a change would have required a new financial strategy—one that did not rely on density financing—to generate sufficient funds to subsidize the public benefits of preserving the theaters and renovating the Times Square subway station complex. There was nothing in the cards at this time, except intense ongoing litigation, to suggest that city officials might rethink their basic approach.

Aesthetic criticism could not stop the project any more than new designs for the office towers could unlock the hold that litigation had on its forward progress. Nor would aesthetic criticism keep city officials awake at night. Koch's primary constituencies in the outer boroughs were likely to be more concerned about cleansing West 42nd Street of pornography and crime (so they might worry less about their children's safety about midtown Manhattan) than about the architectural merits of proposed office towers. The intense critical reaction, however, set in motion influential voices that spoke about their fears that Times Square might be replaced with a second midtown "office canyon," the first being Sixth Avenue only a block east (figure 6.9). The headlines the *Times* chose as leads for these stories, typically placed on the front page of the Metropolitan Section of the paper, indicate how negative publicity during

6.9
The Sixth Avenue "office canyon."
(Gary Hack)

the 1980s came to shape the critical presentation of the proposed architectural vision for West 42nd Street, and by extension the entire Times Square district: "Times Square: Design Problems Remain," "Will Times Square Become a Grand Canyon?" "A Darkened Canyon of Towering Offices [about 52nd Street, viewed as a portent for Times Square], "Times Square: Lurching Toward a Terrible Mistake," "New Times Square Design: Merely Token Changes."

In the course of interviews with many of the involved players, several echoed architect Gregory Gilmartin: "In a way Johnson [and Burgee] inadvertently performed a public service. The miserable quality of [their] design awakened people to the project's deeper flaw: New York City was about to sacrifice its precious entertainment district and replace it with a dreary new world of office buildings."[36] "The designs," recalled architect Hugh Hardy, "were, in retrospect, a great asset to the cause [of renewing the entertainment district]. It was, in fact, a wake-up call to the people that something wrong was about to happen."[37] By setting in motion an alternative vision for what Times Square should be, critical reaction and public opinion forced the issue of entertainment onto the redevelopment agenda, compelling city and state officials to respond, on the defensive, if, at first, in no other way.

The public process by which the new vision for West 42nd Street began to emerge was messy and noisy. Strong controversy prevailed within the ranks of the aesthetic opposition, which, as an interest group, does not speak with one voice any more so than do business interests. The lack of accounting for the unique urban context of Times Square was at the heart of the architectural miscues of the 42DP plan. Missing was what architects call "contextual" development. While most critics agreed that the urban context must be accounted for, the profession's most vocal members were actively disputing the manner and definition of that urban context. Local and state officials seemed to think the urban context could be respected through manipulation of the building's surface and exterior aesthetic. Huxtable, as well as many other architectural critics of the project, felt that a closer and more careful reading of the urban context was necessary. To their way of thinking, the historical, social, and environmental factors could not be reduced to the application of neon lights and signs. Consequently, they saw the new designs as being fundamentally no different from those put forth initially in 1983. The fervor surrounding the renewal of West 42nd Street, and hence Times Square, never diminished. Moreover, a sense of urgency prevailed, for what Huxtable wrote in 1975 still rang true in 1990: "As the symbolic heart of the city, Times Square's condition somehow seems to represent the whole."[38]

LOSING PURITY

The start was favorable. *Design Guidelines* for the 42DP, issued jointly by UDC, PDC, and DCP came out in timely fashion in May 1981, a few months after the initial *Discussion Document* outlining the program for the 13-acre project area. The task had been awarded to Alexander Cooper and Stanton Eckstut of Cooper Eckstut Associates, experienced urban designers and architects with reputations on a rapid rise following their widely praised reworking of the master plan for Battery Park City in lower Manhattan. BPC was perhaps the only large-scale development project in New York's post–World War II memory to have subsequently won unanimous approval from a broad range of critics and urbanists. Just as important, Richard A. Kahan, then president and chief executive officer of UDC, was on record as being a firm advocate of strong urban-design guidelines. A lawyer by training who had taught at Pratt Institute and had earlier worked at UDC for the late Edward J. Logue building housing and later in the private sector for the LeFrak Organization, Kahan spoke from a clearly defined position on the role of the public sector in development—do only what the private market could not do—and made decisions from a bedrock sense of public priorities—urban design and affirmative action. For him, these made up "the public side of the balance sheet." Kahan did not appear, in print at least, to be an expansive booster for the 42DP—"I was pulled into it screaming" he said more than a decade later[39]—yet if his record at BPC was viewed as precedent, he was likely to hold fast to his non-negotiable principles of public policy.

The guidelines sparked a brief-lived momentum of hopeful promise and high expectations because the nearly 150 pages of carefully detailed specifications seemed very much attuned to the task of preserving Times Square's special ambience and visual character as a unique "public room," while controlling the nature of the tall buildings and the huge scale of commercial development they were charged to deal with. In an early editorial on the 42DP, the *Times* called the guidelines "excellent," noting that they "demonstrate the value of public leadership in development."[40] Goldberger responded enthusiastically to Cooper-Eckstut's "sophisticated plan," which he considered to be "more than a set of guidelines . . . most of the way to a real architectural plan." Troubled by the "completeness" of the design guidelines, he asked a philosophical question—is it fair to invite developers to bid on a project that is, in effect, already designed?—which he answered with an unambiguous yes, evoking the old adage about ends justifying means. "For this design is clearly what ought to be built at 42nd Street," he wrote. "It emerges out of a strong understanding of the nature of the existing city, with strong architectural ties to what is best in what is already there."[41]

Compared to comprehensive new development schemes for waterfronts or other large vacant parcels of the urban landscape, setting design controls for congested urban areas like midtown Manhattan is a far more difficult task, especially in strong real estate markets. The role of the urban designer and architect in this type of intervention is, therefore, far more critical. The task is a delicate one because an existing social and cultural fabric exists, as do public spaces laden with memories. A vision of place beyond the two-dimensional site plan or the three-dimensional skyscraper must exist to guide the urban-design plan. Controls for individuals buildings must make sense within a larger existing framework in order to avoid loss of coherence in a large-scale plan when parcels are to be purchased by separate developers and assigned to different architects, a problem common to urban renewal that urban-design expert Jonathan Barnett labeled "parcelitis." As regulatory policy, what design guidelines are supposed to do, Barnett cogently argued, amounts to addressing the policy question: "What is in the public interest in a building, and what are the essential elements of architecture that affect this interest?"[42]

Cooper and Eckstut chose to approach this question by beginning with what existed in a neighborhood. They sought a specific rather than a general solution. They put the emphasis not on the architecture of individual buildings, but rather on understanding the experience urban designers call "place"—the attraction, welcome, and distinctive comfort of being in particular environments. "We believe in two things," Cooper explained: "that every part of the city has its special character, and that there can be certain public benefits to every kind of private development. Our job, as I see it, is to identify principles and goals for each project which are on the public benefit side. Making big private developments work for the public is what we try to do."[43] What the architects identified immediately as characteristic of West 42nd Street was pedestrian activity, its volume and visibility. Between noon and 1 P.M., the block between Seventh and Eighth Avenues typically logged some 4,000 people. This most urban of activities stood out, even amid the squalor, as the outstanding feature of a street whose "excitement and energy," they wrote, "is associated with the uninhibited, flamboyant character of its illuminated signs, billboards, and marquees, and their orientation to key sight lines."[44]

The guidelines set out to achieve three overall design objectives. The first was to maintain and reinforce West 42nd Street's role as a public place; this stemmed from its location, visibility, and function as a nexus of several diverse midtown districts, a transportation node, and an entertainment district and tourist attraction. The second was to preserve the spatial character of West 42nd Street as a low-rise corridor, in particular the mid-block section housing a cluster of historic theaters; this gave the place a pedestrian scale unusual for a wide midtown street. The third was to provide a visual representation of the redevelopment area as a series of three unique places, diverse in commercial uses, aesthetic character, and physical spaces: (1) the high-density office and retail intersection of 42nd Street and Times Square at Seventh Avenue and Broadway, (2) the low-density entertainment cluster of theaters and marquees in the midblock, and (3) the Eighth Avenue corridor. The latter went undefined, except for the impossible-to-miss fact, they noted, that the Port Authority Bus Terminal "dominates" the area.

If maintaining the visual character of West 42nd Street was to be the vernacular of strong design guidelines intent upon keeping it "a lively and public place," Cooper and Eckstut confronted a formidably complex design problem: How does one preserve the ambience of a place while

subjecting it to great changes in scale and use? Their answer: detailed specifications.[45]

The guidelines for the 42DP were unusually detailed, ever more
complex than those crafted for Battery Park City. Building heights and
setbacks were set forth with only small deviations permitted, 5 percent, for
example, in the case of building height. Other specifications controlled
usage, and still others defining circulation and marking ground-floor
entrances and exits governed the relationships between buildings; the
objective was to "produce buildings designed in the spirit of New York's
finest office buildings—Empire State, Chrysler, RCA and Fuller
Buildings." In a "special features" section, Cooper and Eckstut boldly specified the detailing for signage, lighting, materials, and exterior facade
expression to "enhance the lively, visual quality of the street as a setting for
24-hour pedestrian activity." The guidelines, "if followed to the letter," one
commentator pointed out, "virtually designed the buildings."[46]

If these elements seemed to fall into place readily, "a big issue,"
according to Cooper, remained with Site 12, the eastern-most office site
on Broadway between 42nd and 43rd Streets (now Four Times Square and
home of Condé Nast). From a real estate perspective, Site 12 commanded
key value: It was the main recipient of excessive density deemed necessary
to create the "critical mass" for a new office node on 42nd Street at Times
Square. The site's record-breaking FAR would allow the developers to
build 1.45 million square feet piled up in 56 floors. To minimize the massive bulk of the tremendous density on this and the other three office
sites, the guidelines called for maximum heights to define "street walls"
and requirements for building setbacks to reinforce different height zones
of the Times Square intersection.

Operating in flexible space created by UDC's statutory ability to
override city land-use regulations, the design guidelines fashioned by
Cooper and Eckstut, at a reported cost of $370,000, simultaneously func-
tioned as policy, program, and process. They mixed exact prescription with
general intent. They specified the density and uses of sites as would a zoning ordinance. They presented a technical blueprint for controlling development through height and bulk restrictions. They detailed the
architectural outlines of the towers through setback and street-wall
requirements. There would be no formal design-review process, but the
highly detailed document appended to the city and state's *RFP*, in effect,
laid out a procedural framework for ensuring public trust in the alternative
planning process that defined this public-private development venture. A
contractual part of the developer's package, the design guidelines were not
meant to be mere suggestions. Implicitly, they were a political contract
with the public, just as much as a technical blueprint for developers
intending to submit development proposals. As the document proclaimed
on its first page, the requirements "are not discretionary, and proposals
must conform to them to be considered."[47]

Preserving the uniquely diverse and chaotic ambience of Times
Square was not what developer George Klein had in mind, however. In the

cluster of five building sites, including the former Times Tower, he saw an opportunity to develop a new Rockefeller Center, still considered by most design professionals to be *the* preeminent grouping of skyscrapers and defining model of large-scale urban design fifty years after its opening; hence the name Times Square Center, to counter the prior image of Times Square. "What Rockefeller Center did for New York in the 1930s," Klein said, "this [Johnson/Burgee's designs for Times Square] has the potential for doing in the 1980s and 1990s. You cannot build these buildings one at a time because you cannot displace the *garbage* that way." Architects to a world-wide corporate elite with reputations seemingly beyond reproach, Johnson and Burgee were given the task to create the master plan for the complex. "We wanted it to look like a center," Johnson, the project's principal designer, declared. "It's no accident," to which Burgee added: "When you're building a Rockefeller Center, you have to have unity. We're giving Times Square an identity it doesn't have now."[48]

Johnson and Burgee's vision for the four office towers previewed before a select group in October 1983; two months later, after slight revisions, the design scheme debuted before a broader public. The four towers surrounded an open public space—a virtual artifact created by the absence of the former Times Tower, which had been removed from the picture. The visual representation made for a surreal vision of four pristine towers against a Magrittelike background of wispy bright-white clouds reaching down to the sidewalk. The absence of pedestrian activity presented by the vision contrasted starkly with the reality of Times Square; inserting pedestrians into the artificial void of the architectural vision would only have confounded the developer's message by emphasizing their relatively small physical presence against the extraordinary density of the four clustered towers. Once the designs became public, the clash of values embedded in the 42DP came into sharp focus, visually. And as the profound implications of Times Square's future surfaced, so did immediate opposition.

Rockefeller Center may have been every designer's ideal notion of a marvelously urbane place, at once monumental and intimate, formally elegant and ordered, yet still warming and welcoming to tourists and New Yorkers alike, but it was not, in the minds of many vocal New Yorkers, the appropriate model for Times Square. More to the point, the uniform quartet of mansard-roofed towers designed by Johnson and Burgee violated the carefully constructed design guidelines, in detail as well as spirit. Between the first and second unveiling of the designs, the architects' revisions reduced what had been 56 points of difference between their designs and the guidelines to three: setbacks, signs, and building materials. UDC defended its faithfulness to "most of the architectural and design guidelines developed for the project," noting that they were "modified in only three major areas."[49] Yet they were the three elements most critics argued would have the greatest impact on the visual character of the street. Speaking with one voice through the President's Council, a loosely organized group of 11 associations concerned with planning, preservation, and design,[50] the civics assailed the violation of the design guidelines, pointing to the obvious lack of the stepped setbacks and reflective skins of glass and metal called for in the guidelines, as well as bright, large-scale commercial signs that distinguished Times Square. They worried that the plan's concentration of office uses and tremendous densities might destroy the historic character of Times Square, increase real estate pressures on Broadway's economically vulnerable theaters, and jeopardize preservation of the former Times Tower. Other design professionals as well as owners of the major signage companies reinforced this basic critique in the media and professional journals and at the public hearings on the project.

In a *Times* op-ed titled "Ruining Times Square," historian Thomas Bender forcefully appealed for a greater sense of civic responsibility on the part of the government. He argued that the Klein-Johnson scheme blatantly violated the particular guidelines that gave historical significance to West 42nd Street as a public space. By rejecting the five-story street wall and substituting sheer walls rising from the street, the plan, he wrote, "is contemptuous of the public character of the street." The history of the city would also be violated by the developer's plans to demolish the former Times Tower, which, to his way of thinking, was an irreplaceable marker of the role daily newspapers played in the emergence of big-city life. Without the tower, he wrote, "one would have to rename the square and revise the way we think about it: We could acknowledge its privatization and rename it Klein's Square."[51]

In an early appraisal toned by an attitude of ambivalent approval more than critical review, Goldberger accepted the office-center premise of the Johnson/Burgee skyscraper scheme, which he praised as architectural proposals for their "visual appeal" and "historical elements" and likely contribution as "striking additions" to the city's skyline. He chose not see the "shift in bulk" from the lack of setbacks as a major departure in the spirit of the guidelines and went on record as being unconcerned with the demolition of the former Times Tower.[52] Alone in offering approving words, Goldberger voiced some concern about the density and scale of the project. Many, if not most, critics reacted to the banality of the towers—mansards 30 to 50 stories in the air. Johnson and Burgee employed them in the Dallas Crescent project, a complex of office buildings, a shopping mall, hotel, and garage, and people there hated them as well. His AT&T building was not much beloved either. Still others went beyond the violation of guidelines to attack outright the plan's overall density and redevelopment ambitions. Huxtable assailed the underlying travesty of the plan:[53]

> The redevelopment of Broadway's tawdry and tarnished
> Times Square is a case history of the process by which
> the outrageous becomes standard. It also demonstrates
> how political infighting and high economic stakes can
> turn a good plan into a bad one. What was originally a
> sensitive response to the needs and character of the area
> ended as a sanitized exercise in upscale skyscraper real
> estate. . . . The Forty-Second Street plan is a throwback

to urban renewal in its most sterile, insensitive, hack-
neyed, and discredited form; it is as if the hard lessons of
recent decades about the interaction of buildings, people, and cities had never been learned.

While each critique tended to focus on a particular point of contention—the fate of the former Times Tower, lack of setbacks and signage,
awesomely corporate nature of the hulking four mansard towers, loss of
Times Square character—the sharpest critics all spoke in a similar voice,
that of betrayal.

The betrayal was one of vision; the betrayers, the city and state as
stewards of Times Square's role as a place of civic and symbolic importance. The public documents of the project had not hidden the extraordinary density and proposed scale of the plan. Rather, the vision and
discipline of Cooper and Eckstut's design guidelines were intended to
serve as mediating forces in what many accepted as the less-than-satisfacto-
ry trade-off for the large-scale development deemed necessary to privately
finance the desired cleanup and preservation of the midblock theaters.

This compromise, tinged with political connotations beyond what
was immediately apparent in an aesthetic sense, was a familiar one for New
York. It was historically reminiscent of what one real estate historian
termed the "complex bargain" that established "a tradition of the city's
zoning regulations permitting and encouraging very large-scale development while still attempting to accomplish certain important public goals."
To craft its first set of public controls over private building heights in 1916,
the city pioneered a new way to deal with the problem of tall buildings; it
used setback requirements to diminish the effect of the great bulk of tall
buildings, thereby regulating buildings by volume rather than height alone.
"This approach," urban historian Marc A. Weiss concluded, "permitted
development while preserving public open-air space because, as buildings
went higher, the upper stories drew further back from the streets and lot
lines and from surrounding buildings. What was prohibited was *not* tall
buildings per se, just bulky, monolithic fortresses, covering the entire lot,
like the [original] Equitable Building which was built on a scale equivalent
to an FAR of 30 and has been credited with inspiring New York's first
zoning ordinance. Such a compromise made possible the construction fifteen years later of the world's tallest structures, the Empire State Building.
. . ."[54] If it worked so well in the past, one has to ask, why then was this
compromise being forsaken in such a unique place as Times Square?

In a word, marketability. After several months of debate and
negotiation, government officials abandoned the guidelines in deference to
the developer's insistence that the varied shapes called for were economically impractical because they would impair the marketability of the office
buildings. Given the relatively small size of the sites, Klein and his architects argued that following the setback requirements would shrink the
floorplates at higher levels, thereby intensifying the difficulty of leasing to
the banks, law firms, and advertising agencies the developer had targeted as

tenants. These were the prime tenants who took space five, ten, or twenty floors at a time, whose names looked impressive to lenders as well as on a building's ground-floor directory. These tenants, Klein warned, wanted large amounts of contiguous floor space—30,000 square feet "minimum," and, he added, they tend not to favor neon signs blinking outside.[55]

The merits of the marketability issue were open to debate. Eastdil reportedly tested the marketability of the tower floorplates implied in the design guidelines and Cooper walked the plans around to developers. In his view, the only site really constrained was the one south of the former Times Tower, Site 1, an oddly shaped site directly over the subway station, which laid out to floorplates of only 17,000 to 18,000 square feet. "Marketability was a moot issue," he remarked in an interview. "Klein and Johnson wanted to build straight up, and they thought they could pull it off, with a chip off the Chippendale."[56] Whichever way one comes out on this issue, the developers clearly had tremendous leverage in their negotiations with city and state officials. The city was desperate for something to happen on the street. Moreover, nearly all of the public benefits—theater preservation, subway-station renovation, streetscape amenities—were linked to the deal for the office towers. If sacrifice was called for, so be it; the project's urban-design intentions would take second place to the private-financing scheme so fundamental to the project's progress. The future "cost" of this trade-off, however, as one of the early critics of the plan pointed out, would be borne by a permanent encroachment of light, more crowding on sidewalks, and congestion in the streets."[57]

The New York Chapter of the American Institute of Architects (AIA) complained bitterly about its estrangement from the process and the lack of design review. They felt, as did others in the design community including Huxtable, that the project was progressing with a tremendous lack of public discussion. "I find myself facing a fait accompli," Huxtable said.[58] In a city renowned for public posturing, tone as well as substance mattered. In response to charges that it had trampled its own design guidelines, the city displayed an arrogance that might readily have reminded even the friendliest of the project's critics of the city's similarly intense and controversial ongoing struggle over the Westway highway project. When asked to comment on the issue, Mayor Koch snapped, "I, for one, have never felt it necessary to explain why we improve something." CPC chairman Herb Sturz staunchly defended the city's position throughout, arguing that the guidelines were only advisory: They were not standards and "did not mean you can't use genius."[59]

The abandonment of the design guidelines destroyed the fragile state of trust between the city and the civics. At the state level, the high priority UDC previously accorded to urban-design issues had disappeared in a major policy shift triggered by the changeover of administrations from Governor Hugh Carey to Governor Mario M. Cuomo.[60] While UDC's new head, William J. Stern, publicly defended the guidelines, saying he would hold that position over Klein's objections to their restrictiveness, Times Square was city, not state, turf, as the facts of the matter made all too clear. UDC might be the city's partner on the project, but in this case, as in others, the power of decision making implicitly vested in the project's major stakeholder—the city.

If the mayor could forsake the city's own guidelines, which promised to preserve the visual character of Times Square, what else, the civics and critics wondered, might happen to radically alter the plan in ways not yet foreseen? In his balanced yet scathing review of both the 42DP plan and process, Carter Weisman accurately framed the issue:[61]

> But suppose something does wrong after the go-ahead is
> given? For instance, many of Broadway's legitimate theaters
> are already dark much of the year. Can the audience sustain
> nine more? If the renovated theaters fail, and the office
> buildings succeed, the theater sites will begin to look very
> attractive for development. And since major changes will
> have already been made in the project to accommodate a
> developer's estimate of the office market, what guarantees are
> there that others will not follow? U.D.C., it should be
> remembered, makes its own rules. The public is stuck with
> trusting any agency that is to a large degree above the law.

UDC was not above the law. The deals for the 42nd Street theaters would have to pass the upcoming review by the BOE, and any subsequent changes outside the terms of what the BOE approved would have to be taken through another round of review procedures. But the anxiety among the civics, performing-arts interests, and community groups triggered by the abandonment of the guidelines for the 42DP was real. In their view, the city had largely abdicated its planning role in shaping the future of significant places, bowing instead to the needs of private commercial interests. They no longer trusted the city's verbal assurances. Sturz had to find terms of compromise with them, though. Identifiable by its most visible participant, the MAS, the civics functioned as the glue binding together the project's fragile coalition of support.

Two weeks before the BOE public hearings, city officials agreed to the three key concessions put forth by the MAS. The first concession was to reopen the planning of Times Square by undertaking a review of regulations affecting the area short of a "comprehensive" review, meaning a review of zoning. The review process would be monitored by a special Project Advisory Committee, subsequently known as the Bow-Tie Committee, which would include representatives from civic, design, and community groups to ensure that these groups "are involved in the post-Board of Estimate project planning and implementation." The second concession was an agreement to reach a decision over the fate of the Times Tower site through the "consensus of a committee" comprising three city-state-developer representatives and three independents expected to represent architects, designers, and planners. As its third concession, the city agreed to insert into the BOE resolution restrictions prohibiting construction above any of the existing theater structures and the transfer of development rights from the theaters during the 99-year term of the leases, which mollified the civics' fear that the low density of the midblock would be violated by subsequent commercial pressures.[62]

The MAS board of directors was generally pleased with the compromise, though some individual members remained dissatisfied. The package, however, did not reduce their reasoned skepticism and distrust of city actions. Whatever presumption of purity the city might have been entitled to had been lost with its abandonment of the official design guidelines. Violating the key elements of the guidelines was not just a procedural issue of good-government practice, but rather a test of the city's priorities over the conflicting purposes of the 42DP plan: expansion of the central business district versus cultivation of the city's prime entertainment district, which the civics believed should be economically preserved, if not culturally treasured, as a competitive advantage for the city in formulating its strategy for economic development. The MAS did not really believe the advisory Bow-Tie Committee would have an effect. And they did not have guarantees for the agreements they had won, only "promises," as Barwick said.[63] As the minutes of their board meeting revealed, the MAS believed that all it could do at the moment was take Herb Sturz at his word. Its skepticism proved productive because it spurred the society's leaders to mount an extensive and effective campaign to "right" the vision for Times Square. And, as explained in chapter 8, this was a campaign that changed the dialogue of Times Square redevelopment, and, ultimately, the plan for West 42nd Street.

Learning About Symbolism

Intense concern over the fate of the former Times Tower signaled the opening round of the civics' battle, led by the MAS, for the symbolic soul of Times Square. It was the harbinger of high-profile politicized events to come, though this clash had nothing to do with aesthetic merit. Architecturally mutilated in 1964 after the *Times* sold the building to Allied Chemical Corporation, which sought a "showcase for chemistry," the $10-million facelift—hailed at the time in the business press as a hopeful sign that the "decaying travesty" of "once-proud" Times Square was in for a change[64]—covered the historic skyscraper with what Huxtable called "a no-style skin of lavatory white marble with the look of cut cardboard."[65] The 25-story former limestone and terra-cotta building designed in Italian-Renaissance style by Cyrus L. W. Eidlitz remained, nonetheless, to the world at large, the Times Tower. "It could probably be made of marzipan and it wouldn't matter. The odd little icon is universally known by the illuminated signs," remarked Huxtable.[66] Its evocative power was part illusion, yet its signs ensured an enduring iconic status just as its siting, shape, and silhouette had guaranteed its role as the symbolic focus of Times Square when first erected 80 years earlier (figure 6.10).

Not long after the Johnson/Burgee designs debuted publicly, in a move designed to draw widespread attention to the fate of the former Times Tower, the MAS and the Design Arts Program of the National Endowment for the Arts cosponsored an open, international design competition for the site. The goal: "focus attention on imminent large-scale development in the area" and "reflect on the possible meaning of this very special public space for the next generation."[67] It was a "no-build" competition, the society explained, because the building—which no one

6.10
The Times Tower transformed: ca. 1915, 1987, 2001. (© Collection of The New-York Historical Society; David W. Dunlap, *On Broadway: A Journey Uptown Over Time*; Gary Hack)

seemed to reference any way other than by its namesake—was in private hands. For a $45 fee, every entrant was given a kit with background information and photographs; entries were to be judged on the basis of a single drawing, 30 by 40 inches. Responses poured in, 565 of them from 1,380 individuals or teams registered in 17 states and 19 countries, many of whom were young designers seeking an opportunity for recognition in a blind judging.

The diverse entries, which included many buildings similar in shape to the original Times Tower and one, its literal reconstruction, "all made clear the deep, almost passionate commitment of architects to Times Square's traditional, somewhat honky-tonk, identity," wrote Goldberger in a review.[68] Consistent with that view, the entries also revealed a common distress with the radical transformation of Times Square proposed by the Johnson/Burgee designs. A distinguished jury of nine design professionals chaired by Henry N. Cobb, a partner of I. M. Pei & Partners and also at the time chairman of the department of architecture at Harvard University, deliberated over two days. In the end, when it became apparent that no three entries had garnered sufficient support to justify the distinction between "prize" and "commendation" as set forth in the competition guidelines, the jury decided not to award a first-prize winner, but rather eight equal prizes of $2,250, one of them to a poem. Considered from a professional perspective, the terms of the competition lacked an explicit program of action so it was difficult to come to a clear decision on a winner. It was an "idea" competition. Under the leadership of Cobb, the jury issued a public statement:

> The Times Tower site stands at a unique point of confluence; its essential qualities are activity, diversity and accessibility. In planning the future of this site the primary goal should be to reinforce these qualities—to at the very least not diminish them. To achieve this, it is our considered and unanimous judgment that 1) the Times Tower site should be occupied by a building. It is not an appropriate site for an open plaza or monument; 2) the building on this site should respect and reinforce the street walls of Seventh Avenue and Broadway. In this respect it would be difficult to improve on the wedge-shaped form of the present building; 3) the building site should be multi-use, and at least in part accessible to the public. It should include space devoted to those entertainment and communications functions whose continued presence is crucial to the life of the district of which Times Square is the vital center.

Making a public statement was unusual for an architectural jury, though not for the MAS. Indeed, creating public awareness through a PR-type event, even if it turned out to be something of a polemic, was a tactic typical of the society. For planning and aesthetic issues of civic importance, the society's leaders aimed to create media awareness of the policy questions, to get out in front of an issue and present viable alternatives to the public at large and city officials in particular. The winning proposals from the Times Tower site competition, like other events to follow, were exhibited at the society's Urban Center on Madison Avenue at 51st Street. The message: Leave the Times Tower site as it is, even if it is dead.

Creating an open space void of aesthetic interferences that would set off his Rockefeller Center–like ensemble of office towers was a Johnsonian idea. "It is not a distinguished building of any kind," said his partner Burgee, who reportedly added that the former Times Tower ought to be torn down because it does not fit with Johnson's plans.[69] Klein agreed, although he did not have to disagree with that assessment to understand that it was politically necessary to present an alternative centerpiece for the site. Toward that end he retained architects Venturi, Rauch & Scott Brown of Philadelphia as consultants. Asked to design an element for the site that would be in keeping with Times Square's popular references and commercial vitality and that at the same time would be consistent with the scale of the proposed towers to surround it, the principals brought to the task a unique architectural understanding of contemporary American popular culture. Constrained by having to work with Johnson and Burgee's designs as a given, they nonetheless kept to their own signature definition of architecture. With their colleagues, Robert Venturi and John Rauch quickly produced a series of daring iconographic images (plate 10) based on the general idea of a "Big Apple for Times Square," which they described as:[70]

> a piece of representational sculpture which is bold in
> form yet rich in symbolism, realism with a diversity of
> associations. It is popular and *esoteric*. . . . It is stark in its
> simplicity and monumental in scale; but it is also
> ambiguous in scale because of its very simplicity. . . .
> The round form of the Big Apple provides an appropri-
> ate counterpoint to the bulk and angularity of the sur-
> rounding buildings. Despite its size, it promotes also a
> sense of openness and airiness in the space through its
> shape and "floating" quality. This 90 ft.-plus diameter
> apple is the modern equivalent of the Baroque obelisk
> that identifies the center of a plaza.

Times Square is "exceedingly important, if not the most important space in the city—wonderfully exceptional where the diagonal hits the grid," Robert Venturi and Denise Scott Brown later explained in an interview.[71] They wanted to put something there—in the center of Manhattan—that would be as symbolic and imageful to New York as the Statute of Liberty at the island's edge. They wanted it to be civic in character, memorable, and if kids liked it, then they would be on the right track; the inside of the 90-foot apple might hold tourist information facilities, an auditorium, the tkts ticket outlet, or a panoramic museum of Manhattan. Complexity and contradiction, Venturi wrote in 1966 in his now-classic manifesto against modernism, prevailed in Times Square: "jarring inconsistencies of buildings and billboards . . . contained within the consistent order of the space itself," where the "seemingly chaotic juxtapositions of honky-tonk elements express an intriguing kind of vitality and validity, and they produce an unexpected approach to unity as well."[72] The big apple, small in the context of such huge towers, the bright-red glossy surface, the simple silhouette, all these elements reflected their well-studied view that contrasts in scale and unusual juxtapositions "are traditional means of creating surprise, tension and richness in urban architecture." Just as it signified Venturi's love of double meaning, the preliminary design was at the same time a "spoofing" of Johnson. The first but not the last of their brilliant if sometimes jarring visions for New York—Venturi and Scott Brown have yet to see one of their firm's several civic or waterfront designs for the city executed—the "Big Apple" was rejected by Klein.

Fellow architects and critics reacted with no more affection, however much some respected Venturi's courage to tread where others did not dare while others misunderstood his architectural wit. When the plan was denounced at a professional seminar "hundreds in the audience cheered," reported one business writer.[73] In a letter to the *Times* editor, a past president of the AIA and the MAS wrote: "As for Robert Venturi's idea that a giant apple would be a suitable civic monument for Times Square, I think he has it backward. It is more important to have a core in the Big Apple than a big apple in the core."[74] "Would the public grasp the scope and depth of these references?" asked Douglas Davis in his profile of the controversial architect he called "Mr. Post-Postmodern." "The answer has to be no. Venturi's yearning for popular acceptance is probably doomed to frustration during his lifetime. He is still the captive of his intellect; there is nothing 'simple' about his work. And he is surely mistaken in his hope that the deep red apple of apples will be admired on low and high levels at once—by the layman as a pun on the city's nickname, by the cognoscenti as a surreal object in the manner of Magritte."[75] In an appraisal of remaining design problems in the Johnson/Burgee scheme, Goldberger caught the architect's intent—"The Venturi plan is shocking, difficult to accept at first—and brilliant. . . . The genius in this work lies in its ability to manipulate proportion and the element of surprise in such a way as to make us think of the apple as a monumental object, not as a common piece of fruit"—but then Goldberger saw no reason to save the ghost of what was once an "eccentric" landmark.[76]

Venturi's Big Apple was brilliant, but "alien." As expressed in the ideals and entries of the MAS competition, in the opinions voiced at the BOE hearings, and on the pages of the *Times*, New Yorkers did not want iconography for Times Square, or, more specifically, they did not want a new icon. They simply wanted the former Times Tower preserved, whatever the state of its aestheticism, because it was an icon of the city. As John

J. Costonis defined the concept in his cogently argued book about preservation, *Icons and Aliens*, the former Times Tower was an icon because it was "invested with values that confirm our sense of order and identity."[77] It represented the symbolic environment of Times Square, physically. Its embedded associations—as a public place of breaking news announcements, as a civic place of celebration and of protest, as a center of unrestrained commercialism—had made it so. The former Times Tower was synonymous with the "zipper," the ball drop on New Year's Eve, big billboards, and blinking electric signs. Venturi's playful and ironic Big Apple may have been less alien than Johnson and Burgee's awesomely corporate towers, but in the political context of the times, only relatively so. Both threatened the icon and, hence, New Yorkers' "investment in the icon's values." At a time of uncomprehended change, actual and proposed—a description fitting midtown Manhattan during the 1980s' building boom—the bonds between people and icons, Costonis wrote eloquently, become especially compelling. In the face of environmental changes perceived to be a threat to social values, the call for preservation becomes a symbolic call for reassurance and psychological stability, not an aesthetic brief based on notions of beauty. No where was this more so than in Times Square.

Only George Klein, his architects, and the project's most ardent public supporters saw the need for a "centerpiece" for a new Times Square. Using the language of design, the two different sets of architects set out criteria for evaluating what was appropriate for the dense concentration of office towers. The Venturi proposal was the most controversial put forth by the developer, but not the only one. A proposal for a seven-story, Italianate bell tower by Johnson and Burgee quietly circulated around New York about two years later; before that the two partners presented a more reasonable scheme to strip the old Times Tower down to its steel skeleton, paint it white and use it as a base for searchlights.

The skeleton, in fact, has been the icon's most enduring architectural feature. When built, the Times Tower was notable chiefly for its "progressively engineered steel frame and its pedantically designed details"[78] (figure 6.11a). Stripping away those details had done nothing to diminish the tower's appeal as a place to make a statement. In 1968, for example, the artists Christo and Jeanne-Claude, known for their wrapping of civic monuments, focused their intentions on Allied Chemical's "Flat Iron" tower, but to no avail (figure 6.11b). Three decades later, Pritzker Prize–winning architect Frank Gehry would be drawn into the design orbit of the icon when executives of Warner Brothers, which had leased the building for a Warner Brothers Studio store, asked him to let his imagination range freely on a facade design. His proposal, too, would have stripped the tower down to its steel skeleton, then draped it with a layer of metal mesh that would go up and down, billow and gather in folds, the entire "show" manipulated by a giant clockwork mechanism visible through the skin and programmed to provide a continuous animated spectacle day and night. Echoing Venturi's reference to the Statute of Liberty, architectural critic Herbert

6.11
The celebrated skeleton of the
Times Tower: a) under construc-
tion (1903) and b) under wrap by
Christo (1968). (Museum of the
City of New York, Photo Archives;
Christo)

a.

b.

Muschamp described Gehry's design as "a Statue of Liberty for an era
when Times Square had become the city's Ellis Island, a symbolic port of
entry for many of the city's newest arrivals. At least, it's a terrific symbol of
the creative freedom for which the city stands."[79]

In the mid-1980s, among the architects, planners, historians, and
other experts opposed to any kind of radical alteration, no discussion of an
appropriate "centerpiece" was really necessary. The ghost was sufficiently
evocative. Not unexpectedly, given the symbolic importance of the tower,
city and state officials could come to no agreement on an alternative idea
for the site. Having learned their lesson, somewhat reluctantly, they gave in
to the status quo—though not before the leases with TSCA had been
signed in summer 1988.

The symbolic and social meaning of Times Square could mobilize powerful imagery. When deployed skillfully, it could fashion public
opinion and spotlight planning issues of particular importance to special
interests. As a tactic of opposition, however, symbolism could not protect
First-Amendment rights, challenge eminent-domain takings, pose substantive questions about environmental impacts, inject procedural delays on a
continual basis, or threaten the economic feasibility of the 42DP. In short,
it was not a useful tool for those who sought to block the project completely—through litigation.

C H A P T E R 7

THE LITIGATION TRAP

Neither the most brilliantly crafted strategy nor the most ingenious tactics executed by public officials could have shielded the 42DP from the type of lengthy project-deadening litigation that bedeviled forward advances until mid-1989. Since Westway—the controversial highway project that involved demolishing the aging West Side Highway and rebuilding that shoreline, begun in 1972 but continuously delayed and ultimately killed in 1985 by legal challenges—and the Columbus Circle project, intense litigation had become a fact of life for any large-scale development project in New York. The anticipation of litigation loomed large as "a paradox of good and bad," explained Gail S. Port, former UDC general counsel during the early days of litigation over the 42DP. "The good side to this is that we had acknowledged that litigation was to come and this resulted in a very carefully planned project." One of the lessons of Westway, which was blocked from going forward by a federal court judge because the U.S. Army Corps of Engineers had failed to consider the impact of the proposed landfill on the striped bass habitat, was that the public sector could never be too diligent about procedural details nor too precise about data in the all-encompassing environmental-impact statements mandated under city and state law. "Our subsequent assessments and analyses went to new levels of sophistication and depth . . .," Port explained. "We were very sensitive to doing it correctly, to the environmental and urban and social aspects of a government project."[1]

If other high-profile development showdowns prepared UDC for the anticipation of litigation, they could not, however, yield anything close to a reasonable forecast of how much litigation to expect. The 42DP was too significantly different from Westway and Columbus Circle. Litigation over the 42DP went way beyond the expected environmental-impact challenges. Opponents unsuccessfully challenged the project on a wide variety of constitutional and legal grounds, including abridgement of First-Amendment rights and equal-protection rights under the Fourteenth

Amendment; antitrust liability for anticompetitive consequences; violations of eminent-domain taking of an individual property for a "public purpose"; due-process grounds challenging the validity of the BOE approval of the project; favoritism in the selection of developers; absence of competitive bidding in the awarding of the subway-renovation contract by the MTA; UDC's right to award 99-year leases of public property for private development; validity of modifications to the project plan in the absence of resubmission to the BOE for approval; and unfair and adverse competition to an already existing furnishings mart developed with public funds.

Several factors specific to the character and scope of the project contributed to the voluminous trial record: first, the political mandate to cleanup the social environment of West 42nd Street; second, key elements of the implementation strategy; and third, the ingenious complexity of the public payback mechanism. All three offered fertile legal ground for a host of substantive challenges and technical maneuvers. By the time UDC filed its petition for condemnation in May of 1989, the lawsuits numbered 42, seven of which had pressed claims in federal courts. The tally would reach 47 before forward action commenced. In contrast, Westway and Columbus Circle were the subject of only two and three lawsuits, respectively. The initial filings, amended complaints and subsequent motions, discovery proceedings, FOIL (Freedom of Information Law) requests, and judicial appeals continued nonstop over a six-year period once the final environment-impact statement became public in August 1984. In December of that year alone, opponents filed 13 suits—11 on one day.

The range of defendants—UDC, its chairman (William J. Stern, Vincent Tese) and its subsidiary for the project, TSCR and its president (then its successor organization, 42DP, Inc., and its president, Rebecca Robertson); the City of New York; Mayor Edward I. Koch; the BOE and individual members of the board; CPC and chairman, Herbert J. Sturz, and individual members of the commission; DCP; PDC and its president (Steven Spinola, James P. Stuckey, Carl B. Weisbrod); director of the Mayor's OME; the city's Commissioner of Buildings, Commissioner of Finance, Department of Environmental Protection and its commissioner, Corporate Counsel and Law Department; Governor Mario M. Cuomo; the state's Department of Environmental Conservation and its commissioner, MTA (and NYC Transit Authority) and its chairman, the PACB, as well as numerous other municipal and state officials as holders of specific positions; plus designated private developers, individually and as corporate entities— was exhaustive. In all, the cast of defendants totaled 24 government agencies, authorities, or administrative positions, including nine elected officials plus 15 lead individuals and eight designated private developers, most of whom would be represented in court by separate counsel. Just keeping the litigation moving, UDC faced an enormous task. For litigation expertise, the state corporation relied on outside counsel since its own internal legal staff was composed mostly of real estate lawyers who did not have training in litigation.

The strategic effort of the opposition—delay, often without prospect of winning—may have been a foregone conclusion, but, as a counter force of control, UDC's defense effort remained powerless. All it could do was respond; no feasible offense existed to cauterize the flow of litigation. The most public officials could hope for was quick dismissal or a consolidation of cases. The process held them captives to a choreographed campaign of litigation. In New York as elsewhere, lawsuits were no longer, if ever, last resorts, but rather an integral part of the development process for large-scale projects. Winning each confrontation could not assure triumph for the project: As the lawsuits ground their way through the legal system, real estate's cyclic clock ticked away, and the 42DP's economic underpinnings eroded. Ironically, it was a dénouement in which each side could say it had won.

PREDICTABLE MOTIVES

Transparency marks the motives and predictability the tactics when plaintiffs are identified in terms of their interests. As evident from the profile of 42DP litigants presented in table 7.1, the overwhelming majority of legal challenges, 40 in total, were brought directly by those immediately affected by the project—businesses in the project area whose sex shops, bookstores, and movie theaters would be shut down or whose property would be taken by eminent domain, as well as competing real estate interests with property holdings nearby destined to be adversely affected by the proposed new development. The other seven, ostensibly, were brought by community or environmental interests who held the lead-plaintiff position. These "community-interest" lawsuits, however, were not all that they appeared to be; in five of the seven cases, legal counsel for the major economic-interest litigants were also representing community-interest litigants. Accounting for that crossover, the story line is one of vested economic interests' instigation of litigation—45 of 47 of the lawsuits. The social issues and concerns of public policy that gave rise to many of the community-interest

TABLE 7.1. INTERESTS BEHIND LITIGATION OF THE 42DP

INTEREST GROUP AS LEAD PLAINTIFF	NUMBER OF LEGAL CHALLENGES
ECONOMIC INTERESTS:	40
Adult-entertainment operators	2
Theater owners and/or operators	5
Competing real estate interests	12
Property-owner (nontheater) condemnees	21
"COMMUNITY" INTERESTS:	7★
Clinton residents	3
Elected officials	2
Environmentalists	2
TOTAL	47

★For five of the seven community-interest suits, the plaintiffs were represented by the same attorneys representing two of the major economic interests.
SOURCE: Author's files.

lawsuits were certainly genuine and legitimate, yet the coalitions of convenience in which Clinton residents, elected officials, and environmentalists came together, in concert with the financial backing for their lawsuits, readily lent themselves to the supposition that they were being used by the project's vested economic interests.[2]

One notable exception involved a case of environmental litigation, *Jackson v. N.Y.S. Urban Development Corporation*, bought by two elderly, disabled residents of Clinton, designated as a "secondary impact area" of some 15,000 residents. They sought to stop the project on grounds that the *FEIS* was deficient in not giving sufficient attention to the impact of the project on the elderly citizens of Clinton who, along with others, would be forced out of their apartments, and deficient in not adopting effective measures to mitigate their anticipated displacement by gentrification. Unlike others tied to community-based lawsuits, these plaintiffs filed alone and were independently represented by three attorneys affiliated with three well-established legal services organizations: MFY Legal Services, New York Civil Liberties Union, Legal Services for the Elderly. In this highly significant decision finalizing judicial scrutiny of the *GPP*, the court noted that UDC in its *FEIS* "recognized that many of Clinton's residents were of low to moderate income, and discussed their potential displacement due to rising real estate values. Having done so, UDC had no duty to give separate consideration to elderly residents of Clinton." Although there is clearly a duty under SEQRA to mitigate adverse impact, the court went on to opine that there is no obligation for an agency to "impose every conceivable mitigation measure, or any particular one."[3]

A small group of economic interests spearheaded approximately four-fifths of the lawsuits. The most prominent litigant was Rosenthal & Rosenthal, a family-run private firm specializing in factoring (a type of lending commonplace to the garment industry) that, according to court papers, did about a $1 billion a year in business out of an older, well-maintained seven-story building it owned on the north side of West 41st Street within the boundaries of Site 1. Rosenthal & Rosenthal simply wanted to stop the project, or at least the condemnation of their building at 1452 Broadway. Built in 1907, it was, in the words of the U.S. Court of Appeals's opinion affirming the District Court's dismissal of the case, "structurally sound, fully utilized" and "not blighted or substandard." Their first suit challenging the project posed a classic test of taking for a public purpose under the law of eminent domain, and in finding for the defendant, the court reaffirmed well-established precedents underlying implementation of urban-renewal efforts: so long as there was legitimate public purpose underlying the project and so long as the proposed condemnation was rationally related to that purpose, "It makes no difference," the court stated "that the property will be transferred to private developers, for the power of eminent domain is merely the means to the end."[4]

If the ruling affirmed the constitutionality of the taking, it did nothing to quell what became a steady stream of litigation from Rosenthal & Rosenthal, their affiliated interests and counsel, Jacob Friedlander of

LeBoeuf, Lamb, Leiby & MacRae. Over the course of five years beginning in 1984 they brought the single largest number of lawsuits, 17, and they did not give up until the end. "We're completely in favor of the purpose of cleaning up the area of 42nd Street between Seventh and Eighth Avenues, but we're unalterably opposed to destroying our building and its immediate neighbors for the simple reason that there is no blight in this area," said Imre Rosenthal, chairman of the company.[5] Besides Rosenthal & Rosenthal, two nontheater-owning property interests within the project area, Waybro Corporation and Three O. Realty Company (each with a single small parcel subject to condemnation), filed six additional lawsuits.

The 42nd Street theater owners were the most obvious affected property owners. Of the 15 movie theaters in the project area, 14 were controlled by the family-run Brandt Organization, a business force in Times Square since the late 1920s, and Leonard Clark. Together, they brought five lawsuits. During the bidding process, Robert Brandt announced: "We're just not going to turn over a business that's been in our family for 50 years to some other operator." Having failed to win the developer designation for the five theaters on Site 5, he went on record with the statement that his company "will vigorously oppose the project at every level of proceeding on up through the courts."[6] Brandt and Clark's theaters—revenue-generating machines showing primarily low-budget martial arts and horror movies along with some mainstream Hollywood fare and sexually explicit films—typically did "a volume of business second only to the major Times Square first-run theaters," according to the *DEIS*; at the time of their first lawsuit filing, Clark claimed that the 14 theaters drew 10 million customers a year, generating between $30 million and $40 million in admissions.[7] The *DEIS* authors were at a loss to gauge attendance, for they could find "no precise seat occupancy rates" for the 42nd Street movies houses, which together offered more than 7,000 seats; on the other hand, their estimate of attendance, based on an average occupancy of 30 percent, at 10,000 per day (3.65 million per year), stands out as an admittedly conservative figure.

The Durst family interests put their name on five lawsuits directly, but the rumors of their financial backing of many more are legion. Long-time artful assemblers of land, developers, and owners of midtown Manhattan property with extensive holdings in midtown west, the Dursts owned a major land assemblage adjacent to Site 12 comprising 16 of the block's 31 parcels—one of which would be condemned for the 42DP— on which they hoped to erect a major skyscraper. Seymour B. Durst, the family patriarch and president of the Durst Organization, which had been founded by his father in 1915, was a respected figure in the New York real estate industry. He was also a part-time historian of New York, as well as a long-time antigovernment activist, especially when it came to intervention in land markets. He was known for his staunch critical views on New York's city planning department and government regulation, in general, and his eternal readiness to speak out on these issues. Adamantly opposed to earlier public projects (Westway, World Trade Center), Durst had been labeled by one reporter "The Champion of Midtown Laissez-Faire." His views found their way to the op-ed pages of *Crain's* and *Newsday* and in letters to the editor of the *Times,* frequently. Beginning in the 1970s, when the city's fortunes seemed to be falling fast, he had taken to communicating his opinions with the aid of what he called the "attention-attraction method of focusing on urban problems." Among such devices: a New Year's Eve card with the visual message of a "totally gone city"; a 12-foot, black-edged "Scroll of Housing Fatalities" intended to quantify the degeneration of New York City's housing stock; and, in his most public statement, a giant dollar-bill-green debt clock (figure 7.1)—computer-driven to handle the rapidity with which the debt was rising—placed high up on a nondescript building on 42nd Street and Sixth Avenue to broadcast his angst over the rising national debt.

Durst's reputation was that of a no-risk-taking builder. His dreams, however, once included developing a ten-tower office complex larger than Rockefeller Center on a five-block area in midtown west stretching from 42nd to 47th Streets between Sixth Avenue, Broadway,

7.1
Durst's Debt Clock in Times Square. (Courtesy Seymour B. Durst Old York Library at The Graduate Center of The City University of New York)

and Seventh Avenue. While he succeeded in assembling many parcels for his dream, in the early 1970s rising tax bills made them too expensive to hold, so some were sold. Hence, from either of his invested perspectives, property or philosophy, he stood staunchly opposed to the 42DP; he understood only too well that the project would frustrate building plans he had harbored since 1965 for the 42nd Street/Sixth Avenue block, and, at a minimum, would offer more competitively advantaged office space because Klein possessed the most favorable of the city's favorable tax deals for office development.[8]

The interests of the Milstein family, also long-established real estate developers in the city and owners of the Milford Plaza Hotel on Eighth Avenue between 44th and 45th Streets, differed from those of the Dursts: They wanted to participate in the project. In anticipation of being designated as mart developer and to preempt purchase by someone else, in the fall of 1983 they had purchased a 40,000-square-foot parcel of land on the southeast corner of Eighth Avenue and 42nd Street, after the city let lapse the option it had to acquire the site. In 1980 the city had been provided with an option to acquire this site for around $2 million, but chose not renew it, which would have cost between $200,000 or $250,000. Relative to its clear long-term stake in the 42DP and the small sum involved, the city's decision gives "a sense of how reluctant the public was to spend money in mid-Manhattan on development when the city hadn't repaired roads for almost a decade."[9] Unsuccessful bidders for both office and mart development rights in the project, the Milsteins brought at least four lawsuits.

Together, these seven vested economic interests accounted for 37, or 79 percent, of the 47 lawsuits challenging the project. All of the cases were dismissed, but one in which the court found a procedural defect in the *FEIS* technical analysis later reversed on appeal. A winner, the public sector nevertheless remained powerless to control the interminable delays and crippling loss of momentum brought about by so many, continuous lawsuits.

Missing from the list of litigants are the major civic organizations, in particular, the MAS. Watchdog over the city's physical environment, the MAS was no stranger to litigation, especially after its successful all-out legal battle to stop development at the Columbus Circle site. Its executive director, Kent Barwick, was a public personality of sorts, often speaking out on issues of aesthetic concern to the civic group. The decisive lesson coloring the attitude of the MAS about entering the Columbus Circle fray via litigation had been its disillusioning involvement with the 42DP. The group's elite board of directors had accepted Sturz's promise to start the planning and review process for a broad new land-use regulatory framework that would blanket the entire Times Square district, only to feel "burned and lied to."[10] Following this success with their Columbus Circle victory, it was still not too late to join with other litigants in opposition to the 42DP; but by this time the MAS was heavily involved in a lower-profile and ultimately successful effort to recast urban-design regulations for

Times Square, as discussed in chapter 8. Good chance that the MAS's decision to stay out of court on 42DP also turned on an internal issue of organizational politics, as well as a question of balance from an external perspective. In this sense, Barwick made a telling remark at the conclusion of the Columbus Circle fight. After the civic group, according to the *Times* reporter covering the story, agreed to drop the resolved charges in its lawsuit, leaving in limbo some legal issues that might have been resolved by the case; Barwick said that "a more radical institution might have fought this thing to the death. But there comes a point when one wants not to be perceived as pressing litigation just for the sake of delay."[11] Entering into another high-profile litigious arena so soon, especially when its modulated criticism of the 42DP at the BOE hearings signaled ambivalence, might have presented too much internal dissension for an organization known to have conflicting interests among board members who often split on issues of preservation versus development.

THREE ROUNDS OF LEGAL HARDBALL

The first round of cases, so-called "strike suits," numbered 27. These tested the 42DP's legitimacy as public policy. Two challenges based on First-Amendment rights brought by owners of the theaters and operators of stores selling sexually oriented materials were fairly specific to the project with its existing concentration of adult-entertainment uses. Seeking to stop or at least stall the project, other lawsuits filed during this intense two-year period challenged the "findings" of blight under the Eminent Domain Procedures Law (EDPL). Still others challenged the data studies of the project's anticipated environmental impacts under the State Environmental Quality Review Act (SEQRA). In a tactical maneuver, another environmental lawsuit brought by a coalition of activists, economic interests, and Clinton residents under the citizen-suit provision of the Clean Air Act, unsuccessfully aimed to expand standing by circumventing traditional requirements in order to have the case heard in federal court. UDC's judicial success in this round did more than validate the project's policy rationale; it clarified and confirmed the state corporation's expansive powers as a public developer. One decision in particular, *Waybro Corp. v. Board of Estimate*, broke significant new legal ground when it affirmed UDC's ability to override the city's community-based Uniform Land Use Review Procedure (ULURP), hitherto a substantive legal issue because the UDC statute was less than crystal clear on this point.

A second round of lawsuits filed after the lease agreements with TSCA had been signed attacked the project on a variety of procedural fronts. All three of these suits took aim at the public's financial deal with the developers. Opponents, notably a coalition of State Senator Franz S. Leichter, City Councilwoman Carol Greitzer, an area resident, the Times Square Boxing Club and the Dursts, filed suit claiming that the public notice of the "essential terms" of the leases had been defective; they sought full disclosure of the leases between the state and the developers.

Rosenthal & Rosenthal (and counsel) filed two other suits seeking documents pertaining to partnerships or stockholders. However much these lawsuits may have been prompted by the opposition's strategy of delay, by the nature of the complaint these actions also brought forth the issue of accountability in public-private deal making. From that perspective, the state Supreme Court's ruling for UDC in *Leichter v. N.Y.S. Urban Development Corporation*—which held that the UDC statute does not require release of the leases themselves and that "disclosure of the leases in final form would likely hinder negotiations and render the public input less effective"—granted legal recognition to what Vincent Tese, James P. Stuckey, and public officials took as a given—that full disclosure while the process was ongoing would have a chilling effect upon negotiations.

One of the most important episodes in the project spawned a third-round rash of lawsuits. This was the policy decision in mid-1987 to go forward with sequential development of the project. Instead of waiting for agreements on all of the project's sites, UDC and city officials decided to proceed with the eastern portion of the site—the four office towers—letting the western portion slide until a later time. Moving forward on all fronts at once—what Carl Weisbrod metaphorically termed "some sort of harmonic conversion" at a UDC board meeting to consider the amendment to the *GPP*, and what acting chairman William L. Mack jokingly quipped was "a new real estate term"—had always been deemed necessary, but, as events had proved, it was frustratingly elusive. Since the 1984 BOE approval of the project, a lot of discussion had taken place but no definitive private commitments for the "Western Front" of the project had materialized. Tishman Speyer Properties in partnership with Trammell Crow and Equitable had been designated as developers of the mart site, but by early 1987 it was fairly well known among UDC and PDC officials, if not publicly, that the Trammell Crow deal was not going to happen. Crow believed the deal was no longer economically feasible and backed out of the project shortly after. Executives from Tishman Speyer came to UDC and asked to do an office building instead. Tishman Speyer's proposal was within the scope of what the BOE had approved because a little-known provision in the 1984 resolution specifying use for "a wholesale merchandise mart and limited retail" also permitted a "change" in use of the site. Before any switch from mart to office use could take place, however, N.Y. Trade Mart, as the development partnership was known, would have to demonstrate that it had met certain criteria in the BOE deal—one of which was a $5-million spending hurdle for marketing of the mart project. Purportedly, this it could not do.

At about this time, though, representatives of the Kennedy family, owners of the internationally known Chicago Merchandise Mart, along with Chemical Bank's senior real estate professionals, came to UDC and PDC with a proposal for a mart/office building. "This created a lot of tension," recalled Stuckey. "No energies had been focused on this; we were totally focused on the lawsuits and getting the deal renegotiations with Park Tower completed. The focus began to switch."[12] The Kennedy deal was especially attractive to the city for two reasons. First, since it proposed retention of the site for mart use, any potential deal would remain within the BOE-approved terms and, therefore, would be politically easier than a change in use. Second, at a time when the city's economic predominance was being challenged repeatedly by corporate tenants departing the city for cheaper back-office space in New Jersey, Connecticut, and elsewhere, Chemical Bank, which at the time employed approximately 20,300 people and leased more than 3 million square feet of space in Manhattan, ranked high on any senior public official's corporate-retention wish list.

In the context of this set of events, Stuckey recalled, it became clear that they could only do the project in phases. Implementing the plan's ambitions for simultaneous development of the ten sites had become too complex. "The interests of the block were so diverse—hotel, mart, office." He believed that they really had no choice—that they faced a critical urgency "to get things done"—and that having the office towers under construction would end litigation. Opponents who thought litigation could delay the project indefinitely or kill it, he said, would have "no fuel for the fight—we wanted to take away the hope of delay by going ahead."[13] By creating an office-only focus, the change in timing of the condemnation would create a political problem, but, as Tese saw it, conditions made it "impractical" to do the project any other way. And he knew the state and city had a long-term commitment to the project, to getting it all done.[14]

The tactical decision to go forward with a phased development plan shrewdly preempted another potentially serious problem: competition among designated developers for major office tenants. A mart/office building combination or solo office building on Site 8, because of its especially large building footprint, would have been marketable to a broader range of corporate tenants than any of the proposed four towers TSCA could build on its relatively small sites. As explained in chapter 4, the mart deal approved by the BOE was economically disadvantaged compared to what had been approved for the four office sites. While for Stuckey the need to "show action" may have taken precedence in the decision making, not having to work though the economic conflicts of competing developer positions—which might mean reopening deals at the expense of getting the project moving—had to be appealing as a complementary motivation.

Since the original strategy for the project called for simultaneous condemnation, the *GPP* had to be amended to allow for sequential condemnation of the sites. Every such discretionary action, however, provides the predicate for a new round of litigation. That is why the public sector, as one insider noted, "tortures" each deal, in order to avoid going back for a formal review. In this instance, though, there was no way around this review. UDC carefully studied and prepared the necessary reviews of feasibility and a supplementary "Environmental Assessment" of the proposed modifications in the project, in particular, the change in the mart site. Public hearings on the amendments to the plan followed, then UDC board approval of the amendment as well as of the terms of the leases with TSCA, then review of the leases by the PACB. As soon as these procedural steps had been completed, the opposition entered into a third round of litigation, filing 13 new lawsuits within an 18-month period. "The things we were unhappy about weren't things you could sue about," Douglas Durst said later. "But we could sue about the fact that the Eighth Avenue part of the site was being abandoned."[15]

This round of litigation brought an interesting lawsuit by a different competitor, Lazard Realty, Inc., a real estate affiliate of the investment bank Lazard Frères and developer of the International Design Center of New York (IDCNY) in Queens, another city-state coalition project. Lazard Realty claimed that UDC's approval of the supplement to the *FEIS* did not examine the economic impact on IDCNY of the new use for Site 8. The challenge was procedural: The amendment permitting Site 8 to be used as a wholesale or interior furnishing mart, rather than a mart to computer or apparel use as originally contemplated in the *GPP*,[16] Lazard argued, was an "action" requiring de novo review under SEQRA. On a substantive basis, the investment-bank developer claimed that this change in use would have adverse effects on IDCNY and the Long Island City community.

Although the lawsuit had the potential to delay or halt the project, Lazard Realty legitimately objected that its economic interests in IDCNY—fostered through public assistance—would be negatively affected by the public sector's changes in the plan for the 42DP. Other delay-inspired suits similarly claimed that the modifications in the project triggered the need for another round of statutorily mandated reviews—new hearings and determination of findings pursuant to EDPL and a de novo EIS—as well as resubmission to the BOE for approval. The court found otherwise, in each case. In one quick dismissal—*Wilder v. N.Y.S. Urban Development Corporation*—the court found the changes to the *GPP* to be "minimal" and that requiring the project to go through de novo review because of legitimate modifications made to the plan as a result of changing business conditions as various legal challenges to the project wound their way through the courts would "be most inappropriate."[17] The *Wilder* plaintiffs also made the same "change in the use of the mart" claim as Lazard Realty had done only a few months earlier. Even though it had been litigated, the court reaffirmed its position that under SEQRA, no "consideration need be given to the remote effect that potential economic competition might have on an entirely different community located at a considerable distance [from the project]." After having won these round-three cases, finally, in May 1989, UDC successfully filed its condemnation petition for Sites 1, 3, 4, 10, and 12, and a portion of Site 6.

A STRATEGIC EFFORT

Even though the litigation was extensive, no one except Mayor Koch seemed willing to go so far as to openly, even in off-the-record interviews, call the suits "frivolous." The opposition assiduously avoided bringing frivolous litigation, one closely involved attorney noted, though sometimes it came close. More than one public-development official cited the legal papers of Durst's attorney, Gary Rosenberg, as "good," some even as "troublesome," reflecting the fact that he had a clear strategy mapped out for his client. A litigation attorney who managed the appeals section of the firm Rosenberg & Estis, P.C. he had cofounded in 1979, Rosenberg's track record included a successful precedent-setting appeals favorably affecting landlords under New York's rent control and rent stabilization laws. While many of the 42DP lawsuits argued "overlapping issues," Judge Stanley Parness, the judge assigned to these cases who had heard at least eight by early 1989, still saw that "at the bottom each has their own little nuance and you can't give them perfunctory treatment or apply 'stare decisis.'"[18] The delay tactics were obvious: Plaintiffs repeatedly brought newly framed legal challenges and filed multiple challenges—typically at the end of the time period allowed for bringing a lawsuit or filing an appeal. Continuous and repetitive, they became intensely frustrating to public officials—and to the state court as well. In one of several strongly worded opinions, Judge Parness addressed the obvious delay tactic by noting that allowing years of unsuccessful litigation to thwart the completion of the project "renders a baseless challenge as effective as a meritorious one in defeating public development projects and cannot be tolerated."[19]

Personalities and Tactics

Beginning in early 1988, project officials' frustration with the disruption of plans attributable to litigiousness opposition reached something of an emotional crescendo in the news media. Triggering the series of open, intermittent attacks lasting about a year was Seymour Durst's *Newsday* op-ed "Times Square: The Big Con." Voicing consistently strong objections to the 42DP, Durst asserted that the market forces that had brought about development of large office structures in midtown west in the decades before had been "temporarily disrupted" by "only inadequate policing of the areas." He also presented a self-interested claim that "The long unde-veloped block of 42nd Street between Seventh Avenue and the Avenue of the Americas ["his" block] . . . is itself being held hostage to the 42nd Street plan." Weisbrod, who had a professional's perspective on law enforcement from his six years as head of the OME, with Stuckey, offered a seasoned and sharp rebuttal titled "He's Got No Street Smarts," putting forth the rationale for a strong public-development role in the cleanup of West 42nd Street. The name-calling and emotional heat of the rhetoric reached another level when they wrote that leaving Times Square's future to private developers, as Durst had suggested, was "a rather frightening prospect." The next installment came with a diplomatically phrased letter from Mayor Koch to the editor of *Manhattan Lawyer* defending the city's major policy positions from the earliest days of the project; it was followed by a more caustic letter to the editor of that professional journal by the director of communications for the 42DP, who sharply contested bias in the reporting (to UDC's disfavor) about the latest round of lawsuits filed by opponents of the project.[20]

Though no stranger to the Times Square scene, Weisbrod was now in a new position of public leadership. Just ten months earlier, in May 1987, Governor Cuomo and Mayor Koch had appointed him president of UDC's subsidiary for the project, the 42nd Street Development Project, Inc. (42DP, Inc.). The career move shifted him to the state side of politics after more than ten years in city government. He was a protégé of Herb Sturz, and just prior to the 42DP position he had served as executive director of the CPC for three years. He knew the New York real estate market. A native New Yorker who went through the public schools in Queens, spent his undergraduate years at Cornell University's School of Industrial and Labor Relations, and got a law degree at NYU, Weisbrod journeyed the 1960s "caught up in the politics and social change of the decade."[21] He first went to work for Mobilization for Youth, a forerunner of the National Legal Services Corporation, representing squatters, welfare recipients, and other indigents before being recruited into city government by Mayor John V. Lindsay.

Weisbrod's earlier professional experience as head of the OME gave him an insider's view of the history of effort and limitations of law enforcement as a strategy for cleaning up West 42nd Street. He understood the 42DP's mission—intimately, so to speak—and brought to it a fine sense of nuance about the triangular interplay of planning, politics, and economics in redevelopment projects. "Policy is the product of planning and politics," he remarked later with years of perspective on the situation, so the question becomes, "how does the plan get implemented in a political context?"[22] At the time of his appointment, that political context had turned into a quagmire of litigation.

Weisbrod's appointment was greeted with favorable reviews from the *Times,* which earlier in the year had been using its editorial desk as a bully pulpit to redress the governor and mayor for their "flabby dedication to a project they used to brag about," so visible in their failure "even to agree on someone of suitable stature" to lead the 42DP. This was second time that the editors chided both officials for allowing the project to drift bereft of a strong leader, the first being after the departure in August 1984 of Lawrence F. Graham. Though "the antithesis of Mr. Moses in style," the *Times* editors wrote in earnest, he "has demonstrated the same doggedness in other important city positions" that "Robert Moses' presence gave Lincoln Center project in the face of opposition and complications." Weisbrod's mandate from the *Times* was to "carry the 42d Street project through the usual periods of doubt" and rekindle momentum—an ability that depended "above all on the stubborn commitment of the men he reports to, the Governor and the Mayor."[23]

Competent, diligent, and careful when it came to process, the 42-year-old Weisbrod cared about policy at the same time he understood the need for pragmatism. He was persistent. Later, in complaints about the agonizingly slow progress on West 42nd Street, some considered his persistence plodding, but the litigious demands of the project at the time called for his kind of tactical skill, personal patience, and political savvy.

He demonstrated "a terrific ability to mediate between the private and public sector," said Richard L. Schaffer, former CPC chairman under Mayor David N. Dinkins.[24] Though simultaneous condemnation had been the initial policy intent, the project's unwinding string of events put an ever-higher premium on moving forward; Weisbrod would cite the change in policy to sequential condemnation as one of the project's most significant episodes.

Employing strong rhetoric and reasoned argument in defense of the government's intervention to effect a cleanup, Weisbrod was an unwavering public advocate for the project: "42d Street is not just dangerous and menacing; it is also the breeding ground, launching pad and lair for predators who conduct their criminal activities over a broad swath of west midtown and Clinton." He had concluded that the street's "cavalcade of horrors" was impervious to change via traditional approaches of physical and social improvement—law enforcement, municipal service delivery, and economic development. Though progress in the Times Square area, especially Eighth Avenue, had been made during his tenure as head of the midtown enforcement effort, upon leaving office he remarked, "We haven't made a dent on 42d St." In a letter to the editor of the *Times* shortly after the announcement of his appointment as president of the 42DP, Inc., in response to State Senator Leichter's suggestion that the 42DP was unnecessary for the street's cleanup, he cited statistics of rising criminal complaints on West 42nd Street. To Durst's assertion that a revitalization would come as a natural evolution of the area, he challenged in return: "If Seymour Durst, one of the most experienced land assemblers in the city, can't put a site together in this neighborhood after more than a decade of trying, why does he insist someone else will be able to without government intervention?" That same year, in the PANYNJ's house journal *Portfolio*, he wrote the enforcement professional's lament about the block's continuing "frightening" crime statistics: 2,246 crimes (more than six a day), twenty percent of which were crimes of violence (murder, rape, robbery, or assault), and an additional 468 felonies reported in the Times Square subway complex. "Forth-Second Street connects more symbols of New York's preeminence as a world metropolis than any other street in the city." Weisbrod wanted to effectuate its "dramatic revival."[25]

Weisbrod's personal and professional frustration with the litigious quagmire emerged in a searing op-ed in the *Times* titled "42d Street Landlords: Greed Inc." The piece attacked the "small group of well-heeled property owners and operators who have maintained a stranglehold on 42d Street and its immediate environs for 50 years," not only for backing the self-styled activist-oriented "Committee to Reclaim Times Square," but for "engaging in a litigation conspiracy aimed at preventing the reclamation of what was—and should be again—New York's glorious street." Through their obvious delay-driven tactics, these opponents were committed, he charged, only to an apparent position of "business-as-usual-on-42d Street" so as to continue to reap financial rewards or "hope that delay will increase the value of their property before it is ultimately acquired by eminent domain." As to be expected, strong responses and counter-arguments appeared in the *Times* and the industry's *Real Estate Weekly*, which had reprinted the op-ed, by both proponents and opponents of the project: six elected representatives of the residents of the Times Square area speaking collectively; a community activist who had been party to several lawsuits; the chairman of the Shubert Organization; the Dursts; the Brandt Organization; a representative of Park Tower Realty; and the chairman of the Association for a Better New York, developer and civic leader Lewis Rudin.[26] The sides had hardened so over the years of intense litigation that no change in position was conceivable, nor even sought. It was pure posturing, New York style. The barbed restatements of position printed in widely read publications at the height of the project's troubled execution served as just one more indication of momentum lost since the project's approval by the BOE almost five years earlier.

In a 1984 editorial on the 42DP that appeared soon after BOE approval, the *Times* editors warned "The law's delay was deemed by Hamlet a fairly good reason for self-destruction, even before urban renewal. But as the sponsors of Westway and any number of projects have learned, it is a particularly powerful weapon in the cacophony of New York."[27] To wit, UDC may have viewed the extreme multiplicity of lawsuits as merely tactical attempts—"temporary roadblocks," Tese called them—to delay the condemnation petition from being filed, yet notwithstanding a virtually unbroken string of trial and appellate victories, nothing could be taken for granted. Publicly, UDC maintained an ever-ready optimism about its ultimate ability to prevail. Judging from the corporation's public announcements, it appeared to be only a matter of endurance: "Now [after the U.S. Supreme Court had refused to hear an appeal in an environmental-challenge lawsuit] the only place left for these plaintiffs to appeal is the International Court of Justice at The Hague," Tese quipped, "where, by the way, we would also expect to win."[28] The success of the lawsuits' delaying tactics were serious enough, however, for public officials to consider, in private, bringing something like a SLAPP against certain plaintiffs, though the idea was eventually discarded.

SLAPPs, or strategic lawsuits against public participation, are a means real estate developers use to silence critics of their proposed projects. Civil lawsuits filed against private citizens, they aim to push a project forward against strong public opposition. As such, SLAPPs often impede the First-Amendment rights of protestors, as deep-pocketed developers can use the court system to silence critics. State legislators have grappled with the problem of balancing the rights of developers seeking to defend themselves with the Constitutional rights to free speech and public protest. As a result, a number of states, including New York, have passed "anti-SLAPP" legislation in recent years intended to curb baseless lawsuits. In 1992, New York state passed the Citizens Participation Act, which effectively prevented developers from using the court system to silence the opposition. When city and state officials of the 42DP considered bringing a SLAPP in the late 1980s, no such legislation existed. From a tactical perspective, the ability to bring a SLAPP involves deep pockets and a willingness not to back down under pressure. For public officials facing seemingly endless lawsuits of dubious substantive basis, a SLAPP would not have worked as an intimidation tactic. Moreover, it would have extended litigation, something clearly not in the public sector's interest. And, without a doubt, it would have been politically risky.

Klein was frustrated too. At one point, the developer thought about taking out advertisements in the newspaper: "How many kids have been doped in x years the lawsuits have been tied up in the courts? How many tax dollars, tourist dollars [have been] lost?" In retrospect, he believes that the government would have been more strident if its money was at stake. They might have pressured the courts to move the decision. "Government power is persuasive," he said in an interview.[29]

Litigation-driven delay was an especially effective strategy of opposition in the case of the 42DP because under the terms of the agreement with TSCA, as long as there was "significant litigation" pending, the developers would not go forward with their posting of the key L/C necessary for the state to proceed with land acquisition. To do so would have been foolhardy. They could not secure financing for a project if it was being litigated; even if there is only a remote chance that the plaintiffs will win, banks are not going to lend the big sums required for an office tower. "They [the opposition] played it like a harp," Tese said years later in an interview, "pushed it to the limit, each action, then they would begin the next tactic."[30]

Well funded and patient, the opposition could afford to be persistent: It had the luxury of time on its side. Theirs was a effort strategic. Though the motives of activists and vested economic interests might not all be the same, delay would achieve the ends sought by each. Because real estate development is relentlessly a boom-and-bust business, all the opposition had to do was play the real estate cycle. Regardless of the legal outcome of the suits, delays can kill a project, either by an inability to line up prospective major tenants without a guaranteed date for occupancy, or by a lack of demand for new office space, typically, triggered by overbuilding and rising vacancies toward the end of the cycle. "If we can prevent things from happening for any given length of time, we may yet win, not on the merits but on accidents of economics," said Brendan Gill. The time was February 1989, and Gill's reasoning was on target with rapidly deteriorating conditions in the city's office market. "My dream is that if we had another year or so, people would say we don't want to invest several hundred million dollars in yet another office building."[31]

As a preservationist, Gill chaired the Landmarks Conservancy, which he helped found; as an early and ardent opponent of the 42DP, he founded the self-styled Committee to Reclaim Times Square—which sported an adaptation of the readily recognizable prohibition logo: a circle grouping of the four proposed towers crossed with a diagonal slash (figure 7.2)—and joined as a plaintiff in the Clean Air Act suit against the 42DP.[32]

Through his writings and actions, Gill sought vigorously to protect what he viewed as the architectural landscape of the city's greatness, and here he meant Manhattan as the part that stands symbolically for the whole: "hard-driving, short-tempered, romantic, and hazardous—it is New York City distilled and concentrated," as he put it.[33] In his *New Yorker* column "The Sky Line" he cautioned against the "hazards of bigness," the "malady of giantism," and the risks of what he termed Disneyitis, too much cuteness and sanitization in the physical environment. His losing battle to preserve Times Square and his winning battles for Grand Central and the Villard Houses, "each of these emerged out of his certainty," Paul Goldberger wrote, "that we preserve beloved architecture not to take us back into the past but to give us a richer, more resonant present."[34] The intense energy for his preservation battles came from a rock-hard belief that the city was endangered. The places most threatened were West 42nd Street and Columbus Circle.

7.2
Logo for the Committee to
Reclaim Times Square

He considered UDC's plan "grotesquely overscaled," "primarily a real-estate speculation play," a "conspiracy to take away the one sort of village green—open place—we have." He saw the "purported cleanup" as merely driving "the deplorable social evils" further north into the Theater District and west into Clinton: "The idea that you can solve profound sociological problems by building skyscrapers is transparently false," he said. "True that architecture has been the handmaiden of many cultural transformations throughout the course of history, but when has it ever proved capable of eradicating prostitution, petty thievery, and traffic in forbidden substances?" He hated the "exceptionally repellant" towers of Johnson/Burgee, inveighing against them all that he saw wrong with the city and state's commercial-cleanup approach for West 42nd Street: an attempt to turn this unique turf in midtown into a "three-piece-suit imitation of Rockefeller Center." The "remarkably open and airy space" and the bedazzlement and honky-tonk high spirits of the place were "about to be extinguished forever by an unbroken fortress wall on monstrous commercial structures. . . ." His argumentative brief lamented the irrevocable loss of Times Square as "truly a place of entertainment," which at times infused his witty words of criticism with an air of rhetorical romanticism. What "ought," what "*can*" ordinary citizens do? he asked. Go to court, he answered, do battle with "several inconveniently prolonged lawsuits."[35]

In May 1989 Durst challenged UDC's petition of condemnation for his "Toh" parcel, a 25-by-100.5-foot lot that was part of the most valuable of the four office sites. A last-ditch effort to throw yet another obstacle into the path of the 42DP, the legal brief asserted that the condemnation process was invalid. The public did not have the right to take the property, the argument went, when it was the private sector funding condemnation and not the public standing by, ready with its wallet open, to ensure "sure and certain compensation." The privatized-funding arrangement had never been used before; it was novel and untried. Under a conventional scenario, the only reason not to go forward with condemnation, once the petition had been filed, would be if the government "abandons" the project, not if the private developers who were funding the condemnation decide that going forward would be too expensive. The latter was a possibility in the case of the 42DP, Durst's attorney Rosenberg reasoned. The project might also come undone after vesting, when by law UDC would have to do another set of appraisals updating those done beforehand. What if after vesting the market really collapses and, before all parcels have been acquired, Prudential decides it could put no more money into the deal? The state and city would have the big $241-million L/C that the courts required TSCA to post, but where would the rest of the funds come from? TSCA might forfeit its rights to develop, and then the state, which would hold title, would have to figure out a way to complete funding the condemnation. With the collateral in hand, the public sector could sell parcels to fund the rest, if necessary. Hence, notwithstanding the PACB approval, it was possible to argue that the state and city were at risk, that landowners were not guaranteed "sure and certain" payments. The merits of this good-government type of argument fit well with the business benefits of stopping condemnation. No doubt the Dursts liked the way this legal appeal fit symmetrically with their ideological commitment to an unfettered marketplace, but from a calculating competitive perspective, the strategic objective was delay; if TSCA could be kept from getting a tenant, the Dursts would "win" even if they lost the lawsuit—their expectation—because no developer, even Prudential, Douglas Durst and Gary Rosenberg believed, would exercise the option to develop without a tenant. That was the endgame.[36]

A Set Trap

Litigious opposition was a relentless, costly headache for UDC. Litigation-driven delays begat the decision to go forward with sequential condemnation, which triggered an additional set of legal challenges. The delays cost the project its potential office tenants and effectively stalled office development until 1995, when, ironically, the Dursts were the first to build on the prime office site of the 42DP. And, in losing office development, the project could not proceed with the long-planned Times Square subway-station renovations, a real and indisputably significant loss for the public, as discussed in chapter 12. Extensive litigation also ran up a huge legal tab. One newspaper-reported estimate of approximately $4.2 million at the beginning of 1989 had most assuredly been exceeded by the time of condemnation two years later. The lease agreements spoke to the issue of litigation expenses, which when exceeding the specified cap would become part of the ESAC open tab; in the meantime, UDC's subsidiary for the project budgeted for the expense each year.

Litigation became a set trap for the 42DP. Every lawsuit had to be defended, even if it was without merit; public officials could not limit the filings. They could not push litigation along faster than the court-determined calendar for dealing with each individual complaint. They could not sidestep long, exhaustive processes of discovery pursued by plaintiffs or refuse to respond to continual FOIL requests for information.

They could not alter the procedural clock that set the time limits for challenging the validity of a government decision or filing an appeal for review by a higher court. They could not countersue or pursue any tactic other than to be competent and do their homework with diligence— "purposely crossing every *t* and dotting every *i*," as Tese said—to eliminate the chance that the opposition might "beat them" on some technical point, as had been the case with Westway. And, as proven time and time again, litigation did not need to be successful to delay a project almost indefinitely. "New York is one of the few places where litigation, and the threat of litigation, help determine strategy early on in the development process," Weisbrod remarked later.[37] From the start, the city and state entities implementing the project were captives of the legal process: they had to sit it out.

Sitting it out, however, was made even more intolerable by the city's private-funding strategy. In effect, the strategy handed over the timetable for condemnation to the private sector because its dollars were those at risk. If condemnation had been funded directly with city capital-budget funds, as was the case with the second and third condemnations for Site 7 and Site 8, respectively, would the public have gone ahead with condemnation even with significant litigation outstanding? Would public funding have altered the opposition's strategy and tactics in any material way? Might UDC have filed the petition for condemnation earlier? To 42DP officials like Rebecca Robertson, it would have depended, partly, on a determination of whether they would have won any pending or threatened litigation. The question gave Weisbrod pause; he had not considered the issue in those terms and was not sure whether the public sector would have gone ahead in the face of significant litigation.[38] The character of the private-funding arrangement, nevertheless, provided grist for legal challenges. Without the private-funding arrangement, as one anonymous insider put it, "the bottomless pit that is the public sector" would have been standing ready to fund all costs, and it is unlikely that the opposition would have been able to pursue delaying litigation through as many avenues as it did.

The power of litigation is political as well as legal. Continuous litigation keeps the media profile of a project couched in negative terms. Despite winning lawsuits, whether one at a time or in sets, as was the case with the 42DP, government is unable to move the project forward. Such inaction amounts to a test of government competence. Certainly, the haunting legacy of Westway—which Herb Sturz once called "a manhood question"[39] and which Vincent Tese asserted would have gone forward if UDC had been the lead agency, instead of the State Department of Transportation—was just that: a deep political need to prove that the city could still do a big project. As the *Times* editorial opined the day after the state had taken title to two-thirds of the project area: [40]

> The saga of 42d Street means something even more
> profound: It proves that New York has learned from its

costly mistakes how to Build Big. Westway, the proposed
highway on Manhattan's Hudson River shoreline, died
five years ago, a victim of litigation and naive, ill-coordi-
nated political leadership. By contrast, every official
involved in the 42d Street project, led by Gov. Mario
Cuomo and former Mayor Edward Koch, worked to
common purpose.

This is the kind of editorial every politician dreams of. It was to
be expected in this case, because the *Times* had a clear vested interest in
seeing West 42nd Street reclaimed and made into "a dazzling stretch of
urban life" once again. Still, that expectation in no way dimmed the political glory of the editors' praise. In the past the editors of the *Times* had not
withheld sharp criticism of the state and city's highest elected officials for
their failure to prevent the project from drifting into a "development
paralysis." In 1990, the next test of making the 42DP a reality turned on
economics and, as the *Times* editors emphasized, "It won't be easy, given
the troubled real estate market."[41]

MARKET MAYHEM

The *Times* voiced a conservative understatement echoed by the editors of
Newsday, for when UDC finally secured both the legal and financial
wherewithal to take title to nine of the 13 acres of the project area, the
timing could not have been worse. New York was in the midst of a protracted recession, its financial services industry especially hard hit. Leasing
activity mirrored the downward economic trajectory. To make space in a
newly constructed building economically attractive to big tenants, landlords were offering tenants substantial concession packages—temporary
benefits of significant periods of free rent and generous "work letters" for
finishes of interior space. Vacant office space in midtown Manhattan—the
city's largest office area, with more than 159 million square feet of prime
office space at the time—had been on a steady rise since 1985, and by
year-end 1989 the vacancy rate had reached 17.4 percent, a level not
experienced since the trough of the last real estate recession in 1975 (figure 7.3). Even more extreme conditions prevailed in midtown west, the
most intensely overbuilt submarket in the city. With nearly 3.5 million
square feet of additional Class A space in four large towers still under construction—only 9 percent of which was preleased to tenants—the soft
office market in Times Square could only get worse. By year-end 1990,
the vacancy rate in midtown west exceeded 33 percent, before accounting
for sublease vacancies.

Only the magnitude of the office-space glut could have surprised
seasoned real estate professionals who expected a construction boom in
midtown west and saw a bust in the making. City officials, to the extent they
were surprised by the magnitude of new construction, would have been
underestimating the power of zoning incentives to direct the path of com-

mercial development because the 1982 Midtown Zoning Resolution did exactly what it was intended to do—stimulate a lot of new construction in midtown west. The hyper-dynamic of the artificially stimulated market brought 13 new commercial developments—with more than 7.3 million square feet of new office space and over 2,100 hotel rooms—to the area north of Times Square (see figure 7.4 and table 7.2) in an intense two-year building boom that did not begin until early 1988. It was triggered by a rush to beat the "sunset" deadline for securing the 20-percent zoning bonus. Ironically, this date was Friday the 13th of May 1988.

The sunset provision reflected the experimental character of the zoning initiative. The talk at the time was that developers might be reluctant to take advantage of the new incentives. At the same time, the DCP staff worried that too much congestion could "result from long-continued development at exceptionally high density."[42] Given the magnitude of the bonus offered, the sunset provision also made the regulation more palatable politically. If permanent, securing approval for the policy initiative might have been much harder to get. The long-term effects on the development market would have been more unpredictable as well. Set to expire in six years, the sunset provision made it easier for city planners to predict which sites could be developed because the intricate land assemblages needed to develop large towers would most likely already be in place. Three conditions had to be met for a building to qualify for the 20-percent zoning bonus: plans approved by the city's Department of Buildings, finished excavation, and "substantial" completion of the foundation. As the sunset deadline approached, private developers faced the high-risk decision of whether to pull back from development of their sites and forego the special zoning bonus, or build on speculation and risk coming onto a hopelessly overbuilt market. Many went ahead.

While the massive scale of new construction in the relatively tight bounds of the Times Square district north of 42nd Street marked a policy success, the city's planning officials were hardly happy about its

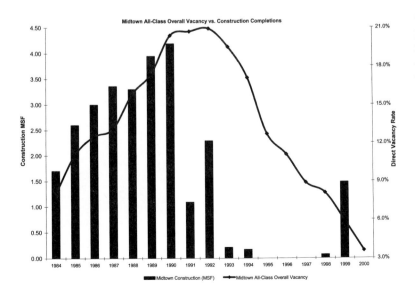

7.3
Profile of a volatile real estate market: vacancy rates in midtown Manhattan, 1984–2000. (Cushman & Wakefield Inc.)

TABLE 7.2 TIMES SQUARE: NEW COMMERCIAL BUILDINGS CONSTRUCTED 1980–1991
42ND STREET TO 52ND STREET, SIXTH AVENUE TO EIGHTH AVENUE

MAP KEY	BUILDING	SIZE (COMMERCIAL SF UNLESS OTHERWISE INDICATED	# STORIES	YEAR COMPLETED
1	Milford Plaza Hotel 700 Eighth Avenue	1,315 rooms	27	1980
2	The Novotel 1651 Broadway	800 rooms	25	1984
3	1155 Sixth Avenue	610,000	41	1984
4	Marriott Marquis Hotel 1535 Broadway	2,020 rooms	50	1985
5	Equitable Tower 787 Seventh Avenue	1,734,000	54	1985
6	830 Eighth Avenue	17,800	10	1986
7	1675 Broadway	752,000	35	1988
8	Worldwide Plaza 825 Eighth Avenue	1,600,000 625 units	49	1988
9	Tower 47 114 West 47th Street	575,000	26	1989
10	Tower 45 120 West 45th Street	432,000	40	1989
11	Holiday Inn-Crowne Plaza Hotel 1601 Broadway	756 rooms 200,000	46	1989
12	Hotel Macklow (Millennium Hotel) 145 West 44th Street	638 rooms 33,000/60,000 conference	52	1990
13	Embassy Suites Hotel (Doubletree Suites) 1568 Broadway	450 rooms	43	1990
14	Morgan Stanley Building 1585 Broadway	1,350,000	42	1990
15	Morgan Stanley Building 750 Seventh Avenue	580,000	36	1990
16	Bertelsmann Building 1540 Broadway	868,868 office 140,000 retail	44	1990
17	The Ritz Plaza 235 West 48th Street	413 units	40	1991
18	America's Tower 1177 Sixth Avenue	1,000,000	48	1991
19	Ramada Renaissance Hotel 1580 Broadway	300 rooms	25	1991

SOURCE: NYS UDC, *42DP: FSEIS*, January 1994, II.B-8, 9; Thomas J. Lueck, "Battling for Tenants in a Slow Market," *New York Times*, March 4, 1990.

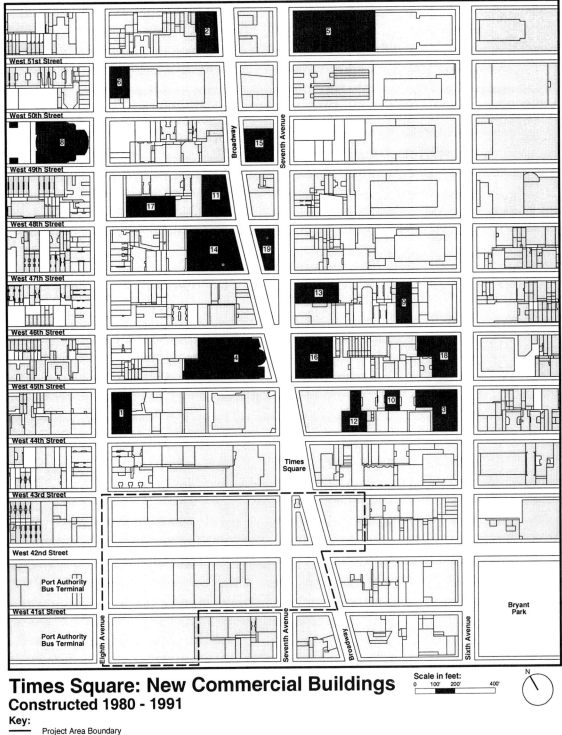

Times Square: New Commercial Buildings
Constructed 1980 - 1991

Scale in feet:
0   100'   200'   400'

N

Key:

— Project Area Boundary

3 New Building Designation

▪ New Buildings 1980 - 1991

▢ Existing Buildings in Midtown

Source: Sanborn Map Company,
New York State Urban Development Corporation,
New York City Development Corporation,
New York Department of City Planning.

7.4
What got built in Times Square during the boom.
(Morgan Fleming for the author)

short-term market impact. Planning goals for renewing Times Square were working at cross purposes: Overbuilding stimulated by the sunset-driven construction frenzy destroyed the handsome economic competitive advantage previously held by the TSCA office sites. The zoning-bonus sites in Times Square also carried subsidies—seven years of deferred property taxes from the city's as-of-right Industrial and Commercial Incentive Program (ICIP)—but the custom-tailored tax-abatement deals for the 42DP towers were vastly superior. The glut of space turned office leasing into a tenants' market. Effective rents on competitive buildings already in place but largely vacant were within the range of 65 percent of what TSCA would have to charge on a break-even basis, before accounting for additional tenant move-in costs. The situation was not economic, and the lack of profitability would press against the developers for a long time, by most analysts' projections. At this point, TSCA could do nothing to repair the damage caused by the litigation-driven delays. The volatile market dynamic was beyond its control—and beyond any set of further incentives the city might devise to move the project forward.

The handwriting on the wall appeared a year earlier, in Chemical Bank's well-publicized pullout as a possible anchor tenant in the project. After negotiating for nearly three years, Chemical finally was unable to see whether the office space would be ready for occupancy when the lease for its current headquarters' space, 1.6 million square feet at 277 Park Avenue, expired in 1994. Several factors had made the 42DP a highly attractive option for Chemical. The first was logistical; space in one of the project's giant towers would have permitted the banking giant to consolidate its administrative operations, then spread out in eight different locations, in a new building with modern mechanical and electrical systems. Second, moving crosstown to the West Side would have produced significant rental savings owing to the favorable tax terms of TSCA's deal with the city. Third, and perhaps most important to the dynamic, as one of the largest tenants in the city with more than 3 million square feet under lease contract, Chemical possessed tremendous negotiating leverage in an imbalanced bargaining situation favoring tenants. It could use the power of its position to press for highly favorable leasing rates, terms, and conditions; TSCA needed a major prime tenant for its development project more than Chemical needed it, as other options were still clearly open to the bank. Chemical was contemplating taking 850,000 square feet in the proposed mart/office building and an option on 1,000,000 square feet in one of the TSCA towers. The complexity of its proposed involvement—tenant in one of the office towers and joint-venture investor with the Kennedy family in the merchandise mart as well as tenant leasing space in the mart—only further compounded the profile of the deal risk for Chemical. After Chemical pulled out, the mart deal also collapsed and, with that, any hope for development of the hotel site across the street disappeared. The project's economic struts collapsed.[43]

In the context of rapidly deteriorating real estate fundamentals, it was not hard for the project's many persistent critics, even its friendly foes, to wonder aloud whether the 42DP had "made itself obsolete." Other well-known New York developers, such as Jerry I. Speyer, president and chief executive officer of Tishman Speyer Properties, had pulled back from proposed major projects in Times Square because of the high hurdle of getting tenants and the obvious development risk of going ahead on a speculative basis when so much space was coming on line at what was assumed to be a high price. And big office deals were falling apart. Where was the demand going to come from? real estate experts asked. Service-sector jobs were shrinking as Wall Street and the banking community underwent a painful restructuring process. When private projects suffer such life-threatening blows they get scaled back or scrapped, argued one influential journalist, using as a case in point Mortimer Zuckerman's much-protested plan for Columbus Circle and the loss of its prime tenant, Salomon Brothers, after the October 1987 stock-market crash. "But the overseers of the Times Square plan are not private," Sydney H. Schanberg wrote; "they are the state and city governments, which have been using tax dollars to drive it onward even though its original rationale has long since disappeared."[44] The all-important change in the perception of the area had already occurred, as newspaper coverage kept reminding readers with enthusiastic headlines ("A Bold, New Face Comes to W. Side"), special reports ("The Changing Face of the Great White Way"), editorials ("A Planner Faces Reality: Watching the West Side Change from Tawdry to Towering") and viewpoint pieces ("We Are on the Threshold of a New Times Square").

POLITICAL PERSISTENCE

From a planning perspective, several decisions and events had seriously weakened the rationale for massive public intervention—elimination of the project's initial strong design guidelines and absence of provisions for reno-vating the midblock theaters, followed by the lack of viable proposals and developer interest for the project's critical western end. When UDC's board amended the *GPP* in August 1987 to permit the start of property condemnation and acquisition in a "sequential process," the project formal-ly lost its balance in terms of public purpose. Simultaneous condemnation was important, politically as well as programmatically. While the change to sequential condemnation signaled a reluctant concession to the practical limits of implementing the complex $2.5-billion redevelopment project all at once, much more was now at stake. Without development along the full stretch of West 42nd Street, the singular, unambiguous, and official objec-tive of the project—for an indefinite future—was office development on the four sites spanning Broadway and Seventh Avenue. To many observers and critics this meant that the state was using its public power to do little more than assemble land for the private sector. Even George Klein—then the principal beneficiary of the change—was already on record for having said: "Our idea Day 1 was that the project works as a whole and not as a part." Richard A. Kahan voiced an opinion commonly shared in certain circles when he remarked: "It should have been an inviolate rule that you can't start the East Side of the project without the West Side."[45]

If a newly transformed Times Square prompted the question—why couldn't the market now pull West 42nd Street out of its social and economic quagmire without the massive 42DP?—it was not one city and state officials were asking, at least out loud. They simply did not see the changed market circumstances affecting the project from that perspective, for reasons both professional and political. For starters, the two top officials running the project day-to-day—Weisbrod, who had recently taken on broader responsibilities for city-wide economic development as Mayor Dinkins's newly appointed president of PDC and Robertson, who took over from Weisbrod as head of the 42DP subsidiary—were experienced professionals with deep-seated views on the efficacy of public intervention to achieve goals of city planning and urban design. Both did not believe the project could have gone ahead in any other way, though Weisbrod volunteered that he had thought hard about the question.[46] While the market context of Times Square had undergone a vast transformation over the past decade, gaining control of the West 42nd Street block with its balkanized ownership and complex layers of leasehold interests and operating businesses remained a jigsaw puzzle of land assembly: 56 parcels and 404 businesses fronting on West 42nd Street, to be precise. This was a key hurdle to comprehensive transformation of the street and the cleanup and elimination of all pornography, adult-entertainment shops, and low-life activities, the project's primary public purpose. "This is an area for runaways, pimps, prostitutes, drug dealing, all the sort of antisocial activities that have created a pox on this part of midtown. It needs radical surgery," Robertson explained in a 1992 interview. "You can't do it piecemeal."[47]

Weisbrod and Robertson were far from alone in believing that exercising the power of eminent domain for public development was the only way to ensure complete redevelopment of the block in a timely fashion, that is, as soon as practicable. The staying power of the city/state institutional coalition had proven its mettle in the unbroken string of legal victories and clearly worded court opinions repeatedly reaffirming UDC's actions. Ideologically, this strengthened the public's position; its condemnation powers were rock solid—a true complement to the deep financial resources of Prudential, which allowed the project to advance at a critical death juncture likely to have felled any other development project.

Politically, it was too late to turn back. Doing so would have been tantamount to admitting the failure of the public plan, and it was inconceivable that either the governor or the mayor would take that risk. The city, still haunted by Westway, desperately needed to show that it could once again accomplish big things. The 42DP had become a test of political will, as the *Times* forecast in 1984. There was just too much political capital at stake for both Cuomo and Koch to throw in the towel. This city initiative was birthed by Koch, and at critical passages or during project-threatening events he stepped into the foreground. With increasing vigor as the litigation filings continued, and in characteristically colorful language, he lambasted the project's critics; those critical of the 1987 amendments to the project plan, among them five Manhattan elected officials threatening to file suit, he reportedly called "cuckoos" and "dogs in the manger," ridiculing their suggestion that the amendments represented significant changes. In word and deed, "reclaiming Times Square from the smut, crime, pornography and child prostitution that currently permeate the area," as he put it, was one of his administration's top priorities—"the single-most-important development project for the City of New York"; it was a "great project because the whole world was looking at it.[48] Mayoral support held firm even after the 1990 change in administrations which brought to power David N. Dinkins, a well-established politician who was not known for his prodevelopment views.

Other than to quell the constant chorus of critics, who were, in fact, small in number and not part of Koch's primary constituency,[49] there was no political need to abandon the project. There was a need, though, to rethink how best to move it forward, and that need grew ever more pressing once businesses had been closed or relocated, tenants evicted, storefronts boarded up, and the theater marquees—those ever-vibrant reminders that West 42nd Street was movie mecca for action films, horror flicks, and grinders—removed (figure 7.5). Once the stores closed, pedestrian activity dropped dramatically. The street morphed into a desolate

7.5
Removal of the Liberty Theater marquee. (© 2001 Maggie Hopp)

7.6
"Post No Bills" Desolation on
West 42nd Street after UDC takes
possession of property, early 1990s.
(42nd Street Development
Project, Inc.)

strip, its vacant state an eerie reminder of its vibrant, then licentious, past:
"Midtown's Ghost Town on 42d Street" was how the *Times* framed one
news caption. Knowing that development was years away, public officials
privately harbored fears that the 42DP would become a "post-no-bills
project," the reference being to the absence of any activity other than the
ubiquitous signs put on every storefront after the state took possession of
the property (figures 7.6).

The collapse of Manhattan's real estate market altered the entire
dynamic of the project—for the better—though this was still a few years
off. The silver lining—recovery in the seeds of economic chaos—was little
recognized at the time. The watershed event was the sale, in March 1992,
of the recently completed but 100-percent vacant office tower at 1540
Broadway by Citicorp to Bertelsmann, A.G., the international media conglomerate, at a price equivalent to a 53 percent discount on the building's
defaulted mortgage—hard evidence of the precipitous drop in property
values and of how implausible new development had become, even if
heavily subsidized. The public understood that the litigiousness opposition
had "won." Delay did abort the high ambitions of the project and silence

its public advocates who could no longer present viable words of encouragement in the face of the market's dramatic deflation. But this was a near-term, temporary state. What the collapse of the market effectively allowed for was a conceptual rethinking of the project—a rare second chance for city planning. From an urban design, architectural, and planning perspective, this was a perversely positive outcome.

The saga of the 42DP's troubled execution reflected the fissured layers of a political struggle over a high-profile planning issue: whether the future of the Times Square district could be separated from the redevelopment of West 42nd Street. As a localized problem of physical planning, the 42nd Street controversy reflected a long-running tension between the low-density character of the theaters and their ever-increasing value as developable commercial real estate (figure 7.7). Were the theaters to be ornaments to the Times Square district or the roots of its attraction? The question epitomized the not-so-new fight between the civics and theater interests on one side and the city and real estate interests on the other over whether the change coming to Times Square would make the neighborhood merely an extension of the midtown office district or whether the change could be managed in such a way as to preserve the unique mix of uses that gave it such exuberant vitality. The neighborhood was a historic mélange of closely packed competing uses—highbrow and high-cost legitimate theaters; small-scale businesses servicing the Theater District's performers and producers; blue-collar pool halls and boxing clubs; low-brow movies and other inexpensive forms of entertainment; adult-entertainment activities; restaurants and nightclubs; electronics and jewelry and souvenir shops among other retail establishments; tourist hotels and office buildings. The legacy of its role as the city's entertainment center, of memory-laden theaters demolished for commercial development and of early misguided zoning initiatives directed toward theater preservation, all bequeathed a highly emotional charge to any form of policy-directed change. Implicitly and immediately, any planning vision of Times Square evoked the highly controversial issue of theater preservation.

At the level of citywide policy making, the impassioned distress over the excessive density of the 42DP office towers simultaneously raised a broader philosophical critique of the build-big direction city planning had taken during the Koch era. The excesses of big development were judged by the civics and other critics to be more egregious in those cases where the city, acting as public developer, appeared more greedy in its quest for financial returns than a private developer, showing no sense of the social costs of gigantic density. By the scale of its declared ambitions, the record-setting densities permitted for the four sites under the 42DP's specially drawn regulatory framework claimed the role of "Exhibit 1" in evidence that the city had lost all sense of planning ("Exhibit 2" being the sale of zoning for the Columbus Circle site). The blurring of the lines between what was the public sphere and what was the private sphere in these projects further contributed to the lack of accepted standards against which to evaluate the appropriateness of "public" behavior.

7.7
The low-rise theaters of West
42nd Street amid the high-rise
midtown business district. (© 2001
Maggie Hopp)

Last, at the political level, the battle over the future of Times Square and subsequent rescripting of the 42DP revealed a new-found influence for the theater-arts and entertainment community, led by the civics. Its role was not expansive in nature, just issue-based; nonetheless, this influence metamorphosed into the power to shape the development agenda. If as a part of its economic-development strategy the city sought to capitalize on its competitive advantage as the national capital of urban entertainment and international capital of live theater, the performing arts obviously were essential. For more than a decade, city and state officials had underestimated the strength of the public's attachment to the symbolic legacy of Broadway, believing as they did that a general disgust with long-festering conditions on West 42nd Street would supersede the highly influential voices of aesthetic criticism and questions about the project's programmatic wisdom—or at least provide a period of tolerance while they worked at getting all the elements of the project lined up. Yet way before the market collapse foreclosed development, that period of suspended disbelief was far gone. Now, giving substance to the rhetoric about new theater and entertainment on West 42nd Street was the yet-to-be declared imperative of the city and state's rescripted plan for renewal.

CHAPTER 8

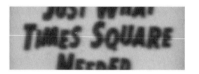

RESCRIPTING RENEWAL

A good-time place that belongs to everybody: democratic, freewheeling, hedonistic. A mix of high and low culture, theater, popular entertainment. An experience for consumers, tourists, families. An aesthetic cacophony of contradictory styles, scales and materials, honky-tonk diversity. Brash bold signage and glitz, unabashedly commercial. Crossroads of the World, an international trademark, an instantly recognizable brand.

These were the set pieces for rescripting the redevelopment of West 42nd Street. The belated task began in earnest in mid-1991, went public in the fall of 1992, then formally debuted in detail a year later. Defined first as "interim," *42nd Street Now!* put forth a dramatically different plan of programmed uses calculated to restore "New York's quintessential entertainment district"—without conceding an inch of ground over the office towers that would "continue to be a major part of the long-term redevelopment." "The focus of the renewed 42nd Street will be theaters and all that goes with them: restaurants and retail establishments related to entertainment and tourism. Once again 42nd Street will be able to take its rightful place among the world's great urban entertainment destinations."[1] In concept, visual imagery (figure 8.1) and language, the plan revealed a shift in values so clear and so startling that a level of disbelief and cautious skepticism accompanied the general enthusiasm with which it was greeted. After rumors of the Walt Disney Company's interest in restoring the New Amsterdam Theater as its New York venue for legitimate theater solidified into a hard financial commitment affirming the new entertainment focus for West 42nd Street, a cartoon by Arnoldo Franchioni in the *New Yorker* titled "Fantasy: The New Forty-Second Street?" captured the inescapable irony of such an improbable transformation of planning values (plate 4).

By 1991, the original plan for the 42DP could have been reasonably considered a "great planning disaster," as put forth by the British geographer and planner Peter Hall. *Great*, because at a projected sum of

8.1
The visual message of the second vision for a new 42nd Street. (© Robert A. M. Stern Architects)

$2.5 billion, this was the nation's largest redevelopment effort, and an enormous amount of money had already been spent on extensive predevelopment work, litigation proceedings, and condemnation awards. *Planning*, because the project involved processes of decision making affecting the physical environment. *Disaster*, because many people perceived the planning process to have gone seriously awry, particularly by the political benchmark established at the start by CPC chairman Herb Sturz: "The biggest risk we perceived was that the project would fail," he said, "that it would be one more articulated plan that would go nowhere."[2] To other observers, especially reporters, the "miscalculations in Times Square" evoked comparison with the failed massive-clearance model of urban renewal put forth aggressively by the federal government during the 1950s and 1960s and reinforced the lesson that "renewal needs more than bulldozers."[3]

The cleanup plan originally sought to make West 42nd Street safe for corporate investment by eliminating the deviant subculture of Times Square. Now the public sector was promoting a new set of values representative of its antithesis in program and design. This was not the first time New Yorkers witnessed such a radical shift in planning vision for a high-profile project, the 1979 reconfigured master plan for Battery Park City being a case in point. Nonetheless, it was a rare event. Unlike the lower Manhattan site, West 42nd Street was not an empty beachhead, but rather part of a congested urban district. What social and political forces influenced the shift in the agenda? How did they come to the fore amid high-profile controversy on turf as contested as Times Square, where long-time efforts to preserve and protect the Theater District had bequeathed a legacy of hostilities among competing factions? What made the timing so right, just when the whole plan for West 42nd Street had to be rethought?

AN INVERSION OF INFLUENCE

The context for promoting entertainment was not especially compelling. A serious recession affected the city economy. Broadway theater business was down, dismally, and the prognosis of its future was not favorable. Real estate interests, philosophically and economically aligned to the corporate-redevelopment strategy, opposed any kind of jazzy commercial aesthetic for the project. Consumed by litigation defense, the project's dedicated advocates—city and state officials at the 42DP, Inc., and EDC—could not function as catalysts for the values of the rescripted plan. Apart from the other major actors, and in a departure from its historic focus on the aesthetics of Beaux-Arts architecture, the Municipal Art Society, with the support of the theater community and other civics, set the stage for the entertainment-based agenda of the new 42DP plan with a tactical campaign aimed at changing the dialogue of planning.

The MAS was an unlikely advocate for glitz. From its founding in 1893 as an organization to advise the city fathers on aesthetic matters, the MAS set out to shift the focus of political debate from individual candidates to specific issues. "By reshaping the political landscape, it can win concessions from candidates of any political stripe," Kent Barwick, the MAS's influential president at the time, wrote in the introduction to Gregory Gilmartin's commissioned history of the society; its greatest achievement, he believed, was that "it introduced the laissez-faire city to a new sense of civicism."[4] A selective catalog published by the MAS to celebrate its first century of civic activism chronicled its achievements, noting "some urban amenities created or retained, some monstrosities avoided or mitigated, and a few mistakes make during the first 100 years of unprecedented urban growth and change." Speaking in the name of the "public interest," the society entered countless debates over the great plan of the city; the design of its municipal buildings, parks, and monuments; the preservation of its landmarks and historic districts; and the public responsibilities of private developers. It was an advocacy group sustained by the elites of the city, one that still exists, notwithstanding the greater diversity and broader base of its current membership. "It could never hope to impress a politician with the length of its membership roll nor could it present itself to Tammany Hall as a loyal constituency that deserved a reward," Gilmartin wrote of its early history with words that would ring true today. "It had access to the newspapers, however; it could criticize, praise, or recommend, and know that its words would find their way into print. . . . The Municipal Art Society soon discovered that in a place like New York, where power over the cityscape was fragmented or evanescent, an articulate voice would carry far."[5]

As an elite organization, the MAS was historically at odds with the values of popular culture. In one of its many struggling campaigns to make New York "an attractive city," the MAS had "won a reputation as the city's leading foe of outdoor advertisement." Billboards were considered visual pollution, a terrible blight on the public environment, and during the first decades of the twentieth century the MAS's dedication to an antibillboard campaign—the first in the nation, beginning in 1902—led the society to numerous tactics. Its members tried to ban sky signs, also known as roof-top billboards (unconstitutional), by controlling their height (willfully violated, unenforced by the city, overturned by state courts, which declared signage to be an aesthetic concern), by getting them taxed (politically dead-ended), and by shaming advertisers, who as Gilmartin noted, proved to be virtually shameless. When the "gaudy electric signs" in Times Square, which the MAS pictured as "the deepest circle of billboard hell," were briefly switched off to save coal during World War I, the society found "some grim satisfaction."[6] In 1918 the New York City Zoning Commission finally ruled that billboards were a "nonconforming" use in residential districts. The self-interest of other groups, in particular the Fifth Avenue Association, which feared that electric signs would spill out of Times Square where they had been allowed under the city's new zoning ordinance of 1916, succeeded in 1922 in getting the city's Board of Alderman to pass a law banning all "projecting and illuminating" signs on Fifth Avenue between Washington Square and 110th Street. Tight controls on signs everywhere around Times Square had the effect of intensifying the glitter and concentrating it in that one sanctioned area, where signage flourished. Even when Times Square was at the height of its glory before the depression, the elites of the MAS, Gilmartin reports, never appreciated the place: "Times Square stood for popular culture, bright lights, billboards, and the messy vitality of commercial culture—for everything the Beaux Arts aesthetes deplored."[7]

The MAS's new-found aesthetic vision centered on the whole Theater District identified with Times Square, an area of some 20-odd blocks (figure 8.2). Persuaded and guided by the influential architect Hugh Hardy, the MAS board sought to preserve the character of the district and, in particular, secure landmark status for the 44 "listed theaters"[8]—for cultural preservation more than architectural preservation. Its characterization of Times Square as an "entertainment district" swayed the City Planning Commission, which subsequently put in place far-reaching design guidelines for the district. It succeeded in no small part because of its ability to accommodate conflicting interests and strike a philosophical balance between preserving as much as possible of the past without precluding development in the future. Once leading individuals within its ranks became galvanized by a new understanding of the diverse vibrancy of the district, the MAS sought to assure its constituents that Times Square's symbolic role and visual character would continue despite the impending development projects and that entertainment activities would not be crowded out in the face of the inevitable expansion of the midtown office district.

During the years litigation kept the project tied up in the courts, Barwick fashioned a savvy media-attention-getting strategy to change the project's "corporate script," meaning a Sixth-Avenue blueprint for Times Square. Using high-profile public-relations tactics and advocacy of traditional land-use regulatory tools—zoning amendments and landmarks designations—the MAS staff scripted what its board members believed would be a reasonable framework within which growth could occur. Because the new regulatory prescriptions put forth by the DCP aroused controversy among different political interests, as was expected, the course of action was not smooth, nor was the outcome certain until the final vote of approval by the BOE.

What made the role of the MAS significant was the power achieved—not formally accorded or willingly given—by the civics and the performing-arts community. Both groups were principally concerned with the preservation of the Theater District, yet their actions came to shape the rescripting of the 42DP. With development shifting to the West Side as a consequence of the 1982 Midtown Zoning Resolution, left hanging was a fundamental issue of planning for midtown: how to accommodate that westward growth of office activity without jeopardizing the unique atmosphere of the Theater District. If the city aimed to capture perpetual economic benefits from the Theater District, resolving this issue meant ensuring the health of the theater industry, not just physically preserving the unique concentration of theaters. What policy prescriptions could mediate the tensions of these two seemingly disparate elements of the city's economic agenda and its cultural identity? How would political considerations play into their implementation? In the dialogue of planning, future zoning regulations and landmark designations would have to coalesce into the common purpose of supporting the development of a mixed-use district of office buildings, hotels, restaurants, theaters, night clubs, comedy venues, and other entertainments as well as ancillary businesses, despite the fact that mixed-use districts have been the exception rather than the rule in the United States.

The policy issue played out in two venues in Times Square, West 42nd Street and the Theater District, each led by a different team of players.[9] Both were politically charged and the focus of highly visible policy initiatives. The situation was choked with irony, however: By the time a collapsed real estate market forced the 42DP's planners to take up the rescripting task in 1991, the surrounding sphere of influence the project had sought to affect had, instead, become the progenitor of the "turnaround" project. This was the programmatic inversion of influence the civics had hoped to achieve. Nonetheless, it upended the conventional wisdom of redevelopment. Typically, an individual project is promoted on the argument that it generates broad-based economic and social benefits that "spill over" beyond the project area and accrue to the collective gain of the city. First, the site-specific project gets done; what follows are broad-based development dividends—which may fail to materialize or turn out to be less than expected. Just the opposite occurred in the case of the 42DP.

The confluence of the two ongoing policy initiatives meant that the innovative 1987 design guidelines for Times Square—born of controversy—imposed an alternative vision for West 42nd Street. This vision reflected a dramatic shift in values. This shift—from corporate business to popular culture—occurred at several levels: *visual*, through legitimization of Times Square's chaotic commercial aesthetic as the place-making character of the district; *land use*, through the belated recognition of the special mixed-use character of the district and the Broadway theaters' role as a tourist attraction and economic generator for the city economy; and *symbolic*, through preservation of the former Times Tower, a seemingly useless piece of real estate but a revered New York icon. From this emerged three planning themes: (1) a program of popular entertainment and legitimate theater uses, (2) site-specific design guidelines aimed at promoting glitz and reaffirming the historic role of Times Square as a public place, and (3) a financial strategy that employed the city's capital budget to acquire the remaining property on the block, thereby eliminating the last vestiges of adult entertainment on West 42nd Street. Together they addressed the problems posed by the collapse of the real estate market and the fortuitous opportunity it presented to replan the 42DP.

CHANGING THE DIALOGUE

It started out as a discrete public-improvement project focused on West 42nd Street, not a remake of the whole of Times Square. Other public-policy initiatives and private-development activities in midtown made the 42DP's planners face larger issues. Clearly, the increased density allowances of the 1982 Midtown Zoning Resolution would put pressure on the Theater District, which theater owners and preservationists alike agreed was irreplaceable. Both sides began calling for amendments and zoning changes the day after its approval. In recognition that more was to be done, Mayor Koch appointed a 14-person Theater Advisory Council (TAC) in the spring of 1982 after the politically costly demolition of the Helen Hayes, Morosco, and Bijou Theaters, and charged it with developing a set of recommendations on how best to safeguard Broadway's Theater District and preserve the remaining 44 legitimate theaters. TAC would meet 44 times before issuing its controversial report two years later. Wary of repeating the serious kerfuffle over theater demolition, the city's Landmarks Preservation Commission (LPC) surveyed every theater in midtown, including those that showed movies, to determine which should be preserved. After the requisite studies and public hearings, the LPC began a review of each theater, for interior as well as exterior designation—a highly controversial tack—and, in halting steps, ultimately granted landmark status to a total of 28 theaters. In addition, the CPC as part of its compromise with the MAS agreed, in principal, to reopen the planning for Times Square as a whole, a concession the MAS considered the "most important of all."[10] Thus, despite their start as two distinct initiatives, Times Square and West 42nd Street became "joined at the hip" by the aesthetic controversy over the proposed office towers for the 42DP and by the fact that the area was the focus of three related planning initiatives.

There was a notion among some MAS board members that planning for the whole of Times Square might be one way of confusing things, but the 45-person board[11] viewed its role in Times Square as "proposing zoning legislation which will preserve its character throughout the impending development."[12] Within months, a greater sense of urgency seized the MAS board—which had supported the 1982 Midtown Zoning

Resolution, but whose impact its members initially underestimated—to "become an aggressive proponent of a master plan for Times Square." The office district's move westward appeared inevitable: 27 "soft sites," large parcels ripe for development, had been identified; land prices were increasing; and substantial tax breaks were available from the city's new tax-abatement program.[13] Even if development proceeded slowly at first, it was obvious that the new skyscrapers were going to be "blockbusters."

Ominously, the Johnson/Burgee designs for the 42DP towers threatened to become a model for the entire district's reconstruction. As the MAS and other civic groups viewed the situation, at stake was nothing less than the permanent scale of the neighborhood, and the diverse character of its commercial uses and entertainment activities; these were economically fragile enterprises that could not afford the high rents in new buildings and would not survive a relocation. Because it feared a "Williamsburg, Virginia type of preservation," recalled architect and MAS director Paul Byard, the board considered it crucial to save the low-rent space in structures like the Brill Building. As the early headquarters for America's popular-music industry, the Brill Building, built in 1931, held symbolic significance; it was, as one historian noted, "a building that had a warren of small gyms and the offices of fight promoters and commission agents, in addition to demonstration rooms for vocalists, songwriters, pluggers, and others. . . ."[14] A hollow prospect haunted the MAS board: "The future may be preserved theaters with nothing around them to support them in a cultural sense, and our theater district could become a kind of Houston."[15]

When the detailed fabric of daily commerce was examined through this refracting lens of awareness, the MAS discovered another dimension of the district beyond the Broadway theater industry: the bars of Eighth Avenue thriving with middle-class black patrons, the lunchtime-frequented boxing clubs, the dwindling pool rooms, the ubiquitous movie theaters with first runs catering to low-income customers from all five boroughs, and the family-owned businesses and restaurants like the Grand Luncheonette—which grabbed its moment of national fame in *Taxi Driver* (1976)—whose longevity in Times Square made them neighborhood fixtures. Under the dedicated joint leadership of architect Hugh Hardy and landscape architect Nicholas Quennell, the MAS formed an Entertainment District Committee to spearhead the organization's new agenda for Times Square—to protect the "bowl of light" created by the low-density buildings that made up the bow-tie; to preserve the glitz of its commercial billboards and electronic signs; and to secure landmark status for its legitimate theaters (figure 8.2). The group worked "feverishly" to make progress on what the society's board minutes noted as "the three *s*'s: Size, Shape and Signage," while struggling with the larger issue of zoning. The committee was convinced, Hardy reported to the MAS board, "that if we clean up Times Square by tearing it all down and replacing it with office towers, we will be doing the wrong thing by eliminating the area's diversity."[16] A few months later, Hardy passionately reiterated the MAS's mission:[17]

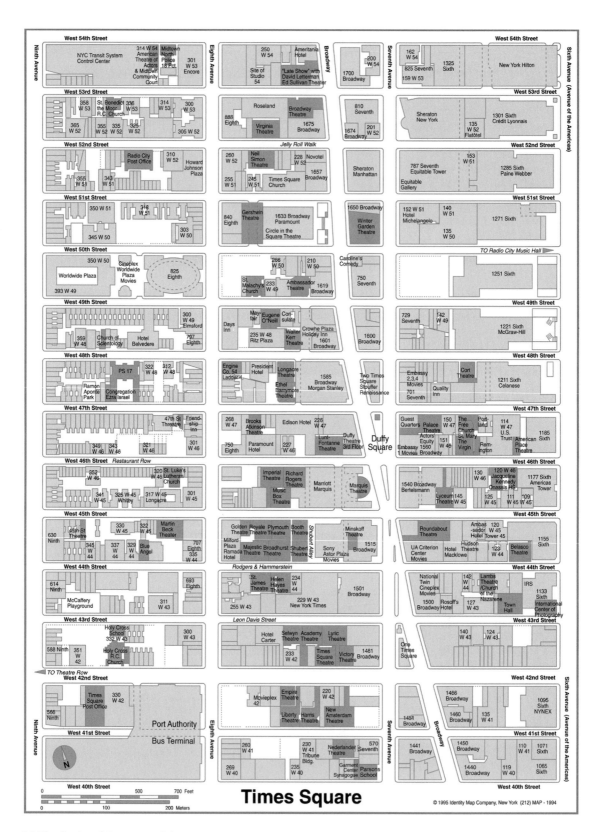

Times Square

© 1995 Identity Map Company, New York (212) MAP - 1994

8.2 The density of theaters remaining in Times Square, 1994. (Reprinted with permission, Identity Map Company, Inc.)

Times Square is overutilized and underappreciated. . . .
We [the Entertainment District Committee] have begun
to counter the argument that you have to abolish Times
Square in order to clean it up. We have become effective
in persuading people that if business continues as usual,
Times Square will disappear. We are making it clear that
we are not opposed to all development. We will address
the issue of density, how much and where. The shaping
of bulk is a primary consideration. In this regard, the
Portman Hotel (Marriott Marquis) has proved to be a
helpful ally by being an example of what not to do. We
will attempt to propose a way to approach our goals
through taxation and zoning rules and regulations, and
we will continue to promote our views zealously. We
will have to identify the coalition that will then go and
do our work. We have to convince interested parties that
they will have to cooperate or lose the neighborhood.

First and foremost, it was Hardy, principal of Hardy Holzman
Pfeiffer Associates, who championed the Times Square "character" issue
within the MAS. While others were fixed on the physical environment of
the district or the cultural significance of the theaters, for him the cause
was all about promoting public culture, theater in particular. "I though
people were missing a lot of what made Times Square the vibrant, diverse
area it was: the breadth of activity and popular culture that the district
attracted." The ancillary activities—voice trainers, instrument suppliers,
prop and costume makers, lighting specialists, makeup and set artists, book-
ing agents, talent brokers, publicists—that support the theater have always
been important, he stressed in an interview, to defining the character of
the Theater District.[18] Little of this might get preserved, but this image
was another form of romanticism about Times Square.

Hardy's infatuation with the city, theater, and Times Square in
particular, began early in his life, as a youngster whose romance with the
place can be traced, he said, to "that tender age when I used to sit alone in
the balcony of just about every theater in Times Square watching second-
run movies."[19] "A star-struck theater devotee from the days of his childhood," he started out as a young architect designing stage sets for designer
Jo Mielziner at the Vivian Beaumont Theater in the 1950s. "The 1950s
was a rare moment in entertainment history," he recalled, "when everybody identified with it, with the musical *Oklahoma!*" Theater came to
define not only his personal experiences and professional work—which by
the early 1980s included designs for the Dance Theater of Harlem, the
Joyce Theater, and the Brooklyn Academy of Music's Majestic Theater—
but his deeply held views on city life.[20]

Hardy and his fellow MAS board members, in particular Philip
Howard and Kent Barwick with staff member Darlene McCloud, set out
to change the public consciousness about Times Square. To convince an

unknowing and skeptical public that the lights, glitter, and tawdry character was worth preserving, Barwick staged PR stunts, developed effective
pamphlet literature, and deployed organizational tactics designed to make
the "character" issue a cause celebre. The board focused the staff's efforts
on what it believed to be the greatest strength of the organization, coalition building, since "The Society, operating by itself, cannot possibly make
any difference: our power comes from being able to spur action."[21] First,
as discussed earlier, it sponsored an international competition for the former Times Tower site in March of 1984, which "worked," Barwick said,
"because it was a prolonged public relations device. It got people talking
and asking questions."[22] To attract an even bigger audience likely to be
sympathetic to the cause, Barwick teamed up with Tama Starr, the third-
generation head of her family's Artkraft Strauss Sign Corporation, which
had built most of the famous Times Square signs, and other civics. On
Saturday evening the weekend before the first set of public hearings on
the 42DP, they staged a half-hour blackout of all signs at 7:30 P.M. The
idea was to surprise and stun the thousands of theatergoers bustling
through Times Square on the way to their 8:00 P.M. curtains, thereby
dramatizing the importance of signage and bright lights in Times Square—
what would be lost in a corporate-dominated redevelopment plan. For
maximum effect, they turned off all the signs, one by one, at two-second
intervals, so the television cameras could pan the spreading darkness from
south to north. The one sign deliberately left lit, the 20-foot-high-by-40-
foot-wide Spectacolor display on the former Times Tower flashed the message: "HEY, MR. MAYOR! IT'S DARK OUT HERE! HELP KEEP THE
BRIGHT LIGHTS IN TIMES SQUARE!" The hugely effective attention-
getting event—nothing like it had happened since World War II—was
repeated in November, on the eve of the BOE's final deliberation of the
42DP.[23]

 The next move may have been one of Hardy's most inspired
ideas to dramatize the case. In the summer of 1985, before the CPC hear-
ings on new planning controls for the Theater District scheduled for
September, he enlisted the aid of Peter Bosselman and his Simulation
Laboratory, or Sim Lab, to depict what would happen if the Theater
District were fully developed under existing zoning. Sim Lab's task was
to suggest an image of what might be possible in Times Square under
Hardy's "ideal world" of "revised zoning controls and stronger signage
and setback requirements." Bosselman, director of the Environmental
Simulation Laboratory in Berkeley, California, had developed Sim Lab
with a grant from the National Science Foundation to provide a realistic
"experience" of what a project would really look like *before* it was built by
moving through a three-dimensional model, and had tested it out with a
simulation of San Francisco's proposed Downtown Plan. The model was
judged to be influential, Hardy and others argued, because it had helped
citizens and civic decision makers understand the consequences of the
rezoning proposal. The effect in San Francisco, one member explained, was
one of horror at the impact on downtown. By applying the same simula-

8.3
Staging the drama of Times
Square's future with a 14-foot
model of Times Square and the
cast of *Big River* before the CPC
and at hearings before the Board
of Estimate. (Marilyn K. Yee, New
York Times)

tion techniques to Times Square, the MAS aimed to tell the city that they
"didn't want Sixth Avenue from river to river."[24]

 Bosselman developed a 16-foot model of every building along
Seventh Avenue and Broadway between 42nd and 53rd Streets, including
signs, billboards, cars, people, statues, and trees around the ticket booths on
Duffy Square, which was capable of portraying three worlds of Times
Square—existing, fully built out, and ideal. Accompanying the model was
a 12-minute film narrated by Jason Robards showing each development
scenario of Times Square from a pedestrian's viewpoint. The impact of
the model, first shown publicly at the CPC hearings—with the cast of the
musical *Big River* for live-entertainment backup—was immediate (figure
8.3). "The dramatic change in scale dazzled the eyes of designers, planners,
and nonprofessionals alike," Bosselman wrote later.[25] Apparently fascinated
by the model's vivid impression of the neighborhood and the alternative
transformations that awaited it, the commissioners subsequently came to
speak of Times Square as an "Entertainment District." Though admittedly
modest, this acknowledgment of the neighborhood's unique role in New
York marked the MAS's first tangible triumph. The change in language in
official circles, Barwick noted in a mood of self-congratulation at a board
meeting, was what changed the argument.[26]

 After viewing the model, an impressed Paul Goldberger led off
his architectural review in the *Times* with the provocative title "Will Times
Square Become a Grand Canyon?" In this article, Goldberger attacked the
city's zoning incentives and policies:[27]

> The light, the energy, the sense of contained chaos that
> have long characterized Times Square are essentially
> incompatible with high-rise office buildings, or with
> stark and harsh modern hotel towers like the Marriott.
> It has been clear since the first of these towers went up
> in this part of town more than 15 years ago: these build-
> ings do not fit. They do not reflect the character of

Times Square and the theater district; they squash it, as firmly as a shoe might flatten an ant.

The Times Square Sim Lab model was a stunning success. Astutely, Hardy and his committee and Barwick had reasoned through how best to use the model, how its message would be received, and what impact it could have on the policy debate. The group wanted to show a lot of affordable signage, the necessity of the "bowl of light"—air space and a view of the sky (figures 8.4a,b,c). It had studied the 1916 Zoning Ordinance, which had been developed with light and air as guiding principles. But as one director remarked, "It doesn't do much good to tell someone who is 25 years old that the 1916 zoning was better. Millions of square feet of typists makes theater-related uses impossible."[28] The model proved to be tactically important because it could convey the significance of FAR in lay terms, without the use of abstract concepts. The MAS leaders used it to take a positive position of what should be there rather than coming out with negative messages about FAR targeting developers, which, Byard stressed at one meeting, from a political perspective, would more likely be perceived as an impossible posture by city policy makers and politicians. From the start they saw the Sim Lab model as a device around which a strong PR campaign could be mounted, and they craftily used the model to promote the society's ideal vision with a choreographed plan of heavy press and media coverage and presentations of the model and the film to the theater unions, all of their professional associates, and the city's other civic organizations. "If you are opening an exhibit on Times Square in the middle of August," advised Jacqueline Kennedy Onassis, who was among those who early on believed that the proposed plan for the 42DP would sterilize Times Square, "and you hope to change the results of anything, it would be wise to plan on generating a barrage of publicity."[29]

Other PR events followed: the inaugural of the new Canon sign with its three miles of neon (November 1985); a *Times* op-ed titled "Times Square's Last Rites" (June 1986) by Philip K. Howard, long-time active MAS director and corporate lawyer who was later elected chairman of the society; and the creation of the Broadway-star-studded "Committee to Keep Times Square Alive" to support the cause and raise voices at public hearings. One such event, a press conference, occurred on the front steps of city hall the day the BOE met to vote on the new design rules mandating signs, lights, and setbacks in Times Square, which the MAS had worked so diligently to birth (January 1987). There were exhibitions on Times Square at the society's Urban Center headquarters on Madison Avenue at 51st Street[30] and a presentation of a Certificate of Merit to Artkraft Strauss (June 1987) "for delighting millions over many decades with extravagant sign displays that wrap Times Square in ribbons of light and color, and for bringing glamour and glitter to the nation's New Year's Eve for the past eighty years by dropping the lighted ball on top of the Times Tower."[31]

a

b

8.4
Bowl of light images over time: a) View north, 1911;
b) Times Square in the rain, view north, 1940s; c)
View north, mid-1980s. (Underhill Foto; © Lou
Stoumen Trust, photograph courtesy of the Barry
Singer Gallery, Petaluma, Calif.; Don Rice, Courtesy
Seymour B. Durst Old York Library at The Graduate
Center of The City University of New York)

c

All of these events were opportunities for the MAS to get its message across, to educate the public as to what the organization was trying to do, which, though not inconsistent with the discarded Cooper-Eckstut design guidelines for the 42DP, was diametrically opposed to the city's current program for the project. Even after the new Times Square design regulations had been legislated into law in February 1987, Barwick pointed out the necessity of continued vigilance. He felt not only that developers might try to elude the legislation, but that the work was far from done: Two other key items on the city's planning agenda for Times Square—rezoning and landmark designations—were still to be decided later that year. The MAS needed to mobilize its constituency, get out in front of its issue, and stay there. It would be the "Passionate Minority," to borrow a term from Anthony Downs.

If the issue of signage struck a dissonant chord with the aesthetic legacy of the MAS, protecting the physical and cultural character of a prized city neighborhood, even Times Square, fit squarely within its organizational mandate to preserve the best attributes of the city's civic appearance, especially after the city passed a Landmarks Preservation Law in 1965. Since the 1950s the MAS had seen its role as erecting a scholarly foundation for the preservation movement; its record of activism in the early days of that movement when lots of glorious buildings in New York fell victim to the wrecker's ball, was mixed. The genesis and character of the society imparted a conservative bent that worked against aggressive advocacy, so its support in several key cases turned out to be too late. Also, the need to avoid outright controversy within the board room lest it cause a split within its own ranks, as was the case in the society's reluctance to come out against the 42DP before the BOE in 1984. In short, the MAS was not always a forerunner in high-profile land-use controversies. But as the campaign to save the character of Times Square revealed, slow entry into the fray did not diminish its ultimate impact.

DEFT IMPLEMENTATION

Having gotten the character issue on the CPC's agenda, it was the task of the DCP, as secretariat to the commission, to develop a design-regulation plan for Times Square, first by identifying those elements that gave Times Square its special character and translating them into technical standards; and second, by drafting regulations that, once approved, would become part of the city's zoning law.

The intent of the design controls was to "ensure that the unique and valuable sense of place of Times Square will be retained and nurtured as new development occurs." Signs and lights, openness and brightness, intense ground-level activity, and entertainment-related uses, "a chaotic liveliness" as Sturz termed it, were the direct concerns of the planners. Yet it was also the case, by interpretation, that the design controls were meant to deal with the negative effects new construction brought about by the 1982 Midtown Zoning Resolution was imposing on the fragile fabric of

Times Square. By implication, the urban-design controls would have to resolve the conflict between the city's efforts to stimulate westward expansion of high-rent corporate-style office buildings and protect the Times Square theater economy and legacy. They would need to ensure the district's identity as a flashy and flamboyant, electrically charged entertainment center—The Great White Way. If on the surface Times Square appeared aged and ill, underneath it possessed neighborhood vitality, kinetic energy, and unusual diversity. Planners could learn from studies of Shibuya and Shinjuku in Tokyo, Piccadilly Circus in London, Kowloon in Hong Kong, and the Strip in Las Vegas, but signage preservation was unprecedented, at least in New York.[32] The act of legislating for chaotic, rambunctious diversity—gaudy bad taste to some—was counterintuitive, certainly ironic, as an objective of city planning. Moreover, the truly vexing problems were how to mandate diversity and how to encourage by legislation an environment that had evolved through the spontaneous actions of competitors trying to outshine one another.

The substantive planning work, initially carried out in the spring and summer of 1985 with updates stretching over 18 months, occupied a team of five planners, including the director of the Manhattan office of the DCP, Con Howe, who in May 1987 was appointed executive director of the whole department. The agency also hired several experts as consultants to assist in the process, including Jules Fisher & Paul Marantz Inc. (lighting), Mayers & Schiff Associates, P.C. (streetscape), and Halcyon Corporation (retailing). The process involved detailed study of the neighborhood's signs and lighting, street-wall heights, building-envelope configurations, ground-floor uses, and district-use patterns, on a bloc-by-block basis. From these results, DCP staff identified "prototypical blocks" characteristic of Times Square and used them as a template for developing closely matching design controls that could function as "as-of-right" zoning regulations applicable to all future developments. The key blocks on Broadway and Seventh Avenues ran between 46th and 47th Streets and between 44th and 45th Streets (figures 8.5, 8.6). The three levels of illuminated signs that the planners mandated—ground-floor small-scale retail signs, mid-level business signs, and higher-up "super-signs"—were based on the finding that the signs themselves functioned as architecture defining the sense of place in Times Square. Taking advantage of the low density of the buildings and low land values during the 1950s and 1960s, sign structures had come to dominate the area; the "low street walls provided elevated platforms on which spectacular super-signs are arrayed in varying geometries to maximize visibility."[33] They also reinforced the scale of the protected legitimate theaters.

Because the planners set out to maintain the *visual* character of Times Square, it was critical to preserve the low building wall of the district, especially in the bow-tie area. The new controls mandated street-wall heights and required substantial building setbacks above those elevations. Although a less flashy design element than signs, setbacks would be the essential tool for preserving some semblance of the "bowl of light." Signs

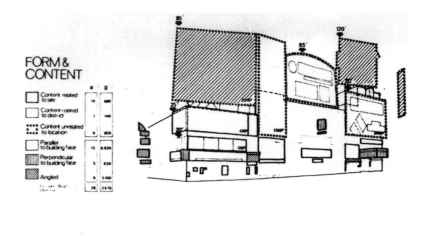

FORM &
CONTENT

	#	①
☐ Content related to site	18	680
☐ Content related to district	1	140
∷ Content unrelated to location	6	850
☐ Parallel to building face	15	6,920
▦ Perpendicular to building face	5	850
▨ Angled	6	5,100
	26	2,670

LIGHTING &
DYNAMICS

	#'	①'
☐ Fixed		
▨ Animated	11	1,290
∷ Traveling		
☐ Day only	#'	①'
■ Brightly-lit openings	4	760
☐ Flood-lit	11	8,910
■ Back-lit	17	2,340
■ Exposed neon	8	600
☐ Exposed incandescent	8	570
☐ Message	1	250
	49	13,430

TOTAL SIGN
AREA | 15,550 ① |

BROADWAY
46 to 47 STS. West

8.5
Prototype block for urban-design analysis of signage and lighting in Times Square, west side of Broadway between 46th and 47th Streets. (NYC Department of City Planning)

come and go depending upon prevailing advertising trends; in periods of economic strength—when they are not prohibited in a district—signs appear in response to a market, spontaneously, as was the case historically in Times Square. In contrast, setbacks create the space and light for the placement of signs; they are the physical framework for ensuring long-term visibility of signs. The mandated building setbacks for Times Square would be much greater than in other parts of the city—over 50 feet above a 50-to-60-foot street wall (about four stories up), compared with a typical setback of 10 feet above 150 feet elsewhere.

8.6
The prototypical block of
Broadway between 46th and 47th
Streets, 2001. (Gary Hack)

Development sites in this area were large, so the DCP staff
believed the big setback would not constrain development. Accommodating office buildings presented less of a problem than hotels, though.
"The signage requirements are O.K. for hotels but not for office buildings,
and the setback requirements are O.K. for office buildings but not for
hotels," remarked Alan Lapidus, an architect who in a year-long dialogue
with the DCP redesigned a hotel for William Zeckendorf, Jr., on the site
of the neighborhood's premier pornographic movie locale, the Pussycat
Lounge and Cinema, to conform with the proposed standards.[34] The
DCP did not want the new design controls to create a bias against hotels
that would lead to an all-office-building district, so the staff listened carefully to the hotel developers who came in with problems asking questions
about how the regulations would affect their building plans. "We had, in
effect, a laboratory for trying untried new concepts—letting developers
know the kinds of regulations we were thinking about," recalled Geoffrey
Baker, who was part of the urban-design team.[35] The process allowed
them to "fine tune" some items; in the case of setbacks, to provide for
alternative "envelope controls," which had the extra benefit of potentially
increasing the openness of street corners.

Packed into eight dense pages of zoning text in sections ZR81-
832 and ZR81-85, the special Times Square signage, street-wall, and setback requirements were specific and inclusive. The controls over signs, for
example, mandated minimum areas, numbers, sizes, and types, controlled
their placement and orientation, and set technical standards for brightness,
animation, and illumination. To clarify the requirements for illumination,
in an amendment staff had to invent a measurement system known as
"Light Unit Times Square" (LUTS) (figure 8.7). The planners tried to
reflect a sensitivity to the place-making ambience of Times Square without dictating specific solutions or styles. Unlike preservationists, they did
not seek to freeze Times Square as it was; they considered change a part of
the neighborhood's dynamic character. To accommodate "diversity, variety

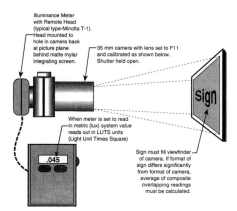

Illuminance Meter
with Remote Head
(typical type-Minolta T-1).
Head mounted to
hole in camera back
at picture plane
behind matte mylar
integrating screen.

35 mm camera with lens set to F11
and calibrated as shown below.
Shutter held open.

When meter is set to read
in metric (lux) system value
reads out in LUTS units
(Light Unit Times Square)

sign

.045

Sign must fill viewfinder
of camera. If format of
sign differs significantly
from format of camera,
average of composite
overlapping readings
must be calculated.

8.7
LUTS (Light Unit Times Square)
Meter, the sign brightness meas-
urement system invented for
Times Square. (NYC Department
of City Planning)

and change," as well as ensure flexibility, the new design regulations, written as performance standards, granted "freedom in the design of signs and
permitted both existing sign types and new technologies." The goal was to
"put the opportunities and responsibilities of interpretation squarely on
the shoulders of the architects and designers of the new Times Square
buildings."[36]

The invention embedded in the groundbreaking regulations for
signage contained things new, things old, things borrowed, things adapted.
The planners were starting from ground zero. The 1981 "Final Report of
the DCP Midtown Development Project" had included a brief passage
acknowledging signage as a special feature of Times Square, yet in keeping
with the corporate-image perspective of that document, it proposed regulations "to control exterior signs, pennants, and displays at grade level
which at the present time give existing shops a blighted, cluttered and
unattractive appearance." The 1982 Midtown Zoning Resolution included
for the first time a mandate for lighted supersigns on all new developments fronting Times Square, from 43rd to 48th Streets, but in keeping
with the thrust of the earlier report's proposal, the zoning text changes
went only so far as to "simply and clarify regulations for signs, store windows, banners and canopies in the Theater Subdistrict."[37]

While the supersign mandate was a step in the right direction,
Howe would later say that these regulations were "hopelessly inadequate."[38] Certainly, no attempt had been made to promote chaotic signage. Hence, while the DCP, MAS, and other friends of the cause were
committed to maintaining "the glow," as Tama Starr and Edward Hayman
described the situation, "nobody knew quite how to go about it. Everyone
knew what a spectacular was when they saw one, but nobody had ever
tried to define the concept before. And zoning regulations, like other laws,
are completely definition-dependent. It was our job to pass them the
ammunition."[39] The task belonged to Artkraff Strauss's Mel Starr, who
defined the essential qualities of a spectacular—which did not depend
solely on size and visibility—in a three-page document widely distributed
among sign allies. The character of a "spectacular," he wrote, came from
having at least three of four other characteristics: light quality, animation,
color and contrast, and extra-dimensional effects. Behind his words was

the experience of a century-old company that had built most of the Times Square spectaculars; that experience formed the basis, Starr and Hayman claimed, not only of the new Times Square sign controls, but also of the sign portion of the design controls governing the rescripted 42DP.

Not everyone was so literal in pursuing the task. The well-known lighting designer Paul Marantz reportedly was on a mission of cultural subversion. He too did not want the neighborhood to be transformed by the professional class, and he too used his expertise to alter the mind-set of planners. By juxtaposing outrageous visual messages flashing words like BEEP, FAST CARS, SEXY MUSIC into the sky against sober commercial towers filled with broadcloth-suited lawyers, bankers, and brokers, he aimed to create a shocking environment that would transform buttoned-up white-collar workers as they left their elegant, restrained offices. "If we have just neat little banker-approved signs, it will be a travesty," he warned. "Unless the culture changes to something like what you have in Tokyo, where it is perfectly acceptable for a lawyer to have his office behind a hot-pink lingerie sign, it's all meaningless."[40] Marantz's sense of humor is such that he wanted to name the new regulatory light unit LUST rather than LUTS.[41]

In the end, development of the new design controls was an iterative process, with feedback from the consultants the DCP had hired, the Times Square Advisory (Bow-Tie) Committee, community boards, and other interest groups who got early briefings on the work. The credibility of the regulations flowed from the professionalism of the DCP staff and the quality of the outside experts supporting that work, work widely viewed as well thought out, skillful, and sensitive. Credibility was essential to the cause, not only because of the high visibility of the initiative, but because opposition to the regulations, principally from developers, was a given, as was the threat of litigation. If the law forced economic penalties on property owners in an arbitrary and capricious manner, it would be susceptible to successful legal challenge.

In a city that has long defined itself by real estate, developers are a highly influential interest group. They are major contributors to the campaign chests of mayors (incumbents and hopefuls), city council members, and, before 1990, members of the BOE—formerly, the key decision-making body (other than the mayor) with respect to zoning variances, tax abatements, leases of city property, the city's own building plans, and the city budget—and local political organizations; their dollars typically lead to top rankings on the donor lists.[42] The networks between elected officials and real estate developers are broad and deep and extend through city-wide real estate organizations such as the Real Estate Board of New York (REBNY) and issue-specific organizations such as the Rent Stabilization Association; through industry-led coalitions like the Alliance for Downtown New York; and through the city's many Business Improvement Districts. "Whoever the mayor is, they want that person to succeed," remarked former Mayor Koch. "I knew I could call on all these people, and I always did."[43]

The established real estate families—the Rudins, Dursts, Roses, Fishers, Speyers, Tishmans, and Resnicks—exercise behind-the-scenes clout. They maintain a low-profile but exert a strong presence and represent an understated permanence. The scions of these families "inherited political networks that had been laboriously built by their fathers with local and citywide political parties, politicians, and elected officials."[44] In the mid-1980s, though they were being challenged by younger, more brash developers from other cities and big foreign players seeking to expand into the United States, it would have been premature to conclude from that boom-period interlude that their influence was fading. "With a few additions and subtractions, these are the same families that dominated the city's real-estate market 40 years ago," wrote David Samuels. "They have survived the assaults of the big insurance companies of the 60's, the near-bankruptcy of the city in the 70's, the entry into the market in the 80's of well-capitalized foreign giants like Sumitomo and Ladbroke and Olympia & York. They have expanded their fortunes as *arriviste* competitors have come and gone. They are as close to a stable ruling class as New York has enjoyed since the beginning of the century, when Manhattan was owned by the Astors and the Rhinelanders. . . ." Likewise, a *Wall Street Journal* reporter called them "Princes of the City." They serve on boards of hospitals, universities, and civic institutions, be it the association for a Better New York chaired by Lewis Rudin whose father helped found the group, the New York City Partnership, or the Citizens Budget Commission. They are often a leading voice for economic development, in general, and infrastructure investment in mass transit, roads, parks, schools, in particular. Leadership in the MAS, though, is usually not part of their biographical profiles.

Real estate has obvious clout because the property tax is the largest single source of revenue for New York—though a much smaller proportion than in any other big American city because scale, powerful unions, and liberal preferences have combined over time to create huge demands on the city treasury that can only be satisfied with broad and diverse sources of funds. But the political influence of real estate, and in particular the real estate families, comes from dynastic savvy, conservative bedrock presence, and wealth. Their influence in the city has prevailed in good times and in bad, the city's 1975 fiscal crisis being the most notable, when they helped the city secure loan guarantees from Congress and prepaid hundreds of millions of dollars in property taxes, as did other major real estate taxpayers. During that crisis, a strong public-private coalition formed; under Mayor Koch, it was fed by specific policies that granted tax abatements and increases in square footage to private developers. "By the end of the 1970s and on into the next decade, the real estate interests reemerged to take command of Manhattan's central business district," political scientist Jewel Bellush wrote in a review of the city's pressure groups and their influence on the political process that updated the classic work of Wallace Sayre and Herbert Kaufman and their colleagues Robert Dahl and Edward C. Banfield.[45]

During the process of formulating the new design controls there were two kinds of questions the DCP's planners needed to address: First, what ought to be done, from a technical perspective, to meet the planning mandate to maintain the Times Square ambience—a lot of signage, kinetic brightness, openness, and mixed uses within district? This was the substantive work. Second, how should this get packaged so there is sufficient political support to secure approval? This was the implementation challenge. The political problems attached to the planning mandate demanded deft management.[46] The signage regulations would be controversial, not just because they evoked the expected opposition from powerful development interests, but because of the juxtaposition of values inherent in mandating that Class A office towers incorporate flashy, brash *advertising* signs—signs that might block windows and discourage high-prestige tenants from making commitments to move to Times Square. This could throw a monkey wrench into Koch's economic-development agenda for midtown, and there was no doubt that potentially blocking windows and hindering marketability would hold more sway than the planning staff. Consequently, the regulations not only had to be "the right thing to do," they needed to show that they were not going to impede new development. Even though style was not the complicating factor for George Klein, whose proposed buildings for the 42DP were the epitome of corporate taste, in the mid-1980s the perception that Times Square was still very much a pioneering location for white-collar financial services held fast within the real estate community. In other words, marketability would be at the top of the agenda.

Technology and invention—thinking that a sign need not be a billboard—eventually produced see-through signs that did not block windows, so the "inoffensiveness" of the incorporated advertising presumably made them compatible with office usage. Constructed of fins, the new signs presented their narrow edges to the window; when looked at straight on, the view of the building was unimpaired, yet when looked at from an angle, the sign made its statement. The cleverness of fin signs, however, made them suspect; some sign companies in New York thought of them as "too discreet, too abstract, too architectural; huge as they were, they seemed designed to not call attention to themselves. Nobody ever made money in the billboard business by worrying about what the neighbors might think," Jerry Adler quipped about the sign-design process for 1540 Broadway.[47]

The lineup of those who testified in favor of the new design regulations at the public hearings before the CPC was impressive and, as has often been the case at these events, provided a form of theater in its own right. Besides the MAS and civics, in attendance was Community Board 5, the sign manufacturers, Actors' Equity Association, set designers and lighting specialists, Local 230 of the Painters' and Decorators' Union, and architects (figure 8.8). Out-of-towners also took seats in the baroque public chamber. Echoing in person what Barwick had said in the press months earlier—"Signs in Times Square are like redwoods in California, they have

8.8
Celebrities showing support for the proposed urban-design rules for Times Square. (Michael Peters, *Newsday*)

to be protected"—members of the Sierra Club from California and Alaska intoned, "Times Square is an advertising park. It is an environment with unique characteristics. It's as American as Yosemite."[48] Dancers and singers used their Broadway talents to present live testimony whose message needed no words. Three concerns, the Shubert Organization, the Nederlander Organization, and the Jujamcyn Company, owned 32 of the 36 theaters operating at the time; while it was hard for these theater owners to take a stand against the character-preserving requirements—lighting, signage, and a use requirement that 5 percent of the floor area in new buildings, or enlargements, be devoted to entertainment-related uses—they wanted to tone down the level of flash. They wanted a less chaotic Times Square, "lighting in lieu of signage, or perhaps more lighting and less signage," as Gerald Schoenfeld said in his testimony on behalf of the Shubert Organization.[49]

The main opposition came from the development community, more specifically, office developers with projects in the final stages of planning who looked at the design regulations and envisioned an economic meltdown. "I would like to see something more moderate—less flamboyant," said Larry A. Silverstein, who had a development site in the area. "I am after good taste, and reasonableness."[50] Gaudy, eclectic signs were seen to mix with new corporate office towers, hotels, or residential towers about as well as oil and water. It would turn out to be a combustible mixture if the mandated features of the building discouraged potential tenants such as Morgan Stanley, the blue-chip investment banking house, which had been in on-and-off discussions with the developers David and Jean Solomon for a new 1.35-million-square-foot tower on a large Broadway assemblage between 47th and 48th Streets, site of the former Strand Theater, one of the original grand movie-picture palaces, and now 1585 Broadway. On the site of another former movie-picture place, the Rivoli Theater, the Solomons were building a second tower, 750 Seventh Avenue. They vociferously opposed the sign regulations every inch of the way, in contrast to most other developers who balked at first but either eventually came to understand what the DCP was trying to do and found ways to go along, even if they spoke against the regulations and the vulgarity of neon at the public hearings, or had plans for a different type of building. Bruce Eichner, for one, was planning a mixed-use development for a Broadway site two blocks south between 45th and 46th Streets, now the Bertelsmann Building at 1540 Broadway, that would include, in addition to offices, theaters and five stories of retail built around an inventive plan by Californian-architect Jon Jerde for an attention-getting "Whiz Bang"—an electronic screen/video wall 20 feet high and 80 feet wide that would hang from the ceiling and display events, advertising, and more. Jerde intended what he described as a "habitable sign" to be the biggest piece of urban theater ever done.[51]

The Solomons, who were from Chicago and newcomers to the development business by the generational standards of New York's real estate families, conceived their project with a mental model of formal dig-

nity and elegance akin to the Champs-Elysées, or perhaps Chicago's but-
toned-down Loop: "Investment bankers and lawyers don't want to work in
an environment surrounded by flashing lights," David Solomon said at
the time. "They want trees and clean streets . . . museums and sidewalk
cafes."[52] The political weighing in came from Morgan Stanley, who was
threatening to leave New York if it had to put signs on its tower. The
prospect of Morgan Stanley moving to Times Square was a major event:
"They had the economic-development muscle to get attention," said
Howe in an interview.[53]

In a *Times* letter to the editor, architect Peter Samton rebutted
the argument that it would be difficult, if not impossible to design a prestigious office building with a substantial amount of signage at its base:
"Look at the Champs Elysées, where elegance and ostentation nearly
coexist. The buildings that line the boulevard contain offices for prestigious companies that peer out from behind white neon signage. The effect
is serene by day and glowing at night."[54] Differences between day and
night were not, however, what the CPC wanted. Later, after the new regulations had been interpreted in just that fashion by the Solomons for 750
Seventh Avenue, the city amended the zoning text to require that at least
50 percent of the minimum aggregate surface area of illuminated signs be
legible during daylight hours from a minimum distance of 60 feet.

Development pressure was intense, and the political pressure to
move the new regulatory proposals, tremendous. "The new rules need to
be rushed to proclamation before builders put construction footings in the
ground. If a single building breaks the proposed 50-foot cornice line, the
openness of the square will be lost. Only haste can avert this waste," the
editors of the *Times* wrote in summer 1986.[55] The new rules had been
proposed by the CPC in January 1986. "For once, it appears to be doing
exactly what city government is supposed to do, and not a minute too
soon," New York urbanist Marshall Berman remarked; yet at the same
time, it appeared to be dragging its heels behind the scenes on details and
letting the big developments proceed.[56] While the big developments had
not committed to steel, plans—which the *Times* editors called "ominous"—were well advanced and, in some cases, demolition was underway;
moreover, in real estate, where perception matters enormously, it was a
well-placed fear that time was rapidly running out. Intensely worried that
"all would be lost," the MAS demanded that the CPC impose a moratorium on construction in Times Square until it formally adopted the new
zoning guidelines.[57]

The political wrangling continued deep into the year. Nineteen-
eighty-six was a year of intense public airing of planning issues, with overlapping public hearings bearing on the Theater District as well as the
new design regulations. The work was being done in public, so, from the
DCP's perspective, it was "let the developers beware." More to the point,
Zeckendorf's hotel project and his voluntary accommodations to the proposed rules were highly visible statements of feasibility; they showed that
commercial development could proceed under the new regulations.

According to Howe, "it knocked out the argument that these regulations would be the death knell to the Theater District. The event had the effect of isolating Morgan Stanley."[58]

By this time, the transformation of values was firming up, with widespread agreement that the Theater District should not succumb to the canyonlike fate of Sixth Avenue. Among some architects, it was also a form of positive rebellion against the banality of commercial development. "In the years since World War II nothing has done more to eradicate distinctiveness of place in American cities than the relentless expansion of office space, standardized in form and overwhelming in scale," architect Henry N. Cobb, of I. M. Pei & Partners, testified at the design-regulation hearings. At the same time, he noted, "nothing has done more to secure the prosperity of the American cities, and especially of New York, than the expansion of office space, with its attendant working population and buying power."[59]

The duality of civic and business interests that Cobb chose to address in his remarks succinctly summarized the tensions of planning for the Times Square district, both political and substantive. Koch needed firm substantive assurances that the design regulations could accommodate what Cobb called "the irreconcilable facts," that is, encourage commercial development within the constraints of a carefully configured regulatory framework designed to protect and enhance the district's "extraordinary distinctiveness of place." This was the political balancing act that would ultimately ensure approval. Sturz succeeded in securing the mayor's support for the lighting and signage controls early on. His good sense of timing was essential, yet holding that support throughout the process was critical; without it, the ending could have been different. Editorial support from both the *Times* ("Signs of Life in Times Square") and the *Daily News* ("Times Square Ain't Vanilla Ice Cream") bolstered the cause, but key votes on the BOE remained uncommitted until the end. Unable to decide at its first sitting on the issue, the BOE put off the vote for two weeks; then, in another of its famous late-night sessions, it approved the legislation at 2 A.M. on February 5, 1987. It was, as Barwick had earlier reported to the MAS board, the first time in a long time that the mayor and the CPC were on the same side of an issue as the MAS (figure 8.9).[60]

PRESERVATION POWER

The Problems of Aesthetic Legislation
Widespread consensus existed that the change in dialogue masterminded by the MAS succeeded in putting in place an innovative aesthetic zoning framework sensitive to the visual legacy of Times Square. To those who never ceased worrying about the peril to Times Square from the scale of new development fostered by the 1982 zoning incentives, the 1987 design regulations were but a "useful first step." The neighborhood was still at stake. Broadway theaters were real estate: small buildings in the midst of large ones, their size nowhere near what the sites could accommodate

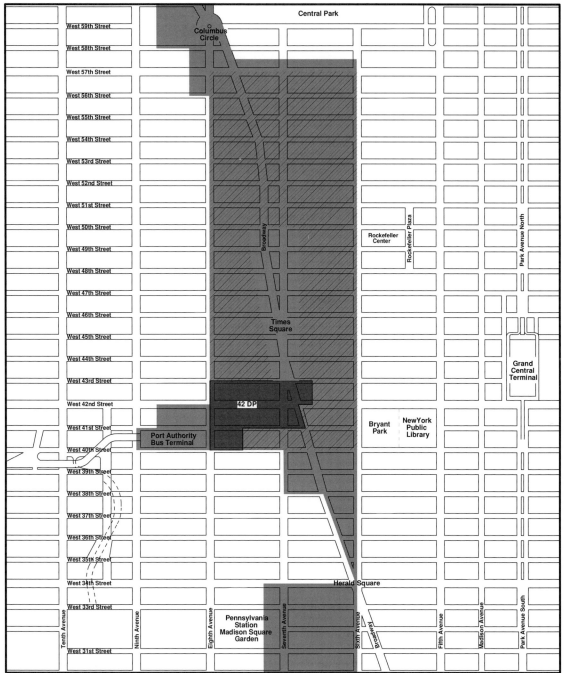

Special Times Square Districts - 1987

Key:

- Theater District
- Urban Design Regulatory District
- 42nd Street Development Project (42DP)
- Upzoned or "Growth" Area

Source: Sanborn Map Company,
New York State Urban Development Corporation,
New York City Development Corporation,
New York Department of City Planning.

8.9
Passage of an amendment to the Zoning
Resolution created special urban-design
regulations for Times Square. (Morgan
Fleming for the author)

under existing zoning if redeveloped for office towers. Without question, office buildings were more profitable investments than theaters. Though obsolete as real estate, the theaters were a prized cultural resource, and only four of the 44 listed theaters were protected by landmark designation. The diversity of activity and the infrastructure of small-scale businesses supporting the entertainment industry remained threatened by displacement and the disappearance of reasonable rents; longtime Times Square personalities had been edged out already. Lost was the excitement of "going out" and the energy of new amusements that had first defined Times Square in the decades before World War I as the center of popular culture and had made it an icon by the 1930s.

To an outsider like Jerde who had little familiarity with the area but was charged with devising a retail entertainment concept suitable for Times Square, the place came off looking a little like Hollywood—outstripped by its legend, where the reality did not fit the iconography of its fabulous past. To Hardy, who wanted to see a populist future for Times Square, the problem not affected by the signage and lighting rules, as strong as they were, was the continual ebb of entertainment life. Times Square's value as an "entertainment marketplace," he argued, came from the density of nighttime activities that drew people to the place. The marketplace value of commercial signage in Times Square was, from this perspective, derivative, "the result of a unique mix of activities." Even the preservation of prized playhouses would not stem the neighborhood's losses if the diversity of activities disappeared under the demolition dust. The narrowness of the legitimate theater audience, he felt, was a "very deep problem," whose solution was not to be found in "just fiddling around with light bulbs."[61]

Ada Louise Huxtable, who for years had been trying to alert policy makers to the same loss of life in Times Square, offered qualified praise for the new urban-design rules in prose characteristically packed with taut insight: "More creative, groundbreaking guidelines through innovative zoning have yet to be devised," she wrote some years later. "Never was a barn more splendidly locked after the horse was out." The situation was ironic, she went on to explain, because New York, as usual, had delivered something special—"important legislation because it is on the leading edge of the heart of place-making through visual and physical means"— and "demonstrated, once again, its absolute mastery of Catch 22":[62]

> The zoning defines the characteristics of the area brilliantly and supplies the criteria meant to protect and preserve those characteristics; but because they are being destroyed by the new construction, and because the new construction is also destroying the place that supplied the characteristics, recreating them is an exercise in artifice and futility. They become a kind of splendid wallpaper, or light show for a performance that isn't there.

The problem of aesthetic legislation, both Hardy and Huxtable were saying, was that it was too limited; all it could do is maintain or cultivate the
recognizable hallmarks of Times Square. It would always fall short of the
real goal because it could never capture the deeper life of the place, which
Huxtable described as a network in which use, character, and economy are
mutually dependent.[63] "It is the activities, mostly affordable, that have created the special scale and ambience, that bring the people who participate
in the range of theatrical and other pleasures, and who form the audience
for the displays and advertising, who *are* the life of the place. Use and
demography create the framework for Times Square, they are intrinsic to,
and definitive of, its visual style."

The critique was stronger than any obvious solution. For sure, the
thornier issues of planning—allowable building density and protection of
legitimate theaters—had not yet been addressed. Land use was the critical
planning issue, and it was, fundamentally, a political issue. Still unclear,
however, was whether regulatory approaches to the problem could address
the task: "We have not figured out how to mandate diversity," Hardy said
to the MAS board, "and it is the most important issue."[64]

A second, unusually quiet, step was taken later in 1987 when the
BOE approved a requirement that developers set aside for entertainment
uses nearly 5 percent of floor space in new or enlarged buildings in a
defined Theater Subdistrict Core, which covered the area between 43rd
and 50th Streets on both sides of Broadway and Seventh Avenue.[65] The
idea for the 5-percent set-aside emanated from the DCP staff. It was supported by surveys of what uses were already prevalent in the area, as well as
what was needed, and conducted by Jack Goldstein, who was chairman of
the planning and zoning committee of Community Board 5 and executive
director of Save the Theaters, Inc. The staff studied a 5-percent and 10-per-
cent requirement. "There was no magic to the five-percent figure," Howe
recalled, "it just seemed right. The goal was to make sure that the new
buildings weren't just office buildings, and it was part of the larger effort by
the city to maintain the character of the Theater District."[66] The regulation
was not especially controversial. The Durst Organization, which was in the
design-and-development stage for a 24-story 550,000-square-foot building
on the midblock site of the former Luxor Baths between Sixth Avenue
and Seventh Avenue on 47th Street, feared the loss of its prime tenant, U.S.
Trust Company, and vocally opposed the rule at first.[67] REBNY stood
opposed to yet "another layer of arbitrary restrictions and limitations that
would make it more difficult to develop property." They also saw it as a
"false solution" to the problems that face theater groups because "the high
costs of construction today will effectively exclude theaters from new
buildings."[68] Theater allies saw it otherwise, and applauded the city's effort
to accommodate "competing interests" in the Theater District. The regulations, however, would apply only until May 13, 1988, when the current
"West Side Growth Area" zoning regulations were set to expire under the
sunset provision—unless replacement regulations were drafted. Just what
regulations would prevail at that time was the major uncertainty.

The dense concentration of theaters in Times Square was unique, a defining contribution to New York's identity and vitality and treasury. Beginning in 1882 and ending fifty years later in 1932, the construction of ninety theaters in the blocks between Times Square and Columbus Circle gave the Broadway Theater District the largest concentration of playhouses in the world. By 1987, only 48 remained, and of these, 41 were concentrated west of Seventh Avenue, as many of those on the east side between 48th and 54th Streets had been razed to make way for office towers. The question of what to do about preserving the Theater District had been its own long-running drama for more than two decades since the DCP's Urban Design Group initiated studies that led to the creation of a Special Theater District in 1969 (figure 8.10), another of the city's zoning innovations. Demolition of the Helen Hayes, Morosco, and Bijou Theaters to make way for the Marriott Marquis Hotel permanently scarred the consciousness of the theater community, preservation groups, theater lovers, and city politicians alike. It did not help matters any that the facade of the Helen Hayes, a third of which was supposed to be preserved because of its architectural importance, collapsed during demolition work on the remainder of the theater. "Sacrificial lambs," Paul Goldberger said later of the three theaters, for their demolition galvanized support for saving what remained.[69] Save the Theaters, Inc., which had been organized to block the razing of the three theaters in 1982, worked intently thereafter to ensure that history did not repeat itself, organizing public events and special exhibitions to commemorate anniversaries of the demolition.

The public mourning for these theaters sparked a complicated and contentious debate about how to save what remained of Broadway's historic theaters. The unanimity behind the preservation effort, however, did not extend to the approach that might best achieve that objective. Theater preservation was "a glamorous rubric disguising a morass of conflicting agendas," Michael H. Zisser wrote in an article describing the problems faced by TAC.[70] Save the Theaters supported the establishment of the Theater District as a registered historic district and the designation of individual theaters as landmarks on a basis that considered a theater's architectural, historical, and cultural value. Theater owners vigorously opposed blanket landmark designation of all theater buildings, favoring instead a continuation of the requirement first put in place in 1982 that owners obtain a special demolition permit before tearing down a theater. Also, they wanted individual theaters to be considered for landmark designation only on the basis of architecturally significant facades above the marquee level, and vociferously objected to landmark designation for interior spaces—unless acceptable arrangements could be made so that theaters could be altered for special productions. Admonishing the preservationists to "Think Hard About Theaters," the editors of the *Times* advised that "some ill-considered rescue schemes . . . should not be allowed to set bad precedents that undermine theater economics or harm urban planning." Arguing quietly for more study and reasoned analysis of

8.10
Cross-section of One Astor Plaza, with the 1,621-seat Minskoff Theater (and separate 1,500-seat movie theater), the first building to be realized (1971) under the city's first special zoning district. Designed to couple office construction in Times Square with the construction of new theaters, the Special Theater District Amendment came to be seen as antithetical to theater preservation efforts. (Mayer, Kahn & Jacobs Architects)

the options, they went on to caution that "the emotions of the preservationists can do harm as well as good."[71]

Any efforts to secure landmark designation of the theaters would yield only a partial solution; it was a self-limiting tactic because it could do nothing to ensure the health of the theater industry. Moreover, making all the theaters landmarks could have a perverse side effect. Under existing law, the unused development rights of a theater with landmark status could be transferred to neighboring sites, and the extra volume—estimated at about 2.8 million square feet by 1987, down from 3.5 to 4.5 million in 1984—could be added to the already large zoning envelopes permitted in the district.[72] In exchange for a commitment to maintain a theater for legitimate theatrical use, TAC proposed a radical liberalization of the rules governing the transfer of development rights by allowing for transfer anywhere within a broad, designated district of midtown west. The proposal worried city officials who considered the precedent-setting character of this recommendation a Pandora's Box of urban planning, and generated a strong response from REBNY, which was, not unexpectedly, sharply critical of the plan. Contending that there would be little market for the rights because the "West Midtown office space market was saturated by the 42d Street development project," a REBNY report of its City Planning and Zoning Committee headed by Seymour Durst, warned that any plan that relied on development rights would be based on "phantom revenues," with the potential to "encourage a crazy-quilt of development."[73]

Another theater-preservation policy option was decreasing the zoning densities in the district, something set to happen automatically in May 1988 if no other discretionary action were taken. This alternative might lessen the potential for development, but it too was not enough to ensure the survival of the Theater District. Much division existed within the theater community and within TAC about how to address what both saw as the underlying economic issue: Broadway theater seemed limited to blockbuster musicals like *Cats!* and other safe, sure hits. Also, ticket costs had risen dramatically, further narrowing the demographic range of theater audiences. Under favorable economic conditions, but more likely through subsidized efforts of a proposed Theater Trust Fund, the legitimate theaters might attract new serious dramatic productions in addition to the musicals that consistently drew big audiences. Still, for electronic entertainment or other yet-to-be developed popular entertainment, the physical character of the historic theaters might be limiting. In short, facilitating the emergence of something new in entertainment in Times Square evolved into another objective separate from theater preservation.

Each approach—landmark designation, zoning, transfer of development rights, and a subsidized theater trust fund—had its allies and opponents, and alignments of interest would shift depending on the specifics of different proposals. Any alliance to preserve, restore, or create anew—the choice of verb itself depending upon one's perspective—the Broadway Entertainment District, however, would have to build upon the power of the preservationists because the political force behind the mandate for diversity in Times Square was solidly lodged in the policy argument for theater preservation, as well as a need to make amends for past transgressions and losses. The ever-present political issue flowed from a basic question: Who would pay the cost of preserving the Theater District? Tried and true, development rights would serve as the city's second currency.

A Tempestuous Triumph

The city's Landmarks Preservation Commission was born in 1965 out of a legacy of neglect during which all kinds of buildings with the power to evoke the city's past—though perhaps none as famous as McKim, Mead, and White's Pennsylvania Station—were lost to the wrecker's ball. Since that time, battles over landmarks have been among the hardest-fought city issues, especially in booming real estate times. The financial stakes are always high and the political maneuvers, typically fierce and Machiavellian. Conservative and initially not controversial, the LPC quickly became an integral part of the development process in New York and a major political as well as cultural force influencing the use and development of land in the city. After a stinging critique of its elite bias by Herbert J. Gans, the LPC's focus moved rather quickly from architectural gems to populist icons, in keeping with a new ideology that celebrated the democratic social history of the ordinary. Since the LPC was free of strict standards of historic or aesthetic value, it could and did exercise its power across a broad range of structures, including, as Joseph B. Rose noted in his discerning review of the issue, "much of the IRT subway station, lower Manhattan's gnarled street plan, and even the abandoned and decaying Parachute Jump at Coney Island."[74]

As a powerful force with its own constituency, the 11-member LPC became a storm center of controversy. With power to designate buildings as landmarks and whole districts as historic being widely and frequently used—in the service of community interests who seek to block development, critics charged—the LPC was operating within the realm of land-use policy, though that was not within its statutory purview. "The commission has enormous power," said former Deputy Mayor Robert F. Wagner, Jr., who was a member of a five-person committee appointed by Mayor Koch in 1985 to reexamine the role of the LPC, "and in the last year or so there has been increasing concern about the predictability of designation and the procedures followed."[75] The LPC appeared to be taking on the planning role ordinarily accorded to the CPC, and the most troubling aspect of this situation was that the administrative decisions of landmarks policy were implemented with virtually no checks and balances, in comparison with the city's other regulatory processes. A landmarks designation became effective immediately after a majority vote of the LPC; it could only be overturned if the BOE voted within 90 days to repeal landmark status. "Though the Planning Commission has an affirmative obligation to gain a three-fourths majority for its proposals, the Landmarks Commission need only obtain a simple majority in those rare cases when its actions come to the attention of the Board (the weighted voting allows this majority to be obtained from as few as three of the Board's eight members)."[76] The "Commission Can Be Faster than a Speeding Builder, More Powerful than a Zoning Board," as one newspaper lead put it.[77]

By the beginning of the 1980s, only one Broadway playhouse, the Lyceum, had been granted landmark status, in 1974. In August 1985, after three years of fierce debate reflected in five hours of arguments by commission members preceding voting, three other theaters (Neil Simon, Ambassador, and Virginia) were designated as landmarks. At issue was whether the interiors and exteriors of the theaters should be given landmark designation on the basis of cultural importance as well as, or in the absence of, architectural merit. "It's not just what's there today," said one commissioner in arguing for the symbolic importance of making landmark declarations, "it's what has been there—the hundreds of theaters that once existed."[78] The decision to go forward and landmark interiors as well as exteriors, which rated a front-page story in the *Times*, elicited the expected outcry from theater owners who argued that in the absence of specific guidelines about what changes would be permitted, the landmark designation, especially of interiors, threatened their ability to survive by subjecting them to a bureaucratic-approval process every time a production called for physical changes.

Only a few days later, the LPC announced that it would postpone the landmark process until guidelines covering the landmark theaters were developed. Writing in support of the decision, the *Times* editors asked, "Why the Rush to Landmark Theaters?" The three designations were approved by the BOE at the end of the 90-day review period, even as the *Times* editors advised that body "to protect theaters from their protectors."[79] The next set of designations was a long time in coming, however. Nearly two years later, in November 1987, in what veteran *Times* reporter David W. Dunlap called the "biggest single step in the effort to create landmarks out of Broadway's legitimate theaters since the process began more than six years ago,"[80] landmark status was accorded to five more theaters (Brooks Atkinson, Barrymore, Martin Beck, Belasco, and Booth), with eight more (Cort, Embassy 1, Forty-sixth Street, Golden, the former Little [now renamed the Helen Hayes], Mark Hellinger, Hudson, and Imperial) two weeks later, and the following month, seven more (Longacre, Lunt-Fontanne, Majestic, Henry Miller, Music Box, Eugene O'Neill, and Plymouth). This brought landmark-status coverage of Broadway playhouses (interior or exterior or both) up to 28 of the 46 theaters on the LPC's list. Victory for the preservationists was but one step away.

In March 1988, the BOE took up the issue of the LPC's designations for the 28 theaters. It was a "tempestuous fight," Dunlap reported, between the LPC, which had the mayor's support, and the three major theater owners. The designations for the exteriors of 21 theaters, most of which had been built between 1910 and 1930, were not likely to be seriously challenged. The heat of the fight, around which there was intense political anxiety and last-minute lobbying, centered on the designations for 26 theater interiors: If the designations were upheld by the board, all of the decorative ornamentation—the fleurs-de-lis, sconces, lunettes, rosettes, sculptural profiles, and architectural details—would have to be preserved intact or restored to their original state at the end of each production run. Reasserting their well-known position, the owners argued that interior designations would inhibit their flexibility in staging shows and jeopardize their economic future. "Unless we get some help," said Robert Nederlander, "somewhere within the next few years we are going to lose one-third of the theaters on Broadway."[81] The chairman of the LPC, Gene Norman, countered: "Theater owners have a regulatory scheme available to them that other owners do not," special guidelines that "provide ways to restore things with economics in mind."[82]

A cast of Broadway luminaries—Colleen Dewhurst, Celeste Holm, Patti LuPone, Sam Waterston, and Lanford Wilson—joined the lobbying. Before the hearings, Save the Theaters placed an advertisement in the Sunday *Times* in which more than 150 signatories—from Actors' Equity Association to developer Mortimer B. Zuckerman—called on the BOE to uphold the designations. After hours of impassioned testimony, the vote, at 3:00 A.M., unanimously approved landmark status for the theaters and rejected the theater owners strong economics-based objections. Reportedly, what broke the deadlock in the preservationists' favor, according to both factions, was the release by the mayor's office of photographs of the interior of the Virginia Theater before and after its alternation twenty years earlier. The photos showed the formerly lavish Italian palazzo interior entirely stripped, looking "like a shoe box." This is an "extreme example of what happens if you don't designate detail," said Deputy Mayor Robert Esnard.[83] While the owners were not without strong support, what enabled the mayor to muster the votes of those board members who sympathized with their position was a last-minute agreement by the chairman of the LPC to form a panel of experts to review the commission's guidelines on altering ornamental decor, with an eye on making them less stringent. The preservationists had scored a decisive victory.[84]

FAR POLITICS

Although important policy directives, the new regulations for signage and lighting and entertainment-use set-asides and the landmark designations for theaters still gingerly skirted the central planning issue: the scale of new development in Times Square. Relative to the question of bulk and density, they came off as superficial addendums to the real problem—the incentives for large-scale development in Times Square put in place by the 1982 Midtown Zoning Resolution. The city's critics were still smarting over what was now viewed as an unnecessary 20-percent density bonus for developers. "It was a puzzling regulation," Goldberger wrote in 1987, "given that there was not much of anyplace else except the West Side for developers to go once restrictions were getting tighter on the East Side. They would have begun to develop sites in west midtown anyway, without the generous bonus that has led to these new buildings being even larger than otherwise permissible."[85] This was a revisionist view fashioned with the benefit of hindsight, for much had happened in five years to dramatically alter the investment climate. Midtown west had gone from being "in the boonies" to being a hotbed of development activity. If there was, as Goldberger put it, "real sadness that the city did not move more aggressively to preserve Times Square long ago by zoning it for smaller buildings," then the debate over what zoning would prevail when the special incentives expired promised to be the most controversial—and political—of all.

The textbook approach to the planning problems of the Theater District called for a district comprehensive plan, not just zoning regulations, to deal with the conflicts and consequences—for design, transportation, theater preservation, economic development—of major new development. Holding to this principled perspective but for varied reasons, the civics and Community Board 5 as well as theater owners found the city's response "agonizingly slow" and its "piecemeal process" lacking. Voicing its frustration at the 1986 hearings on the design controls, the Regional Plan Association, which had as early as 1969 supported an expansion of midtown's commercial district westward, asked when the DCP would have a "firm work program and schedule," complaining that "for more than one year, none has been forthcoming. . . . Logically, development controls follow a plan, not precede it. Is the Commission certain that these controls will implement its planning policy?"[86] Sturz and Howe were "ominously vague about zoning," and it seemed unlikely that the CPC would reach a consensus on the issue anytime soon, one critic reported at about the same time.[87] This reading of the situation was on target, for the political demands of putting in place new zoning for midtown precluded the CPC from taking any other position on timing.

The review processes for landmark designation and midtown zoning were proceeding on separate tracks, and the positions around each were such that a political consensus to move faster on either was never a possibility. The real estate industry would vigorously fight downzoning—they wanted the sunset provision to disappear, the zoning to remain at an FAR of 18. (A zoning text change eliminating earlier bonus provisions meant it was no longer possible to build to a maximum FAR of 21.6.) When the zoning legislation was passed in 1982, developers reportedly did not express much concern about the sunset provision, and little development occurred immediately thereafter. But as the sunset date loomed on the horizon with deals not yet complete, a sense of panic took hold among developers. The economic consequences of unexpectedly getting caught in a downzoning—after land deals had been priced on the basis of existing development rights—were severe. For developers, certainty is typically more important than a specific FAR. At a minimum, they needed certainty until May 1988. What they really wanted was an extension of the bonus provision. "Leave it alone—it's starting to work," said Arthur

Margon, a senior vice president of REBNY. "The city shouldn't be frightened of developers who say they're going to erect a lot of buildings. That's what we need. The only way New York City can be vibrant approaching the year 2000 is to let that kind of growth occur in various parts of the city."[88]

While equally sensitive to the possibility of a downzoning, theater owners, in contrast to developers, were even more sensitive to potential changes in the transferability of development rights. Some, though not all, theater owners stood to make a lot of money from the transportability of FAR; others, in particular those with playhouses on Broadway or Seventh Avenue, were already benefiting from higher building densities than those permitted on midblock sites. As a group, however, they too were strongly against any downzoning and in favor of a more liberal "receiving zone" for their surplus development rights. The MAS as well as others behind the preservation effort were calling for modest downzoning to an FAR of 12 for the avenues. Calling for an FAR of 8 for the midblocks would have been a dramatic policy change, though that seemed to be an implausible option since a number of existing buildings already exceeded that density.

The maelstrom of competing interests surrounding the zoning issue put a premium on pragmatism. Trying to get all the planning for Times Square done at once would have fatally compromised what was so desperately needed in the first place: new controls for the district as soon as possible. "It is just as well that the CPC set it [zoning] aside for now," Marshall Berman wrote, "if it hadn't separated Times Square's immediate needs from its long-range zoning problems, there would soon be no Times Square left to protect."[89] Howe later echoed the sentiment: "If we waited for all to be done in a comprehensive review, it would have been too late."[90] The DCP wanted to put in place new signage and lighting regulations before the new developments got built; it would not help the politics of the preservation cause or enhance the reputation of professionalism they sought to be subject to the charge that the new design controls would take effect "after the horses left the barn."

Zoning was a different matter, however. In a relatively short five years, the CPC achieved what it set out to do with the 1982 Midtown Zoning Resolution, and to mark its victory, it had issued a self-congratulatory report to that effect in summer 1987. Intended to announce to the public that the shift in development to the West Side had occurred, the report also served to lay the ground work for the argument that an FAR of 18 was no longer needed. On the administrative side, the goal of the 1982 resolution was to make zoning as predicable and as-of-right as possible, reversing the CPC's former reliance on discretionary decision making through the practice of negotiated zoning. By specifying performance standards and reducing opportunities for obtaining discretionary approvals, it registered success here as well.[91] Altering the zoning regulations in advance of the scheduled expiration might undo the perception that these administrative gains had made development growth more predicable. More significant was the fact that, unlike the signage and lighting regulations, legislating new zoning rules in advance of the sunset date would definitely impose immediate economic consequences on developers who had already bought and assembled sites. It would destroy the principle of certainty and jeopardize the confidence of the powerful development community, which, in turn, would work against the city's original—and unaltered—goal of encouraging development on the West Side. Given those stakes, it is hard to imagine what forces would have generated the political consensus necessary to accelerate the timetable for a review of midtown zoning.

In the end, the DCP mapped out a quintessential growth-oriented compromise, yet the compromise showed the influence of the theater-preservation movement's unassailable arguments for protecting the lower scale and special character of the Theater District. This it did in several ways. First, the conceptual basis for the staff work continued to be centered on "a key concept enunciated in the Theater Advisory Council report"—that there exists a "core area" of the Theater Subdistrict that has the greatest concentration of theaters, entertainment-related uses, bright lights, and signage, and a lower scale than surrounding areas. This 20-block stretch of Broadway and Seventh Avenues between 43rd and 50th Streets defined the zone of applicability of the design controls as well as the set-aside requirement for entertainment-related uses. Second, in calling for a greater reduction of density in the Core Area—to an FAR of 14 on the avenues and an FAR of 12 on the side streets—the staff went beyond recommending a return to the status quo, which would have been an FAR of 15 when the special zoning regulations expired. "A 1 FAR reduction from the postsunset base FAR of 15," the staff memo argued, "would distinguish this section of the avenues from the sections to the north and south." Third, the new zoning proposals would establish a fixed density in the Core Area, permitting "no zoning bonuses whatsoever—whether presently as-of-right or by special permit." Fourth, the DCP staff rejected the proposals for a more liberalized system of development rights transferability as being "purely economically-based and inconsistent with the Zoning Resolution as a land-use tool." The planners' principled position not to tread into fiscal-policy waters meshed politically with prevailing weak conditions in the real estate market. Widening the arc of development sites would have, in the short-term, exacerbated the problem of overbuilding. To promote the rehabilitation of the 44 listed theaters and allow owners to realize a limited income stream, the staff proposed, in place of the earlier bonuses, a Theater Retention Bonus set at a uniform level (an FAR of 1 but no more than 50,000 square feet of floor area) that could be used in any site within the Theater Subdistrict, yet outside the Core Area where the no-bonus rule applied. In exchange for the bonus, the theater owner would have to record a deed restriction that required proper building maintenance and use as a legitimate theater for the life of the related development.[92] The package received BOE approval near the end of April 1988.

The Theater District's compactness intensified the nature of the planning study as well as the political debate. There was not going to be a philosophical study, Howe noted. The planning staff knew exactly which buildings would be built and which would not. If they needed to assess which theater owners would be more sensitive to one proposal than another, they had only to look at a map of who owned the theaters, and which were on the midblocks rather than the avenues. The small area also seemed to offer greater surety of analysis when assessing the likely impact of various proposed incentives for theater preservation. For example, in "sounding off" at the proposed Theater Retention Bonus, the executive director of the Citizens Housing and Planning Council, argued that the bonus "may cushion the operations of a limited number of theaters" but it would not solve the problem of how to keep Broadway theaters alive because it was unlikely to be used for the most economically distressed theaters. "The arithmetic is simple," said Willa Appel. With approximately 15 potential development sites within the Theater District (excluding possible zoning lot mergers) and some 31 eligible, landmarked theaters, "there are not enough development sites to go around." The limited scope of development opportunity would force theater owners to be selective about which theaters would participate in the bonus transaction and, therefore, come under the protective covenant. "It is reasonable to assume that the safest choice will be to select the more profitable theaters where the bonus incentive will outweigh the risks of foregoing the opportunity to apply for hardship."[93]

For preservationists, landmark designations for the legitimate theaters and lower densities for the Theater Core Area represented extraordinarily significant victories. As policy interventions, their impact was limited, however. These gains could not ensure the future of the Broadway theater industry, nor even a future of entertainment in Times Square. Given the city's earlier decision to encourage commercial development's westward move into the Theater District, the forces of dramatic change were irreversible. The most that zoning or other regulatory policies could achieve was a lessening of the scale of development and an assurance that aesthetic safeguards would define the future look of Times Square—linked visually to an idealized image of its past. Forty-second Street was supposed to represent the base of legitimate theater in New York, and, in 1988, the street's future was still an open question. Though little attention had been directed toward that end, the 42DP planners had not discarded that goal.

CHAPTER 9

THE HOME OF
2 FOR 1 SHOWS

WHERE EVERY DAY
IS A HOLIDAY

Paramount
THEATRE

TIMES SQUARE
NEW YORK CITY
★
LO 3-1100

Inventing an Entertainment Agenda

The continuous entertainment ribbon defining the new 42nd Street was not predetermined by historical condition, nor did it materialize spontaneously. It was not inevitable; it was invented. The bustling cultural scene in Times Square during the 1920s and 1930s, similarly, was "contrived," the result, concluded cultural historian William A. Taylor, of "many different kinds of business decisions that, in turn, succeeded in giving the area its concentrated commercial energy and visual distinctiveness."[1] The contrived invention of the late 1990s, in contrast, reflects the strong and visible hand of public intervention—deliberate tactics and targeted strategies designed to reshape the cultural and commercial prospects of West 42nd Street. Under the leadership of Rebecca Robertson, the 42DP adopted the values of the Times Square design regulations, channeled the untapped consumer-buying power of millions of tourists who continued to flock to Times Square—no matter what locals thought of the place—into commercial prospects, consciously created an enticing visual image of what the street could become, and deployed a smartly crafted public-relations effort attuned to cultivating a constituency for the new vision. All was choreographed: West 42nd Street was being "reimaged" internationally as a unique public place where the pulsating beat of the city never stops and the bright lights never go out.

The planners were not quite sure how the vision would take its final physical form and commercial configuration, but it was part of the new process of "unplanning," which sought to preserve the raucous traditions of the street by prohibiting uniformity and cultivating competitiveness. Robertson's intention was to go forward with an interim plan and not stick to anything on paper. "Anything that can move quickly here is better than requiring that everything be long-term," Cora Cahan, the executive director of 42nd Street's nonprofit theater entity, told the media. "There has to be experimentation and revision. We want the ability to revise."[2] Also, new cultural as well as commercial configurations were supplanting those of the past. With technology advancing new modes of production and broadening the physical horizons of distribution through cyberspace, there was no way to foresee exactly how the street would evolve. One thing did seem clear, though: despite evocative verbal connections and visual linkages to its iconic past, West 42nd Street in the twenty-first century was not likely to repattern itself exactly on that blueprint. Legitimate theater had been the "signature" activity of Broadway, but for decades it had been fading as a pivotal social and economic activity of the area. What mattered to Robertson was programmatic flexibility—broadening entertainment options for the midblock historic theaters as well as a full range of entertainment, recreation, and retail uses for the sites at the western end of the project area. Her new plan had its priorities in order, and it rode the wave of what would subsequently be termed "urban entertainment." You could say its timing was right, though the force of what was happening on West 42nd Street was itself generating much of the hype behind the urban-entertainment trend.

PLANNING AGAINST THE ODDS

There are good reasons that the theater agenda for West 42nd Street languished for more than six years after the BOE approved the 42DP. As explained in chapter 4, the start was programmatically weak and financially nonexistent. Rhetoric rather than hard plans prevailed. And what tentative plans existed self-destructed rather quickly. The renovations planned for the New Amsterdam by the Nederlander Organization, which had gained control of the theater in 1982, collapsed midstream a year later, leaving the dazzling Art-Nouveau theater dark, neglected, and exposed to the elements for many years until UDC finally purchased the badly damaged building in 1992[3] (figure 9.1). There was no question that the once-lustrous New Amsterdam still held great potential as a venue for legitimate Broadway shows, but the street's sordid condition immediately impeded even tentative commitments on the part of producers, as a letter from director Hal Prince—of *Follies* and *A Little Night Music* fame—to Nederlander made clear:[4]

> As per your request . . . I went to see the New
> Amsterdam yesterday.
>
> I will not lie to you: that can be the best legit
> theater in New York City and, of course, would have
> been *ideal* for PHANTOM OF THE OPERA. But there's
> no way that I would go near 42nd Street or ask anyone
> else to.
>
> For example: while we were waiting in front of the theater (all of five minutes) to be shown the place, on one side of us a drug sale took place and on the other, a young girl had her hands in her boyfriend's pockets—need I tell you why. I was seriously concerned for the two women with us.

9.1
The rooftop theater of the New
Amsterdam, a scene of destruction
brought on by private neglect and
a poorly negotiated development
agreement. (© 2001 Maggie
Hopp)

I respect your offer to spend a small fortune putting
private security on the street in front of the theater, but there is
no way I would rehearse on that block or go near that place,
especially in the evening. It's tragic because the New Amsterdam
could so easily be the focal point for the rejuvenation of that
shameful section of the city.

Sorry fellas.

The commitment from the designated developer for the theaters on the
north side of the street, Michael Lazar with Jujamcyn Company, dissolved
within two years, when Lazar was indicted for crimes unrelated to the
42DP. And without firm commitments from the developers of the mart
site, concrete plans for the other theaters on the south side of the street
also failed to materialize.

Part of the problem could be found in the *GPP*'s singular
emphasis on legitimate "Broadway Theater." It was idealistic, a throwback
to the street's glorious past, a 30-year period from the turn of the century
to 1930 when the 17 legitimate theaters on 41st, 42nd, and 43rd Streets
vied for audiences. By 1934, only three of the 42nd Street playhouses
housed legitimate theater. In the ensuring period, the cinema emerged as
a formidable competitor for the average American's entertainment dollar,
capturing ever larger shares of the market for popular entertainment.
Movie theaters became the new symbol of Times Square glamour in the
1920s and 1930s as a succession of grand and ornate "Palaces of the
People" were constructed on or near Broadway (figure 9.2). Despite their
architectural merits, the movie palaces were taken for granted even by the
preservation community, which was so tightly focused on the 44 listed
theaters that even as demolition made them scarce, the grand cinemas
failed to merit any priority. A distinct bias against movie uses in the 42DP
plan existed because developers and city officials alike worried that the
screens might presage the street's return to pornography. Moreover, recreating legitimate theater entertainment was more consistent with the

9.2 Souvenir of "Broadway's biggest stage and screen show" palace. (Collection of the author)

cleanup's bias toward the higher-income demographics associated with the financial-services industry.

Truth be told, no one really knew what to do about the project's theater agenda. The *GPP* required that there be two nonprofit theaters in the project, yet no one believed this was possible without subsidy. The ever-apparent question was, how could these theaters be financed and in a way that would make them self-sufficient? The issue remained unaddressed until Carl Weisbrod hired Robertson in June 1987 with the explicit charge to figure out how to give substance to the theater mandate.

A Canadian-born professional planner, Robertson was 36 at the time. She came to the task from the DCP where she was deputy director of the Manhattan office and senior planner involved with the contextual rezoning of both the Upper West Side and Upper East Side. She was a veteran of the public review process and skilled in the nuances of New York's land-use intricacies. Three years later, on the day the state secured title to two-thirds of the street, she took over as president of the 42DP, Inc., when Weisbrod left to head the city's entrepreneurial development corporation, PDC. By the time of her departure in early 1997 to become a senior executive at the Shubert Organization, she would be widely credited and justly praised as the mastermind behind the new vision for West 42nd Street and the driving force behind its transformation. Robertson deployed focus, high energy, determination, and commitment to push for what was both practical and "right" in terms of what she called the "good bones" that made people love 42nd Street. Ever articulate in promoting the project, she tackled thorny problems during its darkest days—the "D-word era" when articles about the redevelopment effort leaned heavily on the words "dead, desolate, dismal, dreary."[5] For the first seven of the nine years she spent working on the 42DP, Robertson needed to have what she had in abundance: optimism.

To go forward with the theater agenda, Robertson had to devise a funding plan for the operation of the two theaters originally intended for nonprofit entertainment enterprises, the Victory and the Liberty. In terms of physical characteristics and aesthetic attraction, these were the toughest theaters to reconfigure as nonprofit venues—each had two balconies when only one makes sense unless a theater has a large number of seats, which was not the case with either—though that would emerge as a technical problem only later on. To create the basis for a plan, she quickly asked for and received approval from the board of UDC to contract for a planning study of the Apollo, Lyric, Selwyn, and Times Square Theaters. The contract went to Robert A. M. Stern Architects, which would work with consultants Brannigan-Lorelli Associates (theater design) and Robert E. Meadows (historic preservation). An earlier study conducted for the Not-for-Profit Theater Advisory Committee by Hardy Holtzman Pfeiffer Associates covered the Liberty and Victory Theaters.

Stern's involvement in the project would prove to be prescient for his corporate contacts—he is on the board of the Walt Disney Company and played an important role in bringing the entertainment giant to West

42nd Street. A big-name architect best known at the time for designing homes for the wealthy and the upper-class establishment and one of the EuroDisney hotels, he is a traditionalist in style—his signature structure is "a shingle-style house with a big screened porch and a evocation of the past."[6] Stern's calling on the study of the 42nd Street theaters drew on his knowledge of and belief in historic preservation, a field in which he taught and guided as department chair for many years at Columbia University. He better than most other architects understood how to extract the commercial possibilities of historic venues. He knew the role of the "Places of Pleasure," as the city's theaters and roof gardens at the turn of the nineteenth century were called, and of the "City as Theater."[7]

The Stern study, publicly released in October 1988, was instrumental in articulating the agenda in at least two key ways. First, it was intended, Robertson later said, "to galvanize the historic-preservation folks and shake them up as to what was possible and what was not possible. They were not realistic about the possibilities."[8] The report, written with an emphasis on work scope, process, and documentation, infused its discussion of "the alternatives" for the six-theater complex—which ranged in total cost from $60 million to $79 million—with pragmatic rationales. Its reasoning and prose paid homage to the theaters' "fabled past" at the same time it made unequivocal its intent not to re-create that past: "The Street should be restored to glory, not by rolling back the chronological clock," but by seeking formats appropriate to the potential of each building that contribute to the future role of West 42nd Street.[9]

Second, the Stern study articulated a populist approach for the six-theater complex, for that was how Robertson understood West 42nd Street's legendary draw as a place for high- and lowbrow entertainment. "The success of the whole project depends on the soul of the neighborhood," she said at the time. "That means good theater and a cross section of entertainment."[10] No consensus had yet been reached on what forms of entertainment would most appropriately fit the populist mandate: UDC officials were banking on the vision behind the Stern, Brannigan-Lorelli, Meadows designs to stimulate interest and ideas. These, in turn, would be revealed to the project's planners through the RFP process. "There is no final business plan in place," Vincent Tese said that same month the Stern report became public; the only real agreement was that the theaters not be "elitist institutions."[11]

The message of the Stern study was mixed. The emphasis on live-performance arts remained firmly fixed in place, as evident by an architectural model designed by Stern and Hardy of how the restored West 42nd Street might appear (figure 9.3). Festooned with marquees and bright lights driven by fiber-optic technology, the conference-table-size model reflected the historical imagery of West 42nd Street—classic high-class theater entertainment from the first decades of the twentieth century. While entertainment other than legitimate theater was nominally a part of the agenda, the message of the report made visual by the model was that these activities were secondary. Whatever uses took over the theaters, they would have to uphold the high standards of professionalism that defined Broadway entertainment. In keeping with the populist approach, however, UDC's goal of professional-quality entertainment at less-than-Broadway prices was hard to square with the economic realities of the Broadway entertainment business—$65 tickets—especially since the 42nd Street theaters were not slated to receive any special public subsidies. As the first new "image" for the street, the model sent an important visual message.

The most important piece of the theater "solution" Robertson and Weisbrod devised was the creation of a nonprofit entity, the 42nd Street Entertainment Corporation (42EC). Although modeled after the "mother agency" of Lincoln Center, Lincoln Center for the Performing Arts, Inc., the specially designed entity for 42nd Street had a markedly different task—to restore *use* to the street's neglected and outmoded theaters. Its mission would be to recreate the sense of place held by the street at the beginning of the century, with the theaters as places of popular arts and entertainment. Charged with long-term oversight of the renovation and ongoing operation of the street's historic theaters, the 42EC would be managed by an independent board of directors appointed by the governor and given the power to select entertainment uses that would broaden the audience drawn to West 42nd Street. To do this, the 42EC needed "expertise in entertainment, ability to raise funds and credibility to develop the midblock area."[12] This could best be achieved, a PDC memo to the mayor's office argued, if the entity had "the flexibility of a private entity." Given control of the theaters through a sole-source designation, the 42EC's operating powers were broadly defined.[13]

The key element of the funding strategy was legal control over the theaters—first six, then eight with the addition of the Harris and Empire Theaters—through a 99-year lease between the city and the 42EC. Long-term control was deemed essential.[14] TSCA's money would provide only capital contributions for the theaters' renovation; the 42EC's lease with the city would have to ensure the entity's capture of revenue from the theater uses to ensure sufficient funds for ongoing operations and maintenance. In the wake of the Lazar corruption scandal and his dedesignation as developer of Site 5, the 99-year lease became the means of sheltering the 42EC from political interference and budget exigencies—a structure that would prove to be providently important after the mayoral turnover from Dinkins to Giuliani. Forty-second Street's longevity as an entertainment district also required "umbrella management to prevent a recurrence of inactivity, abandonment and blight; to maintain quality operating standards; and to provide an overall marketing and promotional direction for the block."[15] "Held forever in public trust," the theaters would revert back to the city in perpetuity when the lease expired. The strategic function of the lease was to create a self-sufficient financial platform for the theater agenda. Acting as landlord for the theaters, the 42EC would be able generate a self-sustaining revenue stream from rentals to for-profit users of four (later six) of the historic theaters to support itself and cross-subsidize the operations of two nonprofit theaters that the *GPP*

9.3
Architectural model of a new 42nd
Street, south side, built on the ideas
of the planning studies of the street's
theaters by Robert A. M. Stern
Architects and Hardy Holtzman
Pfeiffer Associates. (Wolfgang Hoyt)

required to be in the project. Without funds from the project's commercial
uses to subsidize annual operations, meeting this goal was impossible.[16]

A severe case of Broadway blues made Robertson's task of building a credible structure for the development of entertainment venues on
West 42nd Street daunting. The 1980s were turning out to be the worst
decade in Broadway history, as evident from theater's key business statistics.
In decline for the past 30 years, the number of new productions introduced in the 1985–1986 season reached an all-time low of 33. Only when
considering the decade's record to date did the numbers look slightly
more promising, with new productions averaging 43 a year; still, this contrasted sharply with an average of 60 a year throughout the 1960s. The key
indicator of the health in the theater industry—number of tickets sold—
continued its steady and precipitous decline since the 11-million high of
the 1980–1981 season: only 6.6 million people paid to attend theater during the 1985–1986 season, the worst record since 1973–1974. Dark theaters went hand-in-hand with empty seats. No longer was there talk of
a theater shortage among producers as was the case years earlier when
Broadway was booming. Over the 1984–1987 period, at least half of the
legitimate Broadway theaters had been dark at any one time.

Musicals, the economic lifeblood of the industry, continually
failed to capture the public's excitement, and following poor reviews,
many closed after only days or weeks. Straight theater productions proved
no more successful. The critics complained that the only hits appeared
to be large-scale musical imports from London: *Les Miserables, Starlight
Express, The Phantom of the Opera,* and *Chess.* Strapped for shows they
viewed as potential winners, the venerable Shubert Organization started
producing again after a 40-year hiatus. Cost problems—salaries and
competition with television and Hollywood for star talent, union issues,
soaring technical costs of producing on Broadway, as opposed to Off-

Broadway, economic waste—continued to plague the theater business. Rising ticket prices threatened to drive audiences away. After the October 1987 stock market crash, the vital "angels" who underwrite new productions nearly disappeared, and most affected were independent producers who typically discover new playwrights for Broadway.

Broadway's economic problems veiled only slightly its "product" problems. To many seasoned observers, the industry's myriad problems were, as the proverbial Broadway saying goes, "nothing a few hits couldn't solve." The issue was simple: Broadway was boring. It was not "funk." It was not glamorous. It was not exciting. It was not, in short, what young adults wanted to spend their money on. The irony was that theater as a form of entertainment was alive and well, nationally, in the form of numerous repertory companies and a burgeoning regional theater movement. "People don't go to theater," said Gerald Schoenfeld, president of the Shubert Organization, "they go to see a specific show"[17]—a hit.

In a long magazine profile in the *Washington Post* titled "Bye Bye, Broadway," drama critic John Podhoretz argued that Broadway audiences were trying hard to like what they see, but attendance was sliding anyway. The problem, as he saw it, was that Broadway lacked energy. Spectacular and stunning stage effects were being substituted for genuine excitement and activity—"a play or a libretto or characters or songs." The fact that Broadway could no longer support straight plays, though they are relatively inexpensive to produce and less expensive to keep running than musicals, saddened critics, actors, and long-time theatergoers. Everybody on Broadway, Podhoretz wrote, "concedes that the old theatergoer is disappearing, the fellow who went to the theater as steadily and devotedly as others go to the movies," but he concluded that "the stage's best producers and writers concede they no longer understand the audience, and the performers, who do not know what this nontheatrical audience wants or expects, seem almost loath to entertain it."[18] The future for the typically boom-bust theater industry looked, *Business Week* reported late in 1988, "dim indeed."[19]

The theater industry always had a major stake in what happened on West 42nd Street. That was evident by its consistently strong turnout at the project's major public hearings. However long and hard experts argued over what was causing Broadway's troubles, all perceived the street's threateningly deviant reputation as affecting audience draw, at least among the nontourist market, many of whom lived in the suburbs. On the other hand, given the declining Broadway economy, theater owners worried about potential competition from the six "public-trust" theaters. A national search initiated through a Request for Uses (RFU) issued in October 1988 produced 44 proposals for the six theaters, 31 for nonprofit uses, 13 for commercial uses. An eclectic mix, the proposed uses ranged from popular entertainment to high culture, including a children's theater, cabaret, dance theater, jazz and rock concerts, opera, ballet and tap, movies, improvisational theater, comedy clubs, an indoor high-tech amusement park, and restaurants. "Would You Believe an Indoor Disneyland? *Newsday's* lead on the story asked before stating "From Tap Dance to Redford, Everyone Wants 42nd St."[20] As executive director of 42EC, Cora Cahan's first task would be to review these proposals, but that was still two years off. In the meantime, the sociology of the place prevailed: When project officials took a group of potential users on a tour of the theaters in the spring of 1989, one participant was pickpocketed. The group needed to arrive at one of the theaters before 10 A.M., for at that hour, the Victory showed its triple bill, which included "Hot Saddle Tramp." The place was "smelly, sticky on the floor, and no one was watching the movie; we were bringing part of the Metropolitan Opera board into that space in an attempt to persuade them of the theater's merits," Robertson said of another tour of the Victory."[21]

When created in 1988, the 42EC represented a plausible structure, but it was an empty vessel, just corporate by-laws written by Robertson and a city attorney. It lacked solid financial detail that would confer credibility. Without more substance, it was difficult to believe that the private capital would be forthcoming, especially when the real estate market was rapidly heading south. And how would the hoped-for cross-subsidy revenues from investments in four live-entertainment commercial ventures materialize when Broadway was in such a slump? The 42EC also lacked the leadership that would give it substance. It would come two years later, in the fall of 1990, when Governor Cuomo and Mayor Dinkins announced that Marian Sulzberger Heiskell, part owner of the *Times*, civic leader, and one of the city's leading philanthropists, had agreed to serve as its chairperson. Heiskell had to be persuaded to take on another high-profile position, recalled Carl Weisbrod; she would agree to do so only if someone "special" served as executive director, someone, she said, like Cora Cahan. Cahan had a reputation as a talented doer of the near impossible in the nonprofit performance arena. The combination of Cahan and Heiskell aligned complementary leadership skills, unassailable personalities, and social connections, all of which would prove to be essential to executing the theater agenda. Close friends, they became a tightly knit professional pair. "It was an unusual dynamic," said Weisbrod.[22]

A diverse and distinguished 24-member board of directors drawn from the commercial and nonprofit arts and business communities was announced at the same time.[23] The announcement served multiple purposes, symbolic and real. Held in the Victory Theater, 42nd Street's oldest, city and state officials used the event to showcase the office developers' "continued commitment to the 42nd Street Project" at a time when it was realistically suspect.[24] Using the real stage to accept from TSCA a symbolic check for $9.2 million—the monies committed by the joint venture for rehabilitation and operation of the Victory Theater—the governor and mayor apparently sought to counter what realistic skeptics were saying about dire conditions in real estate markets. Times were tough for New York, in general, and the press conference, a reporter noted, "quickly turned into a pep rally for a city that had been overwhelmed by negative news in recent weeks."[25]

To move the theater component forward, at the end of 1989 UDC advanced funds to the 42EC. Fittingly, this start-up capitalization of approximately $3.1 million came from the "Portman Public Purpose Fund"; it represented one-half of the compensating set-aside designated as the "42nd Street Theater Portion."[26] Having gone unspent since the demolition of the beloved Morosco and Helen Hayes Theaters, the $4-million public-improvement fund had grown from interest earnings, producing extra dollars of which half, $1.1 million, went to the 42EC. The other half of the fund went to the community at large as a result of a compromise designed to clear the political path for the money to be used for the 42nd Street theaters.[27] Targeted to last three to four years until the new uses were producing revenue, this first expectation of self-sufficiency soon collapsed. "That was not to be as 42nd Street was dead, no activity," Cahan said later.[28] A subsequent funding agreement with the city signed in 1992 allowed the 42EC, now renamed the New 42nd Street, Inc. (New42), to access a portion of another special "Theater Reserve Account"—funded with earmarked revenues from postcondemnation tenants on the UDC-owned sites as well as a surcharge to be imposed on tenants in the TSCA office towers—until the year 2000. In short, the New42 now had six years to become self-sufficient. These funds, however, could be used only for 42EC's administrative responsibilities—as landlord, developer, and marketer—not for operating the theaters.

BRING IN THE CHILDREN

The creation of the New42 presaged the development of an entertainment agenda for the entire 42DP. This new programmatic infrastructure, so different in form and conception from regulatory land-use approaches designed to protect and enhance the Times Square entertainment district, pioneered the new vision of popular entertainment on West 42nd Street. A combination of determined leadership in Heiskell and Cahan and fortuitous timing—timing is everything in a competitive business such as real estate—ultimately enabled the New42 to capture the critically needed revenues from commercial ventures. Before that could happen, however, the New42 made a gutsy decision—19 months before Disney was even a rumor on West 42nd Street—to go forward with the creation of the first children's theater in New York by restoring the Victory Theater as its home. This was the catalyst that set future events in play. It became a key factor in getting Disney to commit to a renovation of the New Amsterdam Theater. "We won't be the first on the block," Disney's chairman Michael Eisner told the small group walking around the New Amsterdam with him for the first time at the end of March 1993. "You won't have to," replied Cora Cahan, "we will: the New Victory will open in 1995."[29] It was a date she was not going to miss.

Take a step back. The board's decision to "launch the street's renewal with the renovation of the Victory as a nonprofit theater programmed for the city's youth" came out of the organization's need to make "something out of nothing," Cahan recalled. "We started with the 'archeology' of the place. I paid attention to the 44 proposals which had been sitting in boxes for three years and contacted each of the entities who had submitted a proposal and informed them that the 42EC would be back to them with a set time, by Spring."[30] "The ideas for what to do evolved: this hadn't been done before, we didn't know what exactly to do or how to do it," recalled Heiskell.[31] The group hired Edwin Schlossberg, whose eponymous firm specializes in interactive design for public places, to generate ideas for them, ideas that were slightly different. The process, which paralleled the organization's lease negotiations with the city, was one in which Cahan and the board, most of whom did not know each other nor she them, defined themselves and their job. Cahan explained:[32]

> All we were was someone else's idea. We had to make
> the organization organic, of ourselves. Then we had to
> deal with the harsh landscape, the political administra-
> tions. The changes in political administrations were very
> difficult. It was terrifying—black holes. Remember, we
> were a shell of an organization. The city and the state
> were looking over our shoulders, at plans and budgets.
> We were supposed to be self-sufficient by 1993. But
> then the project was supposed to be built out by then
> too. . . .

The idea for using the Victory as a children's theater came from the board, which wanted action, not another "plan." After a year, the board's activist orientation and dedication galvanized the process. As Cahan recalled the scene, the board said "It's a year now and nothing is going on. We have $18.2 million from the developers whether they build or not. We have to do two nonprofits. Let's prove that something is possible."[33] The staff was asked to come up with three models: One was a black-box the-ater, one was a dance theater, and the last, a children's theater. The choice later seemed evident from the facts: The board did not want to replicate what was already in New York, and there was no children's theater in the city. "We wanted a professional theater, not one that was a gestalt of pover-ty: three steps down and two light bulbs."[34] The demographics of the youth audience also fit well with the problematic "graying of Broadway audiences" much discussed in the papers at the time. The board did not go public with the decision until October 1993, nearly two years later and after Disney's preliminary interest in the New Amsterdam was the talk of the town.

An idea that seems so simple in hindsight—when the former social context of the street no longer intrudes upon reality—was, at the time, bold and momentous: kids on West 42nd Street! The irony of the idea was transparent, but ever more so in 1992 than now since pornogra-phy still dominated the western end of the block where some 20 or so thriving porn shops on Sites 7 and 8 had yet to be condemned.

(Successfully completing the first phase of condemnation had been a firm precondition of Heiskell and Cahan taking on the leadership of the 42EC.) The bigger issue was financial. "Once the board heard the idea for a children's theater," Cahan said, "there was no turning back." But, she explained, there were big implications of going forward in this direction:[35]

> There had to be low-price tickets. The theater had to be for everyone, of all incomes. It had to be popular theater. There had to be educational programs attached to the theater. Kids could not just pass through the theater. And the teachers needed help. A children's theater had to be more than just putting on plays. All this would require big subsidies, about 75 percent to 85 percent of the cost would have to be subsidized.

In addition, the board felt that the New Victory, as the theater was renamed, should be a producing house. "It was our great hope that the public would come to see the theater as a place to see good work." The ambitions of the board spawned other implications less favorable for themselves. Promised when they agreed to take a board seat that no fund raising for the endeavor or personal contributions were involved, board members at first did not react well to the idea of raising an endowment for the New Victory. Here, as in other areas, Heiskell's role as board chairperson, position as a *Times* executive, years of high-profile civic service, and network of social contacts took on great importance. She "pleaded" with each and every one of them to give what they could: For the board to raise money, she argued, it had to show 100-percent commitment itself. "We needed the backing of the whole board," Heiskell said, to raise about $1 million per year, every year; an endowment would come later.[36]

The risk of going forward was what would turn others' attention, get them interested, the board reasoned. "We could have sat back as a landlord," Cahan emphasized in an interview. "Nothing required us to be an operator and manager. Taking on that role meant fund raising because the children's theater had to be subsidized." From a civic perspective, she said, the board understood that "the risk of not doing the New Victory was far greater than doing it." From a practical perspective, they reasoned, "if we got a box office and forced the [entertainment] activity, we might have the benefits from other theaters on the street; we might generate support for the core operation of the New42, as funds from the street could be used to support that theater." It was a gamble. Rental revenue from commercial tenants was still pretty much wishful thinking at the time. "In 1992, we had no idea that this could happen—the cross-subsidy, the commercial tenants," Cahan explained passionately. "We should never have done it. Yet once it seemed that it could happen, it was the thing we should do. We were in a unique position to it. It would be shunning a responsibility not to attempt to make it work."[37]

That attitude personifies the essence of Cahan's professional reputation as a creative doer of the near impossible. Like Robertson, her strength of conviction comes from focus, determination, and commitment to getting things done. "Cora will never, never, never give up," said Weisbrod.[38] Her experience with adaptive-reuse projects—she is widely credited with saving New York's last major rehearsal space for performing artists, 890 Broadway, now known as the Lawrence A. Wein Center for Dance and Theater and the home of two major ballet companies—and her leadership role in founding the Joyce Theater, the city's only theater designed exclusively for dance, made her an obvious candidate to direct the new nonprofit theater entity, to others that is. When Robertson came to her for names of potential directors for the 42EC, it never occurred to Cahan, she said, that they were asking her, that she would be good at it. Her modesty belies an intense underlying drive and intrepid willingness to venture forth. When asked what attracted her to the job, she replied:[39]

> It was one of those moments. I had been at the [Feld]
> ballet job for 17 years. Devoted. I went to high school
> in the area, at Performing Arts. I was a dancer. I was a
> New Yorker. Times Square meant something to me. This
> job was the ultimate challenge. I didn't know anything
> beyond the world of dance. I had been a successful fund
> raiser. I built a dance company which was in great
> financial condition. I built a theater; bought a building;
> fostered community and developed nonprofit space for
> dance and related uses. Still the preparation wasn't
> enough for 42nd Street. There was no microcosm here. I
> hadn't dealt with the city or state or with famous peo-
> ple. The first year was terrifying.

Formal adoption by the New42 board in the spring of 1992 of the $7.9-million plan to restore the Victory Theater for programs and performances designed for youth audiences presented concrete evidence of the shift in planning values that had occurred since the BOE approved the original plan for the street's redevelopment. It would take two years for the restoration to get underway and the cost would total $11.4 million. The planning was complicated by the need to meet historic-preservation requirements—the theater was not designated, but "a hair's breadth away from landmark status"[40]—so the renovation was governed by historic-designation guidelines imposed by the city and state and by the fact that the 92-year old theater had none of the important spaces needed for productions, such as dressing rooms. Such physical constraints were great. Because no lobby existed, one would have to be created by excavating a space underneath the ground floor, at a cost of $1 million. To allow for the reconstruction of the original double staircase, a main feature of the original Theatre Republic, as it was called then, a portion of the sidewalk in front of the theater would have to be taken over.

a

b

The groundbreaking in May 1994 signaled an end to years of
rhetoric surrounding the theater agenda. When complete, the 500-seat
New Victory would be the oldest functioning legitimate theater in New
York, but that romantic promise could not erase the years of go-nowhere
planning that had shaped perception of the project negatively. "A skeptical
public and a wary entertainment industry will be watching West 42nd
Street closely in coming months to see whether there is truly the momentum necessary to rebuild the street after years of failed promises and false
starts," veteran *Times* reporter David W. Dunlap wrote.[41]

Wait they would. But in the meantime, the arts community,
through its most powerful medium—performance—had succeeded in
jump-starting redevelopment of "seedy" West 42nd Street with a project
that signaled an unprecedented turnaround from porn movie house to
legitimate theater for youth entertainment (figures 9.4a–e). When the failure of the original plans for the street became inescapably clear in mid-
1991, so did the corollary irony: The nine historic theaters had become
the most visible surviving aspect of the original redevelopment plan.
Against all odds, the rhetoric disappeared, and the theater agenda emerged
as the leading force of the project some ten-plus years after the city first
announced its first plans for the street's redevelopment.

VISION #3: 42ND STREET NOW!

When the idea of a new "interim" plan for 42nd Street was announced to
the public in August 1992, simultaneous with the formal collapse of the
old plan, the editors of the *Times* called the city and state's decision to sus-
pend construction of the four office towers "A New Opening for Times

c

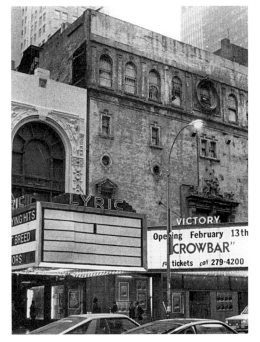

d

e

9.4
The Victory's Five Lives: a) 1900:
The Theatre Republic as a stage
for Lionel Barrymore; b) 1933: The
Republic as a house of burlesque;
c) ca. 1989: The Victory as porn
theater; d) 1990: The Victory reincarnated as a theater venue for
the Obie-winning production of
Crowbar; e) 1995: The New Victory
as a theater for youth. (Museum
of the City of New York; B'Hend-
Kaufman Archives, Academy of
Motion Picture Arts and Sciences;
©2001 Maggie Hopp; © 2001
Maggie Hopp; Elliott Kaufman
Photography)

Square." Those at *Newsday* saw it as "an unexpected benefit from the city's economic doldrums," a "Glad Reprieve for Times Square." At *Crain's*, editors advised "Times Sq. Revival Should Center on Consumer Uses." The "opportunity—for faster restoration of the street-level hurly-burly and empty theaters" and the benefit of a revitalized street "in a manner more in keeping with its ebullient history" came with caveats: "An interim approach is hardly ideal. Why struggle to revitalize 42nd Street only to tear it down later?" It also came with costs: The developers were "relieved of the immediate cost of renovating the sprawling Times Square subway interchange." Relief that the planned towers would not go forward, as designed, was palpable, as was the hope that the alternative plan would hold a silver lining. *Newsday*'s editors were prescient: "There's a good chance that if the entertainment center proves successful, it could influence the design—and aesthetic integration into Times Square—of any office towers that are ultimately built."[42]

Any consensus on the 42DP was rare because the credibility of the public for this project had long since disappeared. "We had become a pariah, politically," Robertson recalled.[43] Even those with objections to individual pieces of the new plan applauded the whole new vision as a sign that a future existed for West 42nd Street. The city and state's real task now was to get from the present empty, desolate street to the new vision of West 42nd Street as a place of lights! signs! dancing! It was "post-no-bills" territory. Something needed to happen, fast. While the formal, more detailed vision was in the process of being worked out, it was "urgent," said the *Times* "that the emptiness be refilled."

Both sides knew that they could not leave the project where it was, boarded up. TSCA, according to George Klein, first recognized this. Weisbrod said the idea was definitely Robertson's. It was, she said, something of an epiphany: "The Gap opened a store at the corner of 42nd Street and Seventh Avenue in the spring of 1992, and they did it all on their own. It was a pivotal moment. Our retail guys said their numbers were incredible, and suddenly we realized what was possible here."[44] The bill would be paid by TSCA under the terms of MOU between the 42DP and the developer in which TSCA finally agreed to spend a minimum of $20 million to fill these empty spaces in adherence with design guidelines being established as part of the new plan; if more than $20 million were spent on interim retail and related obligations, the addition would be put on the ESAC open tab.[45] "The quid pro quo for not having to build is that you have to bring 42nd Street back to life," said Robertson.[46]

The "interim" goal of *42nd Street Now!* was to establish tourist and entertainment-related shops and other "lively late-night venues"—a music store with video theater, nightclubs, restaurants, a ticket agent, even a currency-exchange service center—in the existing buildings where the towers would some day rise. It was a temporary antiblight plan to attract pedestrian activity to the storefronts left vacant from the condemnation; the expectation was that the stores would remain in place for seven to 15 years. For the longer-term "full-build program," in the jargon of the

Supplemental EIS, the rescripted plan presented three revised priorities: an expanded program of entertainment uses for the midblock theater sites under the 42DP's control; exacting design, use, and operating (DUO) guidelines to ensure visual drama through razzle-dazzle lights and signage; and a commitment of public rather than private funds to complete condemnation of the project area's western end—which remained essential to cleanse the street of pornography.

The ideas that gave rise to these priorities came from several sources. These included the public debates and intensive studies of the entertainment district that led up to the 1987 design guidelines for and 1988 rezoning of Times Square and the 44 diverse and creative proposals for reuse of the historic theaters and the role-defining deliberations of the New42. At the same time, Douglas Durst put forth an "antiplan" plan of entertainments for eight historic theaters on the street that his family controlled for a brief period.[47]

Prepared by LucasArts Attractions with the Project for Public Spaces, Inc. and Bolan Smart Associates, Inc., the 33-page document put forth an alternative approach—"intended to be developed privately with limited support and assistance from public agencies"—that made a simple argument: In keeping with its historic legacy, the redevelopment of West 42nd Street should make a "major entertainment statement" that would become a showcase of New York.[48] A plan in concept only, the proposed entertainment center comprised six activity clusters, plus a hotel. Taken together the suggested activities cataloged a vast array of seemingly every possible public amusement, commercial entertainment, theme exhibition, public-purpose museum, and speciality/concession retail store, as well as theaters, other types of performance space, and entertainment-industry studios. It resurrected the concept of the roof garden and speak-easy nightclubs; proposed museums devoted to American Music, the Moving Image, Mystery à la Ripley's Believe It or Not, the Electric Word as in neon and signage, Holography, the Times of New York, and a Children's Museum. It promoted movies, comedy, jazz, variety shows, fine dancing, arcade gaming, billiards (upscale), art galleries, and a "technoplay LBE," which would combine computer graphics, cinema, and storytelling in a themed environment, among other activities. It included a tourist infocenter, the tkts booth, a science and electronic superstore, corporate-sponsored tech exhibits, interactive activities, and all manner of food and beverage service, including a Rube Goldberg–style "investor's club" bar and grill, and a "buffeteria" designed along the lines of the Automat ideal. It aimed to be multicultural and all scale and for all people, changeable and flexible. The mélange of entertainment opportunities would be packaged with corporate sponsorship and thematic advertising.

Some predictable posturing between the adversaries erupted in the media when *Crain's* printed a small blurb on the entertainment-concept plan that inadvertently contained errors. In a letter to the editor, Robertson called it "just another futile public relations ploy" by the Dursts "to protect their assemblage" adjacent to the project area. Durst wrote that "with so many factors preventing movement on 42nd Street, we felt compelled to reach for a new vision for 42nd Street. . . ."[49]

Robertson's task was to meld the many ideas (crazy, out-of-the box, traditional), studies, and reports (theater preservation, visual aesthetics, zoning, financial feasibility, retail development feasibility) and creative thrusts into a feasible plan, then aggressively market the vision and shepherd the plan through various approvals that would ensure its implementation. Asked about the parallels with the project opponents' proposals for a tourist-based entertainment center, she replied: "You know what? Every good idea has its time. The fact of the matter is that this is a good idea, even if we were not necessarily the authors of it."[50]

Like the first big vision for the street, *The City at 42nd Street*, the programmatic essence of *42nd Street Now!* was popular entertainment for the middle class. Both plans specified entertainment-related and tourist-oriented uses—the first, theme-park rides and world's-fair-type exhibits and the second, general entertainment-related uses. Both would be criticized as being "Disneylike." Both called for restoration and reuse of several of the street's legitimate theaters, much retail and many restaurants, and, of course, the financially enabling office towers clustered at the eastern edge of the project area. A careful tally of specifics would likely reveal other broad brush-stroke similarities, despite the passage of more than 13 years. One glaring difference was the disappearance of the infeasible giant mart, effectively dropped out of existence in *42nd Street Now!* and supplanted by more appropriate entertainment venues and cinemas. The dramatic contrasts in approach, tone, and aesthetic vision, however, are what make the comparison between these two programmatic plans striking and notable. Whereas the execution outline in the case of *The City at 42nd Street* was written in terms of financial feasibility, for *42nd Street Now!* it was written in the code of design guidelines, inches-thick comprehensive "Design Use and Operating Requirements."

The goal of Stern and Kalman's design-driven conceptual plan was to re-create the street's legendary luster, with razzle-dazzle honky-tonk details. The images and ideas in their visuals represent a look backward, with modifications for technology and activity options geared to current consumer tastes for pleasure and entertainment. It was nostalgia elevated by state-of-the-art marketing. Nostalgia, though, was not at all what *The City at 42nd Street* was about, however much the visual plan now strikes one as naive—an improbable execution and a "questionable land use for Midtown" as Huxtable said first, as usual. Notwithstanding—or rather because of—its world's-fairish thrust, the visuals of *The City at 42nd Street* now come off looking like 1950s kitsch. But the theme of the century's great world's fairs was forward-looking modernity, and likewise the visuals of *The City at 42nd Street* aimed for more design modernity than can be found in *42nd Street Now!* Times change.

It would take more than two years to line up all the pieces before Robertson could orchestrate the formal presentation of *42nd Street Now!* in September 1993. For earlier changes to the program requiring amend-

ments to the *GPP*, an Environment Assessment had been sufficient, procedurally. But the scope and direction of change embedded in the new plan
finally put it over the top; UDC would have to completely redo the EIS, a
time-intensive and costly—approximately $1.6 million—task as necessary
politically as procedurally.

Not unexpectedly, the new entertainment and tourist-oriented
agenda of the plan garnered strong support from the performing-arts
community, once their greatest fear—competition from additional legiti-
mate-theater entertainment—had been assuaged.[51] This group, in alignment with architects and design professionals, turned out in force for the
public hearings, more so than for the previous events. Together, they
grabbed the most microphone time, 17 spots of the total 53 who testified.
No other set of interests came close; the closest were the property owners
and tenants of West 42nd Street, nine in number. Those representing the
arts and culture spoke in highly positive terms about the new plan—
though the producers were against subsidies to Disney. Five major issues
about the proposed changes to the *GPP* dominated the testimony: broadening the uses for the midblock theaters, especially the return of movies to
the street; traffic and transportation impacts; procedures for the plan's
approval; the financial arrangements with developers and questionable
need for subsidies, now; and, last, social and street conditions—continuing
concern about possible displacement of sex-businesses and crime to nearby Clinton and Chelsea neighborhoods.

The response to the interim plan was overwhelmingly favorable:
"beneficial," "great and brilliant," "will break deadlock on the project
plan," "realistic look at the area and heads project in right direction," "generally sound," "worth doing," "laudable," "imperative now." Though some
voices of dissent could be heard, the overall tone of the hearings was relatively mild compared to past events, as was the overall turnout, as the
numbers testifying indicate (table 9.1).

The intense clash of values so dominant in earlier public forums
was absent from these hearings, though disappear completely it did not.
Many New Yorkers continued to voice dislike for the idea of inventing a
new Times Square, preferring the place as it was: gritty and sinful, a spectacle characterized by unusual street life. This came out most forcefully in
a set of opinions invited by the *Times* and printed on its op-ed page.[52] Luc
Sante, the author of *Low Life: Lures and Snares of Old New York,* cleverly
parodied the idea of recapturing "that eccentric Times Square dazzlement"
when he spoke of the requirement for "colorful characters" and "spontaneous public spectacle:"

> the occasional soft riot, fake ledge-jumper, escaped prize
> bull, inexplicable rain of dollar bills. And let's not forget
> that the experience would be nowhere without a sense
> of sin and consequent expiation. Maybe the city could
> plant used underwear in random visitors' pockets, maybe
> spike every tenth beverage served at the diner, maybe

TABLE 9.1 INTEREST-GROUP REPRESENTATION TESTIFYING AT THE 42DP PUBLIC
HEARINGS

INTEREST GROUP	DEIS 1984	BOE 1984	DSEIS 1993
42DP/development team	0.6%	8.9%	1.9%
West 42nd Street vested interests	11.5%	2.5%	16.9%
Other business	7.1%	5.0%	3.8%
Public-sector officials (non-42DP)	11.5%	17.8%	20.8%
Arts/culture	23.7%	24.2%	39.6%
Clinton community	10.9%	15.3%	3.8%
Construction industry	1.9%	10.9%	0%
Social-service institutions	7.1%	7.9%	7.5%
Garment industry	4.5%	2.5%	0%
Neighborhood associations	3.2%	2.5%	1.9%
Other	18.0%	2.5%	3.8%
Total	100.0%	100.0%	100.0%
	(n=156)	(n=202)	(n=53)

SOURCE: Author's compilations. DSEIS includes written submissions by five who
had not testified in person.

run its own shell games and add to the revenue. For
authenticity, the attraction would hold its own with any
foreign palace and most domestic national parks.

The architectural critic for the *Boston Globe*, Robert Campbell, summed
up the character of New York, as reflected by Times Square as:

the city that doesn't present itself to us, the city where
everything—even the culture palace, even the maverick
person—must tuck into the anonymous grid. It's the
city, therefore, of the risk of the unknown, and so the
turf of the inside dopester, the urban sleuth, the holder
of private knowledge. Let Times Square remain so. Let it
be always the home of entertainment, but never turned
inside out to become, itself, a presented entertainment.

And in a sarcastic plea, Susan Orlean, a *New Yorker* staff writer and author
of *Saturday Night,* called for the old diversity:

If a peddler on Broadway is selling fake cellular telephones, shouldn't others nearby be encouraged with tax
abatements to offer, say, wind-up chattering teeth or
those weird neon tubes? . . . Entertainment should be
various as well. Must every porn theater feature only
women with large breasts? How about a few offering
just average-sized breasts? And lunatic preachers of every
sect must be fairly represented; an aggressive outreach
program is needed. That's my Times Square.

Just as the new plan no longer fought with the street's historic
identity, the city and state's commitment to the original high-density

office program remained solidly in place. In the minds of many, *42nd Street Now!* was enticing but unfortunately interim. The editors of *Newsday* advised public officials "Better rethink those office towers." The project was "out of synch with market reality," they wrote: "the public had swallowed the idea of four bulky towers . . . with great difficulty. What made the idea of these monstrosities somewhat palatable were the public benefits dangled before New Yorkers. Like a brand new mezzanine for the dilapidated 42nd Street subway station . . ." but this was "kissed goodbye" back in 1992. "Redeveloping Times Square is still a worthy venture," they concluded, "but what seemed feasible in 1982 may be obsolete. . . . Fifty-story boxes never did cut it in Times Square."[53] Long-time critics of the 42DP such as Senator Franz S. Leichter and the MAS were quick to forcefully reiterate their objections to a "massive give-away [that] will be New York City's largest taxpayer-financed real estate boondoggle ever," "unbelievably large subsidies . . . that never made sense for the site, and are even worse now."[54] Veteran *Times* reporter Thomas J. Lueck questioned, "Must Show Go On?"[55]

These criticisms of the city's financial deal with TSCA held even less political weight in the new deal climate than they had in the past. This despite the fact that they arose under the Dinkins Administration, which was less friendly to real estate development than the Koch Administration had been. The city could not afford, as the business bi-weekly *Crain's* put it, "angering the company that had invested almost $300 million in the project," nor to lose the 5,000 jobs its subsidiary, Prudential Securities, Inc., had in New York, which "not coincidentally," as *Newsday* pointed out, were in jeopardy. The reason was simple: The city and state needed Prudential to fund the antiblight interim plan and shield the public sector from more potential failure, as further argued in chapter 12. Although they were in a position to default the insurance giant, "A default doesn't do *us* any good," said Tese.[56]

DEAL GYMNASTICS

The original deal had become economically untenable for both sides, and in agreeing to renegotiate, both bowed to reality: The market for new midtown skyscrapers was dead. Given the timing of this renegotiation, the newly opened door allowed for more than just a mutual release of burdensome commitments. It presented an opportunity to amend the deal, for a second time, in ways that could correct past errors, to benefit from past lessons. For TSCA, which had started to chafe at the city's view of the open-tab funding arrangement even before the 1992 renegotiations, this meant getting out from under more big commitments—building a first office tower likely to cost upward of $450 million in the middle of a dramatically overbuilt market and funding a $91-million letter of credit for renovation of the Times Square subway station complex. For the city, this meant cauterizing the hemorrhaging economy resulting from the ever-increasing ESAC and revising the complicated formula defining its financial participation in the project's hoped-for economic success. "The deal strengthened the policy objectives of the project and made them easier to realize," said Weisbrod.[57]

The revised deal, laid out in the 1992 MOU and finalized in the 1994 amendments to the TSCA leases, reflected a dramatically different philosophy: market-driven timing. The risk-aversion that had so driven the city and state's actions from the start had been absorbed by Prudential. The revisions transformed the public-private relationship from an arrangement in which the city and state and the developers were locked together and bound by a contractual obligation to commence construction in phases according the schedule specified in the LADA into one in which TSCA, in effect, got something of an "ownership interest," said Weisbrod, with the right to build—when the developers determined market conditions were favorable. The market-driven timing of construction removed the specter of default. The revised financial arrangements, incorporating changes both little and large, also reallocated the long-term sharing of risk for developing the project.

In relieving all private parties of their respective obligations to fund the Times Square subway-station renovations, the MTA took on this most conventional of public responsibilities—which the public sector should always have borne directly, as discussed in chapter 12. Beside funding the renovations to attract interim retail tenants, TSCA agreed to freeze—"toll" in financial jargon—interest on ESAC during a construction hiatus beginning January 1, 1994, and ending (on an allocated basis for each site) with the start of construction (of the office tower on that site). After tolling, interest would be paid (at 1.1 percent above the yield on the most recently issued ten-year U.S. Treasury obligations), a reworked deal term that promised less volatility and a lower rate than the earlier formula. The city's negotiators rightly viewed these adjustments to the terms of TSCA's "loan" as a big savings. It was the "most important" way in which the deal was significant, said Weisbrod, but the savings were extremely hard to get.[58] Politically important to the city, the concession would ultimately be of little cost to Prudential. Given how unlikely cash returns for the project appeared at that time, it was an accounting issue. For Prudential, the opportunity cost of tolling interest was moot. As a practical matter, the insurance giant had taken a writedown on its books of some portion of the $300 million reportedly then spent on the project. It had become, in other words, economic dead weight.

The long-term risk-sharing changed in other policy-important ways. In terms of the theater agenda, the new deal converted TSCA's obligation to renovate the Liberty Theater into a cash contribution of $9 million—which, at UDC's discretion, could be used for the reconstruction or renovation of any of the theaters on the north (Site 10) or south (Site 5) side of the street—and capped its total obligation for the theaters at $18.2 million. In addition, the agreement called for TSCA to impose an annual "theater surcharge" of 10 cents per rentable square foot on office tenants to support the renovation and operation of the theaters. As with the earlier financial arrangements, a considerable portion of what was presented as TSCA's "contributions" to the project was, technically, substantive fiction because the existing obligations for the theaters ($9.2 million) and streetscape ($2.6 million) as well as a portion of the $3.3 million annual Interim Rent (to be adjusted for inflation) were funding obligations classified as ESAC.[59] The developer benefited, in turn, from the recut deal's extension of the favorable schedule of PILOT payments to 20 years from 15; while now indexed to parallel increases in real estate taxes on comparable buildings, the PILOTs would remain substantially less than what would be paid by competing towers.

The major economic benefit to the city from the renegotiated deal was the revision to the participation formula. The formula for the city's share of percentage rent, previously defined as 5 percent of "net cash flow" (10 percent with rent erosion)—"absolutely meaningless by that stage of the game"—was recast as 2 percent of "adjusted gross revenues" (all revenues other than capital proceeds, minus operating expenses, limited capital expenses, theater surcharges, and PILOTs). Further, the new revenue stream was not subject to ESAC recoupment.[60]

TSCA's real pain came with the programmatic obligations for the interim plan, and, on that front, intense disputes erupted continually during negotiations over the signage and lighting requirements. The design issues became a painful pressure point for each side, a source of natural tension because their respective goals were in conflict. Whereas city and state officials sought to use the plan to create a round-the-clock lively street scene during this "interim" period, Prudential's executives and Klein were principally concerned the protection of TSCA's—Prudential's—enormous investment. This meant, as Crain's pointed out, "keeping costs down on the interim plan and making sure that it doesn't block development of office buildings when that market comes back."[61] The pairing was especially odd under the rescripted plan's vision for West 42nd Street.

The clashes were reportedly monumental, even within the planning team. Graphic designer Tibor Kalman called them "big cat fights."[62] In aesthetic temperament and background, he and Stern were near opposites. Kalman, who died at the age of 49 in May 1999, was a designer whose "innovative ideas about art and society helped change the way a generation of designers and their clients viewed the world," wrote the Times in his obituary.[63] Fondly called the "bad boy" of graphic design, Kalman's mark was all over 42nd Street Now! "I am interested in imperfections, quirkiness, insanity, unpredictability," he said in an interview published in Wired.[64] The forte of his firm, M&Company, which he founded in 1980, was described as "a kind of anti-corporate voice; it had a feel that attracted well-heeled clients like Knoll Furniture, the Limited, ABC News and Lifetime Television, as well as a number of museums and movie studios thrashing about in the 1980's and 90's for some succinct statement of purpose."[65] Kalman was brought onto the 42DP planning team by Paul Whalen, one of Stern's junior associates, who decided that they needed some "craziness." As one who embraced the vernacular, Kalman wanted to keep West 42nd Street the way it was. "It was not a question of big office buildings," he said—"if you want sunlight, go to Kansas." Rather, what he objected to was the bottom of the office towers. "They were overplanned and overdesigned and sterile."[66] In understanding the origins of the vernacular of West 42nd Street, he felt the culture had to be high and low; it could not be just middle class. Kalman wanted "cacophony, excitement and democracy of the sidewalk, where everyone had equal access." "It should be a zoo, like the rest of New York, but a well-maintained zoo, instead of a depressed, unemployed and crack-smoking kind of zoo."[67] Together Robertson and Kalman generated lots of energy: "Tibor is always challenging you," Robertson recalled. "He's always over the top, and that's why he's so good in this type of project. He's really a wonderful person."[68] His cat-fight clashes with Stern were resolved by a simple fact: Robertson was the client. "She liked the vernacular," said Kalman, "which won out."[69]

The developers did not take well to the frenzied, kinetic, and noisy vision of West 42nd Street put forth by *42nd Street Now!* and the large and varied types of signs mandated by its detailed design guidelines. The glitzy neon signs envisioned by the plan were not only the antithesis of corporate culture, they were expensive. Experiencing some degree of déjà vu, Robertson tackled this problem just as she had before, during the 1987 renegotiations of the TSCA deal: using the city's newly passed design regulations as a benchmark, she battled horribly, bitterly, and often with Klein over lighting and signage. Prudential's key negotiators felt no differently about the tenor of these negotiations. Sometimes it was a four-way battle, said a former Prudential negotiator; "the city and state didn't always agree; one would try to upstage the other." For the final buildings, the developers agreed to follow the guidelines they had previously agreed upon in 1988, but for the interim plan, they wanted flexibility in the type of signs, billboards instead of so much light and flash. "It is absolutely essential," said Brian P. Murphy, a senior vice president at Prudential who was the point person on this project, "that we have the ability at any time to take over a complete site when a tenant steps forward, even if it's within a month. The advertisers who would want 'spectacular signs' might require a minimum period of three to five years, or longer, to establish their 'sign presence' and recover the costs of those signs."[70] "Billboards were not expensive to create and they made a statement," said Klein. The diversity—eclectic mix—of the signage requirements, he believed, was "confusing."[71]

As frustration mounted during what became a year and a half of tough negotiations, Robertson and Tese—who steadfastly refused to back off from the new vision or its strict design guidelines—warned that if an agreement was not reached by August 1, 1994, they would force the developers' hand by turning over title to the site on which existing buildings had already been condemned—which would make TSCA legally bound to begin construction within a short period of time or walk away from its huge investment. "T.S.C.A. is tall on buildings and short on signage," Tese said for the record. "We're going to come up with more suggestions but T.S.C.A. knows this is a priority with us, and they've got to start getting real."[72] Robertson threw down the gauntlet: "Enough is enough," she said.[73] In the end, the developers agreed to include 50,000 square feet of retail and electric supersigns in the interim project. The obligations of the interim plan amounted to "the price to get out of the deal's commitments—a date certain for construction and money for the subway. Once the market had turned, these commitments were a constant threat," said a former Prudential executive.

There was no formal plan for *42nd Street Now!*, only 342 pages of detailed DUO guidelines—in fact, several sets, those for individual sites and the historic guidelines for the theaters—and a 25-page executive summary. And while the executive summary was completed by January 1993, it was not released until September of that year, after much haggling with the developers over words. "The developers," *Times* reporter David W. Dunlap pointed out, "were conspicuous by their absence at the news conference."[74] The staunch position on design taken by the public sector came from Robertson: "Aesthetics for 42DP should have the number-one priority; aesthetics are super important," she said. "People come to Times Square to see things. Tourists come to see Times Square, say they've seen it. The pedestrian flow ("count") creates value. With the real estate recession, [we] really felt this."[75] Jettisoning the original 1981 design guidelines was a poor decision, in her opinion. Like Richard A. Kahn, who presided over UDC when those guidelines for West 42nd Street's redevelopment were commissioned, Robertson views aesthetics as one of the essential "returns" the public sector should be getting from public development, the other three being return of existing taxes, a "reasonable" investment return on its dollars in the deal—between 8 and 9 percent, without PILOT and with conservative projections of rent—and upside percentage rents. "As a public-sector negotiator, you don't have to trade off financials and aesthetics," Robertson asserted.[76]

By the strength of her personality, Robertson represented an indefatigable force aiming to make the new vision happen, materialize into new bricks and mortar backed by serious investment commitments. Though in a highly visible hot seat, she was not alone. In Cora Cahan of the New42, she had more than just a strong ally. Personal friends, they were professionally united in their effort to revive West 42nd Street, and the personality dynamics of the two imparted a special measure to the effort (figure 9.5).

9.5
Cora Cahan (left) and Rebecca Robertson on West 42nd Street, 1993. (Jack Manning/New York Times Pictures)

MARKETING THE MESSAGE

Robertson was justly opinionated about the project's aesthetics because she needed to aggressively promote the new vision of tourism and entertainment to a skeptical business community and jaded public, both of which wondered whether this would be yet another articulated plan that would go nowhere. "We hired a public relations firm, something many public development agencies might not like to do. We treated the project like a 'product,'" she explained in an interview. "Before the product was four massive buildings mired in bureaucracy and controversy. It was not a very salable image to the entertainment companies because it said to everybody 'litigation, delay and office towers.' So we hired big people—Robert A. M. Stern, Tibor Kalman—made a big effort." The goal was to market the image to groups like Disney and Viacom by creating "a public relations campaign to say this product is all about great pedestrian traffic, the best tourist market in New York State, a history that no other street can beat and a name with international recognition."[77]

What was the message? "Times Square/42nd Street Means People": 20 million tourists a year; 12,600 hotel rooms accommodating approximately 1.7 million guests; 39 Broadway houses with 7.5 million theater goers; ten first-run movie houses with 1.2 million in annual attendance; 130,000 office and service workers within a four-block radius of the project area; 200,000 commuters a day streaming across midtown from the Port Authority Bus Terminal, and 340,000 daily transit riders who use the Times Square subway station complex of which an estimated 60,000 exit on West 42nd Street. At the key corner locations in the project area, pedestrian counts ranked among the highest in all of Manhattan—between 4,000 and 6,000 per hour, daily. The statistics, they hoped, signaled extraordinary commercial prospects.

The hard facts of pedestrian counts aside, Robertson and her designers and consultants still needed to reestablish the view that the squalid and degraded but vibrant Times Square was the center of the world. "Everybody in New York thought it was . . . so we said it was the center of the world," Stern recalled, "but was it really? Well, it really is . . . at least for a New York tourist."[78] For the corporation commitments Robertson sought to attract, the argument would have to turn on the sweet spot of commercial opportunity—the fact that the Times Square district was under-retailed—revealed by the consultants' feasibility study for retail development. Forty-second Street at Times Square had all the right characteristics for a strong retail market geared to tourists and entertainment seekers, and crime was down significantly on the street. Still, this opportunity was ahead of reality, as one of the consultants, Lee Philips, discovered on his first intercept run for training his people to do focus-group inquiries; the first person to whom he addressed a question said, "I can't talk now—I got to see my parole officer." Philips immediately called Faith Hope Consolo of Garrick-Aug Associates, one of the city's most prominent retail brokers with whom he was working on this consulting assignment, and said, "What are we doing here?" Her reaction to a question Bob Stern asked her earlier at one of the first concept meetings, what did she think of West 42nd Street, revealed the same skepticism: "The minute I cross Fifth Avenue, I get a nose bleed," she replied.[79]

If the retail consultants thought the nose-bleed metaphor appropriate for the area, they did not let that interfere with what they had been asked to do. Out of the demographic data on Times Square they fashioned

1
Times Square in the early 1960s.
(Collection of the author)

3
Disney in its interim space at the
southwest corner of 42nd Street and
Seventh Avenue, 1998. (Gary Hack)

2
The view west of West 42nd Street,
with Richard Haas's mural of the
Times Tower in the left foreground,
early 1980s.(© Peter Mauss/Esto)

4

Inescapable irony. (Arnoldo Franchioni)

5
The north side of the street, Site 7
(before) . . .

6
. . . and E-Walk (after). (42nd Street
Development Project, Inc.; Gary Hack)

7
The south side of the street, Sites 10 and
8 (before) . . .

8
. . . HMV and the Empire as the AMC
Theaters (after). (42nd Street Development
Project, Inc.; Gary Hack)

9
Model of Johnson and Burgee's office towers to be built at the intersection of 42nd Street and Seventh Avenue. (© Thorney Lierberman)

10
Robert Venturi and John Rauch's Big Apple for Times Square set within the Johnson and Burgee model of the 42DP office towers. (Venturi Scott Brown Associates)

11
Pre-preview in Times Square.
(Arnoldo Franchioni)

12
The New 42nd Street Studios.
(Gary Hack)

13
New Year's Eve, 1995. (Times
Square Business Improvement
District)

14
New Victory Theater restored, alone on the desolate street, 1995. (Elliott Kaufman)

15
The adult movie theater transformed into a theater for children. (Elliott Kaufman)

16
The New Amsterdam Theater
orchestra before . . .

17
. . . and after. (© Whitney
Cox Photographer)

18
The New Amsterdam Theater
grande promenade before . . .

19
. . . and after. (© Whitney Cox
Photographer)

20
The New Amsterdam Theater box seats before . . .

21
. . . and after. (© Whitney Cox Photographer)

22
The single neon spectacular created in
the bleak 1970s. (Collection of Artkraft
Strauss Sign Corporation)

23
Postcard of the memorable vision
of the Chicago-based brand, 1936–
1942. (Collection of the author)

24
The Morgan Stanley sign on 1585 Broadway. (Gary Hack)

25
New signs where the Pussycat Lounge used to be, 1998. (Scott Lotokis)

26
The east side of Seventh Avenue at 47th Street newly lit, 1998. (Scott Lotokis)

The world's most expensive video screen, constantly changing. (Gary Hack)

28
One of the established brands returning to Times Square. (Gary Hack)

29
One interpretation of the 42DP design guidelines: signs for the interior food court on the south side of West 42nd Street. (Gary Hack)

30
The postcard site, rebuilt
as a signpost and hotel
by Sherwood Equities.
(Sherwood Equities)

a marketing strategy and a use plan for 320,826 square feet of combined retail/entertainment activities in 61 establishments plus 90,565 square feet of special-purpose uses in six different properties.[80] That is a lot of space, almost twice the retail area of Boston's crowd-attracting Faneuil Hall Marketplace. But the space had to have a street-wide visual identity. "What we had learned most from Times Square," Robertson later said to a group of real estate professionals, "was that aesthetics are good economics, and that if you could create a place as recognizable as the Statute of Liberty, you would make money for the city and the state, forever. So what we wanted to do is create an aesthetic plan that would really become a tourist attraction in itself."[81] The colorful visuals of plan itself, in other words, became a marketing tool for resuscitating the troubled project.

The aesthetics-oriented strategy captured a favorable review—"42d Street Plan: Be Bold or Be Gone!"—from *Times* architectural critic Herbert Muschamp, whose opinions, like those of his predecessors, carried a lot of weight. Muschamp had warmed up to the task of reviewing *42nd Street Now!* with earlier anticipatory pieces in which he laid out his views on "The Alchemy Needed to Rethink Times Square" and announced it was "Time to Reset the Clock in Times Square." He had talked with Robertson on the phone about the new strategy, and was good friends with Kalman, so presumably he had some knowledge of Kalman's germinating ideas for the plan. He was ready to enthusiastically endorse the new proposal since it fit within his framework of how new development could allow Times Square to become "an entertainment center for the year 2000: a place that could energize New York's cultural life for years to come."[82] For him, it illustrated a successful balance between preserving Times Square without antiquating it. "Forty-Second Street Now! . . . is a smoothly choreographed step in exactly the right direction," he wrote. "The plan is important not only because of the historical significance of the site but also because it breaks ground for a fertile exchange between corporate and popular culture." He went on to praise public officials for looking at West 42nd Street "with open eyes," and for making the street's distinctive features central to the plan. Paying homage to Robert Venturi, Denise Scott Brown, and Stephen Izenour's classic 1972 text *Learning from Las Vegas*, Muschamp wrote that the plan "could be called Learning from 42nd Street." Rejecting an easy classification of the plan as "gigantic simulation, an ersatz, corporate urbanism similar to Universal Citywalk in Los Angeles," which others might apply, he went on to praise the corporate character of the plan for what it can potentially achieve:[83]

> In a city where recent real estate development has tended to drive people apart, there is something almost quixotic about the plan's ambition to reunite them beneath the umbrella of popular culture. And at a time when pop's technology (VCR's, Walkmen, virtual reality) tends to reinforce spatial isolation, a public space built on pop is practically a Utopian proposition. And

the fact that the plan is corporate may be the most idealistic thing about it. For it suggests that the corporate and the heterogeneous need not be foes.

One did not have to agree with everything Muschamp put forth to understand that Robertson had scored, big time: "We broadcast [it] everywhere. We made a lot out of this, brought it to everyone's attention. The important thing is to create a sense of activity, of movement."[84] This they generated through a series of marketed events in the theaters: concerts, readings, plays, and art shows.

Robertson's PR machine included the well-publicized "42nd Street Art Project," a contemporary art exhibition organized by Creative Time, Inc., a 20-year-old organization devoted to presenting performing and visual arts in public spaces throughout New York. With $100,000 Robertson raised from leasing a vacant sign on the street, Art Project inaugurated a new vision for West 42nd Street by transforming the block into an outdoor public art display of 17 exhibits by 24 artists asked to create works for spaces left vacant by the condemnation process. The temporary set of installations consisted of irreverent "contextual" projects and word plays, and with these Art Project set out to challenge the public's expectations for and experiences of West 42nd Street. Fashion designer Todd Oldham turned the facade of Peepland into a side-showlike mural. Costume designer Adelle Lutz parodied the fashion industry's marketing slogan—"Make a Statement"—by filling a window of the former American Male shop renamed "American She-Male," with a pair of bright yellow mannequins clad in clothes fashioned from different brands of condoms—"Wear Condoms!!" it proclaimed. Kalman and fellow graphic designer Scott Stowell covered a large billboard with the word EVERYBODY spelled out in black letters against a background of intense yellow (figure 9.6). Conceptual artist Jenny Holzer took over the empty marquees of the street's theaters for thought-provoking aphorisms such as "A Lot of Professionals Are Crackpots," "Raise Boys and Girls the Same Way," "Sloppy Thinking Gets Worse Over Time."[85]

Art Project elicited a generally favorable, if somewhat cynical— "part of a slick urban maneuver"—architectural review by Muschamp, who used his space in the Sunday *Times* cultural section to criticize Elizabeth Diller and Richard Scofidio, architect designers of the exhibit's biggest hit, "Soft Sell." A pair of "glistening red lips" located beneath a theater marquee enticed passers-by with seductive phases in "the juicy tones of a 900-number voice," Soft Sell offered up a tease, as explained in the official brochure for the event:[86]

> Supposedly enticements—the lure of a peep show—
> both lips and words are in fact parodies of what's
> expected. The theater doors are a screen intervening
> between inside and out. Covered with liquid crystal
> panels, the doors—the "plane of enticement"—go from

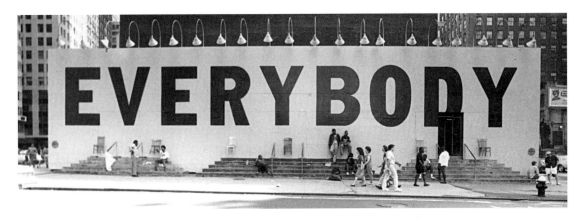

transparent to opaque, drawing you in with glimpses of
pleasures within, then block your view. You are captivated, but you will not be satisfied. Think about it.

9.6
Tibor Kalman and Scott Stowell's
sign for Art Project, 1993. (© 2001
Maggie Hopp)

Praised by some, derided by others as a "new kind of highbrow spectacle"
in which art works were just another part of the cultural process of
repackaging West 42nd Street's troubling images for consumption by a
more upscale crowd, Art Project was all about changing the perception of
the street, reanimating it and, in the process, its sponsor—the "embattled
development arm" of UDC—and the 42DP.[87] Since the market seemed
not to be ready for the vision of entertainment the public sector wanted
to put in place, Robertson's task was to convince it of the rightness of
42nd Street Now! through this high-profile marketing event.

　　Robertson's PR machine has been characterized as "brilliant," a
"seminal event" for the project by friends and foes alike. Durst's attorney
Gary Rosenberg felt that the project should have been disbanded, but, he
said, "This dead dog would not die."[88] Robertson would not let the project die. To her way of thinking, the day had to come when the project
would work. Even during the darkest days, she kept the project alive
through the press—which she used to build a constituency for the plan—
and the press, many believed, allowed itself to be used. "As public officials
in charge of a project, we're courting both the private market for investment, but we are also looking after our politicians and making sure that
they are getting in the headlines," Robertson explained to a conference
of real estate professionals. "Our relationship with the press, therefore, is
extremely symbiotic. We need the press; they need us to fill the columns
of newspapers."[89]

　　The press, she went on, helps move a project along in several
important ways. First, the press functions as "your major marketing tool";
to get budget funding and keep up a flow of favorable reactions for a project, a plan like *42nd Street Now!* needs a high profile, which comes with
continuous coverage. Second, the press can be helpful in getting deadlines
met—the prime example being the July 15th deadline they had with
Disney—and in defining the deal-hanging issues for a project or "softer"
issues with which politicians aren't comfortable, such as aesthetics. "The
press defined this issue of the lights and signs of Times Square, and there-

fore the politicians ultimately responded and took a hard stand on it," she said, "but it took many years to do that." Third, the press helps sell your vision to others. "It [was] our marketing arm. We didn't have any tenants," recalled Robertson. "But the press embraced that vision and helped us get the tenants."[90] After years of nothing but relentless negative news about delays, litigation, and depressed markets, it was not hard for the press to latch onto a change of pace with upbeat news about the long-running 42DP saga, and after the announcement that Disney had signed an MOU with the city and state to redevelop the New Amsterdam Theater in February 1994, the good news came in abundance.

Promoting a specific agenda with substantive flash is not what city planners are typically trained to do, so Robertson's savvy marketing sense combined with her absolute dedication to the task, and to New York, defined a notable persona that won her much praise. She was described as "smart" and "tough," compliments in any developer's lexicon, one reporter remarked.[91] "She was the worst of adversaries and the best friend, as good as an ally as she was bad as an enemy," said Rosenberg from his view as an opposing litigator.[92] Her professional reputation would be made with this project. She was president of the 42DP, Inc., for nearly seven years under both Democratic Governor Cuomo and Republican Governor Pataki, a singular record of political survival. "Rebecca is the real hero of the project," said her colleague, Carl Weisbrod. "There were times in the early 1990s when she was alone. It was really tough."[93] "This project would not have happened without her," said Cora Cahan upon Robertson's departure from the 42DP, Inc., to take an executive position at the Shubert Organization. "She was the shepherd of the street's rejuvenation."[94]

Robertson's marketing of *42nd Street Now!* was skillful for another, unmentioned, reason. As the new public perception of the project took hold—in the media and on the streets—talk about the much-despised program of high-density office development all but disappeared for several years of public bliss—at least until the first office building rose up, a towering structure of glass and metallic sheen. The 42DP did not promote the fact that this essential economic component of the plan was very much in place, but neither did it deny its fundamental existence and strategic importance to making the new entertainment agenda possible. The silent treatment worked because the camera angle had been shifted sharply to the midblock of the street and focused exclusively on an invented program of entertainment. What at first appeared to be a tactical mistake—calling *42nd Street Now!* "interim"—ceased to arouse high-pitch emotion among the civics and other long-time critics as the new plan's programmatic promises came to fruition rather quickly, to everyone's amazement. Blinded by their own love affair with *42nd Street Now!,* then by the design-driven competition for development of the retail/entertainment/hotel opportunity on Site 7, and later by the opening of the New Victory and New Amsterdam Theaters, the architectural critics and urban commentators glossed over their earlier obsession with the catastrophic character of such large-scale density on West 42nd Street.

The gap between the necessity and the invention of redevelopment had been bridged. While not a single practical prayer existed for altering the fundamental financial driver of the project—development density—the new tourist-based agenda nevertheless pushed the pace of change by resetting the public's expectations and altering investors' perceptions with its new focus on popular entertainment (plate 11). Density financing had already succeeded in doing what it was supposed to do: create the economic platform for change without putting the city at direct financial risk. Even if the project's overall development density had not yet changed—it is likely to increase by the time the last sites in the project area are finally developed—the new highly detailed DUO guidelines for each site ensured that what got built on West 42nd Street would be strikingly different from the visual image seared into memory of the justly maligned Johnson/Burgee's corporate towers.

Moreover, by 1994, the transformation of Times Square was well underway. As a consequence of the project area's altered state of social and cultural perception between 1981 and 1994—changes brought about by decreasing crime and city-wide efforts to improve safety, the condemnation and shuttering of the street's sex and porn shops, the triumphs of historic preservation, and the clout of private investors such as Disney—architecture no longer had to serve as a powerful instrument for the reordering of existing physical relationships, as had been the case in the early 1980s. Its role had evolved along with the contentious history of the project. Architecture could now play more of a mediating role linking the fragmented pieces of Times Square's cultural and historical context. But only after the illusions and psychological perception of West 42nd Street had changed could a set of design guidelines allowing for small-scale internally generated transformations find acceptance as an urban reality.

The change in perception of West 42nd Street from an unsafe area in need of a large-scale external transformation to a series of development sites in transition amenable to a subtle set of design guidelines was first articulated by Andrew Mandel and Jacqueline Thaw in a 1990 article, "Teaching Times Square a Lesson." Writing for *Time* two years later, Kurt Anderson followed up with the question "Can 42nd Street Be Born Again?" Next, Paul Goldberger, in "The New Times Square: Magic That Surprised the Magicians," dissected the reasons that allowed Times Square to flourish in an environment previously thought incompatible with such small-scale intervention. Although Goldberger consistently maintained that ideologically this was the correct manner for dealing with revitalization in Times Square, in 1981 when he first wrote about the project, he was skeptical that such a plan was capable of fruition. When it clicked in, the change in perception came fast—faster than what had happened in Manhattan's other distinct district of dramatic change, SoHo. Building on solid economic fundamentals, the changing perception of Times Square was driven by the emergence on Broadway of blue-chip business and global entertainment corporations, which fostered the rehabilitation of 42DP's reputation as a progenitor of a new popular-entertainment culture for Times Square.

CHAPTER 10

Business Buys Broadway

It sits just above Duffy Square on the small, trapezoidal island at the northern end of the Times Square bow tie—Two Times Square. A narrow 25-story tower deftly housing the Ramada Renaissance Hotel behind five vertically stacked supersigns covering its southern face, its signs boldly announce the building's primary commercial purpose—promotion. Prominently placed on the giant, 303-foot signpost is an immense four-story fiber-optic fabrication of the iconic Coca-Cola bottle, its classic message matched to a historical location stretching back to 1932. Two Times Square is five blocks north of One Times Square, the former Times Tower, the icon of Times Square, known for its "zipper" sign, its New Year's Eve ball-drop, and its hitherto singular status as "the Eiffel Tower of outdoor advertising." The address of Two Times Square made little sense in terms of the city's sequential street numbering, which designated the structure as 1580 Broadway; however, the so-called vanity address perfectly captured the marketing logic fueling the new demand for space in Times Square. "What we're selling here is visibility," said Jeffrey Katz, the developer. "When movie-makers want to say, 'This is New York,' *this* is what they shoot"[1] (plate 30).

Place Branding

More than just an address in midtown Manhattan, Broadway between 42nd and 50th Streets was a marketable place. It was the new so-called 100-percent location, but for a different reason than what real estate professionals typically mean by that designation: The location could travel across space and culture to consumers worldwide, through communication broadcasts of every imaginable medium, for one simple reason—Times Square is an instantly recognizable "place brand." Japanese and Korean manufacturers (Sony, Minolta, Canon, Fuji, Konika, Samsung, Aiwa), American consumer products (Coca-Cola, Pepsi, Maxwell House, Eight

O'Clock Bean Coffee, Jell-O), Seventh Avenue fashion makers (Levi's, Kenar Enterprises, Norma Kamali, Boss, Jantzen, Joe Boxer, Calvin Klein), communications giants (MCI, AT&T, ITT) all have sought a presence in Times Square to exploit its "gloriously vulgar" lights-and-billboard advertising tradition. The tradition has not been about selling products, but rather about establishing an image-burnishing brand message and fighting it out with the competition through riotous, shouting signs designed to bring attention to the product and capture the consumer.

For advertisers, media, and entertainment businesses, the value of a Times Square address came not from its physical location as the mass-transportation nexus for the city, but rather from the immediate identification with a place widely seen as an icon for city life (nighttime adventures), entertainment (Broadway theater), creativity (the musical genius of Tin Pan Alley's Irving Berlin, the slang and word play of Damon Runyon, Walter Winchell, and Ring Lardner), communication (the big-city daily newspaper), sex and naughtiness, and a tantalizing, louche living. An estimated 20 million tourists flocked to Times Square each year and, through appearances in movies, TV shows, and tourist photographs, countless millions saw its image daily. Although Broadway seemed far distant from corporate character, blue-chip corporations now lined up to buy the Times Square identification for business purposes. Viacom International (Nickelodeon, Showtime, MTV, Blockbuster Video, Paramount Pictures, Simon & Schuster Publishers), Bertelsmann A.G. (Bantam Doubleday Dell Publishing, RCA Records, Artista Records), the Walt Disney Company, Madame Tussaud's, Virgin Retail Group, Warner Brothers, Ford Motor Company, ABC, and Nasdaq, among others, were not buying space in the sense of real estate, but rather a marketing opportunity made possible by a Times Square address. The place was a branded address.

The iconic image of Times Square sought by corporate marketers evoked a romanticized past that, as a brand, had tremendous value in the global commercial marketplace of the late twentieth century. With condemnation shuttering the adult-entertainment shops and deviant sex activity of West 42nd Street, it once again became acceptable for America's brand names to be associated with Times Square. Now that the place was economically and culturally safe, the marketers aimed to capitalize on the commanding imagery associated with it. Reviving brand-based commercialism not only fit Times Square's history, it filled a surprising gap in the city's retail market: In the early 1990s New York was strikingly underserved in terms of brand-name retailers. The city had been passed over by the new large national chains; its intense street-level retail services were neighborhood domains of local mom-and-pop businesses. If big-box retailers and popular mass merchandisers surfaced, they were the exception rather than the rule, especially in midtown Manhattan. One of the most notable exceptions was The Gap, which had some 30 stores in Manhattan by mid-1992, when it opened a 14,000 square-foot store on the corner of 42nd Street and Broadway (in the old Knickerbocker Hotel building) in space formerly occupied by an Off-Track Betting parlor.

The advertisers, entertainment and media companies that reconfigured the visual nighttime drama of the place with new supersigns, hoteliers and retailers that restaged daytime street-level activity with theme
restaurants (The Official All-Star Café, Ellen's Stardust Diner), multimedia
music stores (Virgin Megastore, HMV), multiplex movie theaters (AMC,
Sony-Loews), entertainment/game centers (Cinema Ride, Alien New
York, VR Showcase, ESPN Sports Zone, Lazer Park), tourist-oriented
superstores selling branded products of animated cartoon characters
(Disney, Warner Brothers, Viacom), and windowed live-production studios
using Times Square as a television backdrop ("MTV News," ABC's "Good
Morning America")—all big corporate names, not surprisingly. However
much Times Square's past may have been associated with personal entrepreneurship, which is less than the myth might suggest, the ability to
exploit the world-wide marketing power of the venue attracted corporations with established brand-name products. It also attracted emergent
growth-oriented companies, such as Viacom, intent on establishing their
identification quickly and with access to the capital to do so.

Entering this market was a high-cost, high-stakes game with
scant opportunity for amateurs. While regulatory constraints were few,
other barriers were substantial. For retailers, the goal was not just to place
an existing outlet in the New York market but rather to use the venue as a
creative opportunity for establishing a special urban prototype. Local
knowledge was needed regarding who owned what real estate under what
terms and what the city and state would do to assist if the venture sought
to be on West 42nd Street, knowledge that could be gained through relationships with experienced local players and that was essential for savvy
bidding on a development site, closing on a prime lease transaction, or
securing favorable tax subsidies. In the small, concentrated district from
42nd to 50th Street between Seventh Avenue, Broadway, and Eighth
Avenue, land for development was extremely limited, and this intensified
the financial stakes of securing a toehold in this market. New York had
always been an expensive city for business; high taxes, above-average operating expenses, and union-labor pay scales added other premiums to the
equation. Reputation—an elusive though more important factor than
many of the quantifiable business costs—was at risk in the highly visible
commercial world of Times Square. "Forty-second Street is not for the
weak and not for dreamers," remarked the 42DP's retail consultant, Faith
Hope Consolo.[2]

Big, well-established corporations with the resources to address
these factors were less likely than others to pioneer risky areas, however. To
spend the big dollars necessary to succeed on the scale of what is typically
needed, the concept and timing of a commercial venture have to be
"right," which by definition includes a "suitable" market. The corporate
approach, especially if the company trades on a public exchange, typically
means taking few chances. That was the case in Times Square, almost
without exception. The first entertainment player to express interest in
West 42nd Street, London-based Madame Tussaud's, of wax museum fame,

started exploring in 1991 whether "The Big Apple" was "essentially rotten at the core or a juicy fruit we should be preparing to pick!" but the investment environment surrounding Times Square and 42nd Street, which the museum maker characterized as "possibly the most undesirable district of mid-town Manhattan," was full of "concerns, pitfalls, dangers and risks."[3] It would not consider making a commitment for what would be its first United States venture without evidence of other comparable business commitments to West 42nd Street. Nor would Disney "go it alone." In the boardrooms of these corporate players, the perceived risks of making a major long-term property-based investment on West 42nd Street remained formidable.

What then finally broke the impasse? First, a recovering economy fueled opportunistic purchases of newly constructed but empty (or nearly empty) Class A office towers at bargain-basement prices. Bertelsmann A.G., the privately held German media conglomerate, and Morgan Stanley, the blue-chip investment banking firm, were the first to make commitments. As owner-users, their high-profile purchases—1540 Broadway, 1585 Broadway, 750 Seventh Avenue—created the critical mass of corporate investment central to transforming Times Square into what it is today. Second, changing trends in entertainment set the industry's leader in family entertainment, Disney, on a strategic quest in search of a Broadway platform for launching its new live-theatrical productions worldwide. Confirmed reports that it was talking with city and state officials about renovating the landmarked New Amsterdam Theater positioned Disney as the draw for the still-somnolent street, yet the entertainment giant's interest symbolized something beyond a marquee tenancy. The Disney announcement marked a turning point for the 42DP because it conferred middle-class respectability on the street, and this triggered intense corporate interest from competing brand-oriented entertainment retailers seeking a similarly visible geographical identity for mass distribution. The pattern was not new, only the players.

Even before Disney's commitment went "hard," as they say in real estate, a gold-rush fever for deals took hold. Journalists exclaimed "42d Street Is Now a Magnet for Merchants" (*Times*); "Times Square Land!" (*New York Post*); "A Star Is Reborn" (*Business Week*); "Times Sq. Lights Are On, and the Glitter Ain't Cheap" (*Crain's*). Retailers, restaurateurs, and hoteliers vied for the opportunity to service the millions of tourists who visited each year and the thousands of white-collar professionals and service workers who streamed in and out of the area's office towers each day. As they had done during heyday of Times Square's "spectaculars" in the 1930s and 1950s, brand merchandisers competed with one another to promote their image using ever-bigger and flashier signs. Cinema chains and purveyors of mass entertainment crowded into Times Square. Faster than most retail experts predicted and sooner than city and state officials dared dream, "The Great White Way 'Suddenly' Looked White Hot," as the *Times* reported. In 1998 Times Square vaulted onto the list of the "World's Most Expensive Streets," right after the Avenue des Champs-Elysées in Paris and just ahead of Rodeo Drive in Los Angeles. As a reporter from the *Wall Street Journal* put it, "Times Square real estate considered dangerous after dark just a few years ago has become some of the most sought-after in the world."[4]

Times Square remained a complex commercial marketplace, an eclectic district unlike any other in the city. Propelled by several engines— franchising, entertainment, tourism—it was not much different from its historic past, except for style. The activities were familiar, only played out in radically new formats of entertainment and on a physical landscape radically reshaped by new skyscrapers. By the early 1990s, the logic of changing land uses was clearer than before. Before any of the four office sites under the control of the Prudential/Klein partnership saw new construction, major corporate tenants would fill the completed, but vacant, office towers. Only after the excess space had been absorbed—which in 1992 real estate analysts estimated would take up to three and one-half years— would speculative office construction in midtown Manhattan begin on the four prime 42DP sites. TSCA did not need to build the towers itself; Prudential could sell the development rights to other developers, since condemnation—and time—had cleared away the sites' earlier marketability problems.

TOWERING BARGAINS

The hangover of distressed property, especially acute in Times Square, merited national attention and its consequences gripped the banking industry especially. *American Banker*, the trade magazine for commercial banks, followed the issue closely, reporting as early as mid-1990 that the "Soft Real Estate Market in Manhattan Worries Bankers" and "Surplus Manhattan Office Space Means Trouble for Banks." Especially worrisome was the potential construction of 4.1 million square feet of additional office space as part of the 42DP, so the official announcement of delay made "Bankers Cheer." By the early 1990s, at least seven of the 19 new developments built in Times Square during the 1980s were "troubled," either foreclosed upon by the lender (or given over to the lender in lieu of foreclosure), or put into bankruptcy by the borrower, or pushed into a workout situation, or on "watch" status because financial problems were probable. The list of distressed assets also included four older buildings, One Times Square among them. Mapped, the big "D" of property distress marked every block of Broadway in the small district of Times Square running from 42nd to 50th Street.

The advantage for early bargain hunting belonged to corporations with a solid balance sheet, not developer/owners. The credit markets had closed their doors to real estate, and lender unwillingness to provide funding for the needed tenant improvements, leasing commissions, and lease assumptions made it hard for landlords to capture tenants with aggressive move-in concessions of free rent and contributions to fit out tenant space. Tenants willing to move in without significant up-front concessions could transact the most aggressive deals. The bargaining edge turned on being able to finance these move-in tenant improvements—at a lower cost of capital than the landlord and in a way that would not adversely affect the tenant's financial position. In this midtown west market of economically driven opportunities, tenants who wanted to own their space held a distinct advantage. Speaking about its purchase, a Bertelsmann senior vice president remarked, "We could finance this at rates that a real estate developer could only dream about."[5]

Bertelsmann's purchase of the 44-story blue-green glass tower at 1540 Broadway between 45th and 46th Streets in March 1992 was a watershed event that brought 1,750 people from the creative fields to Times Square (figure 10.1). Identified by brokers as "an appropriate signature" for the media company's U.S. headquarters, the tower was purchased from Citicorp (lead lender and agent bank for a consortium of 17 Japanese financial institutions) for $119 million—less than fifty cents on the dollar of the outstanding $252-million mortgage. The lending consortium's decision to accept the big loss started the process of market clearing by breaking the logjam at several banks. It also marked an end to the uncertainty about property values that had been in flux since the onset of the property recession. At approximately $118 a square foot, office and retail space combined—a record-breaking price at the time—it was a steal for a building that had cost somewhere in the vicinity of $317 a square foot to develop. A decision like this, said Chris Alpers, the Bertelsmann executive who handled the purchase, "is numbers-driven. . . . The location is a good one. When we set out looking, originally, if we could have gotten the same deal on Sixth Avenue, we would have taken it in a minute."[6] It took the media firm six months to agree to the 1540 Broadway deal.

Eighteen months later the Morgan Stanley Group purchased the 42-story sleek and subtly detailed tower at 1585 Broadway between 47th and 48th Streets from a lending group of eight banks for $176 million, or 55 cents of each dollar of $317 million in outstanding loans. Originally, the tower had been designed for the investment bank. In response to a negotiation dance with Morgan Stanley for tenancy in the building, the developers David and Jean Solomon specified a building with high ceilings and elevators at the back to accommodate trading floors for the investment bank before the firm reportedly backed out of the deal sometime in 1987 because of the city's signage requirements: The management board reportedly did not want to be in a building that was ablaze with honky-tonk blinking lights outside. Subsequently, as noted later, the Hines representatives handling the building's sale ultimately convinced the conservative bankers that a program of financial signage could be created that would proudly redound to their credit. Hailed by the real estate industry, Morgan Stanley's purchase of 1585 Broadway validated Times Square as an office address and endowed it with new respectability. Within six months, the investment bank finalized the purchase of a second building, the 36-story black and steel-gray tower two blocks away at 750 Seventh Avenue for $90 million—less than 50 cents on the dollar of that $187.5-million construction loan—though the pricing, on a per-square-foot basis, was about 10 percent higher than its first purchase. As real estate deals, the acquisitions had been made irresistible not just by lenders' discounted pricing, but by a cumulatively large—$85.5 million—corporate-retention package of abatements for property, sales, and mortgage-recording taxes from the city, which feared the migration of this and other corporations to Westchester County or New Jersey.

Lenders did not need a map of the area to understand the depth of their financial exposure or projected losses. They had become real estate owners, involuntarily. Their execution of this role, though, differed from that of the entrepreneurial or family owner/developer. In one of those ironic twists of business some banks found themselves competing with their loan customers for tenants, at least temporarily. Most significantly,

10.1
The watershed real estate event: Bertelsmann's buy of 1540 Broadway. (Gary Hack)

owning and operating real estate have never been the business of banks, and in the early 1990s when they took over these assets, commercial banks faced significant capital constraints on how much more money (for tenant improvements, concessions, and leasing commissions) could prudently be put in to get a tower fully leased. Constant pressure from bank regulators to do something about their huge portfolios of troubled real estate assets cast a spotlight on the domestic banks' writedown policies and disposition practices. By early 1993, a pricing benchmark for troubled real estate held by financial institutions emerged: "It's 50 Cents on the Dollar, Stupid" exclaimed a research report issued by Salomon Brothers.[7] What mattered most to the future character of Times Square, both short term and long term, turned on how the commercial banks managed the market-clearing disposition process. Through pricing signals the disposition process would affect the pace of market recovery in the short term, and the long-term character of the district would be directly affected by the type of interests buying these distressed assets. The banks' obvious self-interest in protecting their investments would add time to the disposition process, however. The negotiating process would be further shaped, dramatically as it turned out, by the fact that in each case decisions would be made by a consortium of lenders, most, if not all, of whom had to agree on lease deals, the value of tenant-improvement packages, and the terms of sale dispositions.

As the largest, most active real estate lender nationwide throughout the 1980s, Citicorp faced the biggest problem—$6.6 billion of non-performing loans and foreclosed properties in a portfolio of commercial real estate assets that totaled $23 billion at year-end 1991. Its loan exposure in Times Square was relatively small, but highly visible; as lead lender in a loan syndicate, the New York-based bank "held the keys" for developer Ian Bruce Eichner's 1540 Broadway and David and Jean Solomon's 750 Seventh Avenue. Manufacturers Hanover Trust Co. and First National Bank of Chicago also had been active in the West Side office market, as had been foreign banks, who for various reasons—the 42DP and the participation of Prudential, as well as eagerness to finance big deals—bought a presence in the Times Square market by participating in loan syndicates organized by the big underwriting banks. Besides Citicorp, the banks lending to developments in Times Square included Bank of Montreal, Bank of Nova Scotia, Deutsche Bank, Swiss Bank Corp., Toronto Dominion Bank, and a long list of Japanese banks. The small physical size of the market area and high quality of the distressed assets appeared to offer lenders more control to manage the outcome of the process than typically prevails, a situation two banks in particular—Citicorp and Banque Nationale de Paris—used to their advantage. Managing different distress situations independently, both banks quietly forced disposition outcomes that ultimately shaped the market's recovery. The stories are telling.

Citicorp's negotiations with Bertelsmann started off as one thing and ended up another. In search of new space for its 2,000 Manhattan employees, the media company, which was located in two office buildings in midtown, sought the lowest possible cost of occupancy and, initially, refused to consider a purchase transaction. Operating on that agenda, Bertelsmann first negotiated with Citicorp to lease the roughly 870,000-square-foot office component of 1540 Broadway for 27 years. After their brokers ran the numbers and realized how much more beneficial a purchase appeared, Bertelsmann switched gears and offered to buy, but only the office component. Under that scenario, Citicorp would have been left with 140,000 square feet of unfinished retail space, a theater, and a garage.

The bank, known for its bullishness about pricing and refusal to treat 1540 Broadway (or 750 Seventh Avenue, which it was managing) as distressed assets, viewed the market situation through a different lens. Citicorp was leasing more space than anyone else at the time, according to Patricia Goldstein, a seasoned veteran of real estate cycles and a tough negotiator who was in charge of the bank's real estate workouts. Its intensive asset-management approach to the disposition problem was part of the bank's strategy to sell off assets one at a time following repositioning in the market by an experienced in-house real estate team. The up-front costs to prepare the 1.1-million square-foot unfinished building for occupancy and cover leasing commissions, reportedly in the $50-million range, was a daunting hurdle for the bank's real estate executives. At this point, Times Square meant one thing to Goldstein—lots of empty space. There was no economic value to Citicorp if Bertelsmann rented the space under a costly tenant fit-out, so the bank turned down the financially strong company's lease offer, essentially forcing Bertelsmann to buy the building because, as Goldstein knew, the company needed the space.[8] The bank then refused the terms under which Bertelsmann first attempted to purchase the building. Finally, the cost-conscious company closed the deal at a heavily discounted price, but it had to take the whole building. The deal for the Bertelsmann sale won the "Henry Hart Rice Most Ingenious Deal of the Year Award" from the Real Estate Board of New York. In similar behavior designed to extract the most value for the bank, Citicorp refused to sell 750 Seventh Avenue until Morgan Stanley completed the purchase of its first building, 1585 Broadway, according to Goldstein.

If Citicorp's disposition posture was designed to protect its economic interests, the next case posed a bigger challenge. Relative to the big bank players, Banque Nationale de Paris (BNP) held a minor position in the distressed-property drama. Its influence on the second of the three "signal" Times Square dispositions—1585 Broadway—however, proved to be oversized to its position. BNP inherited its real estate interests in Times Square as a result of its takeover of the troubled Paris-based merchant bank, Banque Arabe et Internationale d'Investissement (BAII), yet there was nothing casual about the way it worked the collateral to increase its value as much as possible. The bank held interests in four Times Square properties: One Times Square, 1567 Broadway (a five-story building on a small site prime for redevelopment), 1585 Broadway (the kingpin of the district's new office towers), and the Holiday Inn Crowne Plaza on Broadway (the district's third new hotel, which was completed in 1989).

Its perspective on the disposition of these properties was shaped by the fact that this exposure totaled more than $300 million. Curtis Deane, who as vice president and managing director of the bank's Special Assets Group held responsibility for managing these troubled assets, came to the work-out task from a strikingly different perspective than the original big-bank lenders in Times Square. Whereas the belief in a corporate presence that underlay the original lenders' underwriting of Times Square loans may have been something of a "gamble," he said, to his way of thinking the bank now needed to do everything it could to ensure a corporate presence in Times Square "to offensively protect its downside exposure."[9] Disposition of 1585 Broadway, in which BNP had only a small participation, under terms that would have "unfavorable long-term consequences for Times Square" would have an even greater impact on One Times Square and 1567 Broadway, in which the bank's exposure was considerably larger. Having spent his entire professional life doing workouts, Deane has a finely honed sense of the power of an astute maneuver. He believed BNP had to deal with the "1585 problem," as he put it, to protect its downside risk on the other two assets.

The building was in the process of being sold by the Bank of Montreal on behalf of the eight-bank lending group for $85 million—against which there were $403 million in secured claims—when Deane realized that if BNP, as a small participant, was to get a good deal the bank had to stop the sale at such a low price. BNP also objected to the fact that the prospective buyer was not a corporation committed to Times Square as an owner-occupant of the building. Seeking to divide the three leaders of the bank consortium (Bank of Montreal, Toronto Dominion, and Swiss Bank Corp.), Deane worked to form a block of the smaller creditors, then forced an auction process. At the sealed-bid auction six months later, the highest bid came from Morgan Stanley—$176 million, a price, the *Times* reported, "considerably higher than many real-estate insiders had thought it [the building] would bring." The list of the "also-rans and their bids" also showed a degree of interest in the building far beyond what many had expected.[10]

In pursuit of a critical mass of corporate investment, the real estate market in Times Square was psychologically driven, as the significance of the Bertelsmann and Morgan Stanley purchases revealed. That critical mass took about three years to gel, from 1992 to 1995. The three big "signal" sales to Bertelsmann and Morgan Stanley amounted to more than half of the 5.4 million square feet of available office space at the lowest point of the market in terms of vacancy, 1991. A series of big leasing deals in the area followed: Deloitte & Touche, 80,512 square feet (1633 Broadway); Viacom, 221,131 square feet (1515 Broadway) followed by 500,000 and 183,722 square feet (1633 Broadway), plus its subsidiary, Macmillan Publishing, initially with 255,970 square feet, then another 64,969 square feet (1633 Broadway); Mayer, Brown & Platt, 114,562 square feet (1675 Broadway); American Management Association, 196,684 square feet (1601 Broadway); Virgin Megastore, 65,000 square feet; Sony

Theaters and the Official All-Star Café (1540 Broadway); Condé Nast Publications, Inc., 636,367 square feet (Four Times Square); and Skadden, Arps, Slate, Meagher & Flom, 659,937 square feet (Four Times Square).

The improvement of the market was driven by increasing demand from tenants in the high-growth industries, notably, financial services and entertainment. Viacom's rapid growth into one of the world's largest media companies, for example, fueled a continual appetite for expansion space in two Times Square buildings: 1515 Broadway and 1633 Broadway. Attracted by the area's low-cost space, Viacom first moved to Times Square in 1989 from nearby offices at 1211 Avenue of the Americas by leasing 440,000 square feet in 1515 Broadway for its cable station, MTV, the "arbitrator of youthful coolness" whose network success derived from its ambitious, young, and slightly wacky creative staff. In a short time and on a methodical basis, Viacom grew to occupy approximately 775,000 square feet, or about 53 percent, of 1515 Broadway. Needing still more space to accommodate its acquisition of Paramount Pictures and expectations of growth, it sought space in a second building close by, 1633 Broadway, which with 2.2 million rentable square feet afforded lots of flexibility for expansion. In a series of seven separate lease transactions between 1992 and 1995, Viacom increased its presence by over 1.3 million square feet of space in these two buildings, and by the time the ink had dried on the leases, the media conglomerate's 4,731 employees occupied over 1.8 million square feet in Times Square (plus six floors at nearby 1230 Avenue of the Americas at 48th Street for its Simon and Schuster subsidiary).

More than just a big space user, Viacom symbolized the reemergent status of Times Square—and New York—as home to the new media-based entertainment trend setters. New York had what Viacom's then-president Frank Biondi viewed as having an unbeatable combination of creative people, a concentration of powerful entertainment conglomerates, and access to enormous capital via the financial markets. Those attributes, he said, made it "self-evident that New York and not Los Angeles is the entertainment capital of the world."[11] By 1994, the city was home not only to Viacom but to the ABC, CBS, NBC, and Fox News networks plus dozens of publishing and recording industry giants, including Time Warner, Hearst Publications, Polygram Records, EMI Records, Hachette Filipacchi Magazines, and Bertelsmann. The headquarters and broadcast studios of these firms were collecting force in and around Times Square. In a relatively short period, perceptions of Times Square changed, as Curt Deane put it, from "Gee, wouldn't it be nice" to "Oh, it's a wonder."[12] The new perceptions fit the reality of a growing roster of law firms (Proskauer Rose Goetz & Mendelshon; Lord Day & Lord Barrett Smith; Mendes & Mount; Mayer, Brown & Platt; Cravath, Swaine & Moore; Brobeck Phleger & Harrison; Skadden, Arps, Slate, Meagher & Flom)[13] and advertising and marketing firms (Ogilvy & Mather; D'Arch Masins Benton & Bowles; Frederick Atkins, Inc.), which had also concluded that tenancy in Times Square fit their needs. Ten years earlier, their presence in Times Square would have been unimaginable.

10.2
Gretchen Dystra, president of
the Times Square Business
Improvement District. (The
Atlantic Group)

Much of the credit for the work in changing the perception of
Times Square goes to Gretchen Dykstra, as first president of the Times
Square Business Improvement District (BID) (figure 10.2). Organized as
a not-for profit in 1990 by private interests spearheaded by Arthur Ochs
Sulzberger, Jr., then deputy publisher/chairman of the *Times*, to address
quality-of-life issues that had long plagued the area—sanitation, security,
pornography, social services, and homelessness—the Times Square BID
represents an alliance of an estimated 5,000 businesses and over 400 property owners, several of whom are counted among the city's most powerful.
Physically defined to correspond to the four points of the theatrical com-
pass, the BID's boundaries take in a 32-square-block area stretching from
40th Street to 53rd Street west of Sixth Avenue to the west side of Eighth
Avenue; along 46th Street, the boundary stretches to Ninth Avenue to
include Restaurant Row, which is dependent upon the Theater District.
Because of Times Square's infamous reputation, locally and nationally, at
the time of its creation the BID's backers sought someone skilled in PR
and communications who could dramatically change the perception of the
district. Dykstra came to the job as former director of communications
and community relations for the New York City Charter Revision
Commission and had earlier worked for both the Edna McConnell and
Rockefeller Foundations. "I was attracted to the job for the diversity of its
tasks and the ability to shape a story," Dykstra said in an interview. "I think
of myself as a community organizer with resources. It's a hodge-podge
neighborhood," by which she meant "eclectic, vital, colorful and sort of in
your face, a certain esthetic chaos."[14]

What Dykstra saw as "the gestalt of Times Square" she turned
into a vast and highly effective promotional campaign with the theme:
"There's Even More to Times Square Than You Thought." Spending 19
percent of its annual budget[15] for marketing activities—press relations,
paid ads, publication and distribution of free brochures and pamphlets
(Restaurant Guide, Visitors Guide, BID area map, Hotel Guide, Music
Guide, Marketing Book), tourist assistance, and promotion of highly publicized events such as the New Year's Eve ball drop from One Times Square
and "Broadway on Broadway"—Dykstra aimed to change the perception
of the area, which the BID's 49-person board had clearly identified as the
"fundamental obstacle to improving business"[16] (figure 10.3). City residents posed a particular problem in this regard. While tourists had long
been coming to the area despite the infamous conditions, the BID continued to have a tough time capturing the attention of New Yorkers, who,
Crain's reported, still saw Times Square as "the epicenter of urban blight
and perversion." Early in 1994, Dykstra launched a special campaign targeted to New Yorkers with wry messages attempting "to humanize and
soften the hard-edged perceptions of Times Square by citing some of the
area's quirky features . . . 215,326 light bulbs; 3,537 lawyers; 8.2 miles of
linguine; eight ushers named Alice; and one Dave (Letterman)." The campaign included ads plastered on buses and broadcast on the radio seeking
to communicate the facts of the new Times Square: since the BID started

10.3
The place for city information
in Times Square, 1959, 2001.
(Collection of the author; Gary
Hack)

operations two years earlier, street crime had decreased by 24 percent and
purse-snatching and pick-pocketing, what *Crain's* called the "benchmarks
of criminal activity," had dropped 43 percent.[17]

Even the cleverest marketing campaign could not succeed without a change in the reality of social conditions in Times Square.
Accordingly, making inroads on quality-of-life issues took precedence, as
evident in the fact that the BID's budget priorities have remained consistent from its inception: public safety, sanitation, and marketing. Cleanup
crews in bright red jumpsuits sweep, scrub, and paint from 6:00 A.M. to
10:00 P.M. seven days a week, and the BID's private, unarmed private security force radios the police when it spots street crimes, especially those that
had previously plagued the area, such as the three-card-monte game scam
and drug dealing. (The BID sent its head of sanitation to Disney's hospi-
tality school.) The BID aggressively took aim at pornography concentrated
in the Eighth Avenue corridor and vigorously supported Mayor Giuliani's
antiporn zoning initiative at the same time it devoted considerable
resources to community services, developed outreach services for the dis-

trict's homeless population, and participated in the establishment of a unique Midtown Community Court to handle misdemeanors committed in Times Square swiftly, locally, and visibly, by assigning offenders to community service in the area and social services in the court.

Articulate and effective as the voice of Times Square, Dykstra is widely credited with reshaping its image by marketing the place as a "community." On the occasion of her departure after a six-year tenure as head of the BID, the editors of the *New York Observer* praised her for pushing "against the status quo" and proving "that profound urban revitalization is possible in New York." The key to her success, the editors went on to explain, "was her ability to unite the social service sector and the business community. While city tax breaks and a surging economy certainly played a large part in Times Square's renaissance, it was Ms. Dykstra's personal charisma, quick intelligence and hard work that often kept the ball rolling."[18] Timing also mattered. After approximately 18 months of organizational efforts, the BID finally began operations in 1992, just months before the Bertelsmann purchase of 1540 Broadway broke the bottleneck of new investment in Times Square. As the first head of the BID, Dykstra seized upon the good fundamentals. Capitalizing on the right timing for Times Square and a new structure for organizing property owners, she galvanized the latent market demand for Times Square so evident in the expanding neon on Broadway.

NEON SIGNALS

As barometer of the city's competitive condition, the signs of today's Times Square proudly proclaim New York's singular commercial drive, just as not so long ago they sadly registered its urban malaise. Throughout most of the 1970s the most "memorable" skyward visions of Times Square chronicled by the area's photographers singled out images of vacant spaces adjacent to the Coca-Cola sign, the demolished Budweiser and Camel signs, and "for rent" signs on what had been since the 1920s a jungle of billboards along Broadway. Gone were most of the gigantic neon spectaculars previously put up by national advertisers (plate 23), the huge electronic billboards that formerly promoted restaurants and nightclubs as tourist attractions and the movie marquees, which in an earlier time producers regularly festooned with thousands of lights to promote new films. Appearances of "for rent" notices on the former Times Tower heralded decline. The national energy crisis of 1973 with its threatened stoppage of Middle East oil dampened the commercial logic of exuberant advertising spectaculars by making them appear wasteful. This was also the time Lady Bird Johnson led the movement to beautify America's roads through removing outdoor advertising. The lights went out as advertisers canceled their displays.

Even earlier, however, the dazzle had disappeared as sex became the square's best-known industry, even though only a small percentage of the area's legitimate businesses were sex-related. "Firmly associated with their urban environment, Times Square spectaculars began to lose their glitter."[19] The crowds that once gathered for ceremonies inaugurating a new sign now remained securely at home, watching television in their suburban living rooms. In a superficial effort to improve conditions, owners removed billboards and marquees. "They were taking the position that marquees cause crime because they allow criminals to get out of the rain," said Tama Starr, third-generation president of the family business Artkraff Strauss Sign Corporation, which has long dominated the field of Times Square spectaculars. "Everybody knows the primary function of light is to make streets safer."[20] The city's mid-1970s fiscal crisis further exacerbated the area's downward trajectory. In 1977, the owner of One Times Square halted the operation of the famous "zipper," the moving message board wrapped around the icon's second story which had been flashing electronic news headlines since 1928; it remained dark until 1986, when *New York Newsday* signed a five-year lease to operate the sign.

New visuals coming into Times Square tended to be artifacts of despair designed to cover the blank signs and make the area look lively. On the south side of the Crossroads Building, which became the southeast-tower site of the 42DP, New York artist Richard Haas transformed the windowless cinder-block tower into a wondrous image of the Times Tower as it looked in 1904 (figures 10.4, 10.5a,b). His signature trompe l'oeil was intended to serve as a reminder of how Times Square looked in better days and, according to its sponsor, Frederic Papert's nonprofit 42nd Street Development Corporation, which owned the building at the time, what it could be again. The mural remained in place until the building, which had been sold to the city, was demolished in 1984 to make way for a temporary information center. Also, the Public Art Fund commissioned works by notable artists such as Alex Katz and Jenny Holzer. Holzer, who uses the simplest bold statements as her medium to push the public into reflection, placed several provocative selections from her series *Truisms* on the eye-catching Spectacolor screen on the north side of One Times Square: "YOUR OLDEST FEARS ARE THE WORST ONES," "FATHERS OFTEN USE TOO MUCH FORCE," "ABUSE OF POWER COMES AS NO SURPRISE" (figure 10.6). Controlled by computer, the 40-foot-by-20-foot Spectacolor screen of lights also generated animated, cartoonlike images. It was a lively message board, accessible to advertisers as well as individuals who could buy a 30-second spot for $25; Gustavo Alfredo Noguera made news when he proposed to Magda Stella Ossa on August 8, 1977, via the Spectacolor screen, "Magda Stella Will You Marry Me?" Installed in 1976 by George Stonbely of Spectacolor Communications, the Spectacolor screen became another icon of New York during this period, featured on news broadcasts around the world and used for the opening credits of Saturday Night Live. As one of only two exceptions to the void of new advertising spectaculars in Times Square during the 1970s, the inspiration for Spectacolor was almost too ironic for words: "Believe it or not," the *Times* advertising columnist exclaimed, it was inspired by "similar installations in Moscow, Kuwait and Tijuana, Mexico. Talk about carrying coals to Newcastle."[21] It remained in place until 1990, when it was replaced by the more dazzling Sony Jumbotron.

10.4
At the crossroads, 42nd Street and Seventh Avenue, ca. 1965. (Boris Erwitt)

10.5
Evoking the past to create an illusion of change: Mural of the former Times Tower recreated by Richard Haas on the Crossroads Building, 1979, before and after. Commissioned by the 42nd Street Development Corporation, executed by Artkraft Strauss Sign Corporation. (© Peter Mauss/Esto)

The other exception was in keeping with pornography's dominance in Times Square in the 1970s: The singular major neon commission during the 1970s was for the Pussycat Lounge and Cinema, an upscale nude dancing club. The spectacular sign, designed by Artkraff Strauss, had swagged "curtains" nearly 60-feet across with 600 feet of red neon. Between the curtains traveled a message board and a half medallion with 810 feet of neon flashing the figure of a masked woman with a cat's tail. Seeking to entice passersby, the sign held out the promise of sexual thrills. Set against 1,216 feet of blue and gold neon in letters almost six feet tall, the word *Pussycat* reigned until 1986, when it was torn down to make way for the 44-story Holiday Inn Crowne Plaza Hotel being built by William Zeckendorf, Jr. The 89-year old Artkraff Strauss had fashioned many a spectacular, but the Pussycat remained a favorite of the firm's president "because it embodies the Bauhaus ideal of form following function"[22] (plate 22).

The deeply depressed urban condition that gripped Times Square was but a metaphor for a wider retreat from cities taking place across the nation. The myopia of the situation was peculiarly American. It had an

10.6
One of Jenny Holzer's Truisms
alight on the Spectacolor screen
on the former Times Tower, ca.
1985. (Gary Hack)

analogue, however, in the domestic tunnel vision obscuring the latent
power of Times Square as an advertising venue, despite the decay and
decrepitude that prevailed in the 1970s.

Disenchanted by what they perceived to be the quality of the
audience, long-time advertisers had pulled out of Times Square during the
1970s, leaving the billboards blank. Kent, Beefeater, Accutron by Bulova,
Gordon's Gin, Canadian Club, and Woolmark, all there in 1972, were gone
ten years later. When the 14 billboards controlled by Douglas Leigh, creator
of many of the most memorable Times Square spectaculars, including the
famous smoke-ring blowing Camel sign ("I'd Walk a Mile for a Camel")
and the block-long Bond Clothing store sign ("Every Hour 3,490 People
Buy at Bond") with its flowing waterfall flanked by giant nude man-
nequins of a man and a woman (figures 10.7, 10.8) were sold in 1979 to
Van Wagner Communications, 13 were blank. Jason Perline, Van Wagner's
chairman, recalled a salesman for Philip Morris saying, "We don't want a
sign seen only by pimps and prostitutes," to which he responded, "Who
smokes more than pimps and prostitutes?" Seemingly sound, the logic nevertheless failed to make the case: "It wasn't a good sales pitch," he said. Not
long thereafter, however, Perline succeeded in marketing his billboards to
Japanese advertisers and could honestly say "The area is booming."[23]

Japanese consumer-product manufacturers knew the tourist
appeal of the place—the Japanese flocked to the area because they saw
Times Square as the ultimate symbol of America. They also understood
better than any other group of brand merchandisers the transportability of
the icon's branded location. Sony pioneered, in 1965; in the 1970s, Canon,
JVC, Midori, Panasonic, and Suntory broke the darkness of Times Square
with large, bright-neon supersigns full of animation. By the early 1980s,
the ranks of Japanese advertisers included Aiwa, Brother, Casio, Fuji,
Maxell, Minolta, Seiko, TDK, Toshiba, VCX, and Yashica, and for much of
the 1970s and 1980s, most of the district's signs advertised Japanese products (figure 10.9). The proliferation of Japanese advertisers during that
period reflected more than just prescient advertising logic, however. The

10.7
Memorable smoke rings of
a bygone era, 1941–1966.
(Collection of Artkraft Strauss
Sign Corporation, courtesy
Seymour B. Durst Old York
Library at the Graduate Center
of the City University of New
York)

10.8
Memorable nudes with a real
working mini-Niagara on the
roof, 1947–1955. (Collection
of the Artkraft Strauss Sign
Corporation)

10.9
Times Square relit by Japanese firms, 1985. (Charles M. Weiss)

men behind these decisions, like the president of the American subsidiary of Minolta Corporation, Sama Kusumoto, first came to the United States in the 1950s with a mandate to expand Japanese sales "in the world's richest customer market." They shared similar career paths and, as Kusumoto discovered, a nostalgic attachment to Manhattan. Short on money but long on time, they had whiled away many an evening in Times Square, which he called the "neon heart" of the city. "We struck a gentleman's agreement to relight Times Square," he wrote years later. "We considered giant neon signs a good advertising medium and believed Times Square to be perhaps the best location in the United States. Our companies were doing well, thanks to the openness of the American market and the buying power of American consumers; what better way to symbolize our achievements in that market than to revive one of its vernacular art forms."[24]

A culturally based symbolism stimulated the Japanese resurgence of neon in Times Square. To be in Times Square was "the ultimate expression of the [American] dream . . . a statement of being proud of having become a company that could have such a sign in the center of the world . . . pride in the prestige of just being able to be here," remarked Nick Nakahara, vice president for sales for Dentsu Corporation of American, a Japanese advertising agency that represents many of the advertisers. That the square was physically in decline did not seem to weaken the motive: "The image was intact, " he said. "And it looked fine at night, when the signs were lit."[25] American firms, on the other hand, viewed signs as a corporate-image vehicle, and they could not get beyond the grim grimy reality of the place.

Because it was mandated as aesthetic policy the resurgence in riotous commercial signage in Times Square evident by the mid-1990s caught real estate interests by surprise. For all the prescience that George Klein showed in going after the 42DP designation, he, as well as other real estate people, missed the big economic play about Times Square—its value as a marketing opportunity. They all missed the neon signals of Japanese advertisers, except for Jeffrey Katz, president of Sherwood Equities.

Katz is a maverick. Though hardly a real estate novice, he had only one big development project in Manhattan (The Sarasota, a 300-unit East Side residential condominium) to his credit when in 1985 he bought the two parcels on the Broadway median between 47th and 48th Streets. Shifting his interest to the West Side, where activity was less intense, Katz bought the first of two parcels because of the site's potential for signs: "This was the New York postcard site," he explained in an interview. "I wanted to develop the site, but not on spec. We were too small."[26]

At first he envisioned a narrow office tower bedecked with signs, and hired as architects the firm of Mayers & Schiff Associates, designers of the popular tkts pavilion on Duffy Square, where discount theater tickets are sold. Erected in 1973 as a temporary structure, the award-winning red trusswork frame supporting canvas panels proclaiming "tkts" in bold letters achieved permanence and unofficial "landmark" status as a contemporary symbol of Times Square. Their office/sign tower design for Katz won early praise from Paul Goldberger, who cited it as "surely the most serious attempt to integrate commercial signs into high-rise architecture" and for "the potential that exists in this unusual marriage of corporate and commercial priorities that the city is trying to bring into being at Times Square."[27] But for all its prominence, the 14,000-square-foot site was small by the standards for New York's towers, and with cash flow from the existing structures covering the debt, Katz was in no hurry to develop the site. He could see the investment coming to Times Square and decided to let the "big guys go first," figuring he would be fifth or sixth to come onto the market. "If this were to be viable, it would have to wait for the small users that follow large users into an area," he said—in this case, law offices or advertising agencies.[28] He would sit back and watch the neighborhood change, waiting for the right time.

Two Times Square, whether it was to house offices or a hotel behind the signpost, won respect among architectural critics and planners because of the design's sensitivity to Times Square, yet its character was out of sync with other towers being built in the district.[29] Not only did it stand out stylistically, the concept of a signpost, even if it derived legitimacy from the mandate of public policy, posed a risky business proposition. The idea of selling sign space up and down the tower at the southern end of the building was nearly untested. The only other example was One Times Square, and its status—whether it would remain standing or fall to the bulldozers as part of the 42DP—remained uncertain when Katz started to plan his project. (Only in mid-1988 did the city and state, largely by default and a weak political position, finally relent from the earlier, quite real possibility that the site might be cleared. "Nobody has proposed an alternative that people are rallying around," said Vincent Tese defensively.[30]) If not totally mysterious, the seven big sign companies in New York were highly competitive and known for being tight-lipped about the profitability of their business. Even if the broad outlines of the business were clear, information on lease arrangements, revenue figures, and operating costs remained closely guarded. Sign companies typically leased space on rooftops from landlords, then subleased this space to advertisers for whom they custom-constructed signs and from whom they collected fees for erecting the signs and maintaining them, and paid a percent of gross revenues to the agency handling the advertising account. Analyzing the sign-revenue side of the equation in an absolute way was not possible, according to Katz and his architects. From a financial perspective, Katz still faced the familiar problem that the tower might be difficult to market to corporate users. The answer was to prelease supersign space to advertisers (Coca-Cola, Samsung) and the interior to a hotel operator (Ramada) rather than plan for office tenants; with these commitments, the project had enough credit-worthy cash flow to secure a $90-million construction loan from Chase Manhattan Bank.

Katz's success with Two Times Square changed the nature of the sign business, he says. "Now landlords become lessors, directly. We were the first real estate people to capitalize on the signs; we had to: Sign revenue made the development feasible."[31] (The sign revenues were essential to cover finance the project, and they would cushion a drop in hotel vacancy when the economy declined and, hence, tourism dropped.) "It used to be that we would lease space, pay the landlord a net sum, and everything after that, we pocketed," said Van Wagner's Perline, who acted as an agent for Katz on Two Times Square. "Because of the huge cost and value of the new buildings, the owners looked at the signage as a profit center—although, in context, a small profit center. But they said: 'Hey, it's not a nuisance. There's a profit to be made.' It became, frankly, more difficult for us to do a standard deal."[32]

When complete at the end of 1990, the slim tower's surfaces radiated with seven illuminated supersigns covering nearly 20,000 square feet, or approximately 6 percent more than required under zoning rules.[33] Katz maintains that without public policy, there would have not been signs except for One Times Square and Two Times Square: "They're a financial burden," he said. "They're a net plus to the city but they're not a plus for each individual project."[34] Apart from aesthetics, business wise, the issue is how a sign gets integrated into a building in terms of light and air. Once designers solved that problem with a combination of new technology and thinking that a sign need not be a billboard, the new see-through finlike signs became compatible with office usage.

Compatibility with corporate image remained another matter, however. The biggest question at the time was how Morgan Stanley, as the new owner of 1585 Broadway, would comply with the special zoning rules for Times Square. The 1987 design amendments to the zoning resolution required the blue-chip investment bank to install minimum amounts of signage at three different heights: illuminated retail signs at the ground level, illuminated signs at the mid-level, and supersigns at specific building heights. No decisions about the new signage were made for months as executives debated internally how to resolve the seeming conflict between the requirements for big and kinetic signs and the elite firm's preference for understatement.

The surprising, but not shocking, result was half an acre of glittering light-emitting diodes (LEDs) formed into a continuously moving high-tech display of real-time financial information. This was not just riveting and kinetic; it was stunning because it personified the new character, technology, and diverse imagery of the emergent Times Square. Traveling at irregular speeds in three strips along the building front, each 160 feet long and 10 to 12 feet high, are fast-paced ticker data in bright amber letters and numbers. On the side walls of the building are a pair of 30-by-60-foot, 256-color LED video-data boards showing charts, symbols, and other graphics. Anchoring the corners of the building are intensely blue 44-foot cylindrical world maps indicating the time across Morgan Stanley's global network of offices. Ten decorative fins along the Broadway facade, clad with mirrors and blue-neon edges, spell out "1 5 8 5 B'W A Y." The name of the firm is currently in discrete pale letters only eight inches high on the global clock. No more identification is needed. "The information is the building, and the building is Morgan Stanley," said Bob Jackowitz, Artkraff Strauss's project manager. Architects Gwathemy Siegel & Associates designed this stunner. "The idea is that for the information to appear integral to Morgan Stanley, it had to emerge smoothly as if from the heart of the building, travel, and reenter the building smoothly, as if for reprocessing."[35] Brilliantly adapted, Wall Street culture danced in Broadway lights—a new icon for the era of the marketplace, a blue-chip supersign on a once gritty corner. For this iconic place-making sign, the blue-chip investment bank would win one of the MAS's blue-ribbon awards (plate 24).

There was no clearer message about the success of public policy than the market's delivery of pulsating signs in overabundant quantity—25 percent on average and as high as 61 percent beyond the minimums mandated by zoning, as shown in table 10.1. What Morgan Stanley ended up doing takes the prize for irony: in putting more signage on both its buildings than the regulations called for, the staid pin-striped investment-banking firm "outclassed" every other new building. Placing odds on that outcome would have been dicey.

Even though the new office towers in Times Square were all built under the 1987 design regulations, the property recession of the early 1990s delayed the policy's visual impact. (Signs do not have to be installed and operational until an owner applies for a temporary certificate of occupancy, the first when a building is fifty percent occupied and the second, at

TABLE 10.1 SIGNAGE ON COMMERCIAL BUILDINGS CONSTRUCTED IN TIMES SQUARE: 1987–1991

BUILDING	MINIMUM SIGNAGE REQUIRED (SF)★	SIGNAGE PUT IN PLACE AT CERTIFICATE OF OCCUPANCY (SF)	PERCENT OVER MINIMUM REQUIRED
Holiday Inn–Crowne Plaza Hotel 1601 Broadway	14,436	15,194	5.3%
Embassy Suites Hotel 1568 Broadway	8,706	13,111	50.6%
Morgan Stanley Building 1585 Broadway	13,500	20,480	51.7%
Morgan Stanley Building 750 Seventh Avenue	6,100	9,830	61.1%
Bertelsmann Building 1540 Broadway	13,645	15,056	10.3%
Ramada Renaissance Hotel Two Times Square	18,389	19,558	6.4%
TOTAL	74,776	93,229	24.7%

★Illuminated and supersign requirements as specified under 81-732(a) 2 and 81-732 (a) 3 of the Zoning Resolution of the City of New York.
SOURCE: Drawings of the architect of record, NYC Department of Buildings, Illustration of Compliance (microfiche).

ninety percent occupancy. A final regulatory review occurs for issuance of a final certificate of occupancy.) By early 1993—before the big announcements heralding the coming of Morgan Stanley, Disney, Madame Tussaud's, and the Virgin Megastore later that year—it was clear that the quantity and quality of new signs put in place was being driven by a commercial mandate newly unshackled from the district's negative investment psychology (plate 28). Outdoor displays in Times Square numbered 42, up from 29 five years earlier, according to the advertising columnist for *Crain's*. American companies returned as well, accounting for nearly 70 percent of the 42 leases, or double the proportion in 1988. For American brands, Times Square once again became a place to promote with pride. "Times Square is a place where you can make a dramatic statement," said the president of the Anheuser-Busch's media planning and buying unit about the company's return to the district where prominent Budweiser signs had promoted the brand from the 1930s through the 1950s. A new oversized Budweiser spectacular, 40 feet wide by 70 feet high appeared on the north face of One Times Square in fall 1996.[36]

Advertisers' increasing demand for visibility in the premier outdoor emporium of commercial display showed up immediately in rapidly escalating prices for billboard spaces and supersigns in Times Square. In 1991, big billboards reportedly leased at prices ranging from $150,000 to $500,000 annually, depending upon the size and visibility of a location; lease costs for spectaculars like the Coca-Cola sign on Two Times Square weighed in at more than $1.2 million annually, before electric charges and maintenance costs. Availability was tight. Van Wagner Communications then controlled 23 sign locations, with only one available space, while all of Artkraff Strauss's 17 billboards were rented. (By way of comparison, in 1982 the reported annual rents for signs ranged from $60,000 to $180,000.) In 1995, leases at the low end of the range reportedly went for $240,000 annually, though $1.2 million was a more common figure. At these rates, Times Square ranked as the highest-priced outdoor real estate in America, and that was before prices escalated even further; two years later, the reported asking rents for advertising spaces on the Durst's building, Four Times Square, reached stratospheric levels—"between $500,000 to $2.1 million annually, ranging from $139 a square foot to an eye-popping $536 a square foot," as the *Wall Street Journal* described it.[37]

Nothing illustrates the value of signage better than the repeated sales of One Times Square. Over a period of two and one-half years, from the time it was sold at a foreclosure auction in 1995 to mid-1997 when it was purchased by a German investment group, the selling price of the mostly vacant tower skyrocketed to $110 million from $25.2 million. At nearly $1,000 per square foot, based on interior space, this was double the highest price ever paid for a commercial building in New York. But the building had long outlived its usefulness as office space, so the square-feet metric was obsolete. The signpost collected something in the vicinity of $7.1 million for ten massive billboards, two gigantic video screens, and an electronic news zipper, all visible to 20 million visitors annually and 250 million television viewers on New Year's Eve. The seller, Lehman Brothers Holdings, Inc., had been ridiculed by many real estate investors when it bought the signpost from BNP for $27.5 million within 24 hours of the foreclosure auction. But Lehman's astute investment made with the firm's own money contributed handsomely to its bottom line. "Lehman made out like a bandit," said one broker. "Nobody understood at the time how much signage income could mean to a transaction."[38]

Signage prices went higher still. "Outside Walls Fetching More Than Offices," a *Crain's* headline pointed out later that year, in reference to the fact that billboards had almost become "the tail wagging the dog."[39] In 1998, the income the Durst Organization expected to take in from signs on Four Times Square, estimated by the firm at more than $10 million, up from an earlier estimate of $7 million, had become comparable to that expected from the building's 120,000 square feet of retail space. While the article went on to note that both brokers and landlords thought these prices "verge on the nutty," the unexpected financial windfall from a growth surge induced by regulatory policy that developers bitterly opposed during travails of implementation was rich with irony. But then, the sign business is not real estate.

With the investment bottleneck broken, old advertising patterns reasserted themselves: brand visibility, competitive rivalries, costly spectacular constructions. Fuji's green-and-white spectacular (40 feet high by 90 feet long, covered with neon tubes) on 43rd and Broadway flashed not far from Kodak's giant promotion (30 feet high by 50 feet wide) on the facade of the Marriott Marquis Hotel (figure 10.10). Squaring off against

10.10
Brand promotion dominates the
facade of the Marriott Marquis.
(Gary Hack)

MCI, AT&T erected a giant technological masterpiece of a fiber-optic
sign containing a 35-foot-diameter globe simulating AT&T data tracking
across oceans and continents on the front face of the Marriott. Across the
street from a steaming 35-foot-high by 22-foot-wide mug of Eight
O'Clock Bean Coffee, General Foods planted a Maxwell House "Good
to the Last Drop" spectacular (40 feet high by 60 feet wide)—a return to
Times Square after a 55-year absence. The new competitor in the cola
wars, Virgin Cola, strategically placed a 40-foot billboard to butt heads
with the famous three-dimensional Coca-Cola sign (65 feet high by 41
feet wide) across the way and the Pepsi logo sign (40 feet high by 40 feet
wide) on the northern face of One Times Square, forming something of
a "cola triangle." Playfully sporting a giant spoon and the theme "Smile
More," Kraft Foods's Jell-O billboard (55 feet high by 105 feet long),
joined other food purveyors, Nabisco's 40-foot-high by 102-foot-wide
Oreo promotion and Nissin Food Products' 60-foot-high red neon steaming cup of noodles. Levi Strauss challenged Calvin Klein Jeans on billboard turf. Joe Boxer squared with Jockey International and Calvin Klein
(figures 10.11 and 10.12), prompting the company's chief executive to
remark in reference to his rivals, "What's an underwear company without
a Times Square presence?"[40] At the corner of 42nd Street on the Condé
Nast building the largest and most expensive video screen in the world—
a $37-million, eight-story turret spectacular (plate 27)—for Nasdaq, the
electronic stock market, faced a sign for Reuters broadcasting images from
its photographers around the world on its headquarters tower across the
street and the Dow Jones electronic zipper on One Times Square. All three
clustered five blocks south of two other sources of flashing real-time financial information, Morgan Stanley's three tiers of traveling stock and financial tickers and the electronic bulletin boards for Dow Jones and
Bloomberg.

10.11

Establishing a competitive presence in Times Square. (Gary Hack)

While the new financial-news content of these message boards appropriately reflected the dominance of the marketplace at the close of the twentieth century—"Wall Street has come to Main Street," said Frank G. Zarb, the chairman of the National Association of Securities Dealers, owner of Nasdaq[41]—the power of the glittering medium had not changed in more than 80 years. Whether made of neon, incandescent lights, fiber optics, or light-emitting diodes, the spectaculars in Times Square commanded immediate attention, whether or not people wanted to read them. The power of this advertising, the entrepreneur O. J. Gude wrote in 1912, "literally forces its announcement on the vision of the uninterested as well as the interested passerby. . . . Signboards are so placed that everybody must read them, and absorb them, and absorb the advertiser's lesson willingly or unwillingly."[42] In the early part of the twentieth century, the visiting G. K. Chesterton wrote: "When I look at the lights of Broadway by night, I said to my American friends, 'What a glorious garden of wonders this would

10.12

Brand visibility in Times Square. (Brian Thesis)

10.13
Old-style advertising spectacular.
(Courtesy of Artkraft Strauss Sign
Corporation)

be, to anyone who was lucky enough to be unable to read.'"[43] Times
Square eureka redux! (plates 25, 26).

The new signs are not like the old, though, in one notable way: In
place of "seductive fantasies, many simply offer corporate logos," wrote Dan
Bischoff, art critic for the *Newark Star Ledger*. "There is nothing that com-
pares, for example, to Kleenex's animated spectacular featuring the cartoon
character Little Lulu. From 1952 to 1965, its 10-foot-tall letters spelled out
'Kleenex' in neon, and another series of lights made Lulu jump from one
letter to the next. Each time she landed, the letter would come alive with
glowing neon. When she turned the corner, the neon Lulu grabbed a neon
Kleenex and slid down the length of it to its neon box, and the cycle
would begin again" (figure 10.13). A similarly vivid description might have
been written about the Corticelli sign with its kitten chasing a spool of
thread, the moving Pepsi waterfall sign, or the Camel smoke-puffing sign,
all of which touted consumer products, from the golden age of the Times
Square spectacular. Bischoff traces the lack of true animation in today's
signs to advertisers who, he believes, benchmark signs by the more animated mediums of television and the video screen. "Times Square is significantly diminished by being treated as a roomy couch, with weather," he
reasons, going on to conclude that "few have dared criticize this new face
of advertising, because it is the victory of the marketplace that we are supposed to be celebrating here in the first place"[44] (figure 10.14).

Times Square was no longer outside the mainstream, for brand
advertising, for corporate headquarters, for commercial real estate investment. Yet sex still commanded a strong presence. The area's most notable
and high-class sex emporium, Show World on Eighth Avenue and 42nd
Street, owned and operated by Richard Basciano, the undisputed king of
Times Square porn, was still going strong. On West 42nd Street, sex-related businesses had become more concentrated at the western end, which

was not yet under UDC's control. And after nearly a decade of decline, the Mayor's Office of Midtown Enforcement reported sex-related establishments reappearing in midtown, almost entirely on the West Side. Sex shops, adult movies, adult book and video stores, peep shows, live sex shows, lap dancing, and topless/bottomless bars and clubs had never ceased opening in the area, though a 1993 map of their locations showed a considerably less dense concentration than its counterpart of twenty years earlier. The *Final Supplemental Environmental Impact Statement* [*FSEIS*] for the 42DP issued in 1993 reported 59 sex-related businesses in midtown west (21 in the project area). Nevertheless, their days as a concentrated force were numbered, though not because of an impending decrease in the economic energy fueling the sex business. Indeed, if past demographic patterns provided a reasonable guide to the future, with the increase in white-collar employment in the immediate area, it was plausible to think that demand for sex-related uses might increase, if not in Times Square, somewhere nearby in midtown west. Instead, change would come from continued development pressure complemented by public policy. Antipornography zoning was high on the agenda of the city's new mayor, Rudolph W. Giuliani, who took office on New Year's Day 1995.

If Times Square was no longer marginalized as a real estate location, what would that mean for the development of West 42nd Street? How would market forces interact with the city and state's new ambitious vision for what had been the Deuce? Timing matters a lot in real estate. And the time was now right for change culturally in sync with the street's iconic legacy. The market for popular entertainment was heating up. Cora Cahan's New42 had taken the first step with its decision to recast burlesque's former house, the Victory, as a children's theater. Disney would take the next step, paving the way for other corporate entertainers.

10.14
Corporate logos prevail. (Scott
Lotokis)

DISNEY DELIVERANCE

If the city and state no longer needed to convince the business community of Times Square's locational merit, what then did they have to do to ensure the success of *42nd Street Now!*? Through labored persistence, public policy had finally succeeded in fostering this promising plan for entertainment and retail activity. The outcome, however, could not have materialized during the project's first go-around, regardless of how carefully the city and state planners might have tried to incorporate a vision of popular entertainment into the *General Project Plan*. The real estate market in 1994 differed from the one the planners faced in 1980. Service-sector employment was the driver of commercial real estate development in the 1980s; since the mid-1990s, the driver has been appetites for middle-income consumption of retail and entertainment activities. As a venue for what the industry now calls urban entertainment, New York offered unparalleled potential for capitalizing on this trend and a historical competitive advantage few cities could match. With its rescripted plan, the 42DP planners acted to take advantage of emerging commercial opportunities. "If we had tried to do this back in 1982," Rebecca Robertson explained in an interview, "I'm not sure where we would have ended up, because I'm not sure that the industry was ready to develop in this way." "We got lucky," she explained a year later. "The theater business was changing and Disney and Drabinsky [Livent] were part of it. No amount of good planning would have put them there."[1]

In terms of rampant commercialism, Tokyo has its Shibuya and London, its Piccadilly Circus. West 42nd Street is distinctively different. By historic legacy, it was a place for popular entertainment—for "going out," as social historian David Nasaw termed the turn of the twentieth-century entertainment revolution in public amusement.[2] With substantial promotional efforts for *42nd Street Now!* and the fortuitous timing of Disney's decision to restore the glory and glamour of the street's most prized his-

11.1
Disney's desire. (© 2001 Maggie Hopp)

toric theater, the New Amsterdam (figures 11.1, 11.2), this legacy reasserted itself. In the process, the policy landscape shifted dramatically, as did the implementation agenda confronting city and state officials: business politics asserted its primacy, as in the early deal-making days of the project. The policy questions now were different only in degree. How would the city and state leverage Disney's commitment in ways calculated to achieve its goals and ensure the complete transformation of West 42nd Street? In a changed market context of obviously heightened real estate stakes, what did each side of the public-private alliance bring to the negotiating table? See as major risks? Want as rewards? In an environment no longer shaped by intense opposition to the project—under new business-friendly admin-istrations, a Republican mayor and Republican governor—would the poli-tics of deal making change, and, if so, how? The bottom line: What impact would the deal with Disney have on the revitalization of West 42nd Street?

Handwritten note (partial, cursive): "Dear Julie:— I have sent you under cover two..." / "Sept. 26 '08" / "Saturday evening posts, last week and this. Bill is selling them now and wants to know if you will buy one every week. He is quite anxious about the scheme so we are letting him go ahead. Florrie"

NEW AMSTERDAM THEATRE
"The House Beautiful" | Kla v & Erlanger, Managers
West 42d Street, New York City
Mural Decoration over the Proscenium by Robert Blum
THE DRAMA

11.2
Postcard image of the mural decoration over the proscenium of the New Amsterdam Theater, 1908. (Collection of Bruce J. McCuen)

"Live from New York"

Timely is the best way to describe Disney's entrance onto the development stage of West 42nd Street. With the vision of *42nd Street Now!* essentially complete by the beginning of 1993, the project's sponsors needed a big fishing lure to attract development, and that lure was Disney. Disney too was looking afield at this time. Fresh from success with its record-breaking film *Beauty and the Beast* and in search of a way to leverage its world-wide brand, the entertainment giant decided to launch stage productions of its animated movie features. The strategy demanded a Broadway theater: "We decided that the legitimate theater was a very desirable business for us," said Disney chairman and chief executive officer Michael D. Eisner. "And to be a really legitimate theater producer, you have to be in New York."[3] The choicest venues capable of mounting musical productions, however, were all locked up by other long-running musical spectacles, and as had been the case since the development of the "road show" in the last decades of the nineteenth century, nothing other than a Broadway location would do. Like David Belasco, Martin Beck, the Shubert Brothers, and Florenz Ziegfeld, Disney recognized Broadway's cachet and saw it as the essential channel for launching theatrical productions on an international scale. Although its plans to redo the New Amsterdam would eclipse the staging of its $12-million production of *Beauty and the Beast,* which opened at the Palace Theater in April 1994 (to tepid reviews but strong advance ticket sales), Eisner emphasized that the New Amsterdam "will be the home of our second show, whatever that might be, and our third and our fourth . . . and maybe by that time, our first three will be playing all over the world."[4]

Extending its reach into live-theater entertainment fell within the orbit of a bigger set of strategic decisions being considered by Disney executives in their quest for new sources of revenue to sustain the company's long-held aggressive growth target of 20-percent annual-compound earnings growth. Equally ambitious and high profile, the list of other ventures included Euro Disney outside Paris, plans for two major theme-park-and-resort projects in Southern California (WESTCOT and Disney Sea) and one in Virginia (Disney America), development of a time-share business (Disney Vacation Club) and a planned residential community in Florida (Celebration), the acquisition of Miramax (a small independent production studio making low-budget "art films"), and the rapid expansion of Disney Stores, the company's "retail-as-entertainment" concept. Disney's earnings target reflected an assumption that the entertainment industry was unique in its potential for growth, yet, as a 1994 Harvard Business School case on the company pointed out, "continuing success challenged leadership to maintain its creativity and control across a range of increasingly diverse ventures."[5]

A darling of Wall Street analysts, Disney stock had by year-end 1990 increased sevenfold (on a split-adjusted basis) in the six years Eisner had held the positions of chairman and chief executive officer following an intense four-month takeover battle. Under the new management team, which in addition to Eisner included President Frank G. Wells and Disney Studios' chairman Jeffrey Katzenberg, the company's revenue vaulted to $5.76 billion in 1990 from $1.46 billion in 1984, while profit jumped to $824 million from $97.8 million. The profit growth rate of 42 percent per year reflected expansionist strategies in each of Disney's three divisions: theme parks and resorts, movie making, and merchandising operations.

By the early 1990s, however, growth no longer came easily. Disney faced increasing competition from rival entertainment/media giants—MCA (Universal Studios), Paramount Communications (Viacom), and Time Warner (50-percent owner of Six Flags). New rides remained tremendously expensive while their drawing power wore off quickly. New theme parks took years of planning and increasingly seemed to generate intense environmental issues or high-profile political battles, as was the case with Disney's aborted venture to build a historical theme park and resort complex near Civil War battlefields in rural Manassas, Virginia. Stacked against the performance of Disney's other divisions, its reputation-making core business lagged. In 1993 operating income from theme parks and resorts remained below its high following a dramatic drop in income in 1991—before accounting for a $515-million pretax loss from its troubled investment in Euro Disney, now called Disneyland Paris. In contrast, income from consumer products had increased more than 52 percent during the three-year period and film-entertainment earnings nearly doubled. Moreover, from a business perspective, how many more theme parks could the entertainment giant build before it started cannibalizing its own market? "The draw of Walt Disney World and of Disneyland is so big that if we build a third billion-and-a-half-dollar theme park somewhere in the U.S., it would be like eating our young," remarked Peter S. Rummell, then-chairman of Walt Disney Imagineering, the business unit responsible for developing theme parks and all other real estate projects for Disney. "So if you're a public company and you're committed to growth and you have an expertise in storytelling and placemaking, are there ways you can do that at less than a billion-dollar level?" Considering its plans for a theater platform in New York, Rummell explained, the corporate goal was to create "a series of entertainment products that are Disney-branded—smaller-than-a-theme-park products you can put on a 42nd Street anywhere in the world"[6] (plate 3).

Thinking smaller came reluctantly to Disney—and only after a series of well-publicized setbacks. After two years of efforts to get past regulatory delays, in 1990 the company scrapped its plans for "Disney Sea," a waterfront theme park to be built around the "Queen Mary" ocean liner and the "Spruce Goose" flying boat on a block of waterfront property in Long Beach, California. At Disneyland Paris, it struggled for two years (1992–1994) with lower-than-expected attendance and severe financial losses resulting from cultural blunders rooted in its adamant adherence to the Disney formula for family recreation, which it believed had universal appeal. Disney eventually recovered, but not before a financial restructuring reduced its stake to 39 percent from 49 percent. In October 1994, despite months of unwavering public commitment to go forward with its proposed $650-million development of "Disney America" and support from local government, including $163 million in subsidies, the company exited the historic battlefield at Manassas, Virginia, in a rout. Under a barrage of criticism from property owners, environmentalists, and historians who vehemently opposed the proposed historical theme park, Disney chose to abandon the project and search for another site elsewhere rather than face a costly battle. That same year, Disney suspended plans for the $2 billion WESTCOT addition, saying costs were too high.

Following the West 42nd Street announcement, the public memory of Disney's high-profile setbacks dissolved in an orgy of press coverage and media hype. The announcement scored a publicity coup that capitalized on the irony of the all-American family-oriented entertainment giant on "naughty, bawdy 42nd Street"—what *Times* columnist Frank Rich called the "least Disneyesque thoroughfare in America."[7] Disney injected adrenalin into the beleaguered project, and the press positioned the entertainment juggernaut as a savior. Disney metaphors proved irresistible: "A Prince Charming?" "Disney's Magic Wand," "Disney Leads Cinderella Transformation of 42nd Street," "Disney Wished upon Times Sq. and Rescued a Stalled Dream." Even Rich, who was not known for words of praise when it came to the entertainment giant's corporate behavior, hailed Disney's commitment to renovate the New Amsterdam as "a smart move that marks the beginning of the company's comeback as a civic Aladdin." What led Rich beyond his usual sharp criticism of the entertainment company was a deep understanding of New York's cultural scene and Broadway theater in particular, about which he had written for 13 years as the chief drama critic for the *Times*. "The sleeping 42d Street block intersecting with Broadway requires Disney-style commerce if Times Square is ever again to be the crossroads of the world," he wrote. "By relighting the New Amsterdam, Disney will attract more tenants to the other dark theaters on the street and more customers to the other struggling theaters throughout the Broadway district. Just as valuably, Disney will shake up both the management and labor status quo in the New York theater."[8]

Though he was skeptical at first, when Eisner finally toured the abandoned New Amsterdam with architect Robert Stern in March 1993, it was not a hard sell. Earlier appeals to consider opportunities on the street from both Marian S. Heiskell, who knew Eisner since his childhood, and Stern, who sits on the Disney board, had failed to crack his preconceptions about how bad Times Square was. Amid the ruin, water-soaked from holes in the roof, with its stairways half buried in rubble, and mushrooms sprouting out of the main floor—which Eisner said was like "going through a dark, damp and musty cavern"—he could make out the haunting beauty of the theater's extravagant Art-Nouveau decor and could envision the potential for Disney to be a catalyst in the revitalization of the street.[9] Eisner wanted to be a part of the rejuvenation as an executive of the Disney company and as a former New Yorker, as did Jeffrey Katzenberg, a fellow New Yorker who had worked in the Lindsay administration. They wanted to put their mark on the street in a way that would be remembered forever. But before glory, business. Disney's immediate concerns centered on the feasibility of recreating a sufficiently large theater for its musical productions: Could the seating be expanded from 1,600 to 1,800? the company asked Rebecca Robertson. Could this be done through Landmarks Preservation Commission without a public hearing? Was restoration feasible, and at what cost? How much assistance would the government give them?[10]

Two months later, when David Malmuth, Disney Imagineering's 38-year old executive who took charge of the project, visited the site, his reaction in blunt terms: "fabulous theater, but the street needs a lot of help."[11]

> One of the things the company came to understand
> very quickly, is that we could, with enough money, do a
> marvelous theater, but that was not the solution for
> 42nd Street. The solution was a much larger solution
> which had to do with the redevelopment of the entire
> street. . . . We felt it was important to make this whole
> street come back to life, and so we cajoled and arm
> twisted and used whatever leverage we had to try and
> bring some other potential entertainment tenants to the
> street.

In seeking to affect the whole of West 42nd Street, Disney executives were following a corporate script credited with being hugely successful largely because of the company's ability to control the environment, what they call the "guest experience." But as anyone who has visited a Disney theme park could readily project, being on West 42nd Street would directly challenge the script's core principles—control and regulation. In the orange groves of Anaheim where it built Disneyland and the swampland of central Florida where it built Disney World and Epcot Center, Disney created environments from scratch—consciously far removed from urban centers and accessible only by car. Orderly, clean, safe and sound, and cheerful, they represent the antithesis of city life, by design. "The highly regulated, completely synthetic vision provides a simplified, sanitized experience that stands in for the more undisciplined complexities of the city," architectural critic Michael Sorkin wrote. It represents "a utopia of leisure" whose physical organization and scale—compacted, reduced and internally ordered into a summary tableaux surrounded by peripheral transport systems—Sorkin likened to Englishman Ebenezer Howard's modernist physical model of the "garden city." The Disney theme park relinquishes its power to draw, he argued, "if it fails as an alternative to daily life."[12]

If the idealized leisure environment of Disney's theme parks emerges better than reality—no dirt, no rudeness, no mischance—pervasive control exercised through ownership of vast raw acreage and an emotionally neutral tableau makes this physical conception possible. Through meticulous and detailed design Disney deftly controls the visitor's experience within the park. Disney theme parks, for example, are built on giant platforms. Underneath, an elaborate system of tunnels provides service and staff circulation for the public activities above. Inconspicuous yet indispensable, this labyrinth makes the parks "clean" because, Sorkin explained, "it divides labor into its clean public face, and its less entertaining, less 'magic' aspects." This separation is no different from the typical suburban shopping center. Yet control beyond the entertainment core of the park in Disney World, for example, comes from the complete overlap of private land ownership and governmental power, which is even more critical to its business profitability. For the development of the Florida theme-park domain, Disney purchased approximately 27,500 acres, and through persuasive politics formed its own municipal utility district through which it exercises unprecedented regulatory control as a private company. Directly through ownership of hotels and restaurants or indirectly through ground-lease arrangements with other providers servicing visitors to the park, Disney controls the peripheral lands, thereby preempting the type of aesthetic chaos and disorderly strip development that would otherwise develop in the absence of full corporate control. Most important, total control over the environment maximizes capture by Disney of the economic benefits created by the magnetism of its own drawing power, a widely reported frustration at Disneyland in Anaheim.[13]

In an urban environment such as West 42nd Street could Disney ever have enough corporate control to work its brand of magic? Formerly, Disney shunned cities, their attitude being: We don't do urban entertainment, especially where we can't control the environment. This was the company's reaction to a request in the late 1970s to participate in *The City at 42nd Street*. Not only was the spontaneous cultural landscape of a real city street far removed from the carefully disciplined environment of a Disney "main street" where their full control left nothing to chance, but firm physical boundaries limited the potential for a makeover and political and market forces beyond the control of any single player—public or private—continuously intervened in the process. It was not just that cities were unfamiliar terrain. By the corporate standards applied to Disney's privatized sanctums, the urban environment was undisciplined, messy, chaotic. "One fact captures the gulf between Disney and New York," *Fortune*'s Frank Rose wrote in a feature article on the pending urban event: "Three years ago [1993], when Disney planners first looked at 42nd Street, their initial impulse was to gate it. They forgot that just across Eighth Avenue is the Port Authority Bus Terminal, a point of entry for 180,000 daily commuters." Rummell's candid response: "We do have some genetic instincts. But then we realized that half of New Jersey has to travel 42nd Street to get to work."[14] Another idea—also rejected, but only after "quite a bit of discussion and with an extraordinary amount of risk," Malmuth explained—was that the street become Disney's 42nd Street with everything on it Disney. Alternatively, the company's executives reasoned they could "try to bring in a diverse group of tenants to the street and make it, once again, the center for popular entertainment in the country and the world, and then Disney would be just one of the voices on the street." In time, said Malmuth, they came to realize that in New York they could not control the guest experience. "You don't do that on 42nd Street. It's a public place." The 'guest experience' from Disney's perspective can only start inside the theater, it doesn't happen on the street."[15]

THE ROAR OF RISK AVERSION

The American icon with what one reporter called "a gold-plated reputation for family entertainment" was taking a calculated gamble with its image in coming to West 42nd Street, as was evident in the early conceptual thrashing about. And not every senior executive, according to Robertson, was in favor of the move. The question for city and state officials guiding the 42DP was: What would it mean—in terms of making a deal—for Disney to be on the famously chaotic turf of Times Square where just about the only signs of predictability hung high above ground, in the syncopated rhythm of Broadway's computer-controlled flashing marquees, illuminated advertisements, and standard-issue traffic lights?

It would mean risk aversion. Negotiating a deal with Disney pivoted around the company's efforts to lay off every type of conceivable risk involved with renovating the New Amsterdam Theater. Company executives were especially concerned about the theater's condition. "We met in May 1993, and we very quickly laid out ground rules for Disney's participation in the project," Malmuth explained later to a large audience of real estate professionals:[16]

> Those were that the bulk of the dollars for the restoration of the theater had to come from the public section. We frankly didn't know at that time, nor did Rebecca

[Robertson], how much it was going to cost to do the
theater, but one thing we knew for sure, that restoration
of a historic theater is a very, very expensive proposition,
and it was not something for which Disney wanted to
take the bulk of the risk on. Nor was the company prepared to take the development risk. We, very early on,
started to talk about the "black-hole risk," meaning you
get into one of these historic buildings and you may
find that there's no steel, and it could be not a million
or ten million, but literally $20 million to fix in order to
make the theater usable. So we didn't want to take the
black-hole risk. We also said that, going forward, the soft
costs for the project needed to be covered by the public,
meaning all the design work.

Disney might be willing to put its reputation at risk, but not its money.
Company executives wanted to spend as little as possible, especially in the
early periods when they had not yet committed to the project. And they
did not want to pay government taxes; they were used to having counties
build entire transportation facilities for them, said Robertson. Eisner's
marching orders, according to Malmuth: "Look! If you could get it for
nothing, probably it makes sense to do it."[17]

Between June and December of 1993, city and state officials
worked through a lengthy negotiating agenda to reach agreement on the
broad outlines of a deal with Disney, and they spent all of the next year
arduously working through its details. The negotiations were exhausting,
exasperating to the point of complete frustration for both sides, and occasionally acrimonious. Reviving the faded glory of the New Amsterdam—
which included removing asbestos and reestablishing its structural
integrity—was going to be costly, and with the state and city taking the
direct risk for that renovation—with cash—negotiations over the budget
proved to be complex and contentious. While they were ongoing, Disney
proceeded with construction-and-restoration drawings and budgets
involving a cast of hundreds, if not thousands: architects; conservators;
mechanical, electrical, and plumbing engineers; structural engineers;
acoustical engineers; theater-craft and lighting cost estimators. The 42DP's
owner's representative was "selectively invited to meetings," said
Robertson, "but not kept informed."[18]

By November 1994, after submission of the 80-percent design-
development documents and accompanying cost estimate submitted to the
42DP, Robertson knew serious disputes with Disney were at hand. The
budget had been growing steadily. At $32.8 million, the revised estimate
was up nearly 17 percent from the earlier estimate of $29 million at the
time of the MOU (December 1993) and up 30 percent from the original
figure of $26.1 million (July 1993). How much of the budget increase,
42DP officials wondered, could be traced to Disney's desire to renovate to
a higher-than-Broadway standard, on the government's nickel? The gov-

ernment's commitment was to fund a "first-class Broadway live musical theater," nothing more. Disney wanted a high-tech theater with more expensive custom-quality production items and top-of-the line finishing touches such as grand drapes with mouse ears. Robertson and other 42DP officials objected because these disputed "scope" items, as they came to be called, were either beyond the terms of the MOU or outside the scope requirements of the project. With their own shadow team of engineers, the 42DP estimated that the "restoration of the New Amsterdam Theater as a first-class Broadway musical theater is achievable within a target budget of $30.6 million."[19] However the disputed items ultimately would be resolved—Disney agreed to pay scope and disputed items totaling $1.9 million—the deal's initial provision for a $5-million overrun fund now looked insufficient.

Months later, when final cost estimates came in, just days before the deal's July 15 drop-dead date, the numbers looked more ominous. The budget now totaled $40 million. Once again the parties returned to the negotiating table. Earlier, Disney's haggling over details had been continuous and to effect. Now, however, the solution to escalating costs could not be extracted directly from the public sector as was the case in earlier rounds of talks when Disney negotiators succeeded in getting an additional $5-million loan (at 3.5 percent for 30 years) from the city and state. Under the terms of the lease and funding agreements approved at the end of December 1994 by the four public entities involved in the transactions— the board of directors of UDC, the board of directors of EDC, the PACB, and the Port Authority of New York and New Jersey (PANYNJ)—the city and state were authorized to lend $26 million. The deal had to stay within that amount; neither the city nor the Port Authority could add monies to the pot without holding a public hearing. To accommodate the higher projected costs without changing any of the essential terms of the approved transaction, the recast deal provided for two levels of contingency: a "standby-loan amount" of $3.5 million and another $1.9-million black-hole "contingency loan amount," both of which Disney could fund in the form of a loan (at 3.5 percent for 10 years) to the public entities.[20] In a fashion reminiscent of the TSCA funding arrangement, the public funds to repay these "advances" would come from the theater's payment of percentage-rent revenues via a rent-credit mechanism. In effect, public funds would cover the overrun, but these would be booked as reduced revenues in the future; in other words, they would be invisible, once again. In the end, when the cost came in at $36.7 million (a figure reconciled by the state corporation), the deal's financial expansion joints proved useful, though the "loan" advanced by Disney never hit the maximum $5.4 million.

The toughness of these negotiations stretched beyond economic concessions. In addition to taking little up-front risk, Disney wanted to be shut off from any liability or obligation and to structure incentives for the public entities to keep moving forward while holding on to its own exit strategies in the event the project became undoable. The hardest issue to negotiate, according to Robertson, revolved around the rights of Disney and the public entities to terminate the project.[21] Disney negotiators were no less insistent that the company be protected against any lawsuits involving the project. In light of the 42DP's legacy of litigation, this was a sensitive issue for the project's top public officials, but they gave in after a protracted fight, agreeing to this "duty to defend" formalized in a side letter of agreement to the MOU. "As a general premise, when you are dealing with government, government wants you to be responsible," Vincent Tese later remarked in an interview. "As a result, UDC and the city had a hard time negotiating these two points, and it took a long time."[22] In another instance that revealed how difficult it was for the company to relinquish its well-honed strategies for total control, Disney negotiators pushed hard for, but failed to get, a right of first refusal for every property on the street—an exclusive option that would have allowed them to match any offer the city and state received from any company to develop property on the street.

Known for its unyielding attitude about all business dealings, tough negotiating tactics, intense attention to details, and aggressiveness, Disney's executives held most of the bargaining power. The entertainment giant was dealing from an obvious position of strength. Its size and success meant that its negotiating partners needed Disney more than Disney needed them, as was the case on West 42nd Street. Disney brought to the table, all by themselves, the possibility that the project would get done, and that it would be done by the most important entertainment company in the world, remarked Robertson. "Disney wanted to be on 42nd Street," Tese said. "We were not going to let them go. This was the first really big nonoffice deal."[23]

THE SWEETHEART DEAL

The final terms of the deal provided Disney with a low-risk means of buying a Broadway platform and testing the market for urban entertainment. It was "a very good deal," Robertson wrote Charles Gargano in the first of several briefing memos on the deal during the last feverish days of final negotiations, this one in preparation for the UDC chairman's lunch with Disney's chief negotiator, Frank Iopollo. To the city and state's direct $26-million capital investment made in the form of a subsidized 30-year loan, Disney had agreed to put in $8 million in equity and advance an additional $5.4 million in the form of a loan to the public entities. After accounting for a 20-percent federal historic tax credit for the cost of rehabilitation,[24] its net investment in the deal, less than $3 million, would amount to a tiny fraction (less than 8 percent) of what the renovation finally cost—$38.6 million, including the production-oriented scope items on Disney's tab. With a AA– credit rating on its bonds at the time, the blended rate on the public's below-market rate loan offered the entertainment giant annual interest savings of as much as $1.1 million. In addition, another capital subsidy—a full exemption from state and city sales tax covered the purchase of eligible items and tenant improvements related to the redevelopment of the theater—Robertson estimated, would save the company approximately $1 million.

Equally advantageous is the base rent (equivalent to PILOTs) Disney pays to the city. Starting one year after the substantial completion date, in 1998, this annual payment of $331,401 remains constant during the first five years of the 49-year lease term (which carries options to extend for another 50 years).[25] This is 77 percent of what would have been due on the theater parcels in the absence of tax abatements in the 1998–1999 tax year and 59 percent for tax year 2000–2001; as assessments go up, this subsidy will increase in value. It is, however, higher than what was being paid in property taxes on the Majestic Theater where *Les Miserables* was playing at the time—in other words, the PILOTs were higher than taxes at a competitive theater. "This was probably the one thing that Disney missed," remarked Robertson in an interview some time later.[26]

Substantially, the deal's biggest source of direct return to the city was pegged to the success of Disney's theatrical productions. Defined in financial terms as annual percentage rent, this provision of the deal delivers "upside," in real estate parlance, if and when the theater's "net gross revenues" (including sales of food, beverage, and audio, musical, or video reproductions of performances performed at the theater) meets certain targets of commercial success: 2 percent of the first $20 million of all net gross revenues and 3 percent above that. Projecting net gross revenues on the basis of its wildly successful production of *The Lion King*—1998 winner of the coveted best-musical Tony award—which has been playing to sold-out audiences, the city's annual percentage rent in 1998 would have been more than two and a half times the base rent, or approximately $873,000—nearly twice what the 42DP staff had initially projected in late 1994.

What made this deal distinctive relative to the TSCA deals was the city and state's commitment of hard cash. Initially, the state's money was to come from the Fund for Regional Development, a special pool of discretionary monies for economic development within the PANYNJ's regional realm. Created out of political compromise, the spending pool had been funded by a portion of the incremental rental income resulting from higher rents charged on more than two million square feet of office space in the World Trade Center in lower Manhattan vacated by New York State in the mid-1980s, space that it occupied under a long-term lease at rents well below the market at the time. When Tese and Robertson went to tap it for the Disney deal, however, they found that the spending pool had been overspent. Fortunately, there was another way for Governor Cuomo to tap the Port Authority for the state's $13.5-million share of the Disney deal. The Port Authority's expansive powers allow investments in a project area that will directly benefit or constitute improvements to its investments, in this case, the nearby Port Authority Bus Terminal (PABT). Spending Port Authority funds also meant that state officials did not need to process this decision through public hearings or hold it up to other forms of public scrutiny. In exchange for the funds, UDC promised to convert the PABT's dollars into subway-entrance improvements or a pedestrian bridge over Eighth Avenue connecting the terminal entrance with one of the project sites; streetscape and lighting improvements were among other possibilities, any of which would be agreed upon by the Port Authority and the 42DP. "The lesson here," Robertson noted, "was that there is always money in government if you look hard enough and need it enough. It's a question of being creative."[27] To cover its share, the city simply allocated capital-budget dollars.

For Robertson, the deal offered up another lesson: The public sector should never do complicated deals. "Developers believe government will do anything, that they have no bottom line." That's one reason they feel they can outdeal the public sector through time alone, by exhausting the public negotiators. But more than time is involved, she emphasized in an interview. The public side cannot have the same level of experience and expertise. Typically, the public's negotiators are younger. In defining technical definitions such as "adjusted gross revenues," for example, it is easy for public negotiators to get taken to the cleaners. She believed there was no way the public could win on this one. To her way of thinking the TSCA deal was too complicated, in part, because items in the lease were set up to cause renegotiation.[28]

The deal's largesse made perfect sense to the project's public promoters. "We did a sweet deal in order that Disney would bring others in," Tese said. "We didn't worry about political problems or precedents. We knew this would be the *only* sweet deal. And we had a mission. . . . Also, in the event of objections, the city could place the blame on the other party, say, 'it is the state.'"[29] From the city's top economic-development official: "I'm not going to claim we'll get a market return on the deal," said Clay Lifflander, Mayor Giuliani's president of EDC who replaced Dinkins appointee Carl Weisbrod. "But we subsidized it to get the other activity on the street. In the retail business, it's what you call a loss leader."[30] With Disney committed, public officials' confidence was running high. At the exuberant press conference announcing the Disney deal, Cuomo reportedly went after a "hapless" reporter who questioned the 3-percent subsidized loan. What does it matter if it is 2 percent, or 0 percent, or 10 percent when you are talking about rescuing the soul of our city, its very heart—what price do you put on that?

While the heavily subsidized deal caused public officials no lost sleep, the promised capital subsidy initially raised the vocal ire of Broadway interests, especially theater owners who thought of themselves as having subsidized dark landmarked theaters for years. They saw Disney as gaining an unfair advantage in offering "legitimate attractions that would otherwise be presented in non-subsidized theaters."[31] To those familiar with theater lore, the cry of unfair competition echoed the historic tension between Broadway and Hollywood that developed following the film industry's long-ago move to the West Coast. To the owners' way of thinking, theater was the primary reason tourists came to New York. Unlike corporations, the theaters could not locate anywhere else, which is one reason Mayor Koch during his administration saw no need to give theater owners any coin. The solution was easy: As soon as Governor Cuomo broadened state support for Broadway theaters with a new loan program "dedicated to preserving commercial theater on Broadway," theater owners dropped their opposition to the Disney deal.[32]

However tight Disney squeezed the city and state, no set of financial terms could eliminate what its executives most feared: tarnishing the Disney image. As part of the deal, the company insisted that the adult book store in the adjacent Candler Building had to go and that the 42DP issue a "Policy Statement" excluding sex-related businesses (SRBs) from the project. Doing so required UDC directors to formally adopt "Findings" and make a determination that the policy would have no significant effect on the environment. Robertson felt this was unnecessary. For many years, as a matter of policy, project officials had maintained a neutral position on the issue of whether SRBs would be allowed to return to (or remain in) the project area, and had stated so in litigation. As an agent of the state, the UDC subsidiary did not want to be seen as sweeping away all porn; it was a First-Amendment issue. Then, once the state began to take title to the properties on the street, as a practical matter, it appeared redundant. The eastern portion of the block had been cleared of SRBs in the first phase of condemnation, and the state was in the process of vacating businesses from parcels on the north side of the western end comprising Site 7 (now the E-Walk complex), including what at the time accounted for a third of all SRBs in midtown Manhattan. Only the four parcels making up Site 8E (now AMC Cinemas and Madame Tussaud's) remained in private hands, and the city recently had announced a $13-million commitment to fund this phase of condemnation. Mayor Giuliani was actively pushing for citywide antipornography zoning, and in a first step toward that goal, the city council enacted just before Thanksgiving that year a one-year moratorium on the establishment of any new SRBs within the city. The moratorium was an amendment to the city's Zoning Resolution, but "because the Zoning Resolution has no application to this Project," Tese told UDC directors in one of his many memos on the project, "the moratorium technically may not apply to the Project area, thereby creating the paradox that the Project area may be one of the few (or only) places within The City of New York that SRBs might be able to open or relocate."[33] While the moratorium appeared to give technical cause for UDC's action, it provided political cover to do what the state really did not want to do: give in to Disney's insistence, driven by intense risk aversion, that the New Amsterdam lease agreement include a prohibition on leasing to certain types of uses, namely SRBs.

The growing reality of Disney on West 42nd Street induced other major entertainment corporations to venture forth with proposals for a site on the street, but intervening political forces complicated the deal-making process while the demands of managing fluid negotiations with several major companies devoured months. By the end of 1994,

Robertson was in advanced negotiations with the Kansas City–based AMC Entertainment Inc. for a $53-million development of a 29-screen movieplex on the south side of the street just west of the Candler Building and with the London-based Tussaud's Group for a $55-million tourist attraction in the former Times Tower. She was also evaluating four proposals from some of the biggest names in the hotel industry, who were vying for the opportunity to develop the large site on the western edge of the project area on the north side of the street, while eviction proceedings were commenced on the last occupied site on the street. At the New42, Cora Cahan was negotiating with Viacom's MTV, which had taken a six-month option on three theaters (Apollo, Times Square, Lyric) across the street from the New Amsterdam to explore the development of a multi-media studio-and-entertainment complex.

At the state capitol in Albany, timing became a matter of urgency. At the turn of the New Year, the reigns of government would pass to Republican governor-elect George E. Pataki from Democratic governor Mario M. Cuomo. Fearful that the new administration might decide not to honor the deal with Disney, an intense sense of urgency set in among state officials and Disney executives, all of whom sought to complete binding documents prior to the changeover. After what Malmuth described as "frantic activity" for three days—December 28th–30th—city and state officials were ready to sign separate lease and funding agreements with Disney executives at the end of the work day on the last day of the year. This was a big step from the nonbinding MOU signed a year earlier—also at the time of a political changeover, at city hall. Still it was not a done deal. At the family entertainment giant's insistence, the 400-plus pages of documents included three "conditions precedent" aimed at minimizing the reputation risk of committing to West 42nd Street, which, by UDC's count (in late 1994) still housed 20 SRBs now concentrated at the western end of the project area, only slightly less than the 22 that lined the street in 1984 (figure 11.3). One, the budget of the project had to work, meaning final bids for the renovation, which had not yet been submitted by contractors, could not exceed the $34 million specified in the Funding Agreement. Two, all adult uses had to be removed from the street, a condition in keeping with Disney's early insistence that it would not open the New Amsterdam with XXX-rated establishments on the block. Three, at least two "nationally recognized and reputable companies who are actively engaged in the entertainment business" had to sign letters of intent for at least 35,000 square feet of ground floor space on the street in order for Disney to go forward with its preliminary commitment. If these three, as well as more technical, conditions were not met by July 15, 1995, Disney had the right to walk from the deal.

This drop-dead date 42DP officials "cooked up" with Disney. It was used—successfully—to effect a sense of urgency and pose the possibility of lost opportunity.[34] Negotiations with Disney, AMC, and Tussaud's had reached a point where closure was necessary. State officials believed that the project would only succeed if a critical mass of significant elements were put in place simultaneously. Few of the players wanted to risk going forward without some certainty on the other components, so the project's sponsors pushed for the deals to be concluded within the same time frame. As the perceived linchpin of the pending success or failure of *42nd Street Now!*, Disney was politically essential. With Cuomo leaving office, Robertson felt they had to ensure that the project would get done, that momentum would not be lost. It was old-fashioned politics—as Democrats, they all assumed they would be gone: Republicans would control both the governor's mansion and city hall. As everyone cleared out for the last time, Robertson sat in her office waiting for a call from Charles A. Gargano, the man Pataki had designated as the new head of UDC. Tese had left her signature pages, but what, she wondered, was the purpose of signing if the new administration did not want to go ahead? The call to sign came at 4:20 P.M. (plates 16–21).

11.3
Sex-related uses in the project area, 1993. (42nd Street Development Project, Inc.)

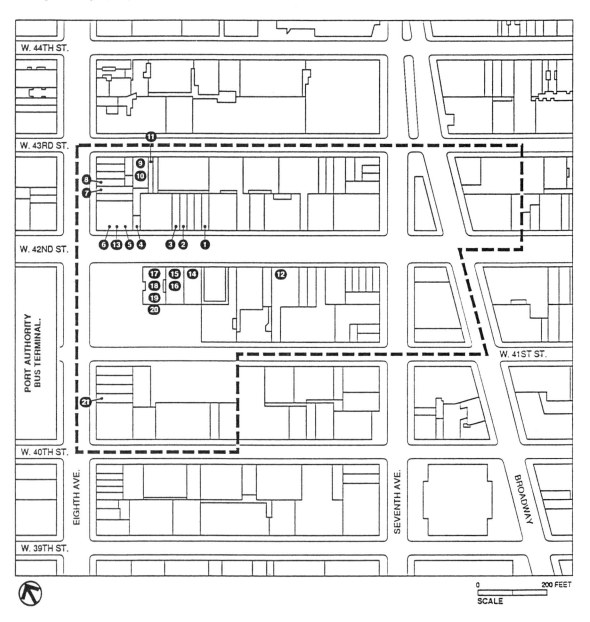

In spite of considerable momentum and a change in perception, the project was still precarious, although the situation was not as dire as in 1991. Following the February 1994 announcement of the MOU a period of guarded optimism prevailed, but during the next six months leading up to the "drop-dead" date, newspaper leads reporting on the status of negotiations signaled a creeping wariness as to whether city and state officials would succeed in meeting the crucial deadline. "Madame Tussaud's Loses Bidding War and Drops Times Square Plan," "42nd Street Scramble! Will Disney's Deadline Melt Madame Tussaud's?" "Times Square Scramble! Disney Gets Jittery, MTV Mulls Pullout," "Efforts to Save 42nd Street Intensify." Deals with two significant brand-name entertainment companies came tantalizingly close to fruition but collapsed, to the chagrin of 42DP officials, Tussaud's in March and MTV in May. In the meantime, the state's exploratory talks with AMC fell captive to intense turf disputes between the project's political partners.

With the project on the cusp of success, one might have expected city and state officials to push in a coordinated way, if not for the greater public good, then for the political credit each elected top executive could claim. But the changeover in city hall from Dinkins to Giuliani the previous year upset a continuity of party leadership that had prevailed across the city/state coalition for more than 13 years, even withstanding the mayoral changeover from Koch to Dinkins. Despite alignment on broad-based goals, fractured relations between city and state players at odds with one another over policy and tactics seriously threatened progress. The tensions ultimately resolved themselves in the deals packaged to meet the Disney deadline, but the pressure to produce revealed the power and willingness of the city to offer highly favorable terms, though no cash, to desired tenants and drive through a sole-source designation, a procedure fraught with political risk given the project's tortured history. The episode also revealed how both public and private players used Disney's magnetic ability to draw others to the project, and how, in this high-profile environment of constant flux, the power of such corporate leverage substituted for the entertainment giant's usual tactics of control.

The political dispute—which did not appear in the news until the beginning of May 1995 and then only in the *New York Observer*—surfaced over sharp differences in the type of deals the city was willing to make with potential users, all of whom were angling for public subsidies to offset the high costs of renovating the deteriorated historic theaters. As expected, AMC and MTV reportedly wanted Disney's deal: The public would put in cash, ask for only a low-cost payback plus an upside pegged to performance, and proffer handsome tax subsidies. Despite being told by city and state officials that no one would get the type of sweet deal that had gone to Disney, AMC, which did not have a New York presence and had been trying to strike a deal for a spot on West 42nd Street since sometime in 1993 (they submitted a formal proposal in February 1994),

tirelessly persisted in seeking some form of subsidy. Lifflander was reported
to be unimpressed by the amount of rent the national movie-theater chain
offered and was desirous of soliciting competitive bids for the south-side
theaters from other potential users through an RFP process. Also, he
reportedly questioned the wisdom of subsidizing a retail operation that
would draw visitors to the street yet fell short of being a true daytime
leisure operation that would attract other tenants the way Disney would.

Since the city was the capital player supplying the funds ($13 mil-
lion, possibly more) needed to condemn and acquire the four parcels that
would be added to the Empire, Harris, and Liberty Theaters and related
parcels acquired by the state as part of the first phase of condemnation to
make up the site, Lifflander's logic was policy correct: "We believe in competition," said Lifflander, a former investment banker. "That's how we maximize value and protect the public interest. The values on the street are
increasing with each successive deal. We firmly believe there's going to be a
lot of interest in the south side. We should see what the market has to say. I
think the state agrees with us."[35] Robertson tactfully declined to comment
to the press; silence made her point. In fact, as reported, the RFP for the
development site, which had been prepared by 42DP staff and was scheduled for release in January, languished for months; it was never released, as
explained below. What the city objected to, in no small part according to a
close confidential source, was the use of the theaters for movies.

Movies on West 42nd Street—60-plus years spanning glamorous
first-runs to popular-action flicks to pornographic grinders—had
bequeathed a controversial legacy. Throughout the 1970s and 1980s, mixed
messages sallied forth from marquees advertising constantly changing fare:
mainstream Hollywood—*Fifth of July, Gremlins, License to Kill, Of Human
Bondage, Stir Crazy, Thief of Hearts;* action fare and martial arts—*Buried
Alive, Borderline, Kung F;* sexploitation—*Hot Saddle Tramp, Ginger's Wet
Dreams, Scent of Sex, The Filthy 5, Ultimate Sensation.* The *DEIS* for the
original plan described the theaters as the core of a low-income entertainment district unlikely to be reestablished elsewhere. Respected intellectuals
such as Herbert J. Gans (who was also a consultant for the Brandt
Organization at the time) went on record in opposition to the project, in
part, over the bias against low-income entertainment inherent in the original plan (figure 11.4).

But the 42nd Street movie houses were part of a symbol of urban
decay, as Weisbrod argued in a letter to the editor responding to a *Times*
op-ed by an attorney representing the theater owners. Weisbrod believed
the owners were being disingenuous when they claimed that the project's
intended elimination of the movie theaters was discriminatory. The owners
did not "offer good, clean, safe venues at bargain-basement prices to provide low-cost entertainment for poor families and couples on dates," but
rather, he argued, the $7 admission price was higher than many first-run
Times Square-area movie theaters. Citing two homicides that occurred
inside project-area theaters that year (1988), he wrote "The theaters maybe
statistically less dangerous than 42nd Street itself, but they are hardly safe

by movie theater standards."[36] As was clear in this public exchange, if allowed as part of the redevelopment, the project's supporters believed movies would once again bring pornography and its accompanying crime back to West 42nd Street. Movie use was omitted from the initial *GPP* and over the years of amendments to that plan only gradually, and in a limited way, sanctioned as a permitted use.[37]

Whether it was a pragmatic afterthought or a response to strong opposition that emerged at the public hearings on the *DEIS*, movie uses first entered the plan through a 1984 amendment that provided that "one or two" of the midblock theaters could be used for "first-run movies," but only "on an interim basis while being renovated or until theater use

11.4
First-run movie theaters operating in Times Square. (42nd Street Development Project, Inc.)

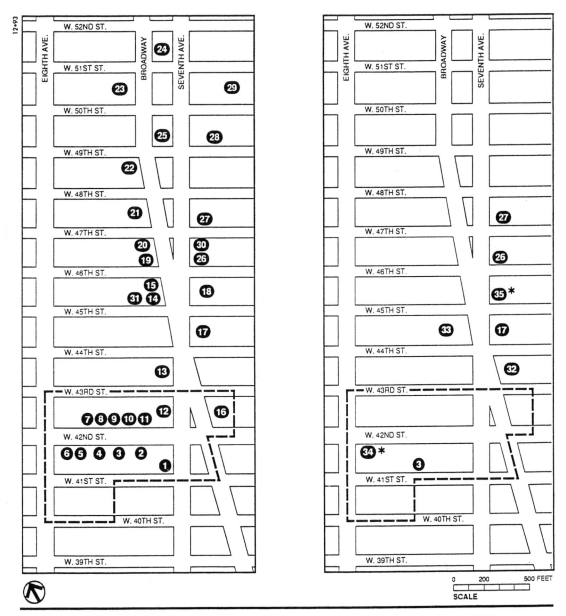

First-Run Movie Theaters Operating in Times Square Area: 1951 and 1993

becomes feasible." Movies became more of an accepted use with the reconfiguration of the entire plan, *42nd Street Now!*, which permitted movie use as an option for all of the project midblock theaters, but, again, with a limit: no more than two cinemas on the north-side theaters (Site 5). On the south side the 42DP planners remained neutral, simply calling for "a popular entertainment and/or tourist venue." A real change in attitude came only in response to specific proposal such as the one put forth by AMC in February 1994 for a 29-screen multiplex.[38]

Firm in her belief that the street needed a western anchor, and fully aware of the ability of a multiplex cinema to draw thousands of people daily, Robertson wanted AMC. Not completing a deal with AMC before Dinkins left office, she said later, created a problem. As the press reported correctly, Giuliani's people would not move on the deal, and AMC walked away angry. "If they want the damn block done," the *New York Observer* quoted a top AMC executive as saying several months later, "somebody's got to step up and say, 'Go.' The city seems to be the main obstacle to closure on this right now. I don't understand the dynamics between the city and the state."[39] Real estate experts were baffled as well, but one in particular, AMC's representative Benjamin Fox, executive vice president of New Spectrum Realty Services, who had seen deals come and go too many times to count, seemed to understand the underlying political tangle. Speaking in reference to a proposal by the Milstein/Weiler Arrow Management Company (which owned the parking-lot parcel at the southeast corner of 42nd and Eighth Avenue) to link AMC's plan to renovate the historic theaters with its proposal for a hotel on Site 7 across the street, Fox said: "We see this as an opportunity for the entire street to be cleaned up and the project to be done. To kick a gift horse in the mouth, I can only assume other agendas [are taking] precedence."[40]

Even more than their reputed dislike of the movie houses for the theater site, the new administration disliked the independence of the theaters' landlord—the New42—a nonprofit entity set up to ensure that the historic theaters would remain in the public domain in perpetuity. This control-focused mayor and his top officials wanted the lease revenues to flow to the city, not to something they could not control. The theater group, they argued, should have to go through the Department of Cultural Affairs for its budget funds. Why should it be different from other interests?[41] When they first learned about the New42's special structure—under the terms of its master lease for the theaters, it paid a nominal $10 base rent to the city, after which it kept all of the lease revenues from the theaters; only 15 years after the New42 received delivery of the first vacant theater would the City of New York, as lessor, receive directly any revenues[42]—the new administration's top officials sought a way to undo it or, as a second-best move, take away its second nonprofit theater (the Liberty, on the south side of the street). Negotiations for the south-side theater sites proved to be especially complex because they involved three landlords: the city, the state, and the New42 (which was, at the time, in the process of renegotiating its master lease with the city and UDC). The city asked that the RFP be written without the Liberty theater, but given its configuration in the center of the site, Robertson pointed out that taking it away would have made any kind of development of the south-side theaters physically impossible. And zealously guarding the long-term interests of her theater mandate, New42 president Cora Cahan vowed not to give an inch. City officials backed off from their demands after a stormy confrontation, but not without residual anger. Cahan explained in understated fashion:[43]

> The changes in the political scene were difficult because of the administrative and staff changes—getting the new people to understand who we were and why we were in place. The hardest was the Giuliani administration with whom we had a particular problem. At the time he took office, the project was already shifting into what it is now. They knew Disney was coming to the street—it was Cuomo and Giuliani who made the announcement in February 1994—so they saw us differently than the Cuomo or Dinkins administration.

Robertson and her staff went ahead and prepared the RFP, but the city would not respond to any communications. As political collateral, holding up the RFP served the city's purpose as a means of control over the site, and the New42. Robertson believed Lifflander had something of a "penchant for re-trading and not closing deals"; he was taking time in signing the EDC/New42 agreement, for example. As the time to close on the Disney deal approached, Robertson advised Gargano to close up one of the key final points with John Dyson, deputy mayor for economic development.[44]

Robertson's job also hung in the balance at the beginning of 1995. As a Cuomo administration holdover, the question was whether she would survive the staff cuts planned by Pataki's new chairman of UDC, Charles A. Gargano, the governor's top fund raiser and a former Long Island contractor who had held posts in the Reagan and Bush administrations. Disney executives were reported to be "jittery" about the new Republican administration and its commitment to the project. The phenomenal box-office success of the Broadway version of *Beauty and the Beast* accelerated its interest in capturing the New Amsterdam for its permanent theater home in New York. Malmuth stayed neutral when asked to comment on the issue, but seeking assurances that there would be no reversals or changes in the redevelopment plan, the company reportedly lobbied the Pataki administration behind the scenes to keep Robertson. On the other side of the issue was George Klein, a major Republican contributor, who had tangled frequently with Robertson over the project's many years of negotiations; he made no secret of wanting her gone.

Robertson had power, however. She also had friends in the press, judging from the timely appearance of a brief by *Times* columnist Frank

Rich titled "The Key to the City." "The best way to preserve the momentum and continuity of the deal-making at this crucial pass," he wrote, "is to retain the current state employees, led by Ms. Robertson, who have gotten so close, know the history and command the other players' trust." By the end of his first month in office Gargano had reportedly axed more than 100 people from the agencies under his command, including 60 at UDC. But with success so close, the new governor would be risking the collapse of the project if Robertson were to leave. Keeping her on was the best way for the newly installed administration to capture immediate credit for a high-profile success. The changeover in city hall the year before had aptly illustrated the power of image control. Shortly after taking office, Mayor Giuliani hosted a press conference with Governor Cuomo to announce the signing of the MOU between Disney and the city for the renovation of the New Amsterdam Theater, which, in fact, had been signed at the twilight of the Dinkins administration by Deputy Mayor Barry Sullivan—on a metal detector at city hall as he was leaving the building for the last time. Under the old protocol, the governor did not announce 42DP events at city hall. The act of holding the press conference at city hall simultaneously announced Giuliani's new protocol—on-my-terms-only. This was "amazing," said Robertson, "given the nonexistent role this city [administration] had had in the deal."[45]

The political logjam of Disney's condition precedent broke on the back of failed expectations for Madame Tussaud's acquisition of the former Times Tower. There the queen of wax fame[46] had planned to install a twenty-first-century museum featuring a "celebration of New York " with robotics and electronic gadgetry depicting the city's history and diversity. Tussaud's, then part of Pearson P.L.C., one of the world's largest media companies and owner of the *Financial Times,* the *Economist,* and Penguin Books, was the first entertainment company to recognize that the special qualities of Times Square were highly marketable. Its analysis of the demographics revealed the strong fundamentals of West 42nd Street's drawing power, especially for tourists, and it influenced others, notably Disney. (Eisner conferred with executives at Tussaud's during a trip to London.) Robertson courted Tussaud's. In December 1994, following more than two years of negotiations with city and state officials—and a number of false starts, including a plan for an overhead bridge across West 42nd Street to one of TSCA's building sites to the south,[47] which would carry visitors through interactive wax and audioanimatronic exhibits about New York—a tentative deal on terms seemed at hand. These included PILOT payments equal to existing taxes, a share in sign revenues, and a percentage participation in gross revenues from ticket sales and concessions. Also included was a $12.5-million loan from the city and state, subject to the new state administration's approval, to be repaid from project revenues (through the percentage of gross revenues from the attractions). Tussaud's originally asked for a $30-million grant from the city and state, reasoning that they needed a property deal that would be "advantageous" in the short term as well as long term. Once Tussaud's acquired the tower at a bankruptcy auction expected to take place in late January, the state planned to condemn the property, then lease it back to Tussaud's, saving the firm the state transfer tax on an otherwise private transaction (figure 11.5).

These plans unraveled the next month when Lehman Brothers won a bidding war for the tower by offering $27.5 million to Banque Nationale de Paris, which had gained control of the asset by way of a first mortgage on the bankrupt property.[48] The high price and the identity of the purchaser surprised everyone, government officials, developers, landlords, sign companies doing business in Times Square who also bid on the icon, and, especially, executives at Tussaud's. Evaluating it not as real estate but as a billboard, Lehman bet big on the tower's underexploited potential to generate millions in sign revenues, a bet validated two years later when it sold the icon at a record-breaking price and reported a gain of $53 million.

In the meantime, after several rounds of intense negotiations urged on by anxious city and state officials, Lehman and Tussaud's could

11.5
Madame Tussaud's proposal for the former Times Tower.

not come to an agreement on price: Lehman reportedly offered to sell at $37.5 million, but the gap between asking and offering prices proved unbridgeable despite a substantial narrowing from the $30-million preliminary target Tussaud's had determined to pay for the tower. The property values implied by these figures amounted to "a very strong vote of confidence in the future of Times Square," said Douglas Durst, who bid $22 million at the BNP auction.[49] Nonetheless, Tussaud's pullout rippled through the project, threateningly. "There was no progress on finding tenants," recalled Malmuth, "because there was no way to put deals together."[50] When the state once again tried in May to broker a deal for the museum, an angry Tussaud's refused to meet Lehman.

The loss to the project of Tussaud's seriously worried Disney executives. From their view, it was untenable to be the only major tenant on the still-tawdry thoroughfare who had only 25 feet of frontage on West 42nd Street. Built during the golden era of the street's acclaim as a venue for theater and high land values, the New Amsterdam's main auditorium like others on the street (the Lyric, Apollo, Selwyn, Harris, Liberty), sat deep into its lot with only a narrow thread of access on West 42nd Street; it relied on the visual drawing power of an impressive facade, an elaborate entrance, and a glittering marquee. Disney cajoled the players behind the scenes, urging Tussaud's to look elsewhere on the street. The entertainment giant's most effective tool for shaping the outcome of the development project was also the most visible: its name. Nowhere did this turn out to be more important than in the competition for the rights to develop Site 7, the large (57,500 square feet) L-shaped set of parcels straddling the northeast corner of West 42nd Street fronting the gritty side of Eighth Avenue diagonally across the traditional point of entry for runaways, the Port Authority Bus Terminal.

Tishman Urban Development Corporation, whose parent Tishman Realty & Construction Co., Inc. (TR&C) is an experienced and widely recognized New York-based firm,[51] won the developer designation with a striking and highly acclaimed design vision by the Miami-based firm Arquitectonica with D'Agostino Izzo Quirk for the luxury hotel portion of the project; the announcement was made May 11, 1995, just four weeks short of Disney's impending drop-dead date. Operating under the newly minted corporate name, Dream Team Associates, Tishman's affiliate would "develop, own and manage" the hotel-and-entertainment complex—with Disney as a tenant. The name change came just days prior to the public announcement and quietly signaled a downsizing in the entertainment giant's participation in the $303-million project to potential anchor tenant from equity partner, or as the 42DP's carefully worded press release put it, to "exploring concepts for retail entertainment either for itself, or with third parties. . . . In addition, Disney has an option to own and operate time share units."[52] Much of the press glossed over the significant change, as the headlines made clear: "Disney Complex Corners 42nd Street," "Disneyland's Megadeal in Times Square," "Disney and Developer Are Chosen to Build 42nd Street Hotel Complex." One got it right:

Charles V. Bagli, then writing for the *New York Observer*, who had been covering the project insightfully for several years and was often the first to break key stories about the project. He saw the issue as a significant point of departure for a broader debate about the nature of the city's public-private partnership. His story's headline was critically on point: "Disney Dream Gang Mugs New York City: A Hard Look at the 42nd Street Hustle." The next week the editors of the paper hit harder, saying the deal looked "flimsy" because Disney could "pull out relatively painlessly," and they criticized the city and state for giving Tishman a "free option."[53]

Several plausible reasons can be advanced for Disney's pullback. One, the sudden reversal was a negotiating tactic to remind city and state officials that the company could pull out of the still-fragile redevelopment project if it did not get what it deemed necessary to venture onto West 42nd Street. Two, the financial commitment ceased to fit the business strategy for its time-share Vacation Club business or retail stores (at the time Disney was also negotiating a lease with TSCA for an 18,000 to 20,000-square-foot Disney store next door to the New Amsterdam Theater). Three, sensitivity to increasing public criticism of its "inroads" in the New York marketplace—on Broadway (*Beauty and the Beast*), on Fifth Avenue (Disney Store), on West 42nd Street (New Amsterdam Theater), in Times Square (banners for the BID extolling "Don't Be a Beast"), in Central Park (premier of *Pocahontas* on the Great Lawn)—led the company to seek a lower profile. Whatever the reason, the perception of Disney's participation in the project, in whatever form, continued to matter a lot. "If they're the lead tenant," remarked John T. Livingston, president of Tishman Urban Development Corporation—who had a strong background in city planning as well as real estate finance and had served in the public sector as James Stuckey's right-hand man for two and a half years at PDC—"that's as good as equity. The currency is in the name. That's what attracts the investors."[54] For Disney, the other side of that currency was control. "Control is what Disney got by joining Tishman on its bid to develop the Eighth Avenue end of 42nd Street," *Fortune* emphasized. "But it wasn't an equity partner, and it was making no commitments as a tenant. Essentially, Disney offered Tishman its name—a not inconsiderable resource—in exchange for a hand in shaping the proposal."[55]

The link between the hotel and the theater was important to Eisner, an architecture buff from childhood; their business arrangement reportedly gave Disney approval over Tishman's choice of the architect. "Building the hotel," Malmuth said at the time of the initial submission, "would fit our business objective to have a New York urban location for [the Disney] Vacation Club and it would work with the timing and the location of another major investment we are making with the New Amsterdam."[56] (Disney operated time-share apartments near Disney World in Orlando and Vero Beach, Florida, and was building them in South Carolina and Southern California.) In general, Disney's move into the live-entertainment business and onto West 42nd Street offered promising synergistic opportunities for cross-merchandising of its branded products.

Time was running short. The deadline loomed. Ultimately, the deal pivoted on Madame Tussaud's. Since 1991 the British company had been exploring opportunities to secure a place in Times Square for its premier entry into the United States. Frustrated and angered by the turn of events, Tussaud's executives did not want to meet with anyone, and agreed to talk to public officials once again only in response to a highly credible behind-the-scenes effort. Disney was also pushing Tussaud's to negotiate directly with the city. The negotiations did not become public until about six weeks later, in mid-June, as all the deal makers scrambled to complete the final language of letters of intent in time to meet the July 15th deadline. The new arrangement brought Brooklyn-based Forest City Ratner Companies (FCR) into the project as developer of what had become an expanded retail-and-entertainment complex fashioned out of the Empire, Harris, and Liberty Theaters (Site 10) and the four parcels comprising Site 8E. This would entail moving the 3,700-ton Empire Theater along steel rails in a tortoiselike roll 168 feet closer to Eighth Avenue, or, as Jimmy Breslin put it, "Taking the Show Out on the Road" (figure 11.6).[57] The 335,000-square-foot development would be anchored by Tussaud's and AMC. Bagli reported that sometime in May "the city reconsidered its plans to start from scratch and solicit proposals from potential developers for the south side site; set aside its differences with the state; and concentrated on getting a deal with Tussaud's and AMC in time to meet Disney's 'drop dead date.'"[58] Through no lack of oversight on his part, that report was only one side of the story.

The overture to Tussaud's sought to keeep politics at bay—by reopening talks with the city. Without informing the state, for five weeks city officials had been negotiating with Tussaud's, according to a close source, promising it could deliver the site. Afterward, Tussaud's executives told 42DP officials it had a deal with the city. City officials followed suit, presenting a fait accompli and demanding that the state take the deal: a sole-source designation. When the smoke cleared, Gargano and Robertson decided not to let egos get in the way, but rather to use the event to demand a quid pro quo: AMC as part of the FCR project. From then on it was a done deal, with just the forever-vexing details to attend to.[59]

It was Tussaud's who brought Forest City Ratner into talks with the city, having hired the firm as a fee developer for its earlier proposals for the former Times Tower. Typically FCR did not do fee development projects, preferring instead to hold property for the long term in its own portfolio. In the relationship presented by a Tussaud's project, however, its executives saw a strategic opportunity. They were involved in one major entertainment project, the Showcase in Las Vegas, and considered New York underserved in this dimension; also, they had no project in Manhattan. An affiliate of the well-known Cleveland-based Forest City Enterprises, FCR is headed by Bruce C. Ratner, whose path to the family business came by way of public service. He began his career in the Consumer Affairs Department during the administration of Mayor John V. Lindsay and later served for four years as Mayor's Koch's consumer affairs

11.6
Moving the 3,700-ton Empire
Theater 168 feet down 42nd
Street. (Dan Hogan Charles/New
York Times Pictures)

commissioner. To his credit, FCR had almost single-handedly revitalized downtown Brooklyn with MetroTech, a 16-acre office/academic complex, and the company had a host of diverse urban projects in its pipeline. Even more important, as a local developer, its project-management staff included a cadre of people with public-development experience—Paul A. Travis, James P. Stuckey, Mary Anne Gilmartin, among them—all of whom had previously worked at PDC. "We knew what the public parties could and couldn't do," said Gilmartin, FCR's project manager for West 42nd Street project. "We knew how far we could push and when we had to, sort of, pull back. We'd all gone through that experience."[60] The deal was put together in a short six weeks, "in large part," said Robertson, "because of FCR's familiarity with government, their loose approach to these deals, and a tremendous excitement by all parties that this thing was finally happening."[61]

It was a highly favorable deal for the developer and Tussaud's. The relatively low minimums for both base rent and PILOTs for the first 20 years of FCR's 49-year lease with the 42DP, Inc., appear to reflect a perception that the financial risk of developing retail and entertainment on West 42nd Street was still quite high. As is typical, the public sector traded off current revenues for future returns figured on the performance of the project and the developer's profitability. Based on specific benchmarks of developer profitability, the FCR project will deliver percentage rents for the 42DP, Inc., the city, and the New42 before the 20-year abatement period ends; this will, in part, offset the fixed base rent of $3.50 a square foot (per the space program at the time of lease negotiation), which is not set to increase in any preset fashion until year 21; the PILOT payment is $4.61 a square foot, approximately 60 percent of which will increase at 3.5 percent each year. The deal required no special contributions for public improvements, as had been the case with the original TSCA deal; rather the public amenities delivered by the project would come in the form of adherence to the heavy-duty design requirements. In structure, the deal was relatively simple and reasonably transparent. The Tussaud's piece, however, appears especially sweet: Passed through FCR, the wax museum pays a base rent of $11.33 a square foot (a "joke," said one former public-sector insider), plus a percentage rent above gross revenues of approximately $22.7 million. "FCR could be getting $75 a square foot at this point in time; it is the 'deal of the century.'"[62]

In the end, Tussaud's loss of the former Times Tower turned out to be a benefit in disguise for the 42DP. By agreeing to build a major brand-name tourist attraction as part of FCR's larger development of a midblock site—a location with much less visual power than the stand-alone presence afforded by that heralding signpost—Tussaud's propelled investment westward, an achievement that had frustrated the comprehensive planning goals of the project's planners from the start. Absent the set of events following Lehman Brothers' purchase of the tower icon, would the midblock have developed as quickly? Tussaud's probably would not have moved to a midblock site, given a choice. By this time, its executives were willing to go it alone, independent of what was to happen on West 42nd Street. They wanted to move into the former Times Tower, not to be held up by delays from the 42DP. Development was on the way, it was just a matter of time, because the market fundamentals of West 42nd Street— off-the-charts foot traffic—were perceived by these major players to be so extraordinarily positive for entertainment.[63] Yet just as the drop-dead date loomed on the calendar, the web of business connections circling around Disney accelerated the pace of investment. Its influence spanned the block and its several players.[64]

Though it would not end up this way, Disney's mark on the street appeared overwhelming to observers considering the pieces put together in mid-1995. "Disney can stage entertainment at the hotel," wrote *Times* reporter Brett Pulley, "have motion pictures produced by Disney Studios playing at the A. M.C. theaters, provide time shares for Disney Vacation Club members, have a Disney musical running at the New Amsterdam and cash registers ringing up T-shirts and mouse ears at the Disney store—all at the same time, on the same midtown block."[65]

Disney did not create the conditions for success on West 42nd Street as much as give spark to them. "Never underestimate the effect of an anchor tenant with clout like Disney," Robertson wrote in her teaching notes on the experience:[66]

> No politician was going to be the one to lose Disney,
> and we used this leverage over and over again: to get the
> last city condemnation dollars, to get the city to sign
> with New42, to get the city to go along with AMC.
> The new state government went along with a Cuomo
> project (while they scuttled others) in large part because
> Disney represented success. [Figure 11.7.] On the other
> hand, I believe the project would have happened with-
> out them. The long history of Times Square as a tourist
> and entertainment market, the amazing pedestrian statis-
> tics, even in bad times, the extraordinary pall of security
> issues. Once that went away, Times Square was going to
> come back and so was 42nd Street. It could have been
> Livent [in place of Disney].

From governor to governor, mayor to mayor to mayor, the conti- nuity of support over what had become a 15-year odyssey of endless hope and continuous effort made the incalculable difference between success and failure. In the mid-1990s, just when events had turned most promis- ing, relations between the city and the state broke down once again, as the behind-the-scenes negotiations over the Tussaud's/AMC commitments made only too clear, though not in a tussle as public as the 1984 mart flap. Notwithstanding the real tensions over whose sphere of influence would dominate, the need to see something materialize on West 42nd Street—the pressure not to let Disney's serious interest in having a Broadway presence

11.7
Explaining progress on West
42nd Street to the new governor:
(l to r) Cora Cahan, Rebecca
Robertson, Governor George E.
Pataki, unidentified bodyguard.
(© 2001 Maggie Hopp)

and its powerful endorsement slip away—ultimately prevailed over issues of political turf. In a first for this high-profile project, the governor brought the hard-cash resources of the Port Authority to bear on the objectives of the 42DP, and his UDC chairman moved out of the way when intergovernmental tensions threatened the project's immediate corporate commitments. Unlike the early days of the project when Mayor Koch called the political ultimatum and walked away from the project, the stakes were now too high for the same kind of theatrical high jinks. Tangible success was too near at hand. In what would become a myth of magical proportions, "the Disney factor" transmuted time, creating the perception of an overnight transformation. Before Disney's hard commitment, the possibilities of West 42nd Street were, as it is said in the real estate business, "all options." As long-time UDC-director William L. Mack put it, "Disney gave value to these options."[67]

With the Disney deal sealed and delivered, the momentum of the street's redevelopment became unstoppable. In the most fundamental sense, the critical task—changing the perception of possibilities—was complete (figure 11.8). The week Disney's commitment went hard with AMC and Madame Tussaud's signed on for the West 42nd Street express, the 42DP's leadership announced that impresario Garth H. Drabinsky's Livent, the Canadian company focused on large-scale musical productions, had signed a letter of intent to combine the Apollo and Lyric Theaters to form a 1,850-seat Broadway musical theater (subsequently renamed the Ford Center for the Performing Arts). It was a triple-play week. Completion amounted to finishing-touches execution—filling out the street's few remaining unclaimed sites: the Selwyn Theater (redeveloped and leased by

11.8
(Robert Grossman)

the Roundabout Theater, subsequently renamed the American Airlines Theater) and its adjacent infill site (built out by the New42 as a 10-story not-for-profit rehearsal facility and 199-seat black-box theater, the New 42nd Street Studios), the Times Square Theater (uncertain), and the western "Milstein" site (uncertain). Also waiting was market-driven development of the TSCA office sites. It would not be a long wait, however. Within a year, the Durst Organization announced it had reached an agreement with Prudential to purchase the development rights to build the first office tower on the northeast corner of Broadway and 42nd Street (Four Times Square); the Rudin Organization and Reuters America, Inc., followed suit the year after (Three Times Square), and the year after that, the last two sites went to Boston Properties (Five Times Square, headquarters for Ernst & Young; Times Square Tower, home to the New York practice of Arthur Andersen). An extra hotel—which was not part of the 42DP program—was soon added to the Forest City Ratner development. By 1998, only the Times Square Theater and the large site making up the south side of the project area between 41st and 40th Streets (Site 8S) remained unclaimed (figure 11.9).

If business was buying West 42nd Street for the location's branded address, city and state officials likewise had bought the participation of Disney and other brand-name corporations (figure 11.10). The tourist-and-entertainment vision of *42nd Street Now!* mandated the move, while the economics of playing on that world-wide urban stage precluded any players other than international corporate giants. Before the Disney

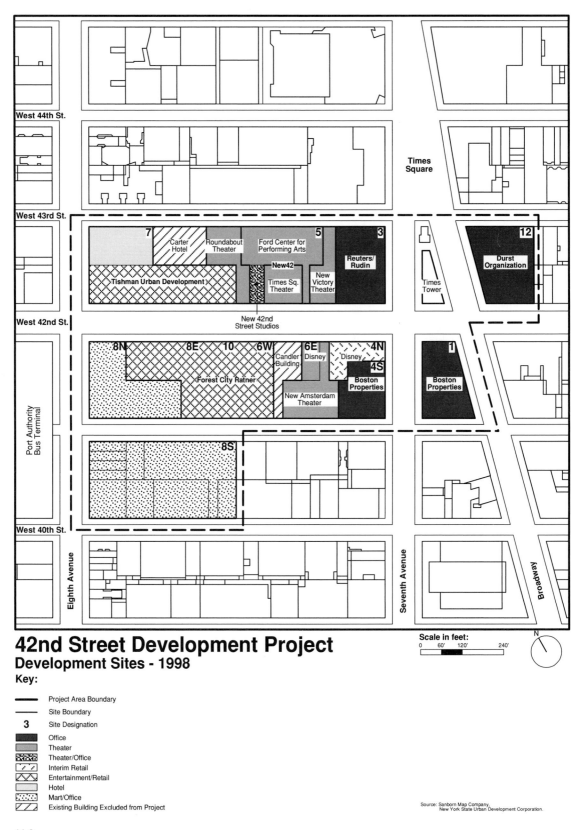

42nd Street Development Project
Development Sites - 1998

Key:

———	Project Area Boundary
———	Site Boundary
3	Site Designation
▓	Office
▒	Theater
▒	Theater/Office
▒	Interim Retail
▒	Entertainment/Retail
▒	Hotel
▒	Mart/Office
▒	Existing Building Excluded from Project

Scale in feet:
0   60'   120'   240'

Source: Sanborn Map Company,
New York State Urban Development Corporation.

11.9
Progress on development: The
pieces fall in place, 1998. (Morgan
Fleming for the author)

11.10
The corners of 42nd Street
and Seventh Avenue (ca. 1984),
transformed (2001). (American
Institute of Architects; Gary Hack)

announcements, the types of tenants Robertson and Cahan were talking to included mud-wrestling operators and retailers wishing to sell pets in the lobby of the theaters. These were not, Robertson recalled, considered legitimate businesses for that iconic venue. To enter this type of branded (though still marginal) location as a market leader as Disney did, corporations always look for some means of lowering the risks. They can either buy in at a bargain price, setting conditions that limit the risks of their capital commitments, or force political assurances of "best efforts" to eliminate perceived barriers to business success such as XXX-rated entertainment. For city and state officials, buying corporate interest to resuscitate West 42nd Street meant finding ways to meet these business needs. The timing was right for the plan's revival-oriented vision of entertainment and the new consumer demand for "going out" finally fit with the street's historic larger-than-life legacy of mass entertainment. While the city's negotiators could not hope to compete on an equal footing with private negotiators in striking economic parity, neither did they have to: The bottom line for public-sector development is inherently different, as discussed in the following chapters. What they could not risk was failure. This was the main reason the stakes have always been so high for the public sector. Consequently, neither the city nor the state could afford the political risk of the untried, especially at this point in the project's history. How the city-state coalition managed the risk of the untried speaks to the tactics of survival behind the strategy of public development.

PART III

POLICY SCORECARD: ASSESSING THE GAMBLE

C H A P T E R 1 2

THE RELUCTANT RISK TAKER

Despite an avowed position that the city would take no financial risk, Mayor Koch bet heavily on a concerted effort to redevelop West 42nd Street. The strategy of public development demanded aggressive public action, including condemnation of private property for private commercial development. For what the mayor aimed to accomplish—sanitization and simultaneous redevelopment of the entire block—and what he strived to avoid—failure—there was no detour around the risk taking. Sticking to a regulatory role would have been a safer posture, though unlikely to effectuate the type of dramatic change he and other government officials desired, at least in the political time frame accorded even the most successful politician. After the all-important approval by the BOE, risks surfaced everywhere in a never-ending sequence—fractious civic opposition, continuous litigation, repetitive delays, market fragilities, collapsed deals, and delayed public benefits, not to mention the ever-present potential liability of fraud and corruption that accompanies most every form of investment behavior, which with the Michael Lazar municipal corruption scandal indirectly tainted the 42DP. Project-threatening tensions between city and state officials surfaced at intervals throughout the two decades it took to transform the Deuce. In retrospect, managing the financial risks of this precedent-breaking project appeared relatively easy in comparison to the political risks that accumulated in sync with ever-increasing delays over the years.

Savvy politicians are reluctant risk takers. Even the best of plans may not reach fruition. The rewards of betting on long-term large-scale projects are distant and uncertain, especially in the early years. How do public officials manage political exposure when thinking big requires taking equally large risks?

Complex agreements serve to shield a city's risk taking from public view, and the 42DP offers many lessons. At the start, to avoid politically vulnerable project failures that might result from ever-escalating costs—the total cost of land acquisition for West 42nd Street is likely to exceed $400 million when condemnation is complete[1]—the city sweetened the deal for the office developers in exchange for their agreement to absorb the front-line financial risk of "excess site acquisition costs." The premium took the form of higher imputed interest rates the public sector agreed to pay on the advance from the developers, but taxpayers would never understand this since the loan repayment date was so far in the future. The city and state later buried the cost of its additional loan commitment for the renovation of the New Amsterdam Theater, as well as its coverage of other project contingencies, in rent credits against Disney's lease payments. These off-budget financing mechanisms, in effect, masked the city's risky long-term financial commitments to the project in technical details far removed from general oversight by the Board of Estimate and later, postcharter-reform, the city council.

Because cities are not supposed to gamble with taxpayers' (current or future generations') dollars, public risk taking almost always requires some form of political camouflage. The use of confidential side agreements—common to both the TSCA and Disney deals—allowed public officials to offer sweeteners and indemnities to the private investors without the appearance of doing so. At the same time, confidential side agreements protected the public position when negotiating with other developers who also wanted equally favorable deals. These mechanisms sustained the city's gamble to clean up West 42nd Street, but even the best talent and legal acumen drafting these mechanisms could not protect city and state officials from unforeseen contingencies that threatened political disaster.

The essence of public development is the open-ended nature of the commitments—financial and political—necessary to keep a project moving forward, especially once large amounts of money have been invested. Each side may have to make new commitments or follow through with existing obligations when, if operating unfettered and independently, its economic interest would best be served by not doing so. The reduced degrees of freedom inherent in a public-private partnership affect both sides of the agreement, if unevenly. Private developers benefit from greater maneuverability because they face few political risks. For city and state officials, however, the combined economic and political costs of severing ties are often unpredictably high, so new compromises must be found in revised deals.

The fundamental asymmetry, however, is that the developer can generally leave the project and even the city, while politicians cannot. When a project-threatening crisis emerges, the politics of pragmatism commands that public officials search for a solution by finding ways to recast a deal, amend a plan, or take on additional risk by investing more dollars (directly or indirectly) to salvage a project in the hopes of moving forward.[2] As developers rather than regulators, public officials cannot afford to be passive. Waiting for a market-driven revival of private development is not a politically feasible option because neither mayor nor governor can risk the charge that he failed to act to achieve the promises of a high-priority project. The political imperative is the bottom line and forces the search for a solution. With many technical sources of camouflage, public officials generally have options for restructuring a deal. From a policy perspective, what matters is whether the solution afforded some protection for the taxpayer, or whether the gamble of political and economic resources is discoverable, and, if so, passes the "smell test" when challenged by opponents. In the case of the 42DP, the gamble of additional financial and political commitments made possible Disney's magical renovation of the New Amsterdam Theater and the subsequent cascade of private investment to rebuild the legend of 42nd Street. But how did the politics of pragmatism finesse the pending political disaster from an aborted project? What are the lessons of the public sector's risk taking? The unrecorded costs? With the benefit of hindsight, did the public sector take sufficient risks or did its reluctance to put money out directly limit its ability to meet the goals of redevelopment more effectively? Were there other, less cumbersome ways for the city to redirect what the market was likely to deliver to West 42nd Street?

THE POLITICS OF PRAGMATISM

Real estate development is persistently cyclical. This character creates a window for implementing a publicly initiated project, especially when plans call for simultaneous development of several sites as did the 42DP at the start. In city districts considered risky from an investment perspective, large-scale ambitions impose further demands on the redevelopment process because investors must be persuaded that the environment will change fast enough to allow them to promote their projects—which may take longer than a single cycle. Public development promotes long-term and complex plans, but in the end, the market cycle commands that progress be made within a relatively narrow window.

That window is framed by a number of factors. In a large and complicated project, especially one involving condemnation, legal challenges are inevitable. On the construction front, building a large skyscraper requires lead time of two to three years, and delivery of the project must mesh with favorable supply and demand conditions at the time it is marketed. Increasingly, developers must line up sufficient tenant commitments to obtain construction financing. As the cycle matures, tenant commitments become more important, but harder to get. Demand has already been absorbed by projects built early in the cycle, meaning that late-in-the-cycle projects always entail greater speculation.

Missing the window for development is a common nightmare. The roster of big-city public developments stalled in 1990 awaiting the next real estate cycle listed well-known public-private projects in New York, including Renaissance Plaza, South Ferry Plaza, and the Columbus Circle site; in San Francisco, Yerba Buena Gardens; in Boston, Commonwealth Center, Boston Crossing, One Lincoln Street, and air-rights development at South Station. In each of these projects, the objectives of public development fell hostage to market dynamics—overbuilding, tight credit conditions, economic recession—that neither public officials nor private developers could control. Expertise in managing the economic risks of development is one reason the public sector seeks a partnership with private developers for high-profile initiatives. Officials attempt to manage these risks through the structure of a negotiated business agreement. But if the fundamental feasibility of a project is undermined by changing market conditions, hedging tactics or inventive details afford only limited protection. Public participation in real estate development rarely insulates a project from market cycles, unless the city restricts new supply by rationing permits, as in San Francisco.

In the case of the 42DP, the 1980s real estate cycle laid bare the risks of the city's primary strategic policy decision: shift the funding of condemnation costs to the project's private developers. Interestingly, the near-fatal risks of the private-funding arrangement were not the ones foreseen by city officials at the time, but rather others that grew like barnacles on the hull of a long-submerged ship. The business terms of the deal would be hard to explain to city officials and citizens at large—that was expected. That there would be numerous legal complications and lengthy negotiations and costly document preparation, all these were anticipated. The possibility of an ever-escalating ESAC was a known hazard; so too was the economic risk that the cost of this borrowing would be greater than if the city had issued debt directly. What was unanticipated, however, were the ways in which the private-funding arrangement created near-fatal risks of delay that ultimately froze the timetable for *any* new investment in the area until the market cycle once again started up. These remained the Achilles' heel of the project.

Since private dollars were underwriting the acquisition of land for the office sites and the theaters, the condemnation process did not begin until all vestiges of "significant litigation" had been eliminated, more than five years after the BOE approved the project. As a practical matter, private investors would not put capital at risk if great uncertainty surrounded the legal authority of the public sector to take title to the land. As a fiduciary, lender, and institutional investor, Prudential reasonably kept to this position. Whether the same duration of delay would have occurred if public money financed land acquisition and the city had more control over the timetable is debatable.[3] But public funding would have guaranteed "sure and certain compensation," thereby removing the basis for the last round of litigation challenging the project.

When office demand evaporated in the late 1980s and property values plummeted, most real estate observers understood that the only rational response would be to put the project on hold until the next cycle. Rational decisions by private developers to delay the start of development, however, exacerbate the political risks for public officials who are accountable to less patient constituencies. In public-private projects, public officials' calculus typically weighs current costs against future benefits. When the future is delayed or effectively aborted, they then find themselves publicly faced with explaining why investments have gone sour. Given the relatively short time horizon of most elected officials, this political exposure is considerably more conspicuous than if their development strategy involved only regulatory incentives.

Much as it afforded city and state officials a reprieve from pending political disaster, Prudential's enormous financial commitment did not resolve the transparent development crisis. It did finally allow condemnation to move forward, but because the decision was so obviously illogical in the context of an extraordinarily overbuilt real estate market, development lagged. Public denials by both Prudential and 42DP officials—"we are not conceding in the least that in a soft real estate market the project has to be abridged or slowed"[4]—kept up appearances but convinced no one. Whether the project went ahead in accord with the terms of the original deal hinged on two pending make-or-break dates: UDC turning two of the four sites in "vacant possession" (meaning the last tenants had departed) and TSCA delivering a $91-million letter of credit for the subway renovations. Both commitments proved untenable since going forward with development was economically suicidal.

"Fortunately for the developers," *Crain's* reported in early spring of 1991, "clearing the sites has become a lengthy process."[5] Progress had been rapid, at first. Within six months of when UDC took title to the 34 parcels making up eastern portion of the project area, nearly 42 percent of the reported 164 tenants (the final count reached 184) on the two sites being prepared for delivery had moved out; five months later at the time of the above-noted report in *Crain's*, more than 75 percent of the site had been cleared, with only 40 businesses left to go. The number dropped to six by July and to four a few months later. Within the real estate community, rumor had it that UDC was not rushing to complete the job—the 42DP had the writs of eviction for the last parcels, but to delay the process they did not go the sheriff and have them served upon the tenants, according to one official. When in early fall Park Tower fired its manager for the project, Richard M. Rosan, real estate professionals assumed the project was on long-term hold, if not dead, though media reports that TSCA was seeking a delay in the project did not surface until mid-November. When the revised deal with TSCA was formally announced in August of the following year, those last four tenants on the two sites yet to be delivered to TSCA still remained in place.

Technically, project officials could have pushed TSCA to deliver on the terms of the Land Acquisition and Development Agreement or default. With a TSCA default and forfeiture, the city and state would, in effect, have acquired the land "free" and have had in its possession four development sites, ready to go on the upswing of the next cycle. Practically speaking, however, if project officials had aggressively forced the issue with TSCA and triggered a default, the project would have been cast into a twilight zone of litigation. Uncertain issues of liability loomed ominously. It is not inconceivable that Prudential might have pressed an "equitable claim," charging unfair behavior on the part of the city and state if it could prove that government deliberately accelerated a process that forced TSCA to perform in an adverse situation, that is, when real estate markets were so depressed. Forfeiture of the land might have amounted to an "extraordinary penalty." It was not a matter of which side might win in the end, but of time lost. What each understood for sure was that litigation would have frozen progress for an indeterminate number of years, which was not likely to benefit anyone but the attorneys handling the lawsuits. Politicians would be called to account for their promises; there would be finger-pointing in all directions. Though the situation differed from the mart flap of 1983 when some developers "balked" at their minimal roles in the project, the advice from the city's leading "process broker," Howard Rubenstein, would have just as aptly applied to Prudential in 1991: "You have a long life to live in this city—don't be a warrior."[6] This is why most developers do not sue the city. Prudential commanded a major economic position in the city, and, as a result, collateral business issues surfaced immediately. The city's perennial fear was that playing hard ball with Prudential would seriously hinder its ability to get other developers to partner projects, the experience of Columbus Circle notwithstanding. The needs of both created grounds for the inevitable compromise.

The lever for a solution to this development crisis was Prudential Securities, Inc. (PSI), the insurance giant's Manhattan-based subsidiary. The third largest brokerage firm in the United States, PSI was also a comanager of the underwriting syndicate for the city's bond issues. With 11 locations in the city, PSI had been planning to consolidate its space in a new headquarters. Although PSI was an obvious tenant for the 42DP, its executives did not want to move to Times Square, into one of TSCA's office towers. At a rental of $35 a square foot (net of the 42DP subsidies), the new tower was too expensive, especially when compared to the likely financial packages in downtown Manhattan where a 17 percent (and climbing) vacancy factor gave tenants seeking large amounts of space tremendous bargaining power. Other factors weighed in negatively: The floorplates on the largest site (Site 12, on the corner of 42nd Street and Broadway) were too small,[7] and a new tower could not have been ready for occupancy when PSI needed it, at the end of 1994. More to the point, the brokerage giant did not want to be the first tenant in a project continually bedeviled by an uncertain finish date. Under heavy pressure to produce the makings of a "construction announcement," Prudential would have scored a coup if PSI had agreed to anchor the project.

Whether PSI would anchor one of the 42DP towers surfaced as a point of tension between city officials and 42DP officials. It was in the city's interest for PSI to move to Times Square, to save the project from total collapse, and Carl Weisbrod, who had moved to the city side of the political partnership as president of EDC, would have put PSI into the project, according to Rebecca Robertson, if the insurance giant had agreed. From where she sat as head of the 42DP, Inc., however, putting PSI into a new tower would have jeopardized the new entertainment-oriented vision of *42nd Street Now!* because building before the interim retail was in place would have meant the collapse of the interim efforts. Even had PSI had made a commitment to the 42DP, though, it would not have solved the economic problem facing Prudential. Under the terms of the LADA, the $91-million subway letter of credit had to be posted when the state delivered vacant possession of two sites (or, if earlier, at the start construction of the first tower). This would be hard to swallow. The numbers could not possibly pencil out if that development cost was being amortized only over one building. And in the real estate market of the early 1990s, starting a second tower on speculation would have amounted to double economic suicide, which is why city officials let PSI slip away from West 42nd Street—so long as the brokerage firm relocated somewhere within one of the city's five boroughs. Without a commitment to stay in the city, Weisbrod reportedly told Prudential negotiators, the insurance company would receive no help on its 42DP obligations.

By early 1992, PSI's choice had come down to Manhattan or New Jersey. After months of intense and intricate negotiations with city officials, in early August Prudential announced it would consolidate its 5,000 Wall Street-area employees into two principal locations in Manhattan's downtown financial district—One New York Plaza and One Seaport Plaza. The city's aggressive corporate-retention package of $106.2 million over 20 years included $48.8 million in energy savings and $57.8 million of tax incentives ($16.7 million of which would come from the state) covering sales taxes, property and commercial-rent taxes, and mortgage-recording taxes. It was, at that time, the city's largest corporate retention deal.

Described by Mayor Dinkins as "the second-largest lease transaction in the history of the city,"[8] the PSI retention agreement hit the news wires just three days after city and state officials formally announced the project's collapse and the signing of a new MOU with TSCA covering the terms of its future involvement in the 42DP. City officials formally denied any direct link between PSI's decision to stay in New York with the near simultaneous decision by the city and UDC to relieve TSCA of its big financial obligations for the 42DP, while requiring it to invest between $20 million and $30 million in renovations for *42nd Street Now!* but Deputy Mayor Barry F. Sullivan said: "I have to tell you that the good will from one negotiation washed over to the other, and vice versa."[9]

The interlocking pieces of the 42DP/PSI agreement led back to Prudential's collateral real estate interests in lower Manhattan. As one of the nation's largest commercial lenders, Prudential held mortgages on several office buildings in the area. Its decision to stay in lower Manhattan generally helped stabilize that marketplace, but more to the point, renewing its lease of 500,000 square feet at one of its interests, One Seaport Plaza, PSI's headquarters since 1985, specifically propped up its $195-million mortgage on that 1-million-square-foot building.[10]

If the city's interests were clear—protect its tax base from failing real estate values, retain 5,000 PSI employees, and salvage the troubled and highly visible 42DP—so were Prudential's—cut its losses on the 42DP, protect its mortgage assets in downtown Manhattan, and gain a favorable retention package for PSI. Each side was trying to play the PSI lever for what it was worth. Whether the threat of taking PSI across the river was real or not—and it appears to have been at least in the early stages of the search[11]—much was at stake for Prudential in New York. The relocation decision went all the way to the top to Prudential's chairman, who decided PSI would stay in New York. "It was awkward," recalled one negotiator. "We were players wherever we turned: on the mortgage, in Times Square, in the interim deal negotiations."[12]

With the collapse of the property market, political and financial risk intersected. The 1991–1992 crisis reflected the practical problems of moving forward with development of the office towers under the terms of the original deal. Neither the city nor TSCA could take a step backward. Both sides were locked into highly visible positions. Prudential was heavily exposed on several fronts. So was Mayor Dinkins, with an election year just around the corner. With more than $270 million already committed to the deal, Prudential needed to salvage the opportunity for development at some future date, preferably unhinged from any contractually driven timetable. The city's position was more complicated. Over the years, the initial policy mandate to avoid direct financial risk for land acquisition had unwittingly intensified the project's political risks. But unlike in the private sector, the city could not readily initiate a change of partners, especially since both sides were heavily invested in a project. With the benefit of hindsight, this crisis lesson defined one of the most salient differences between public and private development: Too many practical considerations as well as financial and political costs intervene as inhibitions on changing partners. Often the best that can be done is to nudge the developer along to a next-best solution.[13]

TSCA's revised deal with the city and state held benefits and costs for each side, but the fundamental financial premise remained unchanged: Prudential had to carry the funding obligation for site acquisition costs and bring new, interim retail activity to the vacant, desolate street. Indeed, TSCA would continue to fund (up to a preset limit) a wide range of public-sector costs beyond the direct costs of site acquisition, including third-party costs (legal, planning, environmental work) arising from the restructuring of the agreement, as well as any third-party litigation costs occasioned by any challenge to the restructuring. The new agreement was laced with tradeoffs.[14] Nonetheless, moving forward with the project required the public sector to publicly commit to two new direct budget allocations: from the MTA, $60 million to fund the renovations of the Times Square subway station complex and from the city, $48 million for the acquisition of most of the street's remaining parcels.

In the public sector, the essence of political risk is the inability of the mayor and governor to walk away from a development project for fear that the action will be perceived as an admission of failure, an example of administrative incompetence. Reputation is as prized an asset in the public arena as it is within the private arena; "saving face" is the operative political dynamic. "It's too bad that the adversarial nature of the development process [can allow a project] to become calcified," explained Weisbrod. "It would be nice to be able to say that maybe we should do something differently, to say that *that* was right four years ago, but it's not today."[15] That was 1989, and governmental officials could not back away from the project as proposed. Ultimately, they did "admit" to a mistaken vision, implicitly, in their decision to recast the use program. That was more than saving face, however. In making big decisions with long-term implications, public officials cannot anticipate all of the needs and problems of a development project no matter how finely crafted their agreements with private developers. It may not possible to get it all right, but it is terribly risky to get it too far wrong. Three mayors and two governors supported the 42DP without loss of continuity for twenty years. While it might have been hypothetically possible for Dinkins to walk away from Koch's commitment to the 42DP by blaming the project's deep-seated problems on his predecessor, the city's financial dependence on Prudential and the project's importance—real and symbolic—to the city made the politics of doing so impossible. Then on the cusp of success with Disney, Giuliani had no reason to jettison the preliminary path-breaking deal with the entertainment giant for which he could, and would brazenly, take full credit.

Was Condemnation the Only Way?

When the state gained legal control of the four office sites and midblock theaters in April 1990, the cast of credits published in the *American Lawyer* totaled 56—29 lawyers representing the public side and 27 representing the private side of the condemnation. The extraordinary number of lawyers at work on these proceedings reflected not merely its duration of five and a half years, but the complicated nature of the legal interests involved, individual and joint. To avoid any conflict of interest between the state and the city, for example, UDC called on outside special real estate counsel (4) in addition to its own internal legal staff (2); in turn, the city relied on PDC's economic development counsel and condemnation counsel from the city's Office of the Corporation Counsel (2), as well as outside special real estate counsel (9). To handle specialized issues of eminent domain, they jointly turned to outside litigation and condemnation counsel (12). On the private side of the table, TSCA hired special litigation and condemnation counsel (2), apart from individual counsel for the two parties of that development joint venture. As a player with dual roles, Prudential brought to the table its regional division counsel (1) as well as outside special real estate counsel (4) to cover its development company's joint-venture interests and another team of counsel (9) to cover its mortgage company's interest as the project's main financier. If one ranks the individual stakeholders in this process by their lawyer count, Prudential comes out on top, though not by much: Prudential, 14; the city, 11; Park Tower, 11; UDC, 6.

The trail of litigation and procedural detail attached to eminent domain, when overlaid on the complexity of the project's unique private-funding arrangement, kept the legal clock running at a healthy clip. Yet getting to the point of vesting was, in a procedural sense, just the beginning of other patience-enduring processes required to relocate tenants,[16] secure possession of premises, then settle ownership interests. Not all tenants would leave voluntarily, so writs of eviction and sheriff's orders would have to be served on several of the retailers, fast-food and counter restaurants, sex-related establishments, movie theaters, game arcades, office tenants, residents, and signs that occupied space within the project area. "Taking possession was a difficult, arduous process," said Robin Stout, senior counsel at UDC for the 42DP. "From among the three takings, the last tenant to leave was out on April 1, 1996—April Fool's Day."[17]

Contested valuations would, undoubtedly, trigger another lengthy set of procedures, as owners could take the state's good-faith offer based on the prevesting appraisals while litigating for greater payments. To settle valuation disputes, expert opinions as to valuation would be submitted by the state's appraiser and the condemnee's appraiser, with the final condemnation award resolved either through negotiated settlement or through trial, a process two noted legal scholars characterized as "a battle of wits between experts."[18] Angst prevailed among Prudential's people who worried about how the parcels would be valued: on the basis of existing use or on development potential. Most, but not all of the TSCA-funded 42DP valuations settled through negotiation. "The theaters were the hardest, most unusual piece of the condemnation," explained Stout. "Claimants tried to argue that these were developable sites, then they tried to argue that one could develop [on air rights] over the theaters. In the end, the judge did not have to rule on this because the owners, six of whom where elderly women represented by one attorney, settled."[19] Measured in time, tenants moved and owners compensated, eminent domain appears to be a clumsy instrument, as the numbers in table 12.1 attest.

Relying on eminent domain to assemble the project's 13 acres of land, city and state officials were following the conventions of urban renewal as commonly practiced in the United States during the decades following World War II. That process coupled government's sovereign power to seize private property—for a "public purpose" with payment of "just compensation"—with its police power to control what and how new land uses would be put in place, and it packaged those powers in a special-purpose entity such as UDC designed to facilitate public-private development ventures. For urban redevelopment, government is often redistributing property rights among private interests. The political power to do so comes from an evolved legal system that countenances a broad standard as to what constitutes "public purpose" and bestows judicial deference to agency execution of public/private endeavors. While government tends to prevail in contests of condemnation, the process is not without its legal and political costs. "Federal and state legislation is primarily aimed at utilizing private initiative and establishing a broad framework

TABLE 12.1 42ND STREET DEVELOPMENT PROJECT CONDEMNATION STATISTICS

| TAKING | TAX LOTS[1] | | TENANTS MOVED | | MONTHS LAPSED UNTIL: | |
	NUMBER	PERCENT	NUMBER	PERCENT	POSSESSION[2]	AWARD[3]
#1: Sites 1, 3, 4, 5, 6, 10, 12	34	61%	290	72%	89	116
#2: Site 7	18	32%	100	25%	13	ongoing[4]
#3: Site 8E	4	7%	14	3%	8	ongoing[4]
TOTAL	56	100%	404	100%	110	

Notes:
1. The project area comprises 74 tax lots, two of which—the former Times Tower and the New Amsterdam Theater—would not need to be condemned. Sixteen lots that comprise the original configuration of Site 8 (now referenced as 8N and 8S) remain in private hands. See figure 3.3.
2. The time between vesting and the departure of the last tenant.
3. The time between vesting and settlement of last ownership valuation claim.
4. As of January 2001.
SOURCE: Author's files.

within which private energies can be effectively released," Charles M. Haar and Michael Allen Wolf wrote in their widely used legal casebook on land-use planning. "It is this uneasy combination that has raised constitutional and practical problems of a unique type: urban redevelopment and renewal, like Tennyson's flower, present in concentrated focus the whole range of questions evoked by eminent domain."[20]

Though relied upon repeatedly, compulsory purchase—condemnation is an American term—employed for urban renewal and economic development remains fraught with political controversy. The policy arguments for the use of eminent domain were rational, proven, and, given the ambitions of the 42DP, practical. The "taking" was also within the scope of UDC's statutory authority, as attested to by the project's successful rebuff of all legal challenges. Yet continuous litigation laid bare the risks of this second strategic policy decision. Given that the condemnation process is so cumbersome and costly, inherently litigious, and full of political risks, was there another way to effectuate comprehensive redevelopment? Weisbrod, for one, kept posing this question in a series of private interviews in the mid-1990s. What realistic and workable alternatives might offer potentially greater efficiencies and expanded equity under a standard that gives existing property owners potential long-term economic rights beyond those of "sure and certain compensation"?

Consider a system in which the public sector creates a legal entity to redevelop land within a defined project area, some type of joint-stock corporation whose shareholders include cash investors (private and governmental) and existing property-rights interests (owners, tenants, leaseholders) who are issued shares in proportion to the value of their property rights as determined by a fair and just system of valuation.[21] Share interests in the larger redevelopment venture allow existing property interests to benefit from the expectations of future capital appreciation and can be monetized at the holder's discretion—through sale, barter, or hypothecation—via the marketplace for real estate development investments and on the holder's own timetable. At a minimum, because the shares issued are based on appraised fair market value, existing property interests theoretically would receive "just compensation" as under eminent-domain procedures, yet if held for long-term investment, the shares' value hold the promise of an upside—returns from owning a piece of the whole project being of greater market value than that of any particular individual component. Earnings in the form of dividends and capital gains might, as a matter of public policy, be exempt from local taxation for some specified time, similar to the tax abatements cities commonly give to corporations and developers to further economic-development goals.

The main activities of the joint-stock corporation would be financing and ensuring the execution of infrastructure improvements, property development, and management of the redevelopment in accordance with the approved master plan and a development strategy submitted to the appropriate governmental bodies. The principal roles of the public sector would be broad: to define the project area, approve articles of incorporation for the joint-stock corporation, develop the master plan of land uses and infrastructure, set out and manage the system for appraisal valuations, hold priority rights to the subscription of capital, and maintain a voting presence in corporation through representation on its board of directors.

This scheme is, in fact, the outline of the redevelopment structure put in place by the government of Lebanon in the early 1990s to implement an ambitious plan for rebuilding the war-torn central district of Beirut after 15 years of intense civil strife caused devastation of buildings and the city's infrastructure and public facilities. Redevelopment implied the restoration and construction of 4.4 million square meters of built-up space and the installation of modern infrastructure in the historic core of the city. The ambitions of the endeavor required a comprehensive legal, financial, and executive approach to implementation. Many complications affected the reconstruction plans: extreme fragmentation of property rights, entangled relationships between tenants and landlords, and a large number of lots small in size, conditions not unlike those of the typical American urban center. In an oversubscribed initial public offering (IPO), the government-backed Lebanese Company for the Development and Reconstruction of Beirut Central District, popularly known as Solidere, raised $926 million—142 percent of the initial subscription target—representing perhaps a third of the project's estimated cost, from some 20,000 investors. Contributions from existing property-rights owners of approximately 1,650 real estate lots for a fixed amount of $1.18 billion compromised the other piece of Solidere's initial capitalization. In a dramatic privatization of the reconstruction process, Solidere is gambling on the capital markets to finance Beirut's redevelopment.[22]

If such a system could have been put in place in New York to carry out the city's ambitious goals for West 42nd Street, would a Solidere-type model have been more efficient or afforded the city a more modest risk exposure? Put another way, having privatized the funding arrangement for condemnation could the city have taken the next big step and privatized the entire execution of redevelopment in a format at once bold and innovative that relied on some hybrid strategy between public development and regulatory control?[23]

Several policy-related questions present themselves. Abstracting from legislative hurdles and judicial questions as to whether it would violate the "takings" provision of the U.S. Constitution, how would a Solidere-type model alter the political risks of effectuating a transfer of land among private interests? Considering the political calculus of potential failure, would a Solidere-type model decrease the probability of "doing it wrong?" Operating within the framework of a Solidere-type enterprise whose stock trades on a public exchange, would the type of disclosure required by the Securities and Exchange Commission and demanded by private investors raise the standards of financial accountability for public-private ventures which in New York, as discussed in the next chapter, are uncommonly low? In short, what does the Solidere model of privatized redevelopment have going for it, from a governmental risk-taking perspective?

To begin with, no model of implementation can immunize an ambitious development scheme from civic opposition, litigation delays, budget uncertainties, conflicts of interest and business fraud, vagaries of the real estate cycle, collapsed deals and renegotiations, partnership tensions, and negative media coverage. Nor can it eliminate the problems linked to tenants being uprooted and priced out of neighborhoods experiencing gentrification. In short, it does not redefine the characteristics of development risk taking: coping with uncertainty, managing unforeseen difficulties, and gambling on the future without knowing the outcome. The Solidere model is an intriguing and innovative experiment in public-private development, but it is not an insurance policy against failure. What it does guarantee, however, is a broader sharing of urban redevelopment's inevitable risks.

Through the structure of its capitalization, the Solidere model of a joint-stock corporation can access diverse source of funds, both private and public, from large and small investors without being dependent upon a single deep-pocketed partner. A broader and deeper base of private investment capital might ease the implied fall-back on the public treasury, though it is naive to believe that it would eliminate completely the political need for government to camouflage its risk taking. The constituencies to which the redevelopment entity is accountable would undoubtedly change. Under a Solidere-type model, the framework for long-term decision making is removed from the immediate political arena by a corporate-governance structure. Although this would not shield the corporation's public directors from being accountable to their voter constituencies, the avenues of influence and control for public-sector directors of a Solidere-type entity would differ and likely diminish—therein lies the key political reluctance to try any new model.

One of the most compelling characteristics of the Solidere model is its promise of ongoing, direct economic benefit—dividends and capital appreciation of shares—to existing tenants, owners, and leaseholders from the redevelopment of land. Moreover, public markets are transparent and unambiguous in valuing economic interests, and they afford liquidity to investors, big and small. These benefits aside, the social situation on West 42nd Street differed so drastically from that in Beirut that it casts serious doubt on the likelihood of a Solidere-type model as an alternative to condemnation. Elected officials in New York evoked images of battle to describe their efforts to rid the street of crime, pornography, and moral despair, but the deterioration of that single street could not compare with the bombed out landscape of what had once been a flourishing and sophisticated Middle Eastern capital city. The extensive damage resulting from the Lebanese civic war created a strong political consensus to rebuild the rich heritage of Beirut, a pressing imperative absent from the fragmented political turf of West 42nd Street.

Could a Solidere-type model, with its promise of enhanced economic benefits, have furthered the development of a stronger political consensus and eliminated much of the litigation and delays that marked opposition to redevelopment of this contested turf? Phrasing the question another way, was the first script's corporate vision more at fault than the model of implementation, or were both equally problematic? While the corporate script failed on the merits, an entertainment-focused plan more attuned to the street's historic legacy would not have eliminated the necessity for eminent domain. A Solidere-type mechanism might have worked in theory, but the economics of property ownership and tenantry on West 42nd Street—profitable, if not praiseworthy, businesses—precluded any approach that did not mandate closures of existing business and compulsory sales of property. In the end, would it have been realistic of city and state officials to expect the vested interests of West 42nd Street to put aside proven short-term profits for a promise of capital gains sometime in the uncertain future?

LOST IN ITS OWN LABYRINTH

Physically improving the Times Square subway station complex, a nexus of four separate stations with passage to a fifth and a shuttle adding up to 11 subway lines making up the system's main transfer point for commuters, had been on the top of the city's priority list from the start of the project for good and obvious reasons. Decades of decay and neglect mixed with intense use had created squalor (figure 12.1). Severe congestion and crowding were legion in a station the first part of which first opened in 1904 but grew haphazardly over four decades through the actions of two competing private subway companies. It had never been designed to handle the estimated 74,250 passengers that passed though it daily (22.5 million annually) in 1982. Nor had it been designed with an eye to control the crime that had erupted in the subways in general, and the Times

Square station in particular offered numerous blind passageways, stairways,
and nooks, which the Transit Authority Police viewed as abetting violent
criminal activity. Conditions below "currently exhibit the same social conditions as 42nd Street above," the *DEIS* reported in 1983.

Though the summary section of the report merely termed the
station's rank and deplorable physical conditions "poor," a fuller description in a chapter devoted to transportation impacts revealed the planners'
honest assessment: "The Times Square station is one of the most complicated in the City and ranks among the most dangerous. The labyrinth of
platforms, concourses, stairs, and ramps has grown incrementally over a
long period of time. When the subway system is called 'the most depressing public environment found anywhere,' this station is often cited as evidence." A decade later when a Supplemental EIS was prepared as part of
the review process for *42nd Street Now!*, the indictment remained just as
valid, for nothing had changed in the festering and squalid underground
pit that made up the station complex except that a number of unsafe
entrances to the station had been closed and most of the concession space
removed, which, in turn, provoked something of a controversy. What was
said a decade before was still true in 1993: "The improvements are not
merely overdue but at this time absolutely necessary."[24] The supplemental
report did not say this, though, because the subway improvements had
been deleted from the project.

A consensus has long prevailed in New York among city officials,
business interests, and civic groups that to a large degree the life of the city
depends on its subways. In keeping with the rare opportunity for reconstruction presented by the overall scope of the 42DP, the original plan to
renovate the Times Square subway station complex ran to the ambitious,
perhaps to a fault, but not unreasonably so given the existing circumstances of the complex interchange and the scale of the proposed office
development. The station renovations comprised several pieces, each a

significant construction undertaking in its own right. A new expansive "fare-zone" mezzanine over Seventh Avenue between 41st and 42nd Streets would be created to ease congestion and provide adequate capacity for transfer movement among the eight subway lines. A large "free-zone" rotunda would be created to provide direct passageways to all four office towers. Filled with "significant new retail space" and a computerized city-wide transit information center, the design of the rotunda aimed to define a grand central focus for the station and integrate it with the office complex "in much the same way that the transit concourses at Rockefeller Center and the World Trade Center unite those developments," as an early project document explained.[25] Following that well-established pattern, the free-zone area would be maintained by the office developer "under an agreement similar to that in effect in Rockefeller Center." A new 24-hour entrance (the only one to be open continuously) on the Crossroads site (the present main entrance to the station) would direct light and air from the street to this free-zone rotunda. Four entrances (of the seven existing within the project area) would be removed from the sidewalks and six new ones placed within building property lines; escalators would be added, and both stairs and escalators would be oriented to provide clear views between sidewalks and station levels. Access for elderly and handicapped patrons would be provided for the first time at the station. The tracks of the crosstown Shuttle would be cutback, ostensibly to improve circulation in the Shuttle area, but, most important, to allow for the easternmost office tower in the complex to tie into the free-zone network (figures 12.2, 12.3). A "complete program of new finishes, lighting, signage, security features, artwork and retail facilities" would enhance the visual environment underground. The cost in 1984 was an estimated $64.2 million, nearly 60 percent of which was to be funded by developers.

As policy, there was nothing unusual about the fact that the Times Square subway station improvements had been inextricably linked to the private development project, through funding as well as integration of architectural design and function. The pattern was commonplace throughout the 1980s, as New York sought to benefit widely from the strength of its development boom by leveraging zoning policy in a number of different ways to coordinate the motives of private development with the needs of public transit.[26] (Alternatively, the policy could be viewed as a "continuation of the bankruptcy mentality";[27] the deals for the Columbus Circle project, Riverside South, and South Ferry Plaza all carried this quid pro quo.) The opportunity for transit-based public gain also meshed well with the MTA's chronic budget problems and perpetual capital needs, while its poor track record on station renovations strongly suggested the authority could benefit from developer-built capital improvements. Moreover, the MTA had neither the entrepreneurial skill nor the legal authority to take advantage of development-based opportunity. Its jurisdiction over land use covers only stations and rights-of-way so it has had to rely on the legal authority of the City Planning Commission to create the regulations and incentives for cost-sharing of station

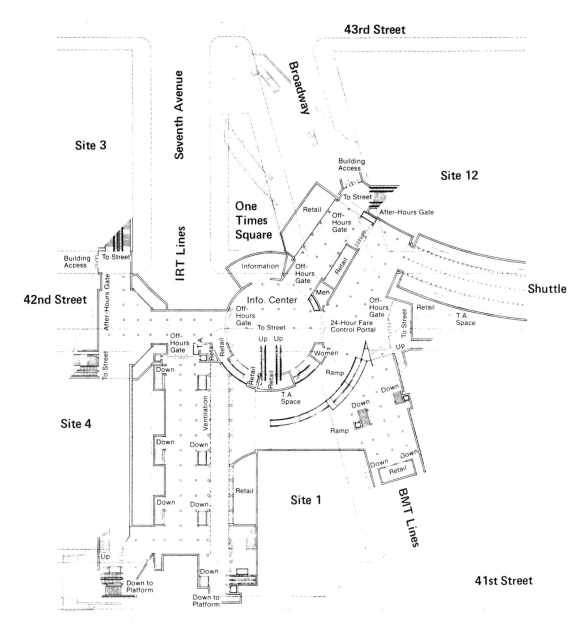

Figure labels (clockwise and throughout):

43rd Street

Broadway

Seventh Avenue

Site 3

Site 12

One Times Square

Building Access

To Street

Retail

Off-Hours Gate

After-Hours Gate

IRT Lines

Passage

Building Access

To Street

After-Hours Gate

Information

Off-Hours Gate

Retail

Shuttle

42nd Street

To Street

Off-Hours Gate

Info. Center

Men

Off-Hours Gate

Retail

T.A. Space

Off-Hours Gate

24-Hour Fare Control Portal

To Street

T.A. Space

Off-Hours Gate

T.A.

Retail

To Street

Up   Up

Women

Ramp

Down

Down

Site 4

Retail

Retail

Ventilation

Down

Down

T.A. Space

Ramp

Down

Down

Down

Down

Retail

Site 1

BMT Lines

Down

Retail

41st Street

Up

Down to Platform

Down

Down to Platform

improvements. Consequently, the CPC became a "full partner" with the Transit Authority on the rehabilitation of transit stations.[28] Within this policy infrastructure, New York became the most active city in the nation pursuing such transit-related joint-development, according to a nation-wide study on transit joint development by two University of California–Berkeley researchers. Forty-five such projects were completed or underway by 1990, 39 of which were in Manhattan, and seven of these, including the 42DP, were in midtown.

It is not hard, in retrospect, to argue that the 42DP's renovation plan for the Times Square subway station complex was seriously limited by its intentions. It was a developer-oriented plan designed to enhance the value of the office towers, and, as such, went substantially beyond the city's regulatory requirements expressly set out in the Special Midtown Zoning district. Still, the program of improvements selectively focused on the IRT

12.2
Subway mezzanine improvement below Times Square, 1984 plan. (42nd Street Development Project, Inc.)

12.3
Visual representation of rotunda
below Times Square, 1984 plan.
(42nd Street Development
Project, Inc.)

mezzanine and realignment of the Shuttle tracks—only two of four major
lines converging in the complex but the ones most closely aligned to the
four office sites. The bulk of dollars would have been spent on the rotunda
directly connected to the office complex that, as a later MTA's Staff
Summary Sheet pointed out, "if completed would have provided only
marginal benefits to our customers."[29]

Making that argument in the 1980s—and I could find no evidence that anyone did raise this issue at any of the major public hearings
on the project or in the press[30]—would have been tantamount to
whistling against the wind of prevailing public policy and respected models of urban design. The models for such a grand central space included
the city's most prestigious large-scale projects: Rockefeller Center, Grand
Central Station, the World Trade Center. All three linked direct access to
office towers with public transit in an aesthetically pleasing and functional
way. The idea had a pedigree, too. Using concourses to link buildings with
adjacent subways was first promoted by the Regional Plan Association
(RPA) in 1969 in *Urban Design Manhattan*, its book-length exposition
demonstrating the application of urban-design principals to midtown
Manhattan. "These links accentuated the advantages of high-density living,
made pedestrian travel from subway to the office easier and inviting, and
brought to the walking portion of commuters' trips light, comfort, culture,
and shopping," Ross Sandler, Mayor Koch's transit-policy expert, wrote in
1982.[31] In retrospect, the MTA's former director of capital planning, Jay
Walder, remarked: "Maybe it was a flawed design: an underground mall
whose design specifications were based on airport design. But if you step
away from the specifics, the integration of the subway with the office towers is a good idea; many work really well."[32]

The opportunity afforded the MTA by the developer-funded improvements for the Times Square subway station complex is not hard to understand. Under the philosophy of how to rebuild the system prevailing in the 1980s, capital spending for track and rolling stock held top priority. Since the same train runs through all communities, the reasoning went, if you can get the trains to work—clean and running on time with few breakdowns—then they work for everyone; there is equity of service. Rebuilding stations is not like that, emphasized Walder. There is a big difference in how decisions need to be made:[33]

> There are 468 stations in the New York system. How do you allocate station dollars? By condition? Number of people? If by number of people, you would only do CBD stations as they carry the most people. How do you balance the demands of the CBD against those of the neighborhoods? For subway riders in Brooklyn, the condition of their local station is far more important than the CBD ones; it may be their only association with the system. The MTA does 20 stations a year. That means every year it has 40 stations under renovation. Even though some stations might not get on the program for 10 to 15 years, that's a lot of stations being renovated at any one time. Boston, for example, only has about 60 stations in its entire system! The scale of New York's system creates a problem of mind-boggling proportions.

The rebuilding of the Times Square station was a cost the public sector should always have borne directly (figure 12.4). The city's fiscal situation in the early 1980s precluded that, as did the project's volatile politics thereafter. However, it would have been both the right and most secure way to do it. The collapse of the original corporate script and the TSCA deal exposed the risks of this third strategic policy decision of the 42DP. Neither operational pragmatism, established policy, nor successfully applied

12.4
Original subway mosaic, restored, 2001. (Gary Hack)

design principles could ameliorate a basic fact: The 42DP's plan of renovations for the Times Square subway station complex was risky—in terms of cost and execution[34]—because it yoked this strategic public benefit to the private-investment calculus of the developer definitively going forward with construction of the office towers. The MTA could not even advance its portion of the subway-improvement plan until the office towers got underway. In seeking a long-needed major overhaul of the city's central transportation nexus, city and state officials again gambled on the vagaries of the real estate cycle.

At the start of the project the gamble seemed to promise a smart public benefit. "This was clearly on the developer, and they would make it grand," said Weisbrod.[35] From developer George Klein's perspective, the cost burden did not appear unreasonable—at the beginning—because it matched his aesthetic ambitions for a Rockefeller Center-like complex. As the subway project grew in scope, however, the developer's risk increased. Since a significant part of the subway "contribution" would be charged to the ESAC open tab, the city's financial liability increased too. Costs estimates initially projected at $64.3 million in 1984 had grown to $160 million by 1990 ($175 million including provisions for cost overruns), and TSCA's funding responsibilities had grown from approximately $37.7 million to $87 million ($91 million including $5 million for projected cost overruns), respectively. By the time the deal was recast, the figure was up to $95 million. "The costs were hard to get a handle on," Vincent Tese explained in an interview. "It was a hole to throw money in, and when you dig such a hole, it's usually to fill it with money." In retrospect, he said, the plan was not well thought out; he would have had the public sector do it. Nonetheless, he believed the subway piece of the project was bedeviled by a series of sequential problems: "When we first started the subway, people were talking about how to make it homeless-proof. Afterward they talked about financing. You have to get things going before you could get the subway. . . . About 1990, we were off to a great station. The MTA was interested in going after it. Then the developer was hemorrhaging all over, and it was too late."[36]

Six years passed before a new, detailed—and funded—renovation plan emerged. Between the summer of 1992, when the project fell apart and the MTA released TSCA from its obligation to fund the subway mezzanine work—but not from its obligation to construct and fund in-building subway entrances on each of the building sites—and the summer of 1998, when the MTA released new blueprints for the station's overhaul (figure 12.5), the story line morphed into the "incredible shrinking subway." Initially, the MTA announced plans for a $130-million renovation. Though it had lost TSCA's funding, if it had to prioritize stations for renovations, Times Square was the most important. More people move through that station on any one day—the daily passenger count was up to 470,000 in mid-1993, the busiest station in the system—than most other entire systems in the United States. Only partial funding of $70.2 million was available as a carry-over item from the New York City Transit

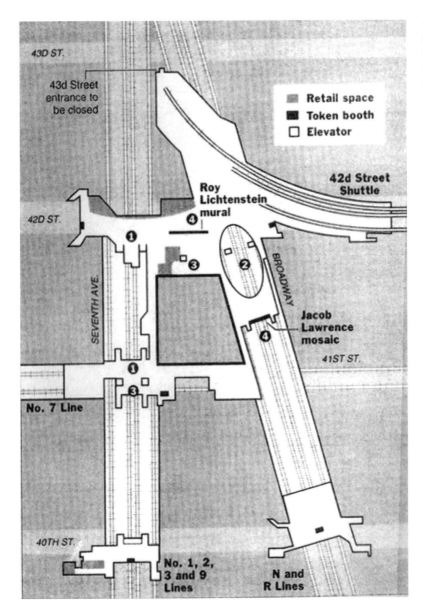

Within the figure:

43D ST.

43d Street
entrance to
be closed

▦ Retail space
▨ Token booth
☐ Elevator

42d Street
Shuttle

42D ST.

Roy
Lichtenstein
mural

❹

❶

❸

❷

BROADWAY

Jacob
Lawrence
mosaic

41ST ST.

SEVENTH AVE.

❹

❶

❸

No. 7 Line

40TH ST.

No. 1, 2,
3 and 9
Lines

N and
R Lines

12.5
Second plan for subway improve-
ment below Times Square, 1998.
(Metropolitan Transportation
Authority)

Authority (TA)'s 1987–1991 capital program. (One of four subsidiaries of
the MTA, the TA is the operating arm of the city's subway system.)

As a matter of policy, the MTA does not permit phased projects
in its capital program unless each phase is a complete and viable project on
its own merit. To go forward with the Times Square station complex redo,
however, they broke with that policy: "It was important enough,"
explained Walder.[37] Still, sources of funding for the $57.9 million balance
of estimated construction work remained uncertain. When the $130-mil-
lion plan was announced in June of 1993, the TA's staff summary sheet
noted: "Construction award is expected to be achieved in the latter part of
1996, at which time the Transit Authority proposes to provide the balance
of the funding from Authority-wide contingency *if available at that time*
[my emphasis]."[38] Walder expected that the funding gap would be closed
with capital-budget funds from the next five-year capital program, which
turned out to be the case. And while the city and state's agreement with

TSCA provided that the MTA receive certain funds generated by future office development if it began construction on the subway renovations within seven years,[39] MTA officials close to the negotiations said they never expected these dollars to materialize.

A year later, station renovations system-wide were put on indefinite hold by Mayor Giuliani's decision to cut the city's $1-billion contribution to the MTA's five-year capital plan by $250 million. Later, at the end of 1995, when the MTA announced with fanfare that the first phase of construction costing $41 million would begin on its "jazzy, razzmatazzy" main entrance—something it never had before—along with underground renovations, funding for the remaining $90 million of projected renovations reportedly was still uncertain, which suggested that the renovations could very well stall out at the $41-million mark. When the new $7.1-million subway entrance opened to acclaim in July 1997 (figure 12.6), the editors of *Newsday* noted that the MTA still had to "scrape up more than $100 million in new money" before the job of renovating thoroughly the "circles of hell" would be finished.[40]

Ultimately, in mid-1998, the MTA produced a complete renovation program pegged at $180 million, and several months later awarded a $82.8-million contract for the first phase of work. The major specifications of the new program included widened corridors to improve sight lines and pedestrian traffic flow; the creation of an oval area cut into the mezzanine level to permit a direct view of the trains below; new elevators to allow additional access to platforms; and, carried over from the original Times Square station plan as part of the MTA Arts-For-Transit Program, new commissioned artwork by Roy Lichtenstein (who completed the 53-foot-

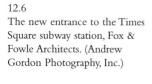

12.6
The new entrance to the Times Square subway station, Fox & Fowle Architects. (Andrew Gordon Photography, Inc.)

long porcelain mural of a futuristic subway shortly before he died) and Jacob Lawrence, among others. The grand mezzanine with its expensive finishes was gone, replaced with new design guidelines more in line with the system's old-fashioned aesthetics: bright white tile highlighted with restored mosaics. The crosstown Shuttle-platform reconfiguration was gone. The $180-million program of renovations promised less, in inflation-adjusted dollars. Though scaled down in ambition, it was more comprehensive in scope. For example, the revised redo addressed at least one visible condition of long-term neglect and abuse not included in original plan—the chewing gum-encrusted platforms of the eight subway lines—and in so doing, bowed to New York's straphangers. Less evident, but more important, the MTA's new blueprints brought full control over project decision making, as well as budget and funding, back in house at the MTA.

The change in control, scope, program, and timing—overall policy—added up to recognition that the previous privatized plan was fatally flawed. It was a policy for a particular time and context, and in its only editorial on the issue, the *Times* made the case for change: "The beguiling concept of having developers 'pay' for zoning concessions [by improving nearby subway stations] succeeded in many instances. . . . It may succeed again. Meantime, in this economy, government must search for other sources—including government."[41] The *Times*, of course, was not unbiased on this issue or on anything else in its namesake district, and its publisher, Arthur Ochs Sulzberger, Jr., was at the time chair of the Times Square BID. The *Times* cared a lot about the subway, and it wanted the MTA to go forth immediately with the improvements, despite the lack of private funds. "The MTA, which spends plenty on renovating stations that are not scheduled for help from developers, says it can't do more because it has higher priorities in its $10 billion capital plan." Recognizing that "critical safety measures . . . indeed deserve to come first," the editors opined that "transit and city officials ought to move station improvement up on their list, rethink the capital plan now pending before the Legislature, and lobby with even more urgency for Federal and state transit funds."[42]

The road to reconstructing an executable station-renovation plan proved bumpy, and it was inefficient when measured in time gone by and design work redone. Without the need to integrate the station complex with the office towers, it was back to square one for the MTA—after five years and $16 million of now-obsolete design and architectural work. To go forward, the station project needed to be redesigned and rescaled to the new financial context. Moreover, the public would have to wait. What was to be a four-and-a-half-year proposition with an anticipated completion date of August 1993 turned into an indefinite delay and uncertain timetable for years, then, in 1998, an eight-year-plus build-out. "The agency moves like molasses," a member of the editorial board of *Newsday* complained. "Even by its own estimate, the remodeling won't be done until 2010."[43]

The public sector had gambled on private development to deliver the funds for a high-priority public benefit—and lost. At the time, UDC understood how dicey the execution would be; humorously, but with dead seriousness, Tese told the board of directors at a meeting in 1988, "We don't want Donald Trump finishing our subway," a reference to Trump's highly publicized rescue triumph in finishing in record time the city's botched and terribly delayed reconstruction of Wollman Ice Rink in Central Park.[44] However sound the policy had been at the time, its execution failed, miserably. The city had given out a handsome package of financial incentives to the developer of the office towers, partly in exchange for a substantial payment toward improving this key transportation nexus, yet as one irate citizen put it, not only is the Times Square station no gift to riders, "the one amenity that is used by New Yorkers must be renovated at taxpayer expense."[45]

The MTA came under more exacting criticism in 1999 when an internal investigation by its Office of the Inspector General (IG) revealed that in a dollars-for-release trade of improvements for the Times Square subway station, the transit authority had shortchanged itself—by some $2.7 to $4.6 million. The deal's bottom line allowed the developers of the Reuters Building (Site 3) to drop a requirement of the 1994 agreement governing the 32-story office tower; instead of installing (and maintaining) two escalators leading from the subway mezzanine to a street-level exit at the northwest corner of 42nd Street and Seventh Avenue—one of the area's most congested—Rudin Management paid the MTA $1.3 million. In asking for the trade the developer claimed that the two escalators were unnecessary; as under the terms of its agreement, it would still provide the required entrance, widened from 12 to 15 feet (figures 12.7–12.9). The company's main concern, the report noted, "did not seem to be the cost of installing and maintaining the escalators, but that they reduced rental space." At a time when retail rates were rapidly escalating, that Rudin would rather use the space for retail stores was not surprising. A conservative value of the agreement, the inspector general concluded, would have ranged between $4 and $5.9 million, meaning the MTA was out "$2.7

12.7
The MTA's "shortchanged" subway entrance. (Gary Hack)

12.8
The negotiated trade: a widened staircase instead of escalators. (Gary Hack)

to $4.6 million more than Rudin paid to be relieved of its obligation." Though the report found no evidence that MTA officials had acted improperly, it detailed the lapses in methodology that led to the resultant shortchange. First, the MTA's cost estimates were based on inexpensive commercial escalators, not the heavy-duty models required by the transit authority's contracts. Second, and more significant, MTA negotiators failed to calculate the opportunity cost of the trade—the rental value of the space the escalators would otherwise occupy. On the basis of an analysis by his own staff, the inspector general concluded that "any figure between $844,566 and $2.8 million would be a reasonable, conservative approximation of the value of the space to Rudin." Moreover, the transit authority "did not use its bargaining leverage to extract other concessions, such as relocating the exit to Seventh Avenue."[46] As the director of the New York City Transit Riders Council said, "This was a bad deal for transit and transit riders."[47]

12.9
The developers' motive for requesting the trade. (Gary Hack)

By the time the MTA announced its cleanup plan for the station, the cost of inaction had led to wretched conditions. If it was a new world above, it was the same old Hades below. "Some of the dust in this station has been here since 1904," the station manager quipped.[48] The city and its straphangers and its coveted tourists would have to endure the "circles of hell" for many more years, plus suffer the inconveniences of major construction activity.[49] How is it, though, that this most visible of denouements did not turn into a political failure, a significant and project-threatening event?

One answer is that being underground, the subway doesn't show, so cheating infrastructure is easy. Only the editors of the *Times* took up the subway loss. When TSCA's new deal with the city and state was announced, *Newsday*'s editorial cheered the "Glad Reprieve for Times Square," without even mentioning that the developers had been released from their obligation to fund the subway improvements. The *Daily News*,

New York Post, New York Observer, and *Crain's New York Business* also were all strangely silent on the topic. Location offers another explanation. "There's no constituency for the Times Square station the way there is for stations in Brooklyn or the Bronx or Queens," explained Walder. "No one within the political process was going to beat you up for not doing the Times Square station. Even the Manhattan borough president did not find this a compelling problem; there are other bigger neighborhood-station concerns in northern Manhattan, for example."[50] In a real sense, the subway renovations became the forgotten public promise of the 42DP, or at best, a promised benefit that the average skeptical New Yorker had trouble believing would ever materialize. "We've heard of such plans before, of course," the editors of *Newsday* penned on hearing of the $180-million revised 1998 station-renovation plan. "But with contracts to be awarded in October and work to begin in the spring, this time it apparently will really happen. It can't be soon enough."[51]

The aborted plans for the subway-station renovations put the city at a double disadvantage; not only was private investment activity on hold until the real estate market rebounded, the public sector could do little to jump-start new activity by fixing up a critical transportation nexus in midtown that confused and alienated straphangers and tourists alike. Whereas the hiatus caused by the recession might have been used to advantage to refurbish the subway station in readiness for the next turn of the cycle, the timing impact of past policy decisions, in effect, precluded that traditional planning approach.

A strong and well-established set of arguments exists for deploying public construction on fundamental infrastructure in the public realm—subways, rail links, tunnels, bridges, schools, and water and sewer lines—when the private economy is in a downturn, between cycles. Public infrastructure investments, in general, enhance a region's economic and social productivity. Moving forth with public-construction contracts during a downturn employs otherwise slack resources, often at lower costs than during the height of the business cycle when demand for labor is greatest. Execution during a downturn overlaps with fewer competing private construction projects, easing the "construction-everywhere" congestion and inconvenience which tends to overtake the tightly circumscribed streets and sidewalks of central business districts. Tying the 42DP's most strategic public-infrastructure benefit to the timetable of private development confounded this opportunity to stimulate the local economy as only countercyclical government spending can.

The onus for not getting something done on the subway, however, did not fall on the city. That political risk belonged to the state through its agent, the MTA. Governor Cuomo understood that. The MTA could be pressured to take over responsibility, though by any criteria its capital planners might select the Times Square subway station complex had long merited a top-priority allocation of dollars. If the MTA had pushed to be made whole on the funding, though, most likely it would have engendered a political battle. In the meantime, the station would have remained in shambles.[52] There was no debating that it had been a hellhole for a long time. But at this policy nexus, the interests of the city and state diverged. The city could wash its hands on the funding problem, adopting the attitude: "Hey, we already put in our dollars for a city-wide capital program. The Times Square subway station is your problem, not ours." How the dollars get allocated is an MTA decision. Politically, it is a hollow defense for the MTA to respond along the lines: "But the plan is connected to the office development, and it's not our fault that the project fell apart." The hellhole would remain a visible example of failed promises. The risks of the subway-improvements' gamble lodged with the state pure and simple. The MTA, as public steward of the system, operates under a social contract to be responsible and accountable for the system's operating performance and condition regardless of who—private developer or public agent—holds the business contract to deliver the physical improvements.

In the end, there was no negotiation over whether TSCA would be let out of the subway obligation, according to Susan Fine, who, as director of real estate for the MTA, was responsible for renegotiating the developer's future subway contribution. From the governor to the head of UDC to the head of the MTA, she was ordered to let TSCA out of the original deal. The real gain for the MTA was political. With the break in the agreement, the state authority gained the ability to spend the $70.2 million budgeted for the Times Square station project. Something might be done, at last, and "getting something done is a powerful thing in the public sector," said Fine.[53] The negotiations were nonetheless combative.[54] The money to fund the gap in dollars needed to complete the remaining phases of the project would be found, somewhere; there was always the next five-year capital program. In the meantime, the state needed to make the commitment, to show good faith by starting phase one of the work plan. At this crucial junction of decision, Governor Cuomo needed a clear path out of the political labyrinth.

Not for the first time, the subway episode revealed the ruling forces of political behavior in the sphere of public development—credit and control: credit for rescue, then credit at the ribbon-cutting ceremony; control over politically sensitive decision making on public-private projects. Governor Cuomo could not back away from nearly a decade of visible commitments to and public promises about the 42DP any more than could Mayor Dinkins when midway into his administration economic reality and political pragmatism forced him to negotiate a generous retention package with PSI and a workout deal with TSCA. Too much political capital was at stake.

The subway project's failure revealed other lessons of public development. First, it clarified any policy ambiguity that might have existed about the limits of the private-funding strategy. Second, it showed that delays brought on by the cycle are always difficult—but seemingly not always fatal—for the public-benefit pieces of large-scale city-rebuilding projects, and it confirmed that delays are costly; the cost estimate for the station's two-phase renovation program had cumulated up to $316 million by the time the MTA took its capital budget for 2000–2004 to Albany. Third, it validated the supposition that the public sector cannot be a passive player once the decision has been made to follow a public-development (as opposed to regulatory) course of action; when market forces threaten to stall a high-profile project indefinitely, cities have no choice but to take additional financial risks along with the private sector to achieve their goals for public development. Some of the risk taking is upfront and deliberate, early in the life of a project. Other decisions come later, when the public sector must step in, reactively. In either case, as long as the policy mandate of the project remains valid, not coming to the rescue becomes inherently self-limiting.

SHOULD CITIES BE HIGH ROLLERS?

The 42DP's three strategic policy decisions—privatized financing, eminent domain, development-based infrastructure delivery—exposed the city and state to project-threatening risks, financial and political. Because the policies were inherently interlocking—joined at the hip in a fashion analogous to the concentration of resources that made the city/state institutional coalition such a political force—the mayor and governor confronted compounded risks when the Times Square gamble hit the uncontrollable force of a recession and market downturn. The very complexity of the project's off-budget financing, for example, made for impossible accountability (discussed in the next chapter), inflexibility in dealing with changing markets, and unreasonable private risks that could only be carried out by naive institutional investors with deep pockets. Most likely, it also cost the city more to structure economic incentives sufficiently enticing to the private sector than if it had directly accepted some significant portion of the financial risk itself, albeit the realities of getting capital funds for the project in the early 1980s. Indeed, the open tab, deferred payback, and rent-credit structure may have created a situation in which both the public and private participants had less than the customary incentives to keep costs down. Where, for example, was the city and state's incentive to go back and contest condemnation awards, especially when relatively few landowners were contesting the awards? What was the private developer's incentive to negotiate for anything less than the highest quality, even grand, public improvements for the project, especially for the subway-station renovations, which would enhance the access and amenities of its four office towers?

Although the city and state joined forces to implement the 42DP, the city bore most of the financial and political risk. By design, UDC was not exposed to any significant financial liability—until the Disney deal—though it did absorb significant front-end costs for development activities and planning to the tune of about $7 million annually during Robertson's tenure as president of the project subsidiary from 1990 through 1997. UDC's role was to act as an intermediary managing the project, brokering relations with developers and running interference for the city. Having a dedicated subsidiary for a project enhanced the state's position within the coalition. Eventually in these endeavors, power shifts to the single-purpose entity where there is 100-percent focus on the project, said Weisbrod, who explained with reference to his shift from president of the 42DP, Inc., to president of PDC. He knew the project better than anyone; still, as head of a city-wide corporation there were many other projects and agendas for him to contend with, which meant that the 42DP got only a piece of his time, not 100 percent of it, as it did with Robertson. Stuckey echoed the political logic. As head of a city-wide agency, a project like this, no matter how important, is only one of many, an issue of balancing priorities.

What was the public good represented by the project? Cleaning up a moral eyesore and civic embarrassment, accelerating commercial development in a key transit location, preserving internationally recognized cultural institutions, improving worn-out infrastructure, and helping develop a mixed cultural/services economy in a unique urban district. Could these have been accomplished by targeting public efforts more cheaply? How critical was the public effort to attracting Disney, Madame Tussaud's, and the cascade of entertainment and retailing investments that followed? The bigger question is whether cities should take on such high-risk ventures as the 42DP. What are the opportunity costs for the use of political and economic resources of city governments? What are the alternatives to high-risk public-development initiatives? Cities can let distressed central areas deteriorate to the point where the private market would revive. They can allow turbulence in development patterns to persist indefinitely. They can focus on preventive measures such as BIDs that attempt to stabilize areas. Or they can focus on areas where they have greater control: fringe areas of the CBD, waterfronts, military bases, and former public lands. These policy alternatives are all important.

The ambitions of public development in New York play themselves out in more projects and on a larger scale than is possible in most other American cities, but they are not atypical. Neither are the strategic policy decisions, implementation structures, and political risks. New York's creation of a private-funding arrangement for the 42DP may have been unique for its time, but it occurred within the broader framework of a trend toward privatization among local government that has been shifting the delivery of basic services and public goods to private-sector providers. The use of market-oriented transit-based development strategies across the country is a trend similarly well documented. And the use of eminent domain to further economic development at the state and local level remains a frequently used tool, not withstanding enduring public controversy over fundamental policy issues raised by condemnation—"to hand one business property of another"—as a page-one feature article in the *Wall Street Journal* recently characterized the issue.[55] Judicial deference to the notion of "public use" has surely broadened since the landmark 1954 U.S. Supreme Court ruling of *Berman v. Parker,* which first established a liberal concept of "public use" relating to a municipality's right to realize the goals of a properly approved plan for redevelopment through the use of eminent domain. Yet, city and state officials cannot assume that all proposed takings for redevelopment or economic development will satisfy the long string of cases that have revalidated our system's expanded notion of "public use."[56]

The strategic fault in the 42DP was the public sector's nearly singular focus on minimizing its financial risk. Political needs continually undermined the economic logic or strategic goal. City and state officials, for example, were always reluctant to put money out; first when they chose not to take the option of tying up one of the western sites even though the cost of doing so was relatively small; second, when they passed up the opportunity to buy the leases for the 42nd Street theaters, which were bought instead by the Durst Organization. The latter instance is instructive.

Operators since the Great Depression who held long-term leases on seven of the street's theaters, the Brandt Organization approached state and city officials with a lease-buyout proposal; Weisbrod was very interested. He saw this as a key strategic opportunity. Buying the leases, even though they would have been extinguished by condemnation, would have given them control over the site. He hoped to speed up the controversial process, establish credibility, and keep condemnation costs down. The state was due to start the condemnation process within a few months. The potential deal, reportedly for around $2 million, fell apart when other family investors who disagreed with the lease sale sought other bidders. It was not well known that the Brandts were selling; by one insider's account, Stuckey announced the government's intentions before the deal was done, possibly costing the city this tactic. Durst had known the Brandts for years, and after hearing of the announcement was soon onto the deal himself. Weisbrod was none too happy. Stuckey to the press: "The last thing I was going to get into with public funds is an Atlantic City roulette game. I don't want to get into a bidding war." The prospect of anyone else buying the leases when condemnation proceedings were imminent angered him because he saw it as "a ploy to rip the government off."[57] Yet there was no means around the lost opportunity: Prudential and Klein had been asked to buy the leases, but they would not do so, even though it was obvious that they could not lose. "The public sector continually got cold feet and let options pass," said Travis. "We were constantly backing away from buying land. Everyone was nervous about the commitment. This is one negative, one downside of the city/state coalition: there were too many people involved into these decisions. In the public sector, people tend to get nervous."[58] Had the city and state been able to purchase the options for the mart site or the leases for the theaters, the 42DP's future, Weisbrod believes, would have been ensured much earlier. This reluctance to commit was one of the project's great mistakes.

In other ways the city did not take financial risks needed to move the project forward in a timely manner. While tax abatements represent real costs to the city treasury, they are not substitutes for direct cash investments. They are, in effect, soft expenditures. They are potent as incentives but they cannot function the same way as hard dollars, which the city should have put in the project as a partner in the deal to provide the strategically critical investment in infrastructure. When the MTA was forced to replan the renovations for the Times Square subway station complex, for example, the new plan turned out to be a better plan—but the developer was off the hook when it had already gotten the density-development incentives and tax abatements that went along with the deal to fund a significant portion of the infrastructure improvements.

Relying excessively on the private sector undercut the pubic sector's bargaining power and policy flexibility, especially when market conditions turned against the project. When the mayor agreed to make the hard commitments to acquire the western sites with capital-budget funds, not only did the city gain a stronger hand to put all the necessary pieces in place, it held a much stronger position when the time came for Tese and Robertson to hold to their nonnegotiable requirement that developers adhere to the complex and stringent design guidelines for the new vision plan, *42nd Street Now!* The lesson embedded in the project's twisting drama and its results is that cities must take financial risks along with the private sector to achieve their goals for public development. Not to do so is inherently self-limiting because there are limits to the privatization strategy.

The risks of implementing ambitious redevelopment goals are such that governmental strategies aiming to ensure their success pose hard questions of policy. Again, the *Wall Street Journal* put the issue on its front page with a story about a downtown renewal planned for the old mining city of Spokane, Washington: "Is Guarantee Proper for a Fancy Mall and What Is City's Risk?"[59] For public officials, the deal making behind redevelopment initiatives turns the spotlight on issues of policy, not because public-private development projects are more complex than untargeted as-of-right zoning incentives—though they are—but because they exist outside a world of known protocols. Because big deals are by definition individualized arrangements, they chafe against the policy norms of uniformity and tax the issue of fairness. Because the process of negotiating with private developers takes place behind closed doors, only the outcomes and not the alternatives are open to review and discussion. Because most of the financing takes place off-budget, these projects are not evaluated in the context of competing uses for public resources. Because projects are typically managed through quasi-independent public-development agencies, accountability often becomes a supercharged political issue. Nevertheless, although public development's deal making entails a myriad of political risks, it is essential for mayors who wish to shape the canvas of city growth.

Just how much risk a city should take is a political decision, ultimately. How much risk taking is needed to ensure success, however, varies with the ambitions of the project, and most particularly, with the economic condition of the local land market targeted for change. If, for example, city officials seek private development of land that is not valuable in market terms, the public has little choice but to assume the substantial financial risk involved in changing the dynamic of current market forces.[60]

No matter how aggressive the actions and how big the total public investment, there are limits to the ability of public development to move ahead of market readiness because demand (from office tenants and local and out-of-town consumers) remains the engine driving commercial success. "The public sector generally starts off ahead of the market on all large-scale projects, then ends up behind," said Weisbrod, "largely because it is not as nimble as the private sector and public processes move so slowly."[61] Alternatively, when cities aggressively seek to define new nodes of commercial employment in less congested areas as New York did with MetroTech in downtown Brooklyn or San Francisco did with Yerba Buena Gardens in the south-of-Market-Street district, a sufficiently large critical mass of development activity is a prerequisite to success. Without exception, pursuing public development to achieve what the market cannot produce on its own in incremental fashion, involves some degree of public risk taking.

If big risks that public officials should not avoid and cannot walk away from inhere in the strategy, should governmental processes be reformed so that this type of negotiated development can occur within the framework of government rather than outside of it? This is the central question of the next chapter. A preview of the argument flows from the 42DP lessons of risk taking. In the United States risk taking for public development relies on an established and well-honed set of mechanisms—the quasi-independent single-purpose entity, off-budget financing mechanisms, and coalitions of governmental powers—that ensure dedicated leadership, aim for more nimble decision making, generate project-specific dedicated revenue streams, concentrate resources, and distribute risks. These mechanisms establish protective distances from political interference and, at times, democratic accountability, but most significantly, they provide protection against short-term political winds of change. The redevelopment of West 42nd Street relied on three specially created entities: UDC's project subsidiary, the 42DP, Inc.; the theater-focused New42; and the Times Square Subway Improvement Corporation. Mayor Giuliani, for example, could not redirect the New42's lease revenues from the theaters despite concerted efforts to do so. The 42DP, Inc., also benefited invaluably from continuity of political and party leadership for a 12- to14-year period crossing the governor's office and city hall. Nonetheless, the visible tensions between the public partners of the institutional coalition erupted dramatically, as the kerfuffles over developer designations for the mart site and a place for AMC and Madame Tussaud's revealed. Notwithstanding the need for procedural safeguards and greater financial accountability, the prognosis for reform is not especially promising. On the basis of the 42DP experience as well as that of numerous other large-scale public-development ventures across the country, politicians' need for camouflage is likely to defeat the best intentions of reformers, unless a project-specific fraud triggers widespread impetus for change.

Coalition deal making sought to protect the city from the political risks of an aggressive redevelopment effort; it proved to be powerful but not omnipotent. It offered a lot of protection, but ironically, it may have served to increase the project's exposure. The controversy and complexity that adhered to the institutional coalition suggests a lesson running counter to its logic: The partnership structure exposed the deal to multiple public hearings, reviews, and repeated criticisms without defeat, opening up the process and the project to wider public scrutiny than if the city or the state or the private sector had done it alone. "Lying down in a partnership" is how one scholar (using a borrowed phrase) described such development deal making in Chicago. "A partnership of almost any kind seems to raise the public standards of performance," wrote Gerald D. Suttles. "It is not just that more is promised of such a partnership but that partnerships tend to open up the number of chinks and cracks through which information is passed, so that deficiencies are notices and opposition aroused."[62]

If joint action opens up the process of review and increases the flow of information—through mandated disclosure or critical media reporting or administrative procedures—then the often-noted problem of accountability associated with deal making needs to be reexamined more closely.

CHAPTER 13

QUIESCENT POLICY DILEMMAS

Policy controversy over deal making arises naturally, even when there is widespread consensus for and legislative approval of a redevelopment project. In big high-profile projects such as the 42DP, controversy over the size and scope of the city's incentive package inevitably surfaces. Public officials anticipate it. Public hearings prime debate. When the terms and conditions of the city's business arrangement with a private developer are negotiated project by project rather than specified in advance by as-of-right policy, the question implicitly thrown open to public debate is: "Is the city giving away too much?" Rarely is there an easy answer to this most fundamental policy question. Measuring a project's immediate benefits in terms of jobs and tax revenues may be relatively straightforward, but gauging redevelopment's transforming force in terms of longer-term social, cultural, and economic impacts—the city's rationale for intervention in the first place—is a combination of factual and subjective assessments based on data that are inherently limited by the unpredictability of future market dynamics. Similarly, accounting for direct cash costs on a project may be relatively easy, but the real task of quantifying the liabilities embedded in complex off-budget financing is not. Technical issues complicating a clear answer to the "give-away" question make for high barriers to public understanding, so emphasis on process and procedure—how the city conducts its deal making and provides for democratic accountability—is crucial.

Deal making for development imposes special burdens on government accountability. First, the real estate offering is specialized and infrequent, so all would-be bidders must be given fair and reasonable access to compete. Second, the city is investing public dollars in selected private investments or transferring public assets, often with subsidies, so it has an obligation to justify its decisions and evaluate the results in terms of the specific public objectives underlying the initiative. Third, the custom-tailored arrangements between the public sector and private firms are financially and legally complex, so special preparations are called for if elected officials, interest groups, and citizens-at-large are to have a reasonable opportunity to review and comment on the deal. And fourth, negotiations between public and private parties cannot take place in public without jeopardizing the public's position, so the timing and substance of disclosure become central features of accountability. More than any other single element, balancing the public's right to know against public officials' need to protect the confidences of the negotiation process creates ongoing policy tensions, seeding allegations that the process is secretive.

Negotiating behind closed doors, however, is not the same as having the entire project proceed in secret. Few would argue with the conventional proposition that deal-based decisions for public development or economic development should be analyzed thoroughly and reviewed openly if they are to meet the test of accountability. The problem may not be one of intent as much as a lack of known protocols for deal making. Accountability is a multifaceted concept. Different procedural standards of performance and substantive agendas of review flow from accountability's multiple meanings—political accountability, judicial accountability, financial accountability, and managerial accountability.

Indeed, when a log of "accountability forums" is tallied for the 42DP (see appendix E), it becomes evident that the project underwent substantial and serious review over the course of years. Numerous formal and informal checkpoints of accountability existed. During the fifteen years it took to line up the pieces of the project, between 1981 and 1996, 11 sets of public hearings were held on the project. Some were mandated by statute or administrative procedures governing a public corporation acting as lead agent for a land-development project, others, by eminent-domain proceedings or a public-lease transaction. Informal processes like the MAS's orchestrated campaign to change the agenda of redevelopment and the media's reports on high-profile project controversies forced political, programmatic, and policy issues into the public arena. In bringing to light the discretionary decision making of nonelected city and state officials, they created additional checkpoints of accountability.

Taken together, the project's legislative approvals, public hearings, judicial reviews, press coverage, professional critiques, and third-party reports add up to a record of intense scrutiny—but one that is highly fragmented, frequently narrow, and void in some important respects. New York's existing protocols for accountability fall short of what are needed for a full-scope policy review because analyses of financial commitments, cost-benefit evaluations, and project audits—the primary forms of financial accountability for deal making—fall outside the procedural and substantive scope of political and judicial reviews. The 42DP experience was not unusual. The details that define the extent of public cost and liability often are not fully negotiated at the time the deal is approved by a city's legislative body because they cannot be known for certain at that time. Rather, they emerge later in the negotiation processes leading up to the signing of project documents, leases, loans, and other agreements.

Greater financial accountability is not impossible to achieve, just unlikely. Suggestions for reform are not hard to come by, just a constituency. The policy dilemma is that the political risks of aggressively pushing public-private development projects toward fruition work against efforts to ensure greater financial accountability because they make the financial risks of the project more apparent. Given the reluctance of public officials to explicitly engage the city in risk taking, such reform is unlikely to come in the absence of some external force. Ultimately, elected officials are accountable, in traditional fashion at the polls. The timing of this final political reckoning extends far into the future, which is what the political bet is all about—producing results in a time frame that lets the public forget about the costs of achieving the benefits. The legacy of the project is the package of public benefits, Rebecca Robertson said more than once in an interview; no one will care about the taxes lost.

FRACTURED CHECKPOINTS OF ACCOUNTABILITY

For 14 years controversy and debate constantly swirled about the 42DP. The issues were diverse, deep-seated, and often meritorious, both on grounds of public policy and planning practice. Was the design and use program of the original corporate script appropriate for West 42nd Street and Times Square? Did the purpose and scope of condemnation contemplated for the project fit the "public-use" rationale of eminent domain? Would private funding of condemnation guarantee "sure and certain compensation" for property owners and tenants, as the meaning of those terms applied to funding from the municipal treasury? Were the subsidies promised developers fair and reasonable? Was the process of public input open and inclusive and disclosure of information on the terms and conditions of the deals sufficient to allow for informed review of the city and state's financial commitments to the project? Is it the function of public hearings to inform or judge the final deals?

In each phase of searching review, the formal process courted the public, though not always to the satisfaction of various interest groups. The first public hearings in 1981 solicited comments on the *GPP*. Major hearings on *DEIS* and *FEIS* followed in 1984. When the political struggle over selecting a developer for the mart site erupted in mid-1983, the *Times* focused attention on the power and politics behind the deal making. Then just prior to the hearings scheduled before the BOE in late 1984, the Milstein Organization challenged the propriety of the office-developer selection process in a "white paper" letter to UDC that once again focused attention on the developer-selection process. Three years later, the loss of developers for both the mart and theater sites caused the city to amend parts of the *GPP*, occasioning a fifth public hearings in 1987. A sixth hearings to air the essential terms of the TSCA leases took place the same year, followed shortly by the PACB's review of the TSCA leases. Between 1988 and 1993, three outside interests reported informally on the subsidies in the deal, generating discussion on a more analytical basis, even though the analyses were flawed. In 1993 public hearings were held again to solicit comment on the *DSEIS* and *FSEIS* proposed amendments to the new vision plan, *42nd Street Now!*, and in 1994, on the new financial deal with TSCA, which was again reviewed by the PACB. This deal too was subject to third-party analysis. More amendments to the *GPP*, the lease deal with Disney, and amendments to the TSCA leases permitting the assignment of the leases to the Durst Organization occasioned still more rounds of public hearings in 1996 and another PACB review. In one form or another, between 1981 and 1996 the project came up for formal public review 14 times.

As required by various statutes, approval by the UDC directors preceded each step—issuance of the *Proposed GPP* and RFPs; selection of developers; publication of the draft and final versions of the EIS and supplemental EIS; findings of blight; amendments to the *GPP*; signing of the leases, petitions for condemnation, amendments and more amendments to the *GPP*; and to existing leases. UDC's role as a planner and implementor of the project meant executive oversight—not adversarial scrutiny. The UDC board of directors was unlikely to veto the deal; perhaps they would modify it, remarked Stephen A. Lefkowitz, who as outside counsel for the city on the project in the early 1980s helped draft the initial MOU:[1]

> One has to look for accountability at the BOE 1984 hearings. Those passing on the deal were all elected officials who had their own constituencies; they were not appointed by the mayor. If the BOE had turned the deal down or required major changes, it would have been dead or modified. They approved it. After that, there was a feeling that the political decision had been made.

Formally or informally, the locus of accountability lodges with elected officials, the most immediate recourse for a policy decision being the chief executive—mayor or governor. Traditionally, this is what political accountability means. Since the 1960s, the standards of political accountability have come to include disclosure of essential information and a process for public review and comment, which is one reason each of the major state statutes governing public-development actions (UDC Act, EDPL, SEQRA) mandates a public hearing in accord with specific procedures. Because UDC acted as lead agency for the 42DP, it was exempt from the city's land-use project review (ULURP), and even though no statutory requirement mandated that the project go to the BOE for approval, political considerations demanded otherwise.

Judicial review occasioned by litigation defines a second level of accountability. Rarely is it taken lightly by public officials. Just knowing that it is there, Carl Weisbrod explained, has a profound effect on administrators. Judicial review acts as a conscience for officials throughout the life of a public project—solicitation of proposals and selection of a developer, regulatory and environmental reviews, land acquisition, financial negotiations. Failing to adhere to correct procedure exposes the agency to the potentially fatal judicial charge that it has abused its discretion.[2] As pointed out by the court in a key and often-cited decision on a 42DP lawsuit, *Jackson v. N.Y.S. Urban Development Corporation,* "Nothing in the law requires an agency to reach a particular result on any issue, or permits the courts to second guess the agency's choice which can be annulled only if arbitrary, capricious or unsupported by substantial evidence."[3] Ensuring that its decision-making procedures meet this legal standard of agency practice is one reason government moves so slowly.

The deals for the 42DP involved at least four essential policy questions, three of which, said Lefkowitz, were viewed at the time as relatively uncomplicated for public review. First, the underlying policy premise of the project: Is it appropriate for the public sector to reach out and condemn such a large amount of land in central Manhattan? "This isn't a complicated question; also, it is one that all of the public can get involved with." Second, the planning question: Is it appropriate to scoop up overall density of the project area and put it on the corners? "This massing could not be done by private initiative (or only under very difficult conditions), but only [by] UDC." Third, on the financial end, the key question: Is the deep tax abatement for these buildings appropriate at all in midtown? "To an extent, the people (though not necessarily the public at large) can have a view on this." The fourth question, he said "is most difficult to pose, yet alone answer: How do you fix a deal when land values are changing so, when the economics of the deal have changed so much over the course of its implementation, going from 'fair' to 'very good' to 'okay for the developer' to 'poor'?"[4]

These policy questions only got debated in the context of specific deals, which were "go" or "no go" propositions. This context of review intensifies the accountability issues attached to public deal making, as does the task of coping with a changing economic context and its implications for already-cut deals. Both issues make apparent the need for financial accountability of public deal making, after initial legislative approval. By the conventional norms of public policy, this means some type of review of the public's financial commitments, an ex-ante evaluation of a deal's costs and benefits or an ex-post audit of financial transactions or both. That the public resources in question may be in the form of off-budget foregone revenues (rent credits or tax abatements) or long-term contingent commitments (ESAC) rather than direct cash grants or loans does not change the logic. It only complicates the tasks of analysis and explanation.

The privatization of public funding for the 42DP did more than complicate the analysis, however. It changed the checkpoints of fiscal review. First, in the absence of direct capital-budget appropriations, the project did not have to compete for funds against other city capital needs. Second, without public borrowing, no independent check by the market (private investors) on the financial feasibility of the business terms with private parties occurred as would have been the case had the project been financed with revenue bonds. Third, without grant funding, no competitive review of funding applications by outside sources or other government investors in the project occurred as would have been the case under the federal urban renewal or the UDAG programs. On the other side of the equation, since UDC's role as land owner and lead agency for the project created a potential state liability, legislative oversight by the state injected itself into the process. Notwithstanding its substantive limits, the PACB's review added a significant checkpoint of financial accountability beyond what would have transpired with a city-only project.

If the city, not UDC, had been the lead agency on the project and condemner of the land, the project would have been required to meet the criteria of EDPL and CEQRA and undergo review through ULURP. That would have meant that the acquisition of the sites would have been voted on by the community board of the project's jurisdiction, the CPC and the BOE. Since UDC did take the 42DP to the BOE, this level of political accountability would not have differed. What UDC did not do, however, was take the lease agreements to the BOE. The BOE Resolution authorized UDC to enter into the leases, but required no further authorization from a politically constituted body.

That was the whole point of having UDC as the lead agency: to cut through all the process that direct city action would imply. For complex public-private development projects, accountability has to be balanced against inaction and red tape. If the city, not UDC, had been the lessor of the sites, the leases would also have been subject to ULURP and a BOE vote. Consequently, there would have been greater political accountability over the terms of the leases because elected politicians, not just UDC directors, would have had to review and endorse the final terms of the deals. Another difference between the UDC- and BOE-approval venues is the role of the city comptroller, an elected official. As the city's "financial-watchdog" on the BOE, the comptroller's office would have taken a serious look at the terms and conditions of the leases before agreeing to approve them. Conversely, in a vote against the leases, the comptroller would have offered a lengthy explanation for why the leases and financial arrangement were inappropriate ways for the city to implement its public-development goals. (According to Lefkowitz, the comptroller's office took an active position in reviewing the deals in 1984, scrutinizing the terms of the agreement prior to the BOE vote. This was not, however, the same as scrutinizing the final leases.) Whether under a city-as-lessor scenario the public at large would have learned more than it did when UDC released the "essential terms" of the TSCA leases in 1987 is unclear. The city may not have been required to disclose much more detailed information about the "essential terms" of the leases than UDC did for its public hearings. In any event, as a forum for feedback, the scope of UDC's disclosure was meaningful, as the judiciary made clear. When the function is oversight, however, the substance of an agreement cannot really be reviewed without seeing the actual leases; essential terms are not sufficient. There is, in real estate, a lot to be said about the proverbial maxim that "the deal is in the details."

The city's new charter that took effect in 1991 abolished the BOE and gave the power of deal making to the mayor. The city council does not have the power to review business terms. This was an enormous change—even in a city such as New York, which has historically been ruled under a strong-mayor form of government—and it goes directly to the heart of the accountability issue. The change in powers was part of a larger set of shifts between the mayor and a newly enlarged city council; the 51-member city council was given decision-making powers over land use, but not much else in the realm of development. (The thinking at the time, according to one insider, was that giving that large and potentially fractious body a say over the business terms of the city's deals would be too risky.) As under the old city charter, the leases would have to go through the ULURP procedure. ULURP, however, is concerned solely with the land-use/environmental aspects of a proposed project, and, as such, is not structured for a review of the business terms of leases. Yet, from the perspective of effective governance, the question remains: How can you make land-use decisions in cases of public-private development when you do not know the business terms of a deal?

When it comes to disposition of city-owned land, the new city charter provides that "the mayor may authorize the sale or lease only for the highest marketable price or rental, at public auction or by sealed bids" and that no such sale or lease could be authorized until a public hearing has been held. If, however, instead of leasing directly to private entities, the city leases the land to EDC or another local development corporation, which in turn leases the land to private entities, the requirements for competitive bidding, preparation of appraisal, advertisement in the *City Record*, and presentation at a public hearing are waived. The revised city charter requires only the mayor and the board of the borough in which the property is located approve the lease. While in practice, broader involvement is sought,[5] EDC does not possess condemnation power, which is one reason the city generally has opted to bring in UDC for complex eminent-domain projects such as the 42DP.

Public hearings do not equate with financial accountability, especially under the mayor's exclusive powers of contracting. In terms of the public protocols of "good government," much is missing. No substantive analysis of the business terms of the lease deals—the city's underlying commitments, the developer's obligations and the project's cost/benefit profile—is made available to city council members or to the public-at-large either to inform the debate at points of decision making or afterward to disclose the status of ongoing obligations or even later to evaluate changes in the deal.[6] While the procedural requirements of holding a public hearing provide for disclosure of the "essential terms" of the leases, this is but one piece of the project's total financial puzzle. More to the point, disclosure is not a substitute for analysis.

The city charter now requires an annual accounting of the city's tax expenditures (for example, tax abatements), a move toward tracking off-budget spending.[7] Yet, there exists no corresponding requirement for such an analysis *prior* to the signing of formal contractual commitments. Moreover, because the data are reported in the aggregate for each tax-exemption program or by public authority operating in the city, it is impossible to identify the foregone revenues attributable to individual deals. Hence, while it is hard to argue that there has been an absence of political accountability for the 42DP, evidence of financial accountability is woefully thin. Formally, the project passed through several checkpoints of accountability, but once approved by the BOE, the process became fragmented by the nature of the review—the deferential scope of judicial review and the limited mandate of the state's legislative oversight.

Once leases are signed and go into effect, who in the city's offices is to monitor performance with the terms of the deals? An accountant? A bureaucrat? A reconciliation with ESAC is necessary, but what happens if no one from the original deal is still at city hall, the comptroller's office, EDC, or ESDC? Such concerns were the subject of a 1993 report by the city comptroller's office on deal-based economic-development projects. The audit focused on the level and type of project documentation supporting decisions for lease arrangements and whether there had been verification of the expected benefits, in particular, the jobs created. In its review of eight projects involving 38 leases executed between 1988 and 1991 and managed by EDC,[8] the comptroller's office strongly criticized the agency for its lack of analysis and evidence. Presenting its findings in a 34-page report, Comptroller Elizabeth Holtzman concluded: "The documentation maintained by PDC and Ports and Trade was extensive, but . . . auditors and the public are not able to obtain sufficient information on assumptions governing EDC's decisions, to evaluate these decisions after the projects are executed and, thus, hold EDC accountable for the projects' results."[9]

The issue for Holtzman was not the lack of success in individual projects—Brooklyn's MetroTech Center was acknowledged and acclaimed as a clear winner for the city—but rather one of process. "This is irrational decision-making to say the least," she commented in *Crain's*. "Here you have a corporation making huge investments of public assets for economic development purposes that can't even tell you its true costs, can't tell you its true benefits, can't even come up with the most primitive rationale for what it's doing."[10] To some extent this was political posturing—Holtzman's remarks came at the beginning of an election year—yet they were on target, and they echoed those of former state comptroller Edward Regan, who wrote in his 1988 report for the Government Research Center of the Government Finance Officers Association:[11]

> With few exceptions, there are not many strategies or guideposts, no accounting, few records and very little knowledge of how the [economic] development process works. The major players—the business community and, especially, elected public officials—either do not want to or do not know the costs versus benefits of playing the development game or how to change the game. Such an evaluation, by default, is now left to finance officials.

Both the city and its comptroller agreed that completed projects should be subject to some form of cost/benefit analysis, but the consensus stopped there. Defining just what constitutes adequate documentation of the deal-making process is a contentious issue. EDC charged that Holtzman's report recommendation calling for the "rationale" behind each of the major elements of a transaction reflected "an incomplete understanding of how real estate transactions are completed" and amounted to an overly simplistic suggestion that "there is a formula or a set of standard questions which should govern the rationale behind many project decisions."[12] EDC objected to such a procedural requirement, stating that it would undermine the city's bargaining position because it threatened to "stifle negotiations" and bring an element of "counterproductive standardization" to its efforts. In response, the comptroller's office acknowledged the uniqueness of each economic-development decision and, hence, the importance for EDC to maintain flexibility during negotiations, but firmly maintained its position:[13]

> It is precisely because each project is unique, and is not based on "standard formulas and procedures," that EDC needs to document the outcome of negotiations and the underlying reasons/rationales. The documentation would provide EDC staff, especially staff who were not involved in the original negotiations, with useful information for renegotiating leases . . . [and] independent evaluators information that would help them evaluate projects after the projects have been executed.

In focusing on the documentation of deals and the evaluation of cost/benefit relationships *after* the political decisions had been made and the projects completed, the comptroller's audit highlighted the issue of managerial accountability, reasonably so. Documentation of the implementation process functions as the counterpart to procedures for community review and public hearing. Generally accepted standards of practice call for internal controls, documentation of decisions, timely performance, and evaluation of results. Documentation also serves to put in place an "institutional memory" of deal-making policy. Because mayoral administrations change and agency staff turns over, thorough documentation of the way deals have been financed and structured is important, especially as the deals become increasingly complex. The city should be able to measure the results of its investments from a bottom line that can be quantified and to evaluate the performance effectiveness of its agents. Accordingly, management audits are but another check on the process of discretionary decision making that defines public deal making. Sometimes pressure from outside interests, good-government watchdog agencies with the skills to analyze deals, increases accountability.[14]

If deal making demands accountability in each sphere—political, judicial, financial, managerial—and current practice, at least in New York, falls short of good-government protocols in the latter two arenas, in the case of the 42DP to what extent has the press—the "fourth estate"—filled the gap? If political accountability, as defined by informed approval of policy decisions by a duly constituted elected body, is necessary but not sufficient to ensure full and timely airing of the issues, how has the press defined the project's policy issues and shaped public opinion? If officials responsible for individual deals should be held accountable for adhering to reasonable levels of documentation and analysis and producing public benefits that meet or exceed the public costs for the project, in what ways has the press acted as a civic conscience by asking the tough questions?

No Press from the Press

Coverage was extensive. In stories designed to appeal to their respective readers, New York's English-language dailies—*New York Times, Daily News, New York Newsday,* and *New York Post*—reported regularly on the project's optimistic plans, milestones of progress, repeated delays, and nagging controversies; its anticipated environmental impacts, design intentions, and architectural miscues; the civics' and performing arts' efforts at theater preservation and landmarking; the city's bright-lights regulations for Times Square; the late Great White Way's rich glory days and its path from ruins to rebirth; midtown west's artificially stimulated real estate boom, overbuilt market distress, and euphoric rebound; advertising's state-of-the-art reglitzing of Broadway. Selected triumphal events and dramatic impacts were deemed worthy by the *Times* of front-page placement: "Six Times Square Theaters to Go 'Populist'"; "Addresses in Times Square Signal Prestige, if Not Logic"; "Disney Wished upon Times Sq. And Rescued a Stalled Dream"; "An Old Jewel of 42d Street Seeking to Dazzle Families"; "That Flashing Crazy Quilt of Signs? It's Art"; "Companies Get Second Helping of Tax Breaks" and "2 Developers Bid Top Dollar for What's Left in Times Sq."; Broadway's Latest Impresario, Canadian Garth Drabinsky, "Gambling on a Trip from 'Ragtime' to Riches"; "Late-Rising New Yorkers Learn Broadway [the 3,700-ton Empire Theater] Has Moved"; "Subway Station to Be Renovated, Keeping Pace with Times Square"; and "Scaffold Collapses, Paralyzing Times Square." With upward of 500 articles over fifteen years (1981–1996), the New York press kept the long-running 42nd Street project alive in the minds of the public at large.[15] This was no small achievement.

Although the *Times*'s coverage of local news has generally been perceived to be a cut below the strength of its international and national desks, this comparative perspective becomes academic when the issue is Times Square; how the *Times* covers the 42DP and what it says on its editorial page carry great weight. Consistently, the paper has held the power to define issues, shape public opinion, and rebuild the image of the project, even though, in retrospect it would be fair to say, as *Times* reporter Brett Pulley did at a session of an Urban Land Institute (ULI) conference focused on "Real Estate and the Press," that the paper is "well-deserving of a fair amount of criticism where our coverage has been concerned."[16] The visibility of news reports; frequency of appearance of news analysis, design critiques, and trend reviews; selective in-depth profiling of issues through special reports, special series of articles, and special photojournalism features in Sunday's *Magazine*—all these forms of news coverage convey a message, though it is not editorial in tone. The *Times*'s message about the 42DP: Cleaning up Times Square is critical to the social and economic health of the City of New York. The tenor of its editorials, their overlap with news stories and the selections of letters to the editor and op-eds— all these forms of editorial voice put pressure on both city and state officials who, after looking at what stories appear on the front page, turn

13.1
The New York Times Annex on West 43rd Street, home for nearly a century. (Gary Hack)

instinctively and immediately to the editorial page. The same content analysis and response pattern holds for the *Daily News, New York Newsday, New York Post, Crain's New York Business, New York Observer,* and *Village Voice,* all of which have covered the 42DP on a consistent basis. In covering events affecting the whole Times Square district, however, only the *Times,* with its headquarters at 229 West 43rd Street (between Times Square and Eighth Avenue), also spoke in the proprietary voice—its third—of a major long-time property owner. It is, after all, "Times Square" (figure 13.1).

The *Times's* imperative message to clean up West 42nd Street was unambiguous; its high-profile coverage of the project's news events, reliable. Its editorial opinions on issues bearing on the redevelopment of Times Square, mostly addressed directly to city and state officials, were numerous and persistent—80 spanning a 20-year period—running the gamut from prodding to goading to encouraging city action, to supporting (sometimes cautiously) policy initiatives, to praising results, to boosterism, to nostalgic recalls and sweet commentaries. Though these editorials spanned the tenure of three editorial-page editors (Max Frankel, Jack Rosenthal, and Howell Raines), their thrust was generally probusiness, at the same time the editors sided with the "public good" and aimed to be "right" on policy questions. Neither in its news reporting nor its editorials, however, did the *Times* coverage of the project explore the policy issues of public-private development or raise questions about the costs and liabilities of the deals underlying the city's most costly redevelopment project.[17] Late in the game when the project fell apart in 1992, it did report, as news, on the release of the MAS's estimate of the project's tax subsidies as well as the city's negotiations to amend the terms of its deal with TSCA. But even in its "news analysis" on the topic, *Times* reporter Thomas J. Lueck gave lip service to the off-budget financing, noting only that the "government incentives were rich," the story's main theme being public officials' "miscalculations in Times Square" brought about by a reliance on the discredited 1960s' strategy of bulldozer urban renewal.[18]

Because of the *Times's* economic interest and emotional investment in Times Square, the question arises whether the void in its coverage of the project's financial dynamics reflected a self-interested position of not criticizing a joint city-state initiative that would simultaneous enhance the paper's image and the value of its real estate while cleaning up West 42nd Street. However logical such a conflict-of-interest hypothesis appears, it lacks convincing proof. The *Times's* news operation is maintained on an independent basis from the tenth-floor editorial-board offices, and a casual look at instances where news coverage overlapped with an editorial statement reveals that its reporters have detailed the project's problems and its critics have commented negatively about the project's planning and architectural flaws, while the paper's editors were promoting the project.[19] For the publisher's views on an issue, the place to turn is the editorial page. The editorials speak for the *Times,* and on that page, despite the sometimes critical tone prodding government to move faster or take greater action, the paper showed unwavering enthusiasm for the 42DP.

The aggressive push of pornography in Times Square constantly concerned *Times* publisher Arthur Ochs (known by the nickname "Punch") Sulzberger who ran the paper from 1964 until his son took over in 1992. In the 1950s, the paper constructed a new printing plant on the West Side of Manhattan "presumably," Gay Talese wrote in his classic account of the paper, *The Kingdom and the Power*, "as the foundation for the skyscraper headquarters of the *Times* in the twenty-first century *if* the Forty-second Street area ever succumbs to the total decadence that has long been predicted by resident clergymen and social reformers."[20]

One argument put forth in defense of the track record of the *Times*, as well as other papers, on this issue involves the longevity of the 42DP. Lacking continuity of coverage, little institutional memory may exist on the news staff. Since the news-clip morgues often contain inadvertent errors, details tend to get repeated until they become part of the conventional wisdom about a project. Errors, in other words, mutate into "facts." This falls short of explaining the true nature of the problem, which lies, in part, with the way the press covers a public-private development project— as a real estate story, when in fact, it is a public-policy story. This, in turn, is part of a bigger long-running problem about the lack of "appeal" in covering the more mundane operations of government. "'Politics' was a fight, sketched in bold strokes, and journalists liked being at ringside to report it. 'Government,' with its bureaus and boards, paper trails, and swollen files, took place in dustier, less glamorous venues," wrote two scholars on the role of the media in New York politics. "American journalism has always been better at paying attention to politics rather than to government."[21]

"It took a long time for the public and for the elected officials to realize that development was not just about making office buildings, but that it was a whole neighborhood" said Robert A. M. Stern, who moderated the ULI's panel "Real Estate and the Press." It was an effort, he recalled, "to get even as enlightened a governor as Mario Cuomo was (and a city person) to recognize that the entertainment business, intangible and weird as it is, is a huge generator of why a city like New York exists, and why everybody hasn't moved to somewhere else." Stern laid a good share of the responsibility for this short-sightedness with the press:[22]

> The newspapers did not play enough of a part to
> explain the interrelationship of all these pieces so that
> the public would understand, at the end, that they were
> not just getting a cluster of office buildings in one place
> or a few poky old theaters, but were really investing in
> one of the major reasons the city exists or can manage
> to exist. . . . Sometime in the late 1980s, a lightbulb
> went off in the press that Times Square was not just a
> piece of geography, that it was a special kind of place.

In addition to the big events, news reporting picks up the quiet cracks and adjustments in plans and policy, two important examples being, 42DP's proposal in 1989 to allow an increase in the height of the four office towers and the MTA's decision in 1998 to allow the developers of one of the sites to exchange their obligation to build escalators for a one-time cash payment to the authority.[23] But it does not look at the totality of a public-private project and how the various pieces that have been reported upon from different "beat" perspectives interrelate to one another. It does not address the cumulative meaning of incremental isolated events, and it leaves the historical perspective to others. And that includes the stories of veteran *Times* metro-desk reporters David W. Dunlap and Thomas J. Lueck, both of whom have been reporting with much acuity on the 42DP since the mid-1980s.

Mayor Giuliani's bypass of a competitive-bid process for Sites 8E, 6W, and 10 should have evoked serious questions of public procedure but the issue never generated critical notice. Though it was within the 42DP's scope of action, the sole-source designation of a developer for this parcel violated the city's own publicly stated policy standards of practice that, as detailed in chapter 11, EDC's Clay Lifflander had righteously (and rhetorically) promoted as being the way "to maximize value and protect the public interest."[24] The political tussle between the city and state for decision-making control over this key site echoed the project's early well-publicized flap over the selection of a developer for the mart site, a part of which had become Site 8E. The fact that the sole-source designation elicited only vague passing notice, however, also seems telling of the desperate drive for tangible results on West 42nd Street and the deep anxiety over the fragility of promising development commitments among those who had anxiously followed the project. Much as the *Observer*'s Charles V. Bagli might question the subsidies of these second-round deals, other likely critics such as the Municipal Art Society or editorial writers seemed reticent to comment. Was this some type of "civic contribution," holding one's silence for fear of jeopardizing hoped-for gains that appeared more real than ever before?

Because the 42DP is a public-private project, it garnered far more scrutiny in the press than an ordinary real estate project would receive, said Pulley of the *Times*. Placement, not frequency of coverage, is the problem, he told the ULI audience:[25]

> These stories can land in one of two places: the real estate pages or the news pages. From a real estate perspective, we've done a fine job in discussing the architecture; we've done a great job in romanticizing the rich history of 42nd Street. But when it comes down to the real details of how this has all come together, the deals . . . what happens, invariably, particularly when a project has gone on this long, is that editors' eyes start of glaze over when you tell them about these stories, when you

start telling them about how the financing for this project is coming together and what it's going to mean for
taxpayers. So what we're increasingly faced with in the
news pages, to want to tell these stores and make them
interesting, is to personify them in some way.

Coverage of stories like the 42DP sometimes can be written as a
civic gesture, an approach akin to "trade-press" boosterism. "You take the
press release, rewrite it, throw in a few quotes and bang! You're done. And
that's it. And . . . the press release doesn't tell half the story," said Bagli, who
focused hard on the project's deal dynamics in the mid-1990s when few
other reporters seemed willing to touch the topic. Reporters did not do
their homework on the public-private partnership story, he complained.
They simplified the complex public-private dynamic and financing relationships. They did not take the time to look into the details of these
deals, dig beyond how the city and state wanted the press to present the
issue. Writing about the Disney deal, both Pulley and Bagli attempted to
address the question, what is the bang for the buck here? "Like the private
sector," said Bagli, "government has got to address these things and say, are
we getting enough back for what we're giving up?"[26] The way he saw it,
part of the problem was rooted in the unwillingness of the government
and the developer to fully engage in that debate. If this type of "routine"
coverage seemed lacking, it was not new. Telling the story of how the
media missed the opening stages of the city's plunge into fiscal disaster,
Diamond and Paine concluded that "budgetary reporting in particular suffered both from media overdependence on official news sources and from
media fixation with politics at the expense of attention to governance."[27]

Local newspapers have the political power and institutional
capacity to press public officials on the issue of financial accountability—
the cost/benefit question. They can knock away at the issue with special
reports, editorials, and op-eds, if they so choose. "In the classic formula-
tion, journalists may not be able to tell their audiences what to think—circumstances of family, class, community, race, religion, peers, occupation,
income, and education all play influential roles in the formation of attitudes and beliefs. But journalists, by dint of repetition and volume, can tell
their audiences what to think about."[28] Most New York dailies, however,
did not have the will—at least until the mid-1990s when the pattern of
Mayor Giuliani's ever-more expensive corporate-retention deals started to
emerge forcefully and become front-page news.

A notable exception was Sydney H. Schanberg, an op-ed columnist for *Newsday*.[29] During the heat of controversy over disclosure of the
TSCA leases (1988–1989), he asked "Why Keep the Times Square Deal in
a Dark Alley?" He then complained loudly that the "Times Square Deal
Remains Shrouded in Mystery" and argued forcefully to "Pull the Plug
on the Bleeding Times Square Plan."[30] Even more than the subsidies,
Schanberg troubled over the public's right to know and the closed-door
nature of the deal-making process. His attacks elicited a conventional

response from UDC chief Vincent Tese: "He demands that we calculate the extent of the tax abatement given the developer of the four office buildings. How can we? Normally, a tax abatement can be measured against what a property would have paid in full taxes. But that assumes someone was willing to pay full taxes in the first place. The fact is, no developer has gone near this stretch of 42nd Street for more than 50 years. That's why government got involved."[31] Tese was right about the analytical methodology for calculating the value of the city's tax abatements and about the lack of development interest on West 42nd Street, but not when he said "To say we are giving away a large amount of money is wrong." Still, his one-sentence justification of public benefits—the promise of forthcoming tax revenues of $200 million and 20,000 full-time jobs—with no accounting for public costs—ended the debate, cold.

That reporters and editors, as professionals, are not analytically trained to answer the cost/benefit question is not material. Using the appropriate forum, their job is to lever the press's political power as a vehicle for accountability from public officials who are responsible for providing forthright answers and full documentation of both costs and benefits. A mandate for broader and deeper investigative review of public subsidies sadly does not exist; seemingly, it has no constituency. At this point, at least, what is missing is a depth of concern about policy implementation—the politics of managing the government's business, process beside results. Process, though, bears heavily on the policy issues of public-private development and public trust of the strategy.

IMPROBABLE PRESCRIPTIONS

The complexity of public-private deals poses problems of analysis, explanation, and disclosure. The full implications of near-term financial commitments and long-term obligations are often hidden in the technical detail of a deal, understandable only to experts. Local officials often face only minimal requirements for reporting on a deal and few, if any incentives, to go beyond those and present a full and detailed accounting of costs. Moreover, complexity is functional. It serves a purpose: The lack of comprehension of complex deals acts as a shield against close scrutiny—what is difficult to understand is more likely to be left alone. As one long-time public fiscal officer for the State of New York remarked, "many policy makers find it easier to leave specific accountability for the success of these [economic development] projects somewhat obscured and diffused."[32]

Greater accountability can, however, be built into the current process in a number of ways. Improving the quantity and quality of information on the city's financial commitments is key. Disclosure of the essential terms of leases, for example, offers a technical glimpse of contracts, but sheds little light on the underlying economic fundamentals of a complex deal and how its many parts fit together. The present process of review should be augmented with an economic evaluation of the business terms of a deal—written in clear, nontechnical terms and available to all interested groups—including an assessment of the risks faced by the city. Such an analysis should clarify the nature and extent of benefits derived by the private sector—including their timing, as well as any costs associated with the delivery of public improvements and other components of the public-benefits package. On the public side of the ledger, it should account for the full set of costs—the present value of projected tax expenditures as well as direct spending by all participating public entities—set against the present value of projected municipal revenues from the project. Even though quantifying some of the costs and benefits presents challenging analytical problems, the current state of affairs leaves much room for improvement.

Consider, for example, the *Summary of Economic and Fiscal Benefits for New York from the 42nd Street Development*.[33] Prepared by consultants for the 42DP in 1994, the 65-page report described the project, its current status, and the development and annual operation of the interim elements of *42nd Street Now!*, as well as the long-range development program. It then presented technically derived estimates of the direct and indirect economic benefits (jobs, wages and salaries, and personal income) and the fiscal value (taxes, other public revenue, and contributions) to the public sector. In objective-sounding tones, the detailed projections and accompanying text presented a profile of "significant positive impact on the City and State." Although carefully carried out, the report was notable for its one-sidedness: a recitation of benefits without corresponding analysis or discussion of the public costs involved in generating those benefits. Likewise, there was no consideration of the timing factor, no analysis, for example, of how the projected benefit profile might reconfigure itself if in the interim the plan ran into delays or its assumptions about future private development failed to materialize, as had happened so frequently in the past. The failure to include the cost side of the equation and a review of risks could only have stemmed from the limited scope of work as specified by UDC and the city. Indeed, the same omissions characterized the seven-year projections of project benefits EDC prepared for the city council, as required under local law, discussed earlier.

Fragmentation of the current procedures for review poses another problem. Expanding a project's EIS to include a financial analysis of deals, for example, might address this issue, yet despite its appeal, a single, comprehensive review is implausible, if not misguided. Typically, deals evolve over time. Even following a defining political decision point such as the BOE Resolution for the 42DP, a deal is not finalized until the detailed business terms of the disposition have been fully negotiated and contracts formally signed. A singular review early in the process might short-circuit approval of the full and final terms and conditions governing a public-private project. Even a later review might not suffice when changing economic conditions and financial reversals upset even the best-laid plans, as Lefkowitz carefully noted, sending both sides back to the negotiating table to revise a deal.

There is a different, potentially problematic issue of process particular to the power of the state development corporation to operate outside the city's existing land-use regulations: creeping density. When plans specifying building densities are approved as part of a *General Project Plan*, typically, they are by necessity "approximate only"; planners expect that the final square-footage numbers are not likely to match one-to-one because as the design-development process evolves the figures will "vary slightly," and a carefully worded EIS will note that, as did the *DEIS* for the 42DP. The same applies for subsequent amendments to the *GPP*. In the case of the 42DP, significant density changes were proposed in three instances, two of which—an increase in height for the Selwyn rehearsal/office building, now known as the New 42nd Street Studios, to 170 feet from 100 feet and the addition of a 270,000-square-foot hotel with up to 470 rooms as part of the Forest City Ratner development—came to pass as *GPP* amendments. This was not the case in the other instance.

As part of their renegotiations with TSCA for an interim plan 42DP officials proposed to increase the allowable heights of TSCA's four office towers—on average, a little more than 100 feet, which would have meant towers 13 percent to 30 percent higher, without accounting for ornamental rooftop features adding between 57 feet and 80 feet, than what was approved under the *GPP*. Though state officials said no increase in overall building area would result, the attempted move touched many a raw nerve of civic groups and local leaders who were closely watching the project; after an immediate outcry, the proposal was quickly shelved before the issue could come up for review at the scheduled public hearing on the *DSEIS*. "To praise UDC for reaching this conclusion would be as pointless as congratulating a lunatic when he stops beating his head against a wall," wrote the editors of *Newsday*. "You don't have to be a real estate mogul to realize that the '90s aren't the time to plan adding more office space to a glutted market—or increasing the height of oversized towers. . . . Don't forget, the public had swallowed the idea of four bulky towers . . . with great difficulty." To propose more bulk was adding insult to injury since the expected public-benefit tradeoff "dangled" before New Yorkers— a brand new mezzanine for the dilapidated 42nd Street subway station— UDC had "kissed goodbye" in its earlier negotiations.[34]

The Selwyn and FCR hotel proposals evoked no such outcry, though the density changes were just as significant. The rational for the Selwyn parcel so clearly met the test of public purpose—a critical need for rehearsal space in the city, the importance of theater as a tourist draw, the fulfillment of a public goal identified for the New42 and required by its lease with the 42DP, Inc. (figure 13.2)[35]—that there was little opposition. The MAS and Community Board 4, however, questioned the appropriateness of further bulk in the midblock, voicing only partial support on the amendment at the public hearings. In written comments for the next review the MAS and Community Board 5 raised the same objection to the FCR hotel (figure 13.3)—which, as an amendment to the *GPP*, seemed to be an afterthought to the use program coming as a request to the 42DP, Inc., only a few months after the public hearing on the lease for the FCR project sites had been held; neither group would support the

13.2
Rehearsal space fulfilling the project's mandate for nonprofit theater activity on West 42nd Street. (Gary Hack)

proposed change in the *GPP* because the public benefits were not significant enough to warrant a change permitting further development in the midblock.[36]

The policy issue here is the cumulative impact of such incremental changes in the *GPP* shifting density around the project area. Both density amendments went forward on the basis of a declaration of "no significant adverse environmental impact." Part of the *GPP*'s initial logic for transferring density from one end of the block to another was to protect the low density of the midblock theaters. Because the amount of theater frontage on the street was small, this objective was vulnerable from the start, but owing to incremental changes—some good, others questionable—when the project is complete, that desired outcome is not likely. Another questionable density-related decision arose when ESDC remeasured the two office sites going to Boston Properties and found additional square footage for the developer—71,442 square feet or the equivalent of a total of three and a half floors. The adjustments, which had been confirmed by the state agency, "may have enabled Prudential to reap an additional $12 million from the deal," wrote a reporter for the *New York Observer*.[37] From an overall project standpoint, the total density allowance has not yet been fully used, but then there are two significant parcels still to be developed—the large parking lot at the southwest corner of West 42nd Street (8N) and another large site (8S) fronting West 41st Street where the *Times,* with Forest City Ratner Companies, plans to build a 51-story tower for its new headquarters with 1.4 million square feet of space. These may well test the durability of the overall buildable limit set by the *GPP* and approved by the BOE.[38] Creeping density is a risk of using the UDC vehicle. While the process is valuable because UDC is often needed to make things happen expeditiously, it must be used carefully, and civic and community watchdogs can never be too observant of proposed changes. They are a fundamental check on the powerful override vehicle.

The multiple venues and formal and informal points of accountability that currently exist subject public-private development projects to different perspectives that bear on the political decision, financial evaluation, and policy rationales for the project. Conceivably, the comprehensiveness implied in multiple points of review might increase public confidence in the process, though not necessarily consensus for the project. For this reason, mayors and governors and their agents have few incentives to increase the frequency of review by going beyond what is demanded by statute or political practicalities. This is one reason third-party reviews and critiques by good-government groups and civic organizations contribute to the accountability process in important ways. Yet without additional checkpoints that address the particular needs of financial and managerial accountability, the public-development strategy continues to run the risk that powerful policy critiques against "secretiveness" and "hidden subsidies" can torpedo its usefulness as a tool for rebuilding cities and promoting economic development. Writing about the issues of Times Square's redevelopment, many of which he considered worrisome, Marshall

13.3
The hotel (West 41st Street entrance) added to the FCR development program. (Gary Hack)

Berman to seemed to have come to an apt conclusion about the importance of deal making for Times Square by drawing on the meaning behind
the song "What I Did for Love," from *A Chorus Line*:[39]

> The city should fight like hell to get the deals it can, but
> it should deal. And people like us should drop our pre-
> tense of purity and unsoiled virtue, and get our heads
> together to live with the deals, because if we love Times
> Square—which has to be very different from the way
> we love Central Park—deals with bright lights are what
> we want. And if you don't believe in making deals,
> Times Square has no reason for being at all.

Besides having to "live with the deals," more can be asked of government.
If it is discomfort with public-private deal making per se, the solution lies
with bettering the standards and procedures of democratic accountability—with new protocols. The fact that "it worked," that the project "succeeded," should not countenance the missing pieces of democratic
accountability.

ARE SUBSIDIES UNFAIR?

Being Opportunistic
"A Spec of Durst on Broadway? Builder Changes Tune on Subsidies."
"Key Developer Seeks a Role in Times Sq." "Times Square Reversal:
George Klein Seethes As Doug Durst Moves In." The headlines said it all.
It was late fall 1995. The supreme irony in the situation was inescapable.
For Prudential, it offered antacid relief. For George Klein, it tasted bitter.
For public officials, it signaled progress, however weird this latest twist in
the long-running 42nd Street saga: Douglas Durst, long-time vocal opponent of subsidies for the Times Square project whose family's continuous
financial backing of oppositional litigation had done much by his own
admission to "delay, postpone or prevent" the public sector's plans for West
42nd Street, "could now be in the paradoxical position of becoming the
first developer to actually build a major office tower in the area," was how
a restrained *Times* put it.[40] "Yes, it's ironic," Durst told Bagli. "But we did-
n't put the tax breaks in place. If they're there, we'll use them. We prefer a
level playing field for everybody."[41]

The Dursts had maneuvered brilliantly. As staunch and vigorous
adversaries, Douglas and his father had thrown every obstacle they could
find or devise into the path of the 42DP (figure 13.4). They had brought
numerous lawsuits and financed others; whether won or lost, the lawsuits
would lead to delays, cause TSCA to lose the market opportunity, and, if
nothing else, foreclose a competitive financial return for Prudential as its
equity in the deal kept escalating. In 1989, when they heard the city was
about to buy the leases on the midblock theaters, they acted quickly.
According to his attorney, Douglas needed only three days to deliberate

13.4
Douglas Durst leading a rally of elected officials, community leaders, and local activists in protest of the 42DP. (© 2001 Maggie Hopp)

before spending $2.5 million to buy a package of seven leases; the eighth he bought separately. Purportedly, he went into the theater business to prove that the market could on its own spur revival on West 42nd Street.[42] But with the theater leases, the Dursts gained greater strategic leverage, and they could make money if the sites were condemned because the terms of the leases entitled the tenant to approximately one-third of the condemnation award. They stood to win either way—with condemnation (reasonable value from an award) or without (competitive position for his intended development of the 42nd Street block between Sixth Avenue and Broadway). In the ordinary course of business, the Durst Organization also had established a relationship with Prudential in the late 1980s when it applied for and secured a $100-million mortgage loan for its 41-story tower at 1155 Avenue of the Americas. This too would become a lever in the negotiation equation with Prudential.[43] On still another front, they considered moving into the limbo of destructive deterioration and inaction that surrounded the New Amsterdam Theater in the early 1990s, and did due diligence on a purchase of the IDA-backed revenue bonds that had been issued in 1983 to finance the Nederlander Organization's planned renovation, but they decided against the purchase.[44] Through these skillfully deployed tactics, they covered all fronts.

The Dursts have a reputation as sharp real estate people. Seymour Durst, who died at the age of 81 in May 1995, built the family's fortune, estimated by *Forbes* at $1 billion in 1989, "by shrewdly anticipating real estate trends. He built office towers on Manhattan's Third Avenue in the 1950s, just before companies began swarming into that area. In the 1960s he jumped to Sixth Avenue, again one step ahead of tenant demand."[45] Being staunch adversaries of the 42DP did not preclude commercial gain from the project. Buying the 42nd Street theater leases was a smart move. Durst claims that the intimate knowledge of the project gained as a by-product of his support of opposing litigation gave him an advantage over other potential acquirers of the office site. But as one Prudential player put it, "anyone could have gotten what was needed to understand the deal in order to negotiate with Prudential." What really made the difference in Douglas Durst's deterministic move into Times Square was his family's control over the "back parcels" to TSCA's prime tower site—two small rectangular lots acquired more than twenty years earlier as part of the senior Durst's monopolylike assemblage of more than half of the 31 lots making up the block. Because of its larger holdings in the immediate area, the Durst Organization always was the most likely builder of a tower on that site. Adding the back parcels (plus a larger lot subsequently purchased from Viacom) to the 33,300-square-foot TSCA site made it more marketable, even if the allowable building size remained the same.[46] Finding their ultimate way into the project may not have come from a fully predetermined game plan, but they knew how to move in many different ways when the opportunity arose.

Whether development subsidies are unfair depends upon perspective. In the real estate business everyone bemoans the unfair advantage a developer receives, yet each and everyone would like it himself. For Douglas Durst, the situation held many potential returns. He decided he wanted to build the tower in early February 1995, about six months after city and state officials signed their new deal with TSCA but before Disney's commitment was locked firmly in place. By being the first to venture forth—before the office market had fully recovered and when others were too afraid to gamble—he stood the best chance of capturing TSCA's prime site at the lowest price. The timing was advantageous; the risks posed by the project's key uncertainties were rapidly disappearing, though not quite gone. He opened negotiations by asking for all four sites, though he did not need (and did not have pockets deep enough for) the other three. The most money would be made from gaining control of the site adjacent to his family's other holdings; the others were not as valuable, even though as the real estate market heated up they would sell for more. The tax abatements attached to the site afforded a way to capture key anchor-tenant commitments, and he was also negotiating to buy the site's pro-rata share of ESAC-rent credits. Combining tax abatements and rent credits, the Durst Organization would be able to write long-term leases at competitively advantageous rates no other developer in the city who wanted to build a new tower could match. In 1990 the Dursts estimated the subsidized advantage at $15 per square foot,[47] and as a result of TSCA's 1994 agreement with the city and state, the advantageous PILOT schedule had been extended to 20 years. By 1995, in a market of firming office rents, super-heated signage rentals, and escalating retail deals, the projected financial returns from this development project looked like a grand slam.

Durst had cash equity to put into the project, a not inconsiderable factor at a time when banks remained terribly gun-shy about lending on real estate. The Durst Organization's conservative ways of running a real estate business—prudent fiscal management and carefully tended tenant relationships—kept its eight office towers relatively low on debt and high on occupancy, which made raising capital from a refinancing of assets relatively easy at a time when it was tough for other developers.[48] Moreover, the Dursts were willing to move ahead on a speculative basis, before major tenants signed leases. All in all, it was an aggressive statement about the younger generation taking charge: Four Times Square would be the family's biggest project ever.

By being the first developer to break ground for a skyscraper that would open in time to usher in the new millennium, the 80-year-old Durst Organization of which Douglas was now third-generation president was positioned for continued leadership in the tight and highly competitive world of New York real estate. Big-time real estate development in New York is unique among the nation's real estate markets in that it is a nearly closed club consisting of a small group of people well known to each other through the generations. Developers in New York play for the biggest stakes in the nation because the real estate market is the largest. To approach George Klein and Prudential in a bid to acquire the leasehold interest in a TSCA site was more than a "stunning turnaround" that "would also break a logjam in the big development scheme."[49] It was a high-profile professional coup establishing the 50-year old scion of a legendary real estate contrarian as a march-to-his-own-beat player in his own right.

"It's been a lifetime of preparation," Durst told a business reporter (figure 13.5). Schooled on his father's real estate philosophy—"Never buy farther than you can walk"—he had been roaming the Times Square area for years since joining the family firm in 1968, not long after receiving his bachelor's degree in economics from the University of California at Berkeley. He knew the area's Zeitgeist better than most other developers, as a significant property owner, patron of the theater arts and eventually a weekday resident with a pied-à-terre on West 43rd Street. (He spent the weekends on his 300-acre organic farm, the largest such farm in New York State, tending his environmental and equestrian interests.) In some not so subtle ways, his moves stood out from the pattern of business practice followed by his father. Where Douglas was willing to build on spec, his father would not go forward without a firm commitment from an anchor tenant. Where Douglas was willing to take on investment partners, his father would do so rarely. Where Douglas was willing to negotiate with city officials on zoning rules, his father would only build on an as-of-right basis. Yet

13.5
Douglas Durst with the model of
Four Times Square. (© Larry
Ford/Ford Foto)

in the areas that made for lasting success and profitability—financial savvy
in deal making, long-term business relationships, prudent risk taking—
Douglas is his father's son. And the son aimed to revive the father's dream
of building out the complete block of 42nd Street running from Sixth
Avenue to Broadway, in due time. First he would build on the Broadway
corner. The ability to link a second major tower to be built on the larger
remainder of the block, he said, eliminated the "speculation" of the Times
Square venture.[50] For making a mark on New York as "the developer who
changed grime into high-rise green"—Four Times Square would be
designed and marketed as a showcase of an environmentally responsible
building—Durst received one of *Crain's* four 1997 All-Stars awards.[51]

The negotiations over the terms and conditions of a sale of the
site's development rights to Durst were tortuous because the past's emotional baggage burdened the three central players: Eugene Heimberg,
George Klein, and Rebecca Robertson. As president of Prudential
Investment Company, Heimberg had been against the decision to go forward with the Times Square project since 1990, when he took over
responsibility for the insurance giant's real estate business. The ultimate end
of its exposure to condemnation costs was still nowhere in sight, five years
after vesting. Prudential was anxious to sell. "Ten years ago," a former
Prudential executive told reporter Bagli, "Prudential wouldn't have
allowed someone who was costing them a lot of money to profit from the
situation. [But] Prudential's attitude at the very top has changed. They're
now saying real estate equity is no longer an appropriate investment for a
large insurance company."[52] In keeping with a radical change in policy
and reorganization of the company, Heimberg aimed to cut back as much
of Prudential's massive development portfolio as he could. He was working 80 to 90 hours a week, all the time dealing with company's broad-
based problems. He wanted to cut Prudential's losses on the 42DP, and
Durst's overture offered a serious start toward a way out.[53] Because they
owned the back parcels and did not need financing, "the Dursts were the
only naturals to speak to," said Heimberg.[54]

George Klein, however, wanted to drop it; he was firmly against a sale. It was not just that Klein disliked Durst intensely. Even before Durst's letter materialized on Heimberg's desk in early spring 1995, Klein was angry that Prudential might not stay with the project for the long haul. The joint-venture partnership had turned into a tense, troubled marriage, and as the economic partner, Prudential was calling the shots. For three years, Klein had been out looking, unsuccessfully, for money to buy the sites himself. No takers could be found. With the market just beginning to turn, he could not fathom Pru's selling out now. He was an entrepreneur, and to his way of thinking, the timing was dead wrong for a sale. But it was over for him. Having gambled money and reputation for fifteen years, Klein had lost position as a player in the 42DP. He had one last move: the ability to exercise his right of first refusal for the property, which brought the insurance company to negotiate a settlement with him.

Approval by the city and state was necessary for a transfer of the development rights to the site, along with the tax breaks that had been pledged to TSCA. It would not come easily. To begin with, bruised feelings made the idea of a transfer to the Dursts hard to swallow for public officials as well, Robertson especially. "For a long time, Rebecca was dead set against this project," one real estate lawyer familiar with the negotiations was reported as saying. "She kicked up a tremendous number of technical objections."[55] Intensely concerned about failure, Robertson wanted safeguards in place so the 42DP would have control in case something went wrong. She wanted guarantees. While Durst agreed to proceed immediately with the construction of the retail portion of the site, he wanted to wait for an anchor office tenant before proceeding with the office tower. The state was reluctant to approve the transfer unless the Dursts guaranteed complete development immediately, with or without a tenant. The Dursts would not promise to build a $400-million office tower immediately. Public officials insisted on having security and guaranty. The developer had to have flexibility on the timing of when to construct a 1.6-million square-foot office tower, financing for which would be impossible to secure without an anchor tenant. Back and forth the negotiations went. Each side pushed for the agenda item that was essential to the feasibility of a transfer, though the bottom line for each differed. Neither side could move off its position, and this impasse stymied negotiations for months. The tax breaks were not at issue, but there were other questions of policy: Would Durst's proposal for the first office tower undermine the energy of the *42nd Street Now!* plan and the entertainment and retail projects of Forest City Ratner and Tishman ready to go forward on the western sites? Should the state and city lease to someone who had sued them over this project? Was Durst a reasonable and credible developer of "commitment and capacity similar to TSCA," which was what the lease agreement required for a transfer of the site's development rights? Would the firm indeed build, or was this just another ploy to thwart the project?

Overriding the technical objections and policy concerns was a simple fact: The state desperately wanted to see something get built. New to the 42DP, ESDC Chairman Charles Gargano was without, as he put it, "that bad taste" and "baggage" others might carry. "I didn't care what had happened in the past. I was looking for a fresh start."[56] The state agreed to the transfer of development rights, in concept, provided Durst built a new office tower or, failing to find a tenant, a new four-story retail building. This was the "fail-safe" solution Durst offered the state.[57] City officials too wanted to see progress on the project, but their warming up to the former project opponent proceeded at a tortoiselike pace. Voicing similar policy concerns, they were reportedly less willing to let go and allow the proposed transfer to move forward. To the existing list of policy concerns, they added another: "Was the city better off with retailers than a never-to-be-built office tower?" asked John Dyson.[58] Dyson, the city's departing deputy mayor for economic development, reluctantly agreed to approve the deal under pressure from the state after several months of negotiations—but only if Durst could come up with an anchor tenant for the office tower.

Although the financial terms of the TSCA lease deal were not up for renegotiation, the parties needed to come to an accord on the size and design of the proposed office tower.[59] On a site that was now 33 percent larger, Durst agreed to maintain the same square footage (1,443,000) as permitted by the lease, which meant that the proposed tower would be shorter, 47, as opposed to 58, stories. (The final configuration topped out at 48 stories and 1,554,000 square feet.) The proposed design also incorporated a number of setbacks, ironically, thereby directly addressing one of the issues that so infuriated the project's earliest critics and allaying the fears of some that the building would have an overbearing impact.[60] Still, Durst was asking for the right to use more of the space for entertainment- and tourist-related retail uses, up to 120,000 square feet, which was almost five times what had initially been approved.

A lot of process had to be attended to: public hearings on the proposed amendment to the *GPP* to expand the footprint of the site and on the essential terms of a proposed amended lease with Durst, related authorizations allowing the state to acquire for a nominal $1 the three Durst parcels (plus a 13-foot strip of land squaring off the site contributed by Durst shortly after), and a return trip to Albany for review of the amended lease by the PACB. All proceeded swiftly. No problems materialized. Opposition was nonexistent. The few people who attended the public hearings held in May (six persons) and June (eight persons) all spoke in support of the project and the proposed changes. While supporting the overall project, the chair of one community board voiced concern that the building facades and signage might be creating "visual overload" and another urged linkage from the development site to the Times Square subway station. Although not present at the hearings, interestingly, the MAS endorsed Durst's plan, despite its long-time opposition to the construction of new office towers on West 42nd Street. The PACB immediately approved the amended lease the same day it was received, which surprised Robertson. The public and the civics had stopped questioning the subsidies (figures 13.6, 13.7).

13.6
Building permits for Four Times Square, 1998. (Gary Hack)

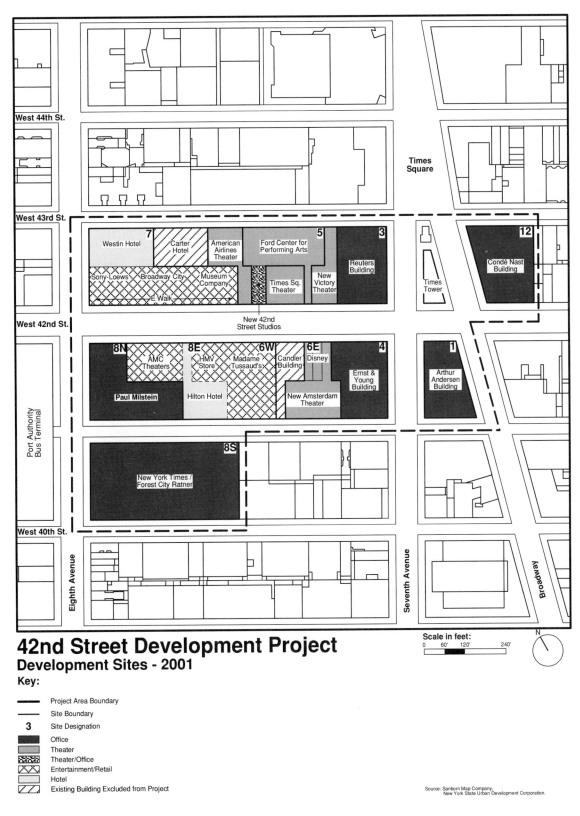

42nd Street Development Project
Development Sites - 2001
Key:

▬▬▬	Project Area Boundary
——	Site Boundary
3	Site Designation
■	Office
▨	Theater
▨	Theater/Office
⧄	Entertainment/Retail
▨	Hotel
⧄	Existing Building Excluded from Project

Labels within map:

West 44th St.
West 43rd St.
West 42nd St.
West 40th St.
Times Square
Times Tower
Times Tower

Eighth Avenue
Seventh Avenue
Broadway
Port Authority Bus Terminal

7 Westin Hotel
Carter Hotel
American Airlines Theater
Ford Center for Performing Arts
5
3 Reuters Building
12 Condé Nast Building

Sony-Loews
Broadway City
Museum Company
E Walk
Times Sq. Theater
New Victory Theater

New 42nd Street Studios

8N AMC Theaters
8E HMV Store
Madame Tussaud's
6W Candler Building
6E Disney
4 Ernst & Young Building
1 Arthur Andersen Building

Paul Milstein
Hilton Hotel
New Amsterdam Theater

8S New York Times / Forest City Ratner

Scale in feet:
0   60'   120'   240'

N

Source: Sanborn Map Company,
New York State Urban Development Corporation.

13.7
The new uses on West 42nd Street.
(Morgan Fleming for the author)

Double-Dipping

Not long into the approval process and a day before the planned formal announcement, city officials leaked to reporters that Condé Nast Publications, Inc., the internationally known publisher of *Vanity Fair, Vogue, GQ, Details, Architectural Digest, Allure,* and ten other upscale consumer magazines, would move its corporate headquarters to Durst's planned tower, Four Times Square. Condé Nast's term-sheet agreement with Durst, signed in April 1996, called for 500,000 square feet of office space and included an option for an additional 150,000 square feet (ultimately, the leased space totaled 740,000 square feet). "The deal is unusual in several respects, not the least of which," wrote *Times* reporter Lueck, "is that Condé Nast, which is part of Advance Publications, is to receive $10.75 million in 'corporate retention' tax breaks from the city and the state, even though its corporate identity is so closely aligned with Manhattan that real estate executives say it is an unlikely candidate to leave."[61] Engineered by city officials, this second layer of corporate subsidies atop of what many perceived to be development subsides no longer needed but irrevocably part of the 42DP—second helpings: tax breaks on top of tax breaks—fulfilled the city's own quid pro quo for approving the transfer of development rights from TSCA to Durst; it made possible the immediate building of an office tower. Dyson reportedly maneuvered the state into contributing $4 million of present-value subsidies when it had no intention of participating in any deal.[62] The character of the deal infuriated Robertson, who believes the city did not have to give Condé Nast what it did in "corporate retention." Unlike the original development-defining incentives, this deal was gilding the lily.

Whether Durst could have secured a similarly large lease commitment at such a favorable time from one of other potential tenants—rumors had it that he been talking with advertising giant Young & Rubicam and the law firm of Skadden, Arps, with whom the developer subsequently did complete a lease deal—remains unknowable. But getting this particular tenant, the swank and trendy publishing company renowned for its concern with style and famous for its perks, to move to Times Square—into a building its artistic director had called "the ugliest building I've ever seen. . . . Armani would never come to such a tawdry location"—required a heavy financial handout.[63]

The idea of moving to Times Square had been rejected by every senior Condé Nast executive only two years earlier after three months of reviewing architectural layouts and financial analyses in response to the idea put forth by the company's long-time tenant representative, Insignia/ESG. Like most of the business community, Condé Nast was skeptical of the potential of Times Square. Four Times Square was one of four buildings on the short-list of plausible headquarters for the publishing conglomerate, the three others being on the East Side in midtown. The consultants at Insignia/ESG would not give up the quest for a serious consideration of Times Square because they believed Durst's office site offered a strong long-term location and competitively advantageous rent for their client.

Consolidation of the 537,000 square feet of dispersed and inefficient space that made up the office editorial and business operations of Condé Nast's publishing empire had been an assignment for Insignia/ESG since 1993. A headquarters in Times Square would be a possibility only, the consultants were told, if the deal was compelling—a "savings of $1 million a year would *not* be nearly enough," remarked Condé Nast's chief financial officer. Despite months of talk that included face-to-face meetings between the Dursts and Condé Nast owner S. I. (Si) Newhouse and president Steven Florio, the upscale publisher remained far from convinced that Times Square would be a suitable new home. A 1996 memo from Florio to Insignia/ESG served as a reminder of just how difficult the challenge would be: "Si reminded me," wrote Florio, "that the *only* way we will put everyone into one building is if you . . . can show us how it will *save us money,* real money, hard dollars. Otherwise, it's a moot point."[64]

On the subject of a city-state incentive package, Newhouse had laid a ground rule: He expressly forbade Insignia/ESG to suggest that Condé Nast would move its operations out of New York. According to the consultants, "Newhouse felt this well-won tactic was deceptive and, thus, inappropriate." No matter how implausible moving beyond Manhattan seemed to anyone familiar with the upscale publisher's well-burnished image,[65] somewhere along the line this ground rule changed, for the "threat factor" became a consistent set piece of the news story, and Florio is on record as saying "I was completely serious about moving some of the back-office operations to New Jersey or down South. We knew we had to have publishers and editors here. But we did not have to have billing or accounting or finance or circulation. We could have moved up to half our company, over 1,000 people, to South Carolina. We looked at real estate down there. We were deadly serious."[66] If there is a tremendous amount of posturing in New York, it is because the stakes are so high.

Judging the seriousness of corporate threats is not the strong suit of city politicians or bureaucrats. Neither the economic criteria for nor sizing of these corporate packages—usually a package of tax incentives, including abatements on property taxes and sales taxes on equipment and machinery; the waiving of mortgage-recording fees; and low-cost electricity from the state—ever seems clear (or consistent), only their durability as a dominant feature of New York's economic-development policy. In terms of concentrated spatial impact, the results of the corporate deals are most striking in Times Square, which has become, as so aptly termed by Bagli, "the Crossroads That Taxpayers Built."[67] The incentives started to flow in the early 1980s with the special deal for the Marriott Marquis Hotel and the as-of-right incentives of the 1982 Midtown Zoning Resolution, which could be financially enhanced with ICIP tax subsidies. In the early 1990s, "retention" packages sweetened the choice of several big corporate moves to Times Square: Bertelsmann A.G. ($11.6 million), Morgan Stanley (two, for a total of $126.1 million), Viacom Inc. ($15 million). Like the Condé Nast deal for its 42DP tower, second helpings went to Reuters America Holdings ($26 million) for its new 30-story U.S. headquarters building being developed by the Rudin Organization and to Ernst & Young ($22 million) and Arthur Andersen ($4.6 million) for new headquarters, respectively, in the 37- and 47-story towers being developed by Boston Properties.[68]

The impact of the city's corporate-retention deal making is far broader than Times Square, however. Since taking office in January 1994, Mayor Giuliani has been willing (if not aggressively eager in some cases) to offer retention/job growth packages to a host of big-name others.[69] This has benefited midtown the most, but the largesse reaches beyond Manhattan to the other boroughs. As reported in the *Times*, as of fall 1999 the Giuliani administration had provided more than $2 billion in tax breaks and other incentives for 50 companies.[70]

The corporate deals have been a particularly volatile political issue for Mayor Giuliani, eliciting a broad range of strong criticism from both the left and right of the political spectrum, academics and business groups, civic and good-government groups. Some criticism is philosophical—these benefits amount to "corporate welfare"; a better way to compete for jobs is to "devote resources to improving the overall business economy by cutting taxes and improving infrastructure and schools." Other criticism is economic—jobs are "just moved around," not created; this is "misspent money," "totally unnecessary given the strength of the city's economy." Still other criticism is based on skepticism of the public sector's capacity to strike a "good" deal—"the city has no top line"; "these deals allow corporations to make suckers out of the public sector," they "beget more such deals, not a stable economy." Or its inherently weak bargaining position—"mediocre but well-intentioned bureaucrats" are no match for "sophisticated deal makers"; given the history of job loss in the recent past, "the city is extremely vulnerable to corporate "economic blackmail." Or bad policy and poor monitoring and accountability—"corporate retention on a case-by-case basis is bad public policy"; "the city is unable to document that companies receiving governments subsidies have in fact created the jobs promised."[71]

If there is a common theme among the critiques, it is that city officials have lost the locking mechanism to the give-away box. At a time of unprecedented prosperity in the city, repeated instances of corporations getting tax breaks and other benefits, sometimes second helpings—even when they have no intention of leaving the city—seem hard to square with economic logic, yet alone norms of good public policy. The "city's sweet deals leave bitter taste," complained the editors of the *Daily News*, who tolerantly credited the tax breaks with "encouraging" firms to stay and, in the case of Disney and AMC on West 42nd Street, with the ability to "restore life not to say decency to seedy Times Square." More concerned with the city's competitive bargaining position than policy correctness, they questioned the practical wisdom of the administration's approach: "With a $2.3 billion budget deficit, all this largess leaves two nagging questions: Can the city afford this? And where will it end?" Without leveling the playing field and making the city a place that business could not afford to leave, the editors warned "Big Business will continue to use New York's weakness as a trump card. And the ante will only go up."[72]

Behind the seemingly irrational corporate packages there is a logic, the logic of political fairness—spreading the benefits around, giving something to all the big players. It may be that a lack of clear standards in these one-off corporate deals makes it politically difficult to turn away from demands based on claims of fairness, especially when competitors have gotten cost-reducing incentive packages: "We never threatened to leave the city," CBS Chairman Laurence A. Tisch said at the time his corporation demanded a deal worth $49.5 million. "I just wanted to be treated like everyone else."[73] If there are no clear rules defining eligibility and new deals set some new precedent, as was the case with the Ernst & Young deal,[74] it may be that when subjected to close comparative scrutiny, analysis would reveal that the pivotal piece of policy discretion in these corporate deals is sizing. If that hypothesis was found to be true, corporate-retention deal making would be following the time-honored political logic of government grants-in-aid programs: Distribute the benefits broadly. That these deals have reportedly gotten somewhat smaller, but continued to increase in number at a time when the domestic and international appeal of New York's urbanity is as strong as its hot economy—a synchronization missing in the 1980s—is anecdotally suggestive of that the political principle has been fully operative.

The Giuliani administration has responded to criticism of its corporate deal making in a consistent fashion by pointing out that the city must deal with the needs of individual companies on a case-by-case basis, not withstanding its agreement in the principle that lower taxes are the best way to improve the business climate of the city. Randy L. Levine, deputy mayor for economic development at the time, argued that the city's prosperity has been due, in part, to the administration's incentive deals that have kept jobs in the city. "All of our deals are tied to job growth," he said. "You get a baseline tax benefit for keeping jobs. The premium is for creating jobs, and that's why, when you look at the numbers, most of our deals are tied to job growth."[75] The political bet behind the corporate-retention subsidies matches that made on West 42nd Street: producing results in a time frame that lets the public forget about the costs of achieving the benefits. And, if not long forgotten, the costs will be less noticeable for being off-budget tax expenditures.[76]

In public development, cities are typically buying private investment ahead of market readiness. Because the public process moves so slowly and the public sector cannot act as nimbly as the private sector, the project often risks ending up behind the market. Over a long gestation period, the "right size" for development subsidies can swing up or down from what was originally agreed upon with changing market conditions, as was the case with the 42DP. Once granted, however, the subsidies cannot be taken back on a change of political mind or economic determination that less is necessary unless there is a default in the contractual agreement. Nor should they. Reneging on such a promise would seriously jeopardize a city's reputation as a reasonable and businesslike partner and, hence, its future ability to secure important long-term private investment commitments. (The lack of maneuverability, though, is asymmetrical; it does not inhibit giving more.) In effect, such pragmatic concerns grandfather the subsidies of past deals, fair or not. In no instance was this more telling than in the final irony of the 42DP subsidy story: With the recovery of the real estate market, ESAC-rent credits—the city's oversized off-budget debt for the acquisition of the four office sites and midblock theaters—became a saleable "asset" for Prudential in each of its negotiations with private buyers who sought the rights to develop a office tower on what had become the city's newest location of prime real estate.

Tax abatement for commercial development in Manhattan has long been a questionable policy to New Yorkers; it is a topic on which many are quick to voice objections, reasonable or not. But this is hardly unique; tax subsidies are often an equally volatile trigger point in large-scale commercial redevelopment projects across the nation, especially in downtowns where the question often arises of whether a city's neighborhoods are getting a fair share of incentives and other public benefits. That these benefits to developers do not get evaluated in the context of competing city priorities, as do direct capital-budget investments, increases the skepticism as to their true worth. Too often the citywide benefits promised by tax abatements seem too abstract to taxpayers and the costs too obvious. When given as part of a uniform as-of-right program, the incentives may seem more equitable. Giving away extra benefits as in the cases of double-dipping in Manhattan's hot market is inherently different than using subsidies as carrots to entice policy-specific private investment in risky long-term ventures. It is different in policy intent from using PILOT-based rent-credits as a form of currency to finance urban renewal. And it is very different in policy practice from sticking to the terms of deals cast when markets were weak despite changes in market conditions over time. The latter—like the subsidies of the 42DP—become a sunk cost of public risk taking, of the gamble on initiating large-scale physical change. It recasts the original question of fairness.

Taxpayers always had a stake in the revival of Times Square, but economics was never the policy driver for the 42DP. It was not the basis on which Koch made the decision to take charge, nor would the project's costs in relation to its benefits become the standard against which the public initiative would be evaluated. The broad economic benefits associated with the cleanup of West 42nd Street—in terms of direct jobs, wages and salaries, and personal income, as well as indirect economic contributions to the city's economy and fiscal returns to the public sector in the form of real estate tax revenues from the project area and other taxes based on retail sales and corporate and business earnings—supported the objective of the city and the state, but the statistics citing these economic benefits served as a defense, to defuse criticism of the project and its subsidies, particularly when the mayor's actions awarded double dips and Times Square had become the hottest piece of real estate in the city. From start to end, the cleanup-turned-transformation aimed to restore civility—real as well as symbolic—to New York's most public of public places.

13.8
Aiming for civility: a place where the middle
class could find "delicious food" and "reasonable
prices," once again, as well as a spot of visual calm
amid the hustle. (Collection of the author)

13.9
Father Duffy Square. (Gary Hack)

CHAPTER 14

THE MESSAGES OF RENEWAL

The transformation of Times Square as described in the media rings with inventive word play: "Apple Just Doesn't Have the Same Bite," "The Great Whitewashed Way," "G-Rated Refurbishment," "From Filth to Fantasia," "pot to pixie dust," "the only hot, steamy thing [Thera-Flu cough syrup] still allowed on this block." The out-of-town travel reports gush promotional: "respectable," "wholesome," "dazzling," "bewildering," "family friendly." In the praise, wonder, hyperbole, photographic messages, telegenic images, and printed criticism—balanced and biased, realistic and nostalgic, superficial and probing—the message writ large in written in capital letters: "NEW NEWS OF THE CITY—TIMES SQUARE."

In the language of superlatives used to describe the transformed place editorialists, reporters, writers, and commentators appear to be searching for an urban romanticism suitable for the twenty-first century. Casting Times Square as "a neon nirvana," "an original multimedia experience," "an outdoor info cathedral," "a global image format," and "a fabrication of the hyperreal" amounts to a redressing of the icon, the start of a new cycle of symbolism. On target with the unbridled optimism of a millennium celebration, the timing of the turnaround turned out to be perfectly choreographed—not as a consequence of visionary foresight but rather as the chance result of a confluence of rare revisionist public policy, accidental market opportunities born of economic distress, and coincident changes in consumer tastes for entertainment particularly beneficial to big cities. Twenty years in the making, the transformation appeared to happen overnight. This is what happens when critical mass materializes (figure 14.1).

As testimonials of change, the many scripts remain semidetached from the urban reality of the place—the impossible traffic, the inescapable noise, the impenetrable sidewalk congestion, the ubiquitous gum-stained pavement. Times Square is still gritty. It may be filled with towering new office buildings and hotels, branded retail emporiums of entertainment,

14.1
The view of Times Square look-
ing south (1979), transformed
(2001). (David W. Dunlap, *On
Broadway: A Journey Uptown Over
Time*; Gary Hack)

theme restaurants, glamorously refurbished theaters, corporate-style movie
multiplexes, and glittering supersigns, but these artifacts of the new physical
environment hardly diminish the ever-present competitive push and shove
in the hub of the nation's largest and most singularly larger-than-life city,
which at times can be as difficult as in the past. Broadway is now full of
suits, but in the face of what some call "remorseless upgrading" and others
call "progress," Times Square remains a destination for the homeless, the
colorful eccentrics, the sadly destitute persons who have always been more
numerous in cities than in the suburbs. It still attracts the vociferous and
shrill groups of activists wanting to exercise their freedom of speech. It still
attracts the local and out-of-town teens seeking immediate thrills, a day of
hooky from school, or a different view of life's possibilities. What has been
pushed away in Times Square, however, is the constant in-your-face behavior that so defined the place from 1960 throughout the early 1990s. "The
salty old flavor of Times Square isn't gone," a reporter for the *Los Angeles
Times* wrote, "just diluted, and unlikely to disappear any time soon."[1]

Tourists are voting favorably, with their feet, in overwhelming
numbers. Architectural critics are penning enthusiastic praise. Cultural
commentators and academics are offering tableaus of modulated ambivalence. Their voices evidence widespread suspicion and ultrasensitivity to

the Walt Disney Company's size and power, which they take to be the prevailing influence on a tourist-oriented gestalt permeating the whole area. Throughout all of these commentaries the focus has been on the physical transformation of West 42nd Street, which programmatically comes off as a "turbocharged" nostalgic redo "largely about the past," in the words of one perceptive critic.[2] Yet the crackling energy of the new Times Square—whether loved, hated, or merely tolerated—derives from the recast and redimensioned economy of the place. Inside the glittering new physical shell that marks the district's transformation lies the real economic transformation: a localized concentration of jobs in the creative fields of media and entertainment built upon the district's legacy to the nation of network radio broadcasting, Broadway theater production, Hollywood-movie distribution, and the image-brokering business of

public relations. On a par with the city's other geographic clusters of specialized businesses known by their informal designations—the Flower District, the Garment District, the former Ladies' Mile and the Meatpacking District—Times Square should be called the Media District. In the jargon of the Internet age, it is the city's headquarters for the production of content—information, entertainment, printed and electronic publishing, and communications—running fast to keep pace with a rapidly evolving global communications industry. It is a microclimate of media creativity based on the nearly century-old trademark of Times Square.

The almost combustible social and economic diversity—seeming chaos—of the place, so different from other city districts where greater visual order and economic or residential homogeneity prevail, marks the true iconic legacy and unchanged reality of Times Square (figures 14.2, 14.3). Times Square is still an irregularity. It is still a public place—locally, nationally, globally—as demonstrated by the unprecedented crowd gathered there to celebrate the millennial New Year's Eve. It is the place where thousands marched in honor of Martin Luther King, Jr., in 1998. It

14.2
Combustible energy. (Alan Batt)

14.3
Density on the ground as well as in the towers. (Gary Hack)

is the place where Jerry Seinfeld unsuccessfully sought to televise his final-episode bash that same year only to be thwarted by Mayor Rudolph Giuliani, who judged that closing down the place for an entire day was likely to create too much confusion, even for Times Square. It is the apocalyptic site for "Military Takeover of New York City," a six-minute work of fiction in film made as a mock lesson of what it would take to provoke a midtown riot. To the astonishment of redevelopment officials, it is also the place where the National Rifle Association plans to open a restaurant and game arcade. However outrageous the advocacy of gun-related entertainment as a means of promoting its anti–gun control position, the NRA has targeted Times Square precisely because it is such a visible public venue. The 10019 and 10036 zip codes that make up the Times Square BID demand 3,500 public telephones—never, it seems, with one working when and where you need it. The identifiable picture-postcard crossroads of New York is the quintessential urban place, which is to say, it is not predicable, however cleaned up it looks, however familylike its new activities.

The journalists' accounts do not fully embrace the new reality of Times Square. Nor do the critics' models always fit; most reveal more personal biases than informed insights. A wistful nostalgic romanticism for what Times Square offered in the past or a skeptical ruefulness toward the inevitable change brought about by development shades many a commentary. In others, a bias against the middle-class attractiveness of the renovation lies beneath the surface, recasting in fresh language a long-standing discomfort among elites with middle-class values in the context of urbane

New York. Ironically, the class-based criticism of the cleanup has come full circle from the class-bias argument initially put forth by Herbert J. Gans that shutting down the many low-cost action movie theaters of West 42nd Street amounted to discrimination against lower and middle-class patrons, especially minorities. Most notably, the existing commentary misses the revisionist story on the politics of urban development post–Robert Moses, and, consequently, one of the most salient messages of renewal.

As the nation's greatest builder of the public realm, Moses and his 50-year legacy cast a gigantic shadow on the processes of public development, even after losing his hold on government in 1968. His methods—arrogant exercise of power, financial secrecy, skillful media-making, ruthless bulldozing—more than his goals provoked intense debate, as did his contempt for too much public discussion, which he contended, as *Times* editorialist Roger Starr put it, "wasted valuable time and could doom a needed development rather than improve it."[3] With the introduction of environmental-impact statements, community-board recommendations, and class-action lawsuits, the process by which New York and other cities was being rebuilt shifted 180 degrees from what had prevailed during Moses's long regime and, with it, the politics of development. "The problem for local government today," Starr wrote on the centennial of Moses's birth, "is not that an official like Robert Moses may wield excessive power so much as whether anyone has the power to complete essential public works, given the complex process of approval, consultation and review." In the same vein, architectural critic Paul Goldberger remarked that "the balance of power in development has moved dramatically away from those who build, whether they are public builders like Moses or private builders, and toward those who oppose building, or least oppose the virtual carte blanche that Moses was known for."[4] In surmounting a set of obstacles that had previously felled other city projects, the ultimately successful execution of the 42nd Street Development Project rewrote the lesson plan on large-scale urban projects. The achievement erased a brooding sense of failure and limiting scope of imagination that had shadowed city hall in the aftermath of Westway and the collapse of the Columbus Circle project. It created a new story line—public-sector success—and definitively marked an era of city building in New York post-Moses that spanned the rest of the twentieth century.

MEDIA MARKETPLACE

Beginning on Broadway between 42nd and 45th Streets (location for Condé Nast, Nasdaq, Reuters America Holdings, Disney, The New York Times, Nickelodeon, Billboard Publications, Bertelsmann A.G., MTV Networks, ABC's "Good Morning America"), moving uptown to 50th Street (Viacom, PolyGram, Hachette Filipacchi Magazines, Children's Television Workshop, Paramount Pictures, Showtime Entertainment Group, Simon and Schuster, Tribeca Communications), then further north (past "The Late Show with David Letterman" in the CBS Studio Ed

Sullivan Theater, Random House's new headquarters under construction, EMI Records) to 59th Street and Columbus Circle (where AOL Time Warner will occupy new headquarters in late 2003), before ending a few blocks still further uptown at the northern edge of Lincoln Center (ABC Television Studios), this mile-plus stretch of Manhattan's longest street, might well be called Communications Mile to denote its economic marquee as the corporate corridor for the city's newest engine of economic growth (figures 14.4a,b).

New York has long enjoyed a concentration of firms in publishing, communications, and advertising, what is now called traditional media, well above the U.S. average. More recently, it has also benefited handsomely from explosive job growth in "new media," defined by the local industry association as combining "elements of computer technology, telecommunications and content . . . to create products and services which can be used 'interactively' by consumers and businesses."[5] New media first achieved elevated status as the boom sector of the city's economy in a spurt of rapid growth between 1995 and 1997 when new-media jobs in New York doubled, reaching 55,973 and accounting for 38 percent of the

14.4
Production studios on Broadway, once again. (Gary Hack)

city's net job creation. During the next two years, new media jobs in New York grew at an even more rapid pace, 147 percent, to reach 138,258. An economic wunderkind born only five years ago, new media appears to be challenging the city's traditional job engine, Wall Street, whose ranking among the fastest-growing job categories dropped to fifth in 1999 and whose job creation accounted for less than one quarter of that year's employment growth in New York.[6]

Silicon Alley—the recently named, funky part of downtown Manhattan radiating from new media's ground-zero location on Broadway at Houston Street and coalescing at 23rd Street in the Flatiron District—is the locus of the Internet-based industry, which draws its workers from a number of professional fields including computer programming, web-site design, systems development, and journalism. The creative-content people for the new-media industry, though, are clustering in the West 50s. That is where the giant content companies like Viacom International and Bertelsmann A.G., among others, are located as well as the smaller companies such as E! Entertainment Television. Boosters for midtown west like the Times Square BID call attention to the fact that the area is attracting a recognizable share of the city's new-media firms, yet as two research economists at the New York Federal Reserve Board have pointed out, new media may well have a bigger influence on the city's economy via job growth within the city's traditional-media firms. These firms, property leasing data show, have been clustering in and around Times Square. By the end of 1999, of the 20 million square feet of office space rented by the largest media-related companies in Manhattan, nearly 60 percent was in the midtown west corridor between Sixth Avenue and Eighth Avenue, from 42nd Street to 66th Street.

The media companies, communications concerns, and advertising firms that "went west" early had no problem with the image of being on Broadway, an address that until only recently marked an off-beat corporate location. The lack of office space in midtown east provided the push and the availability of large blocks of relatively low-cost space in midtown west, the pull. Now the pull is pure location. Architecturally transformed during the 1980s from what journalist David W. Dunlap described as "a heterogeneous mix of old theaters and rag-tag commercial structures into a chilling canyon of hard-edged skyscrapers,"[7] the towers of Times Square cut a skyward profile distinct from the staid discipline and minimalist geometry of the International-Style corporate corridor of midtown's Sixth Avenue. Though high density and commercial in function, Times Square's skyscrapers show the influence, in a subtle fashion toned down for corporate acceptance, of their disorderly and theatrical context—in the blues, greens, pinks, and reds of their facades; sky-piercing finials, far-reaching communication antennas, soaring silver needles, and steeple-sharp peaks—and of the city's design regulations that call for large billboards and glitzy, kinetic supersigns. Constants like the Paramount Building (1501 Broadway), the Art-Deco emblem of Times Square with its setbacks (figure 14.5), great glass globe, and signature clock refurbished and relit; and the music-tenanted Brill Building (1619 Broadway), known as "Tin Pan Alley under one roof," with its strongly geometric relief work and busts of the developer and his son, sit squat and solid amid the fashionable interlopers. The area's architectural stew of notable and nondescript survivors, landmarked theaters, prominent towers of the 1980s, and undistinguished buildings of the 1960s—better today with a camouflage of supersigns—defies easy classification. Its eclecticism fits the cultural legacy of the district and comports with Broadway's diagonal defiance of Manhattan's rigid street grid.

14.5
The enduring sky profile of the Paramount Building. (David W. Dunlap, *On Broadway: A Journey Uptown Over Time*)

The big four—Condé Nast, Reuters, Bertelsmann A.G., Viacom International—account for two thirds of the media industry's real estate presence in Times Square, though this is only part of the story. Media central for the industry giants also serves a myriad of small production companies and specialized business services. A large and intense beehive of small media and entertainment-related firms taking up relatively small amounts of space, each less than 10,000 square feet, has materialized in three office towers (1500, 1501, and 1560 Broadway), two of which stand face-to-face across Broadway. The density of many small service businesses and production companies makes for a physical presence disproportionate to their relatively small command of real estate—at year-end 1999, 59 percent of the 142 media and entertainment-related firms in Times Square accounted for approximately 3 percent of media's leased space in Times Square.[8] As providers of specialized, high-skilled services, these firms are the new infrastructure of the information economy. Their location in Times Square proximate to the media and entertainment giants illustrates the more generalized logic being put forth by a few leading academics that cities hold distinct comparative advantages—agglomeration economies and innovative environments—as key sites for the production of business services.[9]

In an age of advanced information technologies, the concentrated clustering of global media firms and specialized business services presents something of a paradox. Business services—accounting, advertising, legal services, economic consulting, engineering and management services, public relations, design, and printing, among others—along with other traditional sectors of employment might be expected to bypass the high rents, expenses, and congestion typical of big cities such as New York. That logic, however, best suits the older manufacturing economy where business services played more of an ancillary role. In today's information economy, highly specialized services are embedded in value-added processes of production; they are essential inputs and referred to as "producer services." Accordingly, the tendency of specialized business services to cluster holds renewed significance for the future of cities. It means, sociologist Saskia Sassen has pointed out, that the oft-heard argument that high-level professionals need face-to-face interactions calls for some refinement.

Business services are not necessarily dependent upon spatial proximity to the firms they serve, argues Sassen. "Rather, economies occur in such specialized firms when they locate close to others that produce key inputs or whose proximity makes possible joint production of certain service offerings." The accounting firm, and likewise the advertising, economic consulting, or public relations firm, can service its clients at a distance, but the nature of its service depends on proximity to a range of specialists. "Frequently, what is thought of as face-to-face communications is actually a production process that requires multiple simultaneous inputs and feedbacks. At the current stage of technological development, having immediate and simultaneous access to the pertinent experts is still the most effective way to operate, particularly when dealing with a highly complex product."[10] Moreover, this tendency of specialized business services to cluster in cities draws on a calculus beyond cost efficiency and timeliness of delivery. What Sassen argues, and others are beginning to explain with empirical evidence, is that the people who are likely to be employed in these high-skill jobs tend to be attracted to the amenities and lifestyles that large urban centers can offer.

Although advanced communication technologies have made geographic bounds irrelevant and distance a state of mind—and despite the negative prognosis for cities often put forth by technology forecasters—the global media industry continues to concentrate facilities in New York or Los Angeles because that is where the creative professionals are. "The increasingly specialized knowledge necessary for innovation and coordination within the industry heightens the importance of traditional centers," Sassen and coauthor Frank Roost wrote in an article about the global entertainment industry.[11] Increasing globalization has made doing business more complex. Like the finance industry, the media industry demands access to highly specialized inputs: top-level specialists and advanced technology, creative professional talent, the preexistence of a vast business-services sector. All are available in global cities such as New York, where the concentration of talent makes Manhattan the most efficient place for corporate and creative processes that depend on complex face-to-face dealings, especially when time is of the essence. This is why new media executives continue to be optimistic about New York's role as the global content capital of the new media industry. "Consulting and content companies need to be in New York," one industry executive explained. "This is where the talent is, where the intellectual capital is, as well as where traditional media is headquartered." "The work force is extremely driven," remarked another. "New York cultivates this attitude. The culture of New York is particularly well suited to the speed with which this industry is growing."[12] In short, New York has become the strategic site for the global media industry, which relies increasingly on costly cutting-edge information technology. Its economic role, as well as that of other cities, is being redefined by the technological revolution in communications. The new Times Square symbolizes this transformation—in legendary style, with the world's largest and most expensive video screen fashioned in the form of an eight-story cylindrical tower anchoring the Condé Nast building (Four Times Square) at 43rd Street and Broadway (figure 14.6).

As an employment node, the diversity of the new Times Square reflects a highly concatenated mix of the new and the old: new media

14.6
Condé Nast Building, Fox & Fowle Architects. (Andrew Gordon Photography, Inc.)

businesses housed inside traditional media conglomerates, financial services wearing the traditional stripes of blue-chip investment banks while promoting real-time information on state-of-the-technology supersigns, advanced multimedia retail outlets like the Virgin Megastore in trying-to-awe entertainment formats, live-broadcast studios like MTV geared to global distribution, and live-theater from Disney benchmarked in Times Square for the same reason, plus a host of time-tested but newly minted place-based people services for tourists and workers. The business-services infrastructure upon which the global media industry depends accounts for the largest single source of employment in the Times Square BID (11.4 percent), followed by retail trade and banking and finance (each, 9.9 percent) and entertainment services (8.1 percent). When these employment numbers are combined into broader categories descriptive of clusters of economic activity, the leading driver of employment in Times Square, not unexpectedly, is place-based people services—retail trade, hotels, eating and drinking establishments—which account for 21.6 percent of the district's total employment as of 1998, the last year for which data are currently available.[13] Though the "suits"—jobs classified by economic statisticians as FIRE (financial services, insurance and real estate)—housed in the district's towering office buildings dominate the visual image of the new employment pattern, in fact, they make up only 17 percent of the district's employment. Their presence, though, will dramatically increase with the completion and occupancy of the Ernst & Young tower and the fourth office tower above the MTA station entrance.

There is much irony in the identity of who and what makes up the new Times Square. The jobs data indicate the marketplace's expectation for servicing the millions of visitors to Times Square—some 27 million people or more, 74 percent of those who visited New York City in 1999—who spend up to $11.6 billion in the process. The data also suggest a dynamic day-to-day diversity of activity that owes much to the office towers that some critics feel have destroyed the area's character. One has to ask, without the new cluster of media companies and related business services, might not the district have become a singularly tourist-dominated district of consumption and play, an outcome that most undoubtedly would have been subsequently attacked with equal fervor by perhaps the same critics?

TOUCHSTONE SYMBOLISM

As a tourist center Times Square functions much as it did in the early part of the twentieth century when tourism became a conscious pursuit of urban areas in general and stamped an indelible commercial mark on the development of Times Square in particular. As in the past, people from abroad, the tristate area, and elsewhere in the United States come to experience the place and say they've been there, buy souvenirs and other merchandise to bring home, eat or dine, go to theater, or simply walk the crowd-filled streets at night to witness the hustle and bustle of urban life

14.7
Postcard image marketing mid-
town's attractions, ca 1905.
(Collection of Bruce J. McCuen)

(figures 14.7 and 14.8). The venues of today differ but not the enduring
nature of the desire to be entertained: "Urban tourists knew what they
wanted and art museums were not high on the list. The many visitors
patronizing the hotels, restaurants, and roof gardens of midtown New
York, the summer buyers and their entourages had other things on their
minds. And these were dominated by pleasure rather than by culture."[14]

The fact that tourism aided New York's growing economy then
as it does today only sharpened a natural tension that existed between
tourists and local residents. "The urban tourist, out for fun, free-spending,
gullible, more caught up by department stores than museums and libraries,
simultaneously caricatured and nurtured the local sensibility," social historian Neil Harris explained insightfully. "The tourist presence flattered
New York as a world center, and demonstrated the knowledge-ability and
sophistication of the natives. But the tourist was also the whipping boy for
aspects of commercial culture that residents were not proud of, and which
excited occasional envy, contempt, and indignation. Fame brought inconvenience (and traffic jams). And spectatorship meant playing for the crowd.
New York was on stage and Times Square had become the centerpiece.
One's attitude to tourists," Harris concluded, "was, in short, a touchstone
of one's attitude to the new commercial culture generally."[15]

The new Times Square retains all the traits of a "touchstone." The
complexity of cacophonous activity making up the reality of the place
belies the easy assertions that it is an "urban theme park," a "fantasy city," a
"privatized" reserve transplanted from the suburbs only purporting to be a
public place or "like the organizations of consumption everywhere else in
the world," no longer a site of local consumption. Much of this type of

14.8
Luggage memento saying "I've
been there." ca. 1930s. (Collection
of the author)

commentary is being put forth on the basis of casual observation or super-ficial discourse about the place from academic critics who might be expected to look closely and analytically at the results, if not the process, of Times Square's transformation. Another tendency, trying to fit a critique of Times Square into the prevailing analytical construct about the role of tourism in economic development, similarly misses the mark, at least when measured against the political and economic motives that gave rise to the initial set of place-transforming initiatives.[16] Cleaning up West 42nd Street was never an economic-development strategy designed to enhance tourism in New York; cleaning up the social problems and enhancing the growth of the financial services sector was. Although Times Square's dual role as a place of production (media marketplace) as well as consumption (entertainment) is noted by both Sassen and Susan S. Fainstein, two of the more frequently published academic commentators on this topic, neither quite knows what to make of the conflicting images presented by the new Times Square and the new 42nd Street, and this more than anything seems to reflect a bias of perception rooted in many an intellectual's dis-comfort with mass culture and an ideological suspicion of big business.

Sassen and Roost argue, for example, that theme restaurants and corporate stores are artificial because they are marketing avenues for cor-porate profits, notwithstanding what consumers might feel about these places or products, and because their location is not based on the city's inherent attractiveness but rather on its position as a venue for global dis-tribution. Acknowledging that Times Square offers both the artificial (theme restaurants) and the real (television production studios), they remain skeptical of the success of "this unique mixture of media produc-tion and traditional tourist destination." The allure, they conclude, derives from urban culture being experienced as a growing object of consump-tion, with more and more people living in the suburbs, a city like New York has become "an exotic object of tourism increasingly mediated through the entertainment industry," especially when entertainment can be provided in a unique place like Times Square.[17]

In a similar vein, Fainstein and coauthor Robert Stokes put forth a more widespread conception that the legacy of West 42nd Street is threatened by a pervasive corporate presence, in particular Disney's brand of corporate-inspired entertainment which will cater to the tastes of a mass market. "The fact that what is being offered has not just been Disneyfied but, in fact, involves Disney itself means that the sex and sophistication which once characterized the area's theatrical productions will be replaced by productions deemed acceptable for middle America." Imports like Madame Tussaud's, Sony's Cinemax theaters, and London-based musicals such as *Phantom of the Opera, Les Misérables,* and *Miss Saigon* are equally problematic because "rather than New York setting the model of artistic production emulated by the rest of the world, it is being imprinted by the standardized tourist product developed elsewhere."[18] Allowing for some weakness in their argument, they speculate that "New York's seemingly limitless ability to absorb and transmute outside influences may yet triumph over the mundane," and that "the story of 42nd Street redevelopment might, like any Disney production, have a happy ending." Too obsessed with the Disney factor to look beyond the street, they conclude that the city effectively has no other choice: "Maintenance of its position of dominance in the world of popular culture is essential to the future of New York. Disneyfication and multimedia production represents the leading edge of mass entertainment," and "despite the scorn of high-brow critics, New York cannot afford to opt out of this trend." What do they believe augurs West 42nd Street's "happy ending"? "The scale and concentration of activity, which will put it in a class by itself rather than making it a mere replication of other entertainment districts."[19]

Whether intellectual or journalistic, the discourse about the transformation of Times Square comes laden with varying degrees of angst. It is divisively driven on one front by a passionate nostalgia whose "theme is Paradise Lost"[20] and, on the other, by an ultrasensitivity to the high-profile presence of the Walt Disney Company, corporate juggernaut. While entertaining as an ongoing series of opinion pieces written with occasional verve and wit, the polarized debate eliminates the opportunity to understand the reality of change that lies between the two symbolic extremes and their visual imagery.

Nostalgic Angst

For most of the past century, Times Square has been a place of illusion and fantasy, where the view backward conveniently benchmarked the present and not infrequently appeared better. In its own magical way, the "golden age" has advanced decade by decade, from the 1910s and 1920s to the 1930s and 1940s, and, depending upon who is talking, the 1960s, 1970s, and even the 1980s become treasure troves of nostalgic memories. "Indeed, Times Square has the capacity to engender a 'discourse of nostalgia' that floats freely and unites people with radically different views of the Square and the world: people . . . who are nostalgic for the great days of Helen Hayes and Alfred Lunt and Lynn Fontanne; people . . . who are nostalgic for the years of Winchell, Runyon, and *Guys and Dolls*; people . . . who are nostalgic for the pre-AIDS golden age of hustling." Nostalgia, as urbanist Marshall Berman provocatively baited the audience in a keynote speech at a Columbia University symposium on the new Times Square, has been amazingly pervasive "as an organizing force for visions of the place."[21]

Today's voices of lament are many.[22] First, there are the "wistfuls," who reflect fondly on the experiences they had in Times Square. They are nostalgic for what Times Square used to offer; at the same time, they usually realize their memories are time-bound, representative of a finite period that inevitably had to end. They are not bitter about the changes, which some view as progress. "We lose as we gain," one wistful said. "Times Square had grown ugly and squalid and uninviting, but it was never dead. And though new life is being brought to it, as the developers are fond of saying, it bears repeating that what is being replaced, covered up or eased out is also life."[23] "Some of the street has been lost to time," another recalled, but "as much as we mourn Horn & Hardart with its unmatched rice pudding, I doubt that today many of us would plop down, without permission, at an occupied table and have a three-course meal"[24] (figure 14.9).

Then there are the "skeptics." They are suspicious of the changes taking place, and often revert to the old Times Square, which they find preferable to the present. Since their suspicions stem from various sources and take various shapes, this is a diverse group. One laments the loss of military hell-raising in Times Square as a symbol of the area's deadening: "When I first got into the Navy in '83, we'd pull into town, get drunk, raise hell, chase every woman and see what you could get away with. There were always all-you-can-drink parties for us . . . no one even gets a tattoo anymore"[25] Another, suspicious of the powers overseeing the project, is rueful of what he perceives to be irresponsible carelessness in the treatment of the "ornamental terra-cotta facade" of the venerable Selwyn theater that had been "fetishized by the Times Square redevelopment crowd." "The people who dug up the block said, when the dust settled, they they'd never had any warning [about the facade's imminent collapse]. They later revised this story to more closely fit the facts. . . . Over the past decade, architects from the city, and architects from Robert A. M. Stern's office, under contract to the city, meticulously surveyed and measured the Selwyn and other historical theaters on 42nd Street, to what particular effect it's now hard to imagine. . . . Now where the Selwyn once stood, there's a gaping metaphor"[26] (figure 14.10).

Another set, the "retrogrades," voice intense personalized outrage at the intentional destruction of West 42nd Street. They celebrate the

14.9
Postcard image of "The automat as famous as the New York skyline itself." (Collection of Bruce J. McCuen)

14.10
The venerable Selwyn Theater,
1989. (© 2001 Maggie Hopp)

memory of the street as the ideal spot for commercial sex and for the type of "casual" contact that made for "noncommercial" gay encounters as well. They celebrate the memory of Times Square as an "Empire of Tawdriness," lamenting the loss of its "authenticity" and resenting its replacement with a "State of Fun."[27] Fueled by a suspicion of collective action, the retrogrades' anger is directed at the "machinations" of developers who are hell-bent on "doing as much demolition and renovation as possible in the neighborhood, and as much construction work as they possibly can,"[28] or at the government-driven clean-up operation run by a "coalition of moralists, planners, and a nostalgia-driven entertainment giant." Better that Times Square should have "died a 'natural' death."[29]

Nostalgia wafts through other sets of commentary, though not as an indictment of the district's change, but rather as a memory trip designed to recall the associations of people and places that gave identity and life to Times Square and bound people to its legacy of insouciance. There are the "reminders" who bring up undiscussed issues (the havoc that progress can wreak, further marginalizing the marginalized), record human-interest stories (accounts of the "little guy" being pushed out of the impersonal and aggressive new Times Square), and, without histrionics, inform the public of things that otherwise might be lost without so much as a remembrance (pinball arcades, pool halls, Kung-fu movies, boxing clubs, dance auditoriums, architecture gone or going soon, little enterprises that fed the show business world). Also, there are the "resilients" who sometimes lament the losses of New York history and sometimes are skeptical about the new portions, but are ultimately optimistic; their optimism comes from faith in the city's unpredictable ways. They see the New York spirit as more potent that any change occurring in the area. "Times Square is a bratty place, unlikely to obey any official vision, and likely to buck the odds. . . . 'Chaos will take care of itself.'"[30] They truly love the city. Sad over losses and a touch concerned, reporters of this bent have a tendency to interview seasoned veterans of the area, resilients like themselves who "do not miss the human misery so prevalent in the Times Square of a generation ago," believe that "If you live in the past, you might as well go to Frank Campbell's funeral home and say, 'Bury me,'" and feel that "All the activity, all the lights. . . . It just makes you glad to be here."[31]

"And so, yes, Times Square has been drained of its old life," wrote James Traub in a recent *New York Times Magazine* article on the city and psyche Mayor Giuliani will leave behind. "But let's remember what that life had come to be—not the raffish New York of A. J. Liebling and Joe Mitchell but a mean and menacing precinct where you wouldn't even think to take a tourist." The old "street ballet" of urban life that had characterized New York's public places had been degraded into what historian Fred Siegel called "roller derby." The new global-entertainment complex will not restore the street ballet, he concluded, "but it offers an acceptable version of urban life to New Yorkers who had grown weary of roller derby."[32]

The *Times* architectural critic Herbert Muschamp is a borderline "enthusiastic" for the new Times Square. His tack on the Times Square nostalgia is pragmatic and positive:[33]

> Nostalgie de la boue—the sentimental attachment to decrepitude and sleaze—is a venerable urban tradition, and it probably accounts for some of the negative reaction to the retail and entertainment strip now taking shape on 42d Street between Seventh and Eighth Avenues. . . . We had a world class gutter here. Must we trade it in for a shopping strip of chain retail outlets? . . . Already it is evident that more than one kind of nostalgia will be available for those who visit the area.

Muschamp categorizes three types of nostalgia: a "Babes in Toyland" form of childhood innocence, a sentimental ersatz view of New York's past as a kinder, more innocent time, and the infernal Times Square—and admits to being a fan of all three. As a resilient, he sees the soul of New York coming through even the campiest Times Square. "I was delighted to see people like that taking in a part of town that I love. Besides, I found myself thinking, there is always the hope that children might not be fooled by all this innocence stuff, that they'd find a way to be utterly corrupted by city life before nightfall, just as I was when I was their age."[34]

Enthusiasts champion the developments in Times Square. They enter the discourse on nostalgia because they chide it as a luxury of good times, only possible because the destitution and depravity of the past have been eliminated. The most visible spokesperson for this view is Mayor Giuliani. "Some people romanticize the way things were 5 or 10 years ago," he said in a 1998 speech announcing the second phase of his "quality of life" campaign for New York. "They have nostalgia for the old Times Square, for example. They think it was somehow charming to have graffiti on every wall and sex shops on every block. But remember what it was really like. Remember the fear, and the disrespect for people's rights that went unchecked in that climate. . . . We didn't become the city people most want to live in and visit by encouraging an atmosphere of disorder and disrespect for the rights of others"[35] (figure 14.11). A cleaned-up Times Square similarly has brought the luxury of immortalizing versions of the past in theater and anecdote and, most recently, plans for a Museum of Sex (MoSex), all one step removed from reality—sanitized sex turned commercial and stylized. It is not unlike other vices that people "no longer think of as sinful but rather as a way to accessorize," wrote *Times* columnist Maureen Dowd about the broader domestication of vice: Vices as affectations and entertainments "are perfect for our times."[36]

The varied voices of nostalgia reflect Times Square's many layers of symbolic meaning. The roots of this nostalgia stem from both feelings of individual loss and concern with the cultural role of Times Square as a city icon. Also at play is something of Harris's touchstone factor. New York has always stood out from the rest of the country in sophistication, size, intensity, pace—especially in its own mind. Times Square's new status as a "safe designation" can readily make New Yorkers wonder if the city is going "soft," losing some of its legendary toughness.

> As entertainment conglomerates increasingly grasped the mar-
> ketability of the idea of New York itself, some New Yorkers
> feared that Times Square and other talismanic way stations in the
> city were in danger of becoming eerily detached, corporately
> administered simulacra of their former selves—historic spaces
> neutered of all idiosyncracy, cunningly remodeled to fit the idea
> of what they had once had been, then packaged and sold as 'the
> New York experience' to flocks of tourists in a tightly controlled
> commercial environment.[37]

The sentiment caught by Ric Burns and James Sanders is exacer-
bated by increasing tourism, making it more difficult for New Yorkers to establish a pattern or ritual about the place, further alienating those living and working in Times Square. Chronic nostalgia is a crippling, destructive force, however. It too often depends on the disparagement of the present.

"I assume it's a different Rudy."

•

It does not advance our understanding of the history-making in the new Times Square because it does not allow a view of possibilities beyond the past. Even at its best, when sincere and inclusive, nostalgia too often substitutes sentiment for critical analysis. The same affliction affects the discourse about Disney.

The Mouse Demonized

A couple of years before the entertainment giant even consented to talk about a presence on West 42nd Street, the respected preservationist Brendan Gill declared Times Square to be full of new high-rises that "look as if they were intended to serve not as the proud adornments of a great city but as the flashy centerpieces of an instant Disneyland." The eight to ten new skyscrapers, he complained, have made Times Square into a new version of Wall Street; "a calculatedly gimcrack Potemkin village has emerged from the ruin of its lively disorderly predecessor." Gill hated the fact that city-inspired land-use changes had turned what was "truly a place of entertainment" into "a cold-blooded corporate simulacrum of an amusement park designed to contain millions of square feet of offices filled with tens of thousands of office drones."[38] He felt his beloved city was endangered, and what better epithet to employ for dramatic and immediately identifiable imagery?

"Disneyfication" is a powerful and encompassing charge because it triggers many flash points of sensibility among the American public: the age-old American push and pull with big business, as in a suspicion of Disney's sheer size and agenda ("the insatiable global empire that has grown from the parks in Anaheim and Orlando, to Paris and Tokyo, then to major urban projects such as the 42nd Street development in New

York. . . . Mickey's innocent grin barely conceals an insatiable corporate appetite"[39]) and its precedent-setting power ("Disney's interest carries clout beyond the reach of [ordinary] would-be developers"[40]), as well as the fear that omnipotent corporate power will erode individualism ("Square in the middle is where it [Disney] wants us to be, dependable consumers with predictable attitudes"[41]).

A lone voice here and there expressed the belief that the neighborhood was not in jeopardy of being Disneyfied. "Why?" wrote Karrie Jacobs for *New York* magazine. "Because the term implies that an alien force has colonized us and is building amusement facilities against our will, places that express something contrary to what the city is about." The redevelopment, she points out, is "homegrown." Tishman, Ratner, Durst, and now Rudin are New York developers. So too are most of the architects: Robert A. M. Stern, Tibor Kalman, Hardy Holzman Pfeiffer, Platt Byard Dovell, Beyer Blinder Belle, Design Collaborative of New York, Kohn Petersen Fox, David Rockwell. She called the new Times Square "spiffy, but it isn't Disneyland and it never will be." Because it referenced American culture, she saw the place as "New York's only laboratory of twenty-first-century architecture."[42]

Disney is just so easy to target—between the public sensitivity to its formidable impact on American culture and the inescapable irony of its presence on West 42nd Street. In Times Square, it was bizarre enough to think about substituting innocence for depravity; to have Disney involved in the transformation created endless opportunities for hyperbole. And the two have fed off of one another, intensifying the anti-Disney prejudices. A rage-filled charge of Disneyfication in the absence of critical scrutiny, though, represents loose intellectualism. The rage, Marshall Berman pointed out in the revised article of his remarks, but not at the Columbia symposium itself, "is based partly on an accurate view of Walt Disney's racist and xenophobic right-wing career, but also on prejudices of our own: prejudices of many intellectuals against mass culture, prejudices of seltzer against orange juice, of ethnic easterners against middle America, of New York against the world." Admitting that he was likely to "fight for most of them," he argued, not for the first time, that "they could stand some critical scrutiny." As an example, he noted that hard evidence is lacking on the issue of whether Giuliani's "vendetta" against the small sex businesses was one of the concessions the city made to Disney, as rumor has it. Whatever the true story, "We need to look to our house, to New York's own volatile political culture, so receptive to mobilizations of bias and outbursts of bad faith."[43]

The initial apprehension over the "Disney factor" was real, especially in that two-year interim period between the hyped announcement of a firm commitment to the renovation of the New Amsterdam and the actual experience of a live-theater production in the refurbished and newly revered landmark, when, as described in chapter 11, Disney was angling for synergistic business opportunities all over New York. The super-rich, ultra-American, squeaky-clean image of Disney, whose corporate record of theme-park development was one of total control, vaulted homogeneity, and profits-driven synergy—distinguished by a marketing formula for taking content and making it product, "which leaves little room for idiosyncrasy or local flavor"[44]—generated legitimate anxiety even among the most balanced of proponents of the 42DP: Would the family-safe block lack the vibrant and unpredictable heterogeneity that defined its seedy and raffish past?

"That hurly burly is itself erotic," wrote *Times* columnist Frank Rich; "it's what turns us on as we watch those crowds in Times Square each New Year's."[45] The next year he wrote: "Disney is the mouse that swallowed American culture—with culture being defined not just by the media of movies, TV and journalism but by the esthetics of our national life." The mouse's reach was ever-expanding. In signaling the arrival of a "mall sensibility" on what was once a "quintessential urban block," the Disney store on West 42nd Street personified "the essence of Disneyfication—the substitution of what the writer James Howard Kunstler calls 'the tragic falsehood of Hollywood for an indigenous American reality.'"[46] That was the palpable fear of many Manhattan residents, especially intellectuals. Middle-class residents of Queens and Brooklyn and Staten Island and the Bronx, however, were not as likely to have viewed the situation in quite the same way.

The worst fears of Disneyfication are unlikely to come to pass, for several reasons. For starters, the thousands of people who come to Times Square cannot be drawn there solely by Disney; they are coming for pleasures and entertainment beyond what is available at Disney theme parks and beyond what is available more generally in the suburbs. The tens of thousands of suits and workers in the offices of Times Square have little to do with Disney or tourism (figures 14.11, 14.12). Moreover, to criticize the banality of Disney culture or castigate the synergy strategy that puts Disney's live-theater productions "squarely in the middle of the Disney corporate network of consumer performance . . . like theme-park performance"[47] is to miss one of the essential points bearing on the future evolution of Times Square as an entertainment district. This is the "X-factor," Rich argued at the Columbia symposium, "what brought everybody to Times Square in the first place: the theater."[48] That the theater is so troubled a business is the bad news. The good news, he explained, is that tastes are changing and big-production musicals like *Cats!* and *Les Mis* are no longer ensured indefinite tenure as box-office hits. In the light of the emergence of "Broadway's new erogenous zone" with its enormously successful home-grown musicals like *Rent, Bring In da Noise, Bring In da Funk,* and *Chicago,* fears that a Disney-dominated formula would bring only pablum to Broadway are less realistic.[49] Pitched to adults and with more sexuality that Disney or Andrew Lloyd Webber productions, these generationally smart shows amount to the market saying it is not satisfied with a Disney street today. And that, Rich believed, is related to the broader issue of sex in Times Square—which has always been a factor of attraction, even before the Broadway theater industry was built. "When the *New York Times* moved in at the turn of the century . . . people were selling dirty pictures and switchblades, so I'm not convinced that Disneyfication is a foregone conclusion and that sexuality can be stamped out by Giuliani any more than it was by LaGuardia."[50]

Then there is the future of Eighth Avenue and its environs. Forty-second Street is not an island unto itself. The transformation of Times Square, in combination with New York's unprecedented economic resurgence has impacted other neighborhoods and none seem more strategic than the immediate area west (Clinton) and south (the Garment District) of West 42nd Street. What happens in the near term in these areas where new commercial and entertainment activity is already underway will be crucial to assessing whether Disney takes New York or New York takes Disney, the odds on the latter being more favorable. Three large projects on the corners of Eighth Avenue and 42nd Street have yet to be developed, including a proposed office tower atop the Port Authority Bus Terminal (figures 14.13, 14.14). Moreover, not because of intense politics, not because of iconographic power, but rather because of powerful eco-

14.12
The antecedents of mass entertainment in Times Square: postcard images of the Hippodrome (1905) and Ripley's odditorium (1939). (Collection of Bruce J. McCuen; collection of the author)

14.13
Yet to be developed: the northwest corner of Eighth Avenue and 42nd Street. (Gary Hack)

nomic forces being driven by the current vitality of the city's economy, the large amount of acreage west of Times Square, underdeveloped from a real estate perspective, is likely to undergo intense pressure for reuse and redevelopment in the coming decade. The pressure of expansion stretching westward all the way to the Hudson River reflects a powerful momentum because it comes from all possible directions: Times Square to the east; Columbus Circle to the north; and the Garment Center to the south, where expanding new-media businesses are locating. How this potential economic resurgence affects the evolution of the new Times Square in the decade ahead remains to be seen. But the convergent power of economics, consumer preferences, and political will to foster further development is a potent force for market innovation.

The public debate about the new Times Square has been terribly distorted. As set up, the discourse either extols the glories of the old Times Square, including the "celebration of the crummy and degraded sex-bazaar as it is," or decries the coming of "Disneyland, symbolized by that hairless, sexless mouse." This is a "false choice," Michael Sorkin succinctly emphasized. Sorkin was right on point in arguing that this all-or-nothing approach "is anathema to what has been best about Times Square—its complexity, unpredictability, louche charm, and yes, its concentration of sexual energy." In concluding that Times Square's "conversion to another version of the recursion of Vegas . . . must be blamed squarely not simply on the energetic advocates of sanitized fun but on our own failures to propose a better idea," he sidesteps what he rightly recognizes as central to the legacy of the place: defining how to regain the sexual energy and disreputability of the symbolic Times Square—if, in fact, it truly has been lost.[51]

If as an entertainment venue West 42nd Street comes off as being too intensely conventional—a nostalgia-oriented place packed with 38 movie screens, a wax museum, four Broadway theaters, and lots of restaurants and retail activity centers, but missing the kinds of technologically advanced entertainments representative of the twenty-first century—the

14.14
Site of a future office tower atop the Port Authority Bus Terminal. (Gary Hack)

problem stems from the political exigencies of the rescripted plan, *42nd Street Now!* Driven by an immediate need to bring forth a new vision for the street after the project had collapsed along with the market for commercial development, the plan relied almost exclusively on visual aesthetics, rather than outlining a provocative program for innovative content. It was part of a process geared to rebuilding political support for the controversial project through new but comfortably safe images evocative of Times Square's symbolic legacy, carefully and professionally supported by intensely detailed design guidelines. As a political document, the new vision aimed to heal controversy, build anew a coalition of support, and market a set of hopes that, at the time, seemed improbable. In other words, the plan was not a content-driven call for innovative programming that aimed to cultivate cutting-edge entertainments, though Robertson and her colleagues probably would have welcomed such uses. Rather, the visual razzle-dazzle of the images sought to assure key decision makers in government and business and, most important, the civics, that the 42DP was now firmly aligned with the historic symbolism of Times Square. Ironically, therein lay its limitation.

As much as *42nd Street Now!* guaranteed that public officials would be ready to proceed when the market recovered, in hindsight, the entertainment array on the new 42nd Street—relative to technologically empowered entertainment showing elsewhere, at the animated Bellevue Studios in the Music Box at Berlin's Sony Center, for example—represents the status quo. In that sense, it represents a nostalgic redo in new dress. Without diminishing the significance of the project's achievement, in light of the possibility for exciting avant-garde fare, the programmatic build-out of West 42nd Street represents something of a missed opportunity.

Some particularly urban things to worry about remain in the new Times Square: for one, whether the district will retain its social role as a tolerant public place and democratic stomping ground for everybody; another, whether it will remain a creative, trend-setting force of cultural innovation. For black and Latino teenagers who went to Times Square in the mid-1980s, it was "the mall we urban kids never had," recalled Kierna Mayo Dawsey, "one of the few public spots that actually beckoned young people, kids like me." Times Square functioned as "neutral ground—a prized place in an era when territory seemed like everything," a place where they were not the primary targets of suspicion. "The sideshow that was Times Square somehow shielded us from the piercing eyes that made browsing at Macy's or chilling at the South Street Seaport uncomfortable, even impossible." Equally important as an initial draw was the Latin Quarter, "the first seminal, centrally located hip-hop club in the city."[52] Fear of losing this type of cultural innovation might be behind the discourse of distress among critics, but this autobiographic piece stands out in sharp contrast to the familiar mainstream opposition to the new Times Square. The transformation poses pragmatic questions as well: Are the sidewalks wide enough for the crowds? Can people be accommodated on the subway escalators? Is the place too noisy for everyday folks?

14.15
Overseeing presences throughout
the transformation. (Gary Hack)

Criticism of the new Times Square coalesces around the question of whom it is for. As a source of revitalized pride, the new Times Square will fail to live up to its role as a public place if it inhibits, through artifice or cost, the broad range of people who want a place of excitement and play, a place to chill, a place of anonymity, a place to observe others. It should not be a place for any one particular demographic group the way the West 42nd Street of the 1960s through the 1980s functioned as a specialized sexual playground effectively off limits to the city's middle-class residents at large. Some key questions will be answered only with time: Is cultural innovation possible alongside branded entertainment? In what ways will new technology-enhanced forms of entertainment shape the continually evolving legacy of the place? The urban energy of the place, however, is evident on any day or night. "The sheer density, the enormous concentration of people and buildings and signage and things," Burns and Sanders wrote, "was proclaiming once again the city's fundamental reason for being: the infinite potential for interaction within a densely filled, tightly defined finite space—qualities that have been the city's glory since the Dutch settlers first raised their compact outpost at the tip of the island, three and half centuries ago."[53]

As an icon of city life, Times Square represents a symbolism that heralds change as a core identity. That core identity is not frozen in any one frame—neither the roof gardens and nightlife habitués characteristic of West 42nd Street pre-Prohibition, nor the 1930s romantic legend of Broadway, nor the public place of the 1940s where people gathered to listen to the ballgame or wait for war news, nor the 1950s playground of military shore leaves, nor the fleshpots and drug bazaar of the 1960s and 1970s, neither the Black and Latino teenage chill place of the 1980s, nor the last gasp of adult entertainment still present on the edges of the district in the 1990s—it is all these things and more arranged in some time-blurred montage of symbolic imagery (figure 14.15). The cultural identities have so fused together in the meaning of Times Square that the sheer inclusiveness of the place represents a trip across demographic groups, income and status, and race.

REVISIONIST LESSONS

The new Times Square represents a made dynamic fashioned by a set of public policies and market opportunities. It is not an accident, though pieces of its planning vision and execution are the consequence of conflict and controversy; it is an invention. The process was grinding, created as it was out of a highly politicized context that would have been anathema to the man who defined the definitive command-and-control style of public development.

Characterized as "The Power Broker" by his biographer, Robert A. Caro, Robert Moses would have judged the institutional coalition of city and state entities needed to push forward the 42DP as well as other large-scale projects in New York too diffuse a power base from which to operate because it precludes the type of unilateral decision making he exercised continuously through personalized and consolidated control of the city's urban-renewal and building-related authorities. Most likely the deal making would have been familiar, though. Having consolidated power—at the height of his career, he occupied 12 appointed positions simultaneously—Moses did not need to be patiently persevering, as do today's renewal officials. Nor did he need to compromise. The public authorities he controlled could access the weighty financial resources required, beyond the riches he was able to get from Washington, to push through his aggressive building agendas.

Today, as is so evident in the case of the 42DP, public-development officials operate in a far more constrained environment, politically fragmented and financially dependent upon scarce local resources. The region's public authorities are no longer as autonomous as they were during the decades following Moses's handiwork in crafting that quasi-public institution, which operates in an important niche between the purely political and the professional worlds of urban development, as a previously invulnerable power base. And, in the new world of urban-development politics, the traditional build-and-grow coalition of government and business can no longer control the process. Too many interest groups exist, and they are able to gain power and voice, however temporary, by exercising procedural rights of review and leveraging the political system. Through freedom-of-information law (FOIL) requests, they can also access certain types of information that Moses would have kept secret. As a consequence, the ability to build—and sustain—multifaceted coalitions across demanding political circumstances has become a prerequisite for pursuing ambitious urban projects.

If the multibillion transformation of Times Square offers compelling testimony that it is still possible to think big and execute ambitious city-building agendas, the turbulent experience of rebuilding leaves in its wake revisionist lessons about the politics of urban development. First, it has recalibrated the scope of public possibility by reaffirming what was a less-than-certain planning notion—that it is possible for cities to reshape what the market is likely to deliver. It does so, however, only by adding substantive heft to Jane Jacobs's enduring and influential argument that you cannot remake a neighborhood by bulldozing what makes it distinctive in the minds and memories of its residents and frequenters. Jacobs maintained that big schemes for clearance and renewal could never work; only small-scale interventions and private investments could deliver the type of renewal that brought with it urban vitality. Respect for the cityscape—its physical context of place, its street pattern, its older structures and its inherent human qualities—was at the core of her orthodoxy, and it profoundly shaped the planning profession during the late twentieth century. Though it violated most of the premises of this new orthodoxy save for preserving the 42nd Street theaters, the tortured process of rebuilding West 42nd Street vividly demonstrates that if renewal calls for a significant amount of bulldozing, the public's plans must provide for a rebuilding that is consistent with the symbolic legacy of the past. Not to do so is to invite more than the inevitable amount of opposition and controversy signaling the potential for failure, as both a planning initiative and a political program. Selectively chosen and skillfully executed large-scale projects might not be preternaturally doomed to failure. However, to view the cityscape, once again as did Moses, as "fluid, ever alterable, something for him to mold into an efficiently integrated whole"[54] would be to misread this message of renewal.

Second, the means by which project officials maneuvered around fiscal constraints, both budgetary and political, has revealed a latent ability on the part of the city to use public power to command resources not its own. This hidden fiscal muscle is the core of the public-private alliance that has defined the post-fiscal-crisis era of city building in New York, the third and last of the century (the first being the largely unfettered, laissez-faire building curtailed by the 1916 zoning law and halted by the stock-market crash of 1919; the second, the fifty years of Robert Moses ended by his retirement and buried deep by the 1974–1975 fiscal crisis[55]). Tax abatements and incentive zoning had been its primary lubricants, until density financing reached new heights with the 42DP. Privatizing the cost of land acquisition meant forfeiting public control over certain aspects of the project, something Moses most certainly would have resented, and mortgaging almost in perpetuity half the revenues of the project's biggest fiscal engine, which otherwise would have flowed into city coffers. Yet in an era of renewal marked by a dearth of federal dollars for cities, it proved to be an amazingly resilient strategy for "getting things done," a goal Moses most surely would have endorsed. The private sector—that is, Prudential—delivered on its open-ended promise to advance the vast funds necessary to push the condemnation forward at a time of great skepticism, though it did not deliver on the other promised and promoted benefit of funds for a renovated Times Square subway station. A drastically changed climate for development made the mayor and his officials unwilling to enforce the terms of the city's deal for this key public benefit because the politics of pushing for the economically impossible or, alternatively, relying on the extreme remedy of a default posed too risky a scenario. In the end, the private sector was able to do what the city could not, but the public sector could not maneuver completely around the necessity to take on risk itself if it was to achieve its ambitions for rebuilding West 42nd Street. In later rounds of the process, it did not even try.

For more than three decades beginning with LaGuardia's eight-year mayoralty and stretching across the much longer tenure of Robert Moses, the physical rebuilding of New York—its parks, recreation areas, highways and bridges, public housing, and urban-renewal projects—depended upon the largesse of Washington. It was a product of the political moment, both of the New Deal and, later, of the federal government's commitment to slum clearance and urban renewal. LaGuardia, one scholar wrote, "managed to make his city into the New Deal's favorite laboratory for urban and social initiatives."[56] However much he may have agreed with the goals of comprehensive reform that defined his Fusion Party, when it came to obtaining money from Washington, LaGuardia acted on the pragmatic basis that "piecemeal was better than no meal at all," and in his quest for concrete achievement, steered his commissioners "toward what was reasonable and could be sold to Washington." Washington's agenda setting continued to be an especially powerful force for fiscally pressed cities throughout the 1960s and 1970s. Less so in the 1980s. Not at all in the 1990s.

As only one, albeit significant, project in the twentieth-century physical history of New York, the rebuilding of Times Square and West 42nd Street has set a course apart from that long-established model, as did the contemporaneous public development of Battery Park City and MetroTech Center. These projects, as well as several other large-scale public-private efforts initiated by local governments across the nation in the last two decades of the twentieth century, have been realized without any, or in the case of the UDAG era, very few direct resources from Washington. In the realm of place-making urban policy, the federal government has all but ceased to exist as a player. Its role had steadily declined throughout the 1980s, along with the portion of city revenues derived from the federal government; cities ceased looking toward Washington when it came to making their plans. By the 1990s, except for a small program targeted on empowerment zones, the former agenda-setting, rule-making power that reigned from afar for so long had all but disappeared from the local orbit of policy making for city building.

"The impact of the federal urban-renewal program, however, was never as great as some observers assumed, and its physical legacy was limited," wrote urban historian Jon C. Teaford in a recent review of the program and its aftermath. While others, including myself, would question his assessment of minimal physical impact, his overall conclusion on the program's policy image and his insights about its critics are sharply to the point. The program fell short of its supporters' high expectations, despite some successes, while the "hated bulldozer tarnished Uncle Sam's image as a benevolent big brother" and discouraged local officials from fashioning like-type clearance programs. It became "a good 'bad example' that observers with a variety of gripes could cite to support their arguments. . . . Its supposed failure served the interests of a number of malcontents dissatisfied with the status quo." Most significantly, Teaford argued, it was an experiment that became a lesson in what not to do: "Its record influenced later federal revitalization programs that granted local authorities greater flexibility and emphasized rehabilitation and the urban context."[57]

If the political and social disasters of Washington's well-intentioned but cumbersome and bureaucratic ways did away with one model of action, another—the public-private partnership—quickly moved into the vacated space. No time to develop new theories of action or city planning. No time to set too many new policy protocols. The age of cities as entrepreneurs came into being with the boom real estate market of the 1980s. It was learn by doing. Those cities that could draw on public

officials with a bent toward real estate or could hire sophisticated consulting talent moved quickest, took on the boldest initiatives. Others took lessons from a small, experienced cadre of UDAG program officers who
educated city officials on how to bargain with developers, especially for a
share of future financial returns. Deal making became the policy strategy
of choice, a mark of a savvy city. As deals got more complex and the
emphasis on product (versus process) took over, serious questions of policy—levels and amounts of subsidy, slippery sense or absence of accountability—arose in the writings of academic experts. The flexibility and
adaptability of the public-private partnership model to local circumstances,
economic and political, proved impressive, though; and it was hard to
ignore its get-it-done effectiveness—as was the case with the 42DP.

When Koch rejected *The City at 42nd Street* the move sent a signal to the business community that times were changing. The private
coalition backing this first vision might have believed that it would get its
way by presenting carefully prepared plans backed by technical reports and
strong corporate interest and developer commitments. Such progrowth
coalitions were characteristic of rebuilding efforts in cities around the
nation. "The business elite of the city met privately, agreed upon more or
less comprehensive plans for the redevelopment of the central city, and
presented the plans to the press, the politicians and the public as their contribution to the civic welfare."[58] Koch wanted a public process, though
having made the political decision to preserve the 42nd Street theaters, he
most likely did not anticipate the level of influence—through conflict—
the civics and preservationists would eventually have in rescripting the
program for the 42DP. This is the third big lesson of renewal, one that has
revealed a more complex picture of urban-development politics than that
which underlies the prevailing progrowth-coalition theory, which argues
that a solid alliance of business and government governs decision making
for redevelopment. A long list of writings by political scientists, first
advanced by Robert A. Dahl's pioneering study of pluralism and the role
of elites in New Haven in the 1950s, *Who Governs*, and later by John
Mollenkopf and Harvey L. Molotch among others, draw on descriptions
of urban power structures from that era of urban renewal dominated by
federal agenda-setting dollars, whereas the reality of urban-development
politics today differs, in part because the resources to be allocated are local.
Later studies defining the role of interest-group politics and community-
group processes have updated these theories and, in the particular case
of New York, help explain the contentious and tortuous nature of implementing the plan for the 42DP; Norman I. Fainstein and Susan S.
Fainstein's work is one such example. But it is the elevated status of a particular small but vocal interest, the aesthetic opposition—mobilized and
managed by organizations such as the MAS—that stands out as an emergent piece of the coalition essential to the politics of large-scale public
interventions today—not just in New York and the case of the 42DP,
which Alexander J. Reichl discusses, but in other cities like Chicago, San
Francisco, and Boston, where preservationists have been more frequently

winning "tempestuous triumphs."[59] The other significant piece of this big story—the comparative local politics of historic preservation as a force in urban development—remains to be written.

Fourth, the excruciating process of executing the 42DP has attested to how democratic accountability, as a standard for large urban projects, is made up of multiple meanings. Community participatory planning and public review emerged in the 1970s as an integral part of the planning process after the collapse of top-down planning and command-and-control as a strategy for urban renewal. These new procedural elements, however, have proved to be insufficient for the type of financially complex public-private development projects that now characterize city-financed renewal efforts. They do not provide for the type of information elected officials need to make informed decisions about large-scale projects in which the public sector puts itself at risk, directly or indirectly, or for informed open discussion and debate with citizens at large about a project's costs and benefits. Without clear policy protocols, technical obfuscation too easily becomes a political asset for city officials, notwithstanding explicit and pressing questions of accountability raised—usually to no avail—by varied interests who oppose a project. If deal making is to progress as an effective and politically sustainable strategy in the tool kit of development officials and city planners, the protocols for democratic accountability need to be further refined.

Large-scale projects require enormous political capital and an equal amount of persistence. Persistence is needed to surmount the inevitable opposition from varied interest groups, the certain litigation, and the procedural demands for public reviews absent during the Moses era of big public-works projects. The Times Square saga has made visible to the public at large what development officials in the post-Moses era have taken as a given: Successful execution of a large-scale public-development project means finessing the inherent political gamble of possible failure— over time, usually a decade or two. It requires not just political compromise to ensure approval of action, but adaptive accommodation to setbacks and changed circumstances, both economic and political, in order to navigate around the shoals of potential failure. Most significantly, successfully navigating an environment of constraints, ultimately, may pivot on the role of specific individuals as leaders who make things happen apart from market and political forces and institutional context.

"The strength of the old power brokers was largely derived from the institutions they headed," remarked journalist Sam Roberts. "Personality, self promotion, visibility, intelligence and an ability to conceive new ideas and promote them counted too, of course, but they weren't mandatory. Since rank no longer guarantees power, these other attributes have taken on new significance."[60] Roberts was explaining the shifts brought about by the new processes of participatory democracy and the accompanying constraints on public officials' exercise of authority, which had elevated process into power and changed the cast of players. Except for the mayor and governor, the interests of the city's former "urban development repertory company: the Rockefeller family, Robert Moses, labor's Harry Van Arsdale, Tammany's Carmine DeSapio, and Francis Cardinal Spellman, if a Catholic school or hospital happened to stand in the way, or if anyone had the temerity to plan a new store that would open on Sundays," were notably missing from the lineup of the "new power elite" behind the 42DP.

Not having the ability to broker power from a commanding position of influence as did Moses, public-development officials like Rebecca Robertson and Carl Weisbrod typically must operate behind a shield of political power. They can overcome a lack of direct power as well as other limitations "when circumstances are propitious, and sometimes even when they are not. . . ."[61] Using words that seem custom-tailored to the situation Robertson faced when she took over leadership of the 42DP and operative failure seemed imminent, the late Lloyd Rodwin further explained: "They often do so when they have made shrewd assessments of what might be done in a particular environment, or of the changes in opportunity and strategy which might be feasible as the environment changes, and they have managed to exploit the situation to the hilt and make things happen—often things which others did not think feasible." The source of invention in salvaging the 42DP was not the content of the nostalgia-inspired entertainment- and tourist-oriented plan, but rather Robertson's strategy for mobilizing the necessary resources to make it appear that something real might happen when, in fact, the probability of events moving in the opposite direction seemed more likely. In skillfully using the media to keep the project alive and maintain support for her leadership, she seemed to have read the lesson book on public relations written by another of New York's legendary public-authority operatives, Austin Tobin of the Port Authority of New York and New Jersey. Even in an environment of fragmented power and constrained resources, personal motivation "to make a difference" in combination with the opportunity for event-making leadership can have a disproportionate impact on success by giving direction to a floundering project. In the case of the troubled 42DP, it became Robertson's individualized resource for bridging the gap between big vision and little progress. It also became a career-defining success, for which in 1996 she won the AIA's George S. Lewis Award, given annually to someone who helps make New York a better place in which to live and practice architecture. To succeed in the highly political world of public development, today's professionals need to be skilled in managing "soft" resources as well as plans—in other words, to function beyond their core technical competencies.

These then are the elements that made the city's large-scale ambitions for West 42nd Street a reality: the existence of vested stakeholders who could not readily walk away from the project or whose resources endowed them with staying power that could weigh in as powerfully as direct control; a pragmatism on the part of both private developers and public officials that provided for adaptive accommodation to changed circumstances; and an unwavering political commitment enhanced by an unusual continuity of leadership among the project's executive officers over its 20-year history. The 42DP did not suffer the "disease of bureaucracy," nor did it collapse under the weight of continuous litigation. It survived because of the politics of persistence; the public sector's willingness, however reluctantly, to take risks; Prudential's ability and willingness to live up to its commitment; and, in a situation of event-making opportunity, the leadership of specific individuals who did more than just hold a project together.

The forward-looking legacy of the project is just beginning to unfold. If the success of the political gamble is clear, what the ambitions of the transformation have wrought in public benefits beyond the immediate physical changes evident on West 42nd Street and Times Square is just beginning to emerge more clearly. The public costs, on the other hand, remain elusively hidden, though less so the deficiency of the city to deal with the social issues raised by the removal of the "bad uses" that had made West 42nd Street such a civic embarrassment. In a city that long took pride in its tradition of liberal welfare policy, this stands out as either an exception or one of a series of behaviors that marks the end of the broad liberal experiment in New York. Though this shift is part of a bigger set of forces and a story beyond this one, it cannot go unmentioned.

The new Times Square remains synonymous with the city itself, its commercialism, intense energy, urban insouciance, and cultural and economic diversity. The five meanings that over time fashioned the symbolism of place of Times Square for New Yorkers and the world at large—Theater District, Turf of Promoters and Showmen, Great White Way, Testing Ground, Quintessential New York—still fit, with some modifications and one exception. In place of the larger-than-life entrepreneurial impresarios—Hammerstein, Ziegfeld, Klaw and Erlanger, Thompson—the Turf of Promoters and Showmen is now home to the world's giant entertainment conglomerates—Disney, SFX Entertainment—who have brought a corporate approach to theater production at the same time that 42nd Street's other theater marquees carry new names: the Ford Center for the Performing Arts and the American Airlines Theater. If the commercial aesthetic has found new and highly expensive forms of expression once again relighting Times Square, the place has lost its edge as a social testing ground, for now. As is so evident in the hyperbole and the record-breaking numbers of tourists, Times Square continues to embody the quintessential city image for the nation at large. A number of broad economic and social forces are contributing to New York's renewed position as the "Shrine of the Good Time" and its glow as a "spectacle of urban life." As in the past, Times Square takes up its historic role by serving as the symbolic metaphor. As an enduring stage for city life, the transformed Times Square presents itself as a work in perpetual progress.

E P I L O G U E

Midtown west continues to be the "suitable" and most desirable location in Manhattan for adult-entertainment activities—but the adult movie theaters, topless bars, strip clubs, sex shops, XXX video marts and prostitutes no longer concentrate on West 42nd Street or within the bow-tie area of Times Square. They are elsewhere. And if in numbers smaller than in the past, the citywide growth trend of these activities has reasserted itself. As tracked by several studies, including a DCP study undertaken in 1993 to support Mayor Giuliani's antiporn zoning initiative, most of the new adult-use activity—a combination of relocated and new establishments—appears to be taking place on Eighth Avenue and south of 42nd Street. Between 1984 and 1993, adult establishments grew in number citywide from 131 to 177, or 35 percent, a finding attributed in part to the advent of the adult video store and the greater numbers of topless or nude bars going upscale. The biggest increases registered in Manhattan and Queens—Manhattan's share of concentrated adult uses having risen to 61 percent compared to 56 percent in 1984 and 80 percent in 1976. Although as recently as 1998, two people were charged with operating a sex ring near Times Square, by and large the sex activity has moved away, much of it to Chelsea and Clinton—as the *DEIS* had predicted. These survey findings do not, of course, include the more difficult to track migratory activity—the escort services, the prostitutes on the edges of the highway, the young and homeless on the piers, the trade plied on the Internet. Unwanted, unloved, and persistent, if migratory, adult entertainment is still a policy issue common enough to evoke the predictable response: Mayor Giuliani is still trying to do what Mayor LaGuardia aimed to do 67 years earlier—shut down the porn.

In the highly visible bow-tie area of Broadway and Seventh Avenue between 43rd and 50th Streets, the dramatic decline in adult-use establishments—down to five in 1993 from 25 ten years earlier—can be attributed almost exclusively to commercial real estate development. Eleven of the establishments disappeared into the development assemblage for the Holiday Inn Crowne Plaza hotel, three went for the postcard-prominent Two Times Square, two more for 1585 Broadway, and one for 750 Seventh Avenue. By May 1998, the number of remaining adult-use establishments had dropped to three, as tracked by the Times Square BID. Whereas the area's previously depressed property values and marginal building types, along with time and drugs, had helped establish pornography's deep roots in Times Square, the economic Darwinism of higher-value land uses locally and changing fundamentals driving the adult-entertainment industry globally uprooted the trade. As it affected Times Square, the mayor's antiporn zoning policy supplied only the finishing touch on a profound trend that will leave the area with but a few quaint relics of its past, except for Eighth Avenue—which had until the late 1990s witnessed almost no change. In time, development pressures are likely to change that, too (figure E.1).

E.1
Still around, around the corner from the new 42nd Street on Eighth Avenue. (Gary Hack)

A headlong rush of commercial announcements continues to define the new 42nd Street. The B. B. King Blues Club & Grill has brought live blues entertainment to the street, upscale style compared to its decades-old venue in Greenwich Village; if successful, the brand-hopeful will expand the concept to other cities. At the turn of the millennium, the electronic stock market Nasdaq plugged in an eight-story "techno-turret" capable of projecting constantly changing, colorful, swirling images on a 90-by-120-foot screen produced by powerful minicircuitry; located on the pedestrian-packed corner of 43rd Street and Broadway, it is the largest, most colorful, most technologically advanced, and most expensive display in Times Square. The world's largest live-entertainment giant, SFX Entertainment, now a unit of Clear Channel Communications, Inc., moved into its new leased headquarters in the 24-story Candler Building—a historic structure originally built by Atlanta Coca-Cola entrepreneur Asa G. Candler recently retooled with $40 million—receiving in the process $3.5 million in corporate tax breaks from the city and a $500,000 grant from the state (figure E.2). Reuters America Holdings moved into its $360-million office tower, which includes a financial news TV studio, in time for the global news giant's 150th anniversary. In 2002 Ernst & Young is scheduled to move into its 37-story, $600-million headquarters and in 2003 Arthur Andersen will move into the $600-million, 47-story Times Square tower (figures E.3–E.5). The 444-room, $125-

E.2
Candler Building, home of SFX Entertainment. (*Grid*)

E.3
Reuters Building, Three Times Square, Fox & Fowle Architects. (Andrew Gordon Photography, Inc.)

E.4
Rendering of Five Times Square,
headquarters for Ernst & Young,
Kohn Petersen Fox Architects. (©
Kohn Petersen Fox Architects, PC)

E.5
Rendering of Times Square
Tower, Skidmore Owings &
Merrill Architects, LLP for Boston
Properties, Inc. (© pixel by pixel,
renderer)

million Hilton Times Square now draws in crowds as does the $40-million Madame Tussaud's Wax Museum (figure E.6), and the 25-screen AMC Empire multiplex and the HMV Record store that make up the $100-million Forest City Ratner entertainment-and-retail project (plate 29). Across the street, work proceeds on the $320-million, 858-room Westin Hotel designed by Miami-based Arquitectonica and distinguished by a striking curved beam of light slicing through the structure's facade (figure E.7); it joins Sony's 13-screen multiplex center and related $70-million retail complex making up E-Walk (figure E.8). The nonprofit Roundabout Theater Company opened its 2000–2001 season in the venerable Selwyn Theater, rechristened the American Airlines Theater, after a $21.5-million renovation. Opening at the same time on the site of the collapsed Selwyn office building were the $29.6-million New 42nd Street Studios, a deftly detailed 10-story building housing three floors of offices for nonprofit groups, a 199-seat experimental theater known as the Duke on 42nd Street Theater,

E.6
Madame Tussaud's Wax Museum, part of the Forest City Ratner entertainment center. (Gary Hack)

E.7
Rendering of the Westin Hotel behind E-Walk, Arquitectonia. (Luis Vanselow, renderer for Tishman Realty & Construction Company, Inc.)

E.8
Sony Loews Theaters in E-Walk.
(Gary Hack)

and 14 rehearsal studios for actors, dancers, and musicians, who can be seen in practice through a nearly transparent curtain wall (plate 12). The New Victory is a stunning success with the public; subsidized with lease revenues ($2.6 million of its $5.5-million budget for 2000–2001) from the commercial tenants housed in the street's other theaters; the youth theater's $13 average ticket price generates only 25 percent of its annual budget (another 25 percent comes from contributions).

The New York Times Company plans to build a headquarters designed by Italian architect Renzo Piano as part of a larger development with Forest City Ratner. The developer will pay $85 million toward the purchase of the two-acre development site and fund the site's acquisition under a similar ESAC-based arrangement. Knowledge gained from the TSCA experience undergirds its risk taking. "The Park Tower experience allowed us to imagine what might happen in a downturn under this type of funding scenario," said Mary Anne Gilmartin.[1] That leaves only the yet-to-be-developed parking-lot corner of Eighth Avenue and 42nd Street across from the Port Authority Bus Terminal and the renovation of the 100-by-100 foot Times Square Theater. There is also the possibility that Disney will develop the former legendary roof-top theater of the New Amsterdam where Flo Ziegfeld built the Midnight Frolic supper club in 1915 to showcase the "glorified American girl," a.k.a., the eroticized female body (figure E.9).

Early indications of the real estate value created in these 42DP developments can be gleaned from the Durst Organization's refinancing of Four Times Square. Built at a reported cost of $450 million, the property was appraised as of February 2000 at $810 million by real estate consultants—exclusive of the appraised value of the original ESAC credits allocated to this development site ($67 million), which are not expected to be exhausted until 2060; this is an impressive $528 per rentable square foot (with ESACs). At conservative lending ratios (Standard & Poor's valued the asset package at $688 million), such valuations made possible the Dursts' raising of $430 million in securities backed by a mortgage on the 1.66-million square-foot fully leased building. Because of their first-in low acquisition price, bonus returns from extra retail space, and the lucky benefits of signage income—$3 million annually from the Nasdaq sign alone, with a projected total of $13.2 million from signage, retail, and other rental income—the Dursts are likely to score the biggest financial bonanza of any of the 42DP developers. Times Square being the city's hottest real estate market, others are likely to realize handsome financings. Notably, the strength of the appraised values has financial meaning for the public sector as well; under the terms of the MTA's 1993 agreement with the city and TSCA, dollars from the state mortgage-recording tax targeted for the Times Square subway station improvements—dollars that no one quite believed would materialize—began flowing sooner than anyone could have forecast.

Investment activity in the Times Square district has been no less intense than on West 42nd Street. Office rents in the district have skyrock-

E.9
Program cover for Ziegfeld's
Midnight Frolic. (New York
Theater Program Corporation)

eted—asking rents jumped to $42.69 in 1999 from $28.81 in 1996—as has been the case in most of New York's office submarkets; the same for rents for hotel rooms, retail space, and sign locations. The signage count in Times Square in March 2000 hit 157, up from 90 the previous year. Morgan Stanley Dean Witter is building a third office tower on Seventh Avenue at 50th Street on what was known as the Rock West site, and in a move that can only be described as a home run, sold the second of its Times Square towers for a reported $150 million ($264 per rentable square foot), capturing the profit from its fire-sale purchase at $90 million. Starwood Hotels and Resorts, at the last moment, outbid another world-wide chain with an offer reportedly worth an estimated $175 million to lease for 25 years the hotel and retail space of the nearly complete but stalled 562-room hotel once slated to fly the Planet Hollywood flag when its developer was forced to find a new operator after the chain filed for Chapter 11 bankruptcy protection.

More brand-conscious venues keep flocking to Times Square. Having lost out on its bid for a spot on West 42nd Street, the World Wrestling Foundation regrouped and two years later debuted its $25-million, 610-seat theme restaurant, retail store, and entertainment center in the old Paramount Theater site on Broadway and 43rd Street where the young Frank Sinatra crooned to crowds of rapt teenagers. It is also spending $7.5 million to rebuild the famed marquee and monumental arch that once framed the theater, an icon of Times Square night life that disappeared without much notice after the theater closed in 1964, in the belief that the re-creation "will add to the entertainment value of the company."[2] Easy Everything, a London-based chain of Internet cafés—24-hour futuristic-looking "cybercafes on steroids" packed with 650 to 1,000 Internet terminals with high-resolution flat-panel screens—settled on the south side of West 42nd Street. Toys "Я" Us is building the world's largest toy-store and expects to draw more than 20 million visitors a year; as the flagship store for the international toy retailer, the 101,000-square-foot extravaganza is being designed to serve as a focal point for "major toy launches" (see figure E.10). "The deal represents something of a victory for the owner of the building, Charles B. Moss, Jr., who rejected a $92-million deal two years ago to allow Random House to build an office tower over his storefronts," reported the *Times*'s Bagli.[3] That decision, which many believed to be a mistake, Moss considered a valuable option to max out the site's long-term revenues from retail tenants and signage—in a hot market that had not yet peaked.

The prime cue on just how commercially upscale this market has become was in the U.S. armed forces' decision to retire their familiar down-to-earth recruiting station in Times Square—established in this seemingly improbable location in 1946—in exchange for a renovated facility that will have "that Times Square Look" (figure E.11). The next comfy former landmark to go was the pipe-and-canvas "tkts" booth in Father Duffy Square. Installed as a temporary structure in 1973, it is now being replaced with a decidedly significant piece of functional public

E.10
Construction for Toys "Я" Us
store. (Gary Hack)

sculpture—a bright-red grand staircase rising 16 feet to give visitors an equally grand view of public activity in Times Square (figures E.12, E.13). The new discount-ticket booth will be tucked beneath the award-winning structure designed by Australian architects John Choi and Tai Ropiha. Competition jury member Marion Weiss of Weiss/Manfredi Architects predicts the design "will become a new icon of New York." A roster of stars and producers has set up a foundation to create a "Broadway Walk of Fame," not unlike the one in Hollywood. The plan is to "embed a bronze star with a celebrity name at various intervals in the public sidewalk beginning at 48th Street and Broadway in Times Square and running down both sides of the street to 42nd Street, then branching out from there."[4] The Church of St. Mary the Virgin on 46th Street just off Seventh Avenue, whose adjacent mission house has for ten years been the home of SafeSpace, an oasis to runaway, gay, and transgender teenagers, is planning to use the space for an infant day-care center catering to the children of

E.11
The U.S. Armed Services recruit-
ing booth, upscaled to fit the new
Times Square, 2001. (Gary Hack)

E.12
Original tkts discount-ticket booth, Mayers & Schiff Associates. (Gary Hack)

E.13
Award-winning design for new tkts booth by Australian architects John Choi and Tai Ropiha. (© Nathaniel H. Brooks)

Times Square workers and executives when SafeSpace's lease expires in May 2001. Also closing and moving elsewhere is the Lamb's Table, a 20-year-old lunch soup kitchen that is run by the Lamb's Manhattan Church on West 44th Street, which has entered into a partnership with a New York-based chain to build a 120-room hotel, preserving the church's sanctuary and theater but not this social program for the poor. And in what is surely an ironic sign of changing times, Seymour Durst's debt clock, calculating the nation's liability since 1989, has been retired. "The clock's demise is a powerful signal that the fiscally reckless days of the 1980s and early 1990s are over, replaced by a new era of responsible spending," wrote a reporter for the London-based *Financial Times*, though "some feel the debt clock should be preserved in Times Square as a national monument."[5]

Abetted by other favorable conditions, Times Square's gentrification is moving west toward the Hudson River. Formerly an industrial area inhabited by factories, freight yards, warehouses, stockyards, and tenements, the low-density blocks have begun to attract serious large-scale speculative residential towers and corporate office buildings: "Far West 42nd St., Once Scorned, Is Now Much in Demand." Theater Row, that pioneering modest private development between Ninth and Dyer Avenues, is undergoing its own redo: "The stages that saved 42nd Street await the wrecker." The playhouses are being torn down to make way for a $75-million, 40-story apartment tower and collection of eight new or rebuilt theaters seating 1,291 patrons—a transformation the *Times* claims is "the biggest Off-Broadway redevelopment project in New York City history."[6]

Though it rarely gets the credit it deserves, Prudential's name and corporate logo remain in self-promoting bright lights, high on a supersign at the top of Two Times Square and, when it was under construction, on the street-level construction facade of Three Times Square; as a part of its deal with Reuters and Rudin, it retained rights to approximately 6,000 square feet of the tower's signage space, where its name will appear as well. Also, in its traditional role as lender, the insurance company used its knowledge of the 42DP when it underwrote a $270-million construction-to-permanent mortgage loan on the Reuters/Rudin tower.

The insurance giant has sold all four office sites—and their accompanying ESACs—in three separate transactions for a total of approximately $462 million, roughly $27 million more than the commonly reported figure of $435 million put out (though $462 million has also appeared in print) for condemnation, land acquisition, architectural plans and predevelopment expenses, theater renovation, and development of interim retail space. These numbers are at best approximations because the accounting is complicated, and the information not in the public domain. (Indeed, with the breakup of the four sites, tracking the ESACs became "very complicated" even for the 42DP, Inc., which had to put in an accounting system not only to monitor the rent credits, but to make sure that TSCA did not sell more than there were to sell.[7]) At face value, this indicates that Prudential managed to come out of what was widely perceived as a financial debacle better than break-even. Having taken a write-down on its mortgage loan to the venture, Prudential faced a gain on the book value of this asset, an unexpected financial outcome that made the structuring of its deal with Boston Properties for the last two sites especially complicated, because the insurance company wanted a tax-efficient transaction and a way to avoid paying state mortgage-recording and transfer taxes as well. Nonetheless, concluding that an accounting gain constitutes an economic gain ignores the long period of time—nearly ten years—when the money flow only went in one direction—out—and when alternative equity investments like stocks were yielding, on a compounded average basis, 10.5 percent. If someone had invested $200 million, on average, in the S&P stock index over this period that investment should have grown to roughly $550 million.

Subsequent events have not been as kind to George Klein, who was the real pioneer when it came to taking risks in Times Square. The early headlines—"Developer Klein goes quietly into NY night" (*Crain's*, 1996), "George Klein Out in the Cold" (*Wall Street Journal*, 1997)—telling of the dissolution of his real estate holdings were only partially redeemed by the positivism of the next—"'Visionary' Builder George Klein Eyes 42nd Street Return" (*New York Observer*, 1998). While Park Tower had settlement funds from the breakup of its partnership with Prudential, the products of Klein's professional efforts now belonged to others. Even in an industry well inured to the business ravages of boom-and-bust cycles, the post-mortem evoked an unusual amount of empathy. The collapse of his 42DP interests was of a different cast, and his lost opportunity to develop in Times Square, commonly viewed as something of a professional tragedy. After his outrage over Prudential's sale to Durst subsided, he took a step forward step and talked with his former arch-antagonist about a joint effort to secure the second site; when that prize went to the Reuters/Rudin partnership, Park Tower teamed up with the Blackstone Group, which had joined with Boston Properties to bid on the last two sites; with only a small, passive stake, as consulting developer, he would have no say over development decisions. The 42DP experience notwithstanding, Klein remains active in political and philanthropic circles, and 15 years of his unflagging support and efforts made it possible for the city's Museum of Jewish Heritage to come into being. He is not developing new office towers, though.

The key deal makers have moved on to other development agendas. With the changeover in administrations from Dinkins to Giuliani, Carl Weisbrod took a high-profile position as head of the Alliance for Downtown Manhattan, that area's BID. His task—before the advent of new media's ascent accelerated that office market's recovery— was to spearhead business and city efforts to revitalize the area's economic underpinnings. Now much of his efforts are focused on the new stock exchange project. Rebecca Robertson first moved to the Shubert Organization, where she helped develop the new 499-seat Shubert theater being built on Theater Row on West 42nd Street. Then, in the summer of 2000, she took a high-profile position as executive director of the reconstruction committee for Lincoln Center's $1.5-billion rebuilding project, the largest in the cultural center's four-decade history. Robertson is charged with "supervising the master-planning of the complex, its vision and implementation," a task initially expected to take until 2010. The scope of the project covering the 18 acres between Columbus and Amsterdam Avenues and 62nd and 66th Streets, much of which is yet to be determined, presents Robertson with another long-term challenge: Lincoln Center, she described, as "the great urban renewal project of New York City."[8]

For David L. Malmuth, too, the 42DP was a career-making project. As an executive of the TrizecHahn Development Corporation he   currently oversees the development of the company's large retail-entertainment complex next to the historic Mann's Chinese Theater in Hollywood. "I had an experience on 42nd Street that was for me extraordinary. . . . My feeling was: It's really worth it."[9]

The architectural pieces are in place. The quartet of towers is delivering what the plans predicted: density adorned with signs. Critical reaction has been mixed. Four Times Square, for example, has been greeted with high praise "as a piece of urban theater" and neutral acceptance within the tradition of New York commercial high-rises "as an amalgam of stylistic motifs and technical themes that embody concerns and obsessions of late-20th-century architecture" and castigated with the comment that its "most endearing quality is that it *isn't* the tower designed for the same site by architects John Burgee and Philip Johnson."[10] Others have concluded that the dynamic energy has been lost, only to be replaced by "stylistic" energy. Judged on the basis of whether any might achieve icon status, "the new towers in Times Square show us, unambiguously, that the idea of the skyscraper as a pure object is dead," wrote Paul Goldberger. "The skyscraper has become a collection of parts." Bulk is to blame. In contrast, because it is so functional and pristine and "exists to advertise nothing except the building itself, which it does in delicious silence," the New 42nd Street Studios captured his praise as the best new building in Times Square. The real performance is at night, in "a brilliant computerized scheme" that makes the facade glow and flash colors from red to blue and then to yellow, orange, and green. The message of the posticonic skyscraper, he went on to explain, "does evoke a curiously traditional idea . . . that the concept of the city is more important than an individual building. Every one of the new buildings has been designed as a piece of a big, messy whole." Though the buildings are far bigger and bolder than their predecessors, there is nothing to distinguish them from their environment. Rather, the signs "pull the new Times Square together, as the softer, whiter lights of another generation pulled the old Times Square together."[11] In the range of response, criticism, and interpretation of meaning, the transformation of Times Square is generating another cycle of discussion and debate. That was far from the case in the 1960s and 1970s when it served as a metaphor for deep-seated urban malaise.

Irony characterizes a series of counterintuitive outcomes of the much beleaguered 42DP. That Durst, the arch-antagonist of the project, garnered the rights to develop the first office tower dug an especially painful burr into the hardened professional hides of both Klein and Robertson, who could reach mutual agreement on few other aspects of the project. The hyped fact that this developer was contributing to the environment with a "green" building in no way diminished the spoiler turn of events. That Skadden Arps, which had done legal work for Klein, became a key tenant in Durst's building further salted Klein's wound. That Durst, so long opposed to use of eminent domain as a matter of principal, is now reportedly trying to persuade state officials to use condemnation powers to facilitate his family's long-held dream to build a 2-million-square-foot office tower on their frustratingly incomplete assemblage on 42nd Street east of Four Times Square suggests that no outcome is impossible in the world of New York real estate.

That the much-enlarged retail component of Four Times Square serendipitously turned into a financial home run for the developer served to reemphasize the planning lesson that wisdom flows from staying true to the area's special street-level activity. That the four office buildings will be just as dense, towering, and overpowering a concentration crowding the small intersection of Broadway and Seventh Avenue is mitigated only by the fact that they will turn out better than could have been expected—if for no other reason than they will not be four identical corporate monoliths, and that they will be replete with the requisite amount of commercial signage.

That intense sidewalk congestion in Times Square recently prompted the city's transporation experts to implement a three-phase "traffic-calming plan" that included widening the sidewalks in the bow-tie area to ensure the safety of pedestrians and motorists signals an immediate response to one "consequence of our success." That it might call up from the graveyard of policy initiatives the city's long-discarded plans for Broadway Plaza, the controversial pedestrian mall once planned for Times Square that died in the early 1980s, notwithstanding the fact that approvals were in place and funding was in hand, because theater and business interests feared it would become a gathering place for street people, drug traffickers, and peddlers, illustrates the profound impact of changed perceptions possible in cities today.

That the ribbon of entertainment on the new 42nd Street seems to be more like the "orange juice" of *The City at 42nd Street* that Koch, in his quest for "seltzer," rejected as too much like "Disneyland on 42nd Street" is demonstrative of the fluctuations of time and the power of symbolism. In the end, the delays and opposition produced a better project, not because it seems to have come full circle from the late 1970s, but because the focus on West 42nd Street today speaks to the current consumer demand for entertainment in city settings—for the public performance of seeing and being seen.

N O T E S

PREFACE

1. Clarence N. Stone and Heywood T. Sanders, "Reexamining a Classic Case of Development Politics: New Haven, Connecticut," in *The Politics of Urban Development,* ed. Clarence N. Stone and Heywood T. Sanders (Lawrence: University of Kansas Press, 1987), 159–181, at 168.

2. Ibid., 179.

CHAPTER ONE

1. Brooks McNamara, *Day of Jubilee: The Great Age of Public Celebrations in New York, 1788–1909* (New Brunswick, N.J.: Rutgers University Press, 1997), 1–10.

2. Matthew Purdy, "Disney Parade About to Turn Midtown Goofy," *New York Times,* June 13,1997, B1.

3. Ibid.

4. Mike Claffey, Laura Williams, and Anne E. Kornblut, "Dazzling Disney Turns 42D St. into Parade Ground," *Daily News,* June 15, 1997, 3.

5. Douglas Martin, "Its Greeks Bearing Glitz, Disney Parades a Hero," *New York Times,* June 15, 1997, 27.

6. William Cole, ed., *Quotable New York: A Literary Companion* (New York: Penguin Books, 1993), 26.

7. Allen Churchill, "Sex on the Square," *Rouge,* February 1962, 4954, 76, at 76.

8. "Cleaning Up Midtown" [editorial], *New York Times,* July 8, 1971, 34; "Behind the Facade" [editorial], *New York Times,* September 5, 1972, 36; "New Times Square" [editorial], *New York Times,* April 16, 1974, 38; "Times Square Zoning" [editorial], *New York Times,* October 11, 1975, 30; "Zoning 'Adult' Movies" [editorial], *New York Times,* July 8, 1976, 30.

9. "A Place to Meet" [editorial], *New York Times,* January 2, 1977, 4:12.

10. "Zoning out the Porn" [editorial], *New York Times,* November 18, 1976, 42.

11. Charles V. Bagli, "Mayor Claims Credit for Times Sq. Revival," *New York Times,* January 27, 2000, B6.

12. Wayne Barrett assisted by Adam Fifield, *Rudy!* (New York: Basic Books, 2000), 10.

13. Marshall Berman, "Signs of the Times: The Lure of Times Square," *Dissent* 44 (fall 1997): 76–83, at 78.

14. William Kornblum and Vernon Boggs, "Redevelopment and the Night Frontier," *City Almanac* 18 (summer 1985): 16–18, at 18.

15. William Kornblum, et al. *West 42nd Street: The Bright Light Zone,* Graduate School and University Center of the City University of New York, unpublished study, 1978, 17. Herein after referred to as *Bright Light Zone.*

16. William Kornblum and Vernon Boggs, "The Social Ecology of the Bright Light District," in *Bright Light Zone,* 17–51, at 32.

17. Jill Stone, *Times Square: A Pictorial History* (New York: Collier Books, 1982), 141.

18. Josh Alan Friedman, *Tales of Times Square* (Feral Press: New York, 1986), 145; Laurence Senelick, "Private Parts in Public Places," in *Inventing Times Square: Commerce and Culture at the Crossroads of the World,* ed. William R. Taylor (New York: Russell Sage Foundation, 1991), 329–353, at 345.

19. The prostitution system remained left unchanged, even with hyped up mass arrests of prostitutes, because, as Laurence Senelick realistically explained: "the individual pimp was left relatively unmolested, and the thousands of prostitute arrests were ultimately pointless, particularly since their clientele went unscathed." (Senelik, "Private Parts in Public Places," 348.) Moreover, the money men behind the action, especially organized crime, could readily afford bail, court fees, and elaborate litigation. OME turned out to highly successful at closing down massage parlors in no small part because they were not protected under the First Amendment and because they were vulnerable to many health, building-code, and zoning violations. The success only affected indoor activity, though.

20. NYS UDC, *The 42nd Street Development Project: Draft Environmental Impact Statement* [*DEIS*], prepared by Parsons Brinckerhoff Quade & Douglass, Inc., and AKRF, Inc., in association with Urbitran Associates, Inc., February 1984, 2-113.

21. Ibid., 2-113–2-114.

22. In his strong critique of the *DEIS,* Columbia University sociologist Herbert J. Gans argued that the report manipulated the statistics to prove its contention that West 42nd Street was a threatening place. On the basis of his review, the word loitering with its typically menacing connotation did not really fit the data; the number of those loitering was actually small, he said, though their perceived impact was greater. See chapter 3 for more of Gans's critique.

23. Carl B. Weisbrod, author interview, August 15, 2000.

24. Kornblum and Boggs, "The Social Ecology of the Bright Light District," 42.

25. Stanley Bruder, "Forty-Second Street at the Crossroads: A History of Broadway to Eighth Avenues," in *Bright Light Zone,* 53–71, at 75–76.

26. Kenneth T. Jackson, *Crabgrass Frontier: The Suburbanization of the United States* (New York: Oxford University Press, 1985), 274–276.

27. Martin Gottlieb, "Public Projects: Are They Viable in the City Anymore?" *New York Times,* August 14, 1985, B1.

28. Jon C. Teaford, "Urban Renewal and Its Aftermath," *Housing Policy Debate* 11 (2:2000), 443–465, at 459.

29. Ibid.

30. Ibid., 356.

31. Ibid.

32. Clarence N. Stone and Heywood T. Sanders, "Summing Up: Urban Regimes, Development Policy and Political Arrangements," in *The Politics of Urban Development,* ed. Clarence N. Stone and Heywood T. Sanders (Lawrence: University of Kansas Press, 1987), 269–290, at 284.

33. Bernard J. Frieden and Lynne B. Sagalyn, *Downtown Inc.: How America Rebuilds Cities* (Cambridge, Mass.: The MIT Press, 1989).

34. Gerald D. Suttles, *The Man-Made City: The Land-Use Confidence Game in Chicago* (Chicago: University of Chicago Press, 1990).

35. Martin Meyerson and Edward C. Banfield emphasized this in their now-classic book, *Politics, Planning and the Public Interest* (New York: Free Press, 1955).

36. Robert Campbell, "Evaluation: Boston's 'Upper of Urbanity,'" *American Institute of Architects Journal* 70 (June 1981), 24–31.

CHAPTER TWO

1. Laurence Senelick, "Private Parts in Public Places," in *Inventing Times Square: Commerce and Culture at the Crossroads of the World*, ed. William R. Taylor (New York: Russell Sage Foundation, 1991), 329–353, at 329.

2. Ibid., 340, 341.

3. Hammerstein laid the foundations for the modern Theater District in 1895 with construction of the Olympia, a "multiple-theater complex so colossal as to be its own center of gravity." Designed by John B. McElfatrick, the Olympia extended from 44th to 45th Street on Broadway and could accommodate 6,000 patrons. On opening night the place was besieged and mayhem ensued, as Hammerstein had oversold the evening of amusement. Its success was not long-lived, however, because even though Hammerstein could claim credit as the "pioneer" who breached Forty-second Street, the real estate press noted that "even he could not overcome the 'hoodoo' and the result spelt failure. The Olympia was soon in foreclosure and its theaters were turned into separately managed houses." David W. Dunlap, *On Broadway: A Journey Uptown Over Time* (New York: Rizzoli International Publications, 1990), 166.

4. By 1910, with 34 theaters, most of which were new and in Times Square, New York had more theaters than it needed, yet with a pattern of overbuilding seemingly set in place, theaters were constructed at a rapid pace for the next two decades: By the 1919–1920 season, 50 playhouses were operating, and ten years later, 71 were in use.

5. Will Irwin, *Highlights of Manhattan* (New York: Century Co., 1927), 325, quoted in Robert A. M. Stern, Gregory Gilmartin, and Thomas Mellins, *New York 1930: Architecture and Urbanism Between the Two World Wars* (New York: Rizzoli Press, 1994), 229. .

6. Irving Lewis Allen, *The City in Slang: New York Life and Popular Speech* (Oxford University Press, 1993), 60.

7. David Hammack, "Developing for Commercial Culture," in *Inventing Times Square*, 36–50.

8. Ibid. at 36.

9. Neil Harris, "Urban Tourism and the Commercial City," in *Inventing Times Square*, 66–72, at 78–79.

10. Henry Collins Brown, *Valentine's Manual of Old New York*, no. 7, 1923, 114.

11. Attributed to Martin Berger in his history of the *New York Times*, cited in Stanley Bruder, "Forty-Second Street at the Crossroads: A History of Broadway to Eighth Avenue," in *West 42nd Street: The Bright Light Zone,* Graduate School and University Center of the City University of New York, unpublished study, 1978, 53–81, at 61.

12. The **X**-shaped crossing came into being only in the later quarter of the nineteenth century, the direct result of a successful lobbying effort by local realtors who

sought to push forward the growth of the West Side. Compared to the East Side where growth "occurred almost as a matter of course, the development of the West Side above 59th Street due to its highly irregular topography presented special problems." The realtors convinced the city government to widen Broadway between 34th and 59th Street, after which carriage manufacturers with their showrooms soon moved to the area. Bruder, "Forty-Second Street at the Crossroads," 56–57.

13. Ada Louise Huxtable, "Re-Inventing Times Square: 1900," in *Inventing Times Square*, 356–370, at 356.

14. Bruder, "Forty-Second Street at the Crossroads," 64, 66.

15. David Nasaw, *Going Out: The Rise and Fall of Public Amusements* (New York: Basic Books, 1993).

16. Ibid., 227.

17. Bruder, "Forty-Second Street at the Crossroads," 67, 69.

18. Timothy J. Gilfoyle, "Policing of Sexuality," in *Inventing Times Square*, 297–314, at 299.

19. Ibid.

20. Mark Jacobson, "Times Square: The Meanest Street in America," *Rolling Stone*, August 6, 1981, 15ff, at 18.

21. Gail Sheehy, "The Landlords of Hell's Bedroom," *New York*, November 20, 1973, 67ff, at 68. See also "Cleaning Up Hell's Bedroom," *New York*, November 13, 1992, 50–66.

22. An illustrative case is the infamous Lark Hotel owned by Manhattan realtor Irving Maidman, which was leased to the Reise brothers, a pair of chain-restaurant owners. The Reise brothers, in turn, leased to another who was fronting for yet another who actually held the operating lease on the pross hotel. The Lark was demolished for the erection of an office building (810 Eighth Avenue). Maidman, who Sheehy sympathetically described as "one of the self-made casualties" whose real estate hopes had been blighted by midtown vice, had bought the building on the belief that the Uris Brothers were about to construct a major office building on that block; he tried to talk the Reise Brothers into canceling the remainder of their 21-year lease (for which they were paying $25,000 in rent per year), but to no avail. Offered $200,000, they refused to sell the lease at any price (except if Uris would promise them a restaurant in his new building, a condition Uris refused). Maidman's corner parcel was key to the Uris assemblage; he had an opportunity to cash in and receive almost half a million from the Uris Brothers, and lost. Sheehy, "The Landlords of Hell's Bedroom," 72.

23. Bruder, "Forty-Second Street at the Crossroads," 76.

24. The low-cost aspect of milking in part derived from a large increase in the availability of space that occurred in the mid-1960s, as speculators bought up properties in anticipation of office redevelopment. When the boom collapsed in the early 1970s, the porn shops in the area remained, along with substantial vacancies above the first floor. Dick Netzer, "The Worm in the Apple," *New York Affairs* 4 (Spring 1978), 42–48, at 44.

25. Arthur B. Zabarkes, "An Environmental and Economic Survey of Times Square and Mid-Manhattan," undated [newspaper articles reporting on the study place the date at March 1970], 7. See Alfred E. Clark, "Top Film and Shopping Center Is Proposed for West 42d Street," *New York Times*, March 14, 1970, 21.

26. Kornblum and Boggs's sample was not a random or truly representative sample; it was skewed in the direction of professional, middle-class and upper-middle class

persons who were disproportionally young and involved in taking part in Manhattan's entertainment opportunities. They were the people, the researchers reasoned, who if they said they would return for live entertainment, would actually do so. Since their work was commissioned by the Ford Foundation as part of its more comprehensive efforts to assist the business community and government leaders in the revitalization of West 42nd Street at a time when plans to rebuild the street were being actively formulated, they made some key assumptions which shaped their survey. First, they assumed changing the social conditions of the street was desirable; second, they continued to see the area as an entertainment center and so queried respondents on only that type of potentially new activity.

27. Kornblum and Boggs, "The Social Ecology of the Bright Light District," 33, 41.

28. Senelick, "Private Parts in Public Places," 329.

29. Virginia Dajani, *The Livable City,* no. 10/1 (October 1986): 1; Hugh Hardy, "Make It Dance!" Ibid., 6; Marshall Berman, "Signs Square," *Village Voice,* July 18, 1995, 23ff.; Herbert Muschamp, "Smaller Is Better: Condé Nast in Times Square, *New York Times,* May 18, 1996, 24.

30. Margaret Knapp, "Introductory Essay, Entertainment and Commerce," in *Inventing Times Square,* 120–132, at 120.

31. Huxtable, "Re-inventing Times Square: 1990," 360.

32. Knapp, "Introductory Essay, Entertainment and Commerce," 130.

33. As a metaphor for the city, the Big Apple first appeared in print as early as 1909 as a description of the dominant metropolis in the nation—"New York [was] merely one of the fruits of that great tree whose roots go down in the Mississippi Valley, and whose branches spread from one ocean to the other. . . . [But] the big apple gets a disproportionate share of the national sap." Twenty years later it surfaced as a general metaphor for the acme of success in certain endeavors (show business, jazz, horse racing), so many of which (along with their symbolic streets) were in New York that the city itself, Irving Louis Allen wrote, came to symbolize the acme of various fields. The name was all but forgotten, however, until its revival in 1971. Allen, *The City in Slang,* 62–63.

34. Robert A. M. Stern, Thomas Mellins, and David Fishman, *New York 1960: Architecture and Urbanism Between the Second World War and the Bicentennial* (New York: The Monacelli Press, 1995), 442.

35. Kornblum, "Introduction," in *Bright Light Zone,* 1–16, at 6.

36. Ada Louise Huxtable, "Architectural View/Redeveloping New York," *New York Times*, December 23, 1979, 2:31.

37. Terry Williams and Vernon Boggs, "Street Drug Markets and Hustling in the Bright Light District," in *Bright Light Zone,* 127–165, at 164.

38. "Politicians and Porn," *Economist,* April 2, 1977, 59.

39. Jacobson, "Times Square," 18.

40. "What a Drag," *Newsweek,* December 31, 1962, 32.

41. Stern, Mellins, and Fishman, *New York 1960,* 467–468.

42. Ibid., 467.

43. The six properties making up Theater Row I were, in fact, acquired without compensation, subject to existing mortgages that were in default and held by the Federal Deposit Insurance Corporation; all had moderate to serious code violations and taxes had not been paid to the city since December 1974.

44. Hammack, "Developing for Commercial Culture," in *Inventing Times Square,* 36–50, at 36.

45. Frederic S. Papert, author interview, November 5, 1996.

46. Letter to Louis Winnick, Ford Foundation, from Frederic S. Papert, December 17, 1979.

47. Huxtable, "Redeveloping New York," 31.

48. In addition to Elliott and Weinstein, the team of consultants and officers included Martin Stone (vice president of marketing); Frederic S. Papert (consultant); Regina Espenshade (deputy executive director); John C. Hunt (program consultant); Davis, Brody & Associates/Jacquelin T. Robertson, FAIA (architects); Chermayeff and Geismar Associates (exhibit planning and design); Hugh Hardy, of Hardy, Holzman & Pfeiffer Associates (architectural restoration); Economics Research Associates (planning and marketing consultants); Michael Buckley of Halycon, Ltd. (retail consultants); and Robert Brannigan and Robert Lorelli of Brannigan-Lorelli Associates, Inc. (theater consultants).

49. The City at 42nd Street, Inc., "A Proposal for the Restoration and Redevelopment of 42nd Street," January 1980.

50. Ibid., 7.

51. Huxtable, "Redeveloping New York," 32.

52. Philip Lopate, "42d Street, You Ain't No Sodom," *New York Times*, March 8, 1979, 21.

53. Others on the board of directors included: Arthur Barnes (president, New York Urban Coalition), John Chancellor (correspondent, NBC Nightly News), Howard Clark (retired chairman, the American Express Company), Joan Ganz Cooney (president, Children's Television Network), Morris D. Crawford, Jr. (chairman of the board, The Bowery Savings Bank), Aston Glaves (director, Community Services, Broadway United Church of Christ), Jerome S. Hardy (president, Dreyfus Corporation), Mary McFadden (president, Mary McFadden, Inc.), Frederic Papert (president, 42nd Street Development Corporation), Harold Prince (producer/director), Alan Sagner (chairman, Port Authority of New York and New Jersey), Martin Stone (president, VIP Broadcasting Corporation), William Stuhlbarg (executive vice president, Midtown Realty Owners Association), and James Trees (chairman and chief executive officer, Fischer, Francis, Trees and Watts, Inc.).

54. Donald H. Elliott, author interview, February 3, 1997.

55. Ibid.

56. Ibid.

57. Winnick/Papert letter, December 17, 1979, 2.

58. Michael Goodwin, "Roadblocks for a New Times Sq.," *New York Times*, June 8, 1980, 4:6.

59. Edward I. Koch, author interview, October 3, 2000.

60. Robert McG. Thomas, Jr., "Plans for W. 42d St. Area Back on Drawing Boards," *New York Times*, June 28, 1980, 2:23.

61. James Carberry and Daniel Hertzberg, "West Side Story: New York Plans Renewal of Sleazy Times Square, But the Planning Stage Is About as Far as It Gets," *Wall Street Journal*, August 20, 1980, 40.

62. Elliott, author interview; letter to author from Donald H. Elliott, February 4, 1997.

CHAPTER THREE

1. Anonymous, author interview.

2. Martin Gallent, as quoted in Jewel Bellush, "Clusters of Power: Interest Groups," in *Urban Politics New York Style,* Jewel Bellush and Dick Netzer, eds. (Armonk, N.Y.: M.E. Sharpe, Inc., 1990), 296–338, at 317.

3. Ibid., 318.

4. Ibid., 321, 325.

5. Paul Goldberger, "The Limits of Urban Growth," *New York Times Magazine,*
November 14, 1982, 46ff, at 68.

6. Herbert J. Sturz, author interview, December 5, 1991.

7. Steven Spinola, author interview, April 11, 1991.

8. Robert McG. Thomas, Jr., "Plans for W. 42d St. Area Back on the Drawing
Boards," New York Times, June 28, 1980, 2:23.

9. In addition to the 42DP, UDC/PDC projects included the Audubon Research
Center (Manhattan), International Design Center (Long Island City, Queens), Javits
Convention Center (Manhattan), and South Street Seaport (Manhattan);
PDC/PANYNJ projects included Brooklyn Piers 1–5 (Brooklyn), Teleport (Staten
Island), and Bathgate Industrial Park (Bronx); the three-way coalition of
UDC/PDC/PANYNJ initiated the Queens West development project, though the
Port Authority pulled out of the project in the mid-1990s. Other notable projects
of UDC included Roosevelt Island and Battery Park City, both of which were
executed through project subsidiaries.

10. Stephen A. Lefkowitz, author interview, February 27, 1992.

11. "The idea," Logue recalled, "was to create an agency that would have red tape-
cutting ability and that would take a major, strong aggressive role."
Notwithstanding the significance of the emotional context, the legislature
approved the creation of UDC reluctantly. "The reality is that no political entity
could get these powers today," recalled Vincent Tese in an interview. "Even
Rockefeller, who was known as a guy you didn't double cross, had a hard time
getting these powers." Logue believed that they could hold on to the condemnation power only because they never exercised it while he headed the authority.
Under his direction, the agency got roughly half the funds in the largest federal
nationwide housing subsidy program at the time and within a relatively short period had undertaken 113 housing projects with 32,000 apartments, as well as 30
nonresidential projects. Martin Gottlieb, "U.D.C. Chief Steering Agency into New
Area," *New York Times,* April 13, 1983, B1.

12. Vincent Tese, author interview, December 9, 1996.

13. UDC did not need a "real" economic interest in the project to justify its
actions as an intermediary in a city project. The legal precedent for making deals
through such a coalition had been established in the 1977 *Wein v. Beame* decision
by the Court of Appeals of New York upholding UDC's role in the
Commodore/Grand Hyatt Hotel project.

14. The BOE's statutory voting arrangements provided two votes for the mayor,
comptroller, and city council president and one vote each for the five borough
presidents. In March 1989, the U.S. Supreme Court ruled that the BOE violated
the Constitution's one-man, one-vote principle and that its form of governance
had to be changed. A new city charter passed by the voters in 1989 granted many
of the BOE's powers to a newly expanded 51-person city council, and after 92
years, the BOE went out of existence after its last meeting in August 1990.

15. Carl B. Weisbrod, author interview, July 17, 1991.

16. Sturz, author interview.

17. Letter from John J. Walsh, on behalf of Milstein Properties, regarding the 42nd
Street Development Project (including the so-called "White Paper" submitted with
the letter), September 28, 1984; UDC Response to John J. Walsh letter, November
6, 1984, 10.

18. Even though this land was necessary for the project's development and would have to be acquired through condemnation, UDC allowed its option to lapse because it did not have the money for an immediate purchase. Milstein agreed to purchase the parcel, at a bank sale, on two conditions: (1) if the site was assembled per the plan, the group would be allowed to build a mart, and (2) if the site could not be assembled, they would be allowed to build housing. (Robert Berne, author interview, October 24, 1996.) In the long run, this purchase would become a key tactical loss for the city and state, and for the Milstein Organization, its key bargaining lever to become a player in the project.

19. Jonathan Greenberg, "How to make it big in New York real estate," *Forbes*, October 8, 1984, 43ff. In conversation, Paul Milstein repeated the same story to the author.

20. Wayne King, "Trammell Crow Comes to Town," *New York Times*, November 6, 1983, 3:4.

21. Martin Gottlieb, "The U.D.C. under Stern," *New York Times*, January 26, 1985, 23.

22. Gottlieb, "U.D.C. Chief Steering Agency into New Area."

23. Martin Gottlieb, "Times Square Development Plan: A Lesson in Politics and Power," *New York Times*, March 9, 1984, B1.

24. In an interview Koch emphasized that neither he nor Cuomo had anything to do with the plans for the 42DP. "I was concerned that the process be pristine." The awarding of contracts, he also left to Sturz, and though shown the different offers, he did not intervene, until Cuomo wanted to remove George Kein from the mart project. "When 42nd Street started to get progressively better, Mario responded to others' involvement," said Koch, who added that as for himself, he "didn't want the scent of patronage, special interests." "I never overruled a committee [re, developer selection]." Author interview, October 3, 2000.

25. Gottlieb, "Times Square Development Plan."

26. "The City; City-U.D.C. Pact Is Formally Ended," *New York Times*, August 13, 1983, 27.

27. Gottlieb, "Times Square Development Plan."

28. The merger of this final cast of developers, who had never worked together before, was brokered by Benjamin D. Holloway, executive vice president for real estate for the Equitable Life Assurance Society, the nation's third largest life insurance company. Described as the "glue" holding the consortium together, Holloway was no novice investor in the Times Square area. Putting the power of Equitable's purse behind his long-time belief in midtown west, Holloway had backed new initiatives in Times Square in numerous ways. From its start, Equitable had been a prime corporate backer of *The City at 42nd Street*. A giant real estate owner as well as lender with a portfolio of approximately $20 billion at the time, it had $1.9 billion of holdings in New York office buildings and hotels. It was the lead lender for the Times Square Marriott Marquis Hotel and, with Tishman Speyer, owner of One Astor Place; it also owned the Sheraton Centre, the Sheraton City Squire, and the former Taft Hotel (now the Michelangelo Hotel). More interesting, Equitable's historical role had been something of a corporate place-maker. Over a period of 126 years, through the choice of its own NYC headquarters—at 120 Broadway (1870, 1915), on Seventh Avenue between 31st and 32nd Streets (1924), at 1285 Sixth Avenue, west of Rockefeller Center (1961), and most recently at 787 Seventh Avenue—the insurance giant had pioneered new corporate locations in Manhattan, in areas generally considered risky. Michael deCourcy Hinds,

"Equitable Seeks Park Ave. Rents on Seventh Ave.," *New York Times,* February 9, 1986, 8:1.

29. Tese, author interview.

30. Sturz, author interview.

31. Martin Gottlieb, "The Ghost of Robert Moses May Still Haunt City Hall," *New York Times,* August 21, 1983, 4:7.

32. Gerald Benjamin, "The Political Relationship," in *The Two New Yorks: State-City Relations in the Changing Federal System,* Gerald Benjamin and Charles Brecher, eds. (New York: Russell Sage, 1988), 107–150, at 123.

33. Gottlieb, "The Ghost of Robert Moses May Still Haunt City Hall."

34. As they used the term, the ability to concentrate resources refers to the interaction among seven important variables: the extent of formal independence, variety and intensity of constituency demands, control over the use of land, financial resources, political skill, planning capabilities, and the extent of control over subordinate units. See Michael Danielson and Jameson Doig, *New York: The Politics of Urban Regional Development* (Berkeley: University of California Press, 1982), 25–31, 256–285.

35. Weisbrod, author interview, July 17, 1991.

36. Tese, author interview.

37. DCP, Urban Design Group, *42nd Street Study,* January 1978, NYC DCP 78-04; City of New York, *Times Square Action Plan,* August 1978.

38. Martin Gottlieb, "New Times Square," *New York Times,* January 28, 1984, 26.

39. The *DEIS* is referenced in preference to the *FEIS* because it was represents the city and state's first public disclosure of the project's goals and plans. After public hearings, the publication was revised and republished and a second set of hearings held on the project's future impacts.

40. NYC DCP, *Midtown Zoning,* March 1982, DCP 82-03, 21.

41. As reported by the *DEIS,* fewer than 30 percent of the buildings in the project area were in good or better condition; 21 percent of all building space was vacant; and only 24 to 34 percent of potential zoning capacity had been used. Interestingly, the physical inventory of real estate in the area was drawn from the CA42's detailed 1979 study, *Real Estate Documentation and Analysis,* which was updated by a field study conducted by Parsons Brinckerhoff Quade & Douglass, Inc., in June 1983. See 2-8 to 2-24 and in particular tables 2-3, 2-4, 2-5, and 2-7 for detailed data on these existing conditions. Sex-related uses and movie theaters occupied 13 percent of total space, by land-use category; 14 percent of all occupied space; and 22 percent of ground floor space, which, in comparison to just the blockface, is an inclusive measure.

42. Large-scale clearance was no less controversial a strategy for urban redevelopment in other big-city downtowns across the country at this time, the critical difference being that in several of the most high-profile projects the political costs of pushing this strategy had already been paid. For example, in both of California's biggest projects, Bunker Hill (renamed California Plaza) in Los Angeles and Yerba Buena Gardens in San Francisco, city officials were working with large swaths of vacant land, the result of wholesale bulldozing decades earlier under the federal urban-renewal program. The existence of cleared sites, however definitely marked emotionally by community controversy over lost homes and demolished historic structures, made the task officials faced in pursuing plans for new land uses far less risky politically than would otherwise have been the case. The same can be said for another of New York's large-scale Manhattan projects, Battery Park City, though in

this case the 92 acres that many called "the beach" had been created by landfill from the excavations for the development of the World Trade Center.

The North Loop project in Chicago, an area considered to be a prime candidate for massive redevelopment as early as 1973, presents an instructive contrast, though. A seven-block section was scheduled for almost complete demolition as part of a $571-million plan the city's powerful Mayor Richard J. Daley had put before the city council. When his successor, Michael Bilandic, picked up the project and, in 1976, applied to Washington for a $25-million UDAG to cover the cost of acquiring and clearing the site, the federal government rejected the application, twice. Only after the city dramatically cut back the scope of its plan, with an application that called for acquiring and clearing just a two-block area (which became part of a new hotel and convention center owned and operated by Hilton Hotel Corporation), did HUD eventually approve the proposal and fund a $7.9-million grant. Getting to that point had been highly contentious. Intense controversy erupted—over the use of funds for downtown versus neighborhoods; fears of displacement of low-income customers, existing firms and employees, and union jobs; and the proposed tax subsidies. The most sustained issue of all was the preservation of several landmark buildings, four of which were on the National Register and two others of which were being proposed for that status. At least twice, HUD refused to release the grant because of fears that national landmarks would be destroyed. "Despite all their misgivings about landmark buildings and the use of UDAGs, the North Loop's importance to Chicago was quite well recognized among many of those least satisfied with [developer] Rubloff's plan," wrote Gerald D. Suttles. The older Harris, Selwyn, and Woods Theaters were especially important venues for small productions and the Chicago Theater, an excellent facility for rare large productions; a "theater row" connecting the two theater sites through the proposed convention center was possible, but it was nowhere in the developer's plans. Before the UDAG grant was in the clear, a powerful civic coalition emerged to fight for preservation and pressed officials not to grant any tax breaks for the project. Further development of the project did not go forward before guidelines proposed by one of the civics guaranteed the survival of eight historic landmarks, a major victory for preservationists, though these turned out to be only advisory and the controversy waged on for many more years. Theater Row would not become a reality until the late 1990s, under the mayoral administration of Richard M. Daley, who supported the Loop theaters with large tax-increment-financed subsidies. "Chicago brings loop back to life; Billion-dollar plan clearing political, financial hurdles," *Engineering News-Record,* July 2, 1981, 30.

43. Herbert J. Gans, "The 42nd Street Development Project Draft EIS: An Assessment," unpublished report prepared for the New York City Board of Estimate on behalf of the Brandt Organization, 1984, 5.

44. Ibid., 7. [Page references omitted in the quotation.]

45. Ibid., 13.

46. Sturz, author interview.

47. Paul A. Travis, author interview, January 27, 1992.

48. Lefkowitz, author interview.

49. Travis, author interview; Sturz, author interview.

50. Under the 1968 provision to the Zoning Resolution, an owner of a landmark structure could transfer unused development rights to contiguous lots or to lots across a street or intersection, provided that the development potential of the receiving lot was not increased by more than 20 percent and provided that the

CPC found the transfer would do nothing "to the detriment of the occupants of buildings on the block or nearby blocks." Alexander Garvin, *The American City: What Works, What Doesn't* (New York: McGraw-Hill, 1996), 425.

51. *DEIS,* 2-52, 2-54.

52. James S. Russell, "Golddiggers of '84?" *Architectural Record* 172 (October 1984), 125–131, at 127.

53. *Municipal Art Society of New York v. City of New York,* 137 Misc. 2d 832, 837–838 N.Y.S.2d 800, 803–804 (N.Y. Sup Ct. 1987). Donning the hat of entrepreneur, the city had attempted to generate the highest income from the sale of public land while simultaneously approving the use of a discretionary density bonus as part of its regulatory function. The singularity of the city's pecuniary motives was evident in the timing of its actions. The city incorporated the initial proceeds into the fiscal year 1987 budget before final approval of the sale and thus appeared to have granted the bonus to balance the budget. Equally damaging was the city's RFP, which stated that the purchase price offered would be "the primary consideration" and that the developer would be required to "apply for and use its best efforts to obtain the maximum 20 percent Subway bonus." See Lynne B. Sagalyn, "Public Development: Using Land as a Capital Resource," Lincoln Institute of Land Policy, working paper, 1992, 18–22; Richard F. Babcock, "The City as Entrepreneur: Fiscal Wisdom or Regulatory Folly," in *City Deal Making,* ed. Terry Jill Lassar (Washington, D.C.: ULI, 1990), 23–29.

54. In the past, plans for large areas of cities, however rational in form and appealing in urban design, typically floundered because the problem of scale presented, as one well-known critic remarked, "awkward practical problems," typically of a financial nature. If privately financed, the costs of carrying non-producing space in advance of its needs impose heavy demands, while the real estate market cannot absorb the scale of building very big all at once. If publicly financed, "the political problems of government projects increase geometrically with size." Jonathan Barnett, *The Elusive City: Five Centuries of Design, Ambition and Miscalculation* (New York: Harper & Row, 1986), 170–171.

55. Paul Goldberger, "The Legal Hands That Shape Crowded Manhattan Skyline," *New York Times,* July 17, 1980, B1.

56. Not everyone was against the "old zoning concepts" fashioned at a time when crowding and congestion were viewed as positives in a city that physically defined itself by its density. For one, Donald H. Elliott, chairman of the CPC when the discretionary system evolved, considered the revisions a reaction to the density of the three buildings still in construction. "It's a little much to change the world around before you even see how the three buildings work together," he said. "The assumption that the incentive zoning system is a disaster is dead wrong." Alan S. Oser, "Real Estate Arguments Are Assembled on Changing Midtown Zoning," *New York Times,* July 23, 1980, 19.

57. NYC DCP, *Midtown Zoning,* 11.

58. Jonathan Barnett, author interview, January 21, 1997.

59. Michael Kwartler, author interview, February 20, 1997.

60. Oser, "Real Estate Arguments are Assembled on Changing Midtown Zoning."

61. Jeffrey Katz, author interview, April 11, 1997.

62. John Mollenkopf, "City Planning," in *Setting Municipal Priorities, 1990,* eds, Charles Brecher and Raymond D. Horton (New York: New York University Press, 1989), 141–172, at 156.

63. The residents of Clinton had good reason to worry. The *DEIS* concluded that the displacement of sex-related establishments would for the most part be felt in

midtown west, in particular, upper Times Square, along Eighth Avenue north of 42nd Street, and in the Madison Square Garden area south of 35th Street. No area, the report predicted, would emerge as a new West 42nd Street, because limiting factors, such as the office and entertainment centers that are key to the 42nd Street type of uses, were likely to discourage wholesale relocation. Even though the *DEIS* reported that "it is unlikely that more than a few of the displaced establishments would choose or be able to relocate along this stretch of Eighth Avenue [35th to 50th Street]," it went on to conclude that "the resulting impacts will nevertheless be adverse, especially for the neighboring Clinton community." *DEIS*, 2-142

64. Koch, author interview.

65. At the eleventh hour, union interests represented by the International Ladies Garment Workers Union also secured an additional commitment from the city that it would undertake a six-month study of the effect of the 42DP on the Garment District and recommend safeguards to protect the district's manufacturers. The city's compromise with the civic organizations, who questioned the project's mass, density, and overall design guidelines, is discussed in chapter 8. The civics, along with the performing-arts community, were the largest source of opposition to the project, second to Clinton.

66. The data come from the author's analysis and classification of the testimony at both sets of public hearings. The main difference in the composition of vocal opposition at these events was the fact that vested business interests (owners of property in the project area or operators of theaters on West 42nd Street) did not appear in force to testify at the BOE hearings as they had at the *DEIS* hearings; at the *DEIS* hearings, business interests opposed to the project represented 34 percent of all who testified in opposition compared to 5.4 percent of those testifying in opposition at the BOE hearings. Rather, their opposition to the project, manifested itself through individual lawsuits, with five filed in the two months preceding the start of the BOE hearings and another 13 in the month after the project was approved. See chapter 7.

67. H.V. Savitch, *Post-Industrial Cities: Politics and Planning in New York, Paris, and London* (Princeton: Princeton University Press, 1988), 76–77.

CHAPTER FOUR

1. Testimony of Mayor Edward I. Koch at the neeting of the Board of Estimate of the City of New York, October 25, 1984, stenographic record [herein referred to as BOE hearings], 2–3.

2. Richard A. Kahan, author interview, October 16, 1991.

3. Carl B. Weisbrod, author interview, October 31, 1991.

4. Martin E. Gold, "Economic Development Projects: A Perspective," *Urban Lawyer* 1 (Spring 1987), 199–231, at 220.

5. BOE hearings, 134–135.

6. In the case of the 42DP, CPC chairman Herbert Sturz could draw on the expertise of at least two attorneys with deep institutional knowledge of past deals, city counsel for the project Stephen A. Lefkowitz who had been involved in most of the large-scale projects in New York City, including Roosevelt Island and Battery Park City, before he drafted the 42DP MOU, and Martin E. Gold, an economic-development specialist who had set up the economic-development unit within the city counsel's office and had drafted the agreements for the Marriott Marquis Hotel deal.

7. Among the criteria that would be used to select developers for the 42DP, the RFP listed eight: (1) "the willingness and the ability of the developer to make its proposed development consistent with the overall goals of the Project; (2) the nature of the developer's commitment to provide funds needed to pay the costs of acquisition of its proposed Site, including the sources of such funds, the timing of payments and the security that the developer will provide to insure that such payments are made as agreed . . .; (3) the degree to which the proposal furthers the public objectives for the Project Area, including proposed uses and construction of public improvements and rehabilitation and preservation of historically and architecturally significant structures; (4) the amount of rent to be paid by the developer and the timing of the payment thereof . . .; (5) security and guarantees to be provided for the payment of rent and the performance of all other obligations of the developer; (6) the proposed development timetable; (7) the developer's financial, development and management capacity, including experience with similar projects, the development expertise of principal members and consultants of the developer's team and the specific resources to be committee to the Project; (8) the environmental impacts of the proposal. . . ." Preferences would be given for proposals in which the developer would be a master developer, would fund the costs of site acquisition at the time they are incurred by the public sector (and funding of preliminary costs at the time of a developer's conditional selection), and would be prepared to "expeditiously commence and complete their development." NYS UDC, *42nd Street Development Project: Request for Proposals,* June 1981, 6–8, 10.

8. James R. Brigham, "The 42nd Street Development Project: The City's Perspective," *City Almanac* 18 (Summer), 9–11, at 9.

9. Paul A. Travis, author interview, January 27, 1992.

10. UDC, "For Consideration [Board of Directors], 42nd Street Development Land Use Improvement Project, Conditional Designation of Developers," April 6, 1982. Whether to select a master developer for the whole development project or designate individual developers for each of the project's development parcels has been a recurrent policy question of large-scale public development, in New York (Battery Park City), Los Angeles (California Plaza), and San Francisco (Yerba Buena Gardens) alike. There does not seem to be any hard and fast rule about "what works best"; differences in market dynamics, site characteristics, the nature of public objectives for a project, and the legal alternatives for designating developers all factor into the policy decision, making generalizations about the best approach seemingly more conclusive than the experience of the 1980s might suggest.

11. Travis, author interview.

12. Trained as a city planner after receiving a B.A. degree cum laude from the State University of New York at Albany, Travis had come to PDC in 1979 where he served as senior vice president until 1984; he was responsible for numerous commercial and industrial developments throughout the city, in addition to directing PDC's efforts on the 42DP. When the city shifted its efforts from reviewing *The City at 42nd Street* to taking charge of the initiative itself, he was designated as PDC's point person for the project, and he brought to the task a familiarity with public-private deal making, having done a lot of work on the Portman/Marriott Marquis Hotel deal.

13. Travis, author interview.

14. The permissive language of the RFP, however, established a definite policy floor to these payments: "While such payment may include a real estate tax abatement and exemption schedule," the city and state expected "that after a reasonable period

of time" rent would include "an amount equal to the real estate taxes which would otherwise be payable if the Site were not owned by the UDC subsidiary...." Rent under the ground lease was not to be less than the real estate taxes prevailing at the time the site was initially acquired by UDC, NYS UDC, *42DP: Request for Proposals*, 17.

15. Travis, author interview.

16. Anonymous, author interview.

17. "Milstein Opens Throttle As Builder," *New York Times*, October 18, 1981, 8:1.

18. Eastdil Realty, Inc., "Letter Memo to Lawrence F. Graham, Herbert Sturz, Philip E. Aarons," April 5, 1982, 7. Comparing the financial benefits of differently structured bids is rarely easy or clear cut. One way to put them on a level playing field is to recast the numbers in terms of net present values. The two components of Park Tower's proposed lease payment, discounted at 10 percent (to 1982 dollars), constituted $75.3 million in base ground rent and $6.1 million in incentive ground rent. Other payments pledged as part of the bid by Klein included a secured site acquisition price of $88 million; $5.25 million for site acquisition of Site 5, and funding for acquiring the Harris Theater and the infill portion of Site 6; $4.2 million for theater renovations; $21.6 million for subway improvements; and provisions for public profit-sharing from transactions in which Park Tower's interests were either transferred, sublet, refinanced, or sold. These financial terms could be summarized succinctly in two pages. In terms of what was needed to backstop these public and private commitments for development, the deal required 47 pages of a Memorandum of Terms and, ultimately, several thousand pages of lease documents.

19. Paul Goldberger, "An Appraisal: 499 Park, The Intent Is Serious," *New York Times*, February 12, 1981, C24.

20. The innuendo surrounding Klein's designation appeared to be inseparable from his close political ties with Koch. Weisbrod, who was head of the OME at the time, believed the selection of developers for the 42DP was not a political decision, notwithstanding the negative comments about Klein Cuomo had made in his diaries. Likewise, Travis recalled in an interview that Koch stayed out of the developer selection process; the mayor, he said, did not want to be involved and made the point by glibly saying, "I'll see who it is at the press conference." Once the developers had been selected, the mayor, who reportedly has a very good memory, subsequently became involved and familiar with the terms of the deals. Travis, author interview. See also chapter 3, note 24.

21. Jonathan Greenberg, "How to make it big in New York real estate," *Forbes*, October 8, 1984, 43ff.

22. He had helped raise local money for Ronald Reagan's presidential campaign in 1980 and during the mid-to-late 1970s had helped Mayor Koch lobby congressional contacts on behalf of the city when it needed federal aid. So too when it came to the mayor's election efforts: Klein (along with Jack Rudin and Donald Trump) was "at the very top of my campaign contributors when I ran for reelection in 1981 . . . and in 1982 when I was running for Governor," Koch recalled in his first memoir, as characteristically as outspoken as the man. Edward I. Koch, *Mayor: An Autobiography* (New York: Simon & Schuster, 1984), 289.

23. George Klein, author interview, April 4, 1995.

24. Klein, author interview, December 4, 1997.

25. NYS UDC, *42nd Street Development Project: Executive Summary of the Final Environmental Impact Statement*, August 1984, S-3.

26. Known as Broadway Plaza, the $7.5-million project was always highly contentious. It lacked the unqualified support of both theater and business interests who worried that the open space created by the project would become a gathering place for street people, drug traffickers, and peddlers. Some considered that it might become "Needle Park South" in reference to "Needle Park North," the small park, known as a drug hangout, at 66th Street where Broadway crosses Columbus Avenue. Firmly convinced that it was a "misguided effort doomed before it starts," the *Times* editors wrote "It is the kind of dated window dressing that boosters embrace, and someone seems to love at City Hall." They thought it might make a "nice pimp and prostitute promenade." ("When Does a Mall Pall?," *New York Times*, February 5, 1977, 18.) It was, in its last design version, to run between 45th and 47th Streets, and jut out over Broadway in a way so as to create a plaza in front of the Portman hotel. Once opposition to the demolition of the Helen Hayes and Morosco Theaters surfaced, the linkage between the mall project and the hotel project became an issue of public debate. Following the court's final go-ahead for the Portman project, Broadway Plaza appeared doomed, and it was given an early obituary by *Times* critic Paul Goldberger. Notwithstanding the fact that all the approvals were in place and financing was on hand, the plan died—to much applause.

27. Roberta Brandes Gratz, "Cityscape: Save the Helen Hayes," *New York*, November 19, 1979, 74ff, at 75.

28. Michiko Kakutani, "Portman Hotel: Broadway Is a House Divided," *New York Times*, January 24, 1982, 2:1.

29. Bernard Hughes, "On with the Show, Not the Hotel," *New York Times*, February 10, 1980, 21.

30. Michael Sorkin, quoted in Roberta Brandes Gratz, *The Living City* (New York: Simon & Schuster, 1989), 354.

31. NYS UDC, *42nd Street Development Project: Draft Environmental Impact Statement*, February 1984, 2-309.

32. BOE hearings, 204.

33. Ibid., 205.

34. Using development rights as currency was the strategy of choice during the early 1980s for Los Angeles and San Francisco as well, when these cities sought a major public-benefit program as the centerpiece for their large-scale downtown commercial projects.

Seeking elements of a cultural landscape it lacked and sorely needed, Los Angeles bargained for a museum and a hilltop park with an open-space network of gardens, mini-parks, and integrated water elements as part of what would be provided by the developer of California Plaza, the last piece of the city's long-running Bunker Hill urban-renewal project. In addition, the demands of the site's history called for the city to reconstruct, and the developer to provide funds for operation and maintenance of, Angel's Flight, a single-track funicular and tourist attraction that had carried locals and visitors up the eastern slope of Bunker Hill from downtown since the 1890s. A new downtown of office towers built since the mid-1960s had given Los Angeles a skyline, but as a regional focal point for business growth, the downtown lacked an active "heart"—a center that could lure people out of their cubicles and cars with cultural activities after hours and on weekends. To ensure delivery of its priorities, the city demanded that the developer build the free-standing 100,000-square-foot Museum of Contemporary Art, 20 percent of the open-space network, and the first residential phase at the same time as the first office tower, which was a heavy high-risk burden for the developer to carry. The character of the $50.6-million public-benefits package set this $1.2-billion project apart from others in the city at the time. Yet equally ambitious was San Francisco's agenda for its three-block downtown project. Seeking a world-class public-amenity package, San Francisco used the currency of its publicly owned land to generate revenues (both annual lease payments and land-disposition proceeds) that its redevelopment agency, acting as developer, used to build and maintain Yerba Buena Gardens, the largest downtown park since Union Square was presented to the city in 1850. From its inception in the early 1960s as an urban-renewal project, redevelopment of the three central blocks of the Yerba Buena district had been slated for some type of major recreation activity, though the character of this activity changed dramatically over time. (Initial plans for a sports arena to complement a convention center planned for the site were scrapped after nearly two decades of political controversy, lawsuits, and ever-escalating construction costs.) For the city's new public-amenity strategy to work, the San Francisco Redevelopment Authority had to establish a scale of private development that would correspond to the anticipated economics of the desired public amenities, then estimated at $104.5 million. This it could do as owner of the land, and because the urban-renewal project lay outside the conventional land-use approval process. Because the city also wanted to use the project to further its planning objective of shifting new office growth to the area south of Market Street, a territory that historically had been avoided, incentives were necessary to attract a private development team willing to take the risks inherent in meeting the city's ambitious large-scale development objectives (1.6 million square feet), on-site infrastructure needs, and public-amenity package. In negotiating with the different developers of the overall $2-billion mixed-use development, the city sought to maximize the value of the real estate, then extract cash to both construct and maintain the public gardens. As in Los Angeles, the strategy was designed to build on the momentum of a strong real estate market by leveraging the development value of the private commercial uses to deliver extensive public-amenity packages.

35. Anonymous, author interview.

36. Leonard Chazen quoted in Exploring the Metropolis, *Hindsight and Foresight: Planning for Significant City-Owned Sites* (New York: Exploring the Metropolis, October 1988), 32–33.

37. This savings would increase with time, as well. Under the terms of the deal, the developer could count on passing the savings advantage to potential tenants for 15 years because PILOTs were set to escalate at a guaranteed $.27 per square foot compared to an amount in excess of $.80 per square foot projected for other buildings.

38. Landauer Associates, *Marketing and Financial Analysis of the Times Square Redevelopment Project*, prepared for Park Tower Associates, June 1983, 10; see 9–14 in particular for discussion of economic benefits.

39. All four office towers were projected to open at various times through 1992; the combined savings from the differences in land cost and real estate taxes, calculated on an annual basis over the 15-year term, were projected at $18.98 per square foot when compared with a new West Side building and $26.41 per square foot when compared with a new East Side building. From the developer's perspective, the deal's risk-reward relationship appeared sufficiently healthy—until the real estate market collapsed.

40. The interest charge on the loan depended upon the developer's source of funds. If the ESAC was financed over a term of five years or less, interest would

accrue at a rate of 1 percent over the prime lending rate; if financed over a term in excess of five years or paid by the developer with its own funds, the rate would be the yield for 15-year A-rated new issue corporate bonds.

41. David W. Dunlap, "Times Square Plan Is on Hold, but the Meter is Still Running," *New York Times*, August 9, 1992, 44.

42. The 99-year ground lease served as the vehicle for managing the ESAC repayment and abatement of real estate taxes. Because title to the sites would be held by a tax-exempt subsidiary of UDC, real estate taxes would not be payable on the land or the improvements thereon, though through UDC the city would negotiate payments-lieu-of-taxes (PILOTs). Also, materials incorporated into the construction would be exempt from the state sales and compensating-use taxes (SUT). UDC and the city would collect these amounts from developer, and put them into a trust fund which would be first used to reduce the outstanding ESAC. The business terms of the deal specified multiple sources for the repayment of ESAC and established an allocation priority: SUT payments; upside revenues—percentage (or incentive) rents, alternative rents, or transaction payments, and basic rent payments. As a practical matter the funds to repay ESAC ultimately depended upon the PILOT-based lease payments. The rent credit was, to the developer, the most significant because it defined the size of the check he would write to UDC in any one year, and it was limited to 50 percent of the basic rent otherwise payable in that year. This meant that as long as ESAC remained outstanding, only 50 percent of the basic ground rent would flow directly into city coffers; the rest would go to reduce the ESAC balance.

43. Travis, author interview.

44. Veronica W. Hackett, author interview, February 22, 1995.

45. Martin E. Gold, comments to the author on draft report, May 8, 1996.

46. NYS UDC, *42nd Street Development Land Use Improvement Project New York, New York, General Project Plan* [hereinafter referred to as *GPP*], section 5, C.2.

47. Travis, author interview.

48. NYS UDC, *42DP: Request for Proposals*, 2.

49. The language of the BOE Resolution called for renovation and use of the Lyric, Apollo, and Selwyn Theaters (Site 5 theaters), the Harris Theater and the New Amsterdam as "Broadway Theaters"; the Liberty and Victory Theaters were to be used for nonprofit theater. Retail, restaurant, or mart-related conference uses were permitted for the Empire Theater, and retail or restaurant use was permitted for the Times Square Theater. The *GPP* allowed that "one of two theaters could be used for first-run movies on an interim basis while being renovated or until theater use becomes feasible."

50. At the time of its conditional designation in April 1982, the Nederlander Organization had been in business 20 years and controlled the operation of some 25 theaters located in New York, Chicago, Baltimore, San Francisco, Los Angeles, Phoenix, St. Louis, and Detroit; ten of these theaters were in New York. As the Eastdil analysis prepared for UDC's board noted, Nederlander had a contract to purchase the New Amsterdam for $5.2 million and, after closing, would contribute the property to UDC in order to obtain the designation for this site. In addition, Nederlander was designated to develop the Harris Theater at its cost and operate it as a legitimate theater.

51. American Practice Management, Inc. (APM), "Assessing Market Feasibility of Ten Theaters on 42nd Street," report prepared for the NYC Public Development Corporation and the NYS Urban Development Corporation, with the assistance of Brannigan-Lorelli Associates, Inc., and Theater Now, Inc., January 1981, 19.

52. NYS UDC, *42nd Street Development Project: Executive Summary of the Final Environmental Impact Statement*, S-13.

53. NYS UDC, "42nd Street Development Project: Update," October 22, 1984, 9.

54. Jack L. Goldstein, "Development and the Threat to the Theater District," *City Almanac* 18 (Summer 1985), 23–24, at 24.

55. APM, "Assessing the Market Feasibility of Ten Theaters on 42nd Street," 3.

56. James S. Russell, "Golddiggers of '84?" *Architectural Record* 172 (October 1984), 125–131, at 131.

CHAPTER FIVE

1. Peter Grant, "Why Prudential Needs Times Square," *Crain's New York Business*, September 4, 1989, 17.

2. George Klein, author interview, December 4, 1997.

3. State of New York, Executive Chamber, Mario M. Cuomo, Governor and City of New York, Office of the Mayor, Edward I. Koch, Mayor, Press Release, June 21, 1988.

4. Austrian Roth Partners, "Austrian Roth Manhattan Land Price Index," unpublished monograph, March 28, 1991. Land prices in midtown west increased dramatically in 1984, more than doubling according to the City Planning Commission. As reported in its 1987 *Midtown Development Review*, average values of land per buildable square foot rose at an annual average rate of 26 percent between 1982 and 1986, indicating to the CPC "greater market acceptance of the West Side as a development location." On West 42nd Street, the illustrative example was the 24-story Candler Building—the only office building in the project area not slated for acquisition—which sold for $14.75 million in January 1984, an 11-fold increase over the $1.3 million its owner, former City Taxi Commissioner Michael Lazar, had paid for the building in January 1980.

5. Matthew Mayer, author interview, May 18, 1998.

6. Vincent Tese, author interview, December 9, 1996.

7. Richard Levine, "State Acquires Most of Times Square Project Site," *New York Times*, April 19, 1990, 1.

8. James P. Stuckey, author interview, January 23, 1998.

9. Carl B. Weisbrod, author interview, October 31, 1991. Koch liked the renegotiated deal because if values went up, the city would benefit. Not everyone in his administration, he recalled, was happy about redoing the deal, though. Author interview, October 3, 2000.

10. At the time it was fairly well known internally, if not stated in public, that the Trammell Crow deal for the mart site was not going to happen. Tishman Speyer Properties, which had rights to develop with Trammell Crow, came to UDC with a proposal for an office building instead. At about the same time, the Kennedy-mart interests, along with Chemical Bank, came to the city with a joint proposal for a mart/office building.

11. Stuckey, author interview.

12. Ibid.

13. The payback mechanism for the "super" ESAC further pushed the deal into the realm of technical esoterica. Called "nonrecoverable" ESAC in the project's legal documents, the logic of the wording is difficult to grasp at first. Since the new ESAC obligations were linked to the hotel and mart uses, the LADA anticipated their reimbursement by the future developers of those sites. Accordingly, these "private" obligations would not be recoverable by the city. The city, however, actu-

ally would bear the long-term liability to repay these sums (with interest) until such time that private development occurred on those sites.

14. This point was addressed in the 1992 negotiations, as discussed in chapter 9. Carl B. Weisbrod, letter to the author.

15. UDC press releases during 1987–1988 with such language include: "UDC Acts to Speed Acquisition for 42nd Street Development Project," August 20, 1987; "UDC Authorized 42nd Street Development Project to Enter into Leases with Times Square Center Associates and Begin Property Condemnation Process," February 9, 1987; "Public Authorities Control Board Approves 42nd Street Development Project," June 1, 1988.

16. Plaintiffs charged that the public notice did not detail the many fine points of the deal. In particular, they cited missing definitions for "net cash flow," "excess casualty insurance proceeds," and the interest rate on ESAC that would accrue to TSCA; insufficient specification of the identity of the proposed purchasers/lessee, of dates when construction on the four sites must begin; of information on decorative lighting and graphic improvements which the developers would be providing; and of the identity of "related agreements." Complaint, *Franz Leichter et al. v. N.Y.S. Urban Dev. Corp.,* No. 30229/87 (N.Y. Sup. Ct. filed Dec. 8, 1987).

17. Court opinion from *Xerox Corp. v. Webster*, 65 N.Y.2d 131, 132, 48 N.E.2d 74, 490 N.Y.S.2d 488 (1985), as quoted in UDC letter to William J. Robbins, Esq., Rosenberg & Estis, December 3, 1987, 1.

18. "The purpose of the public hearing," Judge Miriam J. Altman opined, "is to give the public the opportunity for comment and input prior to final approval of the leases. Disclosure of the leases in final form would likely hinder negotiations and render the public input less effective." (5) The judge also pointed out the published terms read in conjunction with previously available information [the Memorandum of Terms] provided "sufficient particularity. In fact, it is clear from plaintiffs' papers that they are able to make many meaningful comments and to offer intelligent criticism of the proposed leases." *Leichter et al. v. N.Y.S. Urban Dev. Corp.,* No. 30229/87 (N.Y. Sup. Ct. filed Dec. 8, 1987).

19. In this case, the plaintiffs focused on whether the discrepancy between the actual leases and the proposed leases discussed at the hearing rendered the notice insufficient, ex post facto. *Flynn v. N.Y.S. Urban Dev. Corp.*, 546 N.Y.S.2d 354 (1989).

20. Ibid., at 356.

21. Weisbrod, author interview, October 31, 1991.

22. Gary M. Rosenberg, author interview, May 30, 1990.

23. Michael Moss, "NY Panel Balks at OK for $2B Times Sq. Deal," *Newsday*, March 2, 1988, 9.

24. Anonymous, author interview.

25. The payback pivoted on the relationship between the developer's maximum yearly rent credit (reducing the ESAC) and the city's accrual of interest on the outstanding ESAC (increasing the ESAC), and on the future level and growth of real estate taxes after the 15-year abatement of property taxes burned off. Whether the city's economic liability increased or decreased in any one year depended upon whether the cost of compounding interest exceeded the anticipated revenues (scheduled rents and percentage rents less the maximum rent credit). With rising land values and expanded funding obligations inflating the ESAC, the city's projected interest costs grossly exceeded base rents, even at such time when all four towers might be complete. For instance, with all four buildings complete, a rent credit of $4.5 million (based on the scheduled PILOT payments of $9 million) would be

easily consumed by a $21-million interest accrual (assuming 10 percent interest on a $206-million ESAC), resulting in a $16.5-million addition to the outstanding ESAC balance. Consequently, during the abatement period the net account was sure to be negative, meaning the city faced a growing liability—albeit not a cash cost—from a continuously escalating open tab.

26. Stephen A. Lefkowitz, author interview, March 1, 1992.

27. The three studies are Office of State Senator Franz S. Leichter, "A Public Subsidy Exceeding One Billion Dollars: The Leases for Sites 1, 3, 4, and 12 (Proposed Office Towers) of the 42nd Street Development Project ("Leichter"), memorandum, October 3, 1988; Rosenberg & Estis, P.C., "Economic Calculation of Times Square Redevelopment Project," memorandum, February 1990; Emanuel Tobier and Lisa Roberts, "Calculating the Tax Subsidy Implications of the Times Square Center Associates (TSCA) Project," memorandum to the file, January 15, 1991. Estimates of this cost (interest)-revenue gap over the 15-year abatement period varied from $503 million to $1.3 billion. The huge differentials among the projections can be traced to one key assumption, the point of departure of the ESAC loan, which ranged from $100 million to $214 million. Other critical assumptions included the timing and completion of construction of each of the four towers and the rate of interest charged on the ESAC loan. Despite differences in methodology, the three reviews were in accord on a clear conclusion—the ESAC was not likely to be paid off over the 99-year lease term. After the deal had been recast in 1994, a fourth study by the Municipal Art Society of New York, "Analysis of the 42nd Street Development Project," Memorandum, July 28, 1994, with many of the same methodological problems appeared.

28. Klein, author interview.

29. From a practical perspective, the mortgage company's loan could be considered equity: Could it ever expect to get repaid? Since it was an accrual loan, it could never be considered nonperforming. What security backed this loan? In essence, it was an unsecured line to a venture in which another subsidiary of the parent company was an equity investor. In finance parlance, this is equity.

30. Japanese investors paid the first and second highest prices for Manhattan office properties in 1986: $610 million ($295 per square foot) for the Exxon Building and $301 million ($500 per square foot) for Tower 49. The buying spree continued into next year when the Japanese purchased $3.9 billion of Manhattan office properties—43 percent of their total investment in U.S. office real estate. Their most visible and highly publicized transaction, however, was the purchase of 80 percent of the Rockefeller Group Interests by Mitsubishi in the late 1980s for $1.4 billion.

31. Alan S. Oser, "Falling Inflation Prompts a Shift in Investments, *New York Times*, May 11, 1986, 18; Michael Cassell, "North American Real Estate: The Aftermath of Excess," *Financial Times* (London), April 19, 1986, XIX.

32. Martin Gottlieb, "Developers Looking West of Sixth Avenue," *New York Times*, December 4, 1983, 8:1.

33. Landauer Associates, *Marketing and Financial Analysis of the Times Square Redevelopment Project*, prepared for Park Tower Associates, June 1983, B-3–B-4. In 1983, when the firm's staff did the analysis, the simple economics of the deal looked very favorable: a break-even rent of about $25 to $26 per square foot, which was low by prevailing market rates.

34. In the event TSCA developed only two sites, the cost of the development opportunity (as of 1984 at the time of the BOE approval) per square foot of FAR would increase from $28.76 to a low of $46.52 (Sites 12 and 1) and a high of $74.00 (Sites 3 and 4).

35. "BPT-Associates; Donald R. Knab is named chief of realty venture formed by Bechtel Investments and Park Tower," *Business Wire*, August 13, 1987.

36. Weisbrod, author interview, January 16, 1992.

37. *Jackson v. N.Y.S. Urban Dev. Corp.* [67 N.Y.2d 400], 494 N.E.2d 429, [503 N.Y.S.2d 298] (N.Y. Ct. App. 1986) consolidated four cases by two sets of plaintiffs who either worked or owned buildings in the area. On the significance of this litigation a seminar paper, "Environmental Litigation and Redevelopment Projects," written by Alicia Glen while a Columbia Law Student in 1991 was very helpful.

38. Jeffrey Hoff, "Who Should Pay to Transform Times Square," *Barron's*, September 25, 1989, 64.

39. Klein, author interview, April 4, 1995.

40. Klein, author interview, December 4, 1997.

41. "No one could conceive of a situation in which Prudential, would not be able to get a construction loan. Yet, six months later [early 1989], when they went around for financing, they found they couldn't get lenders to take them seriously," Prudential's Sharon Barnes recalled, painfully. "The lenders would say, 'why should they ever consider Times Square towers when they could go up and down Park Avenue and make loans?'" A state of shock prevailed. "They never thought that the market would collapse and Prudential would not be able to get a loan. They had been confident without understanding that the key variables could change." Sharon Barnes, author interview, November 20, 1997.

42. In the late 1960s and early 1970s, the company had gotten involved with development in response to inflation fears, and only later started to initiate its own projects: "It came down to the question of do you pay retail or do you pay wholesale," said Knab. (Grant, "Why Prudential Needs Times Square.") In 1985, when it had over 100 projects under development nationally, *Corporate Design and Realty*, a trade magazine, ranked it top developer of the year, citing its 31 million square feet under construction. In 1987, *Building Design and Construction Survey* listed Prudential as the fifth largest developer in the county with $850 million of construction in place. In 1989, with a portfolio of direct investments of approximately $18 billion, it was the largest institutional owner of real estate in the United States, a ranking only Equitable Life Assurance Society could challenge. Such size and success Prudential officials attributed to the latitude given the real estate group by the company's board of directors.

The organizational capacity and track record of Prudential's development arm was impressive, especially relative to the more free-wheeling operations of entrepreneurial development firms. In 1986 it was operating in 24 offices across the United States and another in Toronto, each of which exercised responsibility for a full range of development activities—identifying opportunities, selecting and supervising construction teams, securing financing, monitoring accounting procedures, and implementing leasing strategies. Its suburban office parks became noted for their high-end corporate amenities. In big cities like Chicago, Minneapolis, Boston, Dallas, and Houston, speculative investments in signature "Prudential Centers" defined a formidable, sometimes precedent-setting presence, in downtown. Moreover, Prudential customarily built large-scale projects.

Within Prudential's enormous organizational structure in the 1980s, real estate was transacted in one of three areas within the umbrella Prudential Realty Group: the property development company, the equity property group, and the mortgage company, in that order of perceived hierarchical importance. The property development group was a "powerful fiefdom" unto itself, according to one close observer. Overall, the realty group consisted of between 1,300 and 1,400 people.

43. Barbara Selvin, "Klein, Pru Splitsville?" *Newsday,* December 14, 1989, 59.

44. Richard Levine, "State Acquires Most of Times Square Project Site," *New York Times,* April 19, 1990, A1, at B2.

45. The market risks were not unknown at the time of the 1987 formal decision to become a partner in the deal. Prudential had conducted its own analysis of a doomsday-scenario by projecting of the impact of major job losses in the financial-services sector. Under that type of scenario, which indicated that the real estate impact of such would be severe—vacancies in midtown would shoot up into the double-digits, between 18 and 20 percent, with absorption of overbuilt space taking four to five years—projected returns would drop dramatically.

46. Throughout the 1990s, Prudential was beset with a series of deep-seated and widespread business irregularities in its business operations. The first scandal involved real estate limited-partnership investments sold through in its securities subsidiary, Prudential-Bache Securities. As the nationwide scandal unfolded in the early 1990s, the company came under intense scrutiny by the press and insurance regulators of numerous states. In January 1992, the insurance giant's vaulted credit rating was cut by a notch by Moody's Investors Service, from Aaa (or "exceptional") to Aa1 (best of the service's "excellent" ratings). The rating downgrade reflected continued uneasiness among insurance experts about the industry's large investments in junk bonds and holdings in commercial real estate. Later that year, Standard & Poor's lowered its ratings by a notch (to AA+ from the top AAA rating.) In November 1994, Duff & Phelps cut Prudential's rating to AA from AA+, and in mid-1995, the insurance giant was dropped from A. M. Best's elite list of "superior" insurance companies. And that was not the end: Scandal woes surfacing in other business units (insurance sales) continued to tarnish its reputation and tap its deep capital reserves well into the late 1990s.

47. "UDC Acts to Speed Property Acquisition for 42nd Street Development Project" [NYS UDC news release], August 20, 1987, 4.

48. Stuckey, author interview.

49. Tese, author interview.

50. John Mollenkopf, "The 42nd Street Development Project and the Public Interest," *City Almanac* 18 (Summer), 12–13, at 13.

51. "Legislators Release Confidential Developers Report; Expose Billion Dollar Tax Give Away on 42nd Street Redevelopment," joint press release from Senator Franz S. Leichter, Council member Ruth W. Messinger, Assemblyman Richard N. Gottfried, July 1, 1986.

52. Daniel M. Gold, "Times Square Foes Say City Gives Away Too Much," *Manhattan Lawyer,* October 25, 1988, 6ff.

53. NYS UDC, NYC PDC, "Comments on the Piker Subcommittee Report," February 9, 1989. The comments also rebutted the specific economic-return figures. Based upon an ESAC of $73 million, but not taking into account percentage rent, transaction payments, or any rent-recovery payments, at the conclusion of the tax-abatement period, the memo asserted that the city would a) "owe" the office developer nothing; b) will have received $410 million in rent payments; c) will be due an additional $340 million from the developer, and d) the buildings will be paying full taxes. The returns were higher when an upside from percentage rent and transaction payments are taken into account.

54. Weisbrod, author interview, August 15, 2000.

55. These numbers were derived from the Rosenberg & Estis model of project cash flows, in my opinion, the most careful of the three studies. Rosenberg & Estis,

P.C. are legal counsel who represented the Durst Organization. Their unpublished but circulated report of February 1990, "Economic Calculations of Times Square Redevelopment Project," was sent to the city controller as well as other elected politicians. This author's 7.5-percent assumption adjusts for the average historical difference between tax-exempt borrowing rates and the taxable rates used in the third-party analyses; it also closely matches the city's average interest cost between 1986 and 1987. Because it too would depend on tax exemption, this hypothetical reduction is simply another form of tax expenditure but from a different source, the federal government.

CHAPTER SIX

1. Brendan Gill as quoted in "One man's fight over Times Square," *Crain's New York Business,* October 16, 1989, 48.

2. Douglas Durst, "Viewpoints: Times Square's Endless Future," *Newsday*, February 14, 1990, 56.

3. Huxtable quoted in Martin Gottlieb, "Facing Issues of Times Square," *New York Times*, March 26, 1984, B1; Ada Louise Huxtable, "Creeping Giantism in Manhattan" *New York Times*, March 22, 1987, 2:1; Paul Goldberger, "Times Square: Design Problems Remain," *New York Times*, July 5, 1984, B1; Michael Sorkin, "Why Goldberger Is So Bad," *Village Voice*, April 2, 1985, 90; Carter Weisman, "Brave New Times Square," *New York,* April 2, 1984, 34ff; Brendan Gill, "The 'Heinous Misadventure' Facing Times Square" [letter to the editor], *New York Times*, July 11, 1984, A24; Brendan Gill cited in, J. S. R [James S. Russell], "42nd Street: No beat of dancing feet—yet," *Architectural Record* 177 (June 1989), 85; Brendan Gill in, "Verbatim: On Times Square," *New York Times*, 4:6; James S. Russell, "Golddiggers of '84?" *Architectural Record* 172 (October 1984), 125–131, at 131; Douglas David, "Strange Invaders: A controversial face-life for Times Square," *Newsweek*, November 19, 1984, 91–92; Kurt Anderson, "Renewal, But a Loss of Funk," *Time*, February 29, 1988, 102ff; Benjamin Fogey, "Times Square: Putting a Shine on the Apple; At the Crossroads on the Rebuilding Plan," *Washington Post*, October 6, 1984, B1.

4. Franz Schulze, *Philip Johnson: Life and Work* (New York: Alfred A. Knopf, 1994), 404.

5. The Portman hotel style, which even objectively could be called "a formula," meant "a dramatically large 'atrium'; glass elevators; a revolving, view-commanding roof-top restaurant; and a deliberate density of traditional details so often lacking in sterile modern buildings, things like pools and fountains, tapestries and sculpture, patterned paving and a profusion of potted plants." Portman had "put himself on the architectural map," wrote architectural critic Michael Sorkin, "with the construction of the Hyatt-Regency Hotel in Atlanta," which he then "relentlessly" applied across the country. (Michael Sorkin, "Portman's Hotel: Assault on a Mythic Center?" *Wall Street Journal*, January 22, 1982, 9.) It was the Atlanta hotel that in 1971 first captivated Peter Sharp, a New York developer who had assembled the site on Broadway between 45th and 46th Streets years earlier on which he had planned to build an office tower. On the basis of that "Wow!" effect, Sharp determined that he would have Portman build a hotel on the Broadway site.

6. Ada Louise Huxtable, "54-Story Hotel Expected to Revitalize Times Square," *New York Times*, July 11, 1973, 43; Ada Louise Huxtable, "Re-Inventing Times Square: 1990," in *Inventing Times Square: Commerce and Culture at the Crossroads of the World,* ed. William R. Taylor (New York: Russell Sage Foundation, 1991), 356–370, at 362.

7. Ibid.

8. Paul Goldberger, "Architectural View: The Portman Project: Is It An Asset or An Albatross?" *New York Times*, January 31, 1982, D1.

9. Sorkin, "Portman's Hotel, 9.

10. Vance Muse, "Lights Dim on the Great White Way," *Time*, December 1987, 84.

11. Paul Goldberger, "Marriott Marquis Hotel: An Edsel in Times Sq.?" *New York Times*, August 31, 1985, 25.

12. "Broadway Revolution," *Engineering News-Record* [editorial], March 1, 1984, 66.

13. Russell, "Golddiggers of '84?" 131.

14. Ibid., 129.

15. Ada Louise Huxtable, "Architectural View: Today the Cards Are All in the Builder's Hand," *New York Times*, February 2, 1978, 2:29.

16. Ada Louise Huxtable, *The Tall Building Artistically Reconsidered: The Search for a Skyscraper Style* (New York: Pantheon Books, 1982, 1984), 66.

17. Critic Robin Middleton, quoted in James Russell, "The Style Monger," a review of *Philip Johnson: Life and Work*, by Franz Schulze, Knopf, *Village Voice*, December 27, 1994, 50.

18. Paul Goldberger, "Architectural View: Philip Johnson, At 80 Is Dean and Gadfly of the Profession," *New York Times*, June 29, 1986, 2:29.

19. Susan Doubilet, "I'd Rather Be Interesting: Philip Johnson and John Burgee," *Progressive Architecture* 65 (February 1984): 65.

20. Paul Goldberger, "Times Square Lurching Toward a Terrible Mistake? *New York Times*, February 19, 1989, 2:37.

21. Ada Louise Huxtable, "Will Slab City Take Over Times Square,?" *New York Times*, March 25, 1968, 40.

22. Ada Louise Huxtable, "Times Square Renewal (Act II), A Farce," *New York Times*, October 10, 1989, 25.

23. Huxtable, "Will Slab City Take Over Times Square?"

24. Ada Louise Huxtable, "Faith, Hope and Muscle: City Proposes to Save Theater District From Perils of Commercial Blandness," *New York Times*, October 2, 1967, 46.

25. Nicolai Ouroussoff, "The Great Defender" [book review of *The Unreal America: Architecture and Illusions*, by Ada Louise Huxtable (The New Press, 1997)], *Los Angeles Times*, April 6, 1997, Book Review, 6.

26. Huxtable approached architecture from a cultural viewpoint. Aiming to take social, political, and economic issues into account, she was far more pragmatic than other architectural critics or historians, less rigidly bound to formal architectural theory. Urbanism and its social forces served as the main criteria for her evaluation of architecture. She was not seduced by form or aesthetics and, as an early and important advocate of historic preservation, held standards of the historical and urban fabric as sacrosanct. She vehemently disagreed with postmodernism's attempts to reference myths and illusions of the past as means to define the present. Censuring the profession for hiding its flaws under the guise of style, she held fast to the belief that architecture should shape social and cultural conditions, not simply embody what is already there. She cared deeply about the deterioration of public architecture. Her best work, Ouroussoff wrote in a review of one her books years later, "was driven by a deep sense of civic responsibility, by the conviction that architecture can elevate—or diminish—our everyday lives." She was already a seasoned architectural historian when in 1963 the *Times* appointed her as its full-time architectural critic, the first person ever to hold such a position on an American newspaper. She arrived at the *Times*, Ouroussoff said, "with a mission: to

be the great defender of the urban landscape." Having won the first Pulitzer Prize ever awarded to a critic in any field, in 1970, Huxtable's already powerful voice achieved an even more expansive range when, in 1973, she was appointed to the *Times* editorial board, a position from which she wrote unsigned editorials until her retirement from the *Times* in 1982.

27. For this stance, Michael Sorkin mercilessly attacked him personally. Goldberger, Sorkin argued, had a responsibility as a critic to assume informed critical positions rather than to propagate an attitude of ambivalence on controversial issues. "Goldberger artfully presents the existence of conflicting opinions as a means of showing the superiority of having none," Sorkin complained bitterly; "his strategy is to take all the positions." (Sorkin, "Why Goldberger Is So Bad," 91.)

       Sorkin is a critics' critic. "Sorkin knows how to wound his fellow critics," one wrote, yet he has "an urgent sense of what architecture is about; not just styling but the survival and regeneration of cities as fit places to live. And he knows how to disregard transient issues of style in evaluating buildings of real genius. . . ." His writing is "nervy, wisecracking, manic and eloquent," and his critique "consistent, coherent, early, and unequivocal," wrote Kurt Anderson. A sharp rebellious wit who was always in print, Sorkin offered up especially biting criticism of Philip Johnson and John Burgee, two of his favorite targets. Johnson was a dilettante of style in the minds of many critics, and the prime villain of Sorkin's collected essays, *Exquisite Corpse*. Ouroussoff, "The Great Defender"; Kurt Andersen, "The '80s as Spectacle; Exquisite Corpse," *Architectural Record*, May 1992, 50.

28. As a dominant voice in setting the agenda of public debate in New York and beyond by its coverage of the news and its editorials, the *Times* exerts considerable influence, especially in the worlds of culture and entertainment. "The architectural critic for the *New York Times* is read, talked about, and quoted more than any other critic, owing to the reputation and reach of the 'gray lady' [as the *Times* is fondly called]," wrote Suzanne Stephens. "Assessing the State of Architectural Criticism in Today's Press," *Architectural Record* 186 (March 1998): 64ff, at 67.

29. Goldberger, "Times Square: Lurching Toward a Terrible Mistake?"

30. During his first four years of government service, Tese's bureaucratic empire expanded to include four agencies—UDC, Science and Technology Foundation, Job Development Authority, Department of Economic Development—with a total budget of $125 million and 690 employees; he also supervised the economic-development activities of 22 departments. In 1991 he was appointed a commissioner of the Port Authority of New York and New Jersey, and elected vice chairman in 1992.

31. Vincent Tese, author interview, December 9, 1996.

32. Ibid.

33. "Times Square: Towering Troubles," *Economist*, September 30, 1989, 26.

34. Paul Goldberger, "New Times Square Designs: Merely Token Changes," *New York Times*, September 1, 1989, B1.

35. Huxtable, "Times Square Renewal."

36. Gregory F. Gilmartin, *Shaping the City: New York and The Municipal Art Society* (New York: Clarkson Potter/Publishers, 1995), 453.

37. Hugh Hardy, author interview, January 9, 1997.

38. Ada Louise Huxtable, "More Bad News About Times Square," *New York Times,* February 9, 1975, D:2, 32.

39. Richard A. Kahan, author interview, October 17, 1991.

40. "Seize the Time for Times Square" [editorial], *New York Times*, June 23, 1981, A26.

41. Paul Goldberger, "A Renewal As Lively As Times Square Itself," *New York Times*, July 4, 1981, 1:1. Some real estate developers did not respond as enthusiastically as design critics. Bernard H. Mendick, head of the Mendick Realty Company, for one, called the specificity of the design guidelines "kind of arrogant," while Harry Helmsley, in reviewing them, assumed there was room for negotiation on design and more tolerantly commented that "we should really start with something." Carter B. Horsley, "42d Plan Would Add Towers, Theaters And 'Bright Lights,'" *New York Times*, July 1, 1981, B1.

42. Jonathan Barnett, "In the Public Interest: Design Guidelines," *Architectural Record* 175 (July 1987), 114–125.

43. As quoted in Paul Goldberger, "Reinventing the City," *New York Times Magazine*, April 26, 1987, 19ff.

44. NYS UDC, NYC PDC, NYC DCP, *42nd Street Development Project Design Guidelines* [hereafter referred to as, *Design Guidelines*], May 1981, 11.

45. Several other factors contributed to the extra detail in the Cooper-Eckstut guidelines. The land-use program for the 42DP necessitated specifications for preservation of the midblock theaters and direct access into the office sites from the Times Square subway nexus as part of the station's major renovation. The policy decision not to bid out the 13-acre project area to a single, master developer called for detailed specifications "to provide developers assurances of quality control for neighboring parcels." To ensure coordinated development of the separate buildings, each of the four office sites surrounding the Times Square intersection had a orchestrated role to play within the overall design scheme. Most important, the wedge-shaped former Times Tower would have to be preserved, because, as Cooper explained, "Its shape is so much in the memory of the city that if you took it down you would have to build a new building in the same shape." Alan S. Oser, "A Billion-Dollar Plan for West Midtown," *New York Times*, May 30, 1982, 8:7.

46. Russell, "Golddiggers of '84," at 127. For example, they called for a "two-dimensional" skin for the new buildings which took "advantage of the transparent and reflective qualities of either glass or glass and metal panel systems"; this skin was to be "completely transparent" at the first two levels (where the stores would be), becoming "more reflective" as height increased. Also, the building was to change appearance as observers shifted their point of view.

47. *Design Guidelines*, 1.

48. Weisman, "Brave New Times Square," 34.

49. NYS UDC, "Memorandum, Re: 42nd Street Development Project—Response of John J. Walsh," Draft—November 6, 1984, 17.

50. Members of the council included the New York chapters of the American Institute of Architects, American Planning Association, American Society of Landscape Architects, the Architectural League, the Cultural Assistance Center, the Municipal Art Society, the Landmarks Conservancy, the Parks Council, the Public Art Fund, the Regional Plan Association, and the Women's City Club.

51. Thomas Bender, "Ruining Times Square," *New York Times*, March 3, 1984, 23.

52. Paul Goldberger, "4 New Towers for Times Sq.," *New York Times*, December 21, 1983, B1.

53. Huxtable, *The Tall Building Artistically Reconsidered*, 109, 111.

54. Marc A. Weiss, "Density and Intervention: New York's Planning Traditions," in *The Landscape of Modernity*, eds. David Ward and Olivier Zunz (Baltimore: Johns Hopkins University Press, 1992), 46–75, at 58–59.

55. Weisman, "Brave New Times Square," 33–34.

56. Alexander Cooper, author interview, May 6, 1998.

57. Russell, "Golddiggers of '84," at 129.

58. Huxtable quote in Martin Gottlieb, "Civic-Group Leaders Question Times Sq. Plan," *New York Times*, February 29, 1984, B3; George Lewis, "42nd Street/Times Square: A Project in Trouble," *Oculus* 46 (November 1984), 3–6.

59. Weisman, "Brave New Times Square," 32, 33.

60. In 1983, UDC's highly regarded department of urban design and public spaces was, in effect, eliminated through a reorganization that put the function under the aegis of the construction department. By several accounts, Stern wanted to upset the apple cart, to see whether UDC was doing things the right way. Under Herb Sturz's tenure as head of the CPC, the DCP's highly respected urban-design group similarly was dismantled.

61. Weisman, "Brave New Times Square," 35.

62. From a legal standpoint, the theater concessions may have been redundant, as the leases with designated developers for the theaters would contain covenants to that effect. Additional restrictions on the theaters included: purchase options to be available only for the New Amsterdam Theater (after 99 years) and for the Empire (in the event a purchase option is also exercised for the mart). In the case of the Empire, a restrictive covenant would continue to protect the theater after the exercise of the purchase option.

63. Minutes of the board of directors of the Municipal Art Society, November 15, 1984.

64. "Old stage, new stars," *Business Week*, October 24, 1964, 132ff, at 132.

65. Huxtable, "Re-inventing Times Square: 1990," 358.

66. Ibid.

67. Virginia Dajani, "Times Tower Site Competition," *The Livable City* [a publication of the Municipal Art Society], October 1986 (no. 10/1), 2ff, at 3; George Lewis, "Lively Times Square," *Oculus* 46 (November 1984), 21.

68. Paul Goldberger, "Picking a Centerpiece for a New Times Sq.," *New York Times*, September 17, 1984, B1.

69. Arthur Spielgman, "Saving Times Square May Mean End of Its Best Known Building," Reuters North European Service, January 1, 1984.

70. Venturi, Scott Brown and Associates, Inc., "Times Square Plaza Design," description of preliminary design completed in 1984 as provided by VSBA.

71. Robert Venturi and Denise Scott Brown, author interview, December 4, 1999.

72. Robert Venturi, *Complexity and Contradiction in Architecture* (New York: The Museum of Modern Art, 1966, 1977), 104.

73. Graeme Browning, "Architect Robert Venturi," U.P.I. BC Cycle, Domestic News, June 29, 1984.

74. Tim Prentice, "A New Times Square with 'Life After Work'" [letter to the editor], *New York Times,* July 20, 1984, A26.

75. Douglas Davis, "Mr. Post-Postmodern," *Newsweek*, July 9, 1984, 78.

76. Paul Goldberger, "An Appraisal: Design for Time Square: Problems Remain," *New York Times*, July 15, 1984, B1.

77. John J. Costonis, *Icons and Aliens: Law, Aesthetics, and Environmental Change* (Urbana and Chicago: University of Illinois Press, 1989), xv.

78. Huxtable, "Re-Inventing Times Square: 1990," 358.

79. Herbert Muschamp, "Heart of Whimsy in Times Square," *New York Times*, April 7, 1997, C11.

CHAPTER SEVEN

1. Martin Fox, "Litigating Times Square: Eight Years and Counting," *New York Law*

Journal, February 27, 1989, 1. The EIS for the 42DP was only the second one done under the state environmental statute, the first being that for the Convention Center; its unique feature was a chapter on social and demographic factors.

2. One instance of manipulation was the flap over the use of the AIA's mailing list for a questionnaire in 1989. The survey results purportedly indicated that four of five architects believed that the 42DP should go back to the drawing boards. Sponsored by the self-styled Committee to Reclaim Times Square, founded in 1981 by Brendan Gill and supported by the Brandt and Durst organizations, the survey was denounced by the AIA as unauthorized and biased.

3. The final adjudication represented a consolidation of four lawsuits brought on similar grounds. The *Jackson* ruling brought together two distinct sets of plaintiffs: the elderly, disabled Clinton residents and Rosenthal & Rosenthal, the owners of a building slated for condemnation. As to what constitutes appropriate mitigation measures, the court reinforced the deference of the judiciary for leaving such decisions to the agency, in this case, UDC. The expansive nature of judicial deference is such that the agency is permitted to go ahead with a project even if there are some secondary impacts which will not be mitigated. All that is required is that the agency "take a hard look at and consider potential mitigation measures." Despite this hard-look standard of review for the environmental impact of a proposed action, the courts have been reluctant to find that agencies have failed to take the appropriate mitigation measures. Such a finding would mean that a court is second-guessing an agency's substantive expertise in a particular area. Hence, the message of *Jackson*: that the burden on the plaintiffs to establish that an agency has abused its discretion is a heavy one.

4. *Rosenthal & Rosenthal Inc. v. N.Y.S. Urban Dev. Corp.*, 771 F.2d 44 (2d Cir. 1985).

5. Martin Gottlieb, "Financial Concern Sues to Block Times Sq. Plan," *New York Times*, October 10, 1984, B3.

6. Randall Smith, "New York City Again Sets Out to Clean Up Sleazy Times Square, but Obstacles Are Big," *Wall Street Journal*, March 15, 1982, 29; Martin Gottlieb, "Times Sq. Also Beckons with Less Sinister Joys," *New York Times*, May 12, 1984, 25.

7. Martin Gottlieb, "Movie Houses Sue over Plan for Times Square," *New York Times*, October 23, 1984, B1.

8. Another piece of Seymour Durst's professional and civic history bears on the story line. In early 1975, he was appointed by incoming Mayor Abraham D. Beame to be a member of another in a long line of city task forces on the cleanup of Times Square. Later in the year, after a story on Times Square as a "vice capital" appeared on the front page of the *Times*, Durst's ownership of Luxor Baths—named as one of the most notorious massage parlors in the city—became public. His position on the task force seen by some as "an outrage," he was forced to resign. He subsequently sold Luxor Baths to the massage parlor's operators, letting the city take the responsibility for evicting them.

9. Confidential letter to author, not for attribution.

10. Gregory F. Gilmartin, *Shaping the City: New York and the Municipal Arts Society* (New York: Clarkson Potter Publishers, 1995), 462–479, at 465.

11. Thomas J. Lueck, "Citizens Gain in Anti-Developer Wars," *New York Times*, May 14, 1989, 10:1.

12. James P. Stuckey, author interview, January 23, 1998.

13. Ibid.

14. Vincent Tese, author interview, December 9, 1996.

15. David W. Dunlap, "Developers' Hazard: Legal Hardball," *New York Times*, December 8, 1996, 9:1.

16. The 1987 amendments to the *GPP* included sequential condemnation as well as modifications to the parking on the office sites and uses for Site 8. Regarding Site 8, the *GPP* was being amended to make it conform with the provision in the BOE resolution which specified a "merchandise mart" without restriction to a wholesale industry mix; it also permitted conversion from a mart to another use subject to certain conditions. The *FEIS* specified a mart program—"wholesale showrooms," with approximately 70 percent devoted to an "info mart" and an "apparel mart in the remaining 23 percent of the building—which was different from what was specified in the BOE Resolution; this, one insider noted, was one potential lawsuit the opposition missed. A second missed lawsuit involved the PACB's review. In its deliberation, the PACB did not adopt an environment finding, which it is supposed to do for every "discretionary" decision, though the opposition did not press this issue, for unknown reasons that would amount to shear speculation on my part.

17. *Wilder v. N.Y.S. Urban Dev. Corp.* 546 N.Y.S.2d 95 (A.D. 1 Dept. 1989), 96.

18. Fox, "Litigating Times Square," 36.

19. Ibid., as quoted from *Wilder v. N.Y.S. Urban Dev. Corp.*

20. Seymour Durst, "Times Square: The Big Con" [Viewpoints; New York Forum], *Newsday*, February 26, 1988, 86; Carl Weisbrod and James Stuckey, "He's Got No Street Smarts" [Viewpoints], *Newsday*, March 14, 1988, 46; Daniel M. Gold, "Times Square Foes Say City Gives Away Too Much," *Manhattan Lawyer*, October 25, 1988–October 31, 1988, 6; Edward I. Koch, Mayor; "'Joint Initiative' Needed in Times Square," *Manhattan Lawyer*, December 6, 1988-December 12, 1988, 11; Larry Josephs, Director of Communications, 42nd Street Development Project, "Unfair Attack on 42nd Street Project," *Manhattan Lawyer*, January 3–9, 1989, 13.

21. Claudia H. Deutsch, "Commercial Property: The Lower Manhattan B.I.D.'s Chief; A Politically Savvy Leader Jumps in Swinging," *New York Times*, November 20, 1994, 9:9.

22. Carl B. Weisbrod, author interview, August 14, 1996.

23. "Now Playing on 42d Street: Mr. Nobody" [editorial], *New York Times*, March 29, 1987, 4:24; "Reveille on 42d Street" [editorial], *New York Times*, May 15, 1987, A30. The earlier editorials: "Who'll Set the Beat for 42d Street," *New York Times*, October 3, 1984, A26; "The First Step on 42d Street," *New York Times*, November 7, 1984, A26; "Times Square as an Obstacle Course," *New York Times*, December 29, 1984, 20

24. Deutsch, "The Lower Manhattan B.I.D.'s Chief."

25. "Restoring Times Square" [editorial], *Daily News*, June 5, 1984, 41; Carl Weisbrod, "No to a Fast-Food, Fast-Sex, High-Crime 42d St. Historic District" [letter to the editor], *New York Times*, April 29, 1987, A34; Roxanne Tamarkin, "Looking Back," *Daily News*, July 31, 1989, 19; Carl Weisbrod, "A Dramatic Revival: The Future of 42nd Street," *Portfolio* 2 (Autumn 1989), 1–9, at 2.

26. Carl Weisbrod, "42d Street Landlords: Greed, Inc.," *New York Times*, June 17, 1989, 23 and reprinted in *Real Estate Weekly*, July 12, 1989, 4B.

27. "Times Square as Obstacle Course" [editorial], *New York Times*, December 29, 1984, 20.

28. Harry Berkowitz, "Times Sq. Project Gains Ground; High Court Rejects Key Lawsuit," *Newsday*, February 28, 1989, 45.

29. George Klein, author interview, December 4, 1997.

30. Tese, author interview.

31. Berkowitz, "Times Sq. Project Gains Ground."

32. As a writer of fluid style, flippant wit, and constant creativity in a career spanning 60-odd years, Gill penned a vast number of short stories, books, critical reviews of books, architecture, theater, and movies, including what John Updike fondly remembered to be "one of the few thoughtful appreciations of pornographic films—they made him happy, he wrote." ("Citizen Gill: Remembering the quintessential New Yorker," *New Yorker*, January 12, 1998, 70ff, comment of John Updike, at 70.) He was passionately dedicated to the life of the intellect and of art; he relished debate and argument and had a way with words that kindled intense interest among a devoted coterie of readers. The "Gill tone," one of his memorists wrote in the *New Yorker* shortly after his passing, "seemed to have been made in the confident city of the forties and fifties." He loved the city, New York, in a way that did not overshadow his Connecticut roots, Hartford upbringing, and Yale education, but instead permanently defined him as a quintessential New Yorker—a *New Yorker*'s quintessential New Yorker. He liked to socialize with the rich and powerful.

33. Brendan Gill, "The Sky Line: On the Brink," *New Yorker*, September 9, 1987, 113ff, at 113.

34. "Citizen Gill," comment of Paul Goldberger, 72.

35. Russell W. Baker, "Times Square Plan Creates Row," *Christian Science Monitor*, July 25, 1989, 9; Gill, "On the Brink," 118; Howard Kurtz, "American Journal; Transforming Times Square: Can Its Soul Survive in a High-Rise Canyon," *Washington Post*, January 18, 1990, A18; Brendan Gill, "The Sky Line: The Death of the Skyscraper?, *New Yorker*, March 4, 1991, 90ff, at 93; Gill, "On the Brink," at 114, 115.

36. In one sense, dragging out the condemnation may not have been a sure tactic because the longer the court took to decide on the condemnation issues, the longer TSCA's option to develop would be extended; this was too small a consideration to affect the overall strategy, though. Much later, in the summer of 1994 during the condemnation hearings for Site 7, Durst admitted that he delayed and tried to block construction of the TSCA towers because his own buildings would not be able to compete with the subsidized towers. Brett Pulley, "Key Developer Seeks a Role in Times Sq.," *New York Times*, November 21, 1995, B1.

37. Dunlap, "Developers' Hazard: Legal Hardball."

38. Rebecca Robertson, author interview, October 21, 1994; Weisbrod, author interview, August 14, 1996.

39. Sam Roberts, "The Legacy of Westway: Lessons From Its Demise," *New York Times*, October 7, 1985, A1.

40. "Miracle on 42d Street" [editorial], *New York Times* editorial, April 19, 1990, A24.

41. "Reveille on 42d Street."

42. Section 81-214 quoted from memorandum from staff, Department of City Planning to Sylvia Deutsch, director, August 31, 1987, 2.

43. This was not George Klein's first such setback over loss of a potential office tenant. That came in 1986 when one of the city's most prominent Wall Street law firms, Dewey Ballantine, Bushby, Palmer & Wood, withdrew its commitment for approximately 250,000 square feet in one of the office towers, for the same reason. The business advantages of the location augured well for the long term, as evidenced by other big-name blue-chip firms moving to Times Square, among them, U.S. Trust Company; the law firms of Lord, Day & Lord Barrett Smith and Cravath, Swaine & Moore; and D'Arcy Masius Benton & Bowles and Ogilvy & Mather, both advertising firms. Even though Times Square was a difficult area for

corporate tenants to consider in the early 1980s, by the midpoint of the decade the problem for Klein was not finding interested tenants, but nailing down a date of occupancy. It was when "we were into detailed drafts of lease agreements with each party that this problem arose," said Veronica W. Hackett. Challenges to the legality of the project made the timing of condemnation uncertain, so "we could not be certain when we would start construction, and these big tenants needed a date certain because of their existing lease expiration and need for advance planning. Each time we lost the tenant over this unresolvable issue." Veronica W. Hackett, author interview, February 22, 1995.

44. Sydney H. Schanberg, "Pull the Plug on the Bleeding Times Square Plan," *Newsday*, April 25, 1989, 57.

45. D. D. Guttenplan, "Times Square: Saved by the Crash?" *Village Voice*, November 11, 1987, 10, 12; Kahan quote, author interview, October 16, 1991.

46. In 1981, when head of the mayor's OME, Weisbrod expressed some ambivalence to the start-all-over condemnation approach. The city and UDC had just announced its plans for West 42nd Street, which Weisbrod termed "Times Square by press release." At the time his office was heavily involved in advancing a cleanup via an "incremental" approach. "That means you take a small section of the problem and concentrate on it—like massage parlors. . . . We've closed ninety of them. But it's not enough just to close them, then you create a vacant building, which isn't good for the area either. So we look for what we consider 'good use' tenants to move in where the 'bad use' once was." Mark Jacobson, "Times Square: The Meanest Street in America," *Rolling Stone*, August 6, 1981, 15ff, at 18.

47. Robert Hennelly, "Building for the Future on 42nd Street: Interview with Rebecca Robertson," *Newsday*, August 27, 1992, 93.

48. Guttenplan, "Times Square: Saved by the Crash?"; Koch, "'Joint Initiative' Needed in Times Square"; testimony by Mayor Edward Koch at hearing on 42nd Street Development Project, September 30, 1987, 18; author interview, October 3, 2000.

49. Koch and Stuckey's strategy was to isolate these narrow interests, such as Leichter, and show them for being "antidevelopment zealots." The mayor, said Stuckey, wanted to show his constituency how economic development would affect them. Stuckey, author interview.

CHAPTER EIGHT

1. 42DP, Inc., NYS UDC, NYC EDC, *42nd Street Now!: A Plan for the Interim Development of 42nd Street, Executive Summary*, (preliminary), 1993, 2.

2. Herbert J. Sturz, author interview, November 25, 1991.

3. Thomas J. Lueck, "Miscalculations in Times Square: Project Shows That Renewal Needs More Than Bulldozers," *New York Times*, August 10, 1992, B3.

4. Gregory F. Gilmartin, *Shaping the City: New York and the Municipal Art Society* (New York: Clarkson Potter Publishers, 1995), xii.

5. Ibid., 37.

6. Ibid., 234.

7. Ibid., 443.

8. Listed theaters are the predominantly free-standing theaters with full stage and wings located in the vicinity of the Special Midtown District, as defined and listed in May 1982. As discussed later in this chapter, listing imposed certain restrictions, including the requirement of a special permit for most demolitions.

9. I owe this point to Con Howe, who was executive director of the NYC DCP from May 1987 to March 1991 and director of the Manhattan Office of DCP

from March 1982 to May 1987, and before that employed in various capacities by DCP from November 1978 to March 1982. Author interview, September 18, 1998.

10. MAS, minutes of board meeting, November 15, 1984.

11. The board roster read as a who's who in the world of civic culture in New York: Kent Barwick, Jonathan Barnett, Norton Belknap, Paul Byard, Giorgio Cavaglieri, Alexander Cooper, Joan Davidson, Gordon J. Davis, Lewis Davis, John Dobkin, Michael George, Brendan Gill, Harmon Goldstone, John Guare, Hugh Hardy, Benjamin Holloway, Philip Howard, Karl Katz, Ming Cho Lee, Marilyn Levy, Reynold Levy, Ruth McAneny Loud, Richard Menschel, John Merow, the Very Rev. James P. Morton, Jacqueline Kennedy Onassis, Frederic Papert, Charles Platt, David Prager, Tim Prentice, Nicholas Quennell, Carole Rifkin, Robert Rubin, Ross Sandler, Whitney North Seymour, Jr., Carl Spielvogel, Hoyt Spelman, III, Stephen C. Swid, David Teitelbaum, Helen Tucker, William Turner, Cyrus Vance, Margot Wellington, Elliott Willensky, and William H. Whyte.

12. MAS, minutes of board meeting, November 15, 1984.

13. The Industrial and Commercial Incentive Program (ICIP) was created on November 5, 1984. Designed to stimulate economic development, particularly in areas outside Manhattan's central business district, it replaced the Industrial and Commercial Incentive Board (ICIB), which had been established in 1977 during the city's fiscal crisis. Unlike ICIB, which provided benefits on a case-by-case basis, ICIP offered benefits as-of-right if a project met specific eligibility requirements. Based on location, these benefits consisted of an exemption or deferral of the increased tax assessment resulted from new construction or rehabilitation. The part of Manhattan most affected by the program was Times Square, where the benefits of deferred tax assessments went to seven commercial projects: Holiday Inn Crowne Plaza, Worldwide Plaza, 750 Seventh Avenue, 1585 Broadway, Embassy Suites Hotel and theater complex, Hotel Macklowe, and 1675 Broadway. These projects benefited from full deferral from taxes during the first three years, after which the deferral would be phased out over years four through seven at 20 percent annually; during years eight through ten, the owners would pay full taxes. In years 11 through 20, full taxes would be due, plus 10 percent each year of the total deferred taxes. See NYC Department of Finance, *Annual Report to the New York City Council on the Industrial and Commercial Incentive Program*, June 1990; Walter Fee, "Getting All of the Breaks, Plan Gives Tax Relief to Richest," *Newsday*, December 17, 1991, 6.

14. William R. Taylor, "Broadway: The Place That Words Built," in *Inventing Times Square: Commerce and Culture at the Crossroads of the World* (New York: Russell Sage Foundation, 1991), 212–231, at 216.

15. Gilmartin, *Shaping the City*, 455.

16. MAS, minutes of board meeting, July 11, 1985.

17. MAS, minutes of board meeting, October 17, 1985.

18. Hugh Hardy, author interview, January 9, 1997.

19. Julie V. Iovine, "Tenacity in the Service of Public Culture; New Victory Theater Is Latest Icon on Which Architect Leaves His Mark," *New York Times*, December 12, 1995, B1.

20. In a short profile for the *New Yorker*, Brendan Gill explained the nature of the connection: "A principle that Hardy has championed . . . is that a community in which theater flourishes is in good health, while a community in which theater languishes is, whether it's aware of it or not, ill." Times Square was certainly the last

place one would look for "any manifestation of the sacred" he wrote. "For Hardy, however, the theater is an intrinsically sacred activity." (Brendan Gill, "The One-Man City: Hugh Hardy: The Latter-day Stanford White," *New Yorker*, December 9, 1996, 124ff, at 126.) Hardy was a new kind of architect who took the term "arts" seriously in the Municipal Art Society.

21. MAS, minutes of board meeting, October 17, 1985.

22. Gilmartin, *Shaping the City*, 456.

23. This event occurred more than three years prior to the much publicized public extravaganza "Stand against the Shadow" in Central Park, a rally staged by the MAS to protest the much-despised proposal for the redevelopment of the Coliseum at Columbus Circle. For this event, thousands of New Yorkers arrived with black umbrellas in hand and traced the path of "the shadow" that would be cast by the project's two imposing towers (68 and 58 stories tall) across Central Park, shading acres of the city's most prized open space.

24. MAS, minutes of board meeting, July 11, 1985. Also, see Peter Bosselman, *Representation of Places: Reality and Realism in City Design* (Berkeley: University of California Press, 1998), 106–119 (Times Square), 122–137 (Downtown San Francisco).

25. Peter Bosselman, "Times Square," *Places* 4 (1987): 55–63, at 60.

26. MAS, minutes of board meeting, October 17, 1985. In the terms Donald A. Schön used to describe *The Reflective Practitioner*, the change in language reframed the issue.

27. Paul Goldberger, "Will Times Square Become a Grand Canyon? *New York Times*, October 6, 1985, H31.

28. MAS, minutes of board meeting, September 5, 1985.

29. MAS, minutes of board meeting, July 11, 1995.

30. The first, put up in May, posed the question, what should be done about Times Square? The second, on display in September 1985 for four months, exhibited the winning designs for the Times Tower Competition sponsored by the society. A third, put up in February 1987, after approval of the new design regulations, focused on Mayers & Schiff's designs for Jeffrey Katz's new signpost building (Two Times Square). In a chain of continued advocacy, others followed: an exhibit of the 42DP theater exteriors in October 1988 and, between November and December of 1990, a photo exhibit of the New Amsterdam Theater documenting the shocking decay of the once magnificent building.

31. MAS, *The Livable City* 11 (June 1987): 11.

32. In Boston, preserving the red, white, and blue 60-foot-square CITGO sign in Kenmore Square—packed with more than 5,000 neon tubes and visible from more than 20 miles away from its perch atop a seven-story building at a major highway intersection—became a local public-interest issue in the early 1980s, years before signage emerged fully as an issue in Times Square. Though the Boston Landmarks Commission voted against designation in 1983 because of the cost of maintenance, the company, responding to public sentiment, agreed to turn on the sign for at least three years.

33. Office of the Chief Urban Designer, DCP, "Times Square: Summary of Urban Design Study and Proposed Zoning Controls," January 1987, Attachment F.

34. Alan S. Oser, "Planning for a Brighter Times Sq.," *New York Times*, December 14, 1986, R6, at 11.

35. Geoffrey Baker, author interview, February 20, 1997.

36. "Times Square Urban Design Controls, Times Square, New York City," undated five-page "lay" summary from the DCP.

37. NYC CPC, *Midtown Development*, DCP Report 81-8, June 1981, at 58; NYC CPC, *Midtown Zoning*, DCP Report 82-03, March 1982, 40–41.

38. Howe, author interview.

39. Tama Starr and Edward Hayman, *Signs and Wonders: The Spectacular Marketing of America* (New York: Currency/ Doubleday, 1998), 250.

40. Jerry Adler, *High Rise: How 1,000 Men and Women Worked Around the Clock for Five Years and Lost $200 Million Building a Skyscraper* (New York: HarperCollins, 1993), 48.

41. Richard D. Lyons, "Mandating More Glitter on Times Square," *New York Times*, December 27, 1989, D15.

42. One study of campaign contributions from January 1, 1981, through October 31, 1986, for example, revealed that among the top 20 contributors—whose total giving ranged from $113,500 to $350,630—to the mayor and other members of the BOE, 12 were in real estate; they accounted for 61 percent, or approximately $2.4 million of the $4 million given by the top 20; another was a big law firm with a substantial real estate practice. Frank Lynn, "Big Donors to Top City Officials Named," *New York Times*, December 23, 1986, B3, reporting on a study by the staff of State Senator Franz S. Leichter of Manhattan.

43. David Samuels, "The Real-Estate Royals: End of the Line?" *New York Times Magazine*, August 10, 1997, 36ff, at 40.

44. Jewel Bellush, "Clusters of Power: Interest Groups," in *Urban Politics: New York Style*, Jewel Bellush and Dick Netzer, eds. (Armonk, N.Y., and London, England: M.E. Sharpe, 1990), 296–338, at 326.

45. Taking a position contrary to Sayre and Kaufman, who had argued that no single group elite runs New York, Bellush contended that some groups can and do dominate, evidencing distinct and important "clusters of power." Based on the experience of the postcrisis period of Koch's 12-year mayoralty, he concluded that in a growth-oriented city like New York, where real estate naturally is at the forefront, developers became dominate because of the dominance of the build-and-grow policy priority. While this may appear to be particular to that era—much like the community revolution of the 1960s and the fiscal crisis, each of which brought to the fore new clusters of power—real estate is one of those interest groups that "control substantial resources and possess the necessary skills for repeatedly winning substantial prizes provided by the political system." It is a place where power congeals. Developers have been able to "network the governmental arena and provide Manhattan with a new facial, if not spiritual, uplift." Bellush, "Clusters of Power," 325, 334, 331.

46. For insights into this issue, I owe much to Con Howe.

47. Adler, *High Rise*, 293.

48. Barwick quote from James Brooke, "Conserving the Glitter of Times Sq.," *New York Times* May 11, 1986, 2:35; Sierra Club quote, from Starr and Hayman, *Signs and Wonders*, 251.

49. "Statement of Gerald Schoenfeld on Behalf of the Shubert Organization, Inc. to the City Planning Commission Hearing on Design Controls," November 26, 1986.

50. "Planning for a Brighter Times Sq.," 16.

51. Adler, *High Rise*, 188; on the Wiz Bang, see 186–189, 266–269, 295–298, 333–335.

52. Albert Scardino, "Builder Wants Green in Great White Way," *New York Times*, June 13, 1987, 32.

53. Howe, author interview.

54. Peter Samton, letter to the editor, *New York Times*, March 22, 1987, 8:22.

55. "Due Regard for Old Broadway," *New York Times*, July 28, 1986, A14.

56. Marshall Berman, "Taking Back the Night: City Planning Keeps Times Square's Glitz Alive," *Village Voice*, August 19, 1986, 17.

57. The threat of a moratorium, Gilmartin wrote, was enough to convince some developers that they had better redesign their projects, *Shaping the City*, 459.

58. Howe, author interview.

59. Henry N. Cobb, "Statement in Support of the Proposed Zoning Text Change Urban Design Controls in Times Square," November 24, 1986.

60. MAS, minutes of board meeting, December 4, 1986.

61. Hugh Hardy, as vice president of the MAS, "Testimony at Public Hearings on the Urban Design Controls in Times Square," November 26, 1986; Gilmartin, *Shaping the City*, 460–461.

62. Ada Louise Huxtable, "Re-Inventing Times Square 1990," in *Inventing Times Square*, 356–371 at 366.

63. Ibid.

64. MAS, minutes of board meeting, September 5, 1985.

65. The requirement could be satisfied in a number of ways: auditoriums, dance halls, or eating and drinking places where there is entertainment or dancing, motion-picture production studios, studios for music, dancing or theatrical productions, studios for radio or television, theaters. These uses could be anywhere within the building, including basements and sub-basements. Developers could also satisfy the requirement with costume-rental establishments, music stores, musical-instrument repair shops, record stores or ticket sales offices; but these would have to be on the ground floor. Exempt from the regulation were buildings with less than 60,000 square feet of space, a building in which more than half the space is used as a hotel, and a building on a lot more than half of which is outside the core area. At the same time, the CPC approved several other measures affecting the Theater District. It simplified the process through which owners of landmark theaters would have to go to obtain a demolition permit, and it eliminated the zoning bonus of extra floor space that had existed when a developer included a theater in a new building. After BOE approval in late October 1987, the proposals became city law.

66. Howe, author interview.

67. Mark McCain, "Commercial Property: Corporate Corridor; The Pot's Bubbling Along Avenue of the Americas," *New York Times*, August 9, 1987, 8:25.

68. Mark McCain, "Keeping Diversity in the Theater District," *New York Times*, July 5, 1987, 8:9.

69. Paul Goldberger, "Broadway Need Not Become a Doormat for Skyscrapers," *New York Times*, March 13, 1986, 35.

70. Michael H. Zisser, "Theater Preservation: Ideas in Search of a Plan," *New York Affairs* 8, no. 4 (1985): 157–169, at 157.

71. "Think Hard About Theaters" [editorial], *New York Times*, October 3, 1983, A22.

72. The calculation of 2.78 million square feet of air-rights development potential is based on prevailing zoning rules, which were set to expire May 1988, and includes the bonus granted for exterior landmark status, where applicable. Though sizeable, this figure is considerably less than the range of 3.5 to 4.5 million square feet estimated by the LPC and the CPC, respectively, in 1982. Of the three major theater owners, Jujamcyn had already sold the rights to three of its five theaters and still retained 129,524 square feet of current development potential.

Nederlander had not yet sold any of the rights attached to its seven theaters and retained 1,007,761 square feet of current development potential. The Shubert Organization, which controlled the largest number of theaters, had sold the air rights connected with five theaters but still held 1,239,485 square feet of current development potential. Data from individual listings in David W. Dunlap, "The City Casts Its Theaters in Stone," *New York Times*, November 22, 1987, 4:6; 1982 figure from Paul Goldberger, "Architecture View: Theaters and Churches Are the City's New Battlegrounds," *New York Times*, May 30, 1982, 2:1.

73. Martin Gottlieb, "City Panel Near Vote on Save-the-Theaters Proposals," *New York Times*, April 15, 1984, 8:7.

74. Joseph B. Rose, "Landmarks preservation in New York," *Public Interest* 74 (winter 1984): 132–145, at 135.

75. Joyce Purnick, "The Lay of the Landmark Commission; The Latest Fight Is on Fifth Avenue," *New York Times*, April 7, 1985, 4:6.

76. Rose, "Landmarks Preservation in New York," 138.

77. David W. Dunlap, "Landmarks Panel Studies History, Rules on the Future," *New York Times*, November 2, 1986, 8E.

78. Jeffrey Schmalz, "Landmarks Panel Listing Broadway Theaters, *New York Times*, August 7, 1985, A1.

79. "Protect Plays, Not Just Theaters" [editorial], *New York Times,* December 19, 1985, A10.

80. One landmark designation included the auditorium of the Palace Theater on 47th Street, one of the oldest and largest in the Theater District. David W. Dunlap, "5 More Broadway Theaters Classified as Landmarks," *New York Times*, November 5, 1987, B1.

81. Todd S. Purdum, "28 Theaters Are Approved as Landmarks," *New York Times*, March 12, 1988, 33.

82. David W. Dunlap, "Landmark Theaters Are up for Vote," *New York Times*, March 10, 1988, B3.

83. Ibid. Despite the division within the theater community, alliances did attempt to bridge some differences. For example, theater owners and Save the Theaters, Inc., joined together to commission an architectural study that would buttress their case against landmarking surface decorations that are without architectural merit. The report offered to the LPC stressed the overall "geometry of theaters"—their shape, layout and acoustical properties rather—than decorative detail, as standards for landmark designation.

84. Theater owners lost little time in bringing suit to overturn the landmark designation of 22 playhouses as well as a restrictive demolition procedure. The preservationists prevailed throughout a four-year litigation effort when, in 1992, the U.S. Supreme Court refused to hear the theater owners' case.

85. Paul Goldberger, "For Times Square; Light at the Mouth of the Tunnel," *New York Times*, October 25, 1987, 2:42. In first writing about the impact of the new zoning proposals, Goldberger had focused on the East Side; see "Zoning and Midtown" Proposals for Manhattan's East Side, Lauded at First, Now Face Challenge," *New York Times*, April 23, 1982, B3. Nor was there mention of potential problems for midtown west in his other articles about the problems of increasing density in Manhattan; see "Manhattan in Change: A Look Ahead to a Denser City," *New York Times*, July 12, 1982, B1.

86. "Testimony of Richard T. Anderson, executive vice president, Regional Plan Association, to New York City City Planning Commission on Proposed Urban

Design Controls for Times Square Zoning Text Changes for the Special Midtown District," November 26, 1986, 1, 3.

87. Berman, "City Planning Keeps Times Square's Glitz Alive," 23.

88. Quoted in Mark McCain, "Commercial Property: Midtown Development; New Zoning Battles Are Looming for the West Side," *New York Times*, September 13, 1987, 8:37.

89. Berman, "City Planning Keeps Times Square Glitz Alive."

90. Howe, author interview.

91. As evidence of its success, the report noted that of the 35 buildings approved for development in the Special District, 28 (80 percent) were as-of-right, in contrast to 13 (38 percent) as-of-right buildings in the five-year period just prior to the Midtown Zoning Resolution. NYC DCP, *Midtown Development Review*, July 1987, DCP 87-05, 13.

92. NYC DCP, Staff Memorandum to Sylvia Deutsch, director, August 31, 1987. The staff moved away from a fiscally oriented expansion of the system of transfer of development rights because its results were "unpredictable, the implications for density in the area and for existing landmarks regulations, and the precedent that could be set for other classes of buildings or areas."

93. Willa Appel, "Sounding Off at the Theater Retention Bonus," *The Assessor* (newsletter of the Citizens Housing and Planning Council) 6, no. 1 (March 1988).

CHAPTER NINE

1. William R. Taylor, *In Pursuit of Gotham: Culture and Commerce in New York* (Oxford: Oxford University Press, 1992), 93–108, at 94.

2. David W. Dunlap, "Rethinking 42d St. for Next Decade, Interim Project Planned As Office Slump Persists," *New York Times*, June 27, 1993, 10:1.

3. Early attempts to renew the New Amsterdam Theater failed dismally. Rather than condemn the theater, the city and state accepted the best bid in response to its 1982 RFP, which was from the Nederlander Organization. The theater was acquired with $4 million of bond financing from the New York State Industrial Development Authority; Nederlander was responsible for paying off the bonds and making payments in lieu of taxes to the city. The producer had intended to stage Peter Brook's *La Tragedie de Carmen* in the small rooftop theater, but that plan came to a halt when workers discovered structural damage to the roof, and renovation work was stopped with the roof left unsealed, an aesthetic criminal offense. The city then made an unsuccessful attempt at renewal through Frederic Papert and his 42nd Street Development Corporation, which aimed to make the rooftop theater a home for the National Theater Center to stage small, regional theater productions. The agreement with the city and state obligated Nederlander to renovate the theater, but the deal was poorly drafted—it provided no way to force the organization to protect the building. Negative publicity did nothing to effect action and neither could enforcement of the landmarks law, Robertson said, because the landmarks law is not binding on third parties. Only when Nederlander fell behind in his tax payments did the 42DP have an opening to buy back the theater. To effectuate a buyout of the former agreement and acquire the theater, the city forgave Nederlander the delinquent PILOTs, but he was required to pay off the bonds.

4. Letter to James Nederlander and Arthur Rubin from Harold Prince, October 31, 1986, Rebecca Robertson, "Landing the Anchor: The Disney Deal," course preparation materials, Harvard University Graduate School of Design, GCD 5400: Managing Mega-Projects, spring 1999 [herinafter referenced to as Robertson GSD course materials].

5. Bruce Weber, "In Times Square, Keepers of the Glitz: Three Women Overseeing Block's Rebirth Promise to Return Its Splendor," *New York Times,* June 25, 1996, B1, at B6.

6. Elisabeth Bumiller, "From Architectural Showman to Yale Dean," *New York Times,* September 23, 1998, B2.

7. These are themes that would emerge in his gigantic coauthored architectural histories of New York (*New York 1880, New York 1900, New York 1930,* and *New York 1960,* with one more to follow), invaluable troves of development stories and contributions of permanent value to our understanding of urbanism and the architectural evolution of the metropolis.

8. Rebecca Robertson, author interview, August 22, 1996.

9. Robert A. M. Stern et al., *42nd Street Development Project: A Study of the Apollo, Lyric, Selwyn and Times Square Theaters and Related Infill Parcels,* October 1988, 4.

10. Craig Wolff, "On 42d Street, a Tour Back to the Future," *New York Times,* April 14, 1989, B3.

11. Thomas J. Lueck, "Six Times Square Theaters to Go 'Populist,'" *New York Times,* September 18, 1988, 1:1.

12. Memo to Deputy Mayor Sally Hernandez-Pinero from Pamela McKoin, Re: PDC Conditional designation of The New 42nd Street, Inc., as theater sites [Site 5 and 10] developer, December 20, 1990.

13. Its major responsibilities include (1) leasing, renovating, and reconstructing the architecturally and historically significant properties in the midblock; (2) recommending to PDC or UDC the uses of the theaters providing for the mix of for-profit and nonprofit uses; (3) entering into subleases with the users of the theaters that will contain design, use, and operating standards; (4) providing management supervision of the reconstruction of the theaters; (5) overseeing the operations of the theaters once opened, maintaining standards of operation, and enforcing lease obligations. In addition, the 42EC is to provide programmatic and marketing direction to the activities of the 42DP.

14. In general, as a strategic device, the long-term lease agreement gave public officials several tactical levers of control. First, delivery of benefits could be controlled by tying what a city wants (amenities, housing, jobs) to performance-based releases of what a developer needs (development rights, and/or public infrastructure). Second, compliance on an ongoing basis could be managed through the rights of review as a landlord. Third, by building in the ability to escalate returns accruing from rising property values (through rent increases and profit-sharing provisions), a lease's financial arrangements could provide political protection against the charge that city officials "gave away too much." Lynne B. Sagalyn, "Leasing: The Strategic Option for Public Development," Lincoln Institute of Land Policy, working paper, 1993.

15. The New 42nd Street, Inc., press materials.

16. A similar type of revenue-generating structure was used by the San Francisco Redevelopment Agency (SFRA) to ensure that the city would have the necessary funds to carry the full costs of operation and maintenance, including security, for the cultural facilities and open spaces of the "Gardens" of Yerba Buena. These facilities included a Center for the Arts (galleries, forum and theater), a 5.5-acre Esplanade (outdoor performance stage surrounding by a grass meadow seating 3,000, additional gardens, two cafés), and a 22-foot-high, 50-foot-wide waterfall leading to a Martin Luther King, Jr., Memorial, all sitting on top of the roof of the expanded Moscone Convention Center. As in New York, a political imperative existed for a self-financed project, which drove the city's overall financing plan for

the 87-acre redevelopment project, termed the "buckets strategy." The buckets consisted of a series of priorities for funding the project's public amenities; funds in one bucket had to be filled before money could go to the next bucket. Revenues from deliberately timed land sales of office and residential sites would cover the capital costs of the cultural facilities and open-space amenities, while annual funds for ongoing costs would come from long-term leases to other commercial uses, primarily hotels. The operations-and-maintenance funding for the public amenities was dependent not only upon the success of private commercial components, but also on the cultural facilities becoming self-sufficient. The SFRA created "trusteed" operating-and-maintenance funds for the public gardens and cultural facilities, thereby assuring private developers that the funds paid in would in fact be dedicated for these improvements and not moved into the city's general coffers where they might be used for other purposes.

This was similar to the New42's master-lease agreement with the city by the way in which specific project-generated funds from the commercial uses were being legally dedicated to ongoing project-specific priorities and protected from possible political interference or the possibility of changing public policy about what to do with project revenues. Since very few U.S. municipalities can covenant to spend funds in the future, by setting up a segregated account through a redevelopment agency or quasi-public entity, public-development officials are able to come as close as possible to providing that assurance.

17. John Podhoretz, "Bye Bye, Broadway" [a two-part profile in *Insight*] Part 1: "Broadway: The Lights Go Down," *Washington Post*, February 2, 1987, 8ff, at 11.
18. John Podhoretz, "The Decline of Broadway: A Critic's History and Guide," *Washington Post*, February 2, 1987, 12ff, at 15.
19. Donald H. Dunn, "This Year's Show Tune: Broadway Malady," *Business Week*, November 28, 1988, 61.
20. Harry Berkowitz, "From Tap Dance to Redford, Everyone Wants 42nd St.," [Part 2: Would You Believe An Indoor Disneyland?], *Newsday*, May 11, 1989, 2.
21. Patricia Fisher and Paul Marinaccio, "City Gives Up on Buying Theater Leases," *Newsday*, April 14, 1989, 61; Rebecca Robertson, comments on walking tour of 42nd Street with University of Pennsylvania students, April 19, 1999.
22. Carl B. Weisbrod, author interview, August 15, 2000.
23. In addition to Marian Sulzberger Heiskell, the initial members included Frank Biondi, Jr., president and chief executive officer, Viacom International; Lilly Fable, president, Ninth Avenue Association; Henry Guettel, executive director, Theater Development Fund; Ming Cho Lee, set designer; Chita Rivera, Broadway star; Shahara Ahmad-Llewellyn, president, H.A.V.A.; Bill Irwin, performer/director; Charles Bear, retired chairman, Major League Baseball Promotion Corp.; Linda LeRoy Janklow, chairman, ArtsConnection; Walter Corcoran, president, Philips Credit Corp.; Earl Mack, senior partner and chief financial officer, the Mack Company; Henry McGee, senior vice president, programming, HBO Video; Terrence McNally, playwright; Tina Ramirez, artistic director, Ballet Hispanico; Frederic Papert, president, 42nd Street Development Corp.; Brenda Sanchez, trustee, American Red Cross in Greater New York; Charles Platt, partner, Platt and Byard Architects; Donald Platten, retired chairman, Chemical Banking Corp.; Herbert Sturz, president, Trottwood Corp.; Charles Shorter, senior vice president, Real Estate Research Corp.; Martin Stone, president, VIP Broadway Corp.; Mary Ann Tighe, managing director, Edward S. Gordon Co.; Lee Traub, chairman emeritus, Martha Graham Dance Co.; Theodore Wagner, attorney, Carter Ledyard & Milburn. Also serving the board ex-officio included: Kitty Carlisle Hart, chairper-

son, New York State Council on the Arts; Mary Schmidt Campbell, commissioner, New York City Department of Cultural Affairs; Carl Weisbrod, president, Public Development Corp.; Rebecca Robertson, president, 42nd Street Development Project.

24. State of New York, Executive Chamber, Mario M. Cuomo, Governor, "Press Release," September 18, 1990.

25. Kevin Sack, "Leaders Chosen for 42d St. Theaters' Renewal," *New York Times*, September 19, 1990, B4. The reference was to the prior's week *Time* magazine cover story, which questioned whether the Big Apple was rotting, as indicated by a summer-long series of highly publicized crimes in the city.

26. The dollars in the Portman Public Purpose Fund, as would be the case in the 42DP Public Purpose Fund, came from sales and compensating-use taxes associated with the construction of the hotel (office buildings) and paid by the developer of the Marriott Marquis Hotel (office buildings), which the state dedicated to a special fund for capital improvements in the immediate neighborhood (repayment of ESAC), instead of taking the monies into the city coffers.

27. Normally, a community board would only have an advisory role in determining how such funds would be used. But, earlier, when the city contemplated taking over the leases on the theaters, officials decided to offer Community Board 5 a deal that would allow it to decide the uses for half of the fund's money, within specific guidelines.

28. Cora Cahan, author interview, February 21, 1997.

29. Cahan, author interview, December 13, 1996.

30. Ibid.

31. Marion S. Heiskell, author interview, January 7, 1998.

32. Cahan, author interview, December 13, 1996.

33. Ibid.

34. Ibid.

35. Ibid.

36. Heiskell, author interview.

37. Cahan, author interview, December 13, 1996.

38. Weber, "In Times Square, Keepers of the Glitz," B6.

39. Cahan, author interview, December 13, 1996.

40. Ibid.

41. David W. Dunlap, "Theater Restoration Begins on Seedy Times Square Block," *New York Times*, May 18, 1994, B1.

42. "A New Opening for Times Square" [editorial], *New York Times*, August 10, 1992, A16; "Glad Reprieve for Times Square" [editorial], *Newsday*, August 9, 1992, 23; "Times Sq. Revival Should Center on Consumer Uses" [editorial], *Crain's New York Business*, August 10, 1992, 8.

43. Anthony Bianco, "A Star Is Reborn: Investors Hustle to Land Parts in Time Square's Transformation," *Business Week*, July 8, 1996, 102ff, at 104.

44. Paul Goldberger, "The New Times Square Magic: Magic That Surprised the Magicians," *New York Times*, C11–12, at 12, as cited in an unpublished student award-winning paper, Susan Crowl Silberberg, "The Urban Design Politics of the 42nd Street Development Project, or Tweety Bird Meets Donald Duck: How the 42nd Street Development Plan Went to Seed," paper for MIT Urban Design Politics 11.302J, fall 1996.

45. The agreement also provided that TSCA would fund up to $3 million as a ten-year loan for the 42DP to implement *42nd Street Now!* on Site 6 (which was under TSCA's lease control) unless the city and state elected to exercise an option

to purchase the development rights for one or both of the Site 6 parcels, which it did to provide Disney with an enlarged lobby space for the New Amsterdam. For a summary of all the terms of the 1992 revised deal, see NYS UDC, "Memorandum to the Directors, from Vincent Tese, Request for Authorization to Execute Amended Leases for Sites 1, 3, 4 and 12 and the Site 6 Infill with TSCA, the City of New York and Other Entities," September 21, 1994.

46. David W. Dunlap, "Long Delay Likely in Rebuilding Plan for Times Square," *New York Times*, August 3, 1992, A1, at B2.

47. When it looked probable that he would lose his lawsuits against the project, Durst bought the leases to eight 42nd Street theaters in May 1989, after the city gave up an attempt to buy them from the Brandts. It was another tactical lever into the project. Based on his interests as a leaseholder, Durst would be party to any settlement as part of the relocation process once the property was condemned. Before the theaters were condemned, the Durst Organization reported pumped close to $7 million into the first stage of an "alternative" plan for the redevelopment and rehabilitation of the historic theaters. The Obie-Award-winning *Crowbar*, was staged at the Victory and rock concerts were held by Ron Delsener in the Lyric and HBO filmed a Carly Simon special in the Apollo (also known as the Academy).

48. LucasArts Attractions with Project for Public Spaces, Inc., and Bolan Smart Associates, Inc., *42nd Street Entertainment Concept*, draft, October 1991, 2.

49. "Behind the 42nd St. Study" [letters to the editor], Rebecca Robertson, Douglas Durst, *Crain's New York Business*, March 4, 1991, 8, in response to "New York, New York: Times Square Star Wars," *Crain's New York Business*, January 28, 1991, 6.

50. David D. Dunlap, "Times Square's Future May Be Found Back at Its Roots," *New York Times*, August 4, 1992, B1.

51. Reportedly, project officials had made clear their intention to avoid sponsoring direct competition with the Broadway theaters. The 42nd Street theaters were generally smaller and in considerably shabbier shape, Robertson explained; at the time, only the New Amsterdam and the Apollo were considered capable of becoming direct rivals to the major theaters owned by Shubert, Nederlander, and Jujamcyn. Though hardly an iron-clad guarantee, especially with the availability of $18.2 million from TSCA for the renovation of two nonprofit theaters, the public pledges of limited competition appeared reasonable at a time when dismal economic conditions on Broadway made new theater ventures difficult. Even more compelling a factor contributing to their support was the widespread opinion among theater industry interests put forth at the public hearings on the *DSEIS* that the revitalization of 42nd Street was critical to the theater industry since the perception that the area is unsafe "inhibits audiences."

52. Luc Sante, "Sin and Spectacle," Robert Campbell, "Let It Be Itself," Susan Orlean, "Street Life," *New York Times*, October 16, 1993, 23.

53. "Whither 42nd St.; Better Rethink Those Office Towers" [editorial], *Newsday*, October 13, 1993, 50.

54. Press release from State Senator Franz S. Leichter, "Senator Leichter Blasts Times Square Office Tower Deal," August 2, 1994; Thomas J. Lueck, "Financing for Times Square Leads to Harsher Criticism," *New York Times*, July 28, 1994, B3.

55. Thomas J. Lueck, "Must Show Go On?" *New York Times*, August 8, 1994, B3.

56. Dunlap, "Long Delay Likely in Rebuilding Plan for Times Square," B2.

57. Weisbrod, author interview, August 14, 1996.

58. Weisbrod, author interview, December 12, 1992.

59. Since the deal eliminated the concept of Rent Erosion and the differentiation between ESAC and Non Recoverable ESAC, $3 million of nonsubway items which had formerly been classified otherwise were then designated as ESAC, including the $2.6-million streetscape contribution, $130,000 for relocation of Crossroads Users, and $300,000 in theater-related management costs. In addition, three new items related to the renegotiations qualified as ESAC: (1) insurance on the sites for the period from April 1990 until the site was delivered to TSCA; (2) public-sector costs funded by TSCA but incurred by the public sector for legal, planning, and environmental work in connection with the restructuring of the deal, up to a maximum of $2 million, plus third-party litigation occasioned by any challenge to the structuring, up to a maximum of $1 million; (3) legal costs directly incurred by the developer or any tenant for outside counsel in connection with modification of the transaction, including any associated litigation, up to a cap of $3 million. To give a sense of what this adds up to, consider TSCA's commitments to the theater agenda. These compromised (1) obligations to fund the acquisition of Site 5 theaters, at a minimum of $5.25 million, all of which would be considered ESAC; and (2) the $18.2-million "Theater Contributions" for improvements, $9.2 of which would be considered ESAC. In other words, $14.45 million of this subset of costs, more than $23.45 million, would be born by the public sector.

60. Assuming a $40 rent (reasonable at that time), including tenant improvements and operating expenses and PILOTs of $12, the percentage of gross would provide more than $0.50 a foot per year to the city, with its own built-in inflation adjustment; at the full build out of 4.1-million square feet, a reasonable projection would be $2.1 million a year to the city treasury. (Anonymous, letter to the author.) Another point worth noting is that adjusting the participation feature also triggered a change in the terms under which TSCA could purchase the sites in the future, linking it the present value of the 2-percent participation over the remaining term of the lease. Also, how much the public sector would share in developer returns related to a capital transaction (such as a refinancing) increased to 10 percent (up to a cap of $60 million) from seven percent, and was now indexed to inflation over the period prior to office construction.

61. Peter Grant, "Interim Plan for Times Sq. Endangered," *Crain's New York Business*, April 18, 1994, 3; also, see "Hold the Neon: One More Battle on 42d Street," *New York Times*, May 1, 1994, C4.

62. Tibor Kalman, author interview, December 3, 1996.

63. Steve Heller, "Tibor Kalman, 'Bad Boy' of Graphic Design, 49, Dies," *New York Times*, May 5, 1999, B14.

64. Brad Wieners,"Color Him a Provocateur," *Wired*, December 1996, 258ff, at 258.

65. John Hockenberry, "The Splendid Rage of Tibor Kalman," *New York Times*, December 31, 1998, F1.

66. Kalman, author interview.

67. Liz Farrelly, *Tibor Kalman: Design and Undesign* (East Sussex: The Ivy Press, 1998), 46; Peter Slatin, "Architecture: Disney to the rescue in Times Square," *The Independent*, April 6, 1994, 20.

68. Robertson, author interview, December 6, 1996.

69. Kalman, author interview.

70. David W. Dunlap, "Signs Signal Both Profit and Controversy," *New York Times*, February 6, 1994, 10:1.

71. George Klein, author interview, December 4, 1997.

72. Dunlap, "Signs Signal Both Profit and Controversy."

73. Grant, "Interim Plan for Times Sq. Endangered," 20.

74. David W. Dunlap, "Choreographing Times Sq. into the 21st Century," *New York Times*, September 16, 1993, B1, at B3.

75. Robertson, author interview, August 22, 1996.

76. Ibid.

77. Robertson, author interview, October 21, 1994.

78. Robert A. M. Stern, "Real Estate in the Press," transcribed tape, Urban Land Institute fall meeting, Philadelphia, November 3, 1995.

79. Faith Hope Consolo, author interview, February 5, 1997.

80. Garrick-Aug Associates Store Leasing, Inc., and Phillips/Norwalk Company, "Market Feasibility Retail Development Plan, 42nd Street Development Project," June 1, 1993, 35.

81. Rebecca Robertson, "Real Estate in the Press."

82. Herbert Muschamp, "The Alchemy Needed to Rethink Times Square," *New York Times*, August 30, 1992, 2:24 and "Time to Reset the Clock in Times Square," *New York Times,* November 1, 1993, 2:1.

83. Muschamp, "Be Bold or Begone"; Herbert Muschamp, "For Times Square, a Reprieve and Hope of a Livelier Day," *New York Times*, September 19, 1993, 2:33.

84. Robertson, author interview, October 21, 1994; "Reviving Times Square: An Interview with Rebecca Robertson: Disney Saw 42nd St.'s Value, Outsiders Do," *Crain's New York Business*, March 27, 1995, 93.

85. Creative Time, Inc., "The 42nd Street Art Project," undated.

86. Herbert Muschamp, "A Highbrow Peep Show on 42d Street," *New York Times*, August 1, 1993, H34.

87. Thomas Walsh, "NYC's 42nd St. Opens Its Doors and Windows to Ask, 'But Is it art?' The 42nd Street Art Project," *Back Stage*, July 9, 1993, 3.

88. Gary M. Rosenberg, author interview, January 22, 1997.

89. Robertson, "Real Estate in the Press."

90. Ibid.

91. Charles V. Bagli, "Disney Hopes George Will Keep Booster of 42nd Street Plan," *New York Observer*, January 23, 1995, 1, at 1.

92. Rosenberg, author interview.

93. Ibid.; Weisbrod, author interview, November 21, 1997.

94. Peter Grant, "With 42D Well in Hand, She's Moving to Eighth," *Daily News*, November 19, 1996, 53.

CHAPTER TEN

1. David W. Dunlap, "Things That Go Blink in the Night; More Bright Lights on the Way, but Space Is Available," *New York Times*, June 2, 1991, 10:15. On the "Eiffel Tower of outdoor advertising," Glenn Collins, "How do you get your message across among the Times Square throng? Try turning up the steam," *New York Times*, January 18,1996, D8.

2. Faye Brookman, "Turf War: 42nd St.'s Revival May Jeopardize 57th St.'s Outlook," *Crain's New York Business*, April 22, 1996, 35ff, at 37.

3. Michael G. Jolly, "Madame Tussaud's in New York: A Status Report—April 1999," unpublished, 2.

4. "Times Square Gains Spot on List of Costly Streets," *Wall Street Journal*, February 6, 1998, B13F. Based on survey interviews with landlords, tenants, other brokers, and bankers conducted by Manhattan-based Equis Retail Group, Times Square ranked six among the top ten retail venues worldwide. The average annual rent per square foot in Times Square (defined to include properties from 42nd Street to 47th Street on Broadway and Seventh Avenue plus 42nd Street from Broadway to

Eighth Avenues) came in at $340 a square foot compared to $580 for Manhattan's Fifth Avenue, which ranked as the most costly street in the world.

5. Claudia H. Deutsch, "Waiting for Act 2 Around Times Square; A Tale of 3 Buildings Built in Time for the Bust," *New York Times*, May 2, 1993, 10:1.

6. Jerry Adler, *High Rise: How 1,000 Men and Women Worked around the Clock for Five Years and Lost $200 Million Building a Skyscraper* (New York: Harper Collins Publishers, 1993), 387.

7. Salomon Brothers, "It's 50 Cents on the Dollar, Stupid," United States Real Estate Research, Real Estate Valuation, March 1993.

8. Patricia Goldstein, author interview, November 6, 1998.

9. Curtis Deane, author interview, November 6, 1997.

10. Jeanne B. Pinder, "Midtown Building Is Sold for $176 Million, to Cheers of Real-Estate Industry," *New York Times*, August 12, 1993, B3.

11. Tracey L. Miller, "Biondi: NY to Stay Entertainment Mecca," UPI, Domestic News, BC cycle, September 27, 1994.

12. Deane, author interview, October 31, 1997.

13. The movement of law firms to the West Side echoes a 1981 study by seven firms to move en masse into the proposed towers of the 42DP. Two of the seven—Skadden Arps and Proskauer Rose—did move to the district.

14. Gretchen Dykstra, author interview, February 10, 1997; Bruce Webber, "In Times Square, Keepers of the Glitz: Three Women Overseeing Block's Rebirth Promise to Return Its Splendor," *New York Times*, June 25, 1996, B1, at B6.

15. The BID raises revenues from a mandatory assessment on property owners in the district. The assessment, approximately 0.3 percent of the assessed value of commercial buildings (residents pay $1 per year), is collected by the city and returned in full to the BID. Its annual budget rose from $4.7 million in 1992 to $6.8 million in 1998.

16. Information drawn from various briefing and promotional materials from the Times Square BID.

17. Ylonda Gault, "Shop using loaf of wry to lift Times Sq. image," *Crain's New York Business*, January 31, 1994, 5.

18. "Gretchen Dykstra, Queen of Times Square" [editorial], *New York Observer*, May 11, 1998, 4.

19. Text copy accompanying exhibits from "Signs and Wonders: The Spectacular Lights of Times Square," The New-York Historical Society, November 12, 1997, to March 8, 1998.

20. Ken Bloom, *Broadway: An Encyclopedic Guide to the History, People and Places of Times Square* (New York: Oxford/Facts on File, 1991), 348.

21. Philip H. Dougherty, "Advertising: An Addition to Times Square," *New York Times*, October 11, 1976, 44.

22. David W. Dunlap, "Column One: Changes—Curtain Coming Down," *New York Times*, October 9, 1986, B1.

23. On pimps and prostitutes, Charles V. Bagli, "Bullish on Times Square: Wall Street Muscles into Mecca of Commercial Glitter," *New York Times,* August 20, 1998, B1; Philip H. Dougherty, "Japanese Light Up Times Square," *New York Times*, March 2, 1982, D21.

24. Sama Kusumoto, "Japanese Enlightenment," *New York Times*, March 24, 1991, 6:34.

25. Tama Starr and Edward Hayman, *Signs and Wonders: The Spectacular Marketing of America* (New York: Currency/Doubleday, 1998), 31–32.

26. Jeffrey Katz, author interview, April 11, 1997.

27. Paul Goldberger, "New Times Sq. Zoning: Skyscrapers with Signs," *New York Times*, January 30, 1987, B1.

28. David W. Dunlap, "Commercial Property: Times Square Novelty; North of Duffy Sq., a Butler-on-Every Floor Hotel," *New York Times*, June 10, 1990, 10:21. The two parcels had cost $12 million, or approximately $60 a developable square foot. When first purchased, the site could have been built out at a floor-area-ratio of 21.5 (about 301,000 square feet), taking advantage of midtown zoning incentives, plus a subway improvement bonus. Katz said he never intended to beat the sunset date for the incentive which expired in May 1988. Had he built under the earlier zoning, the acquisition cost would have approximately $40 an FAR square foot.

29. Nearby were the two buildings being developed by David and Jean Solomon, whose views on the need for elegance and dignity in the design of office towers could not have been more different that what Katz deemed essential for his Times Square tower. The Solomons were intent on beating the sunset deadline for a construction start. They were trying hard to woo Morgan Stanley as an anchor tenant. Once the design for Katz's project went public, they faced two aesthetic challenges: first, the city's impending mandate for noisy and vibrant signs and, second, the impending reality of a signpost for a neighbor. They could not have been happy developers at this point in time.

30. Thomas J. Lueck, "Reprieve for a Famed Tower in Times Sq.," *New York Times*, July 1, 1988, 25.

31. Katz, author interview.

32. David W. Dunlap, "Signs Signal Both Profit and Controversy," *New York Times*, February 6, 1994, 10:1.

33. Accounting for perhaps 40 percent of pro forma income, the sign tower was more profitable, at least at the start, than the hotel, which began to generate profits only years later, according to Katz. Mayers & Schiff's design aimed to maximize the building's sign surfaces. For example, after research on lines of sight between the building site and the southern part of Times Square, the architects determined that is was possible to make the west-facing plane of the tower also face south by cutting a diagonal stack of slabs out of the smooth west side of the building.

34. Dunlap, "Signs Signal Both Profit and Controversy."

35. Starr and Hayman, *Signs and Wonders*, 289.

36. Stuart Elliott, "The country's biggest brewer renews its defense of that position," *New York Times*, March 19, 1996, D8.

37. Ann Carrins, "Seeing Dollar Signs in Times Square," *Wall Street Journal*, February 28, 1997, B12.

38. Charles V. Bagli, "Tower in Times Sq., Billboards and All, Earns 400% [300%, correction amended] Profit," *New York Times*, June 19, 1997, A1.

39. Jay Levin, "Signs of prosperity in Times Square," *Crain's New York Business*, October 19, 1998, 52.

40. Stuart Elliott, "Joe Boxer Sign in Times Square," *New York Times*, September 8, 1995, D4.

41. Charles V. Bagli, "The Newest Showoff in the Land Where Neon Is King, Times Sq.," *New York Times*, December 29, 1999, B3.

42. William Leach, "Introductory Essay, Commercial Aesthetics" in *Inventing Times Square: Commerce and Culture at the Crossraods of the World*, William E. Taylor, ed. (New York, Russell Sage Foundation, 1991), 234–242, at 235.

43. William Cole, ed. *Quotable New York: A Literary Companion* (New York: Penguin Books, 1993), 29.

44. Dan Bischoff, "signs of the times," *Metropolis* 18 (february/march 1998), 39ff, at 44.

CHAPTER ELEVEN

1. "Reviving Times Square: An interview with Rebecca Robertson; Disney saw 42nd St.'s Value; Outsiders Do," *Crain's New York Business*, March 27, 1995, 76; Rebecca Robertson, author interview, August 22, 1996.

2. David Nasaw, *Going Out: The Rise and Fall of Public Amusements* (New York: Basic Books, 1993).

3. Alan Finder, "A Prince Charming? Disney and the City Find Each Other," *New York Times*, June 10, 1995, 21.

4. Thomas R. King, "Disney Bets Broadway Beast Is Golden Boy," *Wall Street Journal*, February 24, 1994, B1.

5. Harvard Business School, "The Walt Disney Company (B): Sustaining Growth," 1-894-129, March 28, 1994.

6. Frank Rose, "Can Disney Tame 42nd Street?" *Fortune*, June 24, 1996, 95ff, at 102.

7. Frank Rich, "Journal: Mickey Does 42d Street," *New York Times*, January 16, 1994, 4:17.

8. Ibid.

9. David W. Dunlap, "Reviving a True Classic on West 42d Street," *New York Times*, August 14, 1994, 2:1, at 1.

10. Rose, "Can Disney Tame 42nd Street?" 98. Over the next several months, Eisner dispatched teams of Disney personnel to go through the theater and to meet with 42DP and city officials on such issues as renovation costs, seat counts, progress of the project to date, and financial participation by the city and state.

11. Rose, "Can Disney Tame 42nd Street?" 100; further explanation from "The Redevelopment of Times Square," transcribed tape of the concurrent panel session at the Urban Land Institute Fall Meetings, November 8, 1997.

12. Michael Sorkin, "See You in Disneyland," in *Variations on a Theme Park*, Michael Sorkin, ed. (New York: The Noonday Press, Hill and Wang, 1992), 205–232, at 208, 215.

13. Sorkin reports that in the first ten years Disneyland took in $273 million in revenues, while the peripherals servicing Disney's visitors took in $555 million.

14. Rose, "Can Disney Tame 42nd Street?" 96.

15. David Malmuth, "The Redevelopment of Times Square."

16. Ibid.

17. Rebecca Robertson, "Landing the Anchor: The Disney Deal," course preparation materials, Harvard University, Graduate School of Design, GSD 5400: Managing Mega-Projects, Spring 1999 [hereinafter referred to as Robertson GSD course notes]. Malmuth, "The Redevelopment of Times Square."

18. Robertson GSD notes.

19. Letter to Gary L. Mayer from Rebecca Robertson, Re: New Amsterdam Theater Project, Scope of Work and 80% Design Development Package, November 18, 1994; Robertson GSD course notes.

20. With final costs at $36.7 million, as reconciled by ESDC, the "loan" funded by Disney would have been approximately $2.7 million, far less than the maximum $5.4 million as provided for under the terms of its deal with the city and state.

21. These walk-away rights were always linked to the renovation work budget. Under the terms of the nonbinding MOU, the walk-away budget number was $32 million; by the time the Lease and Funding Agreements were signed, the figure had reached $34 million, though these were later amended in ways that provided Disney with right to terminate if the renovation work budget exceeded $39.25 million, while the public entities could terminate at costs exceeding $41.15 million. If Disney walked prior to construction (Phase I), there would be no penalty; with the specs and plans for a classic Broadway theater already complete and paid for under their account, city and state officials believed these were transferrable to another operator. Negotiating termination rights during construction (Phase II) was the most complicated. If Disney walked during this period, it would leave $8 million in the project, 50 percent as a forfeiture and 50 percent as a loan to the public entities (at 3 percent over 20 years). As costs escalated, however, this solution became less satisfactory. None of the parties wanted to revisit this issue during construction, when time really is money. Hence, the high two-tier walk-away numbers in the final documents: If Disney terminated after commencement of operations (Phase III), it would forfeit its $8-million equity investment and pay a termination fee of six months of percentage rent or $200,000 plus $2 million in years one through five and $1 million in years six through ten, plus 33 percent of cost overruns up to $1.5 million.

22. Vincent Tese, author interview, December 9, 1996.

23. Ibid.

24. Since the New Amsterdam is listed on the National Register of Historic Places (in addition to its designation as a NYC Landmark), it was eligible for a 20-percent rehabilitation tax credit. In order to take advantage of this benefit, Disney immediately rejected the city's proposal of grant assistance. Assuming a $26-million investment in improvements, in 1993 Robertson calculated that the tax credit was worth $5.2 million to Disney. Reduced by this tax credit, Disney's cash equity in the deal would be much less than the widely reported $8 million. Also, under a grandfather clause to the Tax Reform Act of 1986 custom tailored for the 42DP through the efforts of George Klein, the theater project qualified for advantageous 19-year accelerated depreciation allowances provided it was able to open by January 1, 1998, which was the case.

25. For years six through 15, the base rent increases at 3 percent each year and thereafter, at the lesser of 4 percent each year or the average increase in assessments and millage for Class IV buildings in the immediately preceding lease year.

26. Robertson, author interview, August 10, 2000. Disney executives did not get everything they wanted. They bargained for an exemption from the state's real property transfer tax, which would be payable since a 99-year lease is treated like ownership; the tax would have been payable upon execution and delivery of the lease. "This was endlessly interesting to the attorneys and the accountants," Robertson said. An exemption would have saved Disney approximately $65,000 in 1995 dollars, based on the 42DP's 99-year analysis of the reversionary interest value. This was a big issue for Disney, Robertson said, but the state never waives the tax, and the company never got the exemption it sought; it did, however, get a rent-credit adjustment for this against percentage rent. It would also get rent credits for emergency repairs, if the 42DP, Inc. did not make timely payment of construction costs and if the public entity did not approve and pay change orders that were ultimately deemed to be "suitable."

27. Robertson, GSD course notes.

28. Robertson, author interview, August 22, 1996.

29. Tese, author interview.

30. Brett Pulley, "A Mix of Glamour and Hardball Won Disney a Piece of 42d Street," *New York Times*, July 29, 1995, 1, at 22.

31. Gerald Schoenfeld, chairman of the Shubert Organization, quoted in David W. Dunlap, "Theater Owners Battle Planned Disney Leap into 42d Street," *New York Times*, November 17, 1993, B2.

32. David W. Dunlap, Cuomo Backs Loan Program for Broadway: Theaters Drop Hostility to Disney Development," *New York Times*, January 7, 1994, B1. In fact, the state ended up doing nothing under this loan program; the administration changed. According to Robertson, the city's rezoning of the Theater District, with its $10-million Broadway Initiative, was to serve as payback for the Disney deal. Initially overturned by the courts, the zoning amendments were ultimately upheld by the appeals court; only the discrete provisions relating to discretionary grants of FAR were annulled. In her teaching notes on the Disney deal, Robertson also remarked that the theater owners' peace with the Disney deal was brokered by the unions, who wanted assurance that the New Amsterdam would be a full-union Broadway house. In fact, the New Amsterdam did not become a union house, despite the "prevailing condition" clause in the Disney deal. The state, under Governor Pataki was not willing to demand it, and Disney made its own deal for the theater workers, a deviation from precedent that Robertson believes will turn out to be significant.

33. There was an ironic circularity to the logic put forth in UDC's memorandum to directors on the issue. Justified as a means of enabling the 42DP to meet its project goals, one of which was "to preserve and restore the Project area's extraordinary theaters, and by doing so, revitalize the Project area as a theater and entertainment center serving tourists and all New Yorkers," the logic inverted causality. It evoked the historic link between the entertainment business and sex by arguing: "The focus on entertainment uses in '42nd Street Now!' may increase the risk that SRBs will try to return to the area and will bring with them deleterious secondary effects." NYS UDC, "For Consideration [Board of Directors], Request for Adoption of Findings and Policy Statement with Respect to Sex-Related Businesses Within the 42nd Street Development Project; Determination of No Significant Effect on the Environment," December 15, 1994, 3.

34. This was neither the first nor the last time state officials set a date for concluding negotiations that might drag on interminably. The first was for TSCA, when they set August 1, 1994, as the deadline for a new deal, without which the developer would have to begin construction under the terms of the LADA or go into default, thereby risking its $241-million L/C. In summer 1996, after more than a year of negotiations, 42DP officials imposed a 60-day deadline for Tishman to conclude negotiations on the lease agreement for Site 7, or the state would scuttle the company's deal to build a $303-million hotel and entertainment complex.

35. Charles V. Bagli, "Disney Dream Gang Mugs New York City: A Hard Look at the 42nd Street Hustle," *New York Observer*, May 22, 1995, 1, at 8.

36. Carl Weisbrod, "42d Street Houses Are Part of a Symbol of Urban Decay" [letter to the editor], *New York Times*, April 18, 1988, A22, in response to Alan H. Levine, "42d Street, in Black and White (Mostly White)" [letter to the editor], March 19, 1988, 27.

37. The "movie issue" was not even on the agenda of analysis for the original environmental-impact statement and was first considered in 1993, as part of the supplemental impact statement required for *42nd Street Now!* "Historically, first-run

movie theaters had been a "major contributing element to the character of Times Square," the 1993 report noted, but demolition of theaters for new office towers and limited new movie-theater construction had "greatly diminished the presence of first-run movie theaters," thereby eliminating their "significant role in defining the character of Times Square" (NYS UDC. *42nd Street Development Project: General Project Plan, Final Supplemental Environmental Statement,* prepared by Allee King Rosen & Fleming, Inc., Parsons Brinckerhoff Quade & Douglas, Inc., Eng-Wong, Taub & Associates, P.A., 1993, II.B-32). Density did not distinguish movie theaters in Times Square the way it did Broadway theater, even historically. Of the 122 legitimate theaters and opera houses in the United States counted by a federal census in 1934, 29 were in Manhattan; no others were in city boroughs and only one other was in the state. If you wanted to see live drama, *the* place to go was Broadway. That was not the case for movies, though. The same survey counted 144 movie theaters in Manhattan, 130 in Brooklyn, 51 in the Bronx, and 48 in Queens. Robert Sklar, "Times Square as a Movie-Goers' Mecca?" unpublished and undated draft, 13–14.

38. AMC's proposal also included restoration of the Liberty Theater interior and exterior, restoration of the Empire Theater facade and proscenium dome, restoration of the Harris Theater facade, restaurants of approximately 15,000 square feet, support space for local legitimate theater, and design and supersigns in the spirit of the *New 42nd Street Now!* plan.

39. Bagli, "Disney Dream Gang Mugs New York City," 8.

40. Bagli, "Disney, Marriott, AMC Get in Line for Sweetheart Deals on 42nd Street," 10.

41. As discussed in chapter 13, this was a plausible question. How often is it that a government entity sets up a nonprofit organization that is not beholden to government, except through the board of directors and then only to a limited extent? Carl Weisbrod asked much later. In addition to the organizational structure, the New42 had an independent source of funds and a 99-year lease on the theaters. Given control of the theaters through a sole-source designation, the New42 was special, though not unique. While the profile suggests the entity is out of scrutiny and accountability, there is a long history of government creating this type of nonprofit setup, for hospitals and museums, to name the most obvious.

42. The New42's agreement with the city and the state also provided for the creation of a Sales Tax Fund. The sales and compensating-use taxes associated with the renovation of the theaters would be deposited in a trust fund to be jointly administered by UDC and the city. Dedicated to theater uses, the specific allocations would be jointly determined. See also note 26, chapter 9.

43. Cora Cahan, author interview, December 13, 1996. Cahan did not win all her battles. Earlier, the New42 had wanted the Disney lease to come under its master lease, and it wanted to be involved in the deal. City and state officials were not prepared to give it to the nonprofit entity as there would be no rents forthcoming to the city and state, except to repay the loans made by these government entities. "It was a PR struggle," Robertson wrote in her teaching notes. "Finally the New42 backed off and stayed out of the negotiation altogether." Robertson GSD teaching notes, February 29, 1999.

44. Memo to Charles Gargano from Rebecca Robertson, "Re: City Response to Disney Renegotiated Terms," July 18, 1995, in Robertson GSD teaching notes.

45. Robertson GSD course notes. As part of the agreements, Eisner had insisted on a confidentiality agreement so as to allow Giuliani, as the new mayor, to make the deal his own. The side-letter agreement prohibited the parties from issuing any

press release, holding any press conference, or making any other public statement.

46. Although its name was synonymous with the wax exhibition, Tussaud's also operated the Rock Circus in London, an exhibition on the history of rock and pop culture, the London Planetarium, and the Scenerama in Amsterdam, which depicts Holland's golden age in the seventeenth century.

47. Fearing that this circuslike tourist attraction would conflict with the corporate image of the four towers he and Prudential planned to build, Klein reportedly blocked the project. Pearson's and Madame Tussaud's then redesigned the museum to fit within the former Times Tower. Bagli, "Times Square Mega-Deal Meltdown," 8.

48. Even before the bankruptcy auction, BNP knew there were many interested bidders, most of whom appeared to be pricing the asset on the basis of its use as an office building. But the tiny floor plates were unsuitable for office space, and the numbers they were hearing undervalued the building's signage potential. At the foreclosure auction, bidding was active (complete with drama that came from a last-minute mystery bidder who called in from a mobile phone). After BNP bought the property for $25.2 million, it was immediately approached by three of the active bidders, including Lehman, but having a good handle on the signage value of the building, the bank decided to sell the tower by means of a sealed-bid process, with bids due at 9 A.M. the next day. Lehman's price had a compelling advantage over Pearson's: It was unconditional, and the investment bank was willing to close the deal in 24 hours. Pearson, in contrast, needed the approval of its board. See infra, 332.

49. Thomas J. Lueck, "Madame Tussaud's Loses Bidding War and Drops Times Sq. Plan," *New York Times*, March 23, 1995, B5.

50. Malmuth, "The Redevelopment of Times Square," transcribed tape.

51. One of the nation's largest builder/owners of real estate projects, TR&C owned or managed at the time over 8,000 hotel rooms, especially in entertainment, resort, and convention settings. These included the 2,270-room Walt Disney Swan and Dolphin Hotel complexes in Florida, the 815-room Hilton at Walt Disney World Village, and the 1,200-room Sheraton Chicago Hotel and Towers. As a nationwide builder, its roster of major construction projects included Epcot Center in Orlando, the John Hancock Center in Chicago, and the World Trade Center and the renovation and restoration of Carnegie Hall and the St. Regis Hotel in New York.

52. State of New York, Governor George E. Pataki, Press Release, "Developer Selected for 42nd Street Hotel Project," May 11, 1995.

53. "Disney and the Developer" [editorial], *New York Observer*, May 29, 1995, 4.

54. Bagli, "Disney Dream Gang Mugs New York City," 1.

55. Rose, "Can Disney Tame 42nd Street?" 102.

56. David Henry, "Disney Wants Hotel on 42nd St.," *Newsday*, July 29, 1994, A47.

57. Jimmy Breslin, "Taking the Show out on the Road," *Newsday,* March 1, 1998, A4.

58. Bagli, "42nd Street Scramble! Will Disney's Deadline Melt Madame Tussaud's?" 8.

59. Robertson author interview, December 5, 1998.

60. Mary Anne Gilmartin, "The Redevelopment of Times Square."

61. Robertson GSD course notes.

62. Anonymous, author interview.

63. 42DP's focus-group research found general disappointment with retail and

restaurant opportunities in Times Square; the majority of respondents said they would have spent more money in the area if there were better stores and eating places. Malmuth echoed these findings: "There are huge numbers of people wanting to spend money. We noticed, when we first started looking at the project, four and a half years ago, that there was this Gap Store at the corner of 42nd Street and [Broadway]. With essentially nothing around it, it was still doing $700 a square foot. Well, why was that? It was because lots of tourists were coming to Times Square and they wanted to buy something, even if it was Gap jeans, at least they can say they bought something in Times Square." "The Redevelopment of Times Square."

64. Through several construction and development projects at Disney World in Orlando, Tishman's links to Disney went way back. AMC, which is the largest distributor of Disney movies, was introduced to state officials by Disney, according to Malmuth. FCR's close hand knowledge of the Disney deal came from Stuckey, who while working as a managing director for the brokerage firm of Dan Gronich & Company before joining FCR, had been hired by Disney to negotiate their deal with the city and state, along with Disney's David Malmuth and Frank Iopollo.

65. Pulley, "A Mix of Glamour and Hardball Won Disney a Piece of 42nd Street," 22.

66. Ibid.

67. William L. Mack, author interview, December 14, 1999.

CHAPTER TWELVE

1. Site acquisition costs for the first phase of condemnation are estimated at $334.5 million (see note 7 in the epilogue); accounting for the allocation of $35 million for Site 7 and $13 million for Site 8E, the costs for both of which are likely to be greater, the total of these three takings comes to $382.5 million. Because the settlements for the last two phases are not yet complete, it is not possible to know the final number, but it is safe to conclude that the costs will be nearly $400 million. A full and final accounting of all land costs for the project would have to take into consideration future acquisition costs for Site 8S (future home of the New York Times) and Site 8N, the Milstein parking lot, which recently transacted in the private market for $111 million.

2. This has been the case in high-profile public developments across the country, most notably San Francisco's Yerba Buena Gardens. When the project hit the force of an economic recession and property depression at the end of 1980s, all did not go according to plan. Both macro events undermined any type of timely commercial development after completion of the project's Marriott Hotel in late 1989. Consequently, the office component never went forward on schedule, and that torpedoed the likelihood of financing the public amenities 100 percent with land-disposition revenues. When the developer, Olympia & York, did not perform in line with the development agreement, the redevelopment agency canceled the contract (and the developer forfeited its development rights), an action that left the agency holding $27 million of up-front advances and option payments for the sites. With heavy political pressure and civic expectations that the SFRA deliver on the promised public-amenity package, the agency reversed the public-private construction priorities of the original strategy and went ahead with the construction of the gardens and arts complex. It did so by drawing on O&Y's forfeited $27 million, $10 million from a renegotiated deal with the Marriott Hotel (to accelerate lease payments) and a $30-million tax-exempt bond issue. A $48-million Children's Center,

to be financed by additional borrowings, was also developed in the late 1990s by the SFRA. Though the benefits had been integrally linked to private commercial development, given the contentious history of this significant site, the SFRA could not take the political risk of failing to act to achieve its agenda. Fortunately, the original buckets strategy and a tightly drafted development and disposition agreement provided sufficient funds to proceed, albeit by taking on more risk. Lynne B. Sagalyn, "Negotiating for Public Benefits: The Bargaining Calculus of Public-Private Development," *Urban Studies* 34 (December 1997): 1955–1970, at 1966.

3. Delays did not mar the acquisition of the Site 7 parcels, where armed with $35 million of city capital-budget monies, UDC relatively quickly finished condemnation proceedings for 18 parcels in October 1994. No litigation bedeviled that process, but UDC would have gone ahead with the action even if lawsuits had been filed, according to Robertson. Generalizing from that single experience is hazardous, however. For UDC to have gone forward in the mid-1980s with the condemnation of the office and theater sites, it would have had to make a determination that the authority would have won any pending or threatened litigation. This would have been a much harder call than it was for the smaller Site 7 condemnation, which followed 47 unsuccessful lawsuits challenging the project on diverse fronts. If history offered any lesson, the disastrous legacy of the federal urban-renewal program—hundreds of acres of vacant land standing idle for years as gaping holes in city centers resulting from acquisition-and-clearance strategies in advance of feasible private development proposals—would have dictated cautious public behavior. See infra, 225.

4. David W. Dunlap, "Times Square Redevelopers Seek Delay in Project," *New York Times,* November 9, 1991, 25.

5. Peter Grant, "UDC seeking order to evict firm from site in Times Square," *Crain's New York Business*, March 3, 1991, 35.

6. Sam Roberts, "Who Runs New York Now?" *New York Times Magazine*, April 28, 1985, 27ff.

7. PSI wanted floorplates of about 50,000 square feet to accommodate its data center, trading floors, and back-office operations. By comparison, the floorplates of a building on Site 12 would have been approximately 40,000 square feet at the lower levels and, after setbacks, 20,000 square feet at most on the upper levels. PSI considered other 42DP sites; though talks were only preliminary, the story is revealing of the hazardous perceptions of West 42nd Street in the early 1990s. The ideal site capable of providing the requisite-size floorplates from a functional point of view, remarked Rodger G. Parker who headed the relocation effort for PSI, was the large western-end site on the southeast corner of 42nd Street and Eighth Avenue across from the Port Authority Bus Terminal (PABT). PSI bankers, however, would not go near the PABT. The next option his group considered was using both sites on Broadway and 42nd Street (Sites 3 and 4) to achieve the large-size floorplates. The idea was to build a base building on each site and bridge over the street with a four-story atrium connecting the two buildings; atop this atrium they would build 10 or 11 stories, then top the two individual sites with towers. Not surprisingly, the city vetoed this cumbersome, street-destroying design scheme.

8. Sharon R. King, "New York Incentives Pact Persuades Prudential Securities to Remain in City," *Bond Buyer*, August 6, 1992, 6.

9. David W. Dunlap, "Rejecting Times Square, Prudential Gets Tax Breaks to Stay in New York," *New York Times*, August 6, 1992, B3.

10. Consolidating its operations in One New York Plaza meant moving out of six downtown buildings, which would leave an especially large vacancy—500,000 of

655,000 square feet—in 100 Gold Street, existing home of PSI's back-office operations. The large nine-story building also housed the headquarters for the city's Housing Preservation and Development Department, which consolidated operations by relocating 2,600 employees from four separate downtown locations to Gold Street after Prudential departed.

The more fundamental political economics of the musical-chairs transaction quietly came to light more than a year later when the city closed on its $37-million purchase of the Gold Street building from Travelers Insurance Company, holders of the second mortgage and involuntary owners after the previous Chicago-based owner of the building filed for bankruptcy. At approximately $56 a square foot, the city paid the highest square-foot price for a major downtown office building that year. By purchasing the 24-year-old building, the city bolstered the weakening downtown market for back-office operations—and those institutions and individuals with investments in it—which was suffering from a flight to quality. "If the city had not done this," *Real Estate Weekly* reported, "the building owner would have been hard pressed to find a user." Robert Martin, "Activity to continue at faster pace in 1994; New York, New York real estate sales and leasing activity; Annual Review & Forecast," *Real Estate Weekly*, January 26, 1994, C2.

The Seaport Plaza linkage surfaced in mid-1995 in a local trade journal article describing in great detail the consolidation gains from the $320-million PSI-headquarters relocation. "The original plan was to consolidate the 11 buildings into one, but it didn't quite work out that way. We just couldn't work out the details," said Parker. One of the details was the Prudential mortgage on One Seaport Plaza, which "was too big to walk away from." John Salustri, "Prudential Securities' HQ Yields Big Dividends," *Real Estate New York*, May 1995.

11. In mid-1990, a tentative verbal agreement had been reached to move PSI to New Jersey, but after considering the broad ramifications of such a move, Prudential's chairman made a decision to delay for at least a year while Prudential reviewed its options from the broader perspective of its complete set of interests in New York.

12. Anonymous, author interview.

13. The prolonged, contentious, and ultimately failed first attempt of the MTA and the city to redevelop the Coliseum site at Columbus Circle stands as a prime example of the public sector's difficulty in cutting loose of initial ties with selected developers. Even compromise could not salvage this public-private project when the trust had disappeared from the partnership.

14. In one, for example, TSCA gained protection for its competitively advantaged financial incentive package in return for waiving any rights to consent to any use of, or financial arrangements for, Sites 7 and 8. As the legal language of the 1992 MOU put it, "UDC and the City agree that any financial incentive package made with the developer of such Site shall not be more favorable than that then offered, as of right, for office buildings in Manhattan, and in no event shall such financial incentive package be more favorable than that provided under the Amended Project Documents to TSCA." For its part, the city improved details of the agreement in its favor.

15. As quoted in Susan Silberberg, "The Urban Design Politics of the 42nd Street Development Project," 21; from James S. Russell, "42nd Street: No Beat of Dancing Street—Yet," *Architectural Record* 177 (June 1989), 85.

16. Under the UDC Act there are clear standards and procedures for relocation assistance for residential displacements; they are voluntary for commercial tenants.

As a policy, 42DP set up a program of assistance for both residential and commercial tenants, tried not to take possession until they needed the site, and used eviction only when necessary.

17. Robin Stout, author interview, January 29, 1998.

18. Charles M. Haar and Michael Allan Wolf, *Land-Use Planning: A Casebook on the Use, Misuse, and Re-use of Urban Land* (Boston: Little, Brown and Co., 1989), 42.

19. Stout, author interview.

20. Haar and Wolf, *Land-Use Planning*, 783.

21. As project-specific entitlements, these shares are passive, meaning they carry no implied rights to actively redevelop the parcels, participate in the direct decision making for such redevelopment, or reoccupy specific sites within the project area. The passive character of these shares does not, however, diminish the long-term economic benefits of the arrangement, especially if the redevelopment corporation is publicly traded on a listed stock exchange. Depending upon the scale of the redevelopment endeavor and the format of the joint-stock corporation, the rights of existing property owners might also include rights of first refusal to redevelop a site as long as the submitted proposal is in conformance with the approved plan for renewal.

22. Soon after the 1994 IPO, *Barron's* reported on one analysis that indicated the company's real estate's assets were worth more than what it paid for them. In fact, those shares available to Arab investors other than the project area's property-rights holders issued at a par value of $10 per share had traded up between $11.25 and $17.75 in the months following the IPO.

23. It is worth noting other arrangements tried abroad that could also serve some of the purposes of the Solidare model. In Japan and much of Asia, land readjustment is used to aggregate properties, finance improvements, and make sites available for development without public takings. Many operate within well-defined statutory agencies. Many European countries, such as Spain, promote public-private share corporations with the right to aggregate interests in property for mutual benefit. See William A. Doebele, *Land Readjustment: A Different Approach to Financing Urbanization* (Lexington, Mass.: Lexington Books, 1982).

24. NYS UDC, *42nd Street Development Project: Draft Environmental Impact Statement, February 1984,* 1-13, 2-309, 2-308.

25. 42DP, "Reconstruction of the Times Square Subway Complex: Status and Summary," October 1984, 3.

26. The transit provisions of the city's Zoning Ordinance fall into three areas: 1) mandatory as-of-right zoning provisions under which developers are required to improve subway facilities that are adjacent to their projects; typically this involves relocating a subway entrance from the sidewalk to within the property line and locating stairs and elevator entrances to the subway in the building lobby or in an adjacent outdoor plaza area; 2) EIS mitigations, though these need not be transit related; and 3) Floor-Area-Ratio (FAR) bonuses of up to 20 percent for significant improvements in station circulation and access determined through negotiations between the developer and the CPC. To further expand the scope and applicability of these zoning-based transit provisions, the DCP established 33 special districts where improvements were needed and where development was likely to occur; under this program, developers and regulators have had greater latitude to negotiate transit improvements. In 1982 the enactment of a Special Midtown Zoning District gave priority to subway connections over covered pedestrian spaces and plazas. It mandated that new buildings relocate adjacent subway stairs from the

public sidewalk to the development lot and continue existing networks of through-block passageways which ease pedestrian movement in the long blocks west of Fifth Avenue. Major subway connection improvements such as opening the station mezzanine to light and air, providing improved connections, escalators or elevators qualified for an FAR bonus up to 20 percent of the base FAR by special permit. While at first the FAR bonuses only applied to the midtown district, in 1984 they were made available to any development in Manhattan (and later extended to downtown Brooklyn and the Court Square subdistrict in Long Island City where Citicorp located a new high-rise tower) with a current FAR of 10 or more.

27. Exploring the Metropolis, *Hindsight and Foresight: Planning for Significant City-Owned Sites* (New York: Exploring the Metropolis, 1988), 35. The strategy has its limits and works best when high land values and rents, as in Manhattan, stimulate developers to take advantage of the density bonuses. In contrast, infrastructure costs for major public-private development projects in Brooklyn, Queens, and Staten Island typically were covered with capital-budget allocations. Since both the land cost and infrastructure cost-sharing will be factored into the price a developer is willing to pay for a development opportunity, the city cannot have it both ways. The real policy question asked in the above-cited report is "What should be planned for and effected by the city and what should be negotiated with the developer?"

28. Ross Sandler, "Private Development/Public Transit: Using Transit's Zoning Tool," *New York Affairs* 7 (1982): 114–120, at 120.

29. NY TA, MTA, "Capital Program Modification: Times Square Subway Station Complex, Staff Summary Sheet," June 9, 1993, 2.

30. Fred I. Kent III, president of Project for Public Spaces, a nonprofit civic advocacy group, is the one notable exception. In an unpublished three-page, single-spaced letter to the editor of the *Times* in response to the article "Picking Up the Pace of Preparing the Site" (July 22, 1990), Kent criticizes the developer-driven agenda of improvements, the developer-set timetable for construction, and the failure of the plan to address what the EIS for the project emphasized were the needs of those who use the station most, transferring subway patrons. His is a balanced and reasoned critique that questions several of the plan's most salient features. First, the real purpose of the free-fare zone: "The sole purpose of the free fare zone is to link the proposed office towers with an underground passageway, but even this is of questionable merit, since most people do not go underground to simply cross the street." Second, moving the Shuttle tracks: while this "may have aesthetic value to the developer in allowing for the continuation of the free fare zone, it is hardly the solution to the traffic and congestion problem for subway passengers." Third, the city's true financial liability for cost of the subway improvements: "The developer is to contribute $92.5 million. However, for this $92.5 million, the developer will receive a rent credit from the City for nearly $40 million, leaving a net cost of only about $50 million. Of that net cost, $12 million is for subway entrances which will be in the developer's own buildings and would be required of any developer of those sites." At the hearings on the *DSEIS*, several people commented on the elimination of the subway improvements as a project element and voiced their concerns over plans for such renovations, but the character of this public space never surfaced as an issue.

31. Sandler, "Private Development/Public Transit," 114.

32. Jay Walder, author interview, June 26, 1999.

33. Ibid.

34. Construction involved extraordinary technical complexity. The entire block of Seventh Avenue would have had to be raised by one foot, the electrical system in the area and the thicket of cable lines moved three times, and a 48-inch water main shifted.

35. Carl B. Weisbrod, author interview, August 14, 1996.

36. Vincent Tese, author interview, December 9, 1996.

37. Walder, author interview.

38. NY TA, MTA, "Capital Program Modification: Times Square Subway Station Complex, Staff Summary Sheet," G-34.

39. To the extent renovation costs exceeded $70 million, the MTA would receive revenues from the office development of up to 50 percent of the "enhanced PILOT"—the increment of renegotiated PILOT over the PILOT schedule approved in 1984—and any payments made by developers in lieu of the state mortgage-recording tax.

40. Bruce Lambert, "Times Square Subway Station: Putting a There There," *New York Times*, December 10, 1995, 13:6; "It's Clean, It's Whimsical: Can This Be Times Square?" [editorial], *Newsday*, July 17, 1997, A46.

41. "Subway Stations; Going Fast" [editorial], *New York Times*, August 20, 1992.

42. Ibid.

43. Joseph Dolman, "All That Glitters in New Times Square Is Surface," *Newsday*, April 2, 1998, A46. The city had spent five years and $12 million trying to renovate the popular skating rink, to no avail. "It was an incredible symbol of incompetence," said Trump who sent a letter to Mayor Koch offering to complete the job with $2 million in city funds and with a promise that it would be done within six months, nine less than what Parks Department officials expected it to take them to complete the job. Samuel G. Freedman, "Trump Feud: Barbs Show Deeper Split," *New York Times*, July 6, 1987, 33.

44. NYC UDC, minutes of the meeting of directors, February 9, 1988, 20.

45. Anthony Feldmesser, "Times Square Station Is No Gift to Riders" [letter to the editor], *New York Times*, July 21, 1998, A14.

46. State of NY, Office of the Inspector General, MTA, *Investigation of Times Square Escalator Buyout*," MTA/IG 99-12, October 1999, at 2, 1, 7, 12. In a footnote, the report noted that these figures were conservative for two reasons: a longer useful life for the tower than upon which the estimates are based and the use of a 10 percent discount rate.

47. Charles V. Bagli, "M.T.A. Shortchanged Itself in Reuters Deal, Report Says," *New York Times*, October 28, 1999, B4. First notice of the trade occurred in Charles V. Bagli, "Retreat on Times Square Subway Plan," *New York Times*, May 14, 1998, B3.

48. David Firestone, "Times Sq. Cleanup Missed Underbelly," *New York Times*, July 19, 1998, 23, at 25.

49. Concerned about this most public of problems, the TA issued a preview of the project's "inconvenience factor" for construction of the large, $9.8-million street-level entrance on West 42nd Street. By the TA's count, 6,200 passengers would be inconvenienced. Community Board 5, whose jurisdiction includes West 42nd Street, contended the count would be higher because the TA's counts, in general, tended to be conservative and because new big-format retail activity like the Virgin mega-store in Times Square was filling the area and, by extension the subway, with many more people. In short, the concerns of pedestrian and subway congestion were paramount.

50. Walder, author interview.

51. "Super Subway Stop" [editorial], *Newsday*, July 18, 1998, A1.

52. I owe this point to Jay Walder, who gamely explained the politics of MTA capital budgeting to me. Author interview.

53. Susan Fine, author interview, June 21, 1999.

54. A key issue was whether there would be a cap on the amount of funds that would come from the office development. Another was whether all the money the MTA received had to go back into the Times Square subway station renovations, or whether some of it could go into the MTA's general coffers. The MTA had no leverage and no political capital to waste on this issue, and whether the money from the office development went to the Times Square station project or the MTA's general coffers was a "distinction without distinction," said Fine. The MTA has a huge capital budget; what it would get from the office towers would be less than what the renovation project would cost, and the MTA agreed to do the project regardless of the future dollars coming in. Author interview, September 15, 2000.

55. Dean Starkman, "Take and Give: Condemnation Is Used to Hand One Business Property of Another," *Wall Street Journal*, December 2, 1998, 1.

56. A recent legal ruling makes that all too clear. In July 1998, a Superior Court judge in Atlantic City, New Jersey, ruled that the state was not allowed to seize three small properties owned by a widowed homeowner and two small businesses in Atlantic City that stand in the way of an expansion of the Trump Plaza Hotel and Casino. The case attracted national attention when the syndicated artist Garry Trudeau drew six "Doonesbury" cartoons needling the owner of the casino, Donald Trump; the homeowner later appeared on ABC's television news show *20/20*. An obvious setback for the state's Casino Reinvestment Development Authority, the ruling marked "the first time a judge had blocked a condemnation on the ground that there was no guarantee for the use of the seized properties," reported the *Times*. "The case could have implications for other eminent domain cases being litigated in Atlantic City and throughout the state. Lawyers for the property owners also said they hope the decision signaled a new nationwide trend in stricter judicial scrutiny of condemnation applications." David M. Herszenhorn, "Widowed Homeowner Foils Trump in Atlantic City," *New York Times*, July 21, 1998, B1.

57. Patricia Fisher and Paul Marinaccio, "City Gives Up on Buying Leases," *Newsday*, April 14, 1989, 61.

58. Paul Travis, author interview, January 7, 1992.

59. Charles Gasparino and Josh P. Hamilton, "Spoken in Spokane: Downtown Revival Plan Relying on HUD Aid Poses Hard Questions, Among Them: Is Guarantee Proper for a Fancy Mall, and What Is City's Risk?" *Wall Street Journal*, January 8, 1999, 1.

60. New York's "Outer-Borough Strategy" initiated in the early 1980s represents a case in point. In a 1988 report requested by Koch evaluating the city's stalled efforts to revitalize downtowns in Brooklyn, the Bronx, Queens, and Staten Island, the RPA reviewed many of the procedural, bureaucratic, and financial problems holding back these projects. Of telling importance was the conflict between the city's development and financial concerns:

> These downtown projects have the type of indirect benefits
> which the City's cost-benefit analysis specifically ignores, but
> City assistance is required precisely because they are inherently

riskier. The bet must be that the City-stimulated projects will
create the critical development mass needed to alter local market forces and reduce developer's risk perceptions and increase
the direct benefits to be gained by future development projects. It seems rather like a Catch 22 argument when the same
reasons are cited both for and against the City's involvement in
these projects.

If the city really wanted to revitalize the outer-borough downtowns, the RPA
concluded, it would have to assume more of those financial risks. Regional Plan
Association, "Expediting Redevelopment Projects in the Outer Boroughs
Downtowns," March 1988, 12, 15.
61. Carl B. Weisbrod, letter to the author, August 18, 1996.
62. Gerald D. Suttles, *The Man-Made City: The Land-Use Confidence Game in Chicago*
(Chicago: University of Chicago Press, 1990), 145.

CHAPTER THIRTEEN
1. Stephen A. Lefkowitz, author interview, February 27, 1992.
2. In 1979, UDC lost a significant case when the court held that the agency had
abused its discretion. The case concerned Syracuse University's attempt to build a
domed stadium. As the chief source of finance and technical assistance, UDC was
deemed the "lead agency" for project review under SEQRA. Acting in this capacity UDC made a determination that the construction of the stadium would not
significantly affect the environment and require the preparation of an EIS under
SEQRA. Local landowners successfully challenged UDC's negative declaration. In
holding that UDC's action was arbitrary and capricious, the court argued in
H.O.M.E.S. v. N.Y.S. Urban Dev. Corp. 69 A.D.2d 222, 418 N.Y.S.2d 827 (N.Y.
App. Div. 1979) that:

> clearly, UDC failed to take a "hard look" at the problems and adverse
> potential effects of the project on traffic stoppage, parking, air pollution
> or noise level damage. Not only did it fail to analyze the traffic and
> parking problems entailed, but it vaguely recognized their existence and
> relied upon general assurances that after the problems developed the
> University and City of Syracuse would adequately mitigate them by
> some unspecified appropriate action. It gave no consideration to the
> effect on the neighborhood of the operation of this facility. . . .

As a result of this decision, those areas cited by the court were subsequently examined in great detail in the EIS for the 42DP.
3. *Jackson v. N.Y.S. Urban Dev. Corp.*, [67 N.Y.S.2d. 400], 496 N.E.2d 429, [503
N.Y.S.2d 298) (N.Y. Ct. App. 1986), at 305.
4. Lefkowitz, author interview.
5. By way of illustration, EDC explained its procedures in response to a 1993 audit
performed by the city comptroller's office of the corporation's lease agreements
with private developers. Besides voluntarily submitting land sales and leases to a
mayoral public hearing, EDC staff "meet on a regular basis with Council members,
Community Board members, and other responsible elected officials on the status
of all projects. . . . EDC's performance is reviewed annually through EDC Master
and Maritime contracts with the City. Every one of EDC's projects is subject to

the approval of both the Deputy Mayor for Finance and Economic Development and the EDC Board of Directors. The City's Office of Management and Budget must also approve projects which involve City funds." City of New York, Office of the Comptroller, Bureau of Audit, "The New York City Economic Development Corporation Should Evaluate and Better Document Its Economic Development Lease Projects," Report K91-05, January 25, 1993, 30. [Herin cited as EDC Audit.]

6. This is, for example, standard practice for San Francisco's and Los Angeles's redevelopment agencies, and was done for both Yerba Buena Gardens and California Plaza, projects with highly complex deals.

7. Pursuant to Section 240 of the city charter, the mayor must submit to the city council a tax-benefit report. The new charter mandates that this report include: a comprehensive listing of city-specific tax-expenditures; the citation of legal authority and the objectives and eligibility requirements for each tax expenditure; data, as available, on the number and kind of taxpayers benefitting from city tax-expenditures programs and the total value of these programs; data on the number and kind of taxpayers carrying forward tax benefits to future years and the total value of these carry-forwards; data, as available, on the economic and social impact of city expenditure programs; a listing and summary of all evaluations and audits of city tax-expenditure programs conducted during the previous two years.

8. These leases were part of five PDC projects (MetroTech, Livingston Plaza, Strand Theater, Jamaica Farmer's Market, and Brooklyn Army Terminal) and three projects of the Department of Ports and Trade (Continental Terminals, MASTAS–Bush Terminal, and Tangent Industries).

9. EDC Audit, 3.

10. Douglas Feiden, "Comptroller asks city: Where are those jobs? Agency hit for not verifying project gains," *Crain's New York Business*, February 1, 1993, 4.

11. Edward Regan, "Government, Inc.: Creating Accountability for Economic Development Programs," Government Finance Research Center of the Government Finance Officers Association, April 1988, 1.

12. EDC Audit, 29.

13. Ibid., 33.

14. For example, the Boston Municipal Research Bureau and the Minnesota Citizens League perform an important purpose by reviewing public deals. In California, counties have used their political power and rights of review in the tax-increment process as levers to bargain for a share of tax increments that would otherwise go to redevelopment agencies, thereby making deal making more accountable by opening up the decision-making process. See Lynne B. Sagalyn, "Explaining the Improbable: Local Redevelopment in the Wake of Federal Cutbacks," *Journal of the American Planning Association* 56 (Autumn 1990): 429–441.

15. The 500 number comes from the author's tabulation of cumulated news clips on the 42DP developed over the decade of research for this book, supplemented with searches on Lexis/Nexis. It covers articles from both daily papers (*New York Times, Daily News, New York Post, New York Newsday*) and weeklies (*Crain's New York Business, New York Observer, Real Estate Weekly, Village Voice*). Other national-circulation papers (*Wall Street Journal, Washington Post*) and widely read trade journals (*American Banker, Back Stage, Engineering News-Record, Manhattan Lawyer, New York Law Journal, Variety*) also regularly reported on the 42DP; adding these would bring the article count to roughly 940.

16. Brett Pulley, "Real Estate and the Press," transcribed ULI tape, fall meeting, November 4, 1995.

17. The topics of the 80 editorials break down into the following categories: the 42DP (28), Times Square cleanup, crime, and renewal (18), Times Square culture and ambience (15), theater preservation (8), Midtown Zoning (4), Portman Hotel (2), Broadway Mall (2), Times Square Hotel (1), other (2). In addition, between 1980 and 1999, the *Times* printed at least 115 letters to the editor and op-eds on these issues.

18. Thomas J. Lueck, "Miscalculations in Times Square; Project Shows That Renewal Needs More Than Bulldozers," *New York Times*, August 10, 1992, B3. This article I am quite familiar with, having been interviewed on the phone at length by Lueck. Pushing for him to discuss the nature of the off-budget financing mechanism and question the cost-benefit relationship proved fruitless; his bulldozer theme was set firmly in place. Apparently, I did succeed in getting him to mention city and state officials "new approach" to the condemnation-cost problem and that the developers would be paid back "not only through tax abatements, but through rent credits." There seemed, however, to be no way to convince him to expand the scope of his critique. Prudently, the news analysis suspended judgment on the ultimate outcome: "Although this financial arrangement may yet prove successful, other roadblocks emerged in the early 1980s."

19. For example, bullish editorials proclaimed, "Get out of the Way of Times Square," "Porn Again or Born Again on 42d Street?," "Who'll Set the Beat for 42d Street?," and offered praise for the new "enlivened" designs for the office towers in "Five Reasons for Transforming 42d Street," while architectural critic Paul Goldberger denounced the project on the arts pages: "Times Square: Design Problems Remain," "Times Square: Lurching toward a Terrible Mistake? "New Times Square Designs: Merely Token Changes."

20. Gay Talese, *The Kingdom and the Power* (New York: Ivy Books, 1971), 346. Under the leadership of John Oakes (1961–1976), the editorial page took highly opinionated positions, according to another *Times* biographer. Oakes insisted on maintaining a strict independence from the news operation, believing that opposition should be expressed on the editorial page, not through slanted reporting. He did not hesitate to comment critically and often on what he considered to be lapses in news judgment. He felt that a newspaper best served its community "by being critical of all the things are wrong with it." (Joseph H. Goulden, *Fit to Print: A. M. Rosenthal and His Times* [Secaucus, N.J.: Lyle Stuart, 1988], 203.) More than what he said, his tone was antibusiness. While his standards of editorial independence continued on with succeeding editorial-page editors, the attacks on business ceased under Max Frankel, whose service as editorial-page editor (1977–1986) spanned the early years of the 42DP.

21. Edwin Diamond and Piera Paine, "The Media in the Game of Politics," in *Urban Politics New York Style*, ed. Jewel Bellush and Dick Netzer (Armonk, N.Y.: M.E. Sharpe, 1990), 339–356, at 345.

22. Robert A. M. Stern, "Real Estate and the Press."

23. David W. Dunlap, "Office Towers in 42d St. Project May Be Getting Taller," *New York Times*, October 6, 1993, B3; David W. Dunlap, "More Height Rejected for Towers in 42d St. Plan," *New York Times*, October 11, 1993, B7; "Whither 42nd St.: Better Rethink Those Office Towers" [editorial], *Newsday*, October 13, 1993, 50; Charles V. Bagli, "Retreat on Times Square Subway Plan: MTA Allows Developer to Pay Rather Than Provide Escalators," *New York Times*, May 14, 1998, B3.

24. Charles V. Bagli and Nicolai Ouroussoff, "Disney Dream Gang Mugs New York City: A Hard Look at the 42nd Street Hustle," *New York Observer*, May 22, 1995, 1, at 8.

25. Pulley, "Real Estate and the Press."

26. Bagli, "Real Estate and the Press."

27. Diamond and Paine, "The Media in the Game of Politics," 349.

28. Ibid., 341–342.

29. Schanberg, a strong reporter with a fierce policy bent, "cared about issues of governmental power and the accountability of the strong." (Colman McCarthy, "The Journalistic Double Standard: The Squashing of Sydney Schanberg," *Washington Post*, September 8, 1985, H8.) At the *Times* for 26 years, he had been one of its journalistic stars, winner of a Pulitzer Prize for his eye-witness-account coverage of the fall of Cambodia (retold in the motion picture *The Killing Fields*). As editor of the *Times* metropolitan section, he wrote about urban affairs in New York in the late 1970s, and later took on many topics sensitive to the *Times* in his op-ed column; one of six regular op-ed columnists, only Schanberg wrote about New York politics and municipal affairs, before being fired in 1985 after a dispute with his editors and the paper's publisher which insiders reportedly attributed to his angry criticism of the *Times*'s own coverage of Westway. Following that exit, he began a column on city affairs for *Newsday*.

30. All Sydney H. Schanberg in *Newsday*: "Why Keep the Times Square Deal in a Dark Alley? March 4, 1988, 89; "Times Square Deal Remains Shrouded in Mystery," November 15, 1988, 71; "Pull the Plug on the Bleeding Times Square Plan," April 25, 1989, 57. Jeffrey Hoff, a writer for *Barron's*, similarly posed the question, "Who Should Pay to Transform Times Square," (September 25, 1989, 64). Even though this was a high-profile national weekly dedicated to financial news, as a one-time issue, the question had become rhetorical.

31. Vincent Tese, "Nothing to Hide," *Newsday*, December 1, 1988, 88.

32. Regan, "Government, Inc.," 8.

33. Allee King Rosen & Fleming, Inc., *Summary of Economic and Fiscal Benefits for New York from the 42nd Street Development Project*, prepared for the 42nd Street Development Project, Inc., October 1994.

34. "Whither 42nd St.; Better rethink those office towers" [editorial], *Newsday*, October 13, 1993, 50.

35. There is a nuance. The New42's master lease provides that if the nonprofit entity makes a new site out of the Selwyn infill parcel, it would be a "theater." The built structure's "predominant use" is for rehearsal and studio space; only the residual is for office use. The language is critical with respect to the New42's mandate and, I would present, that there be no other predominant office uses of the 42DP sites so as to protect the competitive position of TSCA's sites before they are developed and fully leased.

36. At this time, West 42nd Street was no longer a pioneering market. The lease terms for the hotel site were quite favorable to FCR. For the first 20 years, the base rent is $2.68 (calculated on 270,000 square feet), and the minimum PILOT ranges from $.054 to $5.21 per square foot; the deal structure provides for more substantial PILOT revenues to flow to the city, but only on the basis of performance, as set percentages of "adjusted gross revenues," after the developer has earned certain cash-on-cost returns. If not, this PILOT is trivial, and, in effect, the developer has gotten a very low-fixed cost carry during a long start-up period. One has to question the economic logic of this type of deal subsidy—in a hot tourist-oriented city, in a hot hotel market, in a hot location. One former insider who expressed outrage at the deal noted that the city had not been giving tax deals for hotels for the past five years. In short, additional details do not need to be presented to know that with the hotel component, FCR scored a double play.

37. Devin Leonard, "Zuckerman Ends Up with Surprise Space in Times Square Deal," *New York Observer*, April 20, 1998, 1, at 1.

38. The uncertainty involves the size of the building Paul Milstein and his sons, as owners of the L-shaped parcel (Site 8N), will be able to build under the existing terms of the *GPP*. Following ESDC's reallocation of development rights from Site 8N to Site 8S, where the *Times* plans to build its new headquarters as part of a larger tower in a joint venture with FCR, approximately 660,000 square feet of development remain. Because 8S and 8N were originally one site, the development rights were fungible, making ESDC's action discretionary. The question going forward is how much development the Milsteins will be allowed. The government still has the ability, said FCR's Mary Anne Gilmartin, to allocate about an additional 200,000 square feet. Because the project exists outside the city's zoning rules, ESDC could conceivably make a deal involving an even larger development, following a negative declaration of environmental impact and approval of an amendment to the *GPP*, as in the case of FCR's hotel when ESDC reallocated 270,000 square feet from the undeveloped sites (Sites 8N and 8S), which were originally approved for 2.3 million square feet of development. The developer, who talked about building a 35-story tower of up to 1 million square feet a few years ago, is likely to seek a larger building than currently permitted. How much he will actually be able to build, Gilmartin emphasized, would depend upon how good he is at negotiating with public parties, but there exists a strong possibility for a more dense build out of the total project area than that originally approved by the BOE in 1984. Author interview, January 23, 2001. See Steve Cuozzo, "A 'Lot' of Questions: 42nd & 8th—How High Can It Be Built? *New York Post*, August 15, 2000, 45; Charles V. Bagli, "$111 Million for Times Sq. Redevelopment Site," *New York Times*, January 17, 2001, B8.

39. Marshall Berman, "Signs Square," *Village Voice*, July 18, 1995, 23.

40. Brett Pulley, "Key Developer Seeks a Role in Times Sq.," *New York Times*, November 21, 1995, B1.

41. Charles V. Bagli, "Times Square Reversal: George Klein Seethes As Doug Durst Moves In," *New York Observer*, November 27, 1995, 1.

42. As a member of the board of directors of the Roundabout Theater, Primary Stages, and Town Hall, Douglas Durst's involvement in the theater arts was not new. After buying the leases, he staged a production of the Obie-Award-winning *Crowbar* at the Victory. In January 1990 he released an alternative plan for modest redevelopment of the theaters and their return to theater and theater-related use, and announced that three entertainment ventures had signed agreements to operate in the theaters, one for 15 years and the other two for short-term engagements. Reportedly several million was spent for the first stage of the rehabilitation plan, before the state gained title to the properties in April 1990. See infra, 404.

43. At the time the Durst Organization was negotiating with Prudential to acquire the lease for one of TSCA's 42DP sites, it was also negotiating the repayment of the 1155 Sixth Avenue mortgage loan. Just how this loan relationship affected the site-lease negotiations is not evident from the news reporting at the time. By the mid-1990s, prevailing interest rates had dropped far below the rate on Durst's mortgage; the company wanted to repay the loan, but without being held to the note's requirement for yield maintenance. Durst was not likely to default in order to get out of the high-cost loan, this Prudential knew, and the insurance giant would not allow repayment without a penalty. A full or partial waiver of the prepayment penalty would have been worth a lot to Durst, and it is likely to have ecome a factor in the financial equation for acquiring the leasehold interest in the

42DP site. Like any private agreement, though, any such terms would remain confidential.

44. While Nederlander was making the bond payments, he was not making the tax payments. In a default situation, had Durst bought the bonds he would have been able to cure the tax delinquency or cut a deal with the city on this. Possibly he might have gained some leverage into situation, but he would have had to deal with the city on the tax-arrears issue. Would the city have been willing to cut a deal with Durst, the arch-antagonist of its top-priority project?

45. Eric Schmuckler, "From Bad to Durst," *Forbes*, July 10, 1989, 120.

46. Durst, as would have TSCA, faced an economic problem with the existing configuration of the 33,300-square-foot site. In terms of "carpetable" square feet—what the tenant can actually use and, hence, the basis of the building's economic value—the small footprint seriously constrained the potential floor layouts, once space for the elevator bank and other high-rise equipment was taken into account. Adding the additional parcels made for a final footprint of 45,410 square feet and allowed for better-designed floors.

47. Letter to Herbert Berman [Chairman, City Council Finance Committee], Re: 42nd Street Redevelopment Project, from Gary Rosenberg [Durst attorney], June 21, 1990, 2.

48. After several months of negotiations, in November 1995, the Durst Organization announced that it had refinanced three of the company's buildings, 1133 and 1155 Sixth Avenue and 733 Third Avenue, for a total of $215 million.

49. Charles V. Bagli, "A Project 30 Years in the Making; Durst Tries to Revive His Father's Dream, Years Later," *New York Times*, March 16, 1999, B1.

50. Ibid.

51. Amy Feldman, "The developer who changed grime into high-rise green," *Crain's New York Business*, April 14, 1997, 19. For the new tower, building materials are to be environmentally friendly, demolition materials recycled, and shoots for recycling paper and wet trash separately installed.

For a man of few words who shies away from making professional presentations and dislikes small talk, Durst apparently did not have trouble getting used to the new limelight; contradiction and paradox seem to fit his complex personality comfortably. Brokers who have worked with him for years describe him as particularly taciturn. "He doesn't like fluff and he doesn't say a lot, and what he does say, he has thought through," said one. "Seymour's sense of humor was elfin and twinkly, Doug's is ironic and deadpan," said another who has worked with the family. "Douglas is more curt than other developers," remarked a major tenant in a Durst building. Add to that profile economic pragmatism and long-term loyalty to business associates—tenants, architects and construction providers—and personal involvement—the cornerstone of the family's real estate success. "He's more concerned with building a relationship than with getting the last 50 cents on a deal," said a Cushman & Wakefield senior director. Understated and distinctively different from other New York developers, Douglas likes to direct a visitor's attention to the pictures in his office of his days as a long-haired and bearded hippie. Claudia H. Deutsch, "A Savvy Developer Who Marches to His Own Beat," *New York Times*, November 12, 1995, 9:11.

52. Charles V. Bagli and Nick Paumgarten, "Rivals Durst and Klein Embrace on 42nd Street After Long Bitter Spat," *New York Observer*, October 7, 1996, 1, at 26.

53. The deal would close at a price of $75 million, with TSCA having the option to repurchase the ESAC for a fixed amount, $5 million, by December 31, 1997, which it did not exercise. The repurchase option represented a potential upside for

Prudential for, at the time, Prudential's analysts believed the present value of this ESAC buyback could appreciate to $9 million, depending upon when construction might start on its remaining three sites. TSCA also had the right to put the remaining site's ESAC credits back to Durst by December 31, 1997, but chose not to do so.

54. Eugene Heimberg, author interview, December 17, 1996. The day before he was scheduled to present the deal to the Prudential board, Heimberg had a heart attack.

55. Charles V. Bagli, "Times Sq. Giveaway Grants Newhouse A Giant Tax Break," *New York Observer*, May 20, 1996, 1, at 22.

56. Bernice Miles Lucchese, "Durst Melt NYC Office Development Freeze," *Commercial Property News*, July 16, 1996, 1, at 40; Lore Croghan, "Douglas Durst Productions Give Times Square a New Beginning," *Crain's New York Business*, May 16, 2000, 26.

57. Gary M. Rosenberg, author interview, January 22, 1997.

58. Bagli, "Times Sq. Giveaway Grants Newhouse a Giant Tax Break," 22.

59. Between the fall of 1991 and 1992, Johnson had redone his and Burgee's earlier designs for the four towers. At this time, no one was taking the design issue seriously. "These were Johnson's best designs," said Robertson. "At this period, he seemed to be totally disowning the other building designs; he seemed to be working behind Klein. Machiavellian." The 1992 designs were quite sculptural. They lasted until 1997. Although sold with the sites, none of the new designs would be used by the new developers of these sites. Author interview, April 10, 2000.

60. The setbacks were introduced to enhance the aesthetics of the behemoth—the building's bulk approaches about 35 F.A.R.—and the developers' economics. "The setbacks are where they make sense in terms of the building's form, not where the city requires them," said Bruce Fowle, principal of Fox and Fowle, the New York architects who designed the building. Suzanne Stephens, "Projects: Four Times Square, New York City," *Architectural Record* 188 (March 2000): 90–97, at 95.

61. Thomas J. Lueck, "Condé Nast Is to Move to a New Times Square Tower, Officials Say," *New York Times*, May 8, 1996, B3.

62. The state's share of the deal represented a $2.725-million reduction (present value) in Condé Nast's rental payments to Durst, which reduces his lease payments to ESDC, as landlord and a $1.275-million (present value) sales-tax exemption. The city's $6.75 million in incentives comprises sales-tax exemptions on office equipment and electric power discounts.

63. Insignia/ESG, "Case Study: Real Estate Advisory Services, Tenant Representation: Condé Nast Publications, Four Times Square," prepared for the M.B.A. Real Estate Program of Columbia University, Graduate School of Business, March 1998, 3–4.

64. Ibid.

65. Coming from Condé Nast, the threat to move to New Jersey seemed ludicrous to many observers. The editors of the *New York Observer* seemed to take particular delight in spinning words when they wrote: "Magazines do not operate like brokerage houses, where the back office can be tucked away in some suburban backlot. Advertising salespeople can't very well take their Manhattan-based clients to lunch in Fort Lee, N.J. The idea of Armani-and-DNKY-clad Condé Nasters hopping buses each morn to New Jersey is laughable. Imagine Anna Wintour stuck in the Holland Tunnel. Si must be gloating at the naïveté of the officials who threw money his way." Bagli, "Times Sq. Giveaway Grants Newhouse a Giant Tax Break," 22.

66. "Publisher Is Spending Big, But Only to Improve Self, Florio Says," *Daily News*, January 19, 1998, 24.

67. Bagli, "Times Sq. Giveaway Grants Newhouse a Giant Tax Break," 22.

68. For its new headquarters, the New York Times will get a corporate-incentive package reportedly worth about $29 million, but it will not get a break on property taxes; it will pay what city officials call the equivalent of full property taxes. The PILOT will start at about $10 a square foot and increase over time. Charles V. Bagli, "Deal Reached to Acquire Land for the Times's Headquarters," *New York Times,* February 28, 2001, B2.

69. Mercantile Exchange ($183.9 million), Donaldson, Lufkin & Jenrette ($29.5 million), Capital Cities/ABC ($26 million), Travelers Inc. ($22.1 million), CS First Boston ($50.5 million), Depository Trust Co. ($18.5 million), Equitable Companies ($9.3 million), Coffee, Sugar & Cocoa Exchange and the Cotton Exchange ($98.5 million), Bear Stearns & Company ($75 million), American International Group ($55.7 million), Standard & Poor's/McGraw Hill ($34.5 million), News America ($20.7 million), Paine Webber ($14.5 million), NBC ($7 million), Home Box Office ($11 million), and Time Warner, Inc. ($28 million), among others.

70. Philip Lentz, "Rudy Gives $2.1 Billion in Incentives," *Crain's New York Business*, July 26, 1999, 1; Charles V. Bagli, "Corporation Walks Away from Tax Deal," *New York Times*, September 5, 1992, B1, at B27.

71. Among the many articles criticizing corporate retention deals, see Charles V. Bagli, "As Leichter Targets Tax Breaks, Developers Line Up for Handouts," *New York Observer*, April 3, 1995, 1; Thomas J. Lueck, "Lower Budgets Don't Cut Flow of Tax Breaks," *New York Times*, July 5, 1995, A1; Opinions: Subsidizing city businesses (op-ed): John S. Dyson, "Loans Keep Firms Here" and Comer C. Coppie, "Do We Get What We Pay For? *Daily News*, July 23, 1995, 37; Charles V. Bagli, "Commodities Leaders Blackmail City Hall for $100 Million Tip," *New York Observer*, October 23, 1995, 1; Bagli, "Times Sq. Giveaway Grants Newhouse a Giant Tax Break"; Charles V. Bagli, "Skadden Arps Man Sticks Up the City for Many Millions," *New York Observer*, August 5, 1996, 1; Charles V. Bagli, "Companies Get Second Helping of Tax Breaks," *New York Times*, October 17, 1997, 1; Charles V. Bagli, "Reuters Given Big Tax Deal for Its Project in Times Square," *New York Times*, November 1, 1997, B1; Devin Leonard, "N.Y.S.E., NASDAQ Try to Shake Down City for Big Tax Breaks," *New York Observer*, May 11, 1998, 1; Charles V. Bagli, "Ernst & Young Gets Breaks to Stay in New York City," *New York Times*, July 23, 1999, B2.

72. "City's Sweet Deals Leave Bitter Taste" [editorial], *Daily News*, October 14, 1995, 14.

73. Bagli, "As Leichter Targets Tax Breaks, Developers Line Up for Handouts," 19. Tax benefits come with constraints, which made at least one corporation, the German-media company Bertelsmann A.G., walk away from a tentative deal after having negotiated a $25-million package of tax breaks and other subsidies for a new tower at Broadway and 55th Street. Charles V. Bagli, "Office Tower Said to Get Tax Breaks," *New York Times*, June 6, 1999, 43; Bagli, "Corporation Walks Away from Tax Deal."

74. Until that deal, the city had refused to grant subsidies to law firms, architects, and accountants on the theory that those kinds of services would not leave the city because they need to be close to their clients. The law firm of Skadden, Arps, Slate, Meagher & Flom, for example, failed to win any incentives from the city in 1996, despite the fact that the negotiations had been led by Benjamin Needell, head of

the firm's real estate department and a respected rainmaker in this arena. One of the most skilled real estate attorneys in the city, Needell had worked on at least five of the 19 retention deals cut by the Giuliani administration up to that point. Bagli, "Skadden Arps Man Sticks Up the City for Many Millions."

75. Lentz, "Rudy gives $2.1 billion in incentives," 24.

76. Though drawn from the same off-budget tool bag, the subsidies for corporate retention involve different risks from those applied to large-scale redevelopment projects such as the 42DP, from a perspective of policy implementation. They are fewer in number. And while it may be politically more difficult to avoid being "unfair," the problems of execution are less troublesome. City officials have much greater control over their individual, case-by-case corporate deals. The decisions are solely those of the mayor, absent a need for city council approval. There are fewer variables and complexities to contend with, fewer moving parts, and a much shorter gestation period for problems to multiply and trouble the implementation of policy. Also, the degrees of freedom for changing direction are fewer than in development deal making.

CHAPTER FOURTEEN

1. Christopher Reynolds, "New York/New and Improved; A Cleaned-Up Times Square," *Los Angeles Times*, November 2, 1997, L:1:4.

2. Dale Hrabi, "Will the 'New' Times Square Be New Enough?" *Wired*, August 1995, 128ff.

3. Roger Starr, "The Editorial Notebook: Still Debating Robert Moses," *New York Times*, August 18, 1988, A26.

4. Paul Goldberger, "Robert Moses: Patron Saint of Public Places," *Urban Land* 48 (April 1989), 89ff, at 89.

5. Jason Bram and Mike DeMott, "New York City's New-Media Boom: Real or Virtual?" *Current Issues in Economics and Finance*, Federal Reserve Bank of New York 4 (October 1998), 1.

6. Bram and DeMott, 2; Steve Malanga, "New economy propels city to record year," *Crain's New York Business,* December 13, 1999, 1.

7. David W. Dunlap, *On Broadway: A Journey Uptown Over Time* (New York: Rizzoli International Publications, 1990), 164.

8. Data from Cushman & Wakefield. The three percent may represent an underestimate since the inventory tracked does not include the upper stories of small, older buildings on the area's side streets.

9. See in particular the argument put forth by Saskia Sassen in chapter 5 of *The Global City: New York, London, Tokyo* (Princeton: Princeton University Press, 1991) and *Cities in a World Economy* (Thousand Oaks, Calif.: Pine Forge Press, 1994). While some of these services, she argues, may be produced in-house by firms, a large share are bought from specialized service firms because the growing complexity, diversity, and specialization of the services required makes it more efficient to buy them from specialized firms rather than hiring in-house professionals. This, in turn, makes possible a free-standing specialized service sector.

10. Sassen, *Cities in a World Economy*, 66.

11. Saskia Sassen and Frank Roost, "The City: Strategic Site for the Global Entertainment Industry," in *The Tourist City*, eds, Dennis R. Judd and Susan S. Fainstein, *The Tourist City* (New Haven: Yale University Press, 1999), 143–154, at 146.

12. PriceWaterhouseCoopers and New York New Media Association, *3rd New York New Media Industry Survey: Opportunities and Challenges of New York's Emerging Cyber-Industry*, March 2000 (on line).

13. Data from the Times Square BID, *Annual Report 1999*. Available on line at www.timessquarebid.org.

14. Neil Harris, "Urban Tourism and the Commercial City," in *Inventing Times Square: Commerce and Culture at the Crossroads of the World* (New York: Russell Sage Foundation, 1991), 66–82, at 75.

15. Ibid., 81.

16. Proponents of the strategy view tourism as generating better infrastructure and amenities for local residents and boosting the image of the city, while opponents view tourism as producing only low-skill, low-wage seasonal jobs, and posit it as a zero-sum game whose returns often do not justify government investment. Tourism is also criticized as being only about selling cities as a product of consumption rather than as a place to live or work.

17. Sassen and Roost, "The City: Strategic Site for the Global Entertainment Industry," 150, 154

18. Susan S. Fainstein and Robert Stokes, "Spaces for Play: The Impacts of Entertainment Development on New York City," Center for Urban Policy Research, Rutgers, The State University of New Jersey, Working Paper no. 123, 1997, 17.

19. Ibid., 25.

20. Marshall Berman, "Signs of the Times," *Dissent* 44 (fall 1997): 76–83, at 78.

21. Ibid. The Columbia symposium drew together 18 leading urbanists, authors, critics, architects, and academics in early spring 1997. Organized by the Buell Center for the Study of American Architecture (part of Columbia University's School of Architecture, Planning and Preservation), it had major funding from the Overbrook Foundation and additional sponsorship from Skidmore, Owings & Merrill, Virgin Atlantic Airways, Tishman Realty and Construction Company, Inc., and SHAdi. Called "The New Times Square Local/Global," it was organized as a hierarchal exploration of Times Square from the vantage points of New York City, the United States, and the world. Starting in the evening of a Friday, the agenda stretched throughout Saturday in a marathon session.

22. I owe credit for many of the ideas behind these "voices" to one of my research assistants, N. Vanessa Brakhan.

23. Bruce Webber, "Bye, 1996. Bye, Scuzz. Thanks Again," *New York Times*, December 29, 1996, E4.

24. Lorraine B. Diehl. "Neon (Blink) Glow of (Blink) Old 42d," *New York Times*, January 30, 1998, E40.

25. Quoted in Gersh Kuntzman, "Apple Just Doesn't Have the Same Bite," *New York Post*, May 25, 1998, 34.

26. Guy Trebay, "Peepland," *Village Voice*, January 13, 1998, 34.

27. Rem Koolhaas, "Regrets?" *Grand Street* 15 (summer 1996): 137–138, at 137. Also, the photo "42nd Street, North Side, 1979," by Langdon Clay in the same issue.

28. Samuel R. Delaney, remarks at the Columbia conference, and ". . . Three, Two, One, Contact: Times Square Red, 1998," in *Giving Ground: The Politics of Propinquity,* ed. Joan Copjec and Michael Sorkin (London: Verso, 1999), 19–85, at 55.

29. Koolhaas, "Regrets?," 138.

30. Hrabi, "Will the 'New' Times Square Be New Enough?," 173.

31. Dan Barry, "Time Square Grit Peeps through Glitz," *New York Times*, December 31, 1997, B1.

32. James Traub, "Giuliani's New York: The City, and Psyche, He'll Leave Behind," *New York Times Magazine*, February 11, 2001, 62ff, at 64.

33. Herbert Muschamp, "Architectural View: Nostalgia Tripping in Times Square," *New York Times*, August 25, 1996, H36.

34. Ibid.

35. Mayor Rudolph W. Giuliani, "In His Own Words," *New York Times*, February 26, 1998, B4.

36. Maureen Dowd, "Liberties: Vice Takes a Holiday," *New York Times*, December 31, 1997, A15. A generalized nostalgia gripping America acts as a backdrop to the specialized "discourse of nostalgia" about Times Square. It is evident in books that emerged in the early 1990s, among them, James Frazer, *The American Billboard: 100 Years* (New York: Harry Abrams, 1991); Stephanie Coontz, *The Way We Never Were: American Families and the Nostalgia Trap* (New York: Basic Books, 1992); Susan Jonas and Marilyn Nissenson, *Going, Going, Gone: Vanishing America* (San Francisco: Chronicle Books, 1994).

37. Ric Burns and James Sanders with Lisa Ades [picture editor], *New York: An Illustrated History* [the companion volume to the PBS television series] (New York, Knopf, 1999), 553.

38. Brendan Gill, "The Sky Line: The Death of the Skyscraper?" *New Yorker*, March 4, 1991, 90ff, at 93.

39. Nicolai Ouroussoff, "Architectural Review: One Big Fantasyland; An Unusual Exhibit Traces Disney's Search for a Pain-Free Social Environment," *Los Angeles Times,* May 25, 1998, F1.

40. Bob Liff, "Mouse That Roared Eyes Coney Island," *Daily News*, May 7, 1998, 13.

41. Carl Hiaasen, *Team Rodent: How Disney Devours the World* (New York: Ballantine Publishing, The Library of Contemporary Thought, 1998), 9.

42. Karrie Jacobs, "Cityscape: Forty-Deuce Coop," *New York*, April 6, 1998, 62ff, at 63.

43. Berman, "Signs of the Times," 82–83.

44. James S. Russell, "Theming vs. Design," *Architectural Record* 185 (March 1997), 90.

45. Frank Rich, "Journal: Goodby to All That," *New York Times*, December 30, 1995, 27.

46. Frank Rich, "Journal: The Mouse That Ate America," *New York Times*, October 2, 1996, A23.

47. Jayne Merkel, "On Times Square," *Oculus* 59 (May 1997), 9ff, at 11.

48. Ibid., 9.

49. Frank Rich, "Journal: Bring In the Funk," *New York Times*, November 20, 1996, A25. Two years later, Rich sounded less sanguine when he wrote a retrospective piece, "A Detour in the Theater That No One Predicted." He complained bitterly about the "corporatization" of the American theater on Broadway and beyond by the transformation of theater into "'content' suitable for the synergistic annexation and exploitation by our new entertainment conglomerates." The new commercial theater, he concluded, "has more in common with the values of special-effects American movies and network television than did even old Broadway at its most commercial." What was missing was the "theater of language and intimacy and passion," in short, "plays." *New York Times*, October 18, 1998, 2:1.

50. Merkel, "On Times Square," 9.

51. Michael Sorkin, "Status Quo Vadis?," *Harvard Design Magazine*, Winter/Spring 1998, 29ff, at 31.

52. Kierna Mayo Dawsey, "Forty Deuce," *City Journal* 21 (August/September 1996): 20–22, at 21, 22.

53. Burns and Sanders, *New York,* 553.

54. Thomas Kessner, "Fiorello H. LaGuardia and the Challenge of Democratic Planning," in *The Landscape of Modernity: New York City, 1900–1940,* ed. David Ward and Olivier Zunz (Baltimore and London: The Johns Hopkins University Press, 1992), 315–329, at 324.

55. Samuel G. Freeman, 'Trump Feud: Barbs Show Deeper Split," *New York Times,* July 6, 1987, 33.

56. Kessner, "Fiorello H. LaGuardia and the Challenge of Democratic Planning," 321.

57. Jon C. Teaford, "Urban Renewal and Its Aftermath," *Housing Policy Debate* 11(2:2000), 443–465, at 443, 460, 443.

58. Edward C. Banfield and Charles Q. Wilson, *City Politics* (New York: Vintage Book, 1963), 267, as quoted in Paul Kantor, *The Dependent City: The Changing Economy of Urban America* (Glenview: Scott, Foresman & Co., 1988), 259.

59. Costonis's *Icons and Aliens* sets forth a highly persuasive argument about the compelling symbolic and emotional nature of historic preservation as a legal basis for land-use regulation.

60. Sam Roberts, "Who Runs New York Now? *New York Times Magazine*, April 28, 1985, 27ff.

61. Lloyd Rodwin, *Cities and City Planning* (New York and London: Plenum Press, 1981), 245–246.

EPILOGUE

1. Mary Anne Gilmartin, author interview, January 23, 2001.

2. Kenton C. Jenkins, vice president and general manager of W.W.F. New York as quoted in David W. Dunlap, "Reviving Paramount's Marquee and Waldorf's Stars," *New York Times,* April 18, 2001, B7.

3. Charles V. Bagli, "Toys 'R' Us to Build the Biggest Store in Times Square," *New York Times*, August 2, 2000, B6.

4. Robert Osborne, "Rambling Reporter; Great White Walk: Broadway Greats Set for Sidewalk Stars," *BPI Entertainment News Wire*, August 18, 1998.

5. Aravind Adiga, "World News: The Americas: Time Runs Out for National Debt Clock," *Financial Times*, June 2, 2000, 10.

6. Julian E. Barnes, "A Bit Nervously, Theater Row Packs Up," *New York Times*, March 13, 2000, E1ff; Ralph Blumenthal, "Transforming Theater Row: An Unlikely Urban Drama Heads for a Happy Ending," *New York Times*, May 11, 2000, B1.

7. Based on information made available for the Four Times Square refinancing., the implied total ESAC balance for the four office sites had grown to roughly $246.5 million by April 1, 2000 (by which time condemnation awards for this phase of condemnation were complete); adding the $88-million offset amount results in $334.5 million as a derived estimate of the office towers "site acquisition costs. With the transfer of Sites 1 and 4 to another developer, the public-sector entities stood to benefit from any appreciation realized by TSCA; under the terms of the revised deal, the public-sector entities would receive a participation of 10 percent in the transaction (up to a cap of $60 million, adjusted for inflation from

September 8, 1992, to the date upon which construction of the new building on the first site commenced). ESDC did not expect these payments, said Leventer; assuming the sale of the leasehold to Boston Properties closed, she anticipated a transaction payment between $10 and $12 million, which the city and state would split 20/80 as provided for in the City/State Agreements. The state would get the lion's share of the transaction payment, she noted, because of the magnitude of its development costs to date." Wendy Leventer, author interview, March 5, 1999.

8. Ralph Blumenthal, "Chief Is Selected for the Rebuilding of Lincoln Center," *New York Times*, July 29, 2000, B9.

9. After trying to interest Disney executives in plans for projects on Hollywood Boulevard and Chicago's State Street, to no avail—their reaction he recalled: "Boy, these are really complicated, difficult projects . . . much more about real estate development than it is about entertainment"—Malmuth left Disney in 1996 with the intent of starting his own development company. Wooed by TrizecHahn, a Toronto-based real estate company with large holdings of office buildings and shopping malls seeking to branch out into entertainment, Malmuth is again working on a branded place. With strong financial and political support from the city of Los Angeles, he once again hopes to remake a classic. Bettina Boxall, "Special Report: Many Have Failed to Rescue the Boulevard, but a Man Who Helped Save Times Square Is . . . Hoping for a Hollywood Revival," *Los Angeles Times,* May 10, 1998, B1.

10. Herbert Muschamp, "Smaller is Better: Condé Nast Meets Times Square," *New York Times*, May 18, 1996, 21; Suzanne Stephens, "Four Times Square, New York City," *Architectural Record* 188 (March 2000): 91–97, at 91; Karrie Jacobs, "Cityscape: Fat City," *New York*, June 28-July 5, 1999, 38ff, at 38.

11. Paul Goldberger, "The Sky Line: Busy Buildings," *New Yorker*, September 4, 2000, 90ff.

BIBLIOGRAPHY

Listed are only the most pertinent writings that have been of use in the making of this book. Accordingly, the bibliography is by no means a complete record of all the works and sources I have consulted. For example, the hundreds of newspaper articles I reviewed have been excluded from the bibliography; when used for quoted material, specific articles are cited in chapter endnotes. The bibliography indicates the substance and range of reading upon which I formed my ideas and is intended to serve as a convenience for those who wish to pursue the study of public development, planning, and public policy for city building and development politics in New York. The bibliography is divided into three parts corresponding to the type of source material (primary documents, interviews, and selected secondary sources) and organized by topic to provide a guide to the main themes of the book. The primary sources are listed in chronological order; the interviews and secondary sources are listed in alphabetical order.

I. PRIMARY DOCUMENTS

A. 42DP Project Documents

1.a. Planning, Feasibility, Developer Selection

NYS UDC, NYC PDC, NYC DCP. *42nd Street Development Project Design Guidelines*. May 1981.

NYS UDC. *42nd Street Development Project: A Discussion Document*. February 1981.

Eastdil Realty, Inc. *42nd Street Development Project Economic Analysis*. June 1981.

NYS UDC. *42nd Street Development Land Use Improvement Project, New York, New York, General Project Plan*. June 1981. Subsequent attachments and amendments: October 1, 1984. February 9, 1988. January 1991. January 27, 1994. September 21, 1994. June 19, 1996. September 18, 1996. December 19, 1996. January 14, 1998. May 20, 1998. July 16, 1998.

_____. *42nd Street Development Project: Request for Proposals*. June 1981.

_____. *Draft Environmental Impact Statement: The 42nd Street Development Project*, prepared by Parsons Brinckerhoff Quade & Douglas, Inc., and AKRF, Inc., in association with Urbitran Associates, Inc. February 1984.

Gans, Herbert J. "The 42nd Street Development Project Draft EIS: An Assessment," prepared for the New York City Board of Estimate on behalf of the Brandt Organization. 1984. Photocopy.

NYS UDC. *42nd Street Development Project Final Environmental Impact Statement.* August 1984.

Touche Ross & Co. to UDC, attention Lawrence F. Graham [regarding review of the administrative processing procedures relating to proposals received by UDC from prospective developers of the West 42nd Street/Times Square area]. Memorandum. April 5, 1982.

Stern, William J., to the [UDC] Directors. *Recommendation for Site 8 Conditional Designation.* Memorandum. April 5, 1984.

Graham, Lawrence F., Philip E. Aarons, Herbert Sturz to Park Tower Realty Corp. Letter of conditional designation, including *Memorandum of Terms.* April 6, 1982.

Graham, Lawrence F., to the [UDC] Directors. *42nd Street Development Land Use Improvement Project, Request for Conditional Designation of Developers.* Memorandum. April 6, 1982.

Eastdil Realty to Lawrence F. Graham, Herbert Sturz, Philip E. Aarons [regarding developer selection]. Memorandum. April 5, 1982.

Landauer Associates. *Marketing & Financial Analysis of the Times Square Redevelopment Project,* prepared for Park Tower Realty Corp. June 1983.

Stern, William J., to the [UDC] Directors. *Recommendation for Site 5 Conditional Designation.* Memorandum. August 23, 1984.

Walsh, John J. [attorney for Milstein Properties] to Hon. Mario Cuomo, Hon. William J. Stern, Hon. Edward I. Koch, Hon. Herbert Sturz. *Re: 42nd Street Land Use Improvement Project, A White Paper on the Selection of Developers for the 42nd Street Land Use Improvement Project.* September 28, 1984.

Stern, William J., to the [UDC] Directors. *Request for Adoption of Findings Pursuant to (1) the State Environmental Quality Review Act, (2) the New York State Urban Development Corporation Act, (3) the State Historic Preservation Act, (4) the Eminent Domain Procedures Law and an Affirmation of a General Project Plan, as Modified.* Memorandum. October 4, 1984.

[NYS UDC]. *Re: 42nd Street Development Project, response to John J. Walsh Letter.* November 6, 1984.

1.b. *42nd Street Now!*

Dyson, John S. to Vincent Tese. *Re: 42nd Street Development Project Acquisition of Site 7.* February 14, 1993.

Garrick-Aug Associates Store Leasing, Inc., and Phillips/Norwalk Company. *Market Feasibility Retail Development Plan: 42nd Street Development Project*, prepared for UDC. June 1, 1993.

Tese, Vincent, to the [UDC] Directors. *Request for Confirmation of Land Use Improvement Project Findings; Adoption of Amendments to General Project Plan; Authorization to Accept the Draft Supplemental Environmental Impact Statement as*

Satisfactory with Respect to its Scope, Content and Adequacy Under the State Environmental Quality Review Act; Authorization to Publish, Circulate and File the Draft Supplemental Environmental Impact Statement Authorization to Hold Public Hearing(s) Pursuant to Applicable Laws; Ratification of Prior Actions and Authorizations to Take Related Actions. Memorandum. September 15, 1993.

42DP, Inc., NYS UDC, NYC EDC. *42nd Street Now! A Plan for the Interim Development of 42nd Street, Executive Summary (preliminary)*, prepared by Robert A. M. Stern Architects and M & Co. 1993.

NYS UDC. *42nd Street Development Project: General Project Plan Amendment, Final Supplemental Environmental Impact Statement*, prepared by Allee King Rosen & Fleming, Inc., Parsons Brinckerhoff Quade & Douglas, Inc., Eng-Wong, Taub & Associates, P.A. 1993.

Dyson, John. S., to Vincent Tese. *Re: 42nd Street Development Project Acquisition of Site 7.* February 14, 1993.

Weisbrod, Carl, to Rebecca Robertson. *Re: 42nd Street Development Project Acquisition of Site 7.* December 22, 1993.

NYS UDC, NYC EDC. *42nd Street Development Project, Request for Proposals for Site 7.* May 16, 1994.

Allee King Rosen & Fleming, Inc. *Summary of Economic and Fiscal Benefits for New York from the 42nd Street Development Project, draft*, prepared for the 42nd Street Development Project. October 1994.

Gargano, Charles A., to the [UDC d/b/a ESDC] Directors. *Request for Authorization to Hold a Public Hearing on the Proposed Amendment to the General Project Plan* [related to Site 12 and the incorporation of the three Durst parcels]. Memorandum. March 21, 1996.

_____. *Request for Authorization to Acquire Real Property Contiguous with the Project's Site 12.* Memorandum. April 18, 1996.

_____. *Request for Adoption of Amendment to the General Project Plan and Authorization to Hold Public Hearing Thereon; Authorization to Hold a Public Hearing on the Essential Terms of the Proposed Lease and Related Documents for the Project's Site 7 with Tishman Urban Development Corporation or an Affiliate Thereof.* Memorandum. April 18, 1996.

2. Theater Preservation and Reuse

American Practice Management, Inc. *Assessing Market Feasibility of Ten Theaters on 42nd Street*, report prepared for the NYC PDC and the UDC with the assistance of Brannigan-Lorelli Associates, Inc., and Theater Now, Inc. January 1981.

Placzek, Adolf K., and Dennis McFadden for Parsons Brinkerhoff Quade & Douglas, Inc. *42nd Street Development Project, Recommendation for Historic Preservation in the Project Area.* May 1981.

Hardy Holzman Pfeiffer Associates. *Feasibility Study for Non-Profit Reuse of Victory and Liberty Theaters*, report prepared for the Not-for-Profit Theater Advisory Committee. October 1987.

Robert A. M. Stern Architects. *42nd Street Development Project: Study of the Apollo, Lyric, Selwyn and Times Square Theaters and Related Infill Parcels.* October 1988.

Agreement between PDC and The New 42nd Street, Re: Funding for The New 42nd Street. December 1989.

McKoin, Pamela, to Deputy Mayor Sally Hernandez-Pinero. *Re: PDC Conditional Designation of The New 42nd Street, Inc. as Theater Sites Developer.* Memorandum. December 20, 1990.

Theater Project Agreement [UDC, The City of New York, New42]. May 7, 1992.

Theater Development Agreement [UDC and New42]. May 7, 1992.

Tese, Vincent, to the [UDC] Directors. *Forty-Second Street Development Land Use Improvement Project, Request for Authorization to Enter into a Lease with the New 42nd Street, Inc., and Related Agreements with The New 42nd Street, Inc., and The City of New York.* Memorandum. February 20, 1992.

_____. *Forty-Second Street Development Land Use Improvement Project, Request for Authorization to Execute an Amended Lease with The New 42nd Street, Inc., and Related Agreements for Project Sites 5, 10 and portions of Site 6.* Memorandum. December 15, 1994.

New42. *The Manual to The New 42nd Street Master Lease.* August 21, 1996.

Amendment to the Theater Project Agreement. December 13, 1996.

Amended and Restated Theater Development Agreement between 42DP Inc., and The New 42nd Street, Inc. December 13, 1996.

Gargano, Charles A., to the [UDC d/b/a ESDC] Directors. *Forty-Second Street Development Land Use Improvement Project, Request for Determination of No Significant Environmental Impact; Affirmation of General Project Plan, as Amended* [to approve increase in allowable height of the former Selwyn office building and Selwyn infill parcel]. Memorandum. January 14, 1998.

3. Subway Station Improvements

42DP, Inc. *Reconstruction of the Times Square Subway Complex, Status and Summary.* October 1984.

Subway Mezzanine Agreement [The City of New York, NYC PDC, NYS UDC, MTA, NYC TA, TSCA]. June 21, 1988.

Description of Terms of Agreement, Times Square Subway Station Improvements. July 7, 1988.

Times Square Subway Improvement Corporation, William Nicholas Bodouva & Associates/Wollmer Associates. *Times Square: Reconstruction of the Times Square Subway Complex Forty-Second Street, Borough of Manhattan.* 1990.

Amrosino, Edward A., to Gary Rosenberg [Rosenberg & Estis, P.C.]. *Re: Allocation of Funds for The Subway Improvements.* Memorandum. April 3, 1990.

Kent III, Fred I. Letter to the editor of the *New York Times,* July 31, 1990. Unpublished.

42DP, Inc. "$140 Million Reconstruction Promises a Safer, More Efficient Times Square Subway Station," *Crossroads* 1 (January 1991).

NYC TA. *Capital Program Modification: Times Square Subway Station Complex, Staff Summary Sheet.* June 9, 1993.

Tese, Vincent, to the [UDC] Directors. *Forty-Second Street Development Land Use Improvement Project, Request for Authorization to Execute a Memorandum of Agreement among UDC, 42nd St. Development Project, Inc., Times Square Subway Improvement Corporation, The City of New York, New York City Economic Development Corporation, New York City Transit Authority and Metropolitan Transportation Authority of the State of New York; and Authorization to Take Related Actions.* Memorandum. July 20, 1993.

Memorandum of Agreement [UDC, 42DP, Inc., MTA, NYC TA, NYC EDC, The City of New York, Times Square Subway Improvement Corporation]. September 14, 1993.

Subway Contribution Agreement [NYC EDC, The City of New York, 42DP, Inc., NYC TA, MTA]. October 7, 1994.

NYC TA. *Times Square Interim Entrance Construction and Retail Space, Staff Summary Sheet.* October 25, 1995.

NYC TA. *Staff Summary, Consultant Construction Mgr. for Times Square Rehab.* Undated [ca. 1997].

NYC TA. *Staff Summary Sheet, Times Square Complex Reconstruction Phase I.* December 29, 1998.

State of New York, Office of the Inspector General, Metropolitan Transit Authority [Roland M. Malan]. *Investigation of Times Square Escalator Buyout.* MTA/IG 99-12. October 1999.

4. Public Reviews

a. Hearings

Public Comments on the *Draft Environmental Impact Statement* for the 42DP, printed in the *Final Environmental Impact Statement.* August 1984.

Transcript on the public hearing on the *Final Environmental Impact Statement.* September 6, 1984.

Stenographic record of the discussion on *Calendar #86*, held at the meeting of the NYC Board of Estimate. October 25, 1984 and November 8, 1984.

NYC Board of Estimate. *Calendar Item #31.* November 8, 1984.

Stenographic record of the public hearing on the Proposed Amendment to the *General Project Plan* for the 42nd Street Development Project pursuant to Section 16 of the UDC Act. September 30, 1987.

Transcript of public hearing on the Proposed Leases with TSCA. December 10, 1987.

b. PACB Deliberations over the TSCA Leases

Oster, Harry, to Rebecca Robertson and Carl Weisbrod. *Re: Project Build-Out.* Memorandum. January 26, 1988.

Rosenberg, Gary M., to PACB. *Re: 42nd Street Development.* February 29, 1998.

Pleydle, Steven, to Jack Noel. *Re: Questions on Times Square Redevelopment Project.* Memorandum. March 10, 1988.

Noel, Jack, to Steven Pleydle. *Response to Memorandum of March 10, 1988 Regarding the 42nd Street Development Project*. Memorandum. March 16, 1988.

Grinnan, Maureen, and Steven Pleydle to Carl Weisbrod. Memorandum. April 5, 1988.

Weisbrod, Carl, to Maureen Grinnan and Steven Pleydle. Memorandum. April 8, 1988.

NYS PACB. *Resolution No. 88-UDC-196*. June 1, 1988.

Leichter, Franz S., to Hon. John J. Marchi and Hon. Mark Alan Siegel. July 26, 1988.

Weisbrod, Carl, to Hon. Dall Forsythe. August 24, 1988.

5. Deal Making

a. Office Sites

Tese, Vincent, to the [UDC] Directors. *Forty-Second Street Development Project, Request for Adoption of Amendment to General Project Plan and Authorization to Hold a Public Hearing thereon Pursuant to Section 16 (2) of the UDC Act and as may be Appropriate Pursuant to Other Applicable Laws*. Memorandum with attached minutes of the meeting. August 20, 1987.

_____. *Request for Authorization to Hold a Public Hearing on Leases with Times Square Center Associates*. Memorandum with attached minutes of the meeting. November 25, 1987.

_____. *Request for Modification of Proposed Amendment to General Project Plan; Determinations of No Significant Effect on the Environment; Affirmation of Amended General Project Plan; and Authorization to Execute Leases with Times Square Center Associates*. Memorandum with attached minutes of the meeting. February 9, 1988.

Land Acquisition and Development Agreement Between NYS UDC and TSCA. June 21, 1988.

Escrow Agreement [NYS UDC and TSCA]. June 21, 1988.

Side Letters [to Prudential regarding Debt Interests, regarding Escrow Agreement, Liberty Theater, Harris Theater, regarding Acquisition Map]. June 21, 1988.

NYS UDC, NYC PDC. *Comments on the Piker Subcommittee Report*. Memorandum. February 9, 1989.

NYS UDC. *Memorandum of Understanding: 42nd Street Development Project, Sites 1, 3, 4 and 12/Site 6 Infill*. September 8, 1992.

Tese, Vincent, to the [UDC] Directors. *42nd Street Development Land Use Improvement Project, Request for Authorization to Execute Amended Leases for Sites 1, 3, 4, and 12 and the Site 6 Infill with TSCA and Related Agreements with TSCA, The City of New York and Other Entities*. Memorandum. September 21, 1994.

Robertson, Rebecca, to the [UDC d/b/a ESDC] Directors. *Request for Authorization to Execute an Amended Lease and Related Documents for the Project's Site 12 with The Durst Organization or an Affiliate Thereof and Other Parties*. Memorandum. June 19, 1996.

Gargano, Charles A., to the [UDC d/b/a ESDC] Directors. *Request for Authorization to Enter Into Documents to Effectuate the Assignment of the Site 3 Leasehold Interest.* Memorandum. February 6, 1998.

b. The New Amsterdam Theater: Disney Negotiations and Agreements

Tese, Vincent, to the [UDC] Directors. *Authorization to Acquire the New Amsterdam Theater and Enter into Related Agreements with New Amsterdam Nederlander Associates, New York City Industrial Development Agency and The City of New York.* Memorandum. May 21, 1992.

Robertson, Rebecca, to Vincent Tese. *Re: Attracting Disney to 42nd Street.* Memorandum. July 1, 1993.

Draft Term Sheet for Disney Development for the New Amsterdam Theater presented by The City and State of New York. Undated.

42DP, Inc. *42nd Street Development Project Renovation and Operation of the New Amsterdam Theater Public Entity Proposals.* October 27, 1993.

NYS UDC, 42DP, Inc., NYC EDC, The City of New York, Disney Development Company. *Memorandum of Understanding, 42nd Street Development Project Renovation and Operation of the New Amsterdam Theater.* December 30, 1993.

NYS UDC, 42DP, Inc., NYC EDC, The City of New York, Disney Development Company. *Confidentiality Agreement, 42nd Street Development Project Renovation and Operation of the New Amsterdam Theater.* December 30, 1993.

NYS UDC, 42DP, Inc., NYC EDC, The City of New York, Disney Development Company. *Letter Agreement (Re: Duty to Defend), 42nd Street Development Project Renovation and Operation of the New Amsterdam Theater.* December 30, 1993.

Weisbrod, Carl, to Disney Development Company [re: confidentiality agreement]. December 30, 1993.

Letter Agreement (Re: Exclusive Negotiation & Right of First Refusal), 42nd Street Development Project Renovation and Operation of the New Amsterdam Theater. December 30, 1993.

Tese, Vincent, to Disney Development Company [re: Duty-to-Defend Letter Agreement]. December 30, 1993.

NYS UDC, 42DP, Inc., NYC EDC, The City of New York, Disney Development Company. *First Amendment to Memorandum of Understanding.* January 30, 1994.

Tese, Vincent, to the [UDC] Directors. *Request for Authorization to Enter into Contracts with the Port Authority of New York and New Jersey, The City of New York, the New York City Economic Development Corporation and the Disney Development Company Relating to the Funding of an Initial Redevelopment Project within the Forty-Second Street Development Land Use Improvement Project Area.* Memorandum. March 17, 1994.

Agreement between the Port Authority of New York and New Jersey, NYS UDC, 42DP, Inc. [regarding the Disney Deal]. April 8, 1994.

First Supplement to the Agreement between the Port Authority of New York and New Jersey, NYS UDC, 42DP, Inc. [regarding the Disney Deal]. April 10, 1995.

Second Supplement to the Agreement between the Port Authority of New York and New Jersey, NYS UDC, 42DP, Inc. [regarding the Disney Deal]. July 5, 1995.

Robertson, Rebecca, to Gary L. Mayer. *Re: New Amsterdam Theater Scope of Work and 80% Design Development Package.* November 18, 1994.

Tese, Vincent, to the [UDC] Directors. *Request for Authorization to Execute a Lease with the Disney Development Company or Affiliate and Related Agreements for the New Amsterdam Theater and Site 6 East Infill.* Memorandum. December 15, 1994.

———. *Request for Adoption of Findings and Policy Statement with Respect to Sex-Related Businesses within the 42nd Street Development Project; Determination of No Significant Effect on the Environment.* Memorandum. December 15, 1994.

Statement of Rebecca Robertson, President, 42DP, Inc. [re: SRBs]. Undated.

Agreement of Lease between 42nd Street Development, Inc., Landlord and New Amsterdam Development Corporation, Tenant. December 29, 1994.

Phase II Funding Agreement Between 42nd St. Development Project, Inc., and New Amsterdam Development Corporation. December 29, 1994.

Robertson, Rebecca, to Charles Gargano. *Re: Briefing for July 12, 1995 Lunch with Frank Iopollo.* Memorandum. July 11, 1995.

———. *Re: Briefing for July 12, 1995 Lunch with Frank Iopollo.* Memorandum. July 12, 1995.

———. *Re: Proposal for Meeting with Frank Iopollo.* Memorandum. July 13, 1995.

———. *Re: Summary of July 13th Proposal and Iopollo's Response: Suggested Counter Offer.* Memorandum. July 14, 1995.

Robertson, Rebecca, to Anita Romero. *Re: Outline of Disney Terms.* Memorandum. July 17, 1995.

Robertson, Rebecca, to Charles Gargano. *Re: City Response to Disney Renegotiated Terms.* Memorandum. July 18, 1995.

Letter Amendment to the Lease and Funding Agreement between 42DP and New Amsterdam Development Corporation. July 20, 1995.

Second Amended and Restated Promissory Note [New Amsterdam Development Corporation, 42DP, Inc., ESDC, PANYNJ, NYC EDC]. July 20, 1995.

c. Site 7: Tishman E-Walk Project

Gargano, Charles A., to the [UDC d/b/a ESDC] Directors. *Request for Authorization to Amend the Consulting Contract with LaSalle Partners for Financial/Development Advisory Services for the Project.* Memorandum. May 18, 1995.

———. *Request for Adoption of Amendment to the General Project Plan and Authorization to Hold Public Hearing Thereon; Authorization to Hold a Public Hearing on the Proposed Lease and Related Documents for the Project's Site 7 with Tishman Urban Development Corporation or an Affiliate Thereof.* Memorandum. April 18, 1996.

———. *Request for Determination of No Significant Adverse Environmental Impact; Modification of Amendment to General Project Plan; Affirmation of General Project Plan, as Amended; Authorization to Execute a Lease and Related Documents for the Project's Site 7 with the Tishman Urban Development Corporation or an Affiliate Thereof and Other Parties.* Memorandum. September 18, 1996.

_____. *Request for Authorization to Modify the Essential Terms of, and as Modified Execute, a Lease and Related Documents for the Project's Site 7 with Tishman Urban Development Corporation of an Affiliate Thereof and Other Parties.* Memorandum. December 19, 1996.

d. Sites 8E, 6W, 10: Forest City Ratner Entertainment Complex

_____. *Request for Authorization to Hold Public Hearing, Pursuant to Applicable Laws, Regarding the Acquisition by Condemnation of Certain Volumes of Space at Sites 8E, 6W and 10.* Memorandum. February 15, 1996.

Robertson, Rebecca, to the [UDC d/b/a ESDC] Directors. *Request for Authorization to Execute Lease and Related Documents for the Project's Sites 8E, 6W and 10 with Forest City Ratner Companies or an Affiliate Thereof and Other Parties.* Memorandum. June 19, 1996.

Gargano, Charles A., to the [UDC d/b/a ESDC] Directors. *Request for Adoption of Amendment to the General Project Plan* [for a hotel] *and Authorization to Hold Public Hearing Thereon; Authorization to Hold a Public Hearing on the Essential Terms of a Proposed Lease and Related Documents for the Project's Site 6W, 8E and 10 with Forest City Ratner Companies or an Affiliate Thereof and Other Parties.* Memorandum. April 28, 1998.

Leventer, Wendy, to the [UDC d/b/a ESDC] Directors. *Request for Determination of No Significant Adverse Environmental Impact; Authorization to Execute a Lease and Related Documents for the Project's Sites 6W, 8E, and 10 with Forest City Ratner Companies or an Affiliate Thereof and Other Parties.* Memorandum. July 16, 1998.

6. City–State Project Agreements

Memorandum of Understanding between the Urban Development Corporation and the City of New York [MOU]. June 1980.

NYS UDC, NYC PDC, The City of New York. *City-UDC Agreement.* June 21, 1988.

Robertson, Rebecca, to Deputy Mayor Barry Sullivan and Carl Weisbrod. *Re: Joint Funds Application Procedures* [regarding amendment to the City-UDC Agreement concerning "Designated Theater Payments"]. May 7, 1992.

Robertson, Rebecca, to The City of New York and NYC EDC [regarding amendment to the City-UDC Agreement concerning the New Amsterdam Theater]. August 26, 1992.

_____. [regarding amendment to the City-UDC Agreement concerning September 1992 agreement with TSCA]. December 30, 1993.

Tese, Vincent, and Rebecca Robertson to The City of New York and NYC EDC [regarding amendment to the City-UDC Agreement concerning restructuring of TSCA leases]. August 1, 1994.

Robertson, Rebecca, to The City of New York and NYC EDC [regarding amendment to the City-UDC Agreement concerning subway improvements]. October 7, 1994.

_____. [regarding amendment to the City-UDC Agreement adjustments to October 7, 1994 amendment]. December 29, 1994.

Amendment to the City-UDC Agreement [regarding Site 12]. July 10, 1996.

Site 8 East Acquisition Agreement among The City of New York, NYC EDC, NYS UDC and 42DP Inc. December 31, 1994.

7. Press Releases, Updates, Fact Sheets

42DP, Inc. *Theater Preservation/Renovation Program: Status and Summary*. October 1984.

NYS UDC. *42nd Street Development Project: Update*. October 22, 1984.

NYC PDC. *42nd Street Development Project: Summary and Status*. April 1987.

NYS UDC. *News Release: UDC Acts to Speed Property Acquisition for 42nd Street Development Project*. August 20, 1987.

_____. *News Release: UDC Authorizes 42nd Street Development Project To Enter Into Leases with Times Square Center Associates and Begin Property Condemnation Process*. February 9, 1988.

_____. *News Release: Public Authorities Control Board Approves 42nd Street Development Process*. June 1, 1988.

_____. *News Release: 42nd Street Development Project Update*. June 20, 1988.

NYS, Executive Chamber, Mario M. Cuomo, Governor, Press Office. [on signing the TSCA leases]. June 21, 1988.

_____. [on the formation of the 42nd Street Entertainment Corporation]. October 20, 1988.

NYS UDC. *News Release: Report Finds 42nd Street Theaters Historic Yet Adaptable*. October 20, 1988.

_____. *News Release: 42nd Street Development Project Update*. October 1988.

_____. *News Release: 42nd Street Projects Wins Key Legal Challenge Brought By Owners of Manhattan Design Building*. February 16, 1989.

NYS, Executive Chamber, Mario M. Cuomo, Governor, Press Office. [on appointment of Marian Sulzberger Heiskell and Cora Cahan to the New 42nd Street Entertainment Corporation]. September 18, 1990.

NYS UDC. *News Release: 42nd Street Development Project Update*. January 1991.

NYS, Executive Chamber, Mario M. Cuomo, Governor, Press Office. [on NYC's commitment to spend $35 million to fund UDC's condemnation of Site 7 and unveiling of *42nd Street Now!*]. September 15, 1993.

_____. [on the Disney MOU]. February 2, 1994.

NYS UDC. *Update on the 42nd Street Development Project*. Spring 1994.

NYS, Executive Chamber, Mario M. Cuomo, Governor, Press Office. [on the agreement with Prudential to defer construction of the office towers until economically feasible and funding of the interim plan]. August 5, 1994.

NYS UDC. *Update on the 42nd Street Development Project*. Fall 1994.

_____. *Developer Selected for 42nd Street Hotel Project*. May 11, 1995.

8. Litigation Materials

a. Selected Opinions

Cine 42nd St. Theater Corp. v. Nederlander Org. 790 F.2d 1032 (2d Cir. 1986).

In re G & A Books, Inc., 770 F.2d 288 (2d Cir. 1985).

Rosenthal & Rosenthal, Inc. v. N.Y.S. Urban Dev. Corp. 771 F.2d 44 (2d Cir. 1985).

Waybro v. Bd. of Estimate. [67 NY2d 349.] 493 N.E.2d 931. [502 N.Y.S.2d 707] (N.Y. Ct. App. 1986).

Jackson v. N.Y.S. Urban Dev. Corp. [67 N.Y.S.2d 400.] 494 N.E.2d 429. [503 N.Y.S.2d 298.] (N.Y. Ct. App. 1986).

Wilder v. Thomas. 854 F.2d 605 (2nd Cir. 1988).

Lazard Realty, Inc. v. N.Y.S. Urban Dev. Corp. [142 Misc. 2d 463.] 537 N.Y.S.2d 950 (N.Y. Sup. Ct. 1989).

In re N.Y.S. Urban Dev. Corp. [165 A.D.2d 733.] 563 N.Y.S.2d 788 (N.Y. App. Div. 1 1990).

In re Broadway Plus Corp. v. Metro. Transp. Auth. [157 A.D.2d 453.] 549 N.Y.S.2d 23 (N.Y. App. Div. 1990).

Broadway 41st St. Realty Corp. v. N.Y.S. Urban Dev. Corp. 733 F. Supp. 735 (S.D.N.Y. 1990).

b. On the TSCA leases

Franz Leichter, Carol Greitzer, Toh Realty Corp, the Durst Buildings Corporation, the Durst Organization, Inc., Shan Covey and the New York Times Boxing Club v. New York State Urban Dev. Corp. Complaint. December 8, 1987.

Memorandum of Defendant Urban Development Corporation in Opposition to Request for Temporary Restraining Order. December 9, 1987.

Messinger, Ruth W., to Carl Weisbrod [with attached press statement of December 9, 1987]. December 10, 1987.

Memorandum of Defendant in Opposition to Request for Injunctive Relief and Declaratory Judgement on Behalf of the New York State Urban Development Corporation. December 13, 1987.

Affidavit of Carl B. Weisbrod in Opposition to Request for Injunctive Relief and Declaratory Judgement. December 13, 1987.

Memorandum in Support of Plaintiffs' Motion for Injunctive Relief. December 15, 1987.

Reply Memorandum in Support of Plaintiffs' Motion for Injunctive Relief. December 15, 1987.

Reply Affirmation. December 15, 1987.

Leichter et al. v. N.Y.S. Urban Dev. Corp. Denial of Plaintiffs' Motion for a Preliminary Injunction. Index. No. 30229/87. December 24, 1987.

Friedlander, Jacob [for Rosenthal & Rosenthal, Inc.] to Joseph C. Petillo, Esq. *Re: 42nd Street Development Project* [in response to the legal public notice of November 30, 1987 on the "essential terms" of the TSCA leases]. January 5, 1988.

Durst, Robert to Joseph C. Petillo, Esq. *Re: Proposed Leases and Related Agreements for the 42nd Street Development Project* [submitted as written comment in response to the legal public notice of November 30, 1987 on the "essential terms" of the TSCA leases]. January 5, 1988.

Flynn v. N.Y.S. Urban Dev. Corp. 154 A.D.2d 26. 546 N.Y.S.2d 354 (1989).

B. Related Documents

1. Private Actions

a. CA42, Inc.

West 42nd Street: The Bright Light Zone, report of the 42nd Street Study Team, Graduate School and University Center of the City University of New York. 1978.

The City at 42nd Street, Inc. *The City*. Memorandum. October 6, 1978.

Business/Labor Working Group. Meeting Notes. October 27, 1978.

The City at 42nd Street, Inc. *Draft Environmental Impact Statement, The City At 42nd Street Urban Renewal Project,* prepared by Dames & Moore. October 30, 1979.

The City at 42nd Street, Inc. *Fact Sheet*. Undated.

Elliot, Donald E. Letter proposal to Robert Wagner, Jr. [Chairman, City Planning Commission]. August 29, 1979.

The City at 42nd Street, Inc. *Notes on Urban Design*. Memorandum. October 9, 1979.

The City at 42nd Street, Inc. *A Proposal for the Restoration and Redevelopment of 42nd Street*. January 1980.

Elliott, Donald H., to Robert F. Wagner, Jr. *Re: The City at 42nd Street, Inc.* Memorandum. January 30, 1980.

Elliott, Donald E., to the board of directors, The City at 42nd Street, Inc. Memorandum. February 13, 1980.

The City at 42nd Street, Inc. *Draft Letter of Intent for Development* [CA42, Olympia & York Equity Corp., Helmsley-Spear Inc., Rockefeller Center, Inc.]. March 11, 1980.

Elliott, Donald E., to the board of directors, The City at 42nd Street, Inc. *Re: Current Status of the Project*. Memorandum. May 23, 1980.

b. Other

Zarbakes, Arthur B. *An Environmental and Economic Survey of Times Square and Mid-Manhattan*. Undated [ca. 1970].

Vollmer Associates. *Evaluation of the Proposed Times Square Convention Center*. January 1977.

Lucas Arts Attractions with Project for Public Spaces, Inc., and Bolan Smart Associates, Inc. *42nd Street Entertainment Concept*. Draft. October 1991.

2. Planning Proposals

NYC DCP, Urban Design Group. *42nd Street Study*. DCP 78-04. January 1978.

The City of New York. *Times Square Action Plan*. August 1978.

NYC DCP. *Midtown Development*. DCP 81-8. June 1981.

_____. *Midtown Zoning*. DCP 82-03. March 1982.

_____. *Midtown Development Review*. DCP 87-05. July 1987.

_____. [staff on Times Square Zoning Issues]. Memorandum to Sylvia Deutsch. August 31, 1987.

NYC DCP Office of the Chief Urban Designer. *Times Square: Summary of Urban Design Study And Proposed Zoning Controls*. January 1987.

NYC DCP. *Times Square Urban Design Controls* [summary, post passage]. Undated.

Midtown Manhattan: Regulation and Response, a report of the American Institute of American Architects, Regional and Urban Design Committee Meeting, New York, N.Y., May 12–14, 1988.

Times Square Business Improvement District. *Report on the Secondary Effects of the Concentration of Adult Use Establishments in the Times Square Area*, prepared by Insight Associates, April 1994.

NYC DCP. *Adult Entertainment Study*. DCP 94-08. November 1994.

3. Third-Party Estimates of 42DP Subsidies

Office of State Senator Franz S. Leichter. *A Public Subsidy Exceeding One Billion Dollars: The Leases for Sites 1, 3, 4, and 12 (Proposed Office Towers) of the 42nd Street Development Project*. Photocopy. 1988.

Rosenberg & Estis, P.C. *Economic Calculations of Times Square Redevelopment Project*. Photocopy. February 1990.

_____. *A Fresh Look at the Times Square Redevelopment Project*. Photocopy. February 1990.

Tobier, Emanuel, and Lisa Roberts. *Calculating The Tax Subsidy Implications of the Times Square Center Associates (TSCA) Project*. Memorandum to the file. 1991.

MAS. *Analysis of the 42nd Street Development Project*. Working memorandum. July 28, 1994; updated, August 8, 1994, August 15, 1994.

4. Conference Proceedings, Panel Sessions, Exhibits

Real Estate in The Press, transcribed tape of concurrent panel session, Urban Land Institute Fall Meeting, November 3, 1995.

The Redevelopment of Times Square, transcribed tape of concurrent panel session, Urban Land Institute Fall Meeting, November 8, 1997.

Signs & Wonders: The Spectacular Lights of Times Square, an exhibit at the New York Historical Society (November 12, 1997, to March 8, 1998), transcript of exhibit descriptions.

II. INTERVIEWS

Philip E. Aarons, former president, NYC PDC (1980–1983); December 19, 1991.

Deborah Allee, urban planner, Allee King, Rosen & Fleming, Inc.; February 5, 1997.

Richard T. Anderson, former president, Regional Plan Association; December 1, 1992.

Geoffrey Baker, head, urban design, NYC DCP; February 20, 1997.

Sharon Barnes, vice president, Prudential Insurance Company of America; November 20, 1997, July 1, 1999.

Jonathan Barnett, former head, urban design NYC DCP; January 21, 1997.

Robert Berne, real estate developer affiliated with the Milstein real estate interests; December 4, 1996, October 24, 1996, April 15, 1997.

Paul S. Byard, architect, Byard, Platt, Dovell Architects; April 4, 1997.

Cora Cahan, president, The New 42 Street, Inc.; December, 13, 1996, February 21, 1997, September 28, 2000.

Valerie Caproni, former general counsel, UDC; November 21, 1991 (by Alicia Glen), June 15, 1998.

Charles Christella, retail consultant; January 27, 1997.

Barbara Chu, former managing vice president, investment and sales, Prudential Mortgage Capital; January 9, 1997, September 17, 1997, November 14, 1997.

Faith Hope Consolo, vice chairman, Garrick-Aug Worldwide; February 5, 1997.

Alexander Cooper, urban designer, Cooper, Robertson & Partners, Architects and Urban Designers; May 6, 1998.

Curtis Deane, vice president and managing director, Banque Nationale de Paris; October 31, 1997, November 6, 1997, January 7, 1998.

Douglas Durst, president, the Durst Organization (with attorney Gary Rosenberg); May 30, 1990.

Gretchen Dykstra, former president, Times Square BID; February 10, 1997.

Donald E. Elliott, attorney and former president, The CA42, Inc.; February 3, 1997.

Susan Fine, former director of real estate, MTA; December 16, 1993, January 13, 1995, January 21, 1997, July 14, 1998, June 21, 1999, September 15, 2000.

Dall Forthsyth, former budget director for Governor Cuomo; November 6, 1991.

Mary Anne Gilmartin, senior vice president, commercial development, Forest City Ratner Companies; January 23, 2001.

Jeffrey Glen, attorney and former special assistant to the City Corporate Counsel; November 2, 1994.

Martin E. Gold, attorney and former economic development specialist, City Corporate Counsel; December 5, 1991, July 18, 1997; March 22, 2000.

Patricia Goldstein, former executive at Citicorp Real Estate Inc., November 6, 1998.

Maxine Griffith and Eugenie Birch, former commissioners, NYC CPC; July 7, 1994.

Veronica W. Hackett, former vice president, Park Tower Realty Corporation; February 2, 1995.

Hugh Hardy, architect, Hardy Holtzman Pfeiffer Associates; January 9, 1997.

Craig Hatkoff, former consultant to Madame Tussaud's; May 15, 1991, July 15, 1997, December 21, 1998.

Eugene Heimberg, former chairman, Prudential Realty Group; September 20, 1994, September 24, 1996, December 17, 1996.

Marian Sulzberger Heiskell, chairman, The New 42nd Street, Inc., and executive, *New York Times*; January 7, 1998.

Con Howe, former executive director, NYC DCP; September 18, 1998.

Richard A. Kahan, attorney and former president, UDC (1979–1984); October 16, 1991.

Tibor Kalman, graphic designer; December 3, 1996.

Jeffrey Katz, real estate developer, Sherwood Equities; April 11, 1997.

Edward I. Koch, mayor, the City of New York (1978–1989); October 3, 2000.

George Klein, real estate developer, Park Tower Realty Corporation; April 4, 1995, December 4, 1997.

Michael Kwartler, zoning expert and director of the Center for Environmental Simulation; February 20, 1997.

Michael Laginestra, leasing broker representing Viacom, ESG/Insignia; Fall 1998.

Stephen A. Lefkowitz, attorney and former outside counsel for the City of New York; March 1, 1992.

Wendy Leventer, president, 42DP, Inc. (1997-present); March 5, 1999.

John Livingston, former EDC official and president, Tishman Urban Development Corporation; April 11, 1997.

William L. Mack, real estate developer and UDC (d/b/a ESDC) board member; December 14, 1999.

Matthew Mayer, former general counsel, Park Tower Realty Corporation; February 2, 1998, May 18, 1998.

Robert Mayers and John Schiff, architects, Mayers & Schiff Associates, PC; March 3, 1997.

Ruth W. Messinger, former Manhattan Borough President; April 19, 1991.

Robert Paley, former director, real estate development, MTA; March 21, 2000.

Frederic S. Papert, president, 42nd Street Development Corporation; November 5, 1996.

Rodger G. Parker, former senior vice president, facilities management, Prudential Securities, Inc.; July 7, 1999.

Christina Plattner, historic preservation expert, Allee King Rosen & Fleming, Inc.; February 28, 1997.

Alan Pomerance, attorney, Weil Gotshal & Manges; March 5, 1999.

Rebecca Robertson, former president of 42DP, Inc. (1990–1997); October 21, 1994, August 22, 1996, November 5, 1996, December 6, 1996, December 4, 1997, December 4, 1998, April 1, 1999, April 19, 1999, April 11, 2000, August 10, 2000.

Gary M. Rosenberg, attorney, Rosenberg & Estes, PC; January 22, 1997.

Richard L. Schaffer, former chairman of the NYC CPC; January 8, 1997.

Arthur Sonneblick, mortgage broker, Sonneblick-Goldman; December 5, 1991.

Steven Spinola, former president of PDC (1983–1986) and president of the Real Estate Board of New York; April 18, 1991.

Robert A. M. Stern, architect, Robert A. M. Stern Architects; November 19, 1996.

Robin Stout, senior counsel, UDC (d/b/a) ESDC; January 29, 1998.

James P. Stuckey, former president, PDC (1986–1989) and executive, vice president, commercial development, Forest City Ratner Companies; January 23, 1998.

Herbert J. Sturz, former chairman, NYC CPC (1980–1986); December 5, 1991.

Vincent Tese, former chairman, UDC (1985–1994); December 9, 1996.

Paul A. Travis, former project manager, 42nd Street Development Project, PDC; January 27, 1992.

Robert Venturi, architect, and Denise Scott Brown, planner, Venturi, Scott Brown and Associates, Inc.; December 4, 1999.

John Vickers, president, Tishman Hotel Corporation; April 15, 1998.

Jay Walder, former executive director, MTA; June 26, 1999.

Lee Webb, executive vice president, UDC; May 2, 1990.

Carl B. Weisbrod, former president, 42DP, Inc (1987–1989) and president of EDC (1990–1993); July 17,1991, October 10, 1991, October 30, 1991, January 16, 1992, July 23, 1996, August 14, 1996, November 21, 1997, August 15, 2000.

III. Selected Secondary Sources

A. Times Square

1. History, Myth, Nostalgia

Allen, Irving Lewis. *The City in Slang: New York Life and Popular Speech.* Oxford University Press, 1993.

Berman, Marshall. "Signs of the Times: The Lure of Times Square." *Dissent* 44 (fall 1997): 76–83.

Blackmar, Betsy. "Uptown Real Estate and the Creation of Times Square." In *Inventing Times Square: Commerce and Culture at the Crossroads of the World,* ed. William E. Taylor, 51–65. New York: Russell Sage Foundation, 1991.

Bloom, Ken. *Broadway: An Encyclopedic Guide to the History, People and Places of Times Square*. New York: Oxford/Facts on File, 1991.

Bruder, Stanley. "Forty-Second Street at the Crossroads: A History of Broadway to Eighth Avenue." In *West 42nd Street: The Bright Light Zone,* 53–81. Graduate School and University Center of the City University of New York, unpublished, 1978.

Cohn, Nik. *The Heart of the World*. New York: Vintage Books Edition/Random House, 1993.

Dunlap, David W. *On Broadway: A Journey Uptown Over Time*. New York: Rizzoli International Publications, 1990.

Hammack, David C. "Developing for Commercial Culture." In *Inventing Times Square: Commerce and Culture at the Crossroads of the World,* ed. William E. Taylor, 36–50. New York: Russell Sage Foundation, 1991.

Harris, Neil. "Urban Tourism and the Commercial City." In *Inventing Times Square: Commerce and Culture at the Crossroads of the World,* ed. William E. Taylor, 66–82. New York: Russell Sage Foundation, 1991.

Koolhaas, Rem. "Regrets?" *Grand Street* 15 (summer 1996): 137–138.

Lass, William. *Crossroads of the World: The Story of Times Square*. New York: Popular Library, 1965.

Nasaw, David. *Going Out: The Rise and Fall of Public Amusements*. New York: Basic Books, 1993.

Paneth, Philip. *Times Square: Crossroads of the World*. New York: Living Books, 1965.

Rogers, W. G., and Mildred Weston. *Carnival Crossroads: The Story of Times Square*. New York: Doubleday & Company, 1960.

Sclar, Robert. "Times Square as a Movie-Goers' Mecca." Unpublished draft. Undated.

Stone, Jill. *Times Square: A Pictorial History*. New York: Collier Books/Macmillian Publishing Company, 1982.

Stoumen, Lou. *Times Square: 45 Years of Photography*. New York: Aperture, 1985.

The New York Times. *The Century in Times Square*. New York: Bishop Books, 1999.

2. Sex, Pornography and Crime

Buckley, Peter. "Introductory Essay." In *Inventing Times Square: Commerce and Culture at the Crossroads of the World,* ed. William R. Taylor, 286–297. New York: Russell Sage Foundation, 1991.

Delany, Samuel R. *Times Square Red, Times Square Blue*. New York and London: New York University Press, 1999.

Friedman, Josh Alan. *Tales of Times Square*. Portland, Oregon: Feral House, 1986.

Gilfoyle, Timothy J. "Policing of Sexuality." In *Inventing Times Square: Commerce and Culture at the Crossroads of the World,* ed. William R. Taylor, 297–314. New York: Russell Sage Foundation, 1991.

Jacobson, Mark. "Times Square: The Meanest Street in America." *Rolling Stone,* August 6, 1981: 15ff.

Kornblum, William, and Vernon Boggs. "The Social Ecology of the Bright Light District." In *West 42nd Street: The Bright Light Zone*, 17–51. Graduate School and University Center of the City University of New York, 1978.

Netzer, Dick. "The Worm in the Apple." *New York Affairs* 4 (spring 1978): 42–48.

Senelick, Laurence. "Private Parts in Public Places." In *Inventing Times Square: Commerce and Culture at the Crossroads of the World*, ed. William R. Taylor, 329–353. New York: Russell Sage Foundation, 1991.

Sheehy, Gail. "Cleaning Up Hell's Bedroom." *New York*, November 13, 1972: 50–66.

_____. "The Landlords of Hell's Bedroom," *New York*, November 20, 1972: 67–80.

3. Commercial Aesthetic

Bischoff, Dan. "signs of the times." *Metropolis* 18 (February/March 1998): 39ff.

Leach, William. "Introductory Essay [Commercial Aesthetics]." In *Inventing Times Square: Commerce and Culture at the Crossroads of the World,* ed. William E. Taylor, 234–242. New York: Russell Sage Foundation, 1991.

Sorkin, Michael. "See You in Disneyland." In *Variations on a Theme Park,* ed. Michael Sorkin, 205–232. New York: The Noonday Press/Hill and Wang, 1992.

Starr, Tama, and Edward Hayman. *Signs and Wonders: The Spectacular Marketing of America*. New York: Currency Book/Doubleday, 1998.

Taylor, William R. "The Launching of a Commercial Culture." In *Power, Culture, and Place*, ed. John Hull Mollenkopf, 107–133. New York: Russell Sage Foundation, 1988.

Taylor, William R. *In Pursuit of Gotham: Culture and Commerce in New York*. New York: Oxford University Press, 1992.

Venturi, Robert, Denise Scott Brown, and Steven Izenour. *Learning from Las Vegas*. Cambridge: MIT Press, 1972.

4. Theater District: Planning, Preservation, Business

Appel, Willa. "Sounding Off at the Theater Retention Bonus." *Assessor* [newsletter of the Citizens Housing and Planning Council). 6, no. 1 (March 1988).

Gerard, Karen. *American Survivors: Cities and Other Scenes*. San Diego: Harcourt Brace Jananovich, 1984.

Goldstein, Jack L. "Development and the Threat to the Theater District." *City Almanac* 18 (summer 1985): 23–24.

Gratz, Roberta Brandes. "Cityscape: Save the Helen Hayes." *New York*, November 19, 1979: 74–75.

Knapp, Margaret. "Introductory Essay [Entertainment and Commerce]." In *Inventing Times Square: Commerce and Culture at the Crossroads of the World*, ed. William R. Taylor, 120–132. New York: Russell Sage Foundation, 1991.

McNamara, Brooks. "The Entertainment District of the End of the 1930s." In *Inventing Times Square Commerce and Culture at the Crossroads of the World*; ed. William R. Taylor, 178–190. New York: Russell Sage Foundation, 1991.

Rose, Joseph B. "Landmark Preservation in New York." *Public Interest* 74 (winter 1984): 132–145.

Taylor, William R. "Broadway: The Place That Words Built." In *Inventing Times Square Commerce and Culture at the Crossroads of the World*, ed. William R. Taylor, 212–231. New York: Russell Sage Foundation, 1991.

Van Hoogstraten, Nicholas. *Lost Broadway Theaters*. Revised edition. New York: Princeton Architectural Press, 1997.

Zisser, Michael H. "Theater Preservation: Ideas in Search of a Plan." *New York Affairs* 8, no. 4 (1985): 157–169.

5. Architecture: Symbolic and Real

Anderson, Kurt. "Renewal, But a Loss of Funk." *Time*, February 29, 1988: 102–103.

_____. "Can 42nd Street Be Born Again?" *Time*, September 27, 1993: 93.

"Arquitectonica Crashes on 42nd Street." *Progressive Architecture* (July 1995): 25.

Barrenceche, Raul A. "On the Boards: 42nd Street Redevelopment New York City, Robert A. M. Stern Architects." *Architecture* 82 (November 1993): 37.

Cogen, Douglas N. "42nd Street Now! vs 42nd Street Later." *MAS Newsletter*: 3–4.

Crosbie, Michael J. "Times Square Redevelopment Provokes Dispute in New York." *Architectural Record* 172 (May 1984): 54ff.

Davis, Douglas. "Strange Invaders: A controversial face-life for Times Square." *Newsweek*, November 19, 1984: 91–92.

Donhauser, Peter L. "'Populists' Plans for 42nd Street." *Progressive Architecture* (November 1988): 24ff.

"Embassy Suites Times Square." Architectural Digest Citation, *Progressive Architectire* 71 (January 1990): 102–103.

Goldberger, Paul. "Architecture: The New Amsterdam Theater, Hardy Holzman Pfeiffer Revives Broadway's Faded Star." *Architectural Digest* 52 (November 1995): 40ff.

_____. "The Sky Line: Busy Buildings." *New Yorker*, September 4, 2000: 90–93.

Hardy, Hugh. "Make It Dance!" *Livable City* no. 10/1 (October 1986): 6–7.

Hrabi, Dale. "Will the 'New' Times Square Be New Enough," *Wired*, March 3, 1995: 128–133ff.

Hoyt, Charles K. "Times Square Victory." *Architectural Record* 184 (Jan-March 1992): 67–71.

Huxtable, Ada Louise. "Reinventing Times Square: 1990." In *Inventing Times Square, Commerce and Culture at the Crossroads of the World*, ed. William R. Taylor, 357–371. New York: Russell Sage Foundation, 1991.

Jacobs, Karrie. "Cityscape: Forty-Deuce Coop." *New York*, April 6, 1998: 62–64.

Lemos, Peter. "Deficiencies on Times Square." *Progressive Architectire* 67 (June 1986): 26.

_____. "Times Square Air." *Metropolis* 6 (July/August 1986): 14–15.

Lewis, George. "Lively Times in Times Square." *Oculus* 46 (May 1984): 20–21.

_____. "42nd Street/Times Square: A Project in Trouble." *Oculus* 46 (November 1984): 3–6.

_____. "Update on 42nd Street/Times Square," *Oculus* 46 (December 1984): 11.

The Liveable City [A publication of the Municipal Art Society]. no. 10/1 (October 1986): 2–3.

Mandel, Andrew, and Jacqueline Thaw. "Teaching Times Square a Lesson." *Places* 6 (summer 1990): 91–92.

McKee, Bradford. "Times Square Revival." *Architecture* 39 (November 1993): 94–99.

Merkel, Jane. "Fireworks on 42nd Street: As Much About Economics As About Architecture." *Competitions* (fall 1995): 45–49.

_____. "On Times Square." *Oculus* 59 (May 1997): 9–12.

Ouroussoff, Nicolai. "42nd Street's Glitz and Grit Meet Arquitectonica's Punchy (and Punchout) Times Square Design." *Architectural Record* 183 (June 1995): 15.

Russell, James S. "Golddiggers of '84?" *Archtectural Record* 172 (October 1984): 125–131.

_____. "42nd Street: No Beat of Dancing Feet, Yet." *Architectural Record* 177 (June 1989): 85.

_____. "Midtown West: Bright Lights, Big Buildings." *Architectural Record* 179 (June 1989): 83.

Schultz, Franz. *Philip Johnson: Life and Work*. New York: Alfred A. Knopf, 1994.

Slatin, Peter. "Forty-second Street: Part I: What You Might Still Want to Know about 42nd Street." *Oculus* 56 (November 1993): 10–11.

_____. "Forty-second Street: Part II: The Scenario Unfolds," *Oculus* 56 (December 1993): 10–12.

Sorkin, Michael. "The Big Peep Show." *New York Times Magazine*, December 26, 1999: 9–10.

_____. "Too Late for Times Square?" *Progressive Architectire* 65 (October 1984): 23–24.

_____. "Status Quo Vadis?" *Harvard Design Magazine* (winter/spring 1998), 29ff.

Stephens, Suzanne. "Projects: Four Times Square, New York City." *Architectural Record* 188 (March 2000): 90–97.

Weisman, Carter. "Brave New Times Square." *New York*, April 2, 1984, 34ff.

Woldenberg, Susan. "The Future of Times Square: The Portman Portent." *New Criterion* (February 1987), 27–36.

B. Real Estate Development

1. Development Politics, New York Style

Adler, Jerry. *High Rise: How 1,000 Men and Women Worked Around the Clock for Five Years and Lost $200 Million Building a Skyscraper.* New York: HarperCollins, 1993.

Barrett, Wayne, assisted by Adam Fifield. *Rudy!* New York: Basic Books, 2000.

Bellush, Jewel. "Clusters of Power: Interest Groups." In *Urban Politics New York Style,* ed. Jewel Bellush and Dick Netzer, 296–338. Armonk and London: M. E. Sharpe, 1990.

Benjamin, Gerald. "The Political Relationship." In *The Two New Yorks: State-City Relations in the Changing Federal System*, ed. Gerald Benjamin and Charles Brecher, 107–150. New York: Russell Sage, 1998.

Brendle, Mary. "Negotiating for Clinton." *City Almanac* 18 (summer 1985): 25–26.

Brigham, James R., Jr., "The 42nd Street Development Project: The City's Perspective." *City Almanac* 18 (summer 1985): 9–11.

Danielson, Michael, and Jameson Doig. *New York: The Politics of Urban Regional Development.* Berkeley: University of California Press, 1982.

Diamond, Edwin, and Piera Paine. "The Media in the Game of Politics." In *Urban Politics New York Style*, ed. Jewel Bellush and Dick Netzer, 339–356. Armonk, N.Y.: M. E. Sharpe, 1990.

Fainstein, Susan S. "The Redevelopment of 42nd Street: Clashing Viewpoints." *City Almanac* 18 (summer 1985): 1–8.

Fainstein, Norman I., and Susan S. Fainstein. "The Politics of Urban Development: New York City Since 1945." *City Almanac* 17 (April 1984): 1–26.

Gilmartin, Gregory F. *Shaping the City: New York and the Municipal Art Society.* New York: Clarkson Potter Publishers, 1995.

Koch, Edward I. *Mayor: An Autobiography.* New York: Simon & Schuster, 1984.

Lawson, Ronald. "The Political Face of New York's Real Estate Industry." *New York Affairs* 6, no. 2 (1980): 88–109.

McCloud, Darlene. "Preserving the Core of the Big Apple." *City Almanac* 18 (summer 1985): 19–21.

Mollenkopf, John. "The 42nd Street Development Project and the Public Interest." *City Almanac* 18 (summer 1985): 12–15.

Newfield, Jack, and Wayne Barrett. *City for Sale: Ed Koch and the Betrayal of New York.* New York: Perennial Library/Harper & Row, 1989, updated edition.

Reichl, Alex. *Reconstructing Times Square: Politics and Culture in Urban Development.* Lawrence: University of Kansas Press, 1999.

Roberts, Sam. "Who Runs New York Now? *New York Times Magazine*, April 28, 1985, 27ff.

2. City Planning and Public Policy

Barnett, Jonathan. "Onward and Upward with the Art of Zoning," *New York Affairs* 6, no. 3 (1980): 4–14.

_____. *The Elusive City: Five Centuries of Design, Ambition and Miscalculation*. New York: Harper & Row, 1986.

Cervero, Robert, Peter Hall, and John Landis, *Transit Joint Development in the United States*. Institute of Urban and Regional Development, University of California at Berkeley, August 1992.

Costonis, John. *Icons and Aliens: Law, Aesthetics, and Environmental Change*. Urbana and Chicago: University of Illinois Press, 1989.

Exploring the Metropolis. *Hindsight and Foresight: Planning for Significant City-Owned Sites*. New York: Exploring the Metropolis, October 1988.

Fainstein, Susan S., and Robert Stokes. "Spaces for Play: The Impacts of Entertainment Development on New York City." Center for Urban Policy Research. Rutgers, The State University of New Jersey. Working Paper no.123. 1997.

Frieden, Bernard J., and Lynne B. Sagalyn. *Downtown, Inc.: How America Rebuilds Cities*. Cambridge: MIT Press, 1989.

Garvin, Alexander. *The American City: What Works, What Doesn't*. New York: McGraw-Hill, 1996.

Goldberger, Paul. "The Limits of Urban Growth." *New York Times Magazine*, November 14, 1982, 46ff.

_____. "Shaping the Face of New York." In *New York Unbound: The City and the Politics of the Future*, ed. Peter D. Salins, 127–140. New York: Basil Blackwell, 1988.

Grava, Sigurd. "Consequences of the Boom: Strain at the Core." *New York Affairs* 8 (1985): 32–47.

Hall, Peter. *Great Planning Disasters*. Berkeley and Los Angeles: University of California Press, 1980.

Hannigan, John. *Fantasy City: Pleasure and profit in the postmodern metropolis*. London and New York: Tutledge, 1998.

Houston, Lawrence O., Jr. *BIDs: Business Improvement Districts*. Washington, D.C.: ULI, the Urban Land Institute in cooperation with the International Downtown Association, 1997.

Huxtable, Ada Louise. "Stumbling Toward Tomorrow: The Decline and Fall of the New York Vision." *Dissent* 3 (fall 1987): 453–461.

Kessner, Thomas. "Fiorello H. LaGuardia and the Challenge of Democratic Planning." In *Landscape of Modernity: New York City, 1900–1940*, ed. David Ward and Olivier Zunz, 315–329. Baltimore and London: The Johns Hopkins University Press, 1992.

Mollenkopf, John Hull. "City Planning." In *Setting Municipal Priorities, 1990*, ed. Charles Brecher and Raymond D. Horton, 141–182. New York: New York University Press, 1989.

_____, ed. *Power, Culture, and Place: Essays on New York City*. New York: Russell Sage Foundation, 1988.

Ponte, Robert. "New York's Zoning Solution." *Planning* 48 (December 1982): 10–14.

_____. "Manhattan's Real Estate Boom." *New York Affairs* 8 (1985): 18–31.

Regional Plan Association. *Urban Design Manhattan: A Report of the Second Regional Plan*. New York: Viking Press/A Studio Book, April 1969.

Sandler, Ross. "Private Development/Public Transit: Using Transit's Zoning Tool." *New York Affairs* 7 (1982): 114–120.

Sassen, Saskia. *The Global City: New York, London, Tokyo*. Princeton: Princeton University Press, 1991.

_____. *Cities in a World Economy*. Thousand Oaks, Calif.: Pine Forge Press, 1994.

Sassen, Saskia, and Frank Roost. "The City: Strategic Site for the Global Entertainment Industry." In *The Tourist City*, ed. Dennis R. Judd and Susan S. Fainstein, 143–156. New Haven: Yale University Press, 1999.

Savitch, H.V. *Post-Industrial Cities: Politics and Planning in New York, Paris, and London*. Princeton: Princeton University Press, 1988.

Suttles, Gerald D. *The Man-Made City: The Land-Use Confidence Game in Chicago*. Chicago: University of Chicago Press, 1990.

Weiss, Marc A. "Density and Intervention: New York's Planning Traditions." In *The Landscape of Modernity*, ed. David Ward and Olivier Zunz, 46–75. Baltimore: Johns Hopkins Press, 1992.

3. Public Development

Brilliant, Eleanor. *The Urban Development Corporation*. Lexington, Mass.: Lexington Books, 1975.

Board of Founders Solidere. *The Reconstruction of Beirut Central District: The Major Urban Redevelopment Project of the 1990s, Information Booklet,* second edition. October 1993.

Caro, Robert A. *The Power Broker: Robert Moses and the Fall of New York*. New York: Random House, Vintage Books Edition, 1975.

Doig, Jameson W. "Entrepreneurship in Government: Historical Roots," paper prepared for the 1988 Annual Meeting of the American Political Science Association.

Doig, Jameson W., and Erwin C. Hargrove. "'Leadership' and Political Analysis." In *Leadership and Innovation: A Biographical Perspective on Entrepreneurs in Government*, ed. Jameson W. Doig and Erwin C. Hargrove, 1–23. Baltimore: Johns Hopkins University Press.

Gordon, David L. A. "Architecture: How Not to Build a City, Implementation at Battery Park City." *Landscape and Urban Planning* 26 (December 1993): 35–54.

The Lebanese Company for the Development and Reconstruction of Beirut Central District S.A.L. Solidere. *Information Memorandum*. November 1, 1993.

Nahas, Ronald C. "Beruit Rising." *Urban Land* 58, no. 10 (October 1999): 40–46.

Ponte, Robert. "UDC: After a Record of Achievement, A Shift in Course?" *New York Affairs* 8 (1984): 19–34.

Sagalyn, Lynne B. "Public Development: Using Land as a Capital Resource." Lincoln Institute of Land Policy and the A. Alfred Taubman Center for State and Local Government of the John F. Kennedy School of Government, Harvard University, Working Paper, 1992.

_____. "Leasing: The Strategic Option for Public Development." Lincoln Institute of Land Policy and the A. Alfred Taubman Center for State and Local Government of the John F. Kennedy School of Government, Harvard University, Working Paper, 1993.

_____. "Negotiating for Public Benefits: The Bargaining Calculus of Public-Private Development." *Urban Studies* 34, no. 12 (1997): 1955–1970.

Stone, Clarence N., and Heywood T. Sanders. "Reexamining a Classic Case of Development Politics: New Haven, Connecticut." In *The Politics of Urban Development,* ed. Clarence N. Stone and Heywood T. Sanders, 159–181. Lawrence, Kans., 1987.

_____. "Summing Up: Urban Regimes, Development Policy and Political Arrangements." In *The Politics of Urban Development*, ed. Clarence N. Stone and Heywood T. Sanders, 269–290. Lawrence, Kans., 1987.

Teaford, Jon C. "Urban Renewal and Its Aftermath. *Housing Policy Debate* 11, no. 2 (2000): 443–465.

Walsh, Annamarie Hauck. "Public Authorities and the Shape of Decision Making." In *Urban Politics New York Style*, ed. Jewel Bellush and Dick Netzer, 188–219. Armonk and London: M. E. Sharpe, 1990.

4. Fiscal Politics and Policy

Citizens Budget Commission [of New York]. *The Hidden Billions: Tax Expenditures in New York City*. November 1981.

Cockren, Robert W., Maria L. Vecchiotti, and Donna M. Zerbo, "Local Finance: A Brief Constitutional History." *Fordham Urban Law Journal* 8 (1979–1980): 135–183.

Fuchs, Ester R. *Mayors and Money: Fiscal Policy in New York and Chicago.* Chicago and London: University of Chicago Press, 1992.

Gold, Martin E. "Economic Development Projects: A Perspective," *Urban Lawyer* 1 (spring 1987): 199–231.

Leonard, Herman. *The Quiet Side of Public Spending*. New York: Basic Books, 1986.

NYC Office of the Comptroller, Bureau of Audit. *The New York City Economic Development Corporation Should Evaluate and Better Document Its Economic Development Lease Projects*. Report K91-05. January 25, 1993.

Parker, Andrew R. "Local Tax Subsidies as a Stimulus for Development: Are They Cost Effective? Are They Equitable?" *City Almanac* 16 (February–April 1983): 8–15.

Regan, Edward. *Government, Inc.: Creating Accountability for Economic Development Programs.* Government Finance Research Center of the Government Finance Officers Association, April 1988.

Rosen, Bernard. *Holding Government Bureaucracies Accountable.* New York: Praeger Publishers, 1982.

Sagalyn, Lynne B. "Explaining the Improbable: Local Redevelopment in the Wake of Federal Cutbacks." *Journal of the American Institute of Planners* 56 (1990): 429–441.

Shefter, Martin. *Political Crisis/Fiscal Crisis: The Collapse and Revival of New York City.* New York: Basic Books, 1987.

Wolkoff, Michael J. "The Nature of Property Tax Abatement Awards." *Journal of the American Planning Association* 49 (winter 1983): 77–84.

5. New York Architecture, General

Andersen, Kurt. "The '80s as Spectacle; *Exquisite Corpse.*" *Architectural Record* 180 (May 1992): 50.

Dixon, John Morris. "Judging Diversity." *Progressive Architecture* 70 (January 1989): 9.

Gill, Brendan. "The Sky Line: On the Brink." *New Yorker,* September 9, 1987: 113–126.

_____. "The Sky Line: The Malady of Giantism." *New Yorker,* January 9, 1989: 73–77.

_____. "The Sky Line: The Death of the Skyscraper?" *New Yorker,* March 4, 1991: 90–94.

_____. "The Sky Line: Disneyitis." *New Yorker,* April 29, 1991: 96–99.

_____. "The Sky Line: Hazards of Bigness." *New Yorker,* August 31, 1992: 69–75.

Huxtable, Ada Louise. *The Tall Building Artistically Reconsidered: The Search for a Skyscraper Style.* New York: Pantheon Books, 1982.

Stephens, Suzanne. "Voices of Consequence: Four Architectural Critics." In *Women in Architecture: A Historic and Contemporary Perspective,* ed. Susana Torre, 136–143. New York: Whitney Library of Design, 1977.

_____. "Assessing the State of Architectural Criticism in Today's Press." *Architectural Record* 186 (March 1998): 64ff.

Stern, Robert A. M., Thomas Mellins, and David Fishman. *New York 1880: Architecture and Urbanism in the Gilded Age.* New York: The Monacelli Press, 1999.

Stern, Robert A. M., Gregory Gilmartin, and John Massengale. *New York 1900: Metropolitan Architecture and Urbanism 1890–1915.* New York: Rizzoli International Publications, 1995.

Stern, Robert A. M., Gregory Gilmartin, and Thomas Mellins. *New York 1930: Architecture and Urbanism Between The Two World Wars.* New York: Rizzoli International Publications, 1994.

Stern, Robert A. M., Thomas Mellins, and David Fishman. *New York 1960: Urbanism and Architecture Between the Second World War and the Bicentennial.* New York: The Monacelli Press, 1995.

The WPA Guide to New York City: The Federal Writers Project Guide to 1930s New York. New York: The New Press/Random House, 1992 republication of 1939 edition.

6. Developers and Other Players

"The Corporate Developer" [Prudential]. *Progressive Architectire.* 69 (June 1988): 92–95.

Eichenwald, Kurt. *Serpent on the Rock.* New York: Harper Business, 1995.

Greenberg, Jonathan. "How to Make It Big in New York Real Estate." *Forbes.* October 8, 1984: 43ff.

Goulden, Joseph C. *Fit to Print: A. M. Rosenthal and His Times.* Secaucus, N.J.: Lyle Stuart, 1988.

Harvard Business School. *The Walt Disney Company (B): Sustaining Growth.* 1-894-129, March 24, 1994.

Harvard Business School. *The Walt Disney Company (C): A Tumultuous Year.* N9-395-109, January 1, 1995.

Hiaasen, Carl. *Team Rodent: How Disney Devours the World.* New York: Library of Contemporary Thought/Ballantine Publishing Group, 1998.

Robertson, Nan. *The Girls in the Balcony: Women, Men, and the New York Times.* New York: Fawcett Columbine, 1992.

Rose, Frank. "Can Disney Tame 42nd Street?" *Fortune,* June 24, 1994, 95ff.

Samuels, David. "The Real-Estate Royals: End of the Line?" *New York Times Magazine,* August 10, 1997: 36–41.

Scardino, Albert. "They'll Take Manhattan." *New York Times Magazine,* December 7, 1986: 35ff.

Shachtman, Tom. *Skyscraper Dreams: The Great Real Estate Dynasties of New York.* Boston: Little Brown and Co., 1991.

Talese, Gay. *The Kingdom and the Power.* New York: Ivy Books, 1971.

APPENDIXES

42DP	42nd Street Development Project
42DP, Inc.	42nd Street Development Project, Inc.
42EC	42nd Street Entertainment Corporation, Inc.
42RC	42nd Street Redevelopment Corporation
AIA	American Institute of Architects
BID	Business Improvement District
BNP	Banque Nationale de Paris
BOE	Board of Estimate
BPC	Battery Park City
BPCA	Battery Park City Authority
CA42	The City at 42nd Street, Inc.
CEQR	City Environmental Quality Review
CPC	City Planning Commission
CUNY	City University of New York
DCP	Department of City Planning
DEIS	Draft Environmental Impact Statement
DSEIS	Draft Supplemental Environmental Impact Statement
DUO	Design, Use and Operating Guidelines
EDC	Economic Development Corporation
EDPL	Eminent Domain Procedures Law
ESAC	Excess Site Acquisition Cost
ESDC	Empire State Development Corporation
FAR	Floor Area Ratio
FEIS	Final Environmental Impact Statement
FOIL	Freedom of Information Law
FSEIS	Final Supplemental Environmental Impact Statement
GPP	General Project Plan
ICIP	Industrial and Commercial Incentive Program
IDCNY	International Design Center of New York
IRT	Interborough Rapid Transit
LADA	Land Acquisition and Disposition Agreement
L/C	Letter of Credit
LPC	Landmarks Planning Commission
MAS	Municipal Art Society
MTA	Metropolitan Transit Authority
MOU	Memorandum of Understanding

NEW42	The New 42nd Street, Inc.
NRESAC	NonRecoverable Excess Site Acquisition Costs
NY	New York [the city]
NYPAL	New York Public Authorities Law
NYPD	New York Police Department
NYS	New York State
O&Y	Olympia & York
OME	Office of Midtown Enforcement
PABT	Port Authority Bus Terminal
PACB	Public Authorities Control Board
PANYNJ	Port Authority of New York and New Jersey
PDC	Public Development Corporation
PILOT	Payment in Lieu of Taxes
REBNY	Real Estate Board of New York
RFP	Request for Proposals
SAC	Site Acquisition Costs
SEQR	State Environmental Quality Review
SHPA	State Historic Preservation Act
SRB	Sex-related Businesses
SUT	Sales and Use Tax
TA	Transit Authority
TAC	Theater Advisory Council
Times	The New York Times
TSCA	Times Square Center Associates
TR&C	Tishman Realty & Construction Co., Inc.
TSRC	Times Square Redevelopment Corporation
UDC	Urban Development Corporation
UDAG	Urban Development Action Grant
ULI	Urban Land Institute
ULURP	Uniform Land Use Review Process

NEW YORK STATE GOVERNORS

Nelson A. Rockefeller	1959–1973
Malcolm Wilson	1973–1974
Hugh L. Carey	1975–1982
Mario M. Cuomo	1983–1994
George E. Pataki	1995–present

CITY OF NEW YORK MAYORS

Robert F. Wagner	1954–1965
John V. Lindsay	1966–1973
Abraham D. Beame	1974–1977
Edward I. Koch	1978–1989
David N. Dinkins	1990–1993
Rudolph W. Giuliani	1994–present

Strategy/Action	Time period/ Administration
1. Pass licensing laws, antisleaze legislation, curfews, health and safety regulations—legislate it out	
Deny licenses to 14 existing burlesque houses in the city, none new to be issued	1937 LaGuardia
Pass zoning amendment barring open-door "nuisance" establishments such as penny arcades	1947 O'Dwyer
Pass antisleaze law in an attempt to make Times Square a "class" area again	1954 Wagner
Suspend license of one theater as part of License Commissioner's clean-up of "lurid" sidewalk and lobby displays	1962 Wagner
Eliminate licencing requirements that had limited massage parlors	1967 Lindsay
Institute licensing requirements for purported masseuse uses	1973 Lindsay
Enact antiloitering law (modeled after the British State Offenses Act of 1959); as enforced, subsequently declared unconstitutionally vague and overly broad	1975 Beame
Pass zoning amendment to sharply restrict the location of "adult physical cultural establishments" (massage parlors) in the area and amortize nonconforming uses within one year; remainder of the city blanketed with a one-year moratorium on new massage parlors	1975 Beame
Preparation of zoning amendment recommendations to reconcentrate and limit adult uses; legislation flounders, politically	1977 Beame
Pass nuisance-abatement law making it easier to close illegal sex businesses	1977 Beame
Study of antiporn zoning amendment	1993 Dinkins
Pass antiporn zoning amendment	1994 Giuliani
2. Establish citizens committee to study problems and suggest action—political management	
Moralistic suppression by private prevention societies wielding public-like powers	Committee of 15 (1900), of 14 (1905)
Nightly closing of Bryant Park to the public	1944 LaGuardia

Strategy/Action	Time period/ Administration
Political support of independent private groups (during the 1950s and 1960s, the Broadway Association and the Greater Times Square Association; beginning in 1992, the Times Square BID)	Various
Times Square Development Council	1971 Lindsay
Midtown Citizens Committee	1975 Beame
Theater Advisory Council (TAC) (theater preservation)	1982 Koch
Times Square Advisory ("Bow-Tie") Committee (urban design)	1984 Koch
Citizens Cultural Advisory Committee on the 42DP	1986 Koch
Task Force on the Regulation of Sex-Related Businesses	1993 Borough President Messinger

3. Close it down—law enforcement

Institute campaign to clean up louche bookstores and cinemas; seal up "the Hole," the IRT entrance through the Rialto Arcade known as a pickup spot for teenagers	1961 Wagner
Crack down on prostitution	1971 Lindsay
Crack down on peep shows under the state's Obscenity and Related Offenses Statute	1972 Lindsay
Create "super precincts" for midtown law enforcement; raids, closings of bookstores, mass arrests of prostitutes	1972 Lindsay
Create Office of Midtown Enforcement (OME), a special task force for code enforcement based on use of heavy fines, zoning amendments, and Health Department ordinances aimed at closing down nonconforming establishments in order to return the area's real estate to "good commercial uses"	1976 Beame
Establish Operations Crossroads police substation	1978 Koch
Drive to eliminate juvenile prostitution from Times Square by OME	1985 Koch

4. Initiate Projects to Rebuild Area/Stimulate Private Investment—redevelopment[1]

Convention Center (Hudson River at 42nd Street) (Hudson River at 38th Street)	1968 Lindsay 1978 Koch
Portman hotel project/Broadway Plaza (pedestrian mall)	1973 Lindsay 1978 Koch
UDC headquarters moved to 1515 Broadway	1979 Cuomo/Koch

Strategy/Action	Time period/Administration
42nd Street Development Project (42DP)	1980 Koch
Midtown Zoning Resolution	1982 Koch
5. Regulate Building or Character—preservation and aesthetics	
Create Special Theater District	1969 Lindsay
Require special demolition permit for demolition of Broadway theater houses	1982 Koch
Pass design controls for the Bow-Tie District	1987 Koch
Landmark 28 theaters	1988 Koch

Note

1. This approach directly addresses the problem that law enforcement strategies, particularly the OME's real estate-based code-enforcement approach, are ill-equipped to deal with—street behaviors. It generally means public control of property decisions in the area, either through condemnation or regulation or outright public development. Therefore, it is very a different strategy than moral legislation or vice control through law enforcement. It is only politically permissible in an era that has already sanctioned, through extensive land-use controls with an established legal basis, the power of the state to define the marketplace of property transactions.

SOURCES: Norman Marcus, "Zoning Obscenity: Or, The Moral Politics of Porn," *Buffalo Law Review* 27 (1978), 1–46; 42DP, *DEIS*, 1-16–1-20; Timothy J. Gilfoyle, "Policing Sexuality," in *Inventing Times Square*, 297–314; Laurence Senelick, "Private Parts in Public Places," in *Inventing Times Square*, 329–353; newspaper articles.

APPENDIX D
CHRONOLOGY OF THE REDEVELOPMENT OF TIMES SQUARE AND WEST 42ND STREET

1978	Theater Row I opens.
1979	Ford Foundation sponsors The City at 42nd Street, Inc.
1980	The renovated Royal Manhattan Hotel reopens as the Milford Hotel.
June	Mayor Koch dismisses *The City at 42nd Street* plan as "Disneyland at 42nd Street," and initiates the city into a public development project, the 42DP.
July	*Midtown Development Project Draft Report* released for public review and comment.
August	BOE approves the Portman hotel project.
1981	
February	42DP *Discussion Document* issued.
June	Cooper-Eckstut Design Guidelines and the RFP for the 42DP issued.
1982	Theater Row II completed.
March	Helen Hayes and Morosco Theaters demolished.
May	Midtown Special District amendment to the zoning resolution approved.
August	Conditional designation of the first set of 42DP developers.
1983	
August	City and state power struggle over designation of mart developer.
October	Johnson-Burgee designs for Park Tower's four office buildings unveiled.
1984	
March	MAS and the National Endowment for the Arts co-sponsor a design competition for the former Times Tower site.
April	Conditional designation of the second set of 42DP developers.
November	BOE approves the 42DP.
1985	
Summer	42DP litigation accumulates: 20 lawsuits to date.
September	MAS Sim Lab model of Times Square brought to CPC hearings along with Broadway cast of *Big River*.
October	Marriott Marquis Hotel opens.
1986	
April	Conditional designation of Site 5 developer revoked (Lazar corruption scandal).
May	Final judicial scrutiny of 42DP: *Jackson* decision.
October	Prudential joins Park Tower as partner in the 42DP office development.
1987	
February	BOE approves urban-design regulations for Times Square.
August	Proposal to amend the *GPP* to permit sequential condemnation, among other changes to the 42DP.
October	BOE approves a zoning requirement for "entertainment-related use" for 5 percent of the floor area of developments in the "core" area of the Theater Subdistrict

November	Renegotiated project agreements between UDC and TSCA finalized.

1988

March	PACB delays vote on the TSCA leases. BOE unanimously approves landmark designation of 28 Broadway theater houses.
April	BOE approves a new package of zoning regulations for Times Square.
June	PACB unanimously approves the TSCA leases. Major 42DP project agreements executed.
October	The nonprofit 42E formed to oversee theater restoration, and an RFP for six of the theaters issued.

1989

April	Chemical Bank withdraws interest in becoming a tenant in the 42DP after three years of negotiations.
May	Prudential puts up $155-million L/C to secure condemnation proceedings.
August	TSCA unveils new Johnson/Burgee designs for its four office-tower sites.
October	42DP litigation reaches new height: 40 lawsuits to date.

1990

April	Justice Stanley Parness orders TSCA's L/C increased to $241 million; Prudential complies, and UDC takes title to 34 properties on West 42nd Street.
September	Cora Cahan and Marian Heiskell named executive director and chairman, respectively, of the 42EC (New42)

1991

September	The *GPP* amended to authorize wider range of entertainment-related and support activities in theaters, among other changes to the 42DP.
November	TSCA formally seeks delay of its development obligations. Supersigns on Two Times Square redefine the look of the postcard site.
December	Times Square BID created. The board of the New42 votes to launch the street's renewal with the renovation of the Victory Theater as a nonprofit theater programmed for the city's youth.

1992

February	City and state sign lease with the New42 for six historic theaters.
March	Commercial real estate market watershed transaction: 1540 Broadway bought by media-giant Bertelsmann A.G.
May	The GAP opens store at 42nd Street and Broadway.
August	The 42DP collapses, formally; construction of the offices towers delayed indefinitely. Times Square subway station renovations, as financed by TSCA, canceled. *42nd Street Now!* announced, including interim revitalization plan for the office sites, public funding of condemnation of unacquired parcels, and reorientation of plan toward entertainment, tourism and razzle-dazzle aesthetics. New MOU signed with TSCA.

1993

April	Disney CEO Michael Eisner visits the New Amsterdam Theater, and directs staff to begin negotiations with Disney.
August	Morgan Stanley announces purchase of 1585 Broadway.

September	Guidelines for *42nd Street Now!* released publicly and renderings published. City commits $35 million to fund condemnation of Site 7.
October	The New42 announces intention to develop young person's theater.
December	MOU with the Walt Disney Corporation for the restoration of the New Amsterdam Theater signed, on the last day of the Dinkins administration.

1994

February	Governor Cuomo and Mayor Koch hold press conference to announce signing of letter of intent with Disney for restoration of the New Amsterdam Theater.
March	Morgan Stanley announces purchase of a second tower, 750 Seventh Avenue.
Spring	Cascade of corporate interest in Times Square locations.
May	RFP for hotel, retail, and entertainment development of Site 7 issued.
August	Amended lease signed with TSCA which commits $20 million to interim revitalization of the office sites.
October	UDC takes title to all properties on Site 7. TSCA commences construction for interim retail activity.
December	The lease for the New Amsterdam Theater signed, on the last day of the Cuomo administration. City commits $13 million to fund condemnation of Site 8E.

1995

January	Lehman Brothers outbids many others to buy the former Times Tower at a bankruptcy auction.
March	Debut of Morgan Stanley's financial-news supersign.
May	Tishman Urban Development Corporation and Disney Development chosen to develop a hotel and retail-entertainment complex on Site 7.
July	Disney's conditions precedent met: letter of intent signed with Forest City Ratner/American MultiCinema/Madame Tussaud's for entertainment-retail complex on south side of West 42nd Street (Sites 8E, 6W, and 10). Letter of intent with Livent for the renovation of the Apollo and Lyric theaters signed.
October	All remaining adult-use stores on the north side of West 42nd Street officially closed down.
December	The New Victory Theater opens as the first restored theater on West 42nd Street.

1996

March	Remaining adult-use stores on the south side of West 42nd Street officially closed down.
April	Last porn tenant leaves West 42nd Street. The Durst Organization announces intent to buy the development rights for Site 12, and shortly thereafter, a commitment from Condé Nast to anchor the office tower to be called Four Times Square. The three-story Virgin megastore opens in Times Square.
December	A half-scale model of the Concord supersonic plane is erected over Hansen's Brewery on 42DP Site 1.

1997

March	Prudential announces plans to sell the three other 42DP office sites.
	The Roundabout Theater Company announces plans to renovate the Selwyn Theater.
	The New42 announces plans to build a rehearsal building for nonprofits on the Selwyn-infill parcel.

April	The restored New Amsterdam Theater opens.
June	The Hercules Electric Parade takes over West 42nd Street/Times Square.
	The former Times Tower sells for an unprecedented price, as a billboard.
July	Debut of the new Times Square subway station entrance.
August	Plans for an office tower on Site 3 to be developed by Reuters America, Inc., and the Rudin Organization announced.
October	The Grand Luncheonette closes, the last cultural fixture of West 42nd Street.
November	News notice of media-production studios scouting Times Square for prime locations.
December	The Ford Center for the Performing Arts, formerly the Apollo and Lyric Theaters, opens.
	Landmarked globe and clock atop the Paramount Building relit.

1998

February	Times Square gains a spot on list of most costly streets.
March	Boston Properties announces intent to buy the last two 42DP office sites (1 and 4).
November	Morgan Stanley announces plan to build a third tower for itself in Times Square.

1999

June	Design competition for a new "tkts" booth is announced.
	MTA begins phase 1 of its program to renovate the Times Square subway station complex.
October	The *Times* announces intention to build a new tower on 41st Street within the 42DP project area (Site 8S).
November	E-Walk opens.
December	Debut of Nasdaq techno-turret.
	New York–based entertainment giant SFX, which bought Livent, announces it will move its headquarters to West 42nd Street, to the Candler Building.

2000

January	The Van Alen Institute presents winning design for the new tkts booth by Australian architects John Choi and Tai Roipha.
	Second Stage Theater, Times Square's newest theater, opens at Eighth Avenue and 43rd Street.
	Times Square BID opens new full-service Times Square Visitors Center at historic Embassy Theater.
March	News notice that Theater Row to be redeveloped into a large commercial project with eight new or rebuilt playhouses.
April	AMC 25-screen movieplex opens.
June	Hilton Times Square Hotel opens.
July	The New 42nd Street Studios opens.
July	The American Airlines (Roundabout) Theater opens.
November	Madame Tussaud's opens.

2001

March	Three Times Square opens. Reuters America Holdings moves into its new headquarters at Three Times Square.
June	The Gap reopens its newly renovated store at the corner of 42nd Street and Seventh Avenue with an additional 20,000 square feet of retail space.

SOURCE: Author's files.

FORMAL AND INFORMAL POINTS OF ACCOUNTABILITY: 42ND STREET DEVELOPMENT PROJECT, 1981–1998

Date	Event	Executive oversight	Policy approval	Public participation
2/81	Issuance of *Discussion Document*	UDC		
6/81	Approval of *GPP* Findings of Blight	UDC		
8/81	Hearings on *GPP*			UDC Act EDPL
4/82	Conditional developer selection (office mart, hotel, two theater sites)	UDC		
6/82	Conditional developer designation (office)	UDC		
8/83	Controversy over selection of mart developer			Media review
1/84	Issuance of *DEIS*	UDC		
3/84	Hearings on *DEIS*			UDC Act EDPL SEQRA SHPA
4/84	Conditional developer designation (mart, hotel)	UDC		
7/84	MAS design competition for former Times Tower Site			Civic-group intervention
8/84	Conditional developer designation (Site 5)	UDC		
8/84	Issuance of *FEIS*	UDC		
9/84	Hearings on *FEIS*			UDC Act EDPL SEQRA SHPA
9/84	Milstein "White Paper" letter to UDC			Media review
10/84	Adoption of *GPP* and Findings	UDC EDPL		
11/84	BOE approval of *GPP*[1]		MOU	
8/87	Adoption of proposed amendment to to *GPP*[1]	UDC		
9/87	Release of nonprofit Theater Advisory Committee report on programming and management of the Liberty and Victory Theaters			Civic-group intervention
9/87	Hearings on proposed amendment to *GPP*[1]			UDC Act
12/87	Hearings on proposed leases with TSCA			UDC Act
2/88	Authorization of amendment modification to *GPP*[1] and execution of leases with TSCA	UDC		
6/88	PACB approval of TSCA leases	NYPAL		
6/88	Execution of major *Project Agreements*	UDC		
10/88	Leichter analysis of TSCA leases			Media review
7/91	Adoption of proposed amendment to *GPP*[2]	UDC		
8/91	Hearings on proposed amendment to the *GPP*[2]			UDC Act
9/91	Authorization of amendment modification to *GPP*[2]	UDC		

Date	Event	Executive oversight	Policy approval	Public participation
5/92	Authorization to acquire the New Amsterdam Theater and enter into related agreements	UDC		
8/92	Authorization to acquire the New Amsterdam Theater	UDC		
	PACB approval of acquisition of New Amsterdam Theater	NYPAL		
9/93	Adoption of proposed amendment to the *GPP*, *42nd Street Now!*, and issuance of guidelines[3]	UDC		
11/93	Hearings on proposed amendment to *GPP*[3]			UDC Act SHPA
	Hearings on *DSEIS*			SEQRA EDPL
1/94	Adoption of Findings on *FSEIS* and authorization of amendment modification to *GPP*[3]	UDC EDPL		
3/94	Authorization for agreements relating to the funding of the New Amsterdam Theater renovations	UDC PANYNJ		
7/94	MAS analysis of 42DP revised deal with TSCA			Civic-group intervention
9/94	Hearings on proposed amended leases with TSCA[4]			UDC Act
9/94	Execution of amended leases with TSCA	UDC		
12/94	Authorization to execute lease with Disney Development Company and related agreements for the New Amsterdam Theater and Site 6 East Infill	UDC		
12/94	Hearings on essential terms of proposed lease with Disney Development Company			UDC Act
12/94	Adoption of Findings and Policy Statement with respect to Sex-Related Businesses	UDC		
3/95	Questions about "sweetheart" deals for the 42DP (Disney, AMC Tussaud's) and sole-source designation for Site 8E			Media review
3/95	PACB approval of lease with Disney	NYPAL		
3/96	Adoption of proposed amendment to the GPP[5]	ESDC		
4/96	Authorization to acquire Durst parcels contiguous to Site 12 for a nominal payment	ESDC		
5/96	Combined hearings on proposed amendment to the *GPP*[5], proposed lease, and related documents with Forest City Ratner (Site 8E, 6W, 10)			UDC Act
6/96	Combined hearings on proposed amendment to *GPP*[6] and essential terms of lease with Tishman Urban Development Corporation (Site 7) and continuation of 5/96 hearings			UDC Act

Date	Event	Executive oversight	Policy approval	Public participation
6/96	Authorization to execute amended lease and related documents for Site 12 with the Durst Organization	ESDC		
12/96	Adoption of clarification of *GPP*[7]	ESDC		
10/97	Adoption of proposed amendment to the *GPP*[8]	ESDC		
12/97	Hearings on amendment to *GPP*[8]			UDC Act
1/98	Affirmation of *GPP* with respect to amendment[8]	ESDC		
2/98	Authorization to enter into documents to effectuate the assignment of the Site 3 leasehold interest from TSCA to Reuters/Rudin	ESDC		
4/98	Adoption of proposed amendment to *GPP*[9]	ESCD		
6/98	Hearings on proposed amendment to the *GPP*[9] and essential terms of lease with Forest City Ratner			UDC Act
7/98	Authorization to execute lease and related documents for Site 6W, 8E, 10 with Forest City Ratner	ESDC		

NOTES

1. February 1988 amendment: to allow height increases and redistribution of parking spaces among office buildings on Sites 1, 3, 4, 12 and to expand the range of uses permitted on Site 8 to include either office buildings or a general wholesale mart. A portion of the amendment adopted by the UDC board of directors in August 1987 providing for sequential condemnation of sites in the project was shifted to the "Project Status" section of the amendment.

2. September 1991 amendment: to authorize a wider range of entertainment-related and support activities in the theaters on Sites 5 and 10, increase the permitted height of the Selwyn infill building on Site 5.

3. January 1994 amendment: to implement *42nd Street Now!* and other related changes to the midblock sites and the Eighth Avenue Corridor; incorporation of New Amsterdam Theater into the project.

4. September 1994 amendment: to implement September 1992 MOU with TSCA.

5. June 1996 amendment: to expand the footprint of Site 12 to incorporate the Durst parcels.

6. September 1996 amendment: to extend the *42nd Street Now!* plan to Site 7; de minimis modification with respect to closed 42nd Street entrance of the Carter Hotel.

7. December 1996 clarification: to make the project's Design, Use, and Operating Guidelines (DUO) subject to and part of *GPP*.

8. January 1998 amendment: to increase the permissible height of structures on the site of the former Selwyn office building and the former Selwyn infill site. A May 1998 amendment expanded Site 3 and reduced Site 5.

9. July 1998 amendment: to permit a hotel to be built as part of the Forest City Ratner project.

SOURCE: Author's files

New Private Investment on West 42nd Street

Site	Project	Developer	Investment (Millions)
42nd Street Development Project:			
Office Towers:			
12	Four Times Square	Durst Organization	$450.0
3	Three Times Square	Reuters/Rudin	360.0
4	Five Times Square	Boston Properties, Inc.	495.0
1	Times Square Tower	Boston Properties, Inc.	600.0
	tenant improvements (estimate)	Various tenants	516.9
Subtotal: Office			2,421.9
Performance Theaters:			
5	New Victory	The New 42nd Street, Inc.	11.4
5	Ford Center for the Performing Arts	Livent	36.0
5	American Airlines Theater	Roundabout Theater Company	21.5
6	New Amsterdam	Disney Development Company	38.6
Subtotal: Theaters			107.5
North Side Midblock:			
7	E-Walk	Tishman Urban Development Corp.	70.0
	E-Walk tenant improvements	Various tenants	60.0
7	Westin Hotel	Tishman Urban Development Corp.	322.5
5 infill	The New 42nd Street Studios	The New 42nd Street Inc.	29.6
5	Times Square Theater	Not yet determined	--
South Side Midblock and Other:			
6W, 8E, 10	Movie/Retail	Forest City Ratner Companies	100.0
	AMC and other tenant improvements	Various tenants	70.0
6W, 8E, 10	Madame Tussaud's	Forest City Ratner/Tussaud's	40.0
6W, 8E, 10	Hilton Times Square Hotel	Forest City Ratner	125.0
8S	New York Times	Forest City Ratner/New York Times headquarters (estimate)	715.0
8N	Milstein parking lot	Not yet determined	--
Subtotal: North and south sides			1,532.1
42nd Street Development Project			4,061.5
Nonproject:			
11	Candler Bldg renovation	Massachusetts Mutual Life Insurance Company	40.0
Total investment			4,101.5

Source: Individual developers; numbers should be considered close approximations. Author's files.

Index

Hilton Times Square Hotel, *xvii*, 426, 427

Hippodrome, *465*

Hole, The (Rialto Arcade), 31

Holiday Inn Crowne Plaza, 318, pl. 25

Holloway, Benjamin D., 498n28

Holm, Celeste, 271

Holtzman, Elizabeth, 416–417

Holzer, Jenny, 304, 323, *325*

Homosexuality, 31, 44–45

Howard, Philip, 247

Howe, Con, 253, 261, 262, 265, 273, 522n9

Huxtable, Ada Louise, 39, 51, 56, 63, 70
  on aesthetics, 174, 176, 179, 181, 187
  approach of, 183–184, 514n26
  on design, 264–265
  giantism and, 182–184

IBM, 96, 179

I. M. Pei & Partners, 200, 262

Implementation issues
  architectural criticism and, 174–181
  Broadway and, 309–336
  Disney and, 339–372
  entertainment agenda and, 277–307
  litigation trap and, 207–237
  public stake and, 181–189
  purity loss and, 189–198
  renewal and, 239–275
  Theater District and, 171–172
  troubled execution and, 171–204

Industrial and Commercial Incentive Program (ICIP), 230, 522n13

Interborough Rapid Transit Company (IRT), 31, 38–39

International Design Center of New York (IDCNY), 217

Iopollo, Frank, 349

Irwin, Will, 34

Izenour, Stephen, 303

Jackowitz, Bob, 330

Jackson, Kenneth T., 20

Jackson v. N.Y.S. UDC, 154, 210, 413, 511n37, 518n3

Jacobs, Jane, 85, 469

Jacobs, Karrie, 463

Jacobson, Arch K., 151

Jacobson, Mark, 45

Japanese advertisers, 12, 325–326, 328

Javits, Jacob K. convention center, 83, 176

Jerde, Jon, 260, 264

Johnson, Philip, 140

Johnson & Burgee, 101–102, *179*
  alien designs of, 173, pl. 9
  architectural criticism and, 174–181,

200, 223
  Design Guidelines and, 193–194
  office tower project, pl. 9
  redesign of, 554n59
  style of, 201
  zoning amendments and, 145

Joyce Theater, 247

Jujamcyn Company, 260, 279

Jules Fisher & Paul Marantz Inc., 253

Kahan, Richard A., 106, 190, 231

Kalman, Tibor, 299, 304–305, *305*

Katz, Alex, 323

Katz, Jeffrey, 98, 309, 328–329

Katzenberg, Jeffrey, 342, 344

Kaufman, Herbert, 258

Kennedy family, 215–216

Kent, Fred I. III, 545n30

KG Land, 156

Kiley, Robert, 121–122

Klein, George, xiv, 75–77, 106, 114, 156
  architectural criticism and, 186, 194–198, 201
  Bender on, 194
  deal making and, 115–116
  Durst and, 428, 431–433
  entertainment agenda and, 299
  fading of, 487
  499 Park Avenue building, 115–116
  high rollers and, 404
  Koch and, 504n20, 504n22
  liability and, 150
  litigation and, 155, 222, 231
  open-tab policies and, 135–136 (*see also* Open-tab policies)
  ownership issues and, 137
  Prudential and, 151–161
  Rockefeller Center and, 192–193
  subways and, 394
  taxes and, 213
  tenant issues, 520n43

Knab, Donald R., 153–154

Knickerbocker Hotel, 33, 174, *175*

Koch, Edward I., xi–xii, xiv, *14*, 15, *187*, 219, 257, 489
  architectural criticism and, 187–188, 196
  BOE vote and, 99–102
  boldness of, 12
  CA42 and, 66–67, 69, 110–111
  Cobb and, 262
  Cuomo and, 77
  development and, 69–79, 105
  economic issues and, 297
  Klein and, 498n24, 504n20, 504n22
  litigation and, 208, 217–219, 235
  new TSCA deal and, 140–144
  real estate and, 70
  revisionism and, 472

risk and, 375
  Theater District and, 119, 128
  transit system and, 392

Kornblum, William, 16–17, 48, 494n26

Kumagai Gumi, 156

Kusumoto, Sama, 327

Kwartler, Michael, 98

LaGuardia, Fiorello H., 57–58, 470–471

Lamb's Table, 485

Land Acquisition and Development Agreement (LADA), 137, 147, 379, 381

Landauer Associates, 124, 152

Landmarks Preservation Commission (LPC), 128, 222, 244, 252
  Disney and, 344
  triumph of, 269–271

Land values, 138, 508n4

Lardner, Ring, 310

Lark Hotel, 494n22

Las Vegas, 303–304, 364

Lazar, Michael, 129, 279, 375

Lazard Realty, Inc., 217

LeBoeuf, Lamb, Leiby & MacRae, 210

Lefkowitz, Stephen A., 73, 412–413, 502n6

LeFrak Organization, 190

Legal issues
  accountability and, 411–418
  condemnation and, 383–388, 518n3
  definitions and, 509n16
  Disney and, 349
  42DP hearings, *294*
  judicial review and, 412–413
  leasing terms and, 144–148
  litigation and, 145–148, 155, 173, 207–237 (*see also* Litigation)
  market value and, 138
  MAS, 501n53
  new TSCA deal and, 140–144
  nonprofit status and, 539n41
  ownership and, 136–140
  property seizure and, 547n56
  public use and, 403
  restrictive covenant and, 517n62
  subsidies and, 428–441
  title, 140
  UDC and, 154, 197, 548n2

Legal Services for the Elderly, 210

Lehman Brothers, 332, 361–362, 366

Leichter, Franz S., 145, *146*, 163, 214

Leichter v. N.Y.S. Urban Development Corporation, 215, 509n18

Leigh, Douglas, 325

Lenders, 315–318

Les Misérables, 283, 350, 456